EU Food Law

EU Food Law

HANNA SCHEBESTA
Associate Professor, Law Group, Wageningen University & Research (WUR), Hollandseweg 1, Wageningen, Netherlands (the)

KAI PURNHAGEN
Professor and Chair of Food Law, University of Bayreuth, Campus Kulmbach Chair of Food Law Fritz-Hornschuch Str. 13 95326 Kulmbach, Germany

OXFORD
UNIVERSITY PRESS

OXFORD
UNIVERSITY PRESS

Great Clarendon Street, Oxford, OX2 6DP,
United Kingdom

Oxford University Press is a department of the University of Oxford.
It furthers the University's objective of excellence in research, scholarship,
and education by publishing worldwide. Oxford is a registered trade mark of
Oxford University Press in the UK and in certain other countries

Published in the United States of America by Oxford University Press
198 Madison Avenue, New York, NY 10016, United States of America

British Library Cataloguing in Publication Data

Data available

Library of Congress Control Number is on file at the Library of Congress

ISBN 9780198844853

DOI: 10.1093/9780198901570.001.0001

Printed and bound by
CPI Group (UK) Ltd, Croydon, CR0 4YY

Contents

Abbreviations xi

Introduction 1
Part I—The legal foundations of EU food law 2
Part II—The General Food Law Regulation and food law enforcement 3
Parts III-VII—the food law *acquis* 3
Part VIII—international food law 4

PART I EUROPEAN INTEGRATION AND FOOD LAW

1. The Genesis and Evolution of EU Food Law 7
   1.1 Introduction 7
   1.2 The EU Treaties: the political foundations of European integration 8
   1.3 Political paradigms shaping EU legislative harmonization in the area of food 11
   1.4 Conclusions 32

2. The EU Web of Competences and Food Law 34
   2.1 Introduction 34
   2.2 Food and competences 34
   2.3 Food and fundamental rights 50
   2.4 Conclusion 52

3. EU Institutions and Their Role in Food Policy and Law Making 54
   3.1 Introduction 54
   3.2 EU Institutions and their role in policy and law making 55
   3.3 EU law making—who makes what kind of law, and how? 63
   3.4 Reflection 77

4. Internal Market Law and Food 79
   4.1 Introduction 79
   4.2 Food and the free movement of goods: the origins 80
   4.3 An inventory of the case law on the free movement of foods 85
   4.4 Internal market secondary legislation: notification duty and conditional mutual recognition 104
   4.5 Conclusion: is the internal food market complete? 108

PART II FOOD SAFETY UMBRELLA LAWS: THE GENERAL FOOD LAW REGULATION AND THE OFFICIAL CONTROLS REGULATION

5. The General Food Law Regulation (GFLR) and Transparency Amendment 113
5.1 Introduction 113
5.2 Adoption of the GFLR and modification through the Transparency Regulation 113
5.3 GFLR Structure, aim and objective, scope and definitions 115
5.4 Principles of the GFLR, Articles 5–10 (horizontal/transversal nature) 118
5.5 General obligations of food trade (Articles 11–13) 124
5.6 The rules of the general food law requirements of food law (Articles 14–21) 125
5.7 European Food Safety Authority 128
5.8 Risk response: rapid alert system, crisis management, and emergencies (Articles 50–57) 135
5.9 Procedures and final provisions 137
5.10 Reflection on the GFLR 138

6. Official Controls Regulation and Food Law Enforcement 141
6.1 Introduction 141
6.2 Enforcement under the GFLR 142
6.3 Official Controls Regulation 142
6.4 Conclusions 151

PART III FOOD TECHNOLOGY LAW

Exceptions to the 'free marketing of food principle' 155

7. Pre-Market Authorizations of Novel Products: Novel Food Regulation 159
7.1 Introduction 159
7.2 The Novel Food Regulation (NFR) 160
7.3 Legal base and objectives 161
7.4 Scope of the NFR 161
7.5 Consultation process to determine the novel food status 165
7.6 The marketing of novel foods is restricted to inclusion on the Union list 166
7.7 EFSA risk assessment procedures for novel food 170
7.8 The new data ownership turn in novel food authorizations 171
7.9 Reflections 172

8. Genetically Modified Food 174
8.1 Introduction 174
8.2 The EU GMO legal framework 177

8.3 Main requirements of GMO deliberate release and GM food and feed frameworks 181
8.4 Traceability and labelling of GM food 188
8.5 Proposal on plants obtained by certain new genomic techniques and their food and feed 190
8.6 Discussion 191

9. Food Improvement Agents (Additives, Enzymes, Flavourings), and Use of Extraction Solvents 193
9.1 Introduction 193
9.2 Food Improvement Agents Package (Additives, Enzymes, Flavourings) 194
9.3 Food additives 195
9.4 Food enzymes 200
9.5 Food flavouring 204
9.6 Processing aids 213
9.7 Common authorization procedure: Commission Regulation (EU) 234/2011 214
9.8 Extraction solvents 215
9.9 Discussion 218

PART IV FOOD SAFETY LAW

10. Hygiene Legislation and Microbiological Criteria for Food 223
10.1 Introduction 223
10.2 Hygiene legislation 223
10.3 The General Hygiene Regulation 224
10.4 The Hygiene Regulation for Animal Origin 235
10.5 Microbiological criteria for foodstuffs 236
10.6 Discussion 238

11. Chemical Safety of Food Products 241
11.1 Introduction 241
11.2 EU legal framework for contaminants (unintentionally added substances) 242
11.3 'Intentionally added' substances 247
11.4 Discussion 253

12. Food Contact Materials 255
12.1 Introduction 255
12.2 'Food Contact Materials' Framework Regulation 255
12.3 The Regulation on Good Manufacturing Practices 258
12.4 EU legislation on specific materials 258
12.5 Restrictions on the use of specific substances 265
12.6 Discussion 266

PART V FOOD INFORMATION LAW

Information paradigm 272
The 'average consumer' benchmark 273
Charter of Fundamental Rights 278
Other provisions (Articles 168, 169 TFEU) 279
General food law information provisions 280

13. Food Information to Consumers Regulation 282
13.1 Introduction 282
13.2 The Food Information to Consumer Regulation 282
13.3 Objective, scope, and definitions 283
13.4 The principles of food information law 284
13.5 General food information requirements and responsibilities of FBOs 286
13.6 Mandatory food information 288
13.7 Voluntary food information 300
13.8 Discussion 303

14. Nutrition and Health Claims 304
14.1 Introduction 304
14.2 The Nutrition and Health Claims Regulation 305
14.3 Legal base, scope, and objective 305
14.4 Overview of the NHCR and definitions 306
14.5 Definition of claims 307
14.6 Overarching requirements for nutrition and health claims 309
14.7 Nutrition claims 313
14.8 Health claims 314
14.9 The application 319
14.10 EFSA's opinion 321
14.11 Union authorization 322
14.12 General and final provisions 324
14.13 Conclusion 324

PART VI FOOD QUALITY LAW

Conceptual clarifications around food schemes 329
The relationship between public and private standards 331

15. Organic Food 334
15.1 Introduction 334
15.2 Organics Regulation 336
15.3 Additional rules on official controls 344
15.4 Trade with third countries 346
15.5 Procedural aspects 346
15.6 Discussion 346

16. EU Food Quality Schemes 349
16.1 Introduction 349
16.2 Food Quality Systems Regulation 351
16.3 Applications for PDO, PGI, and TSG and their placing on the market 358
16.4 Discussion 359

PART VII FOOD NUTRITION LAW

17. Nutrition and Health in EU Food Law 363
17.1 Introduction 363
17.2 Foods for Specific Groups and Purposes (FSGaP) Regulation 364
17.3 Regulation on Food Fortification 371
17.4 Directive 2002/46/EC on food supplements 375
17.5 Discussion 377

PART VIII INTERNATIONAL FOOD LAW

18. Food in a Globalized World: International Food Law 383
18.1 Introduction 383
18.2 International food law and EU food law 385
18.3 International law under the auspices of the UN 386
18.4 WTO law and food 396
18.5 Discussion 401

Future of Food Law—Conclusions and Outlook 403
Part I—European integration and food law 403
Part II—Food safety umbrella laws: the General Food Law Regulation and the Official Controls Regulation 409
Parts III–VII—the food law *acquis* 409
Part VIII—international food law 414
Future-proofing food law—beyond food law 415

Index 417

Abbreviations

ACP	African, Caribbean, and Pacific
ADIs	acceptable daily intakes
ADME	absorption, distribution, metabolism, and excretion
AGRI	Agriculture and Rural Development Committee
ALARA	as low as can reasonable be achieved
ALOP	appropriate level of protection
ALs	action levels
BSE	Bovine Spongiform Encephalopathy
BPA	Bisphenol A
CAC	Codex Alimentarius Commission
CAP	Common Agricultural Policy
CESCR	Committee on Economic, Social and Cultural Rights
CETA	Comprehensive Economic and Trade Agreement
CFR	EU Charter of Fundamental Rights
CHED	Common Health Entry Document
CJEU	Court of Justice of the European Union
CMO Regulation	Common Market Organization Regulation
CMOs	Common Market Organizations
COOL	country of origin labelling
CoR	European Committee of the Regions
COREPER	Committee of Permanent Representatives
DGs	Directorates-General
EC	Economic Community
ECHA	European Chemicals Agency
ECHR	European Convention for the Protection of Human Rights and Fundamental Freedoms
ECJ	European Court of Justice
ECSC	European Coal and Steel Community
EEC	European Economic Communities
EESC	European Economic and Social Committee
EFSA	European Food Safety Authority
EFTA	European Free Trade Association
ENVI	Environment Public Health and Food Safety Committee
EP	European Parliament
EU	European Union
EURATUM	European Atomic Energy Community
EURCAWs	EU Reference Centres for Animal Welfare
FAO	Food and Agriculture Organization
FBO	food business operator

FCM	food contact materials
FDA	US Food and Drug Administration
FIAP	Food Improvement Agents Package
FICR	Food Information to Consumers Regulation
FSFS	Farm to Fork's legislative framework for sustainable food systems
FSGaP	Regulation Food for Specific Groups and Purposes Regulation
FSMPs	Food for Special Medical Purposes
FSMS	food safety management system
FVO	Food and Veterinary Office
GAPs	good agricultural practices
GATT	General Agreement on Tariffs and Trade
GDPs	good distribution practices
GFLR	General Food Law Regulation
GHPs	good hygiene practices
GHS	Globally Harmonized System of Classification and Labelling of Chemicals
GIs	geographical indications
GMOs	genetically modified organisms
GMPs	good manufacturing practices
GPPs	good production practices
GPSD	General Product Safety Directive
GRAS	generally recognized as safe
GTPs	good trading practices
GVPs	good veterinarian practices
HACCP	hazard analysis and critical control points
HLEG	high-level expert group
IARC	International Agency for Research on Cancer
ICESCR	International Covenant on Economic, Social and Cultural Rights
ICS	internal control systems
ICSMS	Information and Communication System on Market Surveillance
IFOAM	International Federation of Organic Agriculture Movements
IFST	Institute of Food Science and Technology
ILC	International Law Commission
IMCO	Internal Market and Consumer Protection Committee
IMSOC	information management system for official controls
IP	intellectual property
IPFSS	International Platform for Food Systems Science
ISO	International Organization for Standardization
IUBMB	International Union of Biochemistry and Molecular Biology
JECFA	Joint FAO/WHO Expert Committee on Food Additives
JEMNU	Joint FAO/WHO Expert Committee on Nutrition
JEMRA	Joint FAO/WHO Expert Meetings on Microbiological Risk Assessment
JMPS	Joint FAO/WHO Expert Meetings on Pesticide Specifications
JRC	Joint Research Centre

MANCP	multi-annual national control plans
MEEQR	Measure equivalent to a quantitative restriction
ML	maximum levels
MOH	mineral oil hydrocarbons
MRLs	maximum residue levels
NFR	Novel Food Regulation
NGO	non-governmental organization
NGT	new genomic techniques
NHCR	Nutrition and Health Claims Regulation
NIAS	non-intentionally added substances
NUGAG	WHO Nutrition Guidance Expert Advisory Group
OCR	Official Controls Regulation
OECD	Organisation for Economic Co-operation and Development
OML	overall migration limit
OQT	optional quality terms
PAHs	polycyclic aromatic hydrocarbons
PDO	protected designation of origin
PFAS	per- and polyfluoroalkyl substances
PGI	protected geographical indication
POP	place of provenance
PPP	Plant Protection Products
PRAC	Regulatory Procedure with Scrutiny
PRIMo	Pesticide Residue Intake Model
PRPs	prerequisite programmes
QUID	quantitative indication of ingredients
RACE	Rapid Assessment of Contaminant Exposure
RAPEX	Rapid Alert System for non-food products posing a serious risk
RASFF	Rapid Alert System for Food and Feed
REACH	Registration, Evaluation, Authorisation and Restriction of Chemicals
REFIT	Regulatory Fitness and Performance Programme
SAM	Scientific Advice Mechanism
SAPEA	Scientific Advice for Policy by European Academies
SCA	Special Committee on Agriculture
SDGs	sustainable development goals
SEA	Single European Act
SMEs	small and medium-sized enterprises
SMLs	specific migration limits
SPS Agreement	Agreement on the Application of Sanitary and Phytosanitary Measures
SVHC	substances of very high concern
TBR	Trade Barriers Regulation
TBT Agreement	Technical Barriers to Trade Agreement
TEC	Treaty establishing the European Community
TEU	Treaty on European Union

TFEU	Treaty on the Functioning of the European Union
TRIS	technical regulations information system
TSEs	transmissible spongiform encephalopathies
TSG	Traditional Speciality Guarantee
UCPD	Unfair Commercial Practices Directive
ULs	upper intake levels
UN	United Nations
UNCTAD	United Nations Conference on Trade and Development
UTPD	Unfair Trading Practices Directive
WFP	World Food Programme
WHO	World Health Organization
WIPO	World Intellectual Property Organization
WOAH	World Organization for Animal Health
WTO	World Trade Organization

Introduction

> Dis-moi ce que tu manges, je te dirai ce que tu es.
> [Tell me what you eat and I will tell you what you are].
>
> Anthelme Brillat-Savarin, 1826

It has been asserted that 'you are what you eat'. This book, in many ways, challenges this conception—what food ends up on European Union (EU) citizens' plates is determined perhaps more by EU food law than by the personal choice or character of individuals. EU food law regulates what food is available on the EU market, how safe it is, and its quality. EU food law also regulates the information provided about food, which, in turn, shapes citizens' food choices. At the same time, EU food law does not set requirements on, for instance, food environments or food taxation.

This book offers the perspective that how we regulate—or choose not to regulate—food, not only influences what 'we' eat collectively, but also tells us a lot about our society. Food law, in this context, reflects a society's main concerns regarding food—Is food available? Is it cheap? Is it safe? Is it healthy? Is it sustainable?

In the EU, food politics have recently taken centre stage in public discourse. There are many calls for changing our current food system. However, in order to achieve change, one must first understand what the components that make up our food system are. This book is about EU food law. This is because we believe that a thorough legal perspective is indispensable in order to grasp the design of the EU food system. In this way, the book is a statement of the state of affairs of EU food law *de lege lata*. It comprehensively explains the legal architecture of the EU food system, its constitutional foundation, and the applicable legal frameworks.

Looking at the history of European integration, the development of food law at the EU level can be characterized as a constant dialectical relationship between political quests for change, impactful external shocks, and the legal *status quo*.

The enactment of the General Food Law Regulation (GFLR) in 2002 established a food-safety oriented legal architecture, with food safety as a central regulatory goal, and designed rules, processes, and institutions in order to implement it. Food law was gradually consolidated under this umbrella, remedying issues and challenges as they emerged.

For almost two decades, the dedication of EU food law to the food safety paradigm has been stable. Currently, we are at the inception of a new era of food law, where there is an expectation that food law will transition towards prioritizing

EU Food Law. Hanna Schebesta and Kai Purnhagen, Oxford University Press.
DOI: 10.1093/9780198901570.003.0001

sustainability. The European Commission has published the Farm to Fork Strategy (2020) under the auspices of the Green Deal, with a view to shaping a 'fair, healthy and environmentally-friendly food system'. As we show in this book, the contours of this political agenda seem insufficient to reconcile the existing food safety legal architecture with a sustainability paradigm. It is therefore essential to analyse the developments giving shape to this prospective food law.

The book is divided into eight parts, which cover the legal foundations of EU food law (Part I), the GFLR and food law enforcement (Part II), the set of food law *acquis* along topical clusters (Parts III–VII), and lastly international food law (Part VIII). These are structured as follows:

Part I—The legal foundations of EU food law

Part I is dedicated to an analysis of the legal foundations of EU food law. We first explain the genesis and evolution of EU food law through the lens of the history of European integration (Chapter 1). The political foundations of European integration were laid in a succession of international treaties. These founding Treaties are also the foundations of EU food law, and pose the systemic, quasi-constitutional rules governing the operation of the EU. Furthermore, we further show how major political paradigms have shaped what gradually emerged as the area of EU food law. European legal integration initially advanced with a strong focus on the agricultural sector and the creation of the Common Market in parallel, followed by attention to the completion of the internal market (1985), food safety (2000), transparency (2019), and now sustainability (2019). These political paradigms have shaped food legislation, and eventually gave rise to food as a regulatory domain in EU law with a dedicated food framework law: the GFLR and related legal acts.

Although food emerged as a distinct regulatory domain, it has never been formally recognized at treaty level, and this remains the case today. While there is a Common Agricultural Policy and a Common Fisheries Policy, there is no specific food competence or policy. Therefore, food as a domain remains governed and limited by 'a web of competences', most notably agriculture, the internal market, consumer law, the environment, and to some extent health (Chapter 2).

The EU and its institutions can only act in line with the confines of the EU Treaties as constitutional documents, and by exercising competence conferred by the Member States on the EU. It does so my adopting legal acts, that is, secondary law. To understand how EU secondary food law is made, we elucidate the mandate of the respective EU institutions and their role in food policy and law making (Chapter 3). There are distinct legislative and non-legislative law-making trajectories, which we explain, including, inter alia, the important role of the European Commission and technical aspects of the committee procedure. Understanding the policy and law-making processes is not only essential for predicting the future of food law, but also for successful advocacy and lobbying for change.

In terms of the substantive food law, food as a good falls under the Treaty framework on the free movement of goods that constitutes the EU internal market (Chapter 4). We analyse the relevance of the free movement of goods Treaty articles and landmark case law rendered by the Court of Justice of the EU on the relevant Articles 34–36 TFEU. While traditionally cases related to food were often decided under the free movement Treaty articles, we show that the Treaty articles on the free movement of goods in the internal market are becoming less significant within the area of food. Instead, food is largely governed by secondary legislative and non-legislative legal instruments.

Part II—The General Food Law Regulation and food law enforcement

The food regulatory domain is jointly governed by two cornerstone legislative instruments. First, the GFLR of 2002 creates an umbrella legislative framework that is valid for the area of food law as a whole (Chapter 5). The GFLR comprises general principles of food law, food law requirements, responsibilities, risk analysis processes, the European Food Safety Authority, as well as risk response mechanisms. It hereby creates a largely food safety oriented legal regulatory framework. It also institutes the cornerstone rule that unsafe food may not be placed on the EU market. Second, the Official Controls Regulation (OCR) stipulates how the area of food law is enforced (Chapter 6). The ambit of the OCR is even wider than that of the GFLR, as it contains enforcement rules for agri-food chain legislation more widely, and covers plant and animal legislation next to food law. The OCR's approach shows that the EU in the agri-food area is clearly dedicated to public administrative enforcement systems whereby compliance is monitored and enforced by public authorities. In EU food law, private enforcement—for instance through product liability damages claims—take on a residual role only.

Parts III–VII—the food law *acquis*

In addition to the two existing umbrella frameworks, the food law *acquis* is made up of a large number of secondary legal frameworks that cover a diversity of subjects. In this book we present these food laws in topical clusters, namely: food technology law (Part III), food safety law (Part IV), food information law (Part V), food quality law (Part VI), and food nutrition law (Part VII). This categorization is approximate only and certainly non-exclusive, because all food legislation is largely oriented towards food safety and generally pursues a number of objectives simultaneously.

Part III on food technology law clusters the legal frameworks for novel foods (Chapter 7), genetically modified organisms (Chapter 8), and food improvement agents (Chapter 9). The GFLR institutes a general 'free marketing system' for food, whereby foodstuffs can be placed on the market as long as they are not unsafe. However, certain foodstuff categories require pre-market authorization before they may be marketed. The presumption of non-safety is largely due to technical food elements that engage prior authorization requirements.

Part IV on food safety laws groups the legal frameworks on hygiene and microbiological safety (Chapter 10), chemical safety (Chapter 11), and food contact materials (Chapter 12). These legal frameworks address the 'pure' food safety concerns, covering the regulation of biological and chemical food safety hazards, with food contact material being a specifically topical issue of food safety.

Part V on food information law discusses the main food information law, namely the Food Information to Consumers Regulation (Chapter 13) and the regulation of nutrition and health claims (Chapter 14). EU food law aims to enable consumers to make informed choices, and in many ways food law does not prescribe the constitution of products, but rather regulates the food market through information governance, including the provision of verified information for nutrition and health claims.

Part VI on food quality law covers the Organic Food Regulation (Chapter 15) and EU Food Quality Schemes (Chapter 16). These schemes certify that foods have a specific quality, one by prescribing the requirements that organic foods have to meet, and the other by prescribing the processes through which groups of producers can define quality requirements that must be met in order to use a food quality scheme.

Part VII on food nutrition law comprises the legal frameworks for foods for specific groups and purposes, food fortification, and food supplements (Chapter 17). The food nutrition cluster contains a number of compositional requirements for specific foodstuffs. It is characterized by a number of 'incomplete' laws, attesting to the reluctance of legislating at the food for health nexus.

Part VIII—international food law

EU law operates in a global context, and international law influences EU food law. Chapter 18 surveys the impact of international law on food law mainly in two arenas: First, the global governance through the United Nations and other international institutions such as the Codex Alimentarius Commission. Secondly, the EU is particularly embedded into the global world trading order such as the World Trade Organization, as well as a web of trade and investment agreements.

We close the book with an outlook on future developments in EU food law, taking account of the most recent policy changes and their potential impact on EU food law. We take this opportunity to reflect on the future of food law and sustainability beyond the Farm to Fork Strategy.

PART I

EUROPEAN INTEGRATION AND FOOD LAW

1
The Genesis and Evolution of EU Food Law

1.1 Introduction

The genesis and evolution of 'EU food law' is inherently tied to the development of the legal entity that we now know as the European Union (EU); a legal construct based on international treaties that created a supranational, autonomous European Union legal order. Political forces and aims that drive the European integration process will inevitably impact the design of EU food law.

The EU Treaties are political in that they are international agreements, and therefore negotiated, signed, and ratified by Member States. The EU Treaties circumscribe the power of the EU as a political entity, its goals and competencies, and its institutions. The EU Treaties serve as the foundational framework upon which the actions and legislation of EU integration are built. Being quasi-constitutional documents, they impose strict legal constraints on EU actions and policies, including in the area of EU food law. This is why the legal foundations of European integration also serve as the foundations of EU Food Law.

The driving force for European integration originally arose from the aftermath of the war. In this vein, the Treaty establishing the European Economic Communities (EEC) enshrined the objective of achieving a Common Agricultural Policy (CAP) alongside the gradual establishment of the Common Market, which later evolved into efforts to create a single market and finally an internal market).

Legislative harmonization based on these two objectives resulted in several ad-hoc food-specific legal instruments. These laws implicitly recognized that foodstuffs possess unique characteristics that are distinct from other consumer goods, thus justifying their regulation through specific legislation. Examples of this early approach are the CAP 1962 Council Regulation No 23, which postulated the progressive establishment of a common market organization for fruits and vegetables[1] and the Common Market 1962 Council Directive on colouring matter.[2]

Subsequent policy initiatives gradually recognized food as a distinct regulatory sector that deserved separate consideration. For instance, the 1985 White Paper

[1] EEC Regulation No 23 on the progressive establishment of a common organisation of the market in fruit and vegetables [1962] OJ 965/97.

[2] Klaudyna M Terlicka and David J Jukes, 'From Harmonisation to Better, Smart and Fit Food Law: Reviewing the Legislators Attempts to Abolish Barriers to Food Trade in the EU' (2014) 9 European Food and Feed Law Review 302.

EU Food Law. Hanna Schebesta and Kai Purnhagen, Oxford University Press. © Hanna Schebesta and Kai Purnhagen 2024.
DOI: 10.1093/9780198901570.003.0002

Completion of the Internal Market dedicated several paragraphs to the regulation of food specifically.

In policy making, the idea of food law as an autonomous policy domain emerged gradually. The first policy for food was published by the Commission in the Green Paper *General Principles for Food Law in the European Union* (1997), which envisioned 'appropriate measures for the future development of Community food law'. In response to the food scares of the 1990s, the Commission essentially redesigned this approach in the *White Paper on Food Safety* (2000), which proposed the creation of a general food law instrument, along with a large number of other food regulations.

The adoption of the General Food Law Regulation (GFLR) in 2002 marked the formal establishment of food law as a distinct legal domain. The GFLR is an umbrella regulation incorporating overarching principles to govern all food laws. It also defined food law for the first time as:

> the laws, regulations and administrative provisions governing food in general, and food safety in particular, whether at Community or national level; it covers any stage of production, processing and distribution of food, and also of feed produced for, or fed to, food-producing animals.[3]

While the GFLR's definition of food law is widely cast, the rules, risk regulation procedures, and institutions created by it are dedicated to food safety.

Although at the time of writing existing EU food law is largely food safety oriented, a 'sustainability turn' is imminent. The Commission Communication on the Farm to Fork Strategy (2020), as part of the Green Deal of (2019), heralds change by expressing a new concern for 'better food' in terms of fairness, the environment, and health. The extent to which these ambitions will be translated into food law and whether and how the sustainability changes can be integrated in the current food safety architecture remains to be seen.

1.2 The EU Treaties: the political foundations of European integration

The legal foundations of the EU originated in the aftermath of World War II, which—one has to remember—was radically different from the contemporary context. After the war, food shortages and a concern for food security characterized

[3] Regulation (EC) 178/2002 of the European Parliament and of the Council of 28 January 2002 laying down the general principles and requirements of food law, establishing the European Food Safety Authority and laying down procedures in matters of food safety [2002] OJ L31/1 (General Food Law Regulation (GFLR)), art 3(1).

the societal and political climate.[4] Citizens would remember hunger, and farmers the devastating effect of the war on their fields, manpower, production, and income. Fear of war, and a wish for peace, stability, and prosperity were motivating the initial efforts of European integration.

It was in this light that the famous Schuman Declaration of 9 May 1950 advocated for a functional pooling of German and French coal and steel resources to ensure peace. The Schuman Declaration ultimately resulted in the creation of the European Coal and Steel Community (ECSC) in 1951, which is regarded as the first legal predecessor of the EU.

Following the creation of the ECSC, further steps for integration were contested—should integration be pursued on a sectoral basis, or should the European markets be integrated generally? Mansholt, at the time Dutch Minister for Agriculture, in 1952 advocated for sectoral integration by building on the functional approach initiated in the areas of coal and steel and extending it to agriculture.[5] This was at a time when on average 40% of citizens' living expenses were spent on food.[6] His proposal followed up on two governmental initiatives in this line—the Dutch had tabled a proposal in 1950 supporting integration of all agriculture sectors, while the French had proposed a more limited integration of four sectors—wheat, wine, sugar, and dairy—in the Pflimlin Plan of 1951.[7] Ultimately, more ambitious initiatives of general integration were successful—these aspirations were voiced in the highly influential Brussels Report on the General Common Market (more commonly known as the 'Spaak Report' of 1956).[8] The Spaak Report abandoned the idea of sectoral integration, and instead advocated for horizontal integration through the creation of a general Common Market without customs duties or import quotas. It argued that the 'fusion of separate markets is an absolute necessity'.[9] As a result of the Spaak Report, in 1957, the 'Treaties of Rome' (the European Atomic Energy Community (EURATOM) and the Treaty establishing the European Economic Communities (EEC Treaty)) complemented the ECSC. The EEC Treaty was dedicated to the creation of a common market and the gradual alignment of economic policies.[10] Among other goals, this encompassed the elimination of customs duties, quantitative restrictions, and of all other measures having equivalent effect;[11] the implementation of a Common

[4] Paul Brassley, Yves Seger, and Leen Van Molle, *War, Agriculture, and Food: Rural Europe from the 1930s to the 1950s* (Routledge 2012).

[5] Sicco Mansholt, 'Toward European Integration: Beginnings in Agriculture' (1952) 31 Foreign Affairs 106.

[6] ibid.

[7] ibid.

[8] Intergovernmental Committee on European Integration, 'Report of the Heads of Delegation to the Ministers of Foreign Affairs, 'Spaak Report' SG/A (1956) 4 (Spaak Report).

[9] ibid 13.

[10] EEC Treaty, art 2.

[11] ibid, art 3a.

Agricultural Policy;[12] and legal harmonization necessary for the creation of the Common Market.

The EEC made steps towards a gradual liberalization of the market, and prohibited quantitative restrictions and all measures of equivalent effect.[13] It also sets out to create the Common Organization of the Agricultural Market.[14] Agricultural production was defined as primary produce and direct products thereof in their first processing step (*Verarabeitungsstufe*).[15] For the gradual creation of the Common Market, the EEC instituted a transitional scheme consisting of three stages.[16] At the conclusion of each stage, the Commission issued a report, and the Council held a vote confirming the successful completion of the respective stage. The first phase was up to 1962, the second phase lasted until 1964, leading—finally—to the completion of the Common Market in 1968. The creation of the Common Market was hailed as the 'greatest achievement of the European Economic Community during the first twenty years of its existence'.[17]

The first major[18] Treaty reform after the Rome Treaties was the Single European Act (SEA) in 1986.[19] It marks another milestone in the history of European integration. The SEA launched the objective of creating an internal market, described as an 'area without internal frontiers in which the free movement of goods, persons, services and capital is ensured'.[20] The SEA mandated the Community to adopt measures which would progressively realize the internal market by 31 December 1992. The Internal Market was formally launched on 1 January 1993.

The EU as we know it today was formally established by the Maastricht Treaty (1992),[21] which incorporated the EEC, and renamed it the Economic Community (EC). The EC reiterated and expanded the goal of creating an internal market, covering all factors of mobility, including goods: 'an internal market characterised by the abolition, as between Member States, of obstacles to the free movement of goods, persons, services and capital'.[22] The goals relating to the elimination of customs duties and quantitative restrictions, and those relating to agricultural policy remained the same.

[12] ibid, art 3d.

[13] ibid, art 30.

[14] ibid, art 40(2).

[15] ibid, art 38(1).

[16] ibid, art 8.

[17] Stefan Riesenfeld, 'Building the Common Market—And Beyond' (1978) 19 Virginia Journal of International Law 1, 16.

[18] The institutional design was reformed in the Treaty of Brussels Establishing a Single Council and a Single Commission of the European Communities [1965] OJ L152/2 (Merger Treaty), which unified the ECSC, the EEC, and the EURATOM.

[19] Single European Act [1987] OJ L169/1 (SEA).

[20] Wording of the novel art 8a, to supplement the EEC Treaty, see SEA, art 13.

[21] Treaty of the European Union [1992] OJ C191/1 (Treaty of the EC).

[22] Treaty of the EC, art 3(c).

The EU's attempt, in 2004, to take European integration a step further and create a formal Constitution for Europe[23] failed. Treaty changes require unanimous agreement of all Member States, with some national laws mandating ratification by parliament or through a national referendum. The proposed Treaty was rejected in national referenda in France and the Netherlands in 2005. Ultimately, the Constitution was recast into the Lisbon Treaty (2007). The Lisbon Treaty consolidated the EU under a treaty framework comprising the Treaty on European Union (TEU) and the Treaty on the Functioning of the European Union (TFEU). The EU acquired legal personality, and replaced the EC. Furthermore, the Lisbon Treaty was complemented by the EU Charter of Fundamental Rights (CFR) and other Protocols.[24] With the inclusion of fundamental rights as a binding legal document, the Treaty structure of the EU exhibits all the elements of a constitution. However, the Charter neither enshrines a 'right to food' nor directly correlated rights,[25] which means that for food law its relevance is collateral—the 'right to food' is international or national law based, but it is not explicitly incorporated into the EU Treaty framework.

The Lisbon Treaty reform was the last change to the EU Treaty structure. The consensus for stronger European integration and greater European unity, had eroded significantly, marked by the United Kingdom leaving the EU in 2020. The appetite for further treaty changes was then at a historical low, widely regarded as a project too politically risky to attempt. Geopolitical pressures on the EU have brought a Treaty change back onto the agenda; such a reform agenda might be confined to the external relations and internal rule of law elements. However, it might also extend to increasing EU competence in health and enshrining sustainability as an integrative policy goal similar to current environmental ambitions. Consequently, the Treaties constitute a structural legal constraint that imposes firm limits on the possible spheres of action available to the EU, for instance through the competences that are attributed to it.

1.3 Political paradigms shaping EU legislative harmonization in the area of food

Historically, European legal integration began with a strong focus on the agricultural sector and the creation of the Common Market in parallel. To realize these aspirations as outlined in the founding treaties, legislative harmonization was needed to build the necessary legal superstructure.

[23] European Council, Treaty establishing a Constitution for Europe [2004] OJ C310/1, which was adopted by the European Council but not ratified.

[24] Consolidated Versions of the Treaty of the European Union and the Treaty on the Functioning of the European Union [2016] OJ C202/1 (Lisbon Treaty).

[25] Such as 'a freedom from want', 'freedom from hunger', or even 'a right to an adequate living'.

In the history of European integration, four political paradigms that have had the most influence on EU food legislation over time can be identified: (1) agriculture, (2) the creation of the Common Market that later evolved into the completion of the Internal Market (1985), (3) food safety (2000) and (4) transparency, and recently (5) sustainability as a transversal political objective of the EU generally (2019) and EU food policy specifically (2020).

1.3.1 Agricultural origins: the organization of common markets for agricultural products

While the EEC enshrined the idea of horizontal integration, European integration and its Treaties remained characterized by strong sectoral elements. This is especially true in the *sui generis*[26] and exceptional[27] nature of the agricultural sector and the Common Agricultural Policy (CAP) as a joint policy area[28] (alongside the common trade and transport policies). The CAP set out to create the Common Organization of the Agricultural Market, thereby shaping the structure of the agricultural market according to European regulations. In legal terms, agriculture was conceived as part of the Common Market, as explained in Article 38(1) EEC, the rules of which would apply, unless specifically diverted from in the agriculture provisions. As such, agriculture was a distinct subset of the Common Market, with specific sectoral rules.

Rather than choosing to develop the Common Organization of the Agricultural Market gradually, the EEC opted for the immediate adoption of basic regulations establishing common organization for various agricultural sectors and products, while also laying down its principles. These Common Market Organizations (CMOs) were regulations that directly established operative institutional arrangements and provisions. Essentially, CMOs manage production and trade, but also, incidentally, quality and information related aspects on specific products. The full application of some provisions was postponed until the end of the transitional period laid down by the EEC Treaty, and institutional arrangements ensured further progressive implementation.[29] Most of the 'mandated progressive establishment of the common market' was achieved through Council Regulations.[30] The Council Regulations of 1962 led to the 'gradual establishment' of the CMOs. This included

[26] Kai P Purnhagen, 'The Increasing Overlap of Agricultural, Free Movement and Competition Law in the EU' (2021) 46 European Law Review 20.

[27] Carsten Daugbjerg and Peter H Feindt, 'Post-Exceptionalism in Public Policy: Transforming Food and Agricultural Policy' (2017) 24 Journal of European Public Policy 1565.

[28] EEC Treaty, arts 38–47.

[29] Giancarlo Olmi, 'The Agricultural Policy of the Community' (1963) 1 Common Market Law Review 118.

[30] Riesenfeld (n 17) 3.

Regulations Nos 19 to 24[31] relating to the gradual establishment of a CMO in cereals, pigmeat, eggs, poultrymeat, fruit and vegetables, and wine. These product-based CMOs have now been consolidated into a single CMO Regulation for agricultural products and another for fishery and aquaculture.

In subsequent treaty amendments, the wording of the agricultural provisions in the Treaties have remained largely unchanged, although the TFEU established agriculture as a shared, and not partially exclusive, competence.[32]

1.3.1.1 ***Inclusion of common marketing standards in the CMO Regulations***

In addition to rules regarding the market structure, the CMO Regulations contain marketing standards that set minimum quality, sizing, and packaging requirements for agricultural products. This is established through the implementation of mandatory technical product standards and reserved terms that define the quality of products. These quality standards represent a crucial element of EU food law in a narrow sense, as they pertain directly to food products, rather than the organization of the market.

EU legislation on marketing standards aimed to replace 'heterogeneous national standards',[33] thereby contributing to a level playing field for producers across the EU. Regulated product characteristics relate to quality (requirements, classification of classes), sizing (weight, uniformity), freshness, acceptable tolerances, presentation, labelling, and packaging, or specific terms. For example, in 1962, Council Regulation No 23 postulated the progressive establishment of a common organization of the market in fruit and vegetables.[34] It stipulated, for instance, that apricots must be clean, especially of all traces of chemicals, and to be graded as 'Extra' class, no defects are allowed; class II apricots could have defects not exceeding 2cm in elongated shape. Open-air lettuce had to weigh at least 15kg per 100 units, and tomatoes had to specify their district of origin or trade name on

[31] Règlement n° 19 portant établissement graduel d'une organisation commune des marchés dans le secteur des céréales [1962] OJ 30/933; Règlement n° 20 portant établissement graduel d'une organisation commune des marchés dans le secteur de la viande de porc [1962] OJ 30/945; Règlement n° 21 portant établissement graduel d'une organisation commune des marchés dans le secteur des oeufs [1962] OJ 30/953; Règlement n° 22 portant établissement graduel d'une organisation commune des marchés dans le secteur de la viande de volaille [1962] OJ 30/959; EEC Regulation No 23; EEC Council: Regulation No 24 on the progressive establishment of a common organisation of the market in wine [1962] OJ 30/989.

[32] François Nègre, 'Fact Sheets on the European Union—The Common Agriculture Policy (CAP) and the Treaty' (April 2022) <https://www.europarl.europa.eu/factsheets/en/sheet/103/the-common-agricultural-policy-cap-and-the-treaty> accessed 25 July 2022: 'contrary to established legal opinion and the stance adopted by the Commission's legal services [SEC(92) 1990, 27.10.1992] which have hitherto regarded policy on markets (first pillar of the CAP) as an exclusive EU competence'.

[33] Commission, 'Revision of Commission Implementing and Delegated Regulations on EU marketing standards for agricultural products under the Common Organisation of the Market to ensure the uptake and supply of sustainable products, and modernise, simplify, and align them, as well as a proposal to revise the "Breakfast Directives" for the same purposes' (Inception Impact Assessment) Ares (2021) 427166.

[34] EEC Regulation No 23.

the packaging. The 1994 Bananas Regulation stipulated that bananas must have a minimum permitted length of 14cm.[35] Other marketing standard requirements cover the use of specific terms, such as 'free range' for eggs.[36] Common marketing standards therefore create unified EU product standards that combine a number of goals, ranging from food quality to food safety, aesthetics, logistics and packaging, consumer protection, and standardization to create homogenous characteristics.

Marketing standards received a lot of 'negative publicity' (such as the required curvature of cucumbers). The Commission therefore vowed to retain only health and safety requirements,[37] gradually diminishing the significance of marketing standards' by reducing the number of product-specific marketing standards drastically, from 36 to just 11 products currently. However, for these foodstuffs, marketing standards remain highly relevant. Furthermore, under the current Farm to Fork Strategy process, there are discussions about reviving marketing standards for sustainability purposes.

1.3.1.2 ***Contemporary Common Agricultural Policy remains a separate policy track***

From the initial post-war need to secure food security and production, Europe reached a point of overproduction that was addressed in CAP legislation in 1984. In 1992, the CAP first shifted from market support towards producer support, and later in 2003 towards income support, increasingly taking account of sustainability objectives. A major reform in 2013 restructured the CAP. It consolidated the CMO Regulations, so that to date there is only the single Regulation 1308/2013 on the Common Market Organization of agricultural products, complemented by Regulation 1379/2013 on the Common Organization of the markets in fishery and aquaculture products. The newest CAP was agreed at the end of 2021 and created a novel legal framework entirely.[38] The new CAP renationalizes agricultural policy to a significant extent and foresees implementation in all EU countries through national strategic plans that apply from 1 January 2023. In the area of food, this means that CAP policies remain politically and legally a separate policy track, although agricultural competences are sometimes used as a supportive legal base for food regulatory instruments (see Chapter 2).

[35] Commission Regulation (EC) 2257/94 of 16 September 1994 laying down quality standards for bananas [1994] OJ L245/6 (Bananas Regulation).

[36] Commission Regulation (EC) 589/2008 of 23 June 2008 laying down detailed rules for implementing Council Regulation (EC) 1234/2007 as regards marketing standards for eggs [2007] OJ L163/6. 'Free-range eggs' must be produced in systems of production which satisfy at least the conditions specified in Council Directive 1999/74/EC of 19 July 1999 laying down minimal standards for the protection of laying hens [1999] OJ L203/53, art 4.

[37] Katrin Milzow, 'The EU's Marketing Standards for Fruit and Vegetables: The End of a Myth?' (2009) 9 Current Affairs in Perspective 1.

[38] Regulation (EU) 2021/2115 of the European Parliament and of the Council of 2 December 2021 establishing rules on support for strategic plans to be drawn up by Member States under the common agricultural policy (CAP Strategic Plans) [2021] OJ L 435/1.

1.3.2 Dedication to the completion of the internal market—food emerges as a distinct sector

At the outset of European integration, in parallel to the developments of the CAP, efforts for the gradual establishment of the Common Market proceeded (not to be confused with the establishment of the Common Market Organizations under the agricultural policy). Article 8 EEC Treaty mandated the gradual establishment of a common market over a period of 12 years. In 1970, the Common Market was formally completed. Where necessary for the establishment of the Common Market, Article 100 EEC Treaty allowed for the harmonization of national measures at the European level. While Article 43 EEC Treaty allowed voting by a qualified majority for veterinary and phytosanitary measures in agriculture, legislative harmonization for the Common Market was more difficult. This was because, for harmonization purposes, the Council, acting under Article 100 EEC Treaty, required unanimity. For some time during the course of European integration, the harmonization process stalled, and Article 43 EEC Treaty became a 'standard legislative tool (. . .) to adopt rules in areas of food law' in the 1970s and part of the 1980s.[39]

Therefore, legislative food product harmonization initially remained rare: in 1962, the Council passed the first piece of harmonizing legislation related to food within the Community. Diverse national rules on colouring matter were regarded as an obstacle to the free movement of foodstuffs and were harmonized by the Directive on colouring matter[40] (still in force!)—the Directive was based on Article 100 EEC Treaty, as was legislation on preservatives[41] (1964), and antioxidants[42] (1970). Other measures, such as the Directive on fresh meat (1963), were adopted on the basis of agriculture and Common Market harmonization.[43]

In the decades following the completion of the Common Market in 1970, food law developed from two perspectives: first, positive (legislative) harmonization, involving the setting of European harmonized law and, second, negative harmonization through the Court that resulted in the abolishment of national rules that were regarded as obstacles to the free movement of goods.

39 Ferdinando Albisinni, 'The Path to the European and Global Food Law System' in Luigi Costato and Ferdinando Albisinni (eds), *European and Global Food Law* (2nd edn, Wolters Kluwer 2016).

40 Terlicka and Jukes (n 2).

41 Council Directive 64/54/EEC of 5 November 1963 on the approximation of the laws of the Member States concerning the preservatives authorized for use in foodstuffs intended for human consumption [1964] OJ 12/161.

42 Council Directive 70/357/EEC of 13 July 1970 on the approximation of the laws of the Member States concerning the antioxidants authorized for use in foodstuffs intended for human consumption [1970] OJ L157/31.

43 EEC Treaty, arts 43 and 100.

1.3.2.1 From vertical product-based harmonization towards horizontal harmonization

Following the completion of the Common Market, for a short period of time, legislation was inspired by the marketing standards for agricultural products—resulting in the vertical harmonization of products through detailed compositional requirements. This harmonization was based on both agriculture and internal market harmonization measures,[44] and deployed directives as legal instruments. From the late 1970s to the early 1980s, product-specific directives were adopted that are still in force today: the so-called 'Breakfast Directives'. The 'Breakfast Directives' cover rules on the description, definition, characteristics, and labelling of coffee and chicory extracts;[45] cocoa and chocolate products;[46] sugars intended for human consumption;[47] fruit jams, jellies, marmalades, and sweetened chestnut purée intended for human consumption;[48] dehydrated milk;[49] fruit juices;[50] honey;[51] and mineral water.[52] For example, the Marmalade Directive[53] regulates different types of fruit-based spreads and stipulates, for instance, that jam must have a minimum pulp quantity, eg 350g of 1000g as a general rule, but 150g for ginger, and only 60g for passion fruit.

[44] ibid.

[45] Council Directive 77/436/EEC of 27 June 1977 on the approximation of the laws of the Member States relating to coffee extracts and chicory extracts [1977] OJ L172/20.

[46] Council Directive 73/241/EEC of 24 July 1973 on the approximation of the laws of the Member States relating to cocoa and chocolate products intended for human consumption [1973] OJ L/23, now Directive 2000/36/EC of the European Parliament and of the Council of 23 June 2000 relating to cocoa and chocolate products intended for human consumption [2000] OJ L197/19.

[47] Council Directive 73/437/EEC of 11 December 1973 on the approximation of the laws of the Member States concerning certain sugars intended for human consumption [1973] OJ L356/71, now Council Directive 2001/111/EC of 20 December 2001 relating to certain sugars intended for human consumption [2002] OJ L10/53.

[48] Council Directive 79/693/EEC of 24 July 1979 on the approximation of the laws of the Member States relating to fruit jams, jellies and marmalades and chestnut purée [1979] OJ L205/5, now Council Directive 2001/113/EC of 20 December 2001 relating to fruit jams, jellies and marmalades and sweetened chestnut purée intended for human consumption [2002] OJ L10/67.

[49] Council Directive 76/118/EEC of 18 December 1975 on the approximation of the laws of the Member States relating to certain partly or wholly dehydrated preserved milk for human consumption [1976] OJ L24/49, now Council Directive 2001/114/EC of 20 December 2001 relating to certain partly or wholly dehydrated preserved milk for human consumption [2002] OJ L15/19.

[50] Council Directive 93/77/EEC of 21 September 1993 relating to fruit juices and certain similar products [1993] OJ L244/23, now Council Directive 2001/112/EC of 20 December 2001 relating to fruit juices and certain similar products intended for human consumption [2002] OJ L10/58.

[51] Council Directive 74/409/EEC of 22 July 1974 on the harmonization of the laws of the Member States relating to honey [1974] OJ L221/10, now Council Directive 2001/110/EC of 20 December 2001 relating to honey [2002] OJ L10/47.

[52] Council Directive 80/777/EEC of 15 July 1980 on the approximation of the laws of the Member States relating to the exploitation and marketing of natural mineral waters [1980] OJ L229/1, now Directive 2009/54/EC of the European Parliament and of the Council of 18 June 2009 on the exploitation and marketing of natural mineral waters (Recast) [2009] OJ L164/45.

[53] Originally Council Directive 79/693/EEC of 24 July 1979 on the approximation of the laws of the Member States relating to fruit jams, jellies and marmalades and chestnut purée [1979] OJ L205/5, now replaced by the Council Directive 2001/113/EC of 20 December 2001 relating to fruit jams, jellies and marmalades and sweetened chestnut purée intended for human consumption [2001] OJ L10/67 (Marmalade Directive).

This initial 'cookbook/recipe mentality' to trade between Member States was based on the idea that if all products had to comply with one standard, they could circulate freely in the market. However, there are clear drawbacks to making specific legislation for each product category—the sheer amount of laws necessary to regulate all food products individually is daunting, the level of detail of the regulation would be excessive, and resulting products would be homogenous and lack diversity. The vertical approach was therefore largely abandoned, making room for horizontal—not product based—harmonization. However, the 'Breakfast Directives' are still in existence, despite having undergone a reform aimed at simplification.[54]

The gradual shift to a horizontal approach at the end of the 1970s/early 1980s signified a move towards legislation that would govern common aspects of as many different products as possible. Examples of the original horizontal EU laws include labelling,[55] quick-frozen foodstuffs,[56] and food intended for particular nutritional uses.[57] These were all directives, which at the time served as the main legal instrument for approximating laws. Over time, the horizontal measures were modernized, and after 2000 the recast legal instruments were mainly passed as regulations.

1.3.2.2 ***The role of the CJEU: negative harmonization and mutual recognition***

Legislative harmonization is also referred to as positive harmonization because the legal instruments establish positive requirements and obligations. In parallel to the legislative efforts, the Treaty articles on the free movement of goods stipulate important prohibitions that govern food trade, notably the prohibition of quantitative restrictions and any measure of equivalent effect (see also Chapter 4). In testing whether national laws comply with these Treaty provisions, the European Court of Justice (ECJ) has assumed an important role in the European integration process. By invalidating national laws that violate the free movement of goods provision, Court judgments have served as a catalyst for indirect negative harmonization. However, the ECJ went beyond a pure negative integration approach. In *Cassis de Dijon*[58] (1979), it developed the (conditional) Mutual Recognition Approach, which held that all products lawfully marketed in one Member State should—subject to certain limitations—be marketable in all other Member States. Mutual recognition, then, acts as an alternative to positive harmonization. *Cassis*

[54] Bernd van der Meulen and Bart Wernaart (eds), *EU Food Law Handbook* (Wageningen Academic Publishers 2020).

[55] Council Directive 79/112/EEC of 18 December 1978 on the approximation of the laws of the Member States relating to the labelling, presentation and advertising of foodstuffs for sale to the ultimate consumer [1978] OJ L33/1.

[56] Council Directive 89/108/EEC of 21 December 1988 on the approximation of the laws of the Member States relating to quick-frozen foodstuffs for human consumption [1988] OJ L40/34.

[57] Council Directive 77/94/EEC of 21 December 1976 on the approximation of the laws of the Member States relating to foodstuffs for particular nutritional uses [1976] OJ L26/55.

[58] Case C-120/78 *Rewe-Zentral AG v Bundesmonopolverwaltung für Branntwein* [1979] ECR 649 (Cassis de Dijon).

de Dijon was seen as an opportunity to push the integration agenda forward. The mood at the time is captured by one writer who noted, 'by the early 1970s deadlines had been missed and the harmonisation programme was held in disrepute. Under the circumstances, the Cassis de Dijon judgment came as a welcome relief.'[59]

1.3.2.3 ***The White Paper on the completion of the internal market (1985)***

Against the backdrop of the economic slouch of the 1980s, the political pressure to vitalize the Common Market grew. In response, the European Commission published the *White Paper on the Completion of the Internal Market* (1985) ('Internal Market White Paper'), which announced the Commission's ambitious goal of creating a fully united internal market by the end of 1992, and its intention to achieve 'the welding together of the (...) individual markets of the Member States into one single market'.[60] To this end, the White Paper proposed the removal of physical, technical, and fiscal barriers, coupled with a timeline of legislative actions.

On technical barriers, the Commission underlined the importance and the need for a new strategy for the free movement of goods, in particular barriers created by different national product regulations and standards. The White Paper recognized the tension between, on one hand, a market freed by full mutual recognition, and on the other hand, total harmonization, which could be seen as over-regulatory. While the harmonization approach marked the Community's first 25 years, the White Paper argued that the goals of the EEC should not be limited to merely removing technical barriers to trade but should also contribute to industrial efficiency and competitiveness. Therefore, the White Paper called for more efficient harmonization, through the so-called 'New Approach': it proposed that only 'essential' elements should be harmonized, while the remainder should be left to mutual recognition. Legislative harmonization (based on Article 100 of EEC Treaty) would 'in future be restricted to laying down essential health and safety requirements that will be obligatory'. In addition, the White Paper proposed the principle of delegating more law-making powers to the Commission. The Commission, advised by the Scientific Committee for Food, would be responsible for drafting and managing the more detailed and technical aspects of these directives, leaving the Council free to concentrate on the essential safety and health criteria that must be upheld.[61] The New Approach called for an 'essentials-only harmonisation' approach, complemented by a new emphasis on 'executive legislation' by the European Commission.

Foodstuff was singled out as one of the sectors with particular potential for the New Approach.[62] The White Paper noted that efforts to legislate through horizontal

[59] Alan Swinbank, 'Completion of the EC's Internal Market, Mutual Recognition, and the Food Industries' (1993) 9 Agribusiness 509.
[60] Internal Market White Paper, para 10.
[61] ibid, para 65.
[62] ibid, para 71.

directives (such as food additives and labelling) would be continued. Overall, it criticized that 'incorporating detailed technical specifications in Directives has given rise to long delays because of the unanimity required'.[63] Even on technical matters, such as including new substances in the Annex on the Directive on colouring matter (see Table 1.1),[64] it would be the Council's responsibility to amend the law through a unanimous vote. In general, it therefore recommended that the Council 'should off-load technical matters by making more use of its powers of delegation', a general policy which was to be put in practice in the foodstuff sector.[65] Lastly, the White Paper affirmed the mutual recognition principle of the ECJ case law. It also noted that, to *prevent* new obstacles, the notification obligation for new technical regulations of Member States under Directive 83/189/EEC[66] should be extended to the food sector, obliging Member States to notify the Commission in advance of draft technical regulations. The White Paper thereby substantiated an *ex-ante* legality control of national Member State law.

To achieve the removal of technical barriers in Food Law, the Commission proposed a legislative timetable that covered 26 measures to be passed in two phases (1985–1986 and 1987–1992), including a number of general directives.

The main legal instruments proposed in the Internal Market White Paper (1985) are directives. In the area of food, the Commission additionally proposed a number of 'framework directives' or general directives, which would serve as a legal basis for future, more detailed provisions, for example those concerning food hygiene, food additives, foodstuffs for particular nutritional uses, and labelling.[67]

The Internal Market White Paper marks the initial crystallization of EU food law as a distinct legislative arena within the EU, evidenced by the fact that it dedicated a chapter to food law with legislative proposals for the removal of technical barriers, and discussed sector-specific implications of the New Approach to harmonization separately for the food sector.

1.3.3 Food sector-specific risk regulation architecture: the food safety paradigm

The 1990s witnessed several food scandals, such as the BSE crisis, which triggered a significant negative public response due to perceived failures in ensuring food safety across the EU. The concerns for food safety resulted in the political momentum necessary to unify the field of food law as a specific and institutionally

[63] ibid, para 68.
[64] Terlicka and Jukes (n 2).
[65] Internal Market White Paper, para 70.
[66] Council Directive 83/189/EEC of 28 March 1983 laying down a procedure for the provision of information in the field of technical standards and regulations [1983] OJ L109/8.
[67] Terlicka and Jukes (n 2) 305.

Table 1.1 Food Safety White Paper, Annex—Point 2.3. Food Law, 16–17

PERIOD 1985–1986			
General Directive on food additives (in part modification of existing directives)		1985	1986
General Directive on materials and articles in contact with food (amendment)		1985	1986
General Directive on food for particular nutritional uses (amendment)		1985	1986
General Directive on food labelling (amendment)		1985	1986
General Directive on food inspection		1986	1987
General Directive sampling and methods of analysis	COM(84)39	1984	1985
General Directive on quick frozen food	COM(84)489	1984	1985
Management of existing vertical Directives (procedure)		1985	1986
Flavourings*	COM(80)286 COM(82)166	1980	1985
Extraction solvents*	COM(83)626 COM(85)79	1983	1986
Preservatives* (modification)	COM(81)712	1981	1985
Emulsifiers (modification)	COM(84)4	1984	1985
Infant formulae and follow-up milk (diabetic foods)*	COM(84)703	1984	1986
Cocoa and chocolate consolidation*	COM(83)787	1984	1986
Coffee extracts chicory extracts (modification)	COM(84)138	1984	1985
Obligation to indicate ingredients and alcoholic strength*	COM(82)626	1982	1985
Claims in the labelling of foodstuffs*	COM(81)159	1981	1985
Simulants (plastic materials in contact with foodstuffs)*	COM(84)152	1984	1985

Table 1.1 Continued

PERIOD 1985–1986			
Modified starches*	COM(84)733	1984	1986
Fruit juices etc ... (modification)		1985	1986
Jams etc (Modification)		1985	1986
Proposal for a Directive amending Directive 79/581/ EEC on consumer protection in the indication of the prices of foodstuffs	COM(84)23	1984	1985
PERIOD 1987–1992			
General Directive on irradiation of foodstuffs		1987	1988
General Directive on new foodstuffs obtained by a biotechnological process		1987	1988
Additional labelling requirements (Nutrition labelling)		1989	1990
Adaptation of directives on technical progress		1987–1989	1988–1990

Source: Commission, 'White Paper on Food Safety' COM (1999) 719 final (Food Safety White Paper).

distinct area of EU law, culminating in the enactment of the General Food Law Regulation (2002).

The General Food Law Regulation (GFLR) established a comprehensive institutional framework for food (see Chapter 5), incorporating principles of food law, a general safety obligation, food safety procedures, and the establishment of the European Food Safety Authority (EFSA). In terms of policy, the GFLR is the direct product of the 'Food Safety White Paper' (2000).[68] However, two earlier policy initiatives also heavily influenced the design of the food safety system created: first, the 'Communication on Consumer Health and Food Safety'[69] committed to a separation of risk management and science and emphasized the need for excellent science as a basis for decision making. Second, the Commission published the 'Green

[68] Commission, 'White Paper on Food Safety' COM (1999) 719 final (Food Safety White Paper).
[69] Commission, 'Consumer Health and Food Safety' (Communication) COM (97) 183 final.

Paper on the General Principles of Food Law in the European Union'[70] ('from the stable to the table'). It criticized the 'complexity, fragmentation and incoherence'[71] of food laws, and suggested a central unifying text to set out the fundamental principles of Community food law and clearly define the obligations of relevant actors.[72] Interestingly, the Commission Green Paper initially proposed a general directive on food law,[73] instead of what we now know as the GFLR. In addition, it suggested establishing a 'new general obligation of safety and *wholesomeness*'. The reference to wholesomeness, however, was dropped and the focus shifted exclusively to safety in the food obligation.

At the political level, the Helsinki European Council, in December 1999, addressed public health and food safety and called for improving quality standards and reinforcing systems of checks throughout the food chain, from farm to consumers.[74] In the Food Safety White Paper (2000), the European Commission developed this mandate into an 'integrated approach' to bring 'coherence to the corpus of legislation covering all aspects of food products "from farm to table"'.[75] The Food Safety White Paper proposed the creation of a European Food Authority, which in the GLFR was limited to a European Food Safety Authority. The White Paper also proposed better food safety legislation and controls, and enshrines the right to food consumer information regarding food safety. Regarding the international dimensions, the White Paper interestingly proposed that food imports should have to comply with requirements at least equivalent to those set by the EU for its own production.

To implement the food safety policy, the Food Safety White Paper listed 84 legislative proposals in an exhaustive Action Plan (see Table 1.2). The Action Plan covered a total of 19 topical chapters,[76] and—for a majority—the legal actions were to be proposed by the Commission within the very same year.

Only two years after the publication of the policy document, the GFLR was adopted in 2002 and marked the formal creation of 'EU food law'.[77] The GFLR

[70] Commission, 'The General Principles of Food Law in the European Union' COM (97) 176 final (Green Paper on the General Principles of Food Law in the European Union).

[71] ibid, 12.

[72] ibid, 1.

[73] ibid, 3.

[74] European Parliament, 'Helsinki European Council 10 and 11 December 1999 Presidency Conclusions' <https://www.europarl.europa.eu/summits/hel1_en.htm#:~:text=The%20European%20Council%20met%20in,stage%20in%20the%20enlargement%20process> accessed 9 September 2022.

[75] White Paper on Food Safety, 3.

[76] The chapters covered priority measures, feedstuffs, zoonoses, animal health, animal-by-products, BSE/TSE, hygiene, contaminants, food additives and flavourings, materials in contact with food, novel foods/genetically modified organisms, irradiation of food, dietetic foods/food supplements/fortified foods, labelling of food, pesticides, nutrition, seeds, supporting measures, and third country policy/international relations.

[77] The GFLR defines 'food law' for the first time, as 'the laws, regulations and administrative provisions governing food in general, and food safety in particular, whether at Community or national level; it covers any stage of production, processing and distribution of food, and also of feed produced for, or fed to, food-producing animals'.

Table 1.2 Food Safety White Paper, Annex—Action Plan on Food Safety, Chapter 1 Priority measures

No	Action	Objective	REF.IN WP	Adoption by Commission	Adoption by Council/ Parliament
1.	Proposal for setting up a European Food Authority	To set up an independent European Food Authority.	29	September 2000	December 2001
2.	Proposal for laying down procedures in matters of food safety	To introduce a comprehensive safeguard measure covering the whole food chain, including feed. To establish a comprehensive Rapid Alert System covering all feed and food emergencies with harmonised requirements and procedures, including third countries on the basis of reciprocity.	80 18	September 2000	December 2001
3.	Proposal for a General Food Law Directive	To establish food safety as the primary objective of EU food law. To lay down the common principles underlying food legislation (in particular; scientific basis, responsibility of producers and suppliers, trackability along the food chain, efficient controls and effective enforcement)	67	September 2000	December 2001
4.	Proposal for a Regulation on official food and feed safety controls.	To establish a Community framework for official controls on all food and feed safety aspects along the feed and food chain by: - merging and completing existing rules for national controls and Community controls and inspections within the EU, at the borders and in third countries. - integrating existing monitoring and surveillance system so as to establish a comprehensive and effective food safety monitoring and surveillance system from farm to table. - establishing a framework for organising consolidated annual programs for controls of foodstuffs. - merging existing Community rules on mutual assistance and administrative co-operation. - creating a Community approach towards a financial support for official controls.	Ch.6	December 2000	December 2001

(continued)

Table 1.2 Continued

No	Action	Objective	REF.IN WP	Adoption by Commission	Adoption by Council/ Parliament
5.	Proposal for a Regulation on feed	To establish animal and public health as the primary objective of EU feed legislation. To lay down common principles underlying feed legislation (in particular: scientific basis, responsibility of producers and suppliers, systematic implementation of hazard analysis and critical control points (HACCP), traceability, efficient controls and enforcement). To recast all existing measures on feedingstuffs so as to create a comprehensive legislative tool increasing transparency, consistency and legal security.	69	December 2001	December 2002
6.	Proposal for a Regulation on novel feed	To put into a plan a centralised system for the authorisation of use in animal nutrition of non conventional products, in particular of GMOs and GMO derived feedstuffs.	69	September 2000	December 2001
7.	Amendment to the Annex of Directive 96/25/EC on the Circulation of feed materials.	To amend the definitions of feed materials listed in the Annex to Decision 96/25/EC, particularly with regard to oils and fats and animal products.	69	September 2000	
8.	Proposal for a Regulation on hygiene	To recast horizontal and vertical Directives on hygiene of food of plant and animal origin. To clarify responsibility of food operators and to introduce the systematic implementation of HACCP. To apply hygiene rules at all levels of the food chain, including primary production.	72	June 2000	June 2000

9.	Amendment of Decision 98/272/EC on epidemic-surveillance of transmissible spongiform encephalopathies (TSEs)	To reinforce TSE surveillance including a study on mandatory testing (rapid post-mortem test) on targeted groups of cattle. To reinforce TSE surveillance in small ruminants.	71	March 2000 September 2000	--
10.	Decision on the Member State and third country residue programmes.	To ensure efficacy of residue testing in Member States and third countries.	74	December 2000	
11.	Proposal for amending Directive 89/107/EEC on food additives.	To Confer implementing powers for maintaining the list of permitted food additives and to lay down specific provisions in respect of enzymes.	77	December 2000	December 2001
12.	Proposal for amending Directive 95/2/EC on food additives other than colours and sweeteners.	To update and revise the list of food additives other than colours and sweeteners.	77	December 2000	December 2001
13.	Proposal for amending Directive 88/388/EEC on flavourings for use in foodstuffs.	To clarify the scope and update definitions, to set maximum limits for toxic substances and to confer implementing powers to the Commission.	77	December 2000	December 2001
14.	Proposal for amending Regulation 258/97 on novel foods and novel food ingredients.	To make the necessary adaptations in the light of the conclusions of the report on the implementation of the Regulation and in accordance with the new regulatory framework of Directive 90/220/EEC	76	December 2001	December 2002
15.	Regulation on the labelling of GMO-free foodstuffs.	To give operators the possibility to use labelling claims referring to the absence of use of genetic engineering techniques for the production of foodstuffs.	76103	September 2000	

(*continued*)

Table 1.2 Continued

No	Action	Objective	REF.IN WP	Adoption by Commission	Adoption by Council/ Parliament
16.	Proposal for amending Directive 79/112/ EEC on the labelling, presentation and advertising of foodstuffs.	To remove the possibility not to indicate the components of Compound ingredients forming less than 25% of the final product and lay down a list allergenic substances.	100	December 2000	December 2001=
17.	Proposals for Commission Directives to fix maximum residue levels (MRLs) of pesticides in food and agricultural commodities.	To fix MRLs for pesticides residues for, inter alia: 36 pesticides with existing open positions in the residues directives that will automatically go to zero in July 2000 unless the Commission adopts other values. To set MRLs at zero for 8 pesticides that we excluded from Annex I to Directive 91/414/EEC To set MRLs for new active substances included in Annex I to Directive 91/414/EEC	74	June 2000 September 2000 Continuous process	
18.	Communication on an action plan on nutrition policy.	To develop a comprehensive and coherent nutrition policy.	106	December 2000	

Source: Commission, 'White Paper on Food Safety' COM (1999) 719 final (Food Safety White Paper).

was conceived as an umbrella legislation applicable to all aspects of food law, including transversal principles. The risk regulation architecture that was thus devised was largely devoted to food safety: it proposed rules and a general obligation for food to be safe, complemented by procedures and institutions dedicated to ensuring food safety. These notably included the creation of the EFSA, as well as emergency, rapid response, and crisis reaction mechanisms. In this institutional design, the European Commission made several explicit choices: the EFSA would not become a regulatory agency, but would solely provide scientific advice with no risk management responsibilities or regulatory authority. The Commission, on the other hand, would have to retain power over regulation, enforcement, and control. Lastly, the food safety package took an integrated and inclusive approach to responsibility, attributing responsibility for food law compliance to all links in the food supply chain (see Chapter 5).

While still based on the competence norm to establish the internal market,[78] the adoption of the all-embracing GFLR can be understood as a significant emancipation of the food sector from mainstream free movement of goods governance. In 2003, the Commission adopted the Communication *Enhancing the implementation of the New Approach Directives.*[79] This new legislative framework approach excludes food products.[80] Similarly, the Rapid Alert System for Food and Feed (RASFF) pre-empts the Rapid Alert System for non-food products posing a serious risk (RAPEX)[81] to apply to foodstuffs; more widely, the General Product Safety Directive (GPSD)[82] excludes food and pharmaceuticals, for which there is sector specific legislation.

All legislative actions proposed in the Food Safety White Paper were implemented, so that for some time, it was regarded as completed. In this vein, the European Commission limited itself to improving the existing legal framework in the subsequent two decades.

[78] Consolidated Version of the Treaty on the Functioning of the European Union [2012] OJ C326/47 (TFEU), art 114, together with other competence norms.

[79] Commission, 'Communication from the Commission to the Council and the European Parliament on Enhancing the Implementation of the New Approach Directives' (Communication) COM (2003) 240 final.

[80] Regulation (EC) No 765/2008 of the European Parliament and of the Council of 9 July 2008 setting out the requirements for accreditation and market surveillance relating to the marketing of products and repealing Regulation (EEC) No 339/93 [2008] OJ L218/30, art 15(4): 'For the purposes of Articles 16 to 26, a "product" shall mean a substance, preparation or good produced through a manufacturing process other than food, feed, living plants and animals, products of human origin and products of plants and animals relating directly to their future reproduction.'

[81] Commission, 'Safety Gate: The EU Rapid Alert System for Dangerous Non-Food Products' <https://ec.europa.eu/safety-gate-alerts/screen/webReport#weeklyReports> accessed 25 July 2022.

[82] Commission, 'Proposal for a Regulation of the European Parliament and of the Council on general product safety, amending Regulation (EU) No 1025/2012 of the European Parliament and of the Council, and repealing Council Directive 87/357/EEC and Directive 2001/95/EC of the European Parliament and of the Council' (Communication) COM (2021) 346 final (GPSD).

Food law, however, came under the latent influence of the overarching 'Better Regulation Agenda'. In 2010, the so-called 'Fitness Check' identified the food sector as a pilot project. This effort was continued under the Regulatory Fitness and Performance Programme (REFIT),[83] an initiative aimed at making EU law more efficient, more fit for purpose, and less costly.

1.3.4 Making EU food law more transparent—adoption of the Transparency Regulation

The absence of major policy initiatives continued until public opinion forced the European Commission's hand. Over a long period of time, the 'glyphosate' issue started to brew into a perfect storm that rocked EU public opinion and fostered distrust in the independence and functionality of the EU risk assessment processes. Glyphosate is the active substance used in plant protection products such as the Roundup product that was produced by (then) Monsanto. The re-authorization of glyphosate at EU level was heavily contentious,[84] fuelled by the fact that the EFSA and the International Agency for Research on Cancer (IARC) in 2015 had divergent risk assessment outcomes regarding its classification as carcinogenic. This coincided with Greenpeace's successful transparency challenge to the European Commission's decision of non-disclosure in the authorization files.[85] At the same time, court challenges all across the United States against Monsanto's Roundup product uncovered clear evidence that Monsanto had financed scientific studies. On top of this, it emerged that EFSA had directly copied a part of its 2015 Opinion from the application for re-authorization. Public sentiment reached a boiling point, culminating in a 2017 Citizen Initiative to ban glyphosate and reform the authorization system.

Despite initial reluctance, the European Commission reacted to the criticism and proposed several improvements to the risk regulation architecture of the GFLR and the relevant secondary legislation. The Transparency Regulation (TR, 2019) introduced improved transparency rules relating to risk communication and the risk assessment stage (see Chapter 5).

[83] Commission, 'Communication from the Commission to the European Parliament, the Council, the European Economic and Social Committee and the Committee of the Regions on EU Regulatory Fitness' (Communication) COM (2012) 746 final.

[84] Alessandra Arcuri and Yogi Hendlin, 'Introduction to the Symposium on the Science and Politics of Glyphosate' (2020) 11 European Journal of Risk Regulation 411.

[85] Case C-673/13 *Commission v Stichting Greenpeace Nederland and Pan Europe* [2016] EU:C:2016:889.

1.3.5 *Farm to Fork Communication (2020) as part of the Green Deal (2019)*

While the first two decades of the millennium were relatively quiet for food law, major changes are imminent. In 2019, the European Commission adopted the European Green Deal (political priorities of the European Commission 2019–2024), and the EU's strategy for sustainable growth. As part of the Green Deal, numerous policy initiatives in a wide number of sectors were drawn up, broadly implementing the aspiration of the EU to become more 'sustainable' in all sectors. The 'sustainability' paradigm stemming from the Green Deal is overarching and operationalized for the food sector through the Farm to Fork Communication (Farm to Fork Strategy).[86]

The Farm to Fork Strategy can be said to 'bring the sustainability turn to EU food law',[87] and aims to make food systems fair, healthy, and environmentally-friendly. To this end, the Farm to Fork Strategy Communication includes non-binding quantitative targets,[88] a policy outline, and an Annex with 27 legal actions (see Table 1.3).

The cornerstone of the Farm to Fork Strategy is the proposal for a legislative framework for sustainable food systems that will be put forward to support the implementation of the strategy and development of sustainable food policy. While clearly central to the future legislative developments of sustainability food law, the Farm to Fork Strategy remains silent regarding the details of the proposal. In addition, the eventual relationship of 'sustainability food law' and 'food safety food law', particularly the GFLR, remains undefined.

The other legislative actions targeted specific modifications to existing legal food frameworks, which were categorized into proposals relating to sustainable food production, sustainable food-processing and distribution, sustainable food consumption, and food loss and waste prevention. Some noteworthy initiatives are the development of an EU Code of Conduct, a binding corporate governance framework, and sustainable food labelling. Other actions bundle together remaining

[86] Commission, 'Communication from the Commission to the European Parliament, the Council, the European Economic and Social Committee and the Committee of the Regions on A Farm to Fork Strategy for a fair, healthy and environmentally-friendly food system' (Communication) COM (2020) 381 final (Farm to Fork Strategy).

[87] Hanna Schebesta and others, 'Tour de Table: Farm to Fork Law Update' (2022) 17 European Food and Feed Law Review 208.

[88] Reduce the use of chemical and hazardous pesticides in agriculture by 50%; reduce nutrient losses by at least 50%, while ensuring no deterioration on soil fertility; reduce fertilizer use by at least 20%; reduce by 50% the sales of antimicrobials for farmed animals and in aquaculture; enhance the development of EU organic farming (25% of total farmland).

Table 1.3 Farm to Fork Strategy, Annex—Draft Action Plan.

Actions	Indicative time table	N.°
Proposal for a legislative framework for sustainable food systems	2023	1.
Develop a contingency plan for ensuring food supply and food security	Q4 2021	2.
Ensure sustainable food production		
Adopt recommendations to each Member State addressing the nine specific objectives of the Common Agricultural Policy (CAP), before the draft CAP Strategic Plans are formally submitted	Q4 2020	3.
Proposal for a revision of the Sustainable Use of Pesticides Directive to significantly reduce use and risk and dependency on pesticides and enhance Integrated Pest Management	Q1 2022	4.
Revision of the relevant implementing Regulations under the Plant Protection Products framework to facilitate placing on the market of plant protection products containing biological active substances	Q4 2021	5.
Proposal for a revision of the pesticides statistics Regulation to overcome data gaps and reinforce evidence-based policy making	2023	6.
Evaluation and revision of the existing animal welfare legislation, including on animal transport and slaughter of animals	Q4 2023	7.
Proposal for a revision of the feed additives Regulation to reduce the environmental impact of livestock farming	Q4 2021	8.
Proposal for a revision of the Farm Accountancy Data Network Regulation to transform it into a Farm Sustainability Data Network with a view to contribute to a wide uptake of sustainable farming practices	Q2 2022	9.
Clarification of the scope of competition rules in the TFEU with regard to sustainability in collective actions.	Q3 2022	10.
Legislative initiatives to enhance cooperation of primary producers to support their position in the food chain and non-legislative initiatives to improve transparency	2021–2022	11.
EU carbon farming initiative	Q3 2021	12.
Stimulate sustainable food processing, wholesale, retail, hospitality and food services' practices		
Initiative to improve the corporate governance framework, including a requirement for the food industry to integrate sustainability into corporate strategies	Q1 2021	13.
Develop an EU code and monitoring framework for responsible business and marketing conduct in the food supply chain	Q2 2021	14.
Launch initiatives to stimulate reformulation of processed food, including the setting of maximum levels for certain nutrients	Q4 2021	15.

Table 1.3 Continued

Actions	**Indicative time table**	**N.°**
Set nutrient profiles to restrict promotion of food high in salt, sugars and/or fat	Q4 2022	16.
Proposal for a revision of EU legislation on Food Contact Materials to improve food safety, ensure citizens' health and reduce the environmental footprint of the sector	Q4 2022	17.
Proposal for a revision of EU marketing standards for agricultural, fishery and aquaculture products to ensure the uptake and supply of sustainable products	2021–2022	18.
Enhance coordination to enforce single market rules and tackle Food Fraud, including by considering a reinforced use of OLAF's investigative capacities	2021–2022	19.
Promote sustainable food consumption, facilitating the shift towards healthy, sustainable diets		
Proposal for a harmonised mandatory front-of-pack nutrition labelling to enable consumers to make health conscious food choices	Q4 2022	20.
Proposal to require origin indication for certain products	Q4 2022	21.
Determine the best modalities for setting minimum mandatory criteria for sustainable food procurement to promote healthy and sustainable diets, including organic products, in schools and public institutions	Q3 2021	22.
Proposal for a sustainable food labelling framework to empower consumers to make sustainable food choices	2024	23.
Review of the EU promotion programme for agricultural and food products with a view to enhancing its contribution to sustainable production and consumption	Q4 2020	24.
Review of the EU school scheme legal framework with a view to refocus the scheme on healthy and sustainable food	2023	25.
Reduce food loss and waste		
Proposal for EU-level targets for food waste reduction	2023	26.
Proposal for a revision of EU rules on date marking ('use by' and 'best before' dates)	Q4 2022	27.

Source: Commission, 'Communication from the Commission to the European Parliament, the Council, the European Economic and Social Committee and the Committee of the Regions on A Farm to Fork Strategy for a fair, healthy and environmentally-friendly food system' (Communication) COM (2020) 381 final (Farm to Fork Strategy).

legacy REFIT initiatives, for instance those addressing food contact materials and feed additives legislation.[89]

Whether or not the proposed actions will be adequate to translate into the wider policy aspirations remains to be seen.[90] The difference between the 2000 Food Safety White Paper and the Farm to Fork Strategy is certainly striking in institutional and systemic terms; for food safety, a very clear blueprint had been outlined, whereas the Farm to Fork Strategy remains vague and ambiguous. The Strategy also proposes a number of small specific actions, which, together with the REFIT Programme legacy actions, will no doubt be translated into practice. In addition, the 'enabling environment'[91] of food businesses, such as public procurement rules and particularly business responsibilities, is likely to result in significant changes for business operators. However, overall, the current food system architecture is predominantly food safety oriented, and it is unclear how a 'sustainability' reorientation would be put into practice.

A structural weakness of the Farm to Fork Strategy is its connection to the new CAP; here the Commission's powers will be limited to recommending alignment of national strategies with the Farm to Fork Strategy.[92] This reflects the inherent constraints of food law policy within the general confines of the Treaty foundations, such as in this case the division between the agricultural and internal market competencies.

1.4 Conclusions

Food within the EU, to this day, is a distinct domain subject to fragmented regulatory influences, notably the CAP, overarching policies, such as consumer or environmental legislation, and the food sector specific framework, which is historically oriented towards food safety and is increasingly shifting towards food health and sustainability. This book is dedicated to food-sector specific food law in this narrow sense.

Structurally, the least coherent aspect for food law and policy is the CAP, which has a distinct legal Treaty origin and to date follows a separate timeline and policy process. While the internal market efforts are largely consolidated in the Farm

[89] For the progress of the REFIT in Health and Food Safety, see Commission, 'REFIT—Making EU Law Simpler and Less Costly: REFIT Scoreboard—Health and Food Safety' <https://op.europa.eu/webpub/com/refit-scoreboard/en/policy/9/index.html> accessed 25 July 2022.

[90] Hanna Schebesta and Jeroen J L Candel, 'Game-Changing Potential of the EU's Farm to Fork Strategy' (2020) 1 Nature Food 586.

[91] Hanna Schebesta, Nadia Bernaz, and Chiara Macchi, 'The European Farm to Fork Strategy: Sustainability and Responsible Business in the Food Supply Chain' (2020) 15 European Food and Feed Law Review 420.

[92] Commission, 'Commission Staff Working Document—Analysis of Links between CAP Reform and Green Deal' SWD (2020) 93 final.

to Fork Strategy, which as part of the Green Deal spans the period 2019 to 2024, the new CAP covers the period from 2023 to 2027. These two tracks, therefore, unfold in parallel, resulting in possible tensions and the challenge of establishing synergies between the—to date—separate policy sectors.

In literature and politics, voices calling for a holistic approach to the food system are becoming dominant, especially after the United Nations Food System Summit (2021). However, how this approach will be translated legally remains open-ended. At the EU level, there are emerging efforts to reunite food regulation with other areas. The next five to ten years will predictably be dedicated to achieving the sustainability goals in food legislation as set out in the Farm to Fork Strategy. Beyond that, there is a nascent One Health approach aimed at aligning the animal-human-plant nexus more closely.[93] More concrete efforts to integrate food with other policy areas can be found in the Official Controls Regulation that already covers areas beyond food, and recent policy initiatives, notably in the Chemicals Strategy of the Green Deal, that aim to streamline cosmetics, pharmaceuticals, and food.

Given that CAP legislation is now politically more difficult to agree on and may increasingly fall within the sphere of Member State implementation through strategic plans, the European Commission is likely to lean towards addressing food matters through internal market competencies to create EU centralized legislation. However, the lack of integration of the Farm to Fork Strategy with the existing GFLR risks creating a bifurcated food legal framework with parallel tracks for food safety under the GFLR and the Farm to Fork's legislative framework for sustainable food systems (FSFS).

[93] Francesca Coli and Hanna Schebesta, 'One Health in the EU: the Next Future?' (2023) 8 European Papers 301.

2
The EU Web of Competences and Food Law

2.1 Introduction

This chapter elaborates food-related competences across the Treaty on the Functioning of the European Union (TFEU), and how they affect food law in the European Union (EU). The different sub-sections analyse the competence norms and respective legal bases in the Treaty. EU food law is influenced by various policy-making fields (eg agriculture, free movement, environment, consumer, health, and fundamental rights). Therefore, EU food law must strike a balance between often opposing interests. As a result, rather than on a single competence norm, EU food law is based on a 'web of competences', representing the sum of different competence norms, which often combines features of several isolated competence norms. Thereby it enables the regulation of the whole food market as a system.

2.2 Food and competences

The EU can act only within the limits of the competences conferred[1] upon it by the Member States in the Treaties (see Chapter 1). Therefore, the EU is limited to legislating the food market at EU level within the confines of the competence areas conferred to it by the Member States through EU primary law (see also Chapter 3). 'Food' is no such explicitly conferred competence area. Rather, 'food' can form a 'good' and is hence subject to the competence norm governing the internal market, and especially the free movement of goods.[2] This is the default status of foods if one considers foods bought for consumption in the supermarket. Under certain circumstances 'food' can also qualify as 'agricultural product' and hence qualifies under the competence norms governing the agricultural market, defined as 'products of the soil, of stock farming and of fisheries and products of first-stage processing directly related to these products'.[3] 'Food', however, is not only a tradeable product but also has effects on individuals and the environment. Hence, regulating foodstuffs can also target health, consumer protection, and environmental

[1] Consolidated Version of the Treaty on European Union [2012] OJ C326/01 (TEU), art 5(2).
[2] Consolidated Version of the Treaty on the Functioning of the European Union [2012] OJ C326/47 (TFEU), arts 26 and 28–37.
[3] ibid, art 38.

EU Food Law. Hanna Schebesta and Kai Purnhagen, Oxford University Press. © Hanna Schebesta and Kai Purnhagen 2024.
DOI: 10.1093/9780198901570.003.0003

protection purposes. The method of production and the kind of foods we produce and eat impact our health, our environment, and our societies' health-care systems. Food can also be subject to common concerns in public-health matters, for example if our food system causes a pandemic or if a pandemic affects our food system. 'Food' can also be subject to competition law rules and to a customs policy.

Most of these competence regimes belong to the area of shared competence.[4] Within shared competence norms, Member States exercise their competence only to the extent that the Union has not exercised its competence.[5] When food regulations touch upon competition law or the customs union, however, these regulations concern areas of exclusive competence.[6] In these areas, only the Union may legislate and adopt legally binding acts on foods.[7]

As legislation of foodstuffs at EU level often crosses several competence regimes, most acts concerning food law are based on several competence norms; this is elsewhere termed a 'web of competences' approach.[8] The General Food Law Regulation (GFLR), for example, is based on four competence norms, which are Articles 37, 95, 133, and 152(4)(b) of the Treaty establishing the European Community (TEC). However, even in such 'web of competences', the sum of the single competence norms must not go beyond the powers conferred by each competence norm.[9] We will hence investigate each of these areas in turn.

2.2.1 Food and agriculture

EU legislation distinguishes rules relating to agricultural products from those relating to foodstuffs.[10] Respectively, these are linked to different policies and competence regimes in the TFEU. Agricultural products are treated within the provisions on 'agriculture and fisheries',[11] while foodstuffs are 'goods' within the meaning of the provisions on 'free movement of goods'.[12] This distinction is important, as the European Court of Justice (ECJ) has ruled that the common market policy rules applicable to 'agricultural products' take precedence over other rules of the internal market.[13] The borderline between agricultural products and foods seems

[4] ibid, art 4.
[5] ibid, art 2(2).
[6] ibid, art 3.
[7] ibid, art 2(1).
[8] Kai Purnhagen and others, 'More Competences than You Knew? The Web of Health Competence for Union Action in Response to the COVID-19 Outbreak' (2020) 11 European Journal of Risk Regulation 291.
[9] ibid.
[10] Regulation (EU) 1151/2012 of the European Parliament and of the Council of 21 November 2012 on quality schemes for agricultural products and foodstuffs [2012] OJ L343/1, art 1(1).
[11] TFEU, Title III.
[12] ibid, Title II.
[13] Case C-83/78 *Pigs Marketing Board v Redmond* [1978] ECR 02347.

clear-cut at first sight but proves to be more complicated when applied in practice. The distinction is a purely legal one, determined by legislation and the case law of the Court.

The distinction between foodstuffs and agricultural products traces back to the negotiations of the Treaties of Rome (EEC and Euratom). The Spaak Report, which preceded the signing of the EEC, had clarified that agriculture should be included in the rules of the Common Market.[14] The report left open, however, how such an inclusion would work.[15] Despite the numerous arguments for an integral solution for agriculture, many voices in the negotiations in preparation of the Treaties of Rome highlighted that the market for agricultural products in Europe was distinct from other markets for many other goods such as foodstuffs, and hence required special treatment.[16] The French proposal for the formulation of the agricultural provisions in the Treaties of Rome stipulated a compromise. As Barents noted,[17] the French proposal foresaw that both agricultural products and foodstuffs would be subject to the rules of the Common Market, while 'only the former group and some groups of the latter would be subjected to the agricultural treaty provisions'.[18] As a result, agricultural products required a general definition, while a list specified the foods subject to the agricultural legal regime.[19] Foodstuffs that did not fulfil the criteria of 'agricultural products' and were not on the list would be regarded as 'goods' subject to other regimes of internal market law, such as the free movement of goods. Most of the proposal was adopted into the provision known today as Article 38 TFEU. However, for reasons unknown, the reference to food products vanished from the text.[20] The definition of 'agricultural products' has remained in Article 38(1) TFEU.[21] Annex I of the TFEU lists the foods which are exceptionally subject to the agricultural regime (see Table 2.1).[22]

This has resulted in an unclear situation regarding the relationship between these provisions and that between foodstuffs and agricultural products. Is the scope of the agricultural regime only open to agricultural products and foodstuffs on the list? Or is it open to all products that fulfil the criteria of the definition of agricultural products? The Court clarified that the scope of the Common Agricultural Policy (CAP) provisions is only open to products on the list.[23] If the Council were

[14] Intergovernmental Committee on European Integration, 'Report of the Heads of Delegation to the Ministers of Foreign Affairs', 'Spaak Report' SG/A (1956) 4 (Spaak Report).

[15] Rene Barents, *The Agricultural Law of the EC: An Inquiry into the Administrative Law of the European Community in the Field of Agriculture* (Kluwer Law International 1994) 6.

[16] ibid 4–5.

[17] ibid 27.

[18] ibid.

[19] ibid.

[20] ibid.

[21] 'Products of the soil, of stock farming and of fisheries and products of first-stage processing directly related to these products'.

[22] TFEU, art 38(3).

[23] Case C-77/83 *Srl CILFIT and others and Lanificio di Gavardo SpA v Ministero della sanità* [1984] ECR 1257 [11]–[12].

Table 2.1 TFEU, Annex I—List referred to in Article 38 of the Treaty on the Functioning of the European Union, 333–335

(1) No in the Brussels nomenclature	(2) Description of products
Chapter 1	Live animals
Chapter 2	Meat and edible meat offal
Chapter 3	Fish, crustaceans and molluscs
Chapter 4	Dairy produce; birds' eggs; natural honey
Chapter 5	
05.04	Guts, bladders and stomachs of animals (other than fish), whole and pieces thereof
05.15	Animal products not elsewhere specified or included; dead animals of Chapter 1 or Chapter 3, unfit for human consumption
Chapter 6	Live trees and other plants; bulbs, roots and the like; cut flowers and ornamental foliage
Chapter 7	Edible vegetables and certain roots and tubers
Chapter 8	Edible fruit and nuts; peel of melons or citrus fruit
Chapter 9	Coffee, tea and spices, excluding maté (heading No 09.03)
Chapter 10	Cereals
Chapter 11	Products of the milling industry; malt and starches; gluten; inulin
Chapter 12	Oil seeds and oleaginous fruit; miscellaneous grains, seeds and fruit; industrial and medical plants; straw and fodder
Chapter 13	
13.03	Pectin
Chapter 15	
15.01	Lard and other rendered pig fat; rendered poultry fat
15.02	Unrendered fats of bovine cattle, sheep or goats; tallow (including 'premier jus') produced from those fats
15.03	Lard stearin, oleostearin and tallow stearin; lard oil, oleo-oil and tallow oil, not emulsified or mixed or prepared in any way
15.04	Fats and oil, of fish and marine mammals, whether or not refined
15.07	Fixed vegetable oils, fluid or solid, crude, refined or purified
15.12	Animal or vegetable fats and oils, hydrogenated, whether or not refined, but not further prepared
15.13	Margarine, imitation lard and other prepared edible fats

(*continued*)

Table 2.1 Continued

(1) No in the Brussels nomenclature	(2) Description of products
15.17	Residues resulting from the treatment of fatty substances or animal or vegetable waxes
Chapter 16	Preparations of meat, of fish, of crustaceans or molluscs
Chapter 17	
17.01	Beet sugar and cane sugar, solid
17.02	Other sugars; sugar syrups; artificial honey (whether or not mixed with natural honey); caramel
17.03	Molasses, whether or not decolourised
17.05	Flavoured or coloured sugars, syrups and molasses (including vanilla sugar or vanillin), with the exception of fruit juice containing added sugar in any proportion
Chapter 18	
18.01	Cocoa beans, whole or broken, raw or roasted
18.02	Cocoa shells, husks, skins and waste
Chapter 20	Preparations of vegetables, fruit or other parts of plants
Chapter 22	
22.04	Grape must, in fermentation or with fermentation arrested otherwise than by the addition of alcohol
22.05	Wine of fresh grapes; grape must with fermentation arrested by the addition of alcohol
22.07	Other fermented beverages (for example, cider, perry and mead)
22.0822.09	Ethyl alcohol or neutral spirits, whether or not denatured, of any strength, obtained from agricultural products listed in Annex I, excluding liqueurs and other spirituous beverages and compound alcoholic preparations (known as 'concentrated extracts') for the manufacture of beverages
22.10	Vinegar and substitutes for vinegar
Chapter 23	Residues and waste from the food industries; prepared animal fodder
Chapter 24	
24.01	Unmanufactured tobacco, tobacco refuse
Chapter 45	
45.01	Natural cork, unworked, crushed, granulated or ground; waste cork

Table 2.1 Continued

(1) No in the Brussels nomenclature	(2) Description of products
Chapter 54	
54.01	Flax, raw or processed but not spun; flax tow and waste (including pulled or garnetted rags)
Chapter 57	
57.01	True hemp (Cannabis sativa), raw or processed but not spun; tow and waste of true hemp (including pulled or garnetted rags or ropes)

Source: Consolidated Version of the Treaty on the Functioning of the European Union [2012] OJ C326/47 (TFEU).

to decide that the scope should be extended to other products which fulfil the criteria of the definition in (now) Article 38(1) TFEU it may do so by adding to that list.[24] The Council made use of this possibility rather late[25] by adopting Council Regulation 7a.[26] Hence, the relationship between foodstuffs and agricultural products is in principle relatively clear-cut; only those foodstuffs listed in Annex I qualify as agricultural products. Measures based on the agricultural competence norm of Article 43 TFEU may only concern products listed in Annex I; Article 43 TFEU is not applicable for measures concerning products not on these lists.[27]

The borderline between 'agricultural products' (to which the agricultural provisions apply) and 'goods' (to which the rules of the free movement of goods apply) needed clarification. As most agricultural products will be processed and as such will turn into 'goods' within the meaning of the internal market, a decision was needed to determine at which point the shift from an 'agriculture product' to a 'good' takes place. This necessitated a definition of 'agricultural product' to determine the criteria that would turn an 'agricultural product' on the list into a 'good'. The definition requires these to be 'products of first-stage processing directly related to' basic agricultural products.[28] In *Hauptzollamt Bielefeld v König* the Court of Justice of the EU (CJEU) stipulated that 'first-stage processing' did not refer to a productive process (with the consequence that the number of processes involved is irrelevant), but rather required a close economic interdependence between the

[24] ibid.

[25] The respective regulation had been published two years after the expiry of the legal basis for the Council. On the controversy, see John A Usher, *EC Agricultural Law* (OUP 2001) 3.

[26] EEC Council Regulation No 7a adding certain products to the list in Annex II to the Treaty establishing the European Economic Community [1961] OJ 7/71.

[27] The argument can be made in analogous application of Case C-123/83 *Bureau national interprofessionnel du cognac v Guy Clair* [1985] ECR 391 [15].

[28] TFEU, art 38(1).

basic product and the processed product.[29] If the price of the agricultural raw material involved in the productive process of the processed product 'becomes a completely marginal cost'[30] these processed products are not 'agricultural products'.[31]

The Annex I list uses the terminology from a nomenclature introduced in 1950.[32] From today's perspective, the adoption of this old nomenclature results in some interesting observations: Hemp, for example, also in the form of 'cannabis sativa', is considered an agricultural product, while 'cotton' is not included on the list.

The CJEU's strict adherence to a static approach to the definition of 'agricultural products' in its case law has triggered some innovation to overcome it through creative law making and interpretation. Cotton is not on the list but is of great importance to Greek agriculture. When Greece joined the EU, Protocol No 4 was introduced into the Greek accession Treaty, ensuring that cotton would effectively be treated as if it were in the list of agricultural products.[33] Conversely, despite its clear mentioning in Annex I, the CJEU has declared cannabis 'prohibited from being released into the economic and commercial channels of the European Union'[34] if it was not 'strictly controlled by the competent authorities to be used for medical and scientific purpose',[35] in order to effectively fight negative consequences of trade and consumption of drugs in the EU.

Potentially to align its strict case law with the reality of the market, the Court consistently widened its understanding of the criteria for determining what constitutes an 'agricultural product'. While the list in Annex I remains a starting point, the Court has accepted many deviations from the strict application of the wording of Annex I. The Court embraced a flexible interpretation of the many references in Annex I, extending the scope of Article I to include products that have a functional or economic link to them and those needed for their marketing even after processing.[36] With regards to foodstuffs, these cases are relevant in the following situations: foodstuffs are classified as Annex I products if their regulation necessarily requires a regulation of their substitutes, or if non-Annex I products are totally interchangeable with Annex I products.[37] Furthermore, Article 38 TFEU limits the scope of the CAP to production and trade. However, Article 43 TFEU forms a competence norm for measures concerning later stages in the chain, such as human consumption, as long as they relate to Annex I products and fulfil the goals

[29] Case C-185/73 *Hauptzollamt Bielefeld v Offene Handelsgesellschaft in Firma H. C. König* [1974] ECR 607 (*Hauptzollamt Bielefeld v Köni*) [12]–[13].

[30] ibid, [13].

[31] For elaboration on the implications, see *Srl CILFIT and others and Lanificio di Gavardo SpA v Ministero della sanità* (n 23), and Usher (n 25) 3.

[32] The Common Customs Tariffs (known as the 'Brussels Nomenclature'); see Usher (n 25) 3.

[33] Barents (n 15) 28 and Usher (n 25) 4–5.

[34] Case C-137/09 *Marc Michel Josemans v. Burgemeester van Maastricht* [2010] ECR I-13019 [42].

[35] ibid [41].

[36] For a full list, see Barents (n 15) 28–30.

[37] ibid 29.

of Article 39 TFEU.[38] With the adoption of the Unfair Trading Practices Directive (UTPD),[39] the Commission and the Council have started to extend Article 43 TFEU beyond the application of 'agricultural products' to cover all food products, including those with no connection to those listed in Annex I. Elsewhere, this practice has been referred to as a successful application of 'regulatory experimentalism'.[40] It is, however, doubtful whether Article 43 TFEU still covers such an extension.[41]

The UTPD could also be the illustration of a wider phenomenon that started with the expansive interpretation of the term 'agricultural product'. The strict distinction between agricultural products and foodstuffs is blurring. The adoption of the GFLR,[42] which was based on no less than four competence norms, testifies to the difficulties of subsuming food law in distinct policy categories. There is evidence that a number of factors contribute to the different regulatory treatment between agricultural products and food products.[43] Most impactful may be: the chain approach adopted in food law,[44] and EU policy making in the area of food[45] (see Chapter 1); the levelling effect of horizontal clauses in EU law; the increasing application of a 'web of competences' to policy areas rather than single competence norms;[46] and the reform of the Common Market Organisation Regulation (CMO Regulation) towards mirroring more the rationale of the fundamental freedoms.[47] These developments are difficult to reconcile with the fact that the EU is still far from a fully fledged federal state and hence needs control through, for example, the principle of conferral.[48] The realities of the integrated EU market of goods particularly in the area of food, characterized by food chains or food systems, may

[38] ibid 30; Case C-343/07 *Bavaria NV and Bavaria Italia Srl v Bayerischer Brauerbund eV* [2009] ECR I-05491 [50].

[39] Directive (EU) 2019/633 of the European Parliament and of the Council of 17 April 2019 on unfair trading practices in business-to-business relationships in the agricultural and food supply chain [2019] OJ L111/59 (Unfair Trading Practices Directive (UTPD)).

[40] María Paz La Cuesta De Los Mozos and Elena Sedano Varo, 'On Regulatory Experimentalism in European Private Law : The Legal Laboratory of Food and Finance' in Lucila de Almeida and others (eds), *The Transformation of Economic Law* (Hart 2019) 225.

[41] Critical in this respect, see Hanna Schebesta and others, 'Unfair Trading Practices in the Food Supply Chain: Regulating Right?' (2018) 9 European Journal of Risk Regulation 690.

[42] Regulation (EU) 178/2002 of the European Parliament and of the Council of 28 January 2002 laying down the general principles and requirements of food law, establishing the European Food Safety Authority and laying down procedures in matters of food Safety [2002] OJ L31/1 (General Food Law Regulation (GFLR)).

[43] Kai Purnhagen and Peter Feindt, 'Principles-based Regulation: Blueprint for a "New Approach" for the Internal Agricultural Market' (2017) 42 European Law Review 722.

[44] Jessica Vapnek, 'Legislative Implementation of the Food Chain Approach' (2007) 40 Vanderbilt Journal of Transnational Law 487.

[45] Kai Purnhagen, 'The Farm to Fork Strategy from a Perspective of EU Economic Law' (2022) Applied Economic Perspectives and Policies (forthcoming).

[46] Purnhagen and others (n 8).

[47] Kai Purnhagen and Hanna Schebesta, 'A Case moving at the Frontiers of Market Access, Freedom of Goods, the Common Agricultural Policy and Science in Court—Reflections on Scotch Whisky Association' (2017) 42 European Law Review 420.

[48] TEU, art 5.

also need adjusted legal responses.[49] It is too soon to discuss whether and how the Court or the legislator will endorse this trend. From a constitutional point of view, the Treaties do not preclude the usage of several legal bases. In future law making, networks or webs of competence will assume the role of necessary legal brokers in achieving the integrated and holistic approaches propagated by food systems policies.

2.2.2 *Food and the internal market*

The regulation of trade in food products is at the core and origin of internal market law.[50] Harmonizing legislation concerning food was among the earliest laws that the EU passed at the beginning of European legal integration (Chapter 1). The lion's share of EU food legislation is based on Article 114 TFEU (in a 'web of competences'[51] approach often used in conjunction with other legal bases), the so-called 'internal market clause'.[52] It serves as the legal basis for secondary legislation enacted to establish the internal market. The tests for a legal act to comply with the requirements of Article 114 of the TFEU are relatively lax.[53] Only in one case outside the area of food law, the Tobacco judgment, has the Court declared a secondary legal act to be non-compliant with the requirements of (current) Article 114 TFEU.[54]

Any quantitative restriction on food trade in the EU or measures having an equivalent effect are prohibited in the EU and have the potential to hinder the establishment or safeguarding of the internal market. The major requirement of Article 114 TFEU is that the measures achieve the objectives set out in Article 26 TFEU, that is, establishing or ensuring the functioning of the internal market as an area without internal frontiers, which comprises, inter alia, the free movement of goods. 'Foods' that are not categorized as 'agricultural products' fall within the scope of the free movement of goods. Article 114 TFEU hence forms an excellent legal basis for regulating the internal market of foodstuffs.

[49] Purnhagen (n 45). More generally, Ioannis Lianos, 'Updating the EU Internal Market Concept' in Fabien Amtenbrink and others (eds), *The Internal Market and the Future of European Integration* (Cambridge University Press 2019).

[50] Kai Purnhagen, 'The Virtue of Cassis De Dijon 25 Years Later—It is Not Dead, It Just Smells Funny' in Kai Purnhagen and Peter Rott (eds), *Varieties of European Economic Law and Regulation* (Springer 2014).

[51] Purnhagen and others (n 8),

[52] Kai Purnhagen and Hanna Schebesta, 'Food Labelling for Consumers—EU Law, Regulation and Policy Options' (Study commissioned by the PETI Committee of the European Parliament, April 2019) <https://op.europa.eu/en/publication-detail/-/publication/c4868536-7077-11e9-9f05-01aa75ed71a1> accessed 26 July 2022.

[53] Stephen Weatherill, 'The Limits of Legislative Harmonization Ten Years after Tobacco Advertising: How the Court's Case Law has Become a "Drafting Guide"' (2011) 12 German Law Journal 827.

[54] ibid.

The duty to establish and ensure the functioning of the internal market[55] not only comprises regulation based on a free trade or economic rationale, but also comprises the provision of a certain baseline of social protection across the internal market. This is particularly relevant in the area of food regulation, which often aims at achieving health, safety, and consumer protection, and increasingly sustainability goals too. In this respect, the Commission needs to take as a base a high level of health, safety, environmental, and consumer protection in the legislative proposals grounded in Article 114 TFEU.[56] While Article 114(3) TFEU explicitly binds only the Commission in its proposals, Article 169(2)(a) TFEU widens the obligation to take as a base a high level of consumer protection to all 'measures' adopted under Article 114 TFEU that promote the protection of health, safety, and economic interests the consumers. As EU food law also aims to safeguard consumer protection, this provision is of special relevance. These provisions need to be put into the context of EU case law. In *Affish*, the CJEU required that whenever a measure is intended to guarantee the protection of public health 'it must take precedence over economic considerations'.[57] This line of reasoning explains why the Court also requires a more protective yardstick than the protection of the 'circumspect consumer' when public health is at stake.[58] In EU food law, this yardstick is reflected in several provisions which take as a benchmark a more vulnerable consumer than in other areas of internal market law.[59]

Taken together, these provisions could be applied as follows in EU food law: Commission proposals, but also the actions of the European Parliament (EP) and the Council, need to ensure that EU food law realizes a high level of protection for health, safety, and the environment. If economic considerations prevail, this level of protection can be lower, making room, for example, for a circumspect consumer to serve as a protective benchmark in EU food law. When EU food law targets, as in most cases, the protection of the health, safety, and economic interests of consumers, these 'measures' ultimately have to aim at a high level of consumer protection, leading to the application of a different yardstick. When in doubt, preference needs to be given to measures that protect the safety and economic interests of consumers.[60]

[55] TFEU, art 26.

[56] ibid, art 114(3).

[57] Case C-183/95 *Affish BV v Rijksdienst voor de Keuring van Vee an Vlees* [1997] ECR I-4315 (*Affish*) [43]; Case C-221/10 P *Artedogan GmbH v European Commission* EU:C:2012:216 [99].

[58] Case C-220/98 *Estée Lauder Cosmetics GmbH & Co. OHG v Lancaster Group GmbH* [2000] ECR I-117 [28]; see also Case C-99/01 *Gottfried Linhart and Hans Biffl* [2002] ECR I-9375 [31].

[59] Kai Purnhagen and Ellen van Kleef, 'Commanding to "Nudge" via the Proportionality Principle?—A Case Study on Diets in EU Food Law' in Harry Bremmers and Kay Purnhagen (eds), *Regulating and Managing Food Safety in the EU—A Legal-Economic Perspective* (Springer Nature 2018).

[60] TFEU, art 169(a); Jens-Uwe Franck and Kai Purnhagen, 'Homo Economicus, Behavioural Sciences, and Economic Regulation: On the Concept of Man in Internal Market Regulation and its Normative Basis' in Klaus Mathis (ed), *Law and Economics in Europe: Foundations and Applications* (Springer Science 2014).

Recent legislative and judicial developments have started to broadly define consumers' health and interests in normative terms. The Food Information to Consumers Regulation (FICR) serves as an example of how consumers' health and interests encompass a wide range of factors, including 'health, economic, environmental, social and ethical considerations'.[61] In *Organisation juive européenne*,[62] the CJEU defined consumers' interests as also covering the food's country of origin's compliance with international law.[63] This wide understanding of the protective level of the consumer can lead to a more comprehensive application of Article 114 TFEU. This more comprehensive application reflects the post-Lisbon formulation of the internal market, which requires the Internal Market 'to work for the sustainable development of Europe based on balanced economic growth and price stability, a highly competitive social market economy, aiming at full employment and social progress, and a high level of protection and improvement of the quality of the environment'.[64] It is hence to be expected that sustainability will play an equally important role as health in future EU food law.

After the Union has harmonized food law at the EU level, Member States may, in principal deviate from these provisions and 'maintain national provisions on grounds of major needs referred to in Article 36, or relating to the protection of the environment or the working environment'.[65] However, if they do, they 'shall notify the Commission of these provisions as well as the grounds for maintaining them'.[66] The same holds true if it deems it necessary as a response to 'new scientific evidence relating to the protection of the environment or the working environment'.[67] If specific problems of public health arise which makes it necessary to deviate from existing food law at the EU level, Member States have to inform the Council immediately.[68]

[61] Regulation (EU) 1169/2011 of the European Parliament and of the Council of 25 October 2011 on the provision of food information to consumers, amending Regulations (EC) 1924/2006 and (EC) 1925/2006 of the European Parliament and of the Council, and repealing Commission Directive 87/250/EEC, Council Directive 90/496/EEC, Commission Directive 1999/10/EC, Directive 2000/13/EC of the European Parliament and of the Council, Commission Directives 2002/67/EC and 2008/5/EC and Commission Regulation (EC) 608/2004 [2011] OJ L304/18 (Food Information for Consumers Regulation (FICR)), art 1(3).

[62] Case C-363/18 *Organisation juive européenne et Vignoble Psagot Ltd v Ministre de l'Économie et des Finances* EU:C:2019:954 (*Organisation juive européenne*).

[63] Kai Purnhagen and others, 'Beyond Food Safety—EU Food Information Standards as a Facilitator of Political Consumerism and International Law Enforcement Mechanism' (2020) 45 European Law Review (forthcoming).

[64] TEU, art 3(3).

[65] TFEU, art 114(4).

[66] ibid, art 114(4).

[67] ibid, art 114(5).

[68] ibid, art 114(8).

2.2.3 *Food and consumer law*

Consumer protection law had been indirectly touched upon quite early in the history of EU law through the regulation of foodstuffs in the EU, whose primary objective was market integration.[69] Groundbreaking judgments for consumer law in the EU have been decided in food-related cases, in particular involving alcoholic beverages. Cases such as *Dassonville*,[70] *Cassis de Dijon*,[71] and *Scotch Whiskey Association*,[72] to mention a few, have shaped internal market law and policy in the area of consumer protection.

Today, there are two legal bases in the Treaties for realizing consumer protection.[73] EU food law, according to its legacy as a spillover from regulations to integrate the internal market, realizes consumer protection primarily through the application of the internal market clause as a legal basis.[74] Secondary food legislation based on Article 114 TFEU can realize a high level of consumer protection[75] when the institution's margin of discretion is exercised in a way that the resulting food laws favour consumer protection over other economic considerations. This secondary legislation then forms a 'general' balancing exercise to be applied to each and every case within the scope of the respective secondary food law versus its individual treatment under the free movement of goods.[76] Regarding the history of the GFLR, many view this balancing act as largely favouring individual consumer rights, stipulating that after the Bovine Spongiform Encephalopathy (BSE) crisis more emphasis was given to the protection of individual rights in food law. However, a careful study of the GFLR's text illustrates that the GFLR does not deviate much from the old *Cassis de Dijon*[77] regime.[78] As becomes particularly evident in the GFLR,[79] the new regime likewise preferred regulation by information, in order to enable the consumer to make an informed choice.[80] While Article 169 TFEU requires both to 'promote the interests of consumers' and 'to ensure a high level of consumer protection', Article 8 GFLR picks up only one of these

[69] Ellen Vos, 'Responding to Catastrophe: Towards a New Architecture for EU Food Safety Regulation?' in Charles F Sabel and Jonathan Zeitlin (eds), *Experimentalist Governance in the European Union: Towards a New Architecture* (OUP 2010).
[70] Case C- 8/74 *Procureur du Roi v Benoît and Gustave Dassonville* [1974] ECR 837 (*Dassonville*).
[71] Case C-120/78 *Rewe-Zentral AG v Bundesmonopolverwaltung für Branntwein* [1979] ECR I-649 (*Cassis de Dijon*).
[72] Case C-333/14 *Scotch Whisky Association e.a. v Lord Advocate et Advocate General for Scotland* EU:C:2015:845 (*Scotch Whisky Association*).
[73] TFEU, art 169(2); ibid, art 114(3).
[74] ibid, art 114.
[75] ibid, art 114(3).
[76] ibid, art 34.
[77] *Cassis de Dijon* (n 71).
[78] Purnhagen and van Kleef (n 59) 151.
[79] GFLR, art 8(1).
[80] Purnhagen and van Kleef (n 59) 151. For a more detailed analysis of this 'permit but inform' rationale, see Chapter 13.

alternatives, namely the promotion of the interest of the consumer, and defines it as a general principle of food law. This has influenced the interpretation of secondary legislation in this area, as only the interest of consumers has been used as a yardstick to determine whether food is unfit for consumption.[81]

The CJEU has also developed the 'average consumer' concept to determine the protective level of EU food law.[82] The Court had stipulated that the 'average consumer' is a consumer 'who is reasonably well-informed and reasonably observant and circumspect'.[83] Initially, this 'average consumer' had been developed from the rationale of the proportionality principle as a standard of EU primary law confining domestic (food) law which infringes the free movement of goods.[84] It soon developed into a standard to be applied to the interpretation of provisions in secondary law too,[85] especially food law.[86] While the 'average consumer' concept has been around for some time, it has been observed in the literature that the concept of the average consumer is still vague in terms of determining what kind of behaviour is normatively expected from a consumer.[87] In secondary food law, it appears that a more modern concept of the average consumer emerges, informed by insights from behavioural science.[88]

The CJEU has on numerous occasions accepted consumer protection as a valid justification for Member State and Union regulation to interfere with the free movement of foods (see Chapter 4). These cases have concerned foodstuffs which were denied access to the market of another Member State for formal reasons,[89] qualitative reasons,[90] reasons of misleading

[81] Case C-636/11 *Karl Berger v Freistaat Bayern* EU:C:2013:227 [35]; see Kai Purnhagen, 'Beyond Threats to Health: May Consumers' Interests in Safety Trump Fundamental Freedoms in Information on Foodstuffs? Reflections on Karl Berger v Freistaat Bayern' (2013) 38 European Law Review 711.

[82] For more comprehensive treatment, see Chapter 13.

[83] Case C-210/96 *Gut Springenheide GmbH and Rudolf Tusky v Oberkreisdirektor des Kreises Steinfurt - Amt für Lebensmittelüberwachung* [1998] ECR I-4657 [31].

[84] Franck and Purnhagen (n 60); in food law it had first been applied to (now) TFEU, art 34 in Case C-470/93 *Verein gegen Unwesen in Handel und Gewerbe Köln e.V. v Mars GmbH* [1995] ECR I-1923 (*Verein gegen Unwesen in Handel und Gewerbe Köl v Mars*) [24].

[85] Directive 2005/29/EC of the European Parliament and of the Council of 11 May 2005 concerning unfair business-to-consumer commercial practices in the internal market and amending Council Directive 84/450/EEC, Directives 97/7/EC, 98/27/EC and 2002/65/EC of the European Parliament and of the Council and Regulation (EC) 2006/2004 of the European Parliament and of the Council [2005] OJ L149/22 (Unfair Commercial Practices Directive).

[86] Hanna Schebesta and Kai Purnhagen, 'An Average Consumer Concept of Bits and Pieces: Empirical Evidence on the Court of Justice of the European Union's Concept of the Average Consumer in the UCPD', in Lucida de Almeida and others (eds), *The Transformation of Economic Law* (Hart 2019).

[87] ibid.

[88] ibid.

[89] Requirement of a certificate of authenticity, see *Dassonville* (n 70). Requirement to authorize import of foodstuffs for sportsmen and women lawfully manufactured and marketed in other Member States, see Case C-270/02 *Commission v Italy* [2004] ECR I-1559.

[90] eg not meeting a minimum amount of alcohol (see *Cassis de Dijon* (n 71)); a prohibition to use soya flour in meat products (see Case C-274/87 *Commission of the European Communities v Federal Republic of Germany* [1989] ECR 229); a prohibition to sell bread and other bakery products whose

packaging,[91] of misleading advertising on packaging,[92] or misleading product labelling.[93]

2.2.4 *Food and the environment*

Food production and consumption have external effects on the environment. As a consequence, a large number of EU food-law-related fields are environmentally related. Indeed, the legal principles associated with EU environmental policy, such as the precautionary principle, have long determined both EU health policy and EU food law.[94] Some claim that it is environmental policy which determines the legal solutions provided for a variety of problems EU food law has to deal with.[95] The legal basis for the realization of environmental policy could hence serve as an umbrella term to cover food law.[96] Thus far, this has not materialized. This may be in part because a food-specific precautionary principle is enshrined in the GFLR, which pays witness to the legislature's aspiration to pre-empt the effects of the general (environmental) precautionary principle.[97] However, with the EU's shift to provide a more sustainability-oriented internal market (especially through the Green Deal and the Farm to Fork Strategy, see Chapter 1), previous singular claims like these could become more prominent in the future of EU food law.

The increasing number of cases that deal with environmental protection as a reason to interfere with the free movement of foods also pay witness to the increasing prominence of environmental concerns in the internal market of foods. Environmental protection has notably been accepted as an unwritten reason for interference in the free movement of goods, as evidenced by a food-related case: in

salt content is higher than 2% (see Case C-17/93 *J.J.J. Van der Veldt* [1994] ECR I-3537; Case C-123/00 *Christina Bellamy and English Shop Wholesale* [2001] ECR I-2795; and Case C-407/85 *3 Glocken GmbH and Gertraud Kritzinger v USL Centro-Sud and Provincia autonoma di Bolzano* [1988] ECR 4233).

91 Prohibition of marketing of margarine or edible fats where each block or its external packaging does not have a particular shape (see Case C-261/81 *Walter Rau Lebensmittelwerke v De Smedt PVBA* [1982] ECR 3961). Prohibition of sales of wine which does not originate from a specific region in special bottles (see Case C-16/83 *Karl Prantl* [1984] ECR 1299).

92 Using a 10% bonus labelling on a coloured area covering 30% (see *Verein gegen Unwesen in Handel und Gewerbe Köln v Mars* (n 84) and Case C-465/98 *Verein gegen Unwesen in Handel und Gewerbe Köln eV v Adolf Darbo* [2000] ECR I-2297).

93 See Case C-193/80 *Commission des Communautés européennes v République italienne* [1981] ECR 3019 for Fruit Vinegar; Case C-178/84 *Commission of the European Communities v Federal Republic of Germany* [1987] ECR 1227 for Beer Purity; Case C-182/84 *Miro BV* [1985] ECR 3731 for Genever; and Case C-298/87 *Smanor SA* [1988] ECR 4489 for Yoghurt.

94 Kai Purnhagen, *The Politics of Systematization in EU Product Safety Regulation* (Springer 2013) 207.

95 ibid.

96 ibid.

97 An attempt which had been jeopardized by the Court, see Kai Purnhagen, 'You Want it Extra CRISPERY?: Legal Disruption Through New Plant Breeding Technologies in the EU' (2021) 40 Yearbook of European Law 374.

Commission/Denmark, the CJEU accepted that a national regulation requiring the use of reusable containers for beers and soft drinks can be based on the objective of environmental protection.[98] In subsequent case law, the Court has had several opportunities to sharpen its interpretation regarding the fact that the environmental impact of food packaging can justify infringements of the free movement of goods.[99] The Commission likewise emphasized that the environmental impact of beverage packaging can be a reason to justify national measures that interfere with the free movement of goods.[100]

2.2.5 *Food and health*

The provision of health increasingly influences EU food law.[101] Health cuts 'across different areas of EU law, it is found in what may seem to be surprising places . . .'[102] making its legal treatment difficult.[103] The Treaties distinguish between the provision of public health and the provision of human health,[104] without assigning this distinction to clear-cut different legal treatments. Health, like food, is based on a 'web of competences' rather than a clearly delineated competence regime.[105]

Measures in response to threats to public health, such as those that combatted the BSE crisis, were in the past based on the competence norm of agriculture. At that time the Council could implement these measures alone, thus bypassing the European Parliament (EP).[106] As a consequence of this unsatisfactory result, from the perspective of the EP, a special competence regime was introduced.[107] It now serves as the basis for action to protect public health 'in the veterinary and phytosanitary fields' and requires the ordinary legislative procedure as a prerequisite for issuing binding acts. Recommendations in the area of health are still possible without the involvement of the EP.[108]

[98] Case C-302/86 *Commission of the European Communities v Kingdom of Denmark* [1988] ECR 4607 (*Commission/Denmark*) [9].

[99] Case C-463/01 *Commission of the European Communities v Federal Republic of Germany* [2004] ECR I-11705.

[100] Communication from the Commission—Beverage packaging, deposit systems and free movement of goods [2009] OJ C107/1.

[101] FICR (n 61), art 3, which requires food information to take 'into account a high level of protection of consumers' health and interests'.

[102] Tamara Hervey, 'EU Health Law' in Catherine Barnard and Steven Peers (eds), *European Union Law* (2nd edn, OUP 2017) 628. See also, at greater length, Tamara Hervey and Jean McHale, *European Union Health Law: Themes and Implications* (Cambridge University Press 2015).

[103] Purnhagen (n 94) 206–207.

[104] ibid.

[105] Purnhagen and others (n 8).

[106] Joined Cases C-158/79 to 529/79 *Monique Roumengous and others v European Commission* [1979] OJ C304/3.

[107] TFEU, art 168(4)(b).

[108] ibid, art 168(6).

The provision of human health is not attributed to a special competence regime. As with food, measures are often based on a 'web of competences' approach.[109] Within this web, measures intended to increase in particular (individual) human health, as is the case in food law, are often implemented through the 'health' mechanism in Article 114 TFEU, as described in section 2.2.2. Applying this rationale has resulted in a variety of health-related EU food law, which is slowly replacing and/or accompanying EU food law with its traditional focus on 'safety'. The most prominent example is the EU Nutrition and Health Claims Regulation,[110] which in its Recital 1 presupposes a regulatory environment for consumer choice, where '(a) varied and balanced diet is a prerequisite for good health'.[111]

With an expected increase in sustainability-related legislation in EU food law, the legal basis for the realization of environmental policy[112] may become increasingly valuable. This also concerns health, as the protection of human health is part of the environmental policy of the EU.[113]

When food law was enacted to protect either human or public health, the CJEU has on several occasions accepted that such an aim can justify obstacles to the free movement of goods (see Chapter 4). Therefore, minimum pricing of alcohol can, in principle, serve as a reason to interfere with the free movement of goods.[114]

2.2.6 *Food and solidarity*

Under specific circumstances, the Treaties view food as a collective good, governed by the principle of solidarity. The Treaties presuppose that Union law has created functional supply chains as a default in the trade in goods.[115] However, when these supply chains do not function, Member States may ask the EU to use the principle of solidarity[116] to adopt 'measures appropriate to the economic situation'. This suggests a different approach to the Union's competence to control national measures on the basis of proportionality.[117] This approach is based on the

[109] Purnhagen and others (n 8).

[110] For a general account from the perspective of EU food law, see also FICR (n 61), Recital 41. For a more thorough assessment, see Kai Purnhagen, Erica van Herpen, and Ellen van Kleef, 'The Potential Use of Visual Packaging Elements as Nudges: An Analysis on the Example of the EU Health Claims Regime' in Klaus Mathis and Avishalom Tor (eds), *Nudging— Possibilities, Limitations and Applications in European Law and Economics* (Springer International Publishing 2016).

[111] FICR (n 61), Recital 1.

[112] TFEU, art 192(1), in conjunction with ibid, art 191(1).

[113] ibid, art 191(1)(2).

[114] *Scotch Whisky Association* (n 72).

[115] TFEU, art 122(1).

[116] Council Decision (EU) 2014/415 on the arrangements for the implementation by the Union of the solidarity clause [2014] OJ L192/53.

[117] For a requirement to adopt new steering principles to coordinate diversity in the EU which are different from the conventional tools such as proportionality, subsidiarity, and conferral, see Kai Purnhagen, 'From Supranationality to Managing Diversity: A (Re-)New(ed) Paradigm for the

principle of solidarity between Member States,[118] the Union's obligation to protect public health,[119] and the right to health care within Union law.[120] According to this approach, scarce products need to be 'channelled to those who need them most'.[121] This means keeping internal Union borders open for the supply of essential products such as food. In such emergency situations, the internal market is at the service of Europe's population.[122]

2.3 Food and fundamental rights

The EU legal framework on fundamental rights does not explicitly recognize any rights related to food. While we are aware that fundamental rights provisions originate in different sources in the EU, we refer here only to the EU Charter of Fundamental Rights (CFR). The CFR is the only source of human rights that has been of relevance so far in the case law of the CJEU regarding EU food law.[123] The provisions of the CFR are directed at the institutions, bodies, offices, and agencies of the Union and to the Member States when they are implementing Union law. The latter provision needs to be understood widely, as the Court has clarified that '(s)ince the fundamental rights guaranteed by the Charter must therefore be complied with where national legislation falls within the scope of European Union law, situations cannot exist which are covered in that way by European Union law without those fundamental rights being applicable'. This is particularly true for EU food law, which is directly and horizontally applicable to all actors and regulators of the food supply chain acting in the EU, albeit to varying degrees. Weatherill noted with reference to *Weintor*[124] that in the area of EU food law the following provisions may be of particular interest: The right to engage in work and to pursue a freely chosen or accepted occupation, as well as the freedom to conduct a business, can be relied on in the food market by food business operators to protect their business against EU and Member States' regulation. The following provisions are of special interest from the perspective of consumers: ensuring a high level of

Establishment of the Internal Market?' in Sacha Garben and Inge Govaere (eds), *Internal Market 2.0* (Hart 2020).

[118] TFEU, arts 122 and 222.
[119] ibid, art 9.
[120] CFR, art 35.
[121] Coronavirus Response Investment Initiative, Annex 2.
[122] Purnhagen and others (n 8).
[123] In agricultural law, human rights have played a significant role from the early days of the EU; Case C-11/70 *Internationale Handelsgesellschaft mbH v Einfuhr- und Vorratsstelle für Getreide und Futtermittel* EU:C:1970:114 (*Internationale Handelsgesellschaft*). In EU food law, the CFR has been cited as a justification for infringement of the free movement of goods; see Case C-544/10 *Deutsches Weintor eG v Land Rheinland-Pfalz* EU:C:2012:526 (*Weintor*).
[124] *Weintor* (n 123).

human health and consumer protection, as well as in the definition and implementation of EU policies and activities related to consumer protection. In EU food law, *Weintor* constituted the first application of the CFR. In judging whether the use of the expression 'easily digestible' on a wine bottle is protected by European fundamental rights against an EU-wide prohibition of health claims, the CJEU stipulated that 'the requirements of the protection of those various fundamental rights protected by the Union legal order' need to be reconciled and one may 'strike a fair balance between them'.

Lastly, there is an emerging line of reasoning concerning the fundamental and human rights dimension in the case law of the CJEU. Given that food is framed as a trading right, and the fact that the right to food is absent in the Charter, the disputes on food in terms of the Charter are framed as disputes regarding the freedom of expression and information, and the freedom to conduct a business.

In *Neptune Distribution*,[125] an issue arose regarding the Mineral Water Directive[126] and the Nutrition and Health Claim Regulation,[127] which discussed the relevance of 'Freedom of expression'[128]' and 'Freedom to conduct a business'.[129] The Court dealt with the case in a surprisingly detailed and nutritionally technical manner. Although argumentatively interesting, on the merits the Court unsurprisingly found that:

> EU legislature were legitimately entitled to consider that limitations and restrictions, such as those at issue in the provisions which are the subject of the first question, as regards the use of claims or indications referring to the low sodium content of natural mineral waters were appropriate and necessary to ensure the protection of human health in the European Union.[130]

Consequently, it is evident that it is not only trade law that represents a potential legal constraint on the European and national regulation of food products. Companies have also tried to invoke the CFR in the past, in particular the freedom to conduct a business (Article 16), the right to property (Article 17), and the freedom of expression and information (Article 11). These arguments were

[125] Case C-157/14 *Société Neptune Distribution v Ministre de l'Économie et des Finances* EU:C:2015:823 (*Neptune Distribution*).

[126] Directive 2009/54/EC of the European Parliament and of the Council of 18 June 2009 on the exploitation and marketing of natural mineral waters [2009] OJ L164/45.

[127] Regulation (EC) 1924/2006 of the European Parliament and of the Council of 20 December 2006 on nutrition and health claims made on foods [2006] OJ L404/9.

[128] Council of Europe, 'European Convention for the Protection of Human Rights and Fundamental Freedoms' (4 November 1950) ETS 5 (ECHR), art 10; CFR, art 11, which states in paragraph 1: 'Everyone has the right to freedom of expression. This right shall include freedom to hold opinions and to receive and impart information and ideas without interference by public authority and regardless of frontiers.'

[129] CFR, art 16.

[130] *Neptune Distribution* (n 125) [84].

raised, for example, in *Weintor* (ban on advertising with a health claim) before the CJEU, but rejected. According to the European courts, account must be taken of the second sentence of Article 35 CFR, which requires that a high level of human health protection needs to be ensured in the definition and implementation of all Union policies and activities. These different fundamental rights protected by the legal order of the Union must be reconciled and a fair balance must be struck between them. Public interest objectives may justify restrictions on fundamental freedoms.

While the court was not receptive to addressing the economic rights invoked under the CFR in this particular case, in the future one may expect more and more litigation from this corner given that 'food law' increasingly enshrines scientific data ownership rights for applicants in authorization procedures, or in refining the interpretation of the novel transparency balance in the GFLR between access to documents and confidentiality.

2.4 Conclusion

The regulations of the food market cannot be traced to a single competence norm. Food serves a diversity of functions and creates a variety of effects. This reality mirrors the application of food law in the EU, which is based on several competence norms, often applied together, to effectively regulate the EU food market. Rather than on a single competence norm, food law can be understood as based on a 'web of competences', representing the sum of different facets, which often combines features of several isolated competence norms. The 'web of competences' has proven least pliable with respect to the CAP. Historically, harmonization directives were adopted based on the dual legal basis of Article 43 and Article 100 EEC.[131] Today, however, the dual approach between agriculture and the internal market-oriented food policy appears bifurcated. Nevertheless, in the future, the 'web of competence' approach could support an integrated and holistic regulation of the food system.

Competences impose structural legal constraints that delimit EU action due to the principle of conferral of powers. This is also true for the laws that the EU can pass (see Chapter 3). Accordingly, the EU can only act within the limits of the competences that have been conferred upon it by the EU treaties.[132] Competences also entail significant policy implications: first, in shaping 'policy spheres', such as the Farm to Fork Strategy and the Common Agricultural Policy, and, secondly, in

[131] Ferdinando Albisinni, 'Agricultural and Food Law as Innovation Engine of European Law : The New Scenario' in Vicente Rodriguez Fuentes (ed), *From Agricultural to Food Law* (Wageningen Academic Publishers 2014).

[132] TFEU, art 5.

shaping how underlying competences translate at the institutional level, including which Directorate-General is tasked with policy initiatives.

Because EU action, and by consequence policy and legislation, must follow competence norms, certain deep structural changes in the EU can only be achieved by Treaty reform. Calls for a stronger EU health competence have gained traction[133] and garnered (some) political support among the Member States. Similarly, in the best-case scenario, an EU integrated Agri-Food policy would also involve a reshaping of the Treaty articles to create a more synergistic legal environment, rather than the current co-existence of food within the internal market and agriculture. However, the road to a Treaty change is long and will certainly take years to achieve.

133 Vincent Delhomme, 'Emancipating Health from the Internal Market: For a Stronger EU (Legislative) Competence in Public Health' (2020) 11 European Journal of Risk Regulation 747.

3
EU Institutions and Their Role in Food Policy and Law Making

3.1 Introduction

The impetus for change often comes from the political level; but the political will must be channelled into appropriate legal processes in order to translate policy into law. European Union (EU) food law is created, interpreted, and enforced by legal institutions in specifically assigned legal processes. While EU law institutions do not exist at the EU level only (it is for instance, applied in national courts, and enforced by national food safety authorities), in this book we focus on the EU institutions and their role in food policy and law making. The EU and its institutions can only act within the bounds of their competence under the EU Treaties (see Chapter 2). To exercise the Union's competences, the institutions can adopt a range of legal acts, including regulations, directives, decisions, recommendations, and opinions as explicitly mentioned in the Treaty on the Functioning of the European Union (TFEU).[1]

Political actors and policy strategies stimulate the development of EU food legislation. The most recent significant political directions are established by the European Commission for the period 2019–2024 under the Green Deal policy. The Farm to Fork Strategy (2020) is one of many strategies of the Green Deal. It intends to introduce sustainability in the EU's food system. To translate this ambition into law, the EU legislative process, which incorporates supranational and intergovernmental decision makers, must pass legislation. This legislation can then be executed through delegated and implementing acts by the European Commission. Over the next five years, we can expect significant changes in the food law domain due to the proposed sustainability overhaul of food legislation.

When making laws, each EU institution takes on a specific role, which it exercises depending on the selected legal process and its mandate circumscribed by the EU Treaties. The main institutions involved in the EU legislative process are the triad of the European Commission, the Council of the European Union, and the European Parliament. The TFEU further foresees that legislative acts may endow the Commission with powers to adopt non-legislative acts through delegation or

[1] Consolidated version of the Treaty on the Functioning of the European Union [2012] OJ C326/47 (TFEU), art 288.

EU Food Law. Hanna Schebesta and Kai Purnhagen, Oxford University Press. © Hanna Schebesta and Kai Purnhagen 2024.
DOI: 10.1093/9780198901570.003.0004

implementation mandates. Especially in the technically complex area of food law, such kind of acts are very widely used.

This chapter provides a detailed account of the food law-making processes and discusses the conceptual framing of the concepts of risk assessment, risk management, and risk communication. The chapter first outlines the main institutional actors, their legal foundations, and institutional constraints with a focus on food law (section 3.2). It provides an overview of the distinct trajectories through which food law is made, the institutions involved, and their role in the relevant legal procedures (section 3.3), including the role of the European Commission and technical aspects of the committee procedure (section 3.3.5).

3.2 EU Institutions and their role in policy and law making

The EU is founded on the Treaty on European Union (TEU)[2] and the Treaty on the Functioning of the European Union (TFEU),[3] and governed by the Charter of Fundamental Rights of the European Union (CFR).[4] The Treaties circumscribe not only the competences conferred on the EU (see Chapter 2) but also the mandate and constraints on the power of EU institutions in exercising these competences.[5] The Treaties name the European Parliament, the European Council, the Council, the European Commission (Commission), the Court of Justice of the European Union (CJEU), the European Central Bank, and the Court of Auditors as EU Institutions.[6] The European Parliament, the Council, and the Commission are assisted by an Economic and Social Committee (EESC) and a Committee of the Regions (CoR) acting in an advisory capacity.[7] They act in accordance with the procedures, conditions, and objectives set out in the Treaties, and practice mutual sincere cooperation.[8]

This section presents an overview of the EU institutions with a specific focus on their role in food policy and law making.

3.2.1 The European Council: the political lines

The European Council is an intergovernmental body of the heads of state and government of all EU countries and sets the general political directions and priorities

[2] Consolidated version of the Treaty on European Union [2012] OJ C326/13 (TEU).
[3] TFEU.
[4] Charter of Fundamental Rights of the European Union [2012] OJ C326/391 (CFR).
[5] TEU, art 5.
[6] ibid, art 13.
[7] ibid, art 13(4).
[8] ibid, art 13(2).

for future EU policies.[9] The European Council agreed on five priority areas to guide the EU's work over the next five years in its Strategic Agenda for 2019–2024.[10] These political goals relate to protecting citizens and freedoms; developing a strong and vibrant economic base; building a climate-neutral, green, fair, and social Europe (this priority includes food safety and sustainable agriculture); and promoting European interests and values on the global stage. The guidelines provide an indicator of the priorities that will guide the EU in a given political cycle.

3.2.2 The European Commission: legislative initiator, watchdog, and executive organ

The Commission promotes the common interests of the EU, specifically the application of the Treaties and EU law. The Commission initiates, manages, and executes actions of the EU, and, in specific circumstances, represents the EU externally. Currently, there is one member of the Commission from each Member State country. Once in office, however, the Treaty binds the members of the Commission to act only in the interests of the EU, independent from those of Member States, including their own. Consequently, they must not take instructions from any national governments.[11] At present, the Commission has 27 members, who are in office for a five-year term. From its inception, the von der Leyen Commission has pushed ambitious political guidelines,[12] notably the European Green Deal,[13] part of which is the Farm to Fork Strategy on sustainable food.[14] The Farm to Fork Strategy contains a package of legislative actions addressing the sustainability aspects within existing food legislation (see also Chapter 2),[15] which will result in several Commission proposals in the coming years. More practically, the Commission also publishes an annual communication detailing its work

[9] ibid, art 15.

[10] European Council, 'A New Strategic Agenda 2019–2024' <https://www.consilium.europa.eu/en/eu-strategic-agenda-2019-2024> accessed 10 June 2023.

[11] TEU, art 17.

[12] Ursula von der Leyen, 'A Union That Strives for More—My Agenda for Europe: Political Guidelines for the Next European Commission 2019–2024' (*DG for Communication*, 9 October 2019) <https://ec.europa.eu/commission/sites/beta-political/files/political-guidelines-next-commission_en.pdf> accessed 26 July 2022.

[13] Commission, 'Communication from the Commission to the European Parliament, the European Council, the Council, the European Economic and Social Committee and the Committee of the Regions—The European Green Deal' COM (2019) 640 final (Green Deal).

[14] Commission, 'Farm to Fork Strategy: for a fair, healthy and environmentally-friendly food system' <https://ec.europa.eu/food/farm2fork_en> accessed 26 July 2022.

[15] Hanna Schebesta and Jeroen Candel, 'Game-Changing Potential of the EU's Farm to Fork Strategy' (2020) 1 Nature Food 586; Hanna Schebesta and others, 'Tour de Table: Farm to Fork Law Update' (2022) 17 European Food and Feed Law Review 208.

programme, outlining planned legislative actions.[16] These documents give insights into the mid-term policy initiatives.

The Commission's mandate comprises the right to initiate legislation and hold executive legal powers. With a few exceptions, Union legislative acts may only be adopted on the basis of a Commission proposal,[17] which grants the Commission a quasi-monopoly on proposing new laws. The Commission's right to initiative is important in determining the policy choices and institutional design of EU secondary food law. Moreover, the Commission holds executive powers, allowing it to adopt legal delegated or implementing acts. The powers to adopt these executive non-legislative acts always derive from an underlying legislative act. They give the Commission's procedures an important role in the post-legislative phase of law making, for instance authorizing specific substances for the EU market or designing implementing procedures.

The implementation of the Farm to Fork Strategy is likely to result in a number of legislative proposals from the Commission within the period of 2019–2024 in the food sector.

3.2.2.1 ***Commission Directorates-General***

The Commission is home to Directorates-General (DGs), each with their topic-specific portfolios. The DG SANTE for Health and Food Safety is responsible for EU policy on food safety and health and for monitoring the implementation of related laws; the DG AGRI for Agriculture and Rural Development is responsible for EU policy on agriculture and rural development and deals with all aspects of the Common Agricultural Policy (CAP). The management of fisheries (including aquaculture) is under the auspices of the DG for Maritime Affairs and Fisheries (DG MARE), and environmental matters are overseen by the DG ENV. As a result, there is a division of responsibility within institutions. From a policy perspective it is interesting to note that the DGs have developed distinct intra-organizational identities, which tend to protect different interests and can conflict with each other. Therefore, the substantive content of law and policy may vary depending on which DG takes the lead on particular proposals: for instance, DG Agriculture and Rural Development has been regarded as more sympathetic to farmers' interests, and DG Environment, when formulating the 'Green Public Procurement' criteria for food, was reluctant to include social or ethical considerations that extended

[16] For instance, Commission, 'Communication from the Commission to the European Parliament, the Council, the European Economic and Social Committee and the Committee of the Regions—Commission Work Program 2021 a Union of vitality in a world of fragility' COM (2020) 690 final. The Work Programme 2021 lists: Revision of geographical indications, Revision of Directive 94/62/EC on Packaging and Packaging Waste Directive in order to reinforce the essential requirements for packaging to be placed on the EU market, and Revision of Regulation (EC) 1831/2003 on additives for use in animal nutrition. The 2022 Work Programme foresees no new proposals or REFIT initiatives relating to the Farm to Fork actions.

[17] TEU, art 17(2).

beyond its green mandate.[18] The Farm to Fork Strategy, in particular, risks intra-institutional fragmentation as it combines agriculture, internal market, consumer, environment, and health objectives.

3.2.2.2 The Standing Committees

Within the Commission, Committees work on the implementation of existing legislation. These are known as Standing Committees, and they are composed of national experts. The Committees are therefore intergovernmental in nature, and the decision making is based on voting (see 3.4 below). The most commonly convened Committee in the area of food is the Standing Committee on Plants, Animals, Food and Feed (PAFF). Each Committee is divided into different sections. For instance, the PAFF has fourteen different sections, each covering specific topics such as General Food Law, Biological Safety of the Food Chain, and Novel Food and Toxicological Safety. For three Standing Committees (Phytopharmaceuticals, Genetically Modified Food and Feed and Environmental Risk, and the Regulatory Committee 2001/18/EC), there is an Appeal Committee which is convened when no opinion votes are delivered at the Committee level.

3.2.3 The European Parliament

The European Parliament is the voice of the people of Europe and represents the citizens of the EU.[19] The European Parliament shares legislative and budgetary responsibilities with the Council and exercises political control.[20] Each member is directly elected by EU citizens for five years.

Much of the parliamentary work is undertaken within different Committees. For food law, the most relevant committees are Internal Market and Consumer Protection (IMCO); Environment Public Health and Food Safety (ENVI); and Agriculture and Rural Development (AGRI). Again, the various lenses through which food law can be seen are also reflected in the functions of different institutions. When a legislative proposal is tabled, it is initially discussed in the special parliamentary committees where it is first prepared and then brought to the plenary for voting. Unless it concerns a highly politicized issue, the plenary will often follow the Committee recommendations.

The European Parliament can also pass resolutions on its own initiative. For instance, on the Farm to Fork Strategy, the European Parliament published a resolution, which invited the Commission to use the SFSF 'to set out a future-oriented holistic, balanced, integrated and environmentally, socially and economically

[18] Schebesta and Candel (n 15).
[19] TEU, art 10(2).
[20] ibid, art 14(1).

sustainable common food policy' and commented in detail on the proposed legislative actions.[21]

3.2.4 *The Council of the European Union (the Council)*

The Council of the European Union (the Council or Council of Ministers) represents the Member States.[22] It meets in different configurations,[23] the most relevant formations for the area of food being the Agriculture and Fishery Council, the Environment Council, and the Competitiveness Council. There is one minister from each country and the presidency rotates every six months. In the Council, each Member State sends a political representative (usually the minister in a given policy area) to advocate for national interests.

Within the Council, decisions are prepared by different committees. This is often the Committee of Permanent Representatives in the European Union (COREPER),[24] which is a body composed of national representatives from the Member States, usually ambassadors or civil servants. All matters relating to the CAP are prepared by the Special Committee on Agriculture (SCA).

Together with the European Parliament, the Council exercises legislative and budgetary functions, and shares responsibilities for policy making and coordination. The Council votes on legislative proposals of the European Commission. Voting within the Council is based on different thresholds. Where a simple majority is required, 15 Member States must vote in favour of a proposal. Under qualified majority, a decision is passed if at least 55% (16) of the Member States vote in favour, and the proposal has the support of Member States representing at least 65% of the total EU population. In cases where a unanimous voting requirement applies, every Member State must vote in favour.

In terms of agri-food policy, the Council's position represents the plurality of the EU Member States' governments political views, and is therefore determined by national politics and interests.

3.2.5 *The Court of Justice of the EU*

The Court of Justice of the EU (Court or CJEU) is situated in Luxemburg and is the judicial body of the EU. It consists of one judge from each Member State and is assisted by Advocates-General. The Court's major responsibility is to 'ensure that

[21] European Parliament resolution of 20 October 2021 on a farm to fork strategy for a fair, healthy and environmentally-friendly food system (2020/2260(INI)) [2022] OJ C184/2.
[22] ibid.
[23] ibid, art 16(6).
[24] TFEU, art 240.

in the interpretation and application of the Treaties the law is observed'.[25] It rules on legal actions brought by a Member State, an institution, or a natural or legal person; it gives preliminary rulings at the request of national courts or tribunals regarding the interpretation of Union law or the validity of acts adopted by the institutions; and it adjudicates in other procedures as prescribed by the Treaties.[26] Under the preliminary ruling procedure,[27] the Court interprets EU law in cases referred to it by a national court. Cases then move back to the national jurisdiction where the EU law in question is applied by the national court and the case decided on the facts. There is also the procedure for failure to fulfil an obligation,[28] or actions of annulment, for instance, for lack of competence, infringement of an essential procedural requirement, violation of the Treaties or any rule of law relating to their application, or misuse of powers.[29] Lastly, institutions and EU bodies can be challenged at the Court for a failure to act.[30]

The CJEU has been very active in all fields of EU law, including food, which is a widely traded commodity subject to numerous national regulations. Landmark internal market cases such as *Cassis de Dijon*,[31] *Beer Purity Law*,[32] or *Dassonville*,[33] derive from the area of food and have been seminal in shaping the development of EU integration through the development of EU law.[34]

3.2.6 *The Court of Auditors and the European Central Bank*

The independent Court of Auditors audits the EU finances.[35] It consists of one national of each Member State. Its Work Programme specifies priorities, such as, for instance, pesticides or milk and dairy production in 2018–2020.[36] Its 2022+ programme focuses on CAP accountability and on the Fishery and Aquaculture sector. In addition, the Court of Auditors maintains a research programme that often publishes critical studies: for instance, a review of the area of food safety found that the

[25] TEU, art 19(1).
[26] ibid, art 19.
[27] ibid, art 267.
[28] ibid, arts 19 and 258–260.
[29] TFEU, arts 263–264.
[30] ibid, art 256.
[31] Case C-120/78 *Rewe-Zentral AG v Bundesmonopolverwaltung für Branntwein* [1979] ECR I-649 (*Cassis de Dijon*).
[32] Case C-178/84 *Commission of the European Communities v Federal Republic of Germany* [1987] ECR 1227 (*Beer Purity Law*).
[33] Case C-8/74 *Procureur du Roi v Benoît and Gustave Dassonville* [1974] ECR 837 (*Dassonville*).
[34] Mauro Cappelletti, Monica Seccombe, and Joseph Weiler, 'Integration through Law: Europe and the American Federal Experience' in Joseph HH Weiler (ed), *Book 1 A Political, Legal and Economic Overview* (De Gruyter 1986) 3–68.
[35] TFEU, art 285.
[36] European Court of Auditors, '2020 Work Programme' (2019) <https://www.eca.europa.eu/Lists/ECADocuments/WP2020/WP2020_EN.pdf> accessed 9 September 2022.

EU's system for protecting consumers from chemical hazards in food is currently overstretched, and that the European Commission and the Member States do not have the capacity to implement the system.[37]

The European Central Bank[38] has legal personality and consults on proposed areas within its competence. As food falls outside its competence, it is not a relevant actor in the food system.

3.2.7 *The European Union's advisory bodies*

The European Parliament, the Council, and the Commission are assisted by the European EESC and the European CoR.[39] The EESC consists of representatives from employers' organizations, trade unions, and various other civil society groups, representing socio-economic, civic, professional and cultural interests. The CoR consists of representatives from regional and local bodies who either hold a regional or local authority electoral mandate or are politically accountable to an elected assembly. Both of these advisory bodies operate largely autonomously, based on their own institutional statutes, formulating their own political priorities.

The EESC issued an Opinion on the Farm to Fork Strategy,[40] noting that it insufficiently reflects a comprehensive EU food policy, which should deliver:

> [E]conomic, environmental and socio-cultural sustainability; integration across sectors, policy areas and levels of governance; inclusive decision-making processes; and a combination of compulsory measures (regulations and taxes) and incentives (price premiums, access to credit, resources and insurance) to accelerate the transition towards sustainable food systems.[41]

The CoR also issued an opinion.[42] It called for greater cohesion and synergy between different Green Deal Strategies, and more widely that the future CAP, CFP, operational programmes, and national CAP strategic plans, be

[37] European Court of Auditors, 'Special report no 02/2019: Chemical hazards in our food: EU food safety policy protects us but faces challenges' (2019) <https://www.eca.europa.eu/en/Pages/DocItem.aspx?did=48864> accessed 9 September 2022.

[38] TFEU, art 282.

[39] ibid, art 300.

[40] European Economic and Social Committee, '"From farm to fork": a sustainable food strategy' (Opinion NAT/787, 18 February 2020) <https://www.eesc.europa.eu/en/our-work/opinions-information-reports/opinions/farm-fork-sustainable-food-strategy> accessed 26 July 2022.

[41] ibid.

[42] European Committee of Regions, 'From farm to fork—the local and regional dimension' (141st CoR Plenary Session, 8–10 December 2020, NAT-VII/005) <https://webapi2016.cor.europa.eu/v1/documents/COR-2020-00594-00-01-AC-TRA-EN.docx/content> accessed 26 July 2022.

consistently adapted to the objectives set out in the European Green Deal. It also emphasized the role of the regions in the CAP to continue performing their role as managing authorities. They also called for greater emphasis to be placed on short supply chains and for recognition of the diversity of production systems across Europe.

3.2.8 *Additional advisory mechanisms*

A number of institutionally prepared advisory mechanisms on food policy have proliferated and give advice to the Commission on how the future EU food policy should look. The Commission's Joint Research Centre (JRC) conducts research for the Commission and, for instance, published the Food 2050 foresight study.[43] One of the earlier reports is the EU's food research and innovation policy document, EU Food 2030 policy.[44] The Commission is further consulted by a Group of Chief Scientific Advisers,[45] which, together with Scientific Advice for Policy by European Academies (SAPEA), form the Scientific Advice Mechanism (SAM) that published the report, *Towards a Sustainable Food System.*[46] In 2021, the Commission established a high-level expert group (HLEG), whose mandate is to assess the needs, options, impacts, and possible approaches for an International Platform for Food Systems Science (IPFSS).[47] Next to the HLEG the Expert Group on General Food Law and Sustainability of Food Systems advises the Commission on the revision of EU food law from a national perspective.[48] There is thus no shortage of food policy advisors to the Commission.

[43] Kalliopi Mylona and others, *Delivering on EU Food Safety and Nutrition in 2050—Future Challenges and Policy Preparedness* (JCR Science for Policy Report 2016).

[44] Commission, 'Food 2030: Research and innovation policy to make our food systems ready for the future. Main aims, focus areas under Horizon Europe, timeline and publications' <https://ec.europa.eu/info/research-and-innovation/research-area/environment/bioeconomy/food-systems/food-2030_en> accessed 26 July 2022.

[45] Commission, 'Group of Chief Scientific Advisors: How the group works, members, scientific advice topics, news and events' <https://ec.europa.eu/info/research-and-innovation/strategy/support-policy-making/scientific-support-eu-policies/group-chief-scientific-advisors_en> accessed 26 July 2022.

[46] Commission, Directorate-General for Research and Innovation, Group of Chief Scientific Advisors, *Towards a Sustainable Food System: Moving from Food as a Commodity to Food as More of a Common Good* (Independent Expert Report—Scientific Opinion No 8, March 2020).

[47] Commission, 'New Highly Level Expert Group to assess need for an International Platform for Food Systems Science' (News on Research and Innovation, 17 February 2021) <https://ec.europa.eu/info/news/new-high-level-expert-group-assess-need-international-platform-food-systems-science-2021-feb-17_en> accessed 26 July 2022.

[48] Commission, 'Expert Group on General Food Law and Sustainability of Food Systems (E03020)' <https://ec.europa.eu/transparency/expert-groups-register/screen/expert-groups/consult?do=groupDetail.groupDetail&groupID=3020> accessed 9 September 2022.

3.2.9 *Inter- and intra-institutional cooperation*

The Green Deal and the Farm to Fork Strategy are political initiatives led by the Commission, manifesting the idea of a 'political Commission'. By comparison, the European Council has been relatively non-directional in its political guidance and emerged more as a crisis broker reacting to current events such as financial crises, migration, pandemics, and wars.

The European Parliament, the Commission, and the Council operate under inter-institutional agreements that govern their cooperation with one another.[49] The agreement on better law making is one of the most significant inter-institutional agreements.[50] It commits the three institutions to agree on multiannual priorities and to adopt a joint declaration on annual inter-institutional priorities based on the Commission's annual work programme. A key ambition set out in the joint declaration for 2021 is to implement the European Green Deal,[51] which was reiterated in 2022,[52] and for 2023–2024[53].

Nevertheless, in analysing 'EU policy', the EU deserves to be recognized as a complex institutional network, characterized by distinct inter- and intra-institutional interests and relationships. In this vein, the Farm to Fork Strategy has a 'complex institutional embedding', which can give rise to 'bickering over mandates'[54] and conflicting policy ideas.

3.3 EU law making—who makes what kind of law, and how?

EU institutions can only act within the limits of the competences conferred on them in the Treaties to attain the objectives set out therein. Every piece of legislation in the EU is based on a Treaty article that grants competence to the EU to act in a specific matter (see Chapter 2, and section 3.2.1).

The EU legislative process is the most common law-making process. It closely resembles the methods used by national governments to pass legislation. In addition, EU law can be enacted by the Commission, by means of delegated acts, or by the Commission under the oversight of national experts in the Committee Procedure for implementing acts.

[49] TFEU, art 295.

[50] Interinstitutional Agreement between the European Parliament, the Council of the European Union and the European Commission on Better Law-Making [2016] OJ L123/1 (Better Law Making).

[51] Joint Declaration of the European Parliament, the Council of the European Union and the European Commission on EU Legislative Priorities for 2021 [2020] OJ C451/1.

[52] Joint Declaration of the European Parliament, the Council of the European Union and the European Commission on EU Legislative Priorities for 2022 [2021] OJ C514/1.

[53] Joint Declaration of the European Parliament, the Council of the European Union and the European Commission EU Legislative Priorities for 2023 and 2024 [2022] OJ C491/1.

[54] Schebesta and Candel (n 15).

3.3.1 *The cascade of powers conferred and legal competence*

The EU, and therefore EU law making, is constrained by the principle of conferral of powers,[55] and by the principles of subsidiarity[56] and proportionality.[57] Under the principle of conferral of powers, the EU can only act within the limits of the competences conferred upon it by the Member States in the Treaties. Subsidiarity implies that in areas of non-exclusive competence, the Union shall act only if and in so far as the objectives of the proposed action cannot be sufficiently achieved by the Member States. The institutions must apply the principle of subsidiarity, as also laid down in the Treaty Protocol on the application of the principles of subsidiarity and proportionality.[58] National Parliaments furthermore have a role in ensuring compliance with the principle of subsidiarity in accordance with the procedure set out in that Protocol. Under the principle of proportionality, the content and form of Union action may not exceed what is necessary to achieve the objectives of the Treaties. The institutions apply the principle of proportionality, again as laid down in the Protocol on the application of the principles of subsidiarity and proportionality.

By virtue of the conferral of powers, EU legislative actions of the EU are restrained by the division of competence between the EU and Member States (exclusive or shared), by the named objectives of the EU in the Treaty, and the corresponding substantive Treaty legal basis that determines which kind of measures can be adopted using which kind of procedure in order to pass legislation. The selection of a legal basis can significantly impact the procedure for adopting legislation, thereby influencing the law-making possibilities.

In food law, many measures are adopted with the objective of establishing the internal market, as outlined in Article 26 TFEU and Article 3 TEU. Article 114 TFEU serves as the connected legal basis to realize the Article 26 objectives, which in turn prescribes the ordinary legislative procedure for action. For instance, the legal basis of the Novel Food Regulation (NFR) is Article 114 TFEU.

Other legal bases for the EU institutions to act are the application of competition rules to the CAP;[59] legislation concerning the CAP;[60] measures to eliminate distortions in the internal market;[61] public health (measures to tackle common safety concerns in the health sphere);[62] consumer protection;[63] and the environment

[55] TEU, art 5(2).
[56] ibid, art 5(3).
[57] ibid, art 5(4).
[58] Consolidated Version of the Treaty on the Functioning of the European Union—Protocols—Protocol (No 2) on the application of the Principles of subsidiarity and proportionality [2008] OJ C115/206.
[59] TFEU, art 42, which refers to art 43(2).
[60] ibid, art 43(2).
[61] ibid, art 116.
[62] ibid, art 168(4).
[63] ibid, art 169(3).

(Community measures to achieve environmental objectives except for measures of a fiscal nature).[64] The relationship between food law and agricultural policies is the most complex. While the CAP legal basis calls for the ordinary legislative procedure,[65] significant exceptions grant the Council exclusive authority in many respects (see also Chapter 2).

3.3.2 *EU legal acts*

EU institutions can exercise EU competence through various types of legal acts. The major legal acts are enumerated in Article 288 TFEU and comprise Regulations, Directives, Decisions, Recommendations, and Opinions. These acts are not exhaustive; in practice, EU institutions enact all types of legally binding and legally non-binding acts, such as White Papers and Communications. Various categorizations have been adopted to classify the different types of acts. The most basic category distinguishes between legally binding and legally non-binding acts. Article 288 TFEU, for example, distinguishes between legally binding Directives, Regulations, and Decisions and legally non-binding Recommendations and Opinions. Non-binding acts, however, still hold the issuing institution accountable for their content, despite not being legally binding. For example, if an institution or Member State's action aligns with an action or interpretation proposed by the Commission in a legally non-binding document, the Commission cannot initiate an infringement procedure against it.

3.3.3 *Legislative and non-legislative legal acts*

Regulations, Directives, or Decisions[66] are legislative acts, which are drawn up through a designated EU legislative process. However, other types of legal acts can be passed in processes that are outside of the standard legislative procedures; they are executive in nature. The Commission can adopt delegated acts. A legislative basic act may delegate power to the Commission to adopt non-legislative acts of general application that supplement or amend certain non-essential elements of the legislative act. In addition, the Commission, through the Committee Procedure, can adopt implementing acts where uniform conditions for implementing legally binding Union acts are needed and a legislative basic act confers implementing powers on the Commission. Legislative and non-legislative

[64] ibid, art 192(1).
[65] ibid, arts 42(1) and 43(2).
[66] ibid, art 289.

Table 3.1 *Regulatory Framework*

	Legislative Act	Delegated Act	Implementing Act
Purpose	Create legal framework	Supplement or amend non-essential elements of the legislative act	Provide uniform conditions for implementing legally binding Union acts
Actor	Legislative procedure	European Commission	European Commission (or Council in specific cases)
Committees	No	No	Yes, Regulation (EU) 182/2011
Legal basis	Competence derives from Treaty legal basis	Competence derives from basic legislative act	Competence from basic legislative act, Regulation (EU) 182/2011
Oversight	EP and Council participate according to the legislative procedure	EP and Council may object against the delegation or revoke it	Member States' mechanism of control under Regulation (EU) 182/2011, EP and Council right of scrutiny

Source: TFEU, arts 289–291 and Regulation (EU) 182/2011.

(delegated and implementing acts)[67] together form the regulatory framework (see Table 3.1).

Another common terminology to describe the sources of law that together make up the regulatory framework is that of primary, secondary, and tertiary law. The Treaties are considered primary law and establish the distribution of competences between the EU and the EU Member States, and the powers and mandates of the European institutions. Legislative acts are secondary law, in that they derive their validity from the conferred power to act in the Treaties. Delegated and Implementing Acts, in turn, are considered tertiary law as their legal validity is grounded in specific individual legal acts (known as 'basic acts') that confer relatively circumscribed and specific powers on the Commission. Lastly, case law is considered primary law as well.

It has been observed that the area of EU food and agricultural (CAP) law is a mass producer of tertiary, that is, non-legislative law, responsible for over half of the EU output of this kind.[68] Tertiary law is used for a wide range of purposes. It

[67] In 2019, the delegation and implementation powers in a number of laws, including the GFLR, were updated by Regulation (EU) 2019/1243 of the European Parliament and of the Council of 20 June 2019 adapting a number of legal acts providing for the use of the regulatory procedure with scrutiny to Articles 290 and 291 of the Treaty on the Functioning of the European Union [2019] OJ L198/241.

[68] Jens Karsten, 'Lisbon Comitology and Tertiary Law—The Example of Food and Farm Law' in Eljalill Tauschinsky and Wolfgang Weiß (eds), *The Legislative Choice Between Delegated and Implementing Acts in EU Law: Walking a Labyrinth* (Edward Elgar 2018) 93. In 2015, 137 delegated

is commonly employed in food law to create a 'skeleton law with no flesh on the bones'.[69] This means that the broad regulatory conditions are established in a legislative act, while detailed conditions are established by the Commission in delegated acts or through the Committee procedure in implementing acts. An example is the Smoke Flavourings Regulation.[70] This Regulation is set forth in a legislative act, while the compilation of the positive list was delegated to the Commission to establish through the Committee procedure as an implementing act. This approach was challenged in *United Kingdom v Parliament and Council*,[71] the UK arguing that such a two-tiered system would not result in sufficient harmonization as required by the legal base. The Court, by contrast, found that the legislature must determine in the basic act the essential elements of the harmonizing measure in question,[72] but that a system of compiling a list of products authorized throughout the Community to the exclusion of all other products leads to harmonization within the meaning of ex-Article 95 EC Treaty.[73] It is therefore important that the basic act contains the essential elements that characterize a harmonization measure.[74]

Choosing between legislative acts, delegated acts, or implementing acts involves a power-struggle between the Commission and the Council on one side, and the European Parliament on the other. The involvement of the European Parliament is most significant in legislative acts and it retains important oversight functions in delegated acts, while implementing acts are the purview of national review through the Committee Process. Evidently,[75] the European Parliament prefers delegated acts because it retains a veto in that realm.

acts and 1,494 implementing acts were adopted in the EU in total. Of these, over half of the total implementing acts were linked to food and farm: 116 implementing acts came from DG AGRI, and 671 from DG SANTE.

[69] ibid 97.

[70] Regulation (EC) 2065/2003 of the European Parliament and of the Council of 10 November 2003 on smoke flavourings used or intended for use in or on foods [2003] OJ L309/1 (Smoke Flavourings Regulation).

[71] Case C-66/04 *United Kingdom of Great Britain and Northern Ireland v European Parliament and Council of the European Union* [2005] ECR I-10553 (*United Kingdom v Parliament and Council*).

[72] ibid, para 48.

[73] ibid, para 49.

[74] ibid, para 58.

[75] Karsten (n 68) 103, discussing the legislative history of the Food for Specific Groups Regulation (FSGaP Regulation) and the NFR. In the FSGaP Regulation, Parliament was able to impose delegated acts, while in the NFR implementing acts using both the advisory procedure (NFR, art 8) and the examination procedure (NFR, arts 12 and 18).

3.3.4 Legislative acts

The legislative acts or instruments in the EU are Directives, Regulations, and Decisions.[76] Directives are of general application, but they must be transposed by the Member States, that is, each country will pass a national law which implements the requirements and goals of the Directive. Regulations, in contrast, are directly and immediately applicable at the national level, including in national courts. This means they become uniform EU law without the need for additional national implementation measures.

The earlier food law instruments were all passed as Directives, although they contained very detailed obligations. Since the creation of the General Food Law (GFLR),[77] however, the area of food law is largely governed by Regulations, and only a few Directives remain applicable in the field. This highlights that EU food law is becoming more distinctly governed by the EU.

3.3.4.1 ***The ordinary legislative procedure***

The regular procedure to pass EU legislation is the ordinary legislative procedure, which is most commonly used in the area of food. The ordinary legislative procedure[78] consists of the joint adoption by the European Parliament and the Council of a Regulation, Directive, or Decision based on a proposal from the Commission. The procedure is conducted in the following steps.[79] The Commission drafts a proposal that goes to the European Parliament and the Council. There are then two readings: in the first reading, both institutions, that is, the European Parliament and the Council, give their opinion and suggest amendments. In the second reading, voting takes place. Under the ordinary legislative procedure, the Council needs a qualified majority, and the European Parliament needs a majority. The Commission does not participate in the voting, but gives an opinion on the process that influences the voting procedure within the Council. If no agreement can be reached, the proposal is discussed in a third reading in the Conciliation Committee.

3.3.4.2 ***Policy regarding EU law making***

An omnipresent and powerful influence in law making comes from within the Commission itself, through its general policy regarding law making. A highly influential initiative has been the Commission's continued quest for 'better regulation'.

[76] TFEU, art 289.

[77] Regulation (EC) 178/2002 of the European Parliament and of the Council of 28 January 2002 laying down the general principles and requirements of food law, establishing the European Food Safety Authority and laying down procedures in matters of food safety [2002] OJ L31/1 (General Food Law Regulation (GFLR)).

[78] TFEU, art 289.

[79] ibid, art 294.

In 2002, there were initial steps towards a Better Regulation Strategy, which introduced obligatory impact assessments and stakeholder consultations for new proposed initiatives. This was picked up in the Smart Regulation Communication (2010),[80] and lead to a progressively more ambitious approach towards a simplification agenda. As a result, pilot policy evaluations ('fitness checks') were launched in 2010, with the food chain regulation included as one of the sectors in the pilot study. In 2012, the Commission Communication on Regulatory Fitness[81] combined various initiatives into a Regulatory Fitness and Performance Programme (REFIT) aimed at eliminating unnecessary regulatory costs and ensuring that EU legislation is fit for purpose. The Better Regulation agenda (2017) further ensured evidence-based and transparent EU law making based on the views of those that may be affected. The work on Better Regulation and REFIT continued, and the incumbent Commission builds on it.

The 2021 'Better Regulation Communication Joining forces to make better laws'[82] establishes a 'Fit for Future' platform building on the experience with the REFIT Platform. The communication aims to mainstream the United Nations' sustainable development goals (SDGs), pursue a digital by default ambition, and systematically incorporate strategic foresight. It also introduces a 'one in, one out' approach adapted to the policy making. The 'one in-one out' principle implies that for every administrative burden created, an equivalent burden in the same area should be reduced as compensation. This approach will complement the REFIT Programme, which focuses on identifying and removing administrative burdens and unnecessary costs.[83]

When preparing legislation, the Commission works with two instruments: the Better Regulation Guidelines, which set out requirements for the key steps in the policy cycle, and the Better Regulation Toolbox, which provides details on how to fulfil these requirements. The Better Regulation Guidelines (2021)[84] require (i) evaluations and fitness checks, (ii) impact assessments, (iii) input from stakeholders, and (iv) compliance promotion tools. The Better Regulation Toolbox

[80] Commission, 'Communication from the Commission to the European Parliament, the Council, the European Economic and Social Committee and the Committee of the Regions—Smart Regulation in the European Union' (Communication) COM (2010) 543 final (Smart Regulation Communication).

[81] Commission, 'Communication from the Commission to the European Parliament, the Council, the European Economic and Social Committee and the Committee of the Regions—EU Regulatory Fitness' (Communication) COM (2012) 746 final (Commission Communication on Regulatory Fitness).

[82] Commission, 'Communication from the Commission to the European Parliament, the Council, the European Economic and Social Committee and the Committee of the Regions—Better Regulation: Joining forces to make better laws' (Communication) COM (2021) 219 final.

[83] Commission, 'Communication from the Commission to the European Parliament, the Council, the European Economic and Social Committee and the Committee of the Regions—Commission work programme 2022—Making Europe Stronger Together' (Communication) COM (2021) 645 final.

[84] Commission, 'Commission Staff Working Document—Better Regulation Guidelines' SWD (2021) 305 final (Better Regulation Guidelines).

(2021)[85] is a detailed guidance document that prescribes better regulation principles. It provides instructions on conducting impact assessments, identifying impacts, ensuring compliance and monitoring, performing evaluations and fitness checks, conducting stakeholder consultations, and utilizing methodologies for analysing impacts. The two instruments apply internally to all DGs and services involved in the preparation, implementation, and evaluation of EU interventions and are therefore very influential for all areas of law, including EU food law. In addition, the better regulation initiatives instituted a Regulatory Scrutiny Board that assesses the quality of impact assessments, major evaluations, and fitness checks, and issues a positive or negative advice, which may necessitate revision of the document. A negative advice on the impact assessment was given, for instance in the Proposal for a Sustainable Food Systems Framework.

3.3.5 *Delegated acts: non-legislative acts by the European Commission*

The Commission has non-legislative law-making powers. It can exercise delegated powers explicitly conferred upon it. Delegated acts are non-legislative acts of general application,[86] and the authority to delegate must be explicitly granted to the Commission in the basic legislative act. The Commission adopts delegated acts to supplement or amend non-essential elements of a legislative act (therefore also referred to as the basic act). The Treaty further stipulates the limits of this broad discretion: 'objectives, content, scope and duration of the delegation of power shall be explicitly defined in the legislative acts. The essential elements of an area shall be reserved for the legislative act and accordingly shall not be the subject of a delegation of power.'[87] The underlying basic legislative act further needs to explicitly stipulate the conditions for the delegation. For instance, it may specify that the European Parliament and the Council have the authority to revoke the instrument, or that objections from the European Parliament (requiring a majority) and the Council (requiring a qualified majority) can veto such acts. These legal acts are identified by the term 'delegated' in their title.

The GFLR, for instance, lays down the mandate for the European Food Safety Authority (EFSA) to issue scientific opinions at the request of the Commission, on its own initiative, or by the European Parliament or a Member State.[88] The GFLR stipulates that more detailed procedures to be applied by EFSA for scientific opinions are to be adopted by the Commission through delegated acts.[89] The

[85] Commission, 'Better Regulation Toolbox' (November 2021) <https://ec.europa.eu/info/sites/default/files/br_toolbox-nov_2021_en_0.pdf> accessed 26 July 2022.

[86] TFEU, art 290.

[87] ibid, art 290(1).

[88] GFLR, art 29(1).

[89] ibid, art 29(6)(a).

law also contains specific provisions on the exercise of delegation powers by the Commission. These provisions stipulate that the Commission must notify the European Parliament and the Council within a two-month deadline for them to raise objections.[90]

3.3.6 *Implementing acts: non-legislative acts by the Commission with a Committee procedure*

Other types of non-legislative acts are implementing acts, which are used to create 'uniform conditions for implementing legally binding Union acts'.[91] A basic legislative act will confer the implementing powers on the Commission, or in some cases, on the Council. This means that the act does not have to undergo the full legislative process involving the European parliament and the Council; instead it is taken through a Committee procedure.

The meta rules governing the Commission's exercise of its implementing powers are laid down in Regulation (EU) 182/2011,[92] which establishes the rules and general principles concerning mechanisms for Member States to oversee the Commission's exercise of implementing powers. Member State control is conducted through committees composed of the representatives of the Member States and chaired by the Commission, in accordance with one of several specified legal procedures. A basic act may provide for the application of the advisory procedure or the examination procedure, and some older EU laws refer to the so-called Regulatory Procedure with Scrutiny (PRAC).

Under the advisory procedure, the Committee shall deliver its opinion, if necessary by taking a vote. The Commission takes 'utmost account' of the Committee opinion but is not bound by it.[93] For the area of food and other sensitive areas, the examination procedure is commonly applicable,[94] because it is more constraining. In addition, there is a legacy procedure, the PRAC, which is still referenced in several legal instruments until they are formally updated. Under the PRAC, the European Parliament and the Council could veto a Commission draft measure, even if a positive opinion was provided by the Committee.[95]

[90] ibid, art 57a.

[91] ibid, art 291(2).

[92] Regulation (EU) 182/2011 of the European Parliament and of the Council of 16 February 2011 laying down the rules and general principles concerning mechanisms for control by Member States of the Commission's exercise of implementing powers [2011] OJ L55/13.

[93] ibid, art 4.

[94] ibid, art 2(2)(b)(iii), which stipulates that the examination procedure applies for measures relating to the environment, security and safety, or protection of the health or safety, of humans, animals, or plants.

[95] Regulatory procedure with scrutiny was introduced in the 2006 amendment—Council Decision of 17 July 2006 amending Decision 1999/468/EC laying down the procedures for the exercise of implementing powers conferred on the Commission [2006] OJ L200/11.

In the examination procedure, the Commission submits a draft implementing act to one of the Committees. Member States' representatives then decide, usually by voting, on the Commission draft implementing act. If there is a qualified majority of Member States in favour of the Commission's draft act ('positive opinion'), the Commission must adopt the act, while if there is a qualified majority against it ('negative opinion'), the Commission cannot adopt the act. In the absence of a qualified majority for or against ('no opinion'), the Commission may generally[96] adopt the draft implementing act, that is, whether to adopt or not is at the discretion of the Commission. There are important limitations to this rule,[97] namely for (a) specifically sensitive policy areas, (b) where the basic act contains a 'no-opinion clause', or (c) if a simple majority of the comitology Committee members opposes the act.

In the event of a 'negative opinion' or a 'no opinion without Commission discretion', if the Commission deems an implementing act to be necessary, it can present an amended draft, or submit the draft to the Appeals Committee. In these cases, the decision is referred to an Appeals Committee composed of Member State representatives from a higher-level political rank. The Commission is bound by the opinion of the Appeals Committee in the case of both positive and negative opinions. If there is once again a 'no-opinion' outcome, the Commission has the discretion to decide whether or not to adopt an act.

In the current meta-regulation of the process, the Commission can end up exercising strong discretionary implementing powers. By contrast, the European Parliament[98] and the Council have do not have strong roles in Committee procedures, their involvement being limited to the right of scrutiny.[99] This means that they may 'indicate' to the Commission if, in their view, a draft implementing act exceeds the implementing powers provided, and the Commission should express an opinion.

In practice, risk management measures are undertaken through non-legislative measures, and the final outcome of many risk management processes, such as authorizations, takes the legal form of a Commission implementing regulation. For instance, the GFLR is the basic act for implementing acts relating to several issues covered by the GFLR, such as guidelines governing the scientific evaluation of substances, products, or processes which are subject, under Union legislation,

[96] Regulation (EU) 182/2011, art 5.

[97] ibid, art 5: '(a) that act concerns taxation, financial services, the protection of the health or safety of humans, animals or plants, or definitive multilateral safeguard measures; (b) the basic act provides that the draft implementing act may not be adopted where no opinion is delivered; or (c) a simple majority of the component members of the committee opposes it.'

[98] Despite this, the European Parliament emerged as a formidable opponent to the Commission. Influenced by the strong negative public opinion regarding the glyphosate case, it passed several resolutions against the re-approval and organized investigations into the different kinds of allegations tainting the risk assessment.

[99] Regulation (EU) 182/2011, art 11.

to a system of prior authorization or entry on a positive list.[100] For this purpose, the GFLR establishes that the Commission shall be assisted by the Standing Committee on Plants, Animals, Food and Feed,[101] and that the applicable procedure is the examination procedure[102] of Regulation 182/2011.[103]

3.3.6.1 *Implementing acts: contested risk management decisions*

Some policy areas, such as genetically modified organisms (GMOs) and active substance authorizations, are notoriously contentious and regularly leave the risk management choice to the Commission's discretion. This was publicly noted in the case of the glyphosate active substance re-authorization, for example, where the Commission struggled to make a decision due to the divergence of opinions among Member States on this point.

An example of the contested nature of the risk regulatory process is the re-approval process for the active substance glyphosate, which would be carried out through an implementing act. For glyphosate, the responsible committee is the Standing Committee on PAFF, under the auspices of the DG Health and Food Safety, composed of representatives of all Member States and presided by a Commission's representative. The PAFF is divided into 14 different sections, the relevant sections for glyphosate being 'Phytopharmaceuticals-Pesticide residues' (MRLs) and 'Phytopharmaceuticals – Legislation' (PPP placing on the market). The procedure applicable is the examination procedure, and because the protection of the health or safety of humans, animals, or plants is a sensitive policy area, a no-opinion vote will proceed to an Appeal Committee.

Due to the apparent fallibility of the glyphosate risk assessment, the re-approval became highly contested and the risk management phase proved very problematic. The Commission initially put forward an implementing regulation that foresaw a renewal for ten years, subject to some conditions on use, importantly the prohibition on PPP mixtures containing both glyphosate and the coformulant POE-tallowamine. The proposal for an implementing regulation to grant re-approval was discussed in comitology in March for a 15-year extension and in May 2016 for a nine-year extension. These discussions were closed without a formal vote, and in June 2016 the Committee vote resulted in a no-opinion stand-off, failing to muster sufficient support. The proposal then proceeded to the Appeal Committee stage,

[100] GFLR, art 29(6)(b).
[101] ibid, arts 58 and 59.
[102] Regulation (EU) 182/2011, art 5.
[103] The GFLR in its current version still refers to the old comitology procedure that was governed by the Council Decision of 28 June 1999 laying down the procedures for the exercise of implementing powers conferred on the Commission [1999] OJ L184/23, arts 5 and 7. It was replaced by Regulation (EU) 182/2011. Regulation (EU) 182/2011, art 13(1)(c) provides that 'where the basic act makes reference to Article 5 of Decision 1999/468/EC, the examination procedure referred to in Article 5 of this Regulation shall apply and the basic act shall be deemed to provide that, in the absence of an opinion, the Commission may not adopt the draft implementing act, as envisaged in point (b) of the second subparagraph of Article 5(4)'.

where in June 2016 the Committee also failed to support it. In this situation, the Commission unilaterally decided to extend the glyphosate licence until the end of 2017, which it is mandated to do in cases of a no-opinion vote. In the resulting second round, on 9 November 2017, the Standing Committee still could not reach an opinion, with the following formal voting result: 14 Member States in favour, representing a population of 36,95%; 9 Member States against, representing a population of 32,26%, and 5 abstentions, representing a population of 30,79%.[104] The Commission submitted the dossier to the Appeal Committee under an Article 6 procedure on 27 November 2017.[105] This time, the Committee gave a favourable opinion, with 18 Member States in favour representing a population of 65,71%; 9 Member States against representing a population of 32,26% and only 1 abstention representing a population of 2,02%. The glyphosate implementing regulation then entered into force.[106]

While most criticism regarding the EU risk regulatory system has focused on risk assessment and EFSA, it has been noted in the literature that the biggest uncertainty lies, in fact, not in the risk assessment stage, but rather in the risk management stage. Bozzini, for instance, concludes that 'whereas criteria for risk assessment are clearly detailed in the regulation, those informing risk management are largely undetailed'.[107]

3.3.6.2 *The pending proposal to amend the Committee Regulation*

In implementing acts, the meta-regulation rules create a relatively wide discretionary space in which the Commission chooses how to make policy. Empirically, some areas such as GMOs are notoriously exclusively made in this discretionary space.[108] In response, the Commission tabled a proposal for remodelling the Committee procedure at appeals level,[109] thereby addressing risk management in the few (around 2%) highly sensitive decisions made through the Committee procedure. This proposal targets (selective) elements of the risk management phase.

[104] TEU, art 16(4), according to which a 'qualified majority' is defined as at least 55% of the Member States (ie 16) comprising at least 65% of the EU population. A blocking minority must include at least four Member States, failing which the qualified majority will be considered achieved.

[105] Secretariat General, 'DG Sante—Appeal Committee on Phytopharmaceuticals—Pesticides Legislation' CMTD (2017) 1428.

[106] Commission Implementing Regulation (EU) 2017/2324 of 12 December 2017 renewing the approval of the active substance glyphosate in accordance with Regulation (EC) No 1107/2009 of the European Parliament and of the Council concerning the placing of plant protection products on the market, and amending the Annex to Commission Implementing Regulation (EU) No 540/2011 [2017] OJ L333/10.

[107] Emanuela Bozzini, *Pesticide Policy and Politics in the European Union: Regulatory Assessment, Implementation and Enforcement* (Palgrave Macmillan 2017) 50.

[108] ibid.

[109] Commission, 'Proposal for a Regulation of the European Parliament and of the Council amending Regulation (EU) No 182/2011 laying down the rules and general principles concerning mechanisms for control by Member States of the Commission's exercise of implementing powers' COM (2017) 085 final (Commission Proposal for amending Regulation (EU) No 182/2011).

The amendment in particular aims to address the situation where disagreement between Member States results in a 'no opinion' outcome at appeals committee level, resulting in the Commission making decisions without Member States' supporting opinions, and draws attention to the fact that GMO decision making was almost exclusively made in the realm of Commission discretion due to continuous 'no opinion' outcomes at committee level.[110] (1) The proposal foresees a change of the voting rules at the Appeal Committee stage, reducing the occurrence of 'no opinions' under which the Commission then acts without a clear mandate from the Member States. Under the current regime, Member States that are not present or represented are not considered in the overall numbers used to calculate the 55% of Member States and the 65% of the population of the Union. Abstentions, therefore, lead to a higher likelihood of no opinion votes. The draft proposes that abstaining members would not be counted for the purposes of the qualified majority thresholds. The new rules would provide the Commission with a stronger mandate, and means that a positive opinion can be more easily established.[111] (2) A second aspect relates to the involvement of national ministers in the Committee appeals procedure. According to the Commission, participation at appeals level was predominantly limited to Member State representation through their Permanent Representations. A further referral is foreseen to be possible within the Appeal Committee where no opinion is reached, allowing for escalation to a higher political level, namely the ministerial level. Overall, this leads to a politicization of the Committee procedure, which had always been hailed as technical working groups; at the same time, this rule only applies to the most sensitive decisions, and therefore a higher representation may be warranted. (3) With respect to transparency, the proposal suggests making the votes of Member State representatives public, increasing voting transparency at the Appeal Committee. (4) Lastly, the proposal foresees that in the event of a no opinion outcome in an Appeal Committee, a nonbinding advisory opinion by the Council can be requested, 'with a view to obtaining its political orientation on the implications of the no opinion outcome, including the institutional, legal, political and international implications'.[112]

[110] Commission Implementing Regulation (EU) 2016/1056 of 29 June 2016 amending Implementing Regulation (EU) No 540/2011 as regards the extension of the approval period of the active substance glyphosate [2016] OJ L173/52.

[111] Greenpeace has criticized the legislative proposal, arguing that: 'the European Commission presented a proposal to revise the decision-making rules under the so-called "comitology" procedure that is used, among other things, for approvals of products such as pesticides and GMOs. The proposal changes the voting rules for the Appeal Committee, which is invoked when there is no qualified majority of member states for or against in the first committee mandated to vote. Appeal Committee abstentions would not be counted. This could open the door to regulatory approvals even when only a small number of countries support them.' Greenpeace European Unit, 'Commission revises EU decision-making rules in move to avoid blame' (14 February 2017) <https://www.greenpeace.org/eu-unit/issues/democracy-europe/870/commission-revises-eu-decision-making-rules-in-move-to-avoid-blame/> accessed 26 July 2022.

[112] Commission Proposal for amending Regulation (EU) 182/2011.

An issue which is not addressed in the proposal is the latitude granted to the Commission *within* the risk management phase; and, notably, *how* the Commission should exercise its discretion, for instance by clarifying the role of the precautionary principle. Instead, the proposed mechanisms mean that the Commission's position is subject to national politics. The Commission's role thereby changes from one of a supranational institutional autonomous actor into the diligent executor of Member States' combined will. This would lead to strong renationalization and politicization of EU policy making. While the proposal clearly identifies problematic features of the Committee process, it seems politically unlikely that it will be adopted.

3.3.7 The legal status of soft law and case law

The previously discussed legal acts are all legally binding. There are two types of formal legal acts that fall in the realm of soft law: Opinions and Recommendations. They are not binding, but they are authoritative. Alongside these, the food regulatory framework is characterized by a dense array of administrative documents. The European Commission issues 'soft law', such as communications and notices. EFSA, on the other hand, issues, for instance, administrative or scientific guidance. Soft law documents are not legally binding in a strict sense. They explain the law, and provide details and examples in order to clarify EU legal instruments. Soft law acquires a 'quasi-legal' effect based on the general principles of administrative accountability and good administration.[113] Therefore, food business operators may rely on the interpretation given in such documents in good faith.

The case law of the Court is an authoritative and binding legal source. The CJEU itself is not technically speaking bound by its own precedent,[114] but in a wider sense EU case law implies that 'a prior judicial decision which has normative implications beyond the context of the particular case in which it was delivered'.[115] Given the far-reaching implications that CJEU judgments have had on the understanding of legal acts, such as in the case of defining GMOs,[116] the Court can indeed be regarded as a law-making institution.

[113] Fabien Terpan, 'Soft Law in the European Union—The Changing Nature of EU Law' (2015) 21 European Law Journal 68, 74.

[114] Tamás Szabados, '"Precedents" in EU Law—The Problem of Overruling' (2015) 1 ELTE Law Journal 125.

[115] Jan Komárek, 'Judicial Lawmaking and Precedent in Supreme Courts' (2011) LSE Law, Society and Economy Working Papers 4/2011 <http://www.lse.ac.uk/collections/law/wps/WPS2011-04_Komarek.pdf> accessed 26 July 2022.

[116] Kai Purnhagen and others, 'EU Court Casts New Plant Breeding Techniques into Regulatory Limbo' (2018) 36 Nature Biotechnology 799.

3.4 Reflection

The EU institutions each have a specific and circumscribed role in the EU legal system and when transforming policy into law. The institutions' general mandates are prescribed in the Treaties and complemented by specific rules in secondary legislation.

Policy integration is one of the recognized challenges for the transformation of the food system,[117] and calls for the integration of food policy[118] and a move from silo to system are increasingly prominent.[119] At a content level, the functional distribution of the Treaty law competences is largely repeated (although not identical) within the institutional structures. Although the Better Law Making agenda aims to improve inter- and intra-institutional cooperation, it is clear that responsibility for specific initiatives in different DGs in the Commission or the Committees in the European Parliament can lead to opposing directions on implementing policy agendas. The constitutive institutional rules in that sense reinforce functional 'silo-thinking', for instance when it comes to environment, health, trade, and agricultural issues.

In addition, although EU food law is largely set at the EU level with marginal discretion for Member States on specific issues, it is the Member States and their national representatives who ultimately decide which laws are adopted in the first place. In the legislative process, the Commission takes the lead by proposing legislation, which is then most often to be decided on by the European Parliament and the Council. During non-legislative law making, the Commission holds an executive role when using delegated acts. In contrast, in the Committee procedure for implementing acts, the Member States retain an important oversight role through their representation in the Committees. Originally, the Committee procedure was designed as a final mechanism for overseeing residual Commission powers. The governance theories at the time conceived the 'independence of the Commission' from Member State influence as a way of preventing politicization due to too much political Member State involvement, and (largely) as a desirable mechanism. This logic is increasingly being reversed. What was once conceived as a safeguard of the supranational institutions' independence has now been described as a discretionary space lacking the legitimacy deriving from national governments. Therefore, in most cases, Member States have an important role to play not only during legislative law making, but (with the exception of delegated acts) also at

[117] Jeroen Candel and Robbert Biesbroek, 'Toward a Processual Understanding of Policy Integration' (2016) 49 Policy Sciences 211.

[118] Peter Jackson and others, *A Sustainable Food System for the European Union* (SAPEA 9 April 2020) <https://doi.org/10.26356/sustainablefood> accessed 26 July 2022. More nuanced, Jeroen Candel and Laura Pereira, 'Towards Integrated Food Policy: Main Challenges and Steps Ahead' (2017) 73 Environmental Science & Policy 89.

[119] Editorial, 'From Silos to Systems' (2020) 1 Nature Food 1.

the level of post-legislative law making. In this vein, the question raises whether Member States are willing to fully support the ambitious goals of the Commission with respect to the sustainability transition of the EU food system.

The Farm to Fork policy resulted in a number of legislative proposals by the European Commission; these will have to undergo the legislative process, where they are subject to modification, and they must gain the approval of both the European Parliament, representing the EU citizens' will, and the Member States in the Council. In the remainder of the book, we will outline the anticipated legal changes and their timing as a consequence of the ongoing implementation of the Farm to Fork Strategy.

4
Internal Market Law and Food

4.1 Introduction

In terms of regional economic integration models, the European Union (EU) shows a very high degree of integration as it comprises an area of free trade among its members, a joint customs union, and a common, integrated market with mobility across borders of goods, persons, services, and capital. The establishment of a common market, and later the internal market, has been one of the core ambitions during the realization of the European integration project (Chapter 1).

Being essential to the functioning of the EU, these ambitions are enshrined at Treaty level. Article 26 of the Treaty on the Functioning of the European Union (TFEU) sets forth the aim of establishing and ensuring the functioning of the internal market, defined as 'an area without internal frontiers in which the free movement of goods, persons, services and capital'. The internal market will extend to agriculture, fisheries, and trade in agricultural products,[1] but the rules governing the internal market only apply to the extent that they are not expressly divergent from the rules of the Common Agricultural Policy (CAP).[2] The internal market is further shaped by the rules on competition that prohibit cartels, abuse of dominant positions, and illegal state aids. The internal market is an area of shared competence,[3] which means that the EU and the Member States may legislate, although Member States may do so only to the extent that the EU has not already exercised its competence in that area.[4] The main legal basis for achieving the internal market objectives is Article 114 TFEU on the approximation of laws of the Member States (Chapter 3).

This chapter provides an overview of food in the internal market, focusing specifically on the element of the free movement of goods. This comprises, on one hand, the free movement of goods provisions outlined in the Treaty, as well as landmark case law rendered on these provisions by the Court of Justice of the EU (CJEU) in the area of food. On the other hand, it also concerns the codified general internal market legal frameworks, notably for the *ex-ante* obligation on Member States to inform the Commission of their technical domestic laws before they enter

[1] TFEU, art 38.
[2] ibid, arts 39–44.
[3] ibid, art 4(2)(a).
[4] ibid, art 2(2).

EU Food Law. Hanna Schebesta, and Kai Purnhagen, Oxford University Press. © Hanna Schebesta and Kai Purnhagen 2024.
DOI: 10.1093/9780198901570.003.0005

into force, and the codified Mutual Recognition Regulation, which sets up administrative procedures for the decentralized application of the mutual recognition principle at Member State level.

The free movement Treaty articles have lost much of their significance in relation to food. This is for a large part due to the fact that the food sector is widely harmonized. Almost all EU food issues are nowadays covered by secondary legislation, which largely precludes recourse to the free movement Treaty articles. In addition, the obligation on Member States to inform the Commission of their technical domestic laws, including regarding food issues, prevents obstacles to the free movement of goods arising in the first place. Lastly, due to the legislative operationalization of mutual recognition, mutual recognition issues should be resolved at the decentralized level by the authorities of the Member States. It is interesting to note that in this way, the application of the pertinent free movement of goods articles is transferred to the national level. This procedure should be much more accessible and practicable than a long-standing litigation in order to reach the CJEU.

Nevertheless, can we claim that the internal market is now complete? The chapter's conclusions challenge the textbook narrative of the successful completion of the internal market, and instead point to an administratively managed reality of the free movement of foods. In addition, at least for the area of food, we can predict a wave of food sustainability legislation, which is not covered (yet) in existing secondary legislation. This could potentially revive the relevance of the Treaty provisions regarding the free movement of goods.

4.2 Food and the free movement of goods: the origins

Article 26 TFEU sets the aim of establishing and ensuring the functionality of the internal market, defined as 'an area without internal frontiers in which the free movement of goods, persons, services and capital'. The free movement of goods is therefore one of the four freedoms that make up the internal market, and it is fleshed out in Articles 28–37 TFEU. This aspect of the internal market is particularly significant for EU food law, as foods items can be categorized as 'goods' and—as the CJEU has clarified—'foodstuffs lawfully manufactured and/or marketed in other Member States'[5] are within the scope of the free movement of goods.

Components of the free movement of goods (Articles 28–29 TFEU) are the customs union, which prohibits customs duties and measures with equivalent effect on imports and exports between the Member States (Article 30 TFEU) and the fixing of a joint external common customs tariff (Article 31 TFEU), customs

[5] Case C-24/00 *Commission of the European Communities v French Republic* [2004] ECR I-1277 (*Commission v French Republic*), para 60.

cooperation (Article 33 TFEU), and the prohibition of quantitative restrictions between Member States (Articles 34–37 TFEU).

The free movement of goods is designed as a prohibition of quantitative restrictions and measures of equivalent effect between Member States, and is laid down in Article 34 TFEU (for imports) and Article 35 TFEU (for exports). The scope of these provisions is extensive, but not unlimited. Article 36 TFEU allows Member States to introduce justified prohibitions (bans) and restrictions. A trade restriction under Articles 34 and 35 can be justified 'on grounds of public morality, public policy or public security; the protection of health and life of humans, animals or plants; the protection of national treasures possessing artistic, historic or archaeological value; or the protection of industrial and commercial property'. Article 36 TFEU also specifies that such obstacles may not be 'a means of arbitrary discrimination' or a 'disguised restriction on trade'. Under the simple Treaty structure, when evaluating whether a national law violates the free movement provisions, a dual argumentation arises: first, one asks whether a national rule constitutes a trade obstacle (a measure equivalent to a quantitative restriction (MEEQR)) under Article 34, and, if so, whether it's legality can be saved by a justification under Article 36 (or another justification accepted in case law).

Given the concise wording of these Treaty provisions, the CJEU has taken an active role in developing their meaning through interpretation in case law—so important, in fact, that the Court is often called the 'engine of European integration'.[6] The practical application of the free movement provisions by the Court have resulted in a complex system of judicial interpretation, which we can only sketch in its broad contours for the purposes of this book.[7]

In fact, many landmark cases that enshrine major legal principles in EU law stem from the food domain, particularly in the area of the free movement of goods. The CJEU interpretations have clarified and, in many ways, broadened the scope of the basic Treaty provisions. In *Dassonville*,[8] a case regarding whisky, the Court provided an extremely wide interpretation of the scope of Article 34, and of what constitutes a measure having an effect equivalent to an MEEQR, thus ensuring that almost any Member State law could be understood as a restriction of the free movement of goods. In *Cassis de Dijon*,[9] a case involving Cassis liquor, the CJEU established the principle of mutual recognition, although the principle is not explicitly

[6] Andreas Voßkuhle, 'European Integration Through Law: The Contribution of the Federal Constitutional Court' (2017) 58 European Journal of Sociology/Archives Européennes de Sociologie 145; Ulrich Everling, 'Die Zukunft der europäischen Gerichtsbarkeit in einer erweiterten Europäischen Union' (1997) 32 Europarecht 398.

[7] Some general references on this topic include Paul Craig and Gráinne De Búrca, *EU Law: Text, Cases, and Materials* (7th edn, OUP 2020) and Catherine Barnard, *The substantive law of the EU* (5th edn, OUP 2016).

[8] Case C-8/74 *Procureur du Roi v Benoît and Gustave Dassonville* [1974] ECR 837 (*Dassonville*).

[9] Case C-120/78 *Rewe-Zentral AG v Bundesmonopolverwaltung für Branntwein* [1979] ECR I-649 (*Cassis de Dijon*).

mentioned in the Treaty. In addition, the case re-affirmed the idea that the justifications in Article 36 are not exhaustive, and that unwritten 'mandatory requirements', such as consumer protection, can also be accepted. Other famous food cases include the *Beer Reinheitsgebot*,[10] which questioned the legality of a German beer purity requirement, and more recently *Scottish Whisky Association*,[11] which challenged the legality of a minimum unit pricing mechanism on alcoholic drinks.

In the following section, we first explain the relevance of *Dassonville* and *Cassis de Dijon* for the area of free movement of goods law. We then move to a closer examination of how the free movement of goods case law has developed in the area of food law (section 4.3).

4.2.1 Dassonville (1974): the wide scope of the prohibition on trade obstacles

Dassonville[12] is a seminal case from 1974. It is notorious in EU law for providing a very extensive interpretation of what constitutes 'quantitative restrictions', and specifically 'measures having equivalent effect' under (then)[13] Article 30 EEC, which is now Article 34 TFEU.

The case concerned parallel imports of whisky and arose as a preliminary reference by a Belgian court during criminal proceedings against Benoit and Gustave Dassonville. For goods bearing an indication of origin, Belgian law, at the time, required a certificate from the exporting country. The Dassonvilles, however, had bought Scotch Whisky that was freely circulating in France and reimported it to Belgium, making it difficult for them to obtain such a certificate.

The CJEU held that 'trading rules enacted by Member States, which are capable of hindering actually or potentially, intra-Community trade are to be considered as measures having an effect equivalent to quantitative restrictions'.[14] Consequently, a Member State rule requiring a certificate that was less easily obtainable by an indirect rather than a direct importer was regarded as a quantitative restriction, and thus a hindrance to the free movement of goods. The Belgian law thus violated EU law. This interpretation affirmed a very broad scope of the free movement of goods Treaty provisions, capable of capturing almost any trading rule enacted by

[10] Case C-178/84 *Commission of the European Communities v Federal Republic of Germany* [1987] ECR 1227 (*Beer Reinheitsgebot*).

[11] Case C-333/14 *Scotch Whisky Association and Others v The Lord Advocate and the Advocate General for Scotland* EU:C:2015:845 (*Scotch Whisky Association*).

[12] Case C-8/74 *Procureur du Roi v Benoît and Gustave Dassonville* [1974] ECR 837 (*Dassonville*).

[13] With subsequent Treaty changes, the numbering of the articles changed. What is now Article 34 TFEU used to be Article 30 EEC, and then Article 28 EC; Article 36 TFEU used to be Article 36 EEC, and then Article 30 EC.

[14] *Dassonville*, para 5.

Member States, as the trade obstacle did not have to have materialized, and could be purely 'potential'.

4.2.2 *Cassis de Dijon: Mutual Recognition (1979)*

Another classic EU law case is *Cassis de Dijon*,[15] which concerned the interpretation of (then) Articles 30 and 36 EEC. The case is remarkable for instituting—if not inventing—the so-called principle of 'mutual recognition'. The mutual recognition principle, according to the Court, entails that goods that are lawfully provided and marketed in one Member State should in principle be permitted on the market of another Member State, unless the obstacles can be justified under (then) Article 36 EEC or other 'mandatory requirements'.

The case involved the supermarket Rewe, which wanted to import the French liquor *Cassis de Dijon* into Germany. German law, however, required fruit liqueur to contain a minimum alcohol content of 25%, whereas French liqueurs are traditionally weaker, and Crème de cassis only has an alcohol content of about 15–20%.

The CJEU held that 'there is no valid reason why, provided they have been lawfully produced and marketed in one of the Member States, alcoholic beverages should not be introduced in another Member State'. This idea has famously become the principle of mutual recognition. In addition, the CJEU effectively broadened the accepted justifications. In addition to the written justifications of Article 36 TFEU, it recognized 'mandatory requirements' in the general interest as potentially legitimate reasons to justify obstacles under Article 30 TFEU, examples being the effectiveness of fiscal supervision, the protection of public health, the fairness of commercial transactions, and the defence of the consumer.[16] Indeed it is worth noting that the principle of mutual recognition and the extended justifications are not enshrined in the literal wording of the Treaty articles. Nevertheless, in *Cassis de Dijon*, the Court did not accept the justification, as it found that it was a 'simple matter to ensure that suitable information is conveyed to the purchaser'. The measure was therefore found to be in breach of EU law.

4.2.3 *The aftermath of Dassonville and Cassis de Dijon*

The impact of *Cassis de Dijon* was so significant that the Commission published a communication on the implications of the case in 1980,[17] in which it recognized

15 *Cassis de Dijon* (n 9).

16 ibid, para 8. In the literature it had been argued that mandatory requirements could only be invoked when dealing with non-discriminatory obstacles to trade. This distinction is becoming increasingly abandoned; see Craig and de Búrca (n 7) 765.

17 Communication from the Commission concerning the consequences of the judgment given by the Court of Justice on 20 February 1979 in case 120/78 ('Cassis de Dijon') [1980] OJ C256/2.

the need 'to tackle a whole body of commercial rules which lay down that products manufactured and marketed in one Member State must fulfil technical or qualitative conditions in order to be admitted to the market of another' in verifying whether the strict rules by the CJEU had been met. Additionally, the Commission saw the *Cassis de Dijon* ruling as a mandate to enhance its work of harmonization of national laws having an impact on the functioning of the Common Market where barriers to trade to be removed arise from national provisions.

In 1991, in an attempt to curb the expansive scope of the free movement of goods regulations, the CJEU limited its own precedent set in *Dassonville* through *Keck*.[18] The ruling stated that national provisions restricting or prohibiting 'certain selling arrangements' that (1) apply to all relevant traders operating within the national territory, and (2) affect in the same manner, in law and in fact, the marketing of domestic products and those from other Member States, are *not* liable to hinder, directly or indirectly, actually or potentially, trade between Member States within the meaning of the case law initiated by *Dassonville*.

The *Keck* 'exemption' gave rise to intense scholarly debate regarding its utility and operationalization.[19] Nowadays, in surveying general free movement of goods case law it is evident that the *Keck* rule has been largely, but not entirely,[20] replaced by a market access test.[21] Under the market access test, the Court assesses whether a given national measure limits the market access,[22] usually hand in hand with evaluating whether a measure is proportional.

In parallel to this, over time, the Court complemented the dual obstacle-justification framework more systematically with a 'proportionality test'.[23] Broadly speaking, proportionality examines whether a measure is suitable and necessary. Suitability refers to whether the national measure can achieve the pursued (legitimate) aim. Necessity determines if there are no less restrictive measure available.

[18] Case C-267/91 and C-268/91 *Bernard Keck and Daniel Mithouard* [1993] ECR I-6097 (*Keck*), para 16.

[19] For overviews, see Craig and de Búrca (n 7) and Barnard (n 7).

[20] It was, for instance, applied in Case C-198/14 *Valev Visnapuu v Kihlakunnansyyttäjä (Helsinki) and Suomen valtio – Tullihallitus* EU:C:2015:751 (*Alcohol Sale License*).

[21] For an overview, see Barnard (n 7) 102; Kai Purnhagen and Hanna Schebesta, 'A Case moving at the Frontiers of Market Access, Freedom of Goods, the Common Agricultural Policy and Science in Court—Reflections on Scotch Whisky Association' (2016) European Law Review (forthcoming); Kai Purnhagen, 'Anmerkung' (2010) 65 Juristenzeitung 744; Moritz Jesse, 'What about Sunday Trading . . . ?—The Rise of Market Access as an Independent Criterion under Article 34 TFEU' (2012) 3 European Journal of Risk Regulation 437; Astrid Epiney, *Zur Vereinbarkeit der Einführung einer Alpentransitbörse mit den Vorgaben des EU-Rechts – Gutachten im Auftrag der Europaregion Tirol – Sudtirol – Trentino* (Institut Für Europarecht September 2013) 13; Jukka Snell, 'The Notion of Market Access: A Concept or a Slogan?' (2010) 47 Common Market Law Review 456.

[22] In fact, attempts to classify and explain the Court's case laws are divided. Some scholars believe that market access is an overarching principle, whereas others separate discriminatory measures, product requirements, and market access as a separate category within it. See Craig and Búrca (n 7) 750. Barnard (n 7) 105–106 notes the difficulty of establishing whether a *de minimis* rule then applies, that is, whether a substantial market access restriction must exist, and at 140–141 raises criticism.

[23] Wolf Sauter, 'Proportionality in EU Law: A Balancing Act?' (2012) 15 Cambridge Yearbook of European Legal Studies 439.

Sometimes the Court extends this with proportionality balancing testing (known as proportionality *stricto sensu*), in which the balance between different interests is examined. As such, proportionality tends to structure the Court's reasoning, but it does not necessarily lead to more predictable outcomes in case law.[24]

The Court's analysis regarding unjustified obstacles to the free movement of goods has become more complex over time. This section has explained different types of reasoning that are commonly used in general (ie non-food specific) EU law; in this, the summary is far from exhaustive of the subject matter. In the following section we look at the free movement of foods case law specifically.

4.3 An inventory of the case law on the free movement of foods

This section provides a qualitative overview of free movement cases concerning food, separated into the pre- (section 4.3.1) and the post-Lisbon Treaty eras (section 4.3.2). The cases are clustered in subsections based on the type of restrictions involved. The presentation of cases highlights the food products and the national law at issue, the argumentation used by the Court (for instance whether *Keck* or proportionality was applied), and the final outcome (was there a violation of EU law?).

A superficial quantitative analysis of the free movement of goods cases on food that mention 'measures having equivalent effect' shows 2020– present 0 cases; 2010–2020 3 cases; 2000–2009 27 cases; 1990–1999 13 cases; 1980–1989 13 cases.[25]

While *Cassis de Dijon* initiated a series of product requirement litigation in the 1980s and 1990s, followed by 'other issues' in the early 2000s, the post-Lisbon Treaty era sees the number of food law cases based on the free movement of goods provisions significantly decreasing. This is in part explained by the fact that recourse to the Treaty is pre-empted by litigation regarding secondary (harmonized) food legislation (section 4.3.4). In addition, the free movement of goods is nowadays shaped by internal market secondary legislation, notably the duty to notify technical rules and the codification of mutual recognition. The contribution of these pieces of internal market legislation to the fading relevance of the free movement of goods Treaty articles is analysed in section 4.4.

[24] Filippo Fontanelli, 'The Mythology of Proportionality in Judgement of the Court of Justice of the European Union on Internet and Fundamental Rights' (2016) 36 Oxford Journal of Legal Studies 630.

[25] These numbers are based on a search on eur-lex.eu for 'food' and 'measures having equivalent effect', with 78 entries in total, of which 56 were pertinent to the food domain and (now) Article 34 TFEU. The search results are not exhaustive of free movement of food case law, but do give a rough quantitative estimation of the cases concerned. For the purposes of the present chapter, the case selection has been extended using various search strings and case references in literature and policy documents.

4.3.1 Pre-Lisbon case law on food

In the 1970s, we see the Court adjudicating some important free movement of goods cases. In the area of food, *Dassonville* from 1974 (section 4.2.1) and *Cassis de Dijon* from 1979 were among the earliest free movement of food cases. Both find—in no uncertain terms—that the disputed national measure constituted an MEEQR and violated EU law. It is, however, the *Cassis de Dijon* judgment which unleashed an entire series of deregulatory judgments, all of which concluded that national regulations regarding product requirements violated EU law.

Sekt was a prequel to the famous *Cassis de Dijon* case, and forms part of a string of cases that challenged national bans on the importation of products on the basis of specific denominations or product composition requirements. The *Sekt* (alcohol) (1975)[26] case concerned a German rule regarding the reservation of the denominations 'Sekt', 'Weinbrand', and 'Prädikatssekt' exclusively for German products. In this case, however, the German government contended that the rules were justified on grounds of the protection of industrial and commercial property under a national system instituting an indication of origin. The Court disagreed, finding the national measure arbitrary and therefore unjustified. Subsequently, *Cassis de Dijon* (section 4.2.2) and the principle of mutual recognition, in 1979 initiated a series of cases against national product requirements that effectively banned imported foodstuffs from national markets, because foreign products did not correspond to the national product specifications. The impact that *Cassis de Dijon* had is evidenced by the sheer volume of cases on national product requirements that followed (section 4.3.1.1), nearly all of which were deemed to violate the free movement of goods.

4.3.1.1 **Product requirements**

The 1980s witnessed continuous adverse Court jurisprudence around the compatibility of the free movement of goods with different types of national product requirements. These included requirements on product composition (section 4.3.1.2), mandatory product denominations (section 4.3.1.3), packaging (section 4.3.1.4), and labelling (section 4.3.1.5). We see that despite governments increasingly presenting more sophisticated justifications over time, the Court tends to be stringent in accepting these justifications, particularly when it comes to food product requirements. As a result, violations of the free movement of goods are found in almost all product requirement cases.

[26] Case C-12/74 *Commission of the European Communities v the Federal Republic of Germany* [1975] ECR 181 (Sekt).

4.3.1.2 **Product requirements: product compositional requirements**

Typical product requirements of the 1980s are national rules that prescribe a specific compositional product requirement. In the following, various national examples of compositional rules are discussed. *Gilli* (vinegar) (1980)[27] concerned an Italian law stating that vinegar may only contain acetic acid deriving from acetic fermentation of wine. The same provision returned to the Court in *Commission v Italy* (vinegar) (1981).[28] The CJEU established that—although indistinctly applicable to national and foreign products—the Italian law effectively banned all vinegars of agricultural origin from its market. The argument that the 'semantic value' of the word '*aceto*' (Italian for vinegar) would mislead Italian consumers regarding the nature of the product was rejected, and the Court found a violation of EU law. Consistent with the approach taken in *Cassis de Dijon*, the Court relied on the possibility of labelling as a less restrictive alternative to the national law that banned products from domestic markets. Similarly, *Kelderman* (bread) (1981)[29] concerned the legality of a Dutch Bread Order that stipulated a legal quantity of dry matter in bread. The preliminary question was submitted by the national court in criminal proceedings against Kelderman, who had sold 'brioches' exceeding the permissible amount of dry matter. Relying on *Cassis de Dijon* and *Gilli*, the Court confirmed its case law regarding justifications based on imperative requirements relating in particular to the protection of public health, fair trading, and consumer protection. However, once again, the Court concluded that simply labelling the weight and specific composition of the imported product would suffice to meet the objectives of consumer protection, and that the measure therefore breached EU law. *Commission v Italy* (gelatine in confectionary) (1984)[30] concerned another product compositional requirement, namely an Italian restriction on confectionery products containing more than 1% animal gelatine. The Italian government tried to justify this by relying on the imperative reason of consumer protection or even public health—both justifications were curtly dismissed as unsubstantiated: 'as the Court held on numerous occasions, Member States may satisfy such a requirement by adopting an appropriate measure which impedes trade between Member States as little as possible, for example by providing the consumer with suitable information.'[31] Despite the clarity of the line taken by the CJEU, cases continued to be lodged against product requirements, and *Miro* (1985)[32] almost replicated *Cassis de Dijon*. It concerned a Dutch rule stipulating

[27] Case C-788/79 *Herbert Gilli and Paul Andres* [1980] ECR 2071 (*Gilli*).
[28] Case C-193/80 *Commission of the European Communities v Italian Republic* [1981] ECR 3019 (*Commission v Italy*).
[29] Case C-130/80 *Fabriek voor Hoogwaardige Voedingsprodukten Kelderman BV* [1981] ECR 527 (*Kelderman*).
[30] Case C-51/83 *Commission of the European Communities v Italian Republic* [1984] ECR 2793 (*Commission v Italy*).
[31] ibid, para 15.
[32] Case 182/84 *Criminal proceedings against Miro BV* [1985] ECR 3731 (*Miro*).

that Jenever must have a minimum alcohol content of at least 35%, whereas the imported Belgian Jenever only had 30%. Again, the national rule was dismissed. In *Zoni* (1988),[33] an Italian obligation to use only durum wheat for pasta became an issue in criminal proceedings against Zoni, who imported pasta products made from a mixture of common wheat and durum wheat from Germany. The Court held that a general marketing prohibition is contrary to the principle of proportionality. Another case, *Drei Glocken* (1988),[34] again concerned the requirement that pasta should be made exclusively from durum wheat. Although this case had a more extensive treatment of justifications, it nevertheless rejected the public health argument as unsubstantiated. The Court also did not accept arguments relating to additional grounds of certain imperative requirements, notably that suitable labels regarding the nature of the product sold would not be sufficient to make Italian consumers properly aware, or that the Italian government could not guarantee fair trading. The measure was therefore in breach of EU law, much in line with similar cases regarding product requirements.

A specific type of compositional requirements includes purity requirements and substitution prohibitions. The German case *Beer Reinheitsgebot* (1987)[35] concerned the legality of a national purity requirement for beer, namely that beer could only be made from malted barley, hops, yeast, and water, and an absolute ban on the marketing of beers containing any additives. The rule violated EU law and could not be justified on grounds of public health.[36] Less well-known, but with a similar fate, is the case on *Beer Purity* from Greece (1987).[37] Similarly, other (non-alcoholic) products might also be subject to purity requirements at the national level. For instance, *Meat Purity* (1989)[38] concerned a German ban on the importation of meat products that did not comply with German rules instituting stringent requirements on ingredients other than meat. As with other cases concerning the 'purity' of ingredients, the national ban violated the free movement rules. Another variation of purity criteria is the national prohibition of substitutive substances. This was a common type of rule for the dairy sector. *Substitutes for Milk Powder*[39] (1988) and *Milk Imitation* (1989)[40] concerned national rules prohibiting the marketing of milk substitutes in France and Germany respectively. In both instances, these prohibitions on dairy substitutions were regarded to violate the free movement of goods.

[33] Case C-90/86, *Zoni* [1988] ECR 4285 (*Zoni*).

[34] Case C-407/85 *3 Glocken GmbH and Gertraud Kritzinger v USL Centro-Sud and Provincia autonoma di Bolzano* [1988] ECR 4233 (*Drei Glocken*).

[35] *Beer Reinheitsgebot* (n 10).

[36] ibid, para 53.

[37] Case 176/84 *Commission of the European Communities v Hellenic Republic* [1987] ECR 1193.

[38] Case 274/87 *Commission of the European Communities v Federal Republic of Germany* [1989] ECR 229 (*Meat Products*).

[39] Case 216/84 *Commission of the European Communities v French* Republic [1988] ECR 793.

[40] Case 76/86 *Commission of the European Communities v Federal Republic of Germany* [1989] ECR 1021.

The Court, it seems, has spoken. Compositional product requirements that result in a marketing prohibition generally represent an unjustifiable restriction on the free movement of goods. The goals pursued by such marketing restrictions, for instance consumer protection, can be safeguarded equally well by providing adequate food information on the product.

4.3.1.3 ***Product requirements: mandatory descriptions and denominations***

Another type of product requirement relates to mandatory descriptions and denominations of foodstuffs. Product denominations are, in fact, often conceptually intertwined with compositional requirements. *Fietje* (1981)[41] concerned a mandatory description of alcoholic beverages. The Court held that the prohibition on the sale of beverages under a description other than the one prescribed by law necessitates changing the label. Therefore, the national law was to be regarded as an MEEQR, to the extent that the original label supplied the consumers with information on the nature of the product which is equivalent to the description prescribed by law ('information equivalency'). *Deserbais* (Edam) (1988)[42] concerned a product denomination rule. French legislation restricted the use of the name 'Edam' to a type of cheese having a minimum fat content of 40%, whereas Desarbais imported and marketed 'Edam' from Germany with a fat content of only 34.3%. The Court held that Member States were precluded from prohibiting the marketing of products if those products had been lawfully manufactured and marketed under that name within the Member State, and if consumers were provided with proper information. In a variation of this, in *Smanor* (1988)[43] a prohibition on the use of the name 'deep-frozen yoghurt' (because the denomination yoghurt was exclusively reserved for fresh yoghurt) was struck down by the Court.

The culmination of the 'denomination product requirements' saga is evident in later case law, which identifies the way forward for Member States. Member States can enforce stringent domestic requirements, with the understanding that these national laws include a mutual recognition provision. In *Foie Gras* (1998),[44] the Court held that Member State legislation reserving certain trade descriptions to products possessing particular qualities without including a mutual recognition clause for products coming from other Member States, fails to fulfil its obligations under Article 30 EC. This failure occurs because it cannot be justified by imperative requirements of consumer protection or prevention of false descriptions, and it is not proportionate; these aims could be equally achieved through labelling. While a relatively straightforward case in terms of outcome, the Court adds details on the requirements for Member States, and brings to light the relevance of

[41] Case 27/80 *Criminal proceedings against Anton Adriaan Fietje* [1980] ECR 3839 (*Fietje*).
[42] Case C-286/86 *Ministère public v Gérard Deserbais* [1988] ECR 4907 (*Deserbais*).
[43] Case 298/87 *Proceedings for compulsory reconstruction against Smanor SA* [1988] ECR 4489.
[44] Case C-184/96 *Commission of the European Communities v French Republic* [1998] ECR I-6197 (*Foie Gras*).

so-called mutual recognition clauses. Member States may, in fact, enforce strict requirements for their domestic market, but only if they meet the procedural requirement of including a mutual recognition clause.

Overall, in the cases of the 1990s and certainly the 2000s, the Court appears to adopt a less stringent approach, and is more reticent with regards to declaring national rules illegal, often leaving the final assessment to the national courts. For instance, the Court in *Geffroy* (2000)[45]—very typically—held that Member States cannot prohibit alcoholic drinks made from apples, which have been lawfully manufactured and marketed in a Member State under the description of cider, just because they do not comply with legislation regarding the production of cider. This is on the grounds that use of that description would be likely to mislead consumers in that particular Member State. The Court explained that Member States may require producers to alter the description of a foodstuff where a product offered for sale under a particular name is very different, in terms of its composition or production, from the products generally understood under that name. Where the difference is of minor importance, appropriate labelling should be sufficient to provide the purchaser or consumer with the necessary information. It was for the national court to assess this. Overall, the Court held that Article 30 EC did not preclude a national provision from requiring that the labelling of foodstuffs and the labelling methods used must not mislead the purchaser or consumer, especially regarding the characteristics of those foodstuffs. Article 30 EC did, however, preclude a national provision from requiring the use of a specific language for the labelling of foodstuffs, without allowing for the possibility for another language easily understood by purchasers to be used or for purchasers to be informed through alternative means. Whereas the case seems to be in line with earlier rulings on product requirements, it is noteworthy that the Court begins to adopt a more lenient tone. In this instance, the Court refers the decision for a large part to the national level, leaving room for the national measure to be crafted in a manner compliant with the free movement provisions. *Guimont* (Emmenthal) (2000)[46] concerned a national rule prohibiting the marketing of a cheese without rind under the name 'Emmenthal' in that particular Member State. The Court concluded that there was an obstacle to trade because the product conditions (such as having a rind) would make importation more difficult. As the measure was indistinctly applicable to national and imported products, the Court tested the justifications of 'overriding requirements' for fair trading and consumer protection, and whether they were proportionate to the objective pursued and whether less restrictive means could achieve the same goal. Relying on *Geffroy*, the Court reiterated that Member States can require descriptions of foodstuffs to be altered when a product offered for sale under a particular name is so different that it cannot

[45] Case C-366/98 *Yannick Geffroy and Casino France SNC* [2000] ECR I-6597 (*Geffroy*).
[46] Case C-448/98 *Jean-Pierre Guimont* [2000] ECR I-10663 (*Guimont*).

be regarded as falling within the same category anymore. In this specific case, the Court also noted that the Codex Alimentarius allows a cheese without rind to be named Emmenthal, and that other Member States equally market it as such. The Court concluded that Article 30 EC precluded a Member State from prohibiting the marketing of a cheese without rind under the name 'Emmenthal' in that Member State.

Overall, we see a consolidation of the case law in two cases concerning chocolate; one involving a national regulation requiring a change in the sales name for chocolate containing vegetable fat,[47] and another concerning a national requirement to use the name 'chocolate substitute'.[48] In these cases, the Court reinforces the lessons learned: it is legitimate for Member States to ensure that consumers are properly informed (*Smanor*). Member States may require a change in the description of a foodstuff where 'a product offered for sale under a particular name is so different, in terms of its composition or production, from the products generally understood as falling within that description within the Community that it cannot be regarded as falling within the same category' (*Deserbais*, *Geffroy*, and *Guimont*). For minor differences, however, appropriate labelling is sufficient (*Geffroy* and *Guimont*).

4.3.1.4 ***Product requirements: labelling***

While labelling is clearly a preferred alternative to outright bans in the case law, *De Kikvorsch (Beer Acidity)* made it clear that national laws requiring relabelling could equally be regarded as obstacles to trade. In *De Kikvorsch* (*Beer Acidity*) (1983)[49] the Dutch Beer Order challenged the importation of German Berliner Kindl Weisse for exceeding the acidity prescribed for this type of beer in the Netherlands. The Court found a clear impediment to the free movement of goods, and did not accept that the protection of consumers would warrant banning the beer. The Court additionally looked at the obstacle posed by the prohibition of certain information on the label, in this case the prohibition on Kindl's statement of the strength of the original wort (unfermented beer) of beer on the label. The Court found this information requirement made the marketing of imported beer more difficult and more expensive, as the label would need to be altered. It therefore constituted an obstacle to the free movement of goods. While a prohibition on stating confusing information could be justified under consumer protection, it would only be acceptable if consumers were genuinely misled. It was for the national Court, as a question of fact, to ascertain whether the information in the case

[47] Case C-12/00 *Commission of the European Communities v Federal Republic of Germany* [2003] ECR I-9977.

[48] Case C-14/00 *Commission of the European Communities v Italian Republic* [2003] ECR I-523.

[49] Case C-94/82 *De Kikvorsch Groothandel-Import-Export BV* [1983] ECR 947 (*De Kikvorsch*).

would indeed mislead purchasers. This case law further tightened the requirements on national laws.

A requirement to indicate the ingredients used in the compound feedingstuff[50] was deemed justified by the public interest in safeguarding the health of humans and animals, and also by the requirements of consumer protection and fair trading. In contrast, in *German Ham*,[51] a requirement for meat to bear a label stating that it was 'formed shoulder ham composed of ham pieces' under the guidelines for meat and meat products in the German Food Code was regarded as unjustified. Overall, the Court takes a case-by-case approach to labelling. In principle, labelling serves as an information governance solution that is regularly proposed by the Court. At the same time, labelling requirements may themselves constitute an obstacle to trade because of the extra effort involved in changing food product labels. The outcome therefore depends on the national rule in a given case, and the likelihood of the information misleading consumers.

4.3.1.5 ***Product requirements: packaging***

In line with its rulings on product denomination and compositional requirements, the Court regarded packaging requirements for foods as unjustified MEEQRs. *De Smedt* (margarine)[52] (1982) concerned Belgian legislation stipulating that margarine could be sold only in cube-shaped packaging. Belgium argued that the requirement was intended to prevent consumers from confusing butter with margarine and that it was therefore justified. The Court developed an argument on the proportionality principle: the measure went beyond what was necessary to achieve its objective, and the CJEU found—similar to denomination and compositional requirements—that labelling measures would equally achieve this objective, while imposing fewer restrictions on the free movement of goods. *Prantl* (1984) concerned a product packaging restriction on bottles—a German rule that allowed only national producers to use a specific wine bottle shape (*Bocksbeutel*)—was equally regarded as an unjustified MEEQR.[53] Another, similar, packaging requirement was at issue in *Pétillant de raisin*,[54] which concerned a ban on the marketing of 'pétillant de raisin' in traditional champagne-type bottles. The measure clearly constituted an obstacle to the free movement of goods. The Court recalled that in the absence of comprehensive EU legislation on packaging, some disparities between national laws had to be accepted. Nevertheless, none of the justifications sought were accepted and the measure was declared to violate EU law. Packaging requirements were successfully defended only in one, much later, case. In *Schwarz*

[50] Case C-39/90 *Denkavit Futtermittel GmbH v Land Baden-Württemberg* [1991] ECR I-3069.

[51] Case C-383/97 *Criminal proceedings against Arnoldus van der Laan* [1999] ECR I-731.

[52] Case C-261/81 *Walter Rau Lebensmittelwerke v De Smedt PVBA* [1982] ECR 3961 (*De Smedt*).

[53] Case 16/83 *Criminal proceedings against Karl Prantl* [1984] ECR 1299 (*Prantl*).

[54] Case 179/85 *Commission of the European Communities v Federal Republic of Germany* [1986] ECR 3879 (*Petillant de raisin*).

(2006),[55] the Court was faced with an Austrian law that required chewing gum sold in vending machines to be packaged. According to the Court, this did constitute a MEEQR, but was justified by reasons of public health, and proportional in its implementation. The Court accepted Austria's arguments that non-packaged goods were impaired by moisture or insects, in particular ants, within vending machine containers and that contamination by pathogenic germs and their transmission onto the goods was 'by no means merely theoretical'.[56] Overall, however, unless related to a genuine safety concern, packaging requirements tend to meet the same fate as other product requirements and are generally deemed inadmissible.

*4.3.1.6 **Genuine food safety requirements***

One cluster of cases stands out in the jurisprudence; these are cases that show genuine and relatively stringent food safety concerns—either as a specific safety issue, or concerning particular categories of substances—and in which the Court consistently rules in favour of national rules. In this vein, genuine food safety concerns, legislation limiting the import of foodstuffs with additives and colourants, and pesticide limitations were regarded as justified obstacles.

A case at the crossroads of compositional and genuine safety issues, *Van der Veldt* (1994)[57] concerned national legislation prohibiting the marketing of bread and other bakery products with a salt content exceeding 2% by reference to the dry matter. The Court held that it constitutes a MEEQR because it may prevent bread and other bakery products originating in other Member States from being marketed in the State concerned. Belgium tried to justify its rule on the basis of public health or consumer health. The motivation behind the Belgian rule was very succinct, and limited to the assessment that the salt content of the Dutch bread at issue in the case was deemed 'too high' amounting to a daily increase of 0.6g per person on average. The Court dismissed this argument and set high requirements:

> General conjecture of that nature does not prove that increasing salt intake by such an amount poses a risk for public health. It is true that, as the Court has already held (see Case 97/83 Melkunie [1984] ECR 2367), the fact that there is a risk to consumers is sufficient to make legislation of the kind at issue compatible with the requirements of Article 36. However, the risk must be measured, not according to the yardstick of general conjecture, but on the basis of relevant scientific research (see, in particular, Case 178/84 Commission v Germany [1987] ECR 1227) [*Beer Purity Case*].[58]

[55] Case C-366/04 *Georg Schwarz v Bürgermeister der Landeshauptstadt Salzburg* [2006] ECR I-10139.
[56] ibid, para 35.
[57] Case C-17/93, *Van der Veldt* [1994] ECR I-3537 (*Van der Veldt*).
[58] ibid, para 17.

Belgium therefore failed to produce sufficient scientific evidence, and the Court also argued that labelling would have constituted a more appropriate alternative measure. The measure returned in *Bellamy* (2001),[59] and the Court found it in breach of EU law by reference to the *Van der Veldt* judgment. Nevertheless, the case is notable because the Court elaborated criteria for finding food safety risks. The risk must be measured, and substantiated on the basis of scientific research.

Only genuine and specific safety concerns seemed to convince the Court that national measures deserved justification, but in cases in which these were raised, the Court consistently ruled in favour of justifying them. *Koninklijke Kaasfabriek Eyssen* (additive)[60] (1981) is one of the rare product composition cases in which the CJEU upheld a national measure, in this instance a Dutch law prohibiting the additive Nisin in processed cheese. The Dutch government specifically emphasized that the measure was applicable exclusively to domestic goods, and not those for export to other Member States. The Court easily found that the measure at hand constituted an MEEQR, but fully embraced the public health justification:

> ... it follows that whilst it has the effect of hindering trade between Member States in the product concerned, national legislation, such as that referred to by the national court, prohibiting the use of nisin as a preservative in processed cheese intended for the domestic market is included amongst the measures which Article 36 of the Treaty permits Member States to adopt on grounds of the protection of health of humans and for that reason it escapes the prohibitions resulting from Articles 30 and 34 of the Treaty. In view of the uncertainties prevailing in the various Member States regarding the maximum level of Nisin which must be prescribe in respect of each preserved product intended to satisfy the various dietary habits, it does not appear that such a prohibition, although restricted only to products intended for sale on the domestic market of the State concerned constitutes 'a means of arbitrary discrimination' or a 'disguised restriction on trade between Member States' (para 16).

A distinguishing feature, and therefore an explanation for why the national measures was upheld, is the fact that the case is characterized by having a genuine and highly specific food safety concern at issue, and one that had been recognized in several other Member States.

Genuine safety concerns on additives and colourants were also consistently regarded by the Court to justify a national measure. In *Motte* (1985),[61] concerning restrictions on foodstuffs containing colourants, the Court upheld a national rule

[59] Case C-123/00 *Christina Bellamy and English Shop Wholesale SA* [2001] ECR I-2795 (*Bellamy*).

[60] Case C-53/80 *Officier van justitie v Koninklijke Kaasfabriek Eyssen BV* [1981] ECR 409 (*Koninklijke Kaasfabriek Eyssen*).

[61] Case 247/84 *Criminal proceedings against Léon Motte* [1985] ECR 3887 (*Motte*).

that set requirements for foodstuffs to which a colourant had been added (in this case the requirement to be entered on a positive list and subjected to assessment by an expert committee to determine their harmfulness). In *Muller* (1986),[62] concerning restrictions on additives, the free movement of goods provisions did not prevent a Member State from prohibiting the marketing of foodstuffs with additives. The national rule was allowed, but it was for the competent national authorities to demonstrate in each case, taking account of national eating habits and international scientific research, that the rules were necessary to achieve the public health objective.

Genuine microbiological safety concerns have also been assessed favourably by the Court in terms of their justifiability. A successful case was *Melkunie* (1984),[63] which concerned a Dutch law that (a) did not allow active coliform bacteria in pasteurized milk products, and (b) did not allow non-pathogenic micro-organisms in a quantity exceeding 50000 per millilitre. Milk imports from Germany, which were tested by the Dutch authorities, in contrast contained 9000000, 18000000, and 90000000 active micro-organisms per millilitre, and active coliform bacteria. The Court emphasized that Community legislation has not laid down microbiological requirements on the production or marketing of milk and milk products. The Court initially concluded that the Dutch rule prohibiting the importation of products that do not satisfy microbiological requirements constituted a MEEQR. The Netherlands argued that the rules were justified for public health reasons. The Court held (a) that the presence of active coliform bacteria in milk represents a risk of pathogenic micro-organisms being present, and therefore may be a source of real danger to human health. It was, therefore, justified under Article 36 EEC. (b) With regards to the maximum micro-organism level, the Commission and Melkunie argued that it is not possible to establish the maximum quantity that one may absorb without serious risk—they argued that such risks only arise at levels of 1–2 million microorganisms per millilitre, and that the Dutch law, fixing this amount at 50000 was excessively stringent. The Court disagreed, stating that other Member States with microbiological criteria managed similar standards. It further held that the data available did not deliver scientific certainty, and therefore—in the absence of harmonization—it was for the Member States to establish 'the level at which they wish to ensure that human life and health are protected'. Consequently, both rules were permitted because they were justified under public health arguments.

Finally, *Hahn* (2002)[64] is another case involving a genuine food safety issue, as it concerned limit values for the presence of Listeria monocytogenes in smoked fish products. The Court emphasized that the existence of a risk to public health had to be assessed in light of scientific research. However, it argued that 'from

[62] Case 304/84 *Criminal proceedings against Claude Muller and others* [1986] ECR 1511 (*Muller*).
[63] Case 97/83 *Melkunie* [1984] ECR 2367 (*Melkunie*).
[64] Case C-121/00 *Criminal proceedings against Walter Hahn* [2002] ECR I-9193 (*Hahn*).

the available data, (. . .) the current state of scientific research does not make it possible to determine with any certainty the precise concentration of Listeria monocytogenes pathogens above which a fish product poses a threat to human health.' Member States were therefore in a position to decide which level of health protection to pursue. The free movement of goods provisions did not preclude the application of national legislation establishing a zero-tolerance policy for Listeria monocytogenes in fish products that had not undergone chemical preservation.

Interestingly, the Court also positively recognized the food safety component of pesticides—it upheld national restrictions of apples treated with EU unregulated pesticides (*Albert Heijn* (1984)[65]) and a prohibition on importing fruit and vegetables that have been treated with the pesticide maleic hydrazide (*Mirepoix* (1986)[66]).

Overall, free movement of goods cases with a genuine safety concern at heart are likely to withstand the scrutiny of the Court, and be justifiable under Article 36 TFEU as a public health concern.

4.3.1.7 ***Restrictions on nutritional substances, enriched food, and supplements***

Another dense series of cases concerns the topic of restrictions on nutritional substances, enriched foods, and supplements.

Initially, the Court showed a relatively lenient approach to nutritional prohibitions, even though it had, in the early days, emphasized the importance of a 'real' authorization procedure. *Sandoz* (1983)[67] held that an authorization requirement for foods to which vitamins are added is permissible, but that the latter cannot be subject to proof that the product is not harmful to health, or require the producer to prove that the product meets a marketing demand. In similar terms, the Court upheld restrictions on vitamin preparations[68] (1983), as long as authorizations could be granted when they were compatible with the requirements of health protection.

The case law crystallized authorization conditions for finding authorization schemes compliant with EU law;[69] they had to be accessible, provide a reasonable timeframe, be open to challenge, and any refusal had to include an 'assessment of the risk to public health, based on the most reliable scientific data available and the most recent results of international research'.

The 2000s saw a wave of litigation centring around restrictions on enriched food and supplements, largely due to the fact that a number of Member States' authorization systems were compliant with EU law. The Danish prohibition on

[65] Case 94/83 *Criminal proceedings against Albert Heijn BV* [1984] ECR 3263 (*Albert Heijn*).
[66] Case 54/85 *Ministère public against Xavier Mirepoix* [1986] ECR 1067 (*Mirepoix*).
[67] Case 174/82 *Criminal proceedings against Sandoz BV* [1983] ECR 2445.
[68] Case 227/82 *Criminal proceedings against Leendert van Bennekom* [1983] ECR 3883.
[69] Case C-95/01 *Criminal proceedings against John Greenham and Léonard Abel* [2004] ECR I-1333.

marketing of foodstuffs to which vitamins and minerals have been added[70] was too systematic, and did not allow 'the identification and assessment of a real risk to public health, which requires a detailed assessment, case-by-case, of the effects which the addition of the minerals and vitamins in question could entail'. French legislation that exhaustively listed the nutrients which may be added to foodstuffs[71] was also illegal, because the law failed to establish that the marketing of other enriched foodstuffs entails a real risk to public health. A failure to fulfil its obligations was equally established for Germany,[72] Austria,[73] and the Netherlands.[74]

In many cases, national regimes failed to meet the Court's requirements on the authorization systems, for instance in a prior authorization requirement for sports food[75] in Italy. National requirements for food supplements had a very similar fate. The Court emphasized that the absence of a nutritional need in the population of the Member State alone did not suffice to justify a complete ban.[76] The Court also failed an authorization system for food supplements that did not allow, on the basis of the most recent scientific data, account to be taken of the actual risk to public health presented by such products.[77]

The continuing importance of the free movement of goods case law in this area can be explained by the incomplete harmonization of nutritional laws at EU level (Chapter 17). Member States therefore retain the right to make the marketing of these substances subject to an authorization scheme, and authorization schemes, in turn, fall outside of the scope of the Mutual Recognition Regulation (section 4.4.2.1).

4.3.1.8 ***Requirements on origin indications***

A specific pocket of case law formed around the topic of origin requirements. The case law is somewhat erratic, and the Court appears to accept justifications for origin products that would perhaps not have been accepted had they been 'mere' product requirements.

[70] Case C-192/01 *Commission of the European Communities v Kingdom of Denmark* [2003] ECR I-9693.

[71] Case C-24/00 *Commission of the European Communities v French Republic* [2004] ECR I-1277.

[72] Case C-387/99 *Commission of the European Communities v Federal Republic of Germany* [2004] ECR I-3751.

[73] Case C-150/00 *Commission of the European Communities v Republic of Austria* [2004] ECR I-3887.

[74] Case C-41/02 *Commission of the European Communities v Kingdom of the Netherlands* [2004] ECR I-11375.

[75] Case C-270/02 *Commission of the European Communities v Italian Republic* [2004] ECR I-1559.

[76] Joined cases C-211/03, C-299/03 and C-316/03 to C-318/03 *HLH Warenvertriebs GmbH (C-211/03) and Orthica BV (C-299/03 and C-316/03 to C-318/03) v Bundesrepublik Deutschland* [2005] ECR I-5141.

[77] Case C-88/07 *Commission of the European Communities v Kingdom of Spain* [2009] ECR I-1353.

In a case regarding domestic legislation on the use of the description 'mountain' for agricultural products and foodstuffs[78] (1997), the Court found that in the case at hand the denominations had a directly discriminatory effect, and were thus not capable of justification. Similarly, the Court found that awarding the quality label 'Markenqualität aus deutschen Landen' (quality label for produce made in Germany)[79] (2002) to finished products of a certain quality produced in Germany constituted a violation of the free movement of goods provisions. However, in *Spanish Wine Bottling*[80] (2000), a case on a local bottling requirement, the Court decided that designations of origin fall within the scope of industrial and commercial property rights; therefore the requirement of bottling in the region of production, although it precluded the bulk transport of wine, was allowed under EU law despite its restrictive effects on trade. In the same vein, a national requirement that made the use of the Protected Designation of Origin (PDO) 'Prosciutto di Parma' for ham conditional on the slicing and packaging in the region of production was considered justified[81] (2003).

4.3.1.9 ***Certain selling arrangements***

In the 1990s, we see the straightforwardness of the product requirement cases begin to crumble; new subjects enter the litigation arena, and even when the subject matter stays the same (food product requirements), the Court starts to engage in more complex and more accommodating arguments to justify certain outcomes. In 1991, the Court also adopted the *Keck* exemption for certain selling arrangements, which could result in a straightforward exemption from the free movement of goods scrutiny altogether.

Commission v Greece (infant milk)[82] (1995) concerned a Greek law allowing the sale of processed milk for infants exclusively by pharmacies. The Court applied *Keck* and argued that the law merely determined the points of sale where the infant milk products could be distributed. The requirement was therefore regarded as a certain selling arrangement, which falls outside of the scope of (then) Article 30 EC. The case is notable for applying and using *Keck* in order to uphold a national measure. In contrast, in a prohibition on the marketing of deep-frozen pre-baked bread[83] (2003), the Court held that the need to alter the packaging or the labelling

[78] Joined cases C-321/94, C-322/94, C-323/94, and C-324/94 *Criminal proceedings against Jacques Pistre (C-321/94), Michèle Barthes (C-322/94), Yves Milhau (C-323/94) and Didier Oberti (C-324/94)* [1997] ECR I-2343.

[79] Case C-325/00 *Commission of the European Communities v Federal Republic of Germany* [2002] ECR I-9977.

[80] Case C-388/95 *Kingdom of Belgium v Kingdom of Spain* [2000] ECR I-3123.

[81] Case C-108/01 *Consorzio del Prosciutto di Parma and Salumificio S. Rita SpA v Asda Stores Ltd and Hygrade Foods Ltd* [2003] ECR I-5121.

[82] Case C-391/92 *Commission of the European Communities v Hellenic Republic* [1995] ECR I-1621.

[83] Case C-416/00 *Tommaso Morellato v Comune di Padova* [2003] ECR I-9343.

of imported products prevents such requirements from constituting selling arrangements within the meaning of the judgment in *Keck*.

Cases relying on the *Keck* exemption are specific exceptions to the free movement of goods, but more generally, the Court's attempt to curb the *Cassis de Dijon* case law is perhaps also reflected in a parallel shift in the overall mood of the cases.

4.3.1.10 ***Miscellaneous national measures***

Next to these broader themes, the Court had to deal with numerous more specific topics which illustrate that 'food law' issues arise in many spheres of (national) regulation. The question of the legality of inspections[84] was a recurring one, especially in the early days of the free movement of goods case law. Legality here typically depends on the type and systematic nature of the inspection or control carried out. Other topics concerned state aid, which was also regarded as a restriction to the free movement of goods.[85] For instance, in order to receive aid, growers in Extremadura were obliged to sell their production to processors in the region. National provisions prohibiting the importation of alcoholic beverages by private individuals[86] were not justified, as they were regarded as unsuitable for attaining the objective of limiting alcohol consumption generally, and not proportionate for attaining the objective of protecting young persons against the harmful effects of alcohol consumption. In a case concerning a national rule laying down short maximum journey times and distances for live animals being transported to the nearest abattoir,[87] the Court found the national measure constituted an unjustifiable obstacle to international transport.

It is perhaps in these types of free movement cases where we most often see the Court struggling to find a convincing balance between safeguarding the free movement of goods and accepting national justifications, and where from a policy perspective the outcomes of the cases risk failing genuine societal values such as animal welfare.

4.3.2 ***Post-Lisbon case law on food***

For the purposes of providing an insight into the current relevance of the free movement of goods provisions in the Treaty, the post-Lisbon period is the most significant. This is because it represents the period after the adoption of the General Food Law Regulation (GFLR) and its legislative package and therefore best reflects

[84] Case C-272/95 *Bundesanstalt für Landwirtschaft und Ernährung v Deutsches Milch-Kontor GmbH* [1997] ECR I-1905.

[85] Case C-113/00 *Kingdom of Spain v Commission of the European Communities* [2002] ECR I-7601.

[86] Case C-170/04 *Klas Rosengren and Others v Riksåklagaren* [2007] ECR I-4071.

[87] Case C-350/97 *Wilfried Monsees v Unabhängiger Verwaltungssenat für Kärnten* [1999] ECR I-2921.

the unharmonized space left to be governed by the Treaty provisions. Additionally, the approach of the Court to the free movement of goods provisions has changed under general EU law, and this time period gives a more precise impression of the current approach deployed by the Court. Post-Lisbon research shows that the number of cases concerning foodstuffs under the free movement provisions has decreased significantly; our case law research was only able to identify five cases between 2010 and 2023. The reasons for the fading relevance of the Treaty articles are discussed in section 4.3.4.

Only one more 'classic' food free movement case on product requirements has arisen post-Lisbon. *Asociación Nacional de Productores de Ganado Porcino*[88] (2018) contested a Spanish law that reserved the sales designation 'ibérico de cebo' exclusively to products that comply with certain conditions imposed by that legislation. In its argumentation, the CJEU cited *Guimont*, recalling that conditions about the use of the generic designation commonly used for a product do not absolutely preclude the importation into the Member State concerned of products originating in other Member States, but are likely to make their marketing more difficult and thus impede trade between Member States. However, it emphasized that where the production conditions were similar, comparable, or identical to those set out in in the Spanish decree, they could be imported and marketed in Spain under such designations, despite not fully meeting the requirements laid down in the decree. Given these circumstances, the Court held that the measure was not precluded by Article 34 TFEU.

The *Processing aids*[89] (2010) case aligns with the series of cases on nutritional measures (section 4.3.1.7) because—much like the nutrition EU legal frameworks—processing aids are not distinctly regulated in the EU, and therefore share a similar context regarding the necessity for an authorization system that complies with EU law. The case concerned a prohibition on marketing processing aids or foodstuffs in which processing aids have been used. The Court reiterated its case law that such a requirement would be subject to an in-depth assessment of the risk alleged by the Member State. In the circumstances of the case, the Court found that the prior authorization did not comply with the principle of proportionality. The nutritional series of cases is further extended by *Noria Distribution SARL* (food supplements)[90] (2017), which concerned a French prohibition of supplements whose content in nutrients exceeded the maximum daily doses set by that legislation. The CJEU held that the free movement provisions preclude national legislation that does not provide for a procedure for placing on the market food supplements whose nutrient content exceeds the maximum daily doses set by that

[88] Case C-169/17 *Asociación Nacional de Productores de Ganado Porcino v Administración del Estado* [2018] (*Asociación Nacional de Productores de Ganado Porcino*).

[89] Case C-333/08 *European Commission v French Republic* [2010] ECR I-757 (*Processing Aids*).

[90] Case C-672/15 *Noria Distribution SARL* EU:C:2017:310 (*Noria Distribution SARL*).

legislation and which are lawfully manufactured or marketed in another Member State. In doing so, the CJEU reaffirmed its authorization procedure requirement[91] (see also section 4.4.2.1 below).

Looking at future litigation, it is likely that free movement of goods cases regarding national food regulation on topics of incomplete secondary harmonization are going to continue. In the food sector, these notably include the addition of substances to foodstuffs, food supplements, and processing aids.

Lastly, a new type of case seems to appear—cases that concern genuine public (health) policy projects, such as the fight against alcohol abuse, and which are ultimately challenged under the free movement of goods rules. An example is *Scotch Whisky Association*[92] (2015), which challenged a minimum unit pricing mechanism on alcoholic drinks. The Court found that it constituted a measure equivalent to a quantitative restriction under Article 34 TFEU because it prevented the lower cost price of imported products being reflected in the selling price to the consumer, thereby hindering market access. The Court criticized the Member States' choice for a minimum price per unit instead of a less trade-restrictive excise duty, and gave firm guidance on a strict proportionality test that it devised, but ultimately left it to the national court to verify whether the conditions were met. In substance, the case seemed to suggest that the minimum unit pricing mechanism violated EU law, but on procedural grounds the Court showed a high degree of deference to the national level. Interestingly, this case bears resemblance to the (very old) *Van Tiggele* case (1978), which at the time was decided by the Court to constitute a violation of the free movement of goods with much less argumentation. *Van Tiggele* (alcohol)[93] concerned a minimum retail price for alcoholic beverages. The CJEU regarded the setting of minimum alcohol retail prices under Dutch law as a barrier to trade insofar as it prevents the lower cost price from being reflected in the retail price. The Court did not evaluate any justification, but simply found the measure to violate Article (then) 30 EEC that prohibits measures having an equivalent effect to a quantitative restriction.

Another post-Lisbon case on alcohol was *Alcohol Sale License*[94] (2015) regarding a Finish requirement to hold a retail sale licence in order to import alcoholic beverages. The Court argued that the rule prevents traders established in other Member States from freely importing alcoholic beverages into Finland with

[91] ibid, para 22: 'such rules must make provision for a procedure enabling economic operators to obtain the authorisation to market food supplements including nutrients in doses exceeding those authorised. The procedure must be one which is readily accessible and can be completed within a reasonable time, and, if it leads to a refusal, the decision of refusal must be open to challenge before the courts', referring to Case *Commission v French Republic* (n 5) para 26; Case C-95/01 *John Greenham and Léonard Abel* [2004] ECR I-1333 (*Greenham and Abel*) para 35; and Case C-333/08 *European Commission v French Republic* [2010] ECR I-757 (*Commission v France*), para 81.

[92] *Scotch Whisky Association* (n 11) 4.

[93] Case C-82/77 *Openbaar Ministerie (Public Prosecutor) of the Kingdom of the v Jacobus Philippus van Tiggele* [1978] ECR 25 (*Van Tiggele*).

[94] *Alcohol Sale License* (n 20).

a view to their retail sale. The Court found that certain selling arrangements, first, apply to all relevant traders operating within the national territory, and, secondly, affect in the same manner, in law and in fact, the marketing of domestic products and those from other Member States. Since the Finish rules did not apply to all traders equally, the case failed these *Keck* criteria[95] and constituted a barrier to trade. However, the rules were justified by the objective of the protection of human health and life listed in Article 36 TFEU. The Court emphasized that it had already held that legislation aimed at the control of the consumption of alcohol to prevent the harmful effects on the health of humans and society by alcoholic substances, thereby seeking to combat alcohol abuse, reflects health and public policy concerns recognized by Article 36 TFEU. The case was one of the rare instances in which a national measure was upheld for reasons of health and public policy.

In view of the rising sustainability agendas at national level, it is likely that we will see more litigation on the free movement of goods provisions and their relationship to national food regulations that genuinely pursue public policy goals. As food is increasingly framed as a public or common good, food regulation will in the future increasingly cater to the public interest.[96] Since the EU is struggling to adopt or even propose 'sustainable' EU food legislation, it is likely that we will see an increasing number of regulatory sustainability initiatives emerging at national level. These sustainability initiatives are likely to genuinely cater to legitimate interests of public policies, but they might still face some uncertainty regarding their compatibility with the free movement of goods provisions. Alcohol regulation is a case in point, but other examples include the national regulation of sugar, fats, and salt, and national rules regarding the food environment, such as prohibitions and limitations on supermarket promotions of unhealthy foods.[97]

4.3.3 *The instability of case law*

The overview of case law shows that the majority of national food laws contested in the CJEU were ultimately characterized as MEEQR under Article 34 TFEU. It further illustrates the difficulty of trying to justify barriers to the free movement of goods in the food domain under Article 36 TFEU or other mandatory requirements. Whereas early cases sometimes showed relatively unreasoned 'declarations' by the Court, the Court gradually began to engage in more extensive argumentation regarding the justifications involved. Nevertheless, the Court has shown itself very reluctant to accept Article 36 justifications or other mandatory reasons.

[95] ibid, para 107.
[96] Hanna Schebesta, 'How to Save the Farm to Fork Strategy: A Two-Phased Approach' (2023) 18 European Food and Feed Law Review 231.
[97] ibid.

Certainly in terms of product requirements, the main rule, therefore, remains that a Member State cannot ban food if it has been marketed lawfully in another Member State.

Public health and consumer protection are the most commonly invoked justifications.[98] When debating the validity of public health arguments and consumer protection, the CJEU predominantly follows the 'proportionality' line of reasoning. Where product requirements are specifically concerned, the Court consistently held that labelling would protect consumers as much as a prohibition or prescription of the compositional quality of products, while forming less of a trade barrier.

The 'protection of life of humans' was successful in isolated cases,[99] notably when raising 'classic' food safety concerns. This was the case for the additive Nitin in *Koninklijke Kaasfabriek Eysen* (additive)[100] or micro-biological criteria in *Melkunie*[101] and *Hahn*.[102] These cases were scientifically debated by the Court and concerned genuine food safety concerns which had been recognized across several Member States. However, the Court's approach is 'suspicious of attempts by Member States to use health protection as a means of affording a disguised restriction on trade', leading to careful scrutiny by the Court, a general requirement of evidence from the invoking Member State, and even the existence of a well-considered health policy.[103]

Other cases in which national laws withstand Court scrutiny are selling arrangements. *Advertisement of alcoholic beverages*[104] concerned peripheral trading rules (advertisement) and not product compositional requirements directly, as did *Infant milk*[105] on infant milk being sold in pharmacies—in these cases the Court applied the *Keck* exemption on certain selling arrangements.

Despite the scholarly attempts of 'systematizing' the Court's approach to the free movement of goods, a specifically food domain look at the case law confirms that—perhaps—there is no static system or scheme. Alternatively, the Court may be understood as a socially and normatively permeable institution that functions in its role in synchronization with the societal demands of European integration.

[98] Barnard (n 7) 159.

[99] Klaudyna Terlicka and David Jukes, 'From Harmonisation to Better, Smart and Fit Food Law: Reviewing the Legislators Attempts to Abolish Barriers to Food Trade in the EU' (2014) 9 European Food and Feed Law Review 302.

[100] *Kaasfabriek Eysen* (n 60).

[101] *Melkunie* (n 63).

[102] *Hahn* (n 64)

[103] Barnard (n 7) 159.

[104] Joint Cases C-1/90 and C-176/90 *Aragonesa de Publicidad Exterior SA and Publivía SAE v Departamento de Sanidad y Seguridad Social de la Generalitat de Cataluña* [1991] ECR I-4151 (*Advertisement of Alcoholic Beverages*).

[105] C-391/92 *Commission of the European Communities v Hellenic Republic* [1995] ECR I-1621.

4.3.4 Explaining the fading relevance of Treaty law for the food domain: harmonization

The extensive amount of harmonization through secondary legislation in EU food law contributes to the fading relevance of the free movement of goods Treaty law. The internal market is established by the free movement of goods Treaty rules, but Articles 34–37 TFEU apply only to the extent that there has not been any harmonization of the matter.[106] In this vein, the Commission has argued, for instance, that the principle of mutual recognition should not be invoked in order to interpret harmonized rules (such as the Food for Specific Groups Regulation and Delegated Regulation (EU) 2016/128), and an assessment of Food for Special Medical Purposes (FSMPs) should be exclusively undertaken in light of the harmonized EU provisions.[107] Most areas of food law have now been harmonized. In part, therefore, the receding number of cases on the free movement of foods can be explained by the fact that the Treaty rules have become background considerations, with most legal issues being resolved based on interpretations of secondary legislation. This argument is supported by the fact that areas where harmonization remains incomplete, such as food fortification and supplements (see Chapter 17), continue to generate numerous cases that reach the CJEU.

4.4 Internal market secondary legislation: notification duty and conditional mutual recognition

An additional important factor leading to the fading relevance of the free movement of goods Treaty provisions, not only in the area of food, is the gradual *legislative framing* of internal market law. A two-pronged legal framework nowadays operationalizes mutual recognition. First, there is an *ex-ante* notification requirement, that is, Member States must notify other Member States of technical regulations that may pose an obstacle prior to their adoption.[108] The notification framework stems from 1998.[109] Second, a monitoring system for national administrative decisions taken on the basis of technical regulations was started in 1995, and

[106] 'As explained by the Court, where a matter is regulated in a harmonised manner at EU level, any national measure relating thereto must be assessed in the light of the provisions of that harmonising measure and not of the Articles of the Treaty (17).' See Commission Notice on the classification of Food for Special Medical Purposes [2017] OJ C401/1 (Commission Notice FSMP), citing Case C-324/99 *DaimlerChrysler AG v Land Baden-Württemberg* [2001] ECR I-9897, para 32.

[107] Commission Notice FSMP (n 106).

[108] Currently based on Directive (EU) 2015/1535 of the European Parliament and of the Council of 9 September 2015 laying down a procedure for the provision of information in the field of technical regulations and of rules on Information Society services [2015] OJ L241/1.

[109] Directive 98/34/EC of the European Parliament and of the Council of 22 June 1988 laying down a procedure for the provision of information in the field of technical standards and regulations [1998] OJ L204/37, later repealed by Directive (EU) 2015/1535.

replaced by a Mutual Recognition Regulation with rules and procedures for the administrative application of the principle by Member State authorities in 2008.

4.4.1 Ex ante control: obligation to notify technical regulations

Today, Member States must notify the Commission and other Member States of draft national technical regulations prior to their adoption.[110] The Commission informs other EU Member States using the technical regulations information system (TRIS).[111] During a standstill period of three months (extendable), the Member States may not adopt the proposed draft technical regulation. The Commission and the other Member States can provide comments to the notifying Member State, however they may only relate to a hindrance of trade or free movement. The Member State concerned will take the comments 'into account as far as possible'.[112] This system aims to prevent trade barriers before they are established and is therefore an important mechanism for securing the free circulation of goods in the internal market. The system is rendered practically effective by the significant 'teeth' given to the Directive by the CJEU.[113] The Court has stipulated that unnotified measures are not enforceable (*CIA*[114]), and that the Directive is even enforceable between individuals (*Unilever*[115]). A very illustrative example[116] of the far-reaching implications of the *CIA* judgment for governments is the Dutch case: as a consequence of the ruling, the Netherlands identified 400 non-notified measures and withdrew 96 technical regulations unilaterally and an additional 77 after consultation with the Commission. It further notified 227 texts, of which over a third raised an issue of compatibility with EU law.

Under the notification system, since 1984 more than 12000 national rules have been notified.[117] The database TRIS is a useful resource for researching and keeping updated on proposed technical laws of Member States. For foodstuffs specifically, for the time span after 2003, over 800 entries can be found, each accompanied by an explanation of the measure and eventual comments. Overall, while presumably not a perfect, the *ex-ante* notification mechanism is an important administrative mechanism to prevent trade obstacles before they arise.

[110] Directive (EU) 2015/1535.
[111] Commission, 'Prevention of technical barriers to trade' <https://ec.europa.eu/growth/tools-databases/tris/en/> accessed 9 September 2022.
[112] Directive (EU) 2015/1535, art 5.
[113] Stephen Weatherill, 'The Principle of Mutual Recognition: It Doesn't Work Because It Doesn't Exist' (2017) 43 European Law Review 224.
[114] Case C-194/94 *CIA Security International SA v Signalson SA and Securitel SPRL* [1996] ECR I-2201 (*CIA Security*), according to which national courts must decline to apply non-notified national technical regulations. Terlicka and Jukes (n 99).
[115] Case C-443/98 *Unilever Italia SpA v Central Food SpA* [2000] ECR I-7535.
[116] See Barnard (n 7) 112.
[117] See Terlicka and Jukes (n 99) 306.

4.4.2 Mutual Recognition Regulation

Another important shift away from the Treaty was achieved through the codification of the Mutual Recognition principle in secondary law. Consequently, the system of mutual recognition on the basis of the Treaty has been largely superseded by a system of decentralized application of mutual recognition, governed by a Mutual Recognition Regulation (MRR).

In 1995, the first monitoring scheme was instituted by a decision[118] stipulating that Member States were required to notify the Commission of any actions taken to prevent the free movement or placement on the market, especially bans, refusals to market products, modification of a product, or withdrawal of goods from the market.[119] The system was regarded as unsuccessful[120] in achieving a rapid solution to free movement problems and was therefore replaced by the first MRR in 2008,[121] which since then has been repealed by a new 'revised and strengthened'[122] Regulation in 2019.[123]

The MRR creates a decentralized system for the application of the principle of mutual recognition by national authorities. To this end, the Regulation lays down rules and procedures for the application of mutual recognition in individual cases for goods that fall under Article 34 TFEU and which are lawfully marketed in another Member State, having regard to Article 36 TFEU and the case law of the CJEU.[124]

The Regulation codifies and operationalizes the mutual recognition principle. In scope, it applies to any administrative decision at the Member State level that is (a) based on a national technical rule applicable in the Member State and where (b) the direct or indirect effect of the decision is to restrict or deny market access in the Member State of destination.[125] Therefore, the MRR in fact adopts a market access approach to the free movement of goods. The Regulation clarifies what counts as a technical rule and provides a definition for the elements that determine free movement of goods cases,[126] such as different types of obstacles. These definitions

[118] Decision No 3052/95/EC of the European Parliament and of the Council of 13 December 1995 establishing a procedure for the exchange of information on national measures derogating from the principle of the free movement of goods within the Community [1995] OJ L321/1.

[119] Decision No 3052/95/EC, art 1.

[120] Regulation (EC) 764/2008 of the European Parliament and of the Council of 9 July 2008 laying down procedures relating to the application of certain national technical rules to products lawfully marketed in another Member State and repealing Decision No 3052/95/EC [2008] OJ L218/21, Recital (36).

[121] Regulation (EC) 764/2008.

[122] Regulation (EU) 2019/515 of the European Parliament and of the Council of 19 March 2019 on the mutual recognition of goods lawfully marketed in another Member State and repealing Regulation (EC) No 764/2008 [2019] OJ L91/1 (MRR), Recital (8).

[123] MRR.

[124] ibid, art 1.

[125] ibid, art 2(1).

[126] ibid, art 3.

clearly codify, and thereby clarify, the existing conditions created over time in the large volume of case law.

Producers may use a voluntary mutual recognition declaration by businesses to demonstrate that their products are lawfully marketed in another EU Member State.[127] More importantly, the MRR lays down procedural requirements for Member State authorities when assessing goods. A decision on the 'assessment of goods' must be notified[128] to the food business operator (FBO) and to the Commission using the Information and Communication System on Market Surveillance (ICSMS). The decision must also contain arguments on a number of listed points, such as the technical rule at issue and the respective legitimate interest protected, and it must provide evidence demonstrating that the decision is appropriate for the purpose of achieving the objective pursued and that the administrative decision does not go beyond what is necessary in order to attain that objective.[129] FBOs may continue to place goods on the market until they receive an administrative decision denying market access.[130]

The MRR also institutes a 'business-friendly' problem-solving procedure, where on the basis of a SOLVIT procedure,[131] the Commission may be requested to give an opinion.[132] Member States must also create a Product Contact Point for information for cooperation and exchange of information and provide free advice related to the MRR within 15 working days.[133]

'Assessment of goods' administrative decisions and temporary suspension from the market must be fed into the ICSMS[134] to facilitate communication between market surveillance bodies in EU and European Free Trade Association (EFTA) countries. It appears that the ICSMS is designed largely as an internal communication tool; its use for the public is (to date) decidedly limited.

4.4.2.1 ***Prior authorization schemes***

The issue of prior authorization schemes, that is, a requirement to apply for an authorization before placing products on a Member State market, became and remains an oddity in EU internal market law, and a field in which the Treaty retains

[127] ibid, art 4.
[128] ibid, art 5(9).
[129] See the items listed in ibid, art 5(10).
[130] ibid, art 5(3).
[131] European Commission, 'SOLVIT: Solutions to problems with your EU Rights' <https://ec.europa.eu/solvit/index_en.htm> accessed 27 July 2022.
[132] MRR, art 8.
[133] ibid, arts 9 and 10.
[134] Now regulated in Regulation (EU) 2019/1020 of the European Parliament and of the Council of 20 June 2019 on market surveillance and compliance of products and amending Directive 2004/42/EC and Regulations (EC) No 765/2008 and (EU) No 305/2011 [2019] OJ L169/1, art 34 (see table of equivalencies), originally Regulation (EC) No 765/2008 of the European Parliament and of the Council of 9 July 2008 setting out the requirements for accreditation and market surveillance relating to the marketing of products and repealing Regulation (EEC) No 339/93 [2008] OJ L218/30, art 23.

importance. Under the MRR, a prior authorization scheme is not a national technical rule for the purposes of the Regulation,[135] and the compliance of such a scheme with EU law should be assessed in light of the CJEU case law.[136] However, a decision to refuse authorization under a given technical rule must satisfy the procedural requirements of the MRR.[137] National authorization schemes therefore continue to fall under the free movement of goods Treaty articles. Case law has established many administrative conditions that national prior authorization schemes must respect,[138] but they are essentially allowed and therefore to date remain a legal way for national governments to control products on their market. In this way, administrative obstacles to the internal market continue to exist—leading to a 'nationally administered' rather than a 'free' movement of goods between Member States.

4.5 Conclusion: is the internal food market complete?

As will be clear from the remaining chapters of this book, there are very few topics related to the EU food system which are not, by now, subject to EU legislation. As harmonization pre-empts application of the free movement of goods, the importance of the Treaty provisions have gradually diminished in practice. The internal market for foods is therefore now largely constituted by secondary legislation.

The marked decrease in Treaty-based food cases can also be explained by the combination of the secondary law notification duty and the codification of the mutual recognition principle. Here, the notification duty of national technical food law helps to prevent obstacles, while the MRR manages the application of national technical food rules by national authorities in a way that ensures compliance with the free movement of goods provisions.

Today, the principle of mutual recognition is probably better described as conditional or non-absolute mutual recognition,[139] resulting in a 'persistently incomplete nature of the internal market'.[140]

> So, in short, EU law applies a principle of conditional or non-absolute mutual recognition. States are locked into a set of reciprocal commitments, but these do not go so far as to strip them entirely of their competence to regulate domestic markets. The space within which States are allowed to show justification for

135 MRR, art 2(4).
136 ibid, Recital (11).
137 ibid, art 2(4).
138 Lisa van der Meer and Hanna Schebesta, 'The Internal Market, Incomplete: EU, Dutch and Belgian Legislation on Maximum Food Fortification with Micronutrients' (2020) 3 European Food and Feed Law Review 201.
139 Weatherill (n 113).
140 ibid.

> trade-restrictive practices is of crucial importance to ensuring the EU's internal market is not a process of remorseless deregulation, but rather a site within which diversity in national regulatory choices is managed, checked but, provided it is shown to be sincere, respected.[141]

Instead of a free market, the possibility of maintaining national authorization systems and the current MRR system create an administratively managed permeability between Member States markets, yet somewhat distant from the originally conceived idea of a unitary and 'free' internal market.

Due to the pressure of the Farm to Fork Strategy agenda, 'sustainability' currently is in the focus of reform of secondary EU food law. However, as long as no significant changes of secondary law towards providing sustainability are underway, it may well be that primary law—including the free movement of goods articles—will be given more attention in the future when sustainable food laws and free movement rationales clash.

[141] ibid.

PART II

FOOD SAFETY UMBRELLA LAWS

The General Food Law Regulation and the Official Controls Regulation

5
The General Food Law Regulation (GFLR) and Transparency Amendment

5.1 Introduction

The chapter outlines the General Food Law Regulation (GFLR)[1] which is considered the main EU food law umbrella harmonization measure. It discusses the aims and objectives of the GFLR and defines its scope of application. The role of the GFLR as an overarching framework of principles valid for EU secondary food law is explained, in particular in terms of the principles it lays down (science-based risk analysis, the precautionary principle, transparency, and protection of consumers' interests). The chapter details the general requirements on food trade, in particular the prohibition on placing unsafe food on the market, and the corresponding duties of food business operators (FBOs) when placing food on the market. The GFLR further establishes the European Food Safety Authority (EFSA). It also lays down the Rapid Alert System, Crisis Management procedures. Lastly, the GFLR covers procedural aspects.

5.2 Adoption of the GFLR and modification through the Transparency Regulation

To date, the most important overarching European Union (EU) food harmonization instrument is the 2002 GFLR. The Regulation forms the basis of current EU food and feed law. According to some interpretations, the coming into force of the GFLR also establishes the legal field of food law as an autonomous legal domain in the EU.[2] The GFLR followed from the *Green Paper on the General Principles of Food Law in the European Union*[3] (1997) and—more directly—the *White Paper on Food Safety*[4] (2000). As an effort to provide coherence to the fragmented legal

[1] Regulation (EC) 178/2002 of the European Parliament and of the Council of 28 January 2002 laying down the general principles and requirements of food law, establishing the European Food Safety Authority and laying down procedures in matters of food safety [2002] OJ L31/1 (General Food Law Regulation (GFLR)).

[2] Bernd van der Meulen, 'The Structure of European Food Law' (2013) Laws 69.

[3] Commission, 'The General Principles of Food Law in the European Union' COM (97) 176 final (Green Paper on the General Principles of Food Law in the European Union).

[4] Commission, 'White Paper on Food Safety' (Communication) COM (1999) 719 final (White Paper on Food Safety).

EU Food Law. Hanna Schebesta and Kai Purnhagen, Oxford University Press. © Hanna Schebesta and Kai Purnhagen 2024.
DOI: 10.1093/9780198901570.003.0006

landscape of food regulation, the GFLR was enacted to shape a comprehensive architecture of EU food law through principles, rules, processes, and institutions. The Transparency Regulation[5] (2019) made significant amendments to the area of risk communication and transparency of risk analysis processes. The Farm to Fork Strategy (2020) has not suggested any action relating to the GFLR and does not refer to the Transparency Regulation (see also Chapter 1).

The GFLR's overarching paradigm is 'food safety'. It serves as the cornerstone of EU food law by providing a sector-specific instrument dedicated to rules and to the legal governance of EU food law by principles, processes (risk analysis and risk regulation), and institutions (the European Food Safety Authority (EFSA)). Specifically, the GFLR covers:

- **Scope and definitions** (Chapter I)
- **General Food Law** (Chapter II), comprising
  - transversally applicable principles of EU Food Law (Section 1), specifically risk communication (new Section 1a) and principles of transparency (Section 2),
  - obligations of ('international') food trade (Section 3),
  - and general requirements of food law (Section 4)
- **European Food Safety Authority** (Chapter III)
- **Risk response mechanisms**: Rapid Alert System, Crisis Management and Emergencies (Chapter IV)
- **Procedures** (Chapter V)

The Transparency Regulation later made significant amendments to the GFLR to strengthen its 'transparency' dimensions, with a particular emphasis on risk communication, which had been regarded as insufficiently developed. These changes included modifications to risk assessment structures, notably to improve scientific studies, to balance access to documents with the confidentiality of applicants' data, and to give EFSA a more 'active' mandate.

In this foundational function, the GFLR covers an unusually wide array of topics, and creates an overarching and coherent framework for the development of food and feed legislation both at the Union and national levels.

[5] Regulation (EU) 2019/1381 of the European Parliament and of the Council of 20 June 2019 on the transparency and sustainability of the EU risk assessment in the food chain and amending Regulations (EC) No 178/2002, (EC) No 1829/2003, (EC) No 1831/2003, (EC) No 2065/2003, (EC) No 1935/2004, (EC) No 1331/2008, (EC) No 1107/2009, (EU) 2015/2283 and Directive 2001/18/EC [2019] OJ L231/1 (Transparency Regulation).

5.3 GFLR Structure, aim and objective, scope and definitions

The GFLR is regarded as foundational for the area of 'EU Food Law.' It provided the first legal definition of food law:

> 'food law' means the laws, regulations and administrative provisions governing food in general, and food safety in particular, whether at Community or national level; it covers any stage of production, processing and distribution of food, and also of feed produced for, or fed to, food-producing animals.[6]

The definition emphasizes the importance of food safety, while clearly enshrining an all-encompassing understanding of what constitutes food law.

The GFLR sets out to achieve a high level of protection of human health and consumers' interests in relation to food, as well as diversity in the supply of food including traditional products, whilst ensuring the effective functioning of the internal market.[7] Consequently, the Regulation is based on an amalgam of legal bases, namely Article 43 Treaty on the Functioning of the European Union (TFEU) on agriculture; Article 144 TFEU on the approximation of law for the internal market; Article 207 for a common commercial policy, and Article 168(4)(b) TFEU on human health for measures in the veterinary and phytosanitary fields which have as their direct objective the protection of public health. In order to achieve these objectives, the GFLR promised to take 'a sufficiently comprehensive and integrated approach to food safety'[8] that would 'consider all aspects of the food production chain as a continuum from and including primary production and the production of animal feed up to and including sale or supply of food to the consumer.'[9] The GFLR further recognized that it was 'necessary to consider other practices and agricultural inputs at the level of primary production and their potential effect on the overall safety of food.'[10] From this perspective, the GFLR took an important step in bridging the Common Agricultural Policy (CAP) and the internal market areas by regulating aspects both areas within one piece of secondary legislation. It was realized by providing a very inclusive definition of food (including primary produce), as well as a comprehensive definition of the supply chain 'applying to all stages of production, processing and distribution of food and feed'[11]—thus shaping a veritable 'farm to table' approach.[12] Having broadened its scope of application, the GFLR matched it with common principles, food safety

[6] GFLR, art 3(1).
[7] ibid, art 1(1).
[8] ibid, Recital (11).
[9] ibid, Recital (12).
[10] ibid, Recital (13).
[11] ibid, art 1(3).
[12] White Paper on Food Safety (n 4), although the GFLR itself does not refer to this concept.

requirements, and responsibilities on FBOs. In addition, the GFLR aims to design science-based risk analysis processes. The fundamentals of the EU food risk analysis processes are the distinction between risk assessment and management, and the nomination of a distinct process of risk communication. The risk regulatory architecture also included the creation of a novel institution for risk assessment—EFSA—that would take up the role of an independent scientific point of reference in risk assessment. These features were 'means to provide a strong science base' and 'efficient organisational arrangements and procedures to underpin decision-making in matters of food and feed safety'.[13]

The 'General Food Law' (Chapter II GFLR) applies to all stages of the production, processing, and distribution of food, and also of feed produced for, or fed to, food-producing animals. Food is defined as

> any substance or product, whether processed, partially processed or unprocessed, intended to be, or reasonably expected to be ingested by humans. 'Food' includes drink, chewing gum and any substance, including water, intentionally incorporated into the food during its manufacture, preparation or treatment.[14]

The definition works largely in practice, however a substantial amount of case law has emerged which separates food from other regulated products such as medicinal products. Most of these cases, however, have emerged at the national level. The Court of Justice of the European Union (CJEU) has held that there are two definitions that can result in classification as a medicinal product: one definition 'by presentation' and another definition 'by function'.[15] This is to be decided on a case-by-case basis, taking into account 'the characteristics of the product, in particular its composition, its pharmacological properties, to the extent to which they can be established in the present state of scientific knowledge, the manner in which it is used, the extent of its distribution, its familiarity to consumers and the risks which its use may entail.'[16] The 'by function' definition includes 'pharmacological

[13] GFLR, art 1(1).

[14] GFLR, art 2.

[15] Directive 2001/83/EC of the European Parliament and of the Council of 6 November 2001 on the Community code relating to medicinal products for human use [2001] OJ L311/67, art 1(2): 'any substance or combination of substances presented for treating or preventing disease in human beings'. According to the second subparagraph of art 1(2), 'any substance or combination of substances which may be administered to human beings with a view to making a medical diagnosis or to restoring, correcting or modifying physiological functions in human beings' is likewise to be considered a medicinal product.

[16] Joined Cases C-211/03, C-299/03, and C-316/03–C-318/03 *HLH Warenvertriebs GmbH (C-211/03) and Orthica BV (C-299/03 and C-316/03 to C-318/03) v Bundesrepublik Deutschland* [2005] ECR I-05141, (*Orthica*), para 29; Case C-369/88 *Jean-Marie Delattre* [1991] ECR I-01487 (*Delattre*), paras 26 and 35; Case C-60/89 *Jean Monteil and Daniel Samanni* [1991] ECR I-01547 (*Monteil and Samanni*), para 29; Case C-112/89 *Upjohn Company and Upjohn NV v Farzoo Inc. and J. Kortmann* [1991] ECR I-01703 (*Upjohn*), para 23; Case C-290/90 *Commission of the European Communities v Federal Republic of Germany* [1992] ECR I-03317 (*Commission v Germany*), para 17; Case C-150/00 *Commission of the European Communities v Republic of Austria* [2004] ECR I-03887 (*Commission v Austria*), para 64.

properties of a product',[17] as well as a 'risk to health'.[18] However, the CJEU has also held that in preliminary reference proceedings, 'which are based on a clear separation of functions between the national courts and the Court of Justice', the assessment of the facts is a matter for the national court, and it is not for the CJEU to decide the nature of the foods in question.[19] Therefore, it is still possible that differences exist between Member States in the classification of products as medicinal or foodstuffs.[20] That said, on some occasions the CJEU provided 'strict guidance' and—for instance—classified honey and pollen-based food supplements as foodstuff.[21]

A definition of food might traditionally distinguish foods from agricultural products. However, due to the wide interpretation of 'agricultural products' by the CJEU[22] and the similarly wide definition of 'food' in the GFLR, the Regulation effectively includes most agricultural products as well as circulating foodstuff. The GFLR does, however, provide a refined legal food category of 'primary production' as 'the production, rearing or growing of primary products including harvesting, milking and farmed animal production prior to slaughter'. It also includes 'hunting and fishing and the harvesting of wild products'.[23]

The integration of agriculture and the internal market is further reinforced by a comprehensive and inclusive definition of a complete supply chain defining 'stages of production, processing and distribution' as 'any stage, including import, from and including the primary production of a food, up to and including its storage, transport, sale or supply to the final consumer and, where relevant, the importation, production, manufacture, storage, transport, distribution, sale and supply of feed'.[24] In this vein, the description 'farm to table' and 'farm to fork' is a simple expression of the significant achievement of uniting agricultural produce and foodstuffs under one regulatory umbrella.

From a supply chain perspective, the definitional elements of the GFLR equally reinforce a holistic approach encompassing a wide range of food businesses and operators: a food business means any undertaking, whether for profit or not and whether public or private, carrying out any of the activities related to any stage of production, processing, and distribution of food,[25] whereas 'food business operator' means the natural or legal persons responsible for ensuring that the requirements of food law are met within the food business under their control.[26]

17 *Orthica* (n 16), para 53.
18 ibid, para 54.
19 ibid, para 96.
20 ibid, para 56.
21 Case C-442/09 *Karl Heinz Bablok and Others v Freistaat Bayern* [2011] ECR I-07491.
22 See Chapter 2, section 2.2.1.
23 GFLR, art 3(17).
24 ibid, art 3(16).
25 ibid, art 3(2).
26 ibid, art 3(3).

Considering its foundational definitional elements, the GFLR goes a long way to supporting a 'sufficiently comprehensive and integrated approach to food safety'[27] from a legal perspective.

5.4 Principles of the GFLR, Articles 5–10 (horizontal/transversal nature)

The principles laid down in Articles 5 to 10 GFLR form a general framework of a horizontal nature to be followed when implementing measures.[28] These are horizontal principles of food law; they do not impose direct obligations on the FBOs and are used to interpret existing laws and guide the objectives of forthcoming legislation.

5.4.1 *The objectives of the GFLR (Article 5)*

The objectives of food law are a high level of protection of human life and health and the protection of consumers' interests, including fair practices in food trade, taking account of, where appropriate, the protection of animal health and welfare, plant health, and the environment. Food law aims to achieve the free movement of food within the Community. International standards shall be taken into consideration when developing food law.

5.4.2 *The risk analysis principle (Article 6)*

To achieve a high level of protection of human health and life, food law should be based on risk analysis.[29] Risk analysis is one of the most foundational, pervasive, and practically relevant principles, because the different elements of risk analysis are circumscribed by the law in detail, and the risk analysis principle is operationalized through legal processes and institutions. Risk analysis, according to the GFLR, is divided into 'three interconnected components', namely risk assessment, risk management, and risk communication.[30]

The GFLR regulatory architecture is 'risk-based' as it relies on the risk analysis principle. The risk analysis legal processes are elaborated in specific secondary legislation, for instance in the authorization of Novel Foods or Genetically Modified

[27] ibid, Recital (11).
[28] ibid, art 4(2).
[29] ibid, art 6.
[30] ibid, art 3(10).

Organisms (GMOs) in food and the approval of food improvement agents, which detail the institution that acts as risk assessor and how risk management procedures on particular issues. The risk regulation processes are discussed below in section 5.6.

The Transparency Regulation, which responded to the glyphosate scandal, extensively tackled risk communication and risk assessment. However, it left the role and rules of risk management unaddressed, sustaining a largely unregulated discretionary policy area.

5.4.2.1 *Risk assessment*

Risk assessment, as part of the risk analysis principle, must be based on the available scientific evidence and undertaken in an independent, objective, and transparent manner.[31] From a process perspective, the law defines 'risk assessment' as a scientifically based process consisting of four steps: hazard identification, hazard characterization,[32] exposure assessment, and risk characterization.[33] Hazard means a biological, chemical, or physical agent present in, or condition of, food or feed with the potential to cause an adverse health effect.[34] 'Risk' is determined by the probability of an adverse health effect and the severity of that effect, resulting from a hazard.[35] In the EU risk analysis processes, a major risk assessor is EFSA, although some EU food risk regulation processes may involve other risk assessors.

5.4.2.2 *Risk management*

Risk management means the process, distinct from risk assessment, of weighing policy alternatives in consultation with interested parties, considering risk assessment and other legitimate factors, and, if necessary, selecting appropriate prevention and control options.[36] Principally, risk managers are not bound by risk assessors. Risk management takes into account the results of risk assessment, and in particular EFSA opinions, other factors relevant to the matter under consideration, and the precautionary principle (where the conditions laid down in Article 7(1) GLFR are relevant).[37]

5.4.2.3 *Risk communication*

Risk communication will fulfil the objectives and respect the general principles set out in Articles 8a and 8b[38] (see section 5.4.4). It is defined as the interactive

[31] ibid, art 6(2).
[32] Commonly described as the characterization of the nature and probability of adverse human effects.
[33] GFLR, art 3(11).
[34] ibid, art 3(14).
[35] ibid, art 3(9).
[36] ibid, art 3(12).
[37] ibid, art 6(3).
[38] ibid, art 6(4).

exchange of information and opinions throughout the risk analysis process as regards hazards and risks, risk-related factors, and risk perceptions, among risk assessors, risk managers, consumers, feed and food businesses, the academic community, and other interested parties, including the explanation of risk assessment findings and the basis of risk management decisions.[39]

5.4.3 The food-specific precautionary principle (Article 7)

The precautionary principle has attracted wide attention, including in law and politics. Its legal relevance is generally attributed to the German *Vorsorgeprinzip* of the 1970s and the hopes it incorporated for environmental causes.[40] There are numerous formulations to the precautionary principle, so it is also context-specific, and it has been harshly criticized as both too vague and too restrictive. In the EU Treaties, the precautionary principle is referred to only once, in the context of environmental protection (Article 191 TFEU), which also does not define the principle further.

Food, however, is an exceptional domain in that the GFLR incorporates a specific version of the precautionary principle tailored to the food sector:

> In specific circumstances where, following an assessment of available information, the possibility of harmful effects on health is identified but scientific uncertainty persists, provisional risk management measures necessary to ensure the high level of health protection chosen in the Community may be adopted, pending further scientific information for a more comprehensive risk assessment.[41]

There should be reasonable grounds for concern that an unacceptable level of risk to health exists, the available supporting information and data are not sufficiently complete to enable a comprehensive risk assessment to be made, and measures taken may only be temporary.

The precautionary principle has been applied differently by the CJEU in various food-related cases.[42] This results in three different types of application. At times,

[39] ibid, art 3(13).

[40] Sonja Boehmer-Christiansen, 'The Precautionary Principle in Germany—enabling Government' in Timothy O'Riordan and James Cameron (eds), *Interpreting the Precautionary Principle* (Cameron May 1994); Eckhard Rehbinder, 'The Precautionary Principle in an International Perspective' in Ellen Margrethe Basse (ed), *Miljørettens Grundspørgsmål: bidrag til en nordisk forskeruddannelse* (Gad 1994); Kai Purnhagen, 'The Behavioural Law and Economics of the Precautionary Principle in the EU and Its Impact on Internal Market Regulation' (2014) 37 Journal of Consumer Policy 453, 455.

[41] GFLR, art 7(1).

[42] Kai Purnhagen, 'You want it extra CRISPERY?: Legal Disruption Through New Plant Breeding Technologies in the EU' (2021) 40 Yearbook of European Law 374, 387.

the Court directly applies the test in Article 7 GFLR in a straightforward manner,[43] but it also differentiates based on the level of risk recognized in the underlying secondary legal act and whether products need to go through an authorization procedure or not.[44] While Article 7 GFLR applies to the whole area of food law, the precautionary principle needs to be interpreted differently to the GMO Regulations, which stipulate an authorization procedure. Article 7 GFLR hence needs to 'be read in the light of the procedural operation of those provisions'.[45] This also accounts for procedures for taking emergency measures, which can act as a *lex specialis* and therefore pre-empt Member States from taking measures solely on the basis of the precautionary principle.[46] On one hand, the conditions of such provisions must be interpreted in the light of, inter alia, the precautionary principle.[47] On the other hand, this principle cannot result in such provisions being 'disregarded or altered, in particular by relaxing them'.[48]

Queisser Pharma[49] illustrates the link between Article 6 GFLR on risk analysis and Article 7 GFLR on the precautionary principle. In this case, the CJEU held that a German law that generally prohibited the use of amino acids in foods (except where a derogation was issued by the authorities) would not satisfy the precautionary principle of the GFLR. Accordingly, the application of the food precautionary principle requires (1) identification of the potentially negative consequences for health of the substances or foods concerned, and (2) a comprehensive assessment of the risk to health based on the most reliable scientific data available and the most recent results of international research (para 56). Restrictive measures can be adopted if it is 'impossible to determine with certainty the existence or extent of the alleged risk because of the insufficiency, inconclusiveness or imprecision of the results of studies conducted, but the likelihood of real harm to public health persists should the risk materialise'. Here, the principle targets the lowering of risks (precautionary measures), not the lowering of hazards (preventive measures).[50]

The principle has been given more shape in political interpretations,[51] most specifically in the Communication from the Commission on the precautionary

[43] Case C-282/15 *Queisser Pharma GMBH & co. KG v Bundesrepublik Deutschland* EU:C:2017:26 (*Queisser Pharma*); Case C-333/08 *Commission v French Republic* EU:C:2010:44, para 91.
[44] Case C-111/06 *Giorgio Fidenato and Others* EU:C:2017:676 (*Fidenato*), para 52.
[45] ibid, para. 52.
[46] ibid, para. 54.
[47] Cases C-58/10 to C-68/10 *Monsanto and Others* EU:C:2011:553, para 71.
[48] *Fidenato* (n 44) 47–48.
[49] *Queisser Pharma* (n 43).
[50] Kai Purnhagen, 'The EU's Precautionary Principle in Food Law is an Information Tool!'(2015) 6 European Business Law Review (forthcoming).
[51] Commission in the Green Paper on the General Principles of Food Safety and the Communication of 30 April 1997 on Consumer Health and Food Safety, by Parliament in its Resolution of 10 March 1998 concerning the Green Paper, by the Council in its Resolution of 13 April 1999 and by the Joint Parliamentary Committee of the EEA (European Economic Area) in its Resolution of 16 March 1999.

principle,[52] which outlines the Commission's approach to using the precautionary principle and the guidelines for applying it. It also builds a common understanding of how to handle risks that science has not yet fully evaluated, and aims to avoid the abuse of the precautionary principle as a disguised form of protectionism.

The jurisprudence of the CJEU has interpreted the food precautionary principle as a clearly supportive/interpretative principle only, incapable of leading to a situation where existing EU law would be disregarded, altered, or relaxed.[53] In fact, it has been argued that the CJEU has thereby taken away from Article 7 GFLR much of its regulatory force.[54]

5.4.4 *Protection of consumer interests (Article 8)*

Consumer protection is subject to a distinct competence norm in the EU treaties, which, however, relies on the internal market competence norm of Article 114 TFEU, complemented by numerous self-standing pieces of secondary legislation that are generally applicable to contracts or consumer transactions.

In the GFLR there is a positive obligation that food law should protect the interests of consumers and provide a basis for consumers to make informed choices in relation to the foods they consume. Food law should prevent misleading practices in general, as well as fraudulent or deceptive practices and the adulteration of food specifically.[55] These principles are further elaborated by Article 3(1) of the Food Information to Consumers Regulation (FICR),[56] which also provides normative requirements of consumer expectations in areas of consumer information on foods.

5.4.5 *New section 1a on risk communication*

Risk communication was identified as one of GFLR's weaknesses in the Regulatory Fitness and Performance Program (REFIT) evaluation.[57] As a response,

[52] Commission, 'Communication from the Commission on the precautionary principle' (Communication) COM (2000) 1 final.

[53] *Fidenato* (n 44).

[54] Purnhagen (n 42).

[55] GFLR, art 8(a)–(c).

[56] Regulation (EU) 1169/2011 of the European Parliament and of the Council of 25 October 2011 on the provision of food information to consumers, amending Regulations (EC) No 1924/2006 and (EC) No 1925/2006 of the European Parliament and of the Council, and repealing Commission Directive 87/250/EEC, Council Directive 90/496/EEC, Commission Directive 1999/10/EC, Directive 2000/13/EC of the European Parliament and of the Council, Commission Directives 2002/67/EC and 2008/5/EC and Commission Regulation (EC) No 608/2004 [2011] OJ L304/18 (Food Information to Consumers Regulation (FICR)).

[57] Commission, 'Commission Staff Working Document, Executive summary of the REFIT evaluation of the General Food Law (Regulation (EC) No 178/2002) Brussels' SWD (2018) 37 final.

improvement of risk communication is one of the major objectives of the new Transparency Regulation,[58] which amended the GFLR to include a new section on risk communication that covers general objectives (Article 8a), principles (Article 8b), and a general plan of risk communication (Article 8c). Considering the effects that (lack of) risk communication has on both risk management and risk assessment, this is laudable. Examining the general objectives, risk communication must deliver on awareness, consistency, transparency, public understanding, appropriate involvement, the provision of information, and the fight against false information.[59]

The principles clarify that risk communication is to be undertaken by both risk managers and risk assessors in accordance with their respective roles. They both must ensure that 'accurate and all appropriate information is exchanged in an interactive and timely manner with all interested parties, based on the principles of transparency, openness, and responsiveness'.[60] There is a strong emphasis on providing information about every stage of the risk analysis process, along with a duty to justify decisions made at each stage.[61] There is also a new-found emphasis on taking account of the 'risk perceptions' of interested parties;[62] facilitating understanding and dialogue amongst all interested parties;[63] and being clear and accessible, including to those not directly involved in the process or lacking a scientific background.[64]

The Commission is also tasked with drawing up a general plan of risk communication, probably inspired by the US Food and Drug Administration's (FDA) Strategic Plan for Risk Communication.[65] The plan asks for the creation of risk activity communication typologies, tools, and channels; mechanisms of coordination to ensure coherency between risk managers and assessors; as well as appropriate mechanisms to ensure a stakeholder dialogue.[66] To date, there is no further information regarding the details of the plan, although EFSA has started significant internal preparations.[67]

58 Regulation (EU) 2019/1381 of the European Parliament and of the Council of 20 June 2019 on the transparency and sustainability of the EU risk assessment in the food chain and amending Regulations (EC) No 178/2002, (EC) No 1829/2003, (EC) No 1831/2003, (EC) No 2065/2003, (EC) No 1935/2004, (EC) No 1331/2008, (EC) No 1107/2009, (EU) 2015/2283 and Directive 2001/18/EC [2019] OJ L231/1 (Transparency Regulation).

59 GFLR, art 8(a).

60 ibid, art 8b(a).

61 ibid, art 8b(b).

62 ibid, art 8b(c).

63 ibid, art 8b(d).

64 ibid, art 8b(e).

65 FDA, 'Strategic Plan for Risk Communication' (Fall 2019) <https://www.fda.gov/about-fda/reports/strategic-plan-risk-communication> accessed 27 July 2022.

66 GFLR, art 8c.

67 Anthony Smith and others, 'Future Directions for Risk Communications at EFSA' (2021) 19 EFSA Journal 190201.

5.4.6 *Principles of transparency*

Transparency was one of the 'founding principles' of the GFLR, but it has been significantly strengthened by the Transparency Regulation's amendments.

Under general EU law, there is no clear principle of transparency in adjudication, and it could be characterized as a 'misunderstood' EU legal doctrine. In adjudication, transparency is mainly construed as a narrow iteration of access to documents,[68] and there are sector-specific variations, for instance in public procurement or food law. Understood more widely, transparency can potentially encompass many facets, extending to notions of democracy, legitimacy, accountability, realization of individual rights, and market efficiency.[69] Although the Transparency Regulation included many additional provisions of the GFLR that relate to transparency in the wider sense, it did not modify the original transparency section.

The food sector-specific principle of transparency in the GFLR is therefore somewhat limited. It requires public consultation (participatory aspects of transparency)[70] and public information, which is framed through access to documents with an obligation on public authorities to inform the public regarding health risks.[71] *Berger*[72] confirmed that national law may (but EU law does not require it) allow public authorities to inform the public even if food is deemed unsafe not only because it is injurious to health but also because it is simply unfit for human consumption. However, with the introduction of the Official Controls Regulation (see Chapter 6) most questions regarding the legality of inspections will typically be handled under this new legal instrument.

5.5 General obligations of food trade (Articles 11–13)

Food and feed imported into the EU must comply with EU food law, or with conditions recognized as equivalent by the EU, or with requirements agreed in international agreements between the third country and the EU.[73] This provision is one aspect which has led authors to argue that the EU, as an important market player, is imposing its stringent food safety standards in international trade—sometimes called the 'Brussels effect'.[74]

[68] Marianna Vanuzzo, 'Transparency in EU Food Law' (Doctoral thesis, Università Cattolica del Sacro Cuore 2022).

[69] ibid.

[70] GFLR, art 9.

[71] ibid, art 10.

[72] Case C-636/11 *Karl Berger v Freistaat Bayern* EU:C:2013:227 (*Berger*).

[73] GFLR, art 11.

[74] Anu Bradford, 'The Brussels Effect' (2012) 107 Northwestern University Law Review 1; Joanne Scott, 'From Brussels with Love: The Transatlantic Travels of European Law and the Chemistry of Regulatory Attraction' (2009) 57 American Journal of Comparative Law 897; Gregory Shaffer,

Food and feed exported from the EU for placing on the market within the Community of a third country must comply with the relevant requirements of food law, unless other standards are explicitly required by the third country, or the authorities have been informed of reasons preventing compliance with EU standards and expressly agree to products being sold in their market.[75]

With regards to international standards, the GFLR mandates a generally proactive attitude to international standard setting, taking into account the positions of developing countries and supporting consistency between international technical standards and food law when developing Union legislation.[76]

An example of this relationship is the concept of 'food safety culture', which was developed at the Codex Alimentarius level, and is now implemented in various EU food law instruments.

5.6 The rules of the general food law requirements of food law (Articles 14–21)

5.6.1 General safety obligation

The GFLR establishes a general food safety requirement. Article 14 GFLR stipulates that food cannot be placed on the market if it is unsafe.[77] The general requirement is characterized by three aspects: (1) it is a general umbrella provision, in nature wide enough to be able to cover unforeseen and hence unregulated safety risks; (2) it implies a free marketing principle, where as a starting point the main understanding is that all products can be placed on the market, unless they are unsafe; (3) it is based on an *ex-ante* self-assessment by the FBOs, placing a lot of responsibility on them.

The definition of unsafety is strictly legal; it does not follow its meaning in natural language. Accordingly, food can be unsafe for two reasons, either because it is (a) injurious to health, or because it is (b) unfit for consumption.[78] In determining whether food is unsafe, the following factors should be taken into account: (a) the normal conditions of use of the food, and (b) the information provided to the

'Globalization and Social Protection: The Impact of EU and International Rules in the Ratcheting Up of U.S. Privacy Standards' (2000) 25 Yale Journal of International Law 1, 46; Dominique Sinopoli and Kai Purnhagen, 'Reversed Harmonization or Horizontalization of EU Standards?: Does WTO Law Facilitate or Constrain the Brussels Effect?' (2016) 34 Wisconsin International Law Journal 92.

[75] GFLR, art 12.
[76] ibid, art 13.
[77] ibid, art 14(1).
[78] ibid, art 14(2).

consumer.[79] Information can therefore act as a broker of safety, and more information can influence the finding on unsafety, and indirectly liability.

In determining whether a food is 'injurious to health' (a) probable immediate and/or short-term and/or long-term effects, as well as effects on subsequent generations, can be taken into account, along with the (b) likely cumulative toxic effects and health sensitivities of particular categories of consumers.[80]

To determine whether food is 'unfit for human consumption', regard shall be had to whether the food is unacceptable for human consumption based on its intended use, for reasons of contamination, whether by extraneous matter or otherwise, or because of putrefaction, deterioration, or decay. Unfit consumption is more quality oriented; the main question is whether it is unacceptable for human consumption. For instance, a fingernail in a sausage would render a food unfit for consumption, but not hazardous to health.[81] The Commission clarifies this further:

> The central concept of unfitness is unacceptability. Food can be rendered unfit by reason of contamination, such as that caused by a high level of non-pathogenic microbiological contamination (see Article 14(3) and (5) of the Regulation), by the presence of foreign objects, by unacceptable taste or odor as well as by more obvious detrimental deterioration such as putrefaction or decomposition.[82]

There is also 'legal' unsafety, meaning that foods which are part of an unsafe batch, lot, or consignment, are also presumed to be unsafe.[83] Unsafety can also be reached by legal definition; after expiry of the 'use by' date a food shall be deemed to be unsafe.[84] In addition, there is legal safety: if a certain aspect of a food is regulated, compliant food is to be regarded as safe as regards the regulated aspects,[85] unless there are reasons to suspect it is unsafe.

Alongside the strong safety obligation, there is a general prohibition against misleading consumers in the presentation of food.[86]

This general marketing requirement in principle implies that there is a free food market; FBOs can put food on the market subject to a self-assessment of whether the goods comply with the legal requirements, specifically whether it is not safe. There are some areas in which this 'free food marketing' principle is limited, and prior authorization is required (see Chapters 7–9).

[79] ibid, art 14(3).
[80] ibid, art 14(4).
[81] Commission, *Guidance on the implementation of Articles 11, 12, 14, 17, 18, 19 and 20 of Regulation (EC) N° 178/2002 on General Food Law – Conclusions of the Standing Committee on the Food Chain and Animal Health* (26 January 2010).
[82] ibid.
[83] GFLR, art 14(6).
[84] FICR, art 24(1).
[85] Both for EU and national law, see GFLR, art 14(7) and 14(9).
[86] ibid, art 16.

5.6.2 *Basic obligation to comply*

FBOs must comply with all food law obligations.[87] This enshrines the approach of the GFLR to hold FBOs accountable as much as possible for complying with food legislation. The 'farm to fork' inclusive responsibility approach implies that this obligation is applicable to the entire supply chain, that is, food and feed business operators at all stages of production, processing, and distribution, and within the businesses under their control. The provision is transversal in nature, in that it requires FBOs to comply with all food laws, not just with the GFLR.

Member States must enforce food law and monitor and verify compliance with food law. They must have a system of official controls and measures, and penalties for infringements.[88] Measures and penalties must be effective, proportionate, and dissuasive.[89]

Along these lines, under Article 17 GFLR—FBO responsibility,[90] a national legal system may institute a system of strict liability for the violation of microbiological criteria.

5.6.3 *Traceability*

The traceability of food and feed products must be established at all stages.[91] This means they must be able to identify who supplied them,[92] and have a system to identify other businesses that have been supplied.[93] This obligation is commonly interpreted in practice as encompassing the identification of business partners at least one step up and one step down the supply chain. Such a limitation on the legal obligation of traceability, however, has no solid basis in current EU food law.

5.6.4 *Consequences and responsibilities for FBOs*

The GFLR further stipulates consequences and responsibilities. Article 19 GFLR outlines the consequences for an FBO who places unsafe food on the market.

[87] ibid, art 17(1).
[88] On the interplay of public and private enforcement in EU food law, see Kai Purnhagen and Alexandra Molitorisová, 'Public and Private Enforcement of EU Food Law' (2022) 13 European Journal of Risk Regulation 464.
[89] While openly worded, the effectiveness requirement has led the Court to interfere in the Member States' system of remedies in other sectors, and this could easily be applicable here. See Hanna Schebesta, 'Does the National Court Know European Law? A Note on *Ex Officio* Application after *Asturcom*' (2010) 18 European Review of Private Law 847.
[90] Case C-443/13 *Ute Reindl v Bezirkshauptmannschaft Innsbruck* EU:C:2014:237.
[91] GFLR, art 18.
[92] ibid, art 18(1) and 18(3).
[93] ibid, art 18(3).

FBOs who consider or have reason to believe that non-compliant food has reached the market must withdraw the food, and if there is a possibility that the food has reached consumers, they must inform consumers and, if necessary, recall the product to ensure consumer safety. Foods that are classified as injurious to health under Article 14(2)(a) GFLR must therefore be recalled from the market. In addition, FBOs must inform the competent authorities if foods that are injurious to health have been marketed.

The marketing FBO must cooperate with the competent authorities.[94] Other businesses must cooperate in procedures and, for instance, initiate actions to withdraw from the market products that are not in compliance with the food-safety requirements.[95]

The rules of the GFLR implement the 'Farm to Table' approach that intended to capture the entire supply chain, and to establish connections between them. Importantly, the responsibilities attributed under Article 17 GFLR are not legal liabilities.[96] The Product Liability Directive[97] applies in parallel, and therefore defective food products can trigger damages claims under the conditions of that regime.[98] However, the Guidance to the GFLR clarified that responsibility under the GFLR would not equate to liability, rather it must be based on a legal basis found in the national legal order and in the specific food legislation that has been infringed.[99] This is because the main principle of EU law is that in many areas the remedies available for breaches are largely governed by Member States. This is, of course, not absolute, and is already significantly limited in areas such as administrative remedies and the official controls regulation.

5.7 European Food Safety Authority

The GFLR institutionalized food safety governance and created EFSA. On one hand, the GFLR was far-reaching in creating a dedicated agency. On the other hand, whereas the White Paper on Food Safety foresaw the creation of a European Food Authority (with a food safety mandate), the GFLR very clearly delimits the role of EFSA to safety, as indicated by its name. In addition, following the Commission proposal, EFSA was not intended to become a regulatory agency, but merely provide scientific advice without taking on a risk management role. In

[94] ibid, art 19(4).
[95] ibid, art 19(2).
[96] See Guidance (n 81).
[97] Council Directive 85/374/EEC of 25 July 1985 on the approximation of the laws, regulations and administrative provisions of the Member States concerning liability for defective products [1985] OJ L210/29 (Product Liability Directive).
[98] GFLR, art 21.
[99] Guidance (n 81) 13.

terms of scientific advice, EFSA had a largely passive role, in that it aggregates science, but it does not regularly conduct or commission scientific studies.

The GFLR founded EFSA as an independent agency exclusively dedicated to food safety. The legal status of all EU agencies under EU law is controversial, in particular raising questions of democratic legitimacy and how to control the activities of EU agencies.[100] EU agencies curiously lack a dedicated Treaty basis, and they used to be primarily established under Article 308 EC (now Article 352 TFEU), the residual competence clause to attain EU objectives. It has now become common practice to ground agency competence on functional competence. Agencies provide administrative support, and exercise powers delegated to them. Limits to the exercise of these powers were set in the *Meroni*[101] and *ESMA*[102] cases, notably the fact that the principal needs to retain control. In addition, Treaty rules regarding the actions and accountability of institutions have been made applicable to agencies, so that since the Lisbon Treaty[103] agencies are recognized at constitutional level. In the literature, agencies are therefore subject to critiques concerning accountability.[104] EFSA can be regarded as a quasi-regulatory[105] agency, or as a decentralized agency with advisory powers.[106]

The GFLR details the main outlines of EFSA's institutional structures and, in legal terms, functions as the basic act to anchor further tertiary law governing the functioning of the agency. The chapter on EFSA has been significantly amended by the Transparency Regulation.

5.7.1 Mission and tasks of the authority

EFSA's mission is to provide scientific advice and scientific and technical support for food and feed safety legislation.[107] This general mandate is therefore potentially wider than food safety alone, and could be expanded to cover areas such as sustainability. However, currently, EFSA's practical tasks remain confined to food safety.

[100] Miroslava Scholten and Alex Brenninkmeijer, *Controlling EU Agencies: The Rule of Law in a Multi-jurisdictional Legal Order* (Edward Elgar 2020).

[101] Case C-9/56 *Meroni & Co., Industrie Metallurgiche, SpA v High Authority of the European Coal and Steel Community* EU:C:1958:7 (*Meroni*).

[102] Case C-270/12 *United Kingdom of Great Britain and Northern Ireland v European Parliament and Council of the European Union* EU:C:2014:18 (*ESMA*).

[103] Consolidated Version of the Treaty on the Functioning of the European Union [2012] OJ C326/47 (TFEU), arts 15, 228, 263, and 267.

[104] Marios Costa, *The Accountability Gap in EU law* (Routledge 2017).

[105] Elena Madalina Busuioc, 'The Accountability of European Agencies: Legal Provisions and Ongoing Practices' (DPhil thesis, Utrecht School of Governance 2010).

[106] Simone Gabbi, Matthew Wood, and Béla Strauss, 'Controlling the European Food Safety Authority' in Miroslava Scholten and Alex Brenninkmeijer (eds), *Controlling EU Agencies: The Rule of Law in a Multi-jurisdictional Legal Order* (EE 2020).

[107] GFLR, art 22.

EFSA should contribute to the protection of human life and health, and 'in this respect' take into account animal health and welfare, plant health, and the environment, in the context of the operation of the internal market. EFSA's mission is anthropocentric and largely included in an internal market rationale without consideration for agricultural policy topics.

Furthermore, EFSA's activities are risk-based, with its main task being the characterization and monitoring of risks which have a direct or indirect impact on food and feed safety. The scope of EFSA's work extends to human nutrition for EU law and nutritional issues in the framework of the EU health programme. It also covers animal health and welfare and plant health, and it comprehensively covers GMOs, including non-food and feed GMOs.[108] EFSA provides scientific opinions which will serve as the scientific basis for the drafting and adoption of EU measures.[109]

In exercising their tasks, EFSA, the Commission and the competent bodies in the Member States, Member States, and relevant Union agencies, have general co-operation duties.[110]

Specifically, the tasks of the Authority include the following:[111]

- scientific opinions;
- developing uniform risk assessment methodologies;
- scientific and technical support to the Commission;
- commissioning scientific studies if necessary;
- collecting data;
- identifying and characterizing emerging risks;
- establishing a system of networks of organizations operating in the field;
- providing assistance in the crisis management procedures, if requested;
- providing assistance between the Community, applicant countries, international organizations, and third countries, if requested;
- providing information to the public and interested parties;
- expressing independently its own conclusions and orientations;
- undertaking any other task assigned to it by the Commission within its mission.

In order to outline how it will undertake its mission, EFSA prepared its Strategy 2027 'Science, safe food, sustainability',[112] defining key strategic objectives, namely, to deliver reliable scientific advice and communication of risks from farm to fork,

[108] ibid, art 22(5).
[109] ibid, art 22(6).
[110] ibid, art 22(7), (8), and (9).
[111] ibid, art 23.
[112] EFSA, 'EFSA Strategy 2027—Science, Safe food, Sustainability' (June 2021) <https://www.efsa.europa.eu/sites/default/files/2021-07/efsa-strategy-2027.pdf> accessed 28 July 2022.

ensure preparedness for future risk analysis needs, and empower individuals while ensuring organizational agility.

5.7.2 *Organization*

EFSA's internal organization comprises a management board, executive director, an advisory forum, as well as scientific committees and scientific panels.[113]

The new Transparency Regulation (to enhance transparency and the sustainability of risk assessment in the food chain) significantly altered the parts of the GFLR that regulate EFSA governance. Among other things, the proposal targets the internal composition of EFSA bodies. The new regulation changed the composition of the management board of EFSA, including Commission and European Parliament representation and representatives from civil society and food chain interests,[114] as well as the composition and nomination of scientific committees and panels.

The EFSA Management Board ensures that EFSA is carrying out its mission under the conditions of the GFLR. The representation in the EFSA Management Board changed significantly through the new Transparency Regulation, leading to a nationalization of this body; Member States will be able to nominate members that will subsequently be appointed by the Council. In addition, there is a fixed quota that will be nominated by the Commission (two), the European Parliament (two), and one member each from a consumer organization, an environmental non-governmental organization (NGO), a farmers' organization, and an industry organization.[115] This composition of the Management Board is entirely novel and it remains to be seen whether it will improve governance or, conversely, potentially make it a more politicized body. The term of office is four years, and members normally act by majority. The Management Board appoints the executive director.[116]

The Advisory Forum is composed of representatives from competent bodies in the Member States, and is a mechanism for coordination and advice.[117]

The Scientific Committee and Scientific Panels are responsible for providing ESFA's scientific opinions.[118] The Scientific Committee is composed of the Chairs of the Scientific Panels and six independent scientific experts who do not belong to any of the Scientific Panels, appointed by the Management Board. There are ten Scientific Panels with different mandates[119] that are composed of independent scientific experts.

113 GFLR, art 24.
114 Transparency Regulation.
115 ibid, amendment of art 25.
116 GFLR, art 26.
117 ibid, art 27.
118 ibid, art 28.
119 GFLR, art 28(4):

EFSA is dedicated to the idea of independence.[120] Yet, it is one of the areas that has received a number of legal challenges.[121] Gabbi and others note that despite criticism, the EU agency appears to work relatively smoothly.[122]

5.7.3 *Operation*

The actions open to EFSA are detailed in the operations chapter. The tasks have been substantially extended by the Transparency Regulation, creating a more active scientific mandate than was the case before.

EFSA writes scientific opinions,[123] at the request of the Commission, the European Parliament, and on its own initiative. Detailed rules for scientific opinions are established in delegated and implementing acts. In instances where there are diverging scientific opinions, EFSA must try to clarify the contentious scientific issues.[124] In addition, the EFSA can deliver scientific and technical assistance.[125] EFSA can actively commission scientific studies where necessary for its mission.[126] The Transparency Regulation devised a number of mechanisms that could be regarded as exhibiting a 'participatory' approach to science, and certainly EFSA mechanisms reflect a dialectical process. One such mechanism is the pre-submission advice, where EFSA can provide advice to potential notifiers or authorization applicants.[127] This is an example of the more dialogical direction that

[123] GFLR, art 29.
[124] ibid, art 30.
[125] ibid, art 31.
[126] ibid, art 32.
[127] ibid, art 32a.

(a)the Panel on food additives and flavourings;
(b)the Panel on additives and products or substances used in animal feed;
(c)the Panel on plant protection products and their residues;
(d)the Panel on genetically modified organisms;
(e)the Panel on nutrition, novel foods and food allergens;
(f)the Panel on biological hazards;
(g)the Panel on contaminants in the food chain;
(h)the Panel on animal health and welfare;
(i)the Panel on plant health;
(j)the Panel on food contact materials and enzymes and processing aids.

[120] ibid, art 37.
[121] Case C-615/13 *Client Earth and Pesticide Action Network Europe (PAN Europe) v European Food Safety Authority* EU:C:2015:489.
[122] Gabbi, Wood, and Strauss (n 106).

risk assessment is taking. Similarly, scientific studies are now being monitored—they must now be notified by potential applicants and EFSA maintains a database of consultation with third parties. Studies that have not been previously notified result in the inadmissibility or invalidity of authorizations or notifications.[128] In instances of renewal, the potential applicant or notifier must notify the Authority of the studies it intends to perform for that purpose, and EFSA consults relevant stakeholders to provide advice on the content and design of studies.[129] In addition, the Commission may request EFSA to conduct verification studies,[130] 'in exceptional circumstances of serious controversies or conflicting results'. EFSA may also take an active role regarding data, with a mandate to search for, collect, collate, analyse, and summarize relevant scientific and technical data in the fields within its mission.[131] In order to engage proactively with risks, EFSA is required to establish monitoring procedures for the identification of emerging risks in the fields within its mission.[132] It is also the recipient of messages of the rapid alert system, which EFSA is required to monitor for health and nutritional risks.[133] Institutionally, EFSA is tasked with the networking of organizations operating in the fields within the Authority's mission.

Overall, the Transparency Regulation's changes captured in the provisions on EFSA's operation created a more active, diligent, dialogical, and collaborative risk assessment mandate for the Authority.

5.7.4 Independence, transparency, confidentiality, and communication

The section 'Independence, Transparency, Confidentiality and Communication' comprises a relatively diverse combination of provisions that govern EFSA operations. All EFSA bodies undertake to act independently in the public interest.[134] In addition, the Transparency Regulation introduced stronger transparency obligations[135] in terms of transparency in the strict sense, understood as the disclosure and making public of EFSA documents. However, there are disclosure limitations through intellectual property rights and any provisions set out in Union law 'protecting the investment made by innovators in gathering the information and data supporting relevant applications for authorisations' ('data exclusivity rules'). The rules also cover confidentiality, including detailing the balance between public

[128] ibid, art 32b.
[129] ibid, art 32c.
[130] ibid, art 32d.
[131] ibid, art 33.
[132] ibid, art 34.
[133] ibid, art 35.
[134] ibid, art 37.
[135] ibid, arts 38 and 39.

access to documents and applicant confidentiality. Confidential information shall not be made public. However, there are two important public interest limitations to confidentiality, notably for urgent action to protect human health, animal health, or the environment, as well as information which forms part of the conclusions of scientific outputs.[136] Confidentiality can be requested by the applicant if they can demonstrate that making the information public would significantly harm their interests.[137] EFSA's decision on confidentiality can be subject to an action before the CJEU under the conditions laid down in Articles 263 and 278 TFEU.[138] EFSA further reviews the confidentiality of old applications.[139] Upon request, EFSA must make available to the Commission and the Member States all information in its possession relating to an application, although confidentiality towards the public must remain protected. In addition, the staff members are subject to requirements of professional secrecy pursuant to Article 339 TFEU. The names of individuals involved in the scientific outputs will be made public, unless they are not suitable for the protection of personal data.[140] Regarding access to documents, the GFLR further stipulates that other EU legislation remains applicable. This concerns Regulation (EC) 1049/2001[141] for documents held by EFSA. For environmental information, Regulation (EC) 1367/2006 and Directive 2003/4/EC continue to apply. In addition, the practical arrangements for implementing access to documents are defined by a decision of the Management Board.[142] The new confidentiality rules contained in the GFLR have significant impact on other areas of regulation. The Proposal declares the confidentiality rules in the GFLR to apply *mutatis mutandis* in other fields, in parts supplementing area specific reasons that may warrant confidential treatment, that is, 'information, the disclosure of which may be deemed, upon verifiable justification, to significantly harm the interests concerned'.[143] For example, in the area of plant protection products, the confidentiality rules of the GFLR apply, and additional reasons that may justify non-disclosure are laid down.[144] The Transparency Regulation could be seen as having

[136] ibid, art 39.
[137] ibid, art 39d.
[138] ibid, art 39b.
[139] ibid, art 39c.
[140] ibid, art 39e.
[141] Regulation (EC) 1049/2001 of the European Parliament and of the Council of 30 May 2001 regarding public access to European Parliament, Council and Commission documents [2001] OJ L145/43.
[142] EFSA, 'Decision of the Management Board laying down practical arrangements for implementing Regulation (EC) No 1049/2001 and Articles 6 and 7 of Regulation (EC) No 1367/2006' (27 March 2020) <https://www.efsa.europa.eu/sites/default/files/documents/wp200327-a2.pdf> accessed 28 July 2022.
[143] ibid.
[144] In the case of Plant Protection Products (PPPs), information relating to the specification of impurity of the active substance and the methods of analysis for impurities, results of production batches, and information on the complete composition of a plant protection product may enjoy confidentiality privilege.

elements of a Trojan horse—while regulating access to documents, it also establishes strong proprietary protection of data and confidentiality rights for FBOs. In this regard, the provisions on confidentiality have been greatly clarified, without necessarily resulting in greater access to information.

The GFLR in this section further solidifies EFSA's important formal role in risk communication. The Authority shall communicate on its own initiative in the fields within its mission without prejudice to the Commission's competence to communicate its risk management decisions. It will promptly provide objective, reliable, and easily accessible information. This includes, after the Transparency Regulation, public access to all scientific outputs including scientific opinions.[145] Furthermore, the Authority will develop effective contacts with consumer representatives, producer representatives, processors, and any other interested parties.[146]

The section additionally contains provisions on data collection, that is, standard data formats[147] and information systems.[148]

5.7.5 *Strategic plan*

EFSA publishes Strategic plans,[149] the most recent being the EFSA Strategic Plan 2027. The main challenges are Green Deal actions and in particular the Farm to Fork Strategy, the Chemicals Strategy for Sustainability, and the Biodiversity Strategy. Furthermore, the implementation of the Transparency Regulation is a major task, notably the expanded mandate for EFSA in risk communication. Lastly, EFSA intends to tackle new challenges such as methodologies and digitalization, as well as the One Health—One Environment approach.

5.8 Risk response: rapid alert system, crisis management, and emergencies (Articles 50–57)

5.8.1 *Rapid Alert System for Food and Feed (RASFF)*

A rapid alert system for the notification of direct or indirect risks to human health deriving from food or feed is hereby established as a network. It will involve the Member States, the Commission, and the Authority. The Member States, the

[145] GFLR, art 40.
[146] ibid, art 42.
[147] ibid, art 39f.
[148] ibid, art 39g.
[149] EFSA (n 112).

Commission, and the Authority will each designate a contact point, which will be a member of the network.[150] The Rapid Alert System for Food and Feed (RASFF) supports Member States' actions by allowing the rapid exchange of information on risks posed by food or feed and on measures taken or to be taken to address such risks.

The RASFF members can make a notification, and the system allows information sharing regarding risks, tracing of food on the market, as well as measures taken by Member States. RASFF in turn generates information, border rejections, news, and alerts. Alert notifications are sent for serious risks requiring a rapid response. Information on border rejections pertains to consignments that have been intercepted at the borders for health risks, in accordance with the information principle provided for in Article 10 GFLR. In general, the public will have access to information on product identification, the nature of the risk, and the measures taken.

*5.8.2 **Emergencies (Articles 53–54)***

The Commission is entitled to adopt emergency measures for food and feed of Community origin or imported from a third country where it is likely to constitute a serious risk to human health, animal health, or the environment, and cannot be adequately contained or addressed by means of measures taken by the Member State(s).[151]

Member States may adopt interim measures. They must inform the Commission 'officially' of the need to take emergency measures and, where the Commission has not acted in accordance with Article 53 GFLR, they must 'immediately' inform the other Member States and the Commission of the interim protective measures adopted—the term 'immediately' is understood to mean as soon as possible, but no later than when the emergency measures are adopted by the Member State concerned.[152] Within ten working days, the Commission is to bring the matter before the Standing Committee on the Food Chain and Animal Health, with a view to the extension, amendment, or abrogation of the national interim protective measures.[153]

[150] GFLR, art 50.
[151] ibid, art 53.
[152] Joined Cases C-58/10 and C-68/10 *Monsanto SAS and Others v Ministre de l'Agriculture et de la Pêche* [2011] ECR I-07763.
[153] *Fidenato* (n 44).

5.8.3 Crisis management (Articles 55–57)

The Commission will draw up, in close cooperation with the Authority and the Member States, a general plan for crisis management in the field of food and feed safety. The latest of these plans is contained in Decision (EU) 300/2019,[154] which covers situations requiring increased Union coordination as well as situations requiring the establishment of a crisis unit bringing together the Commission as well as relevant Member States and Union agencies.

Furthermore, in cases not sufficiently addressed through emergency response procedures (Articles 53–54 GFLR), the GFLR tasks the Commission with establishing a crisis unit[155] tasked with collecting and evaluating all relevant information and identifying the options available to prevent, eliminate, or reduce to an acceptable level the risk to human health as effectively and rapidly as possible.[156]

5.9 Procedures and final provisions

In terms of its own function as a 'Basic Act', the GFLR contains an article specifying the conditions for delegation.[157] The Commission has been granted the power to adopt delegated acts as regards the number and names of the EFSA Scientific Panels, for establishing the procedure to be applied by the Authority to the requests for a scientific opinion, and criteria for organizations to be included in the network operating in EFSA's field of mission.[158] The Council and the European Parliament must be informed, and may object.

For the purposes of the Committee procedure, the GFLR stipulates that the Commission is assisted by the Committee on Plants, Animals, Food and Feed, a committee that falls under the definition of a committee as outlined in Committee Procedure Regulation (EU) 182/2011.[159][160] The Committee carries out the functions according to the GFLR or other Union law. It may also independently examine any issue falling under those provisions, either at the initiative of the Chairman or at the written request of one of its members.[161]

[154] Commission Implementing Decision (EU) 2019/300 of 19 February 2019 establishing a general plan for crisis management in the field of the safety of food and feed [2019] OJ L50/55, which repealed the Commission Decision 2004/478/EC of 29 April 2004 concerning the adoption of a general plan for food/feed crisis management [2004] OJ L160/98.

[155] GFLR, art 56.

[156] ibid, art 57.

[157] ibid, art 57a.

[158] ibid, arts 28(4), 29(6), and 36(3).

[159] Regulation (EU) 182/2011 of the European Parliament and of the Council of 16 February 2011 laying down the rules and general principles concerning mechanisms for control by Member States of the Commission's exercise of implementing powers [2011] OJ L55/13.

[160] GFLR, art 58.

[161] ibid, art 59.

Lastly, the GFLR provides for a mediation procedure in instances where a Member State believes that a measure taken by another Member State in the field of food safety is either incompatible with the GFLR or is likely to affect the functioning of the internal market. The Member States concerned and the Commission will 'make every effort to solve the problem', and in instances of disagreement, the Commission may request an opinion on any relevant contentious scientific issue from the Authority.[162]

5.10 Reflection on the GFLR

The GFLR is the cornerstone of the risk regulation processes in food within the EU. Risk regulation in EU food law is phrased as 'risk analysis', that is, risk assessment, risk management, and risk communication. This distinction is a key tenet of EU risk regulation, and the strict separation of risk management and risk assessment has been characterized as 'the single biggest innovation in the GFLR'.[163] In comparative terms, it markedly differs from other regulatory regimes;[164] for instance, in the US, risk assessment and management are a combined regulatory function. A prime purpose of the strict separation between risk assessment and risk management is to shield scientific risk assessments from political considerations regarding how to act upon those scientific findings. Outcomes of risk assessments are supposed to be objective facts, on the basis of which decisions can be taken in a political risk management process. Politicization, therefore, is foreseen in the risk management phase, but not in risk assessment.

In the EU, only risk communication is a shared task for both risk assessors and risk managers. Initially a somewhat ambiguous process, it has now been clarified and expanded upon with the implementation of the Transparency Regulation.

The GFLR establishes the EU risk assessment institution (EFSA) as an independent scientific advisor, as well as the applicable risk assessment operations and a number of general principles of risk assessment. The procedural steps for the involvement of EFSA as a risk assessor are laid down in the underlying Basic Act (for

[162] ibid, art 60.

[163] Commission, 'Proposal for a Regulation of the European Parliament and of the Council on the transparency and sustainability of the EU risk assessment in the food chain amending Regulation (EC) No 178/2002 [on general food law], Directive 2001/18/EC [on the deliberate release into the environment of GMOs], Regulation (EC) No 1829/2003 [on GM food and feed], Regulation (EC) No 1831/2003 [on feed additives], Regulation (EC) No 2065/2003 [on smoke flavourings], Regulation (EC) No 1935/2004 [on food contact materials], Regulation (EC) No 1331/2008 [on the common authorisation procedure for food additives, food enzymes and food flavourings], Regulation (EC) No 1107/2009 [on plant protection products] and Regulation (EU) No 2015/2283 [on novel foods]' (Proposal) COM (2018) 0179 final.

[164] Emanuela Bozzini, *Pesticide Policy and Politics in the European Union: Regulatory Assessment, Implementation and Enforcement* (Palgrave Macmillan 2017).

instance, the Novel Food Regulation (NFR)[165]). Upon being given a mandate by the Commission, EFSA will adopt its Opinion. The conditions for risk assessment are regulated within the respective legal framework (Basic Act), and any delegated or implementing acts specifying the procedural details.

Risk management, on the other hand, is predominantly conducted under the auspices of the Commission, either through delegated acts, or in the case of implementing acts following processes outlined in the Committee Regulation,[166] which involves national decision makers. The idea of extending a broader mandate to EFSA that would include risk management was seen as too far-reaching at the time, although it is something that is nowadays seen in supervisory agencies in the financial sector,[167] and may be an (unspoken) option on the table in the sustainability revision under the Farm to Fork Strategy.

The GFLR establishes the outline of risk analysis processes, but must always be read in conjunction with the respective secondary piece of legislation governing a specific issue ('Basic Act'), for example the NFR for new products and production processes. The underlying Basic Act (for instance, the NFR) will stipulate the general procedural steps for different purposes, and in particular which procedure must be used in order to pass a given risk regulatory measure. The NFR outlines the procedure for applying for authorization of novel foods, including the fact that the Union List can be updated by an Implementing Regulation.[168]

One obvious limitation of EFSA is the mandate: EFSA deals strictly with food, and more specifically with food safety. This means that some issues will be dealt with under a very specific mandate that risks overlooking important elements. For example, food safety risk assessments are limited to human health considerations and do not consider wider ecological impacts of substances. Similarly, addressing microplastics in food may neglect other human health risks arising from microplastics. Generally, chemical and medicinal regulation is embedded in a complementary institutional setting separate from EFSA.

EFSA is the risk assessor in food safety law. However, EFSA does not habitually conduct its own studies, rather it is composed of experts in the field that review available science. In that sense, EFSA is not a scientific evidence producer, but a reviewer. While this division is firmly enshrined in EU law, one may question whether restructuring the EU food risk regulation architecture to encompass full scientific assessment capacities would be desirable.

[165] Regulation (EU) 2015/2283 of the European Parliament and of the Council of 25 November 2015 on novel foods, amending Regulation (EU) No 1169/2011 of the European Parliament and of the Council and repealing Regulation (EC) No 258/97 of the European Parliament and of the Council and Commission Regulation (EC) No 1852/2001 [2015] OJ L327/1 (Novel Food Regulation, NFR).

[166] Regulation (EU) 182/2011 of the European Parliament and of the Council of 16 February 2011 laying down the rules and general principles concerning mechanisms for control by Member States of the Commission's exercise of implementing powers [2011] OJ L55/13.

[167] Gabbi, Wood, and Strauss (n 106) 197.

[168] NFR, art 10.

The Transparency Regulation went some way towards creating a more active mandate for EFSA in clarifying and elaborating risk assessment requirements. The need to be transparent and granting public access to documents is in tension with issues of confidentiality and data/privacy protection. There has been an important number of cases at the CJEU that challenge this tension, particularly in food law risk assessment, but also in other areas of EU law, such as environmental law. Following the glyphosate scandals, the new regulation aims to balance these issues through a significant amendment of the initially relatively sparse legal provisions.[169] The conduct of scientific studies may now be subject to consultation with stakeholders regarding the kind of studies to be performed. This shift from the current 'take it or leave it' approach to risk assessment to a more consultative role allows stakeholders to influence the direction of risk assessments before studies are undertaken. This change has positive aspects as it enables criticism to be addressed before studies are carried out. However, it also means an increasing politicization of the risk assessment processes. This is because the research design of studies will be subject to stakeholder consultation, which could result in political pressure being exerted on the scientific process as it unfolds. In addition, the Commission will be able to task EFSA itself with carrying out scientific studies. However, these modifications do in part address the criticism that EFSA was only an oversight body, without a mandate to conduct independent scientific research.

In 2018, the Commission completed the Fitness Check under the REFIT on the GFLR that had been launched in 2014. It evaluated the relevance, effectiveness, efficiency, coherence, and EU added value, and concluded that there were no systemic failures, even though it regarded the GFLR as 'less adequate to address new challenges like food sustainability in general'.[170] In that respect, it is surprising that the Farm to Fork Strategy does not address the GFLR.

Beyond this, it is clear that the current institutional design, notably EFSA, is largely food safety oriented. There are to date no profound changes at institutional or procedural level proposed by the Farm to Fork Strategy, which may constitute an obstacle to the effective implementation and anchoring of the sustainability paradigm into mainstream EU food law.

169 GFLR, arts 38 and 39–39f.

170 Executive summary of the REFIT evaluation (n 57), 1.

6
Official Controls Regulation and Food Law Enforcement

6.1 Introduction

This chapter elaborates on the enforcement regime of food law in the European Union (EU). Food business operators (FBOs) must comply with food law (compliance obligation). In addition, they have an obligation to enforce food law compliance in the businesses under their control. These compliance obligations are flanked by public enforcement.[1] Public enforcement is the *ex-ante* supervision and *ex-post* enforcement by a public authority, empowered by law to perform these actions.[2] In the EU, such public enforcement can be placed at Member State or at Union level. In EU food law, public enforcement rests primarily with Member State authorities, while the rules governing such public control are set at the Union level. Regulation (EU) 2017/625[3] (Official Controls Regulation (OCR)) specifies requirements for the operation of Member State's supervision and surveillance activities in the food market. Private enforcement is the enforcement of substantive law by subjects of private law.[4] For this purpose, subjects of private law can be endowed with special rights, such as a privileged standing or a right to information. Such special rights to facilitate enforcement can be granted at Union or at Member State level.

[1] Kai Purnhagen and Alexandra Molitorisová, 'Public and Private Enforcement in European Union Food Law' (2022) European Journal of Risk Regulation 1.

[2] Franziska Weber and Michael Faure, 'The Interplay between Public and Private Enforcement in European Private Law: Law and Economics Perspective' (2015) 23 European Review of Private Law 525, 529.

[3] Regulation (EU) 2017/625 of the European Parliament and of the Council of 15 March 2017 on official controls and other official activities performed to ensure the application of food and feed law, rules on animal health and welfare, plant health and plant protection products, amending Regulations (EC) No 999/2001, (EC) No 396/2005, (EC) No 1069/2009, (EC) No 1107/2009, (EU) No 1151/2012, (EU) No 652/2014, (EU) 2016/429 and (EU) 2016/2031 of the European Parliament and of the Council, Council Regulations (EC) No 1/2005 and (EC) No 1099/2009 and Council Directives 98/58/EC, 1999/74/EC, 2007/43/EC, 2008/119/EC and 2008/120/EC, and repealing Regulations (EC) No 854/2004 and (EC) No 882/2004 of the European Parliament and of the Council, Council Directives 89/608/EEC, 89/662/EEC, 90/425/EEC, 91/496/EEC, 96/23/EC, 96/93/EC and 97/78/EC and Council Decision 92/438/EEC [2017] OJ L95/1 (Official Controls Regulation (OCR)).

[4] ibid.

EU Food Law. Hanna Schebesta and Kai Purnhagen, Oxford University Press. © Hanna Schebesta and Kai Purnhagen 2024.
DOI: 10.1093/9780198901570.003.0007

6.2 Enforcement under the GFLR

Article 17 General Food Law Regulation (GFLR) establishes a dual system of compliance control by FBOs and enforcement by Member States. FBOs are primarily tasked with controlling compliance with EU food law, and they must ensure 'at all stages of production, processing and distribution within the businesses under their control' food law requirements are met.[5] Whenever an FBO 'considers or has a reason to believe' that a foodstuff under its control is 'not in compliance with the food safety requirements', it has to inform relevant parties, withdraw the product from the market, or recall the product (see Chapter 5).[6]

This obligation on FBOs is complemented by an obligation on EU Member States[7] to enforce and monitor compliance of FBOs with food law. Specifically, they 'shall maintain a system of official controls', and they have the discretion to introduce 'other activities as appropriate to the circumstances', such as measures facilitating private enforcement. Lastly, Member States must lay down rules on measures and penalties applicable for food law infringements that are 'effective, proportionate and dissuasive'.

These general obligations on the Member States are further substantiated in the OCR.

6.3 Official Controls Regulation

Historically, the first OCR dates from 1989; it was revised in several instances, most recently and profoundly in 2017. The OCR significantly expands the area of Member State oversight of the EU food market subject to EU law. Once a strict EU food law instrument, the legislation now covers official controls and other official activities performed to uphold compliance with food and feed law, rules on animal health and welfare, and plant health and plant protection products. To describe this extended scope, the instrument introduces the term 'Union agri-food chain legislation'.[8] The OCR therefore combines the enforcement of food and feed safety, plant health, as well as animal health and welfare. In this way, the OCR already embodies a One Health approach, by integrating the diverse sectors under the umbrella of one enforcement regime.

[5] Regulation (EC) 178/2002 of the European Parliament and of the Council of 28 January 2002 laying down the general principles and requirements of food law, establishing the European Food Safety Authority and laying down procedures in matters of food safety [2002] OJ L31/1 (General Food Law Regulation (GFLR)), art 17(1).

[6] ibid, art 19.

[7] ibid, art 17(2).

[8] OCR, Recital (3); See Maria Jose Plana Casado, *E-FOOD: Closing the Online Enforcement Gap in the EU Platform Economy* (Springer 2021) 85.

'Official controls' are defined as activities performed by the competent authorities in order to verify (a) compliance by the operators with relevant laws and (b) that animals or goods meet the requirements laid down in the rules.

Articles 1 and 2 OCR lay down the general scope of the OCR's application. The OCR applies in particular to 'official controls and other activities by the competent authorities of the Member States',[9] their financing,[10] and 'the performance of controls by the Commission in Member States and in third countries'.[11] The OCR also distinguishes between 'official controls' and 'other official activities'. While 'official controls' relate to activities performed by competent authorities or the respective delegated bodies or persons,[12] 'other official activities' relate to all other activities other than official controls performed by competent authorities or the delegated bodies or persons.[13]

The OCR applies to official controls aimed at verifying compliance with regulations, regardless of whether they were adopted at Union level or by the Member States for the application of Union law.[14] Article 1(2) forms the cornerstone of the Regulation by defining which areas of law the OCR applies to. These include provisions concerning food safety and quality. Specifically, in terms of food safety, they encompass 'food and food safety, integrity and wholesomeness at any stage of production, processing and distribution of food',[15] animal 'feed and feed safety at any stage of production',[16] as well as animal health[17] and welfare[18] requirements. In terms of food quality, the OCR applies in particular to 'organic production and labelling of organic products'[19] and the 'use and labelling of protected designations of origin, protected geographical indications and traditional specialities guaranteed'.[20] The goods subject to control are defined as 'all that is subject to one or more of the rules referred to in Article 1(2), excluding animals'.[21] In the case of imports, inspection takes place in so-called border inspection posts as outlined in Article 3(3) OCR.

Member States must designate a competent authority or authorities for all areas covered by Article 1(2).[22] Article 5 OCR determines the general obligation towards competent authorities and organic control authorities. These obligations are aimed

[9] OCR, art 1(1)(a).
[10] ibid, art 1(1)(b).
[11] ibid, art 1(1)(d).
[12] ibid, art 2(1).
[13] ibid, art 2(2).
[14] ibid, art 1(2).
[15] ibid, art 1(2)(a).
[16] ibid, art 1(2)(c).
[17] ibid, art 1(2)(d).
[18] ibid, art 1(2)(f).
[19] ibid, art 1(2)(i).
[20] ibid, art 1(2)(j).
[21] ibid, art 3(11).
[22] ibid, art 4(1).

at the effectiveness (appropriate to fulfil the goals of the OCR, sufficient resources, and legal certainty) and impartiality (no discrimination and no conflict of interest) of the procedures. They have to have or have access to, for example, 'an adequate laboratory capacity for analysis, testing and diagnosis'.[23] Article 5(4) OCR stipulates the minimum requirements for the quality of inspection staff. Competent authorities will be audited,[24] and the decisions taken by a competent authority are subject to a right of appeal.[25] Certain tasks of competent authorities may be delegated under the conditions specified.[26]

The competent authorities are bound by confidentiality obligations, and they may not disclose information acquired when performing their official duties if that information is protected by professional secrecy.[27] However, competent authorities may publish public information regarding the outcome of official controls concerning individual operators, if (a) the operator concerned is given the opportunity to comment on the information and (b) the information takes into account the comments expressed by the operator concerned or is published or released with such comments.[28]

The OCR also prescribes rules regarding official controls. These are to be conducted under a risk-based approach.[29] They need to be regular, and their frequency must be determined under a risk-based approach that takes account of: identified risks, information indicating a likelihood that consumers may be misled, operators' past record of compliance, and reliability of controls performed by the operator themselves. Controls should be carried out without prior warning. The OCR also establishes an integrated approach, which mandates the control of animals and goods, substances, and operators at all stages of production, processing, distribution, and use.[30] Controls should be transparent while ensuring confidentiality.[31] Controls must follow documented procedures,[32] and written records must be drawn up for official controls.[33]

The OCR lists 'as appropriate' a number of methods and techniques that can be deployed in official controls. These include inspecting operators' control measures, inspections, controls on the hygiene conditions, controls of food safety management procedures, examination of records, interviews, verification of measures, sampling, analysis, diagnosis and tests, audits of operators, and any other activity required to identify cases of non-compliance.[34] The control methods are defined in

23 ibid, art 5(1)(d).
24 ibid, art 6.
25 ibid, art 7.
26 ibid, arts 28–33.
27 ibid, art 8.
28 ibid, art 8(1).
29 ibid, art 9(1).
30 ibid, art 10(2).
31 ibid, art 11.
32 ibid, art 12.
33 ibid, art 13.
34 ibid, art 14.

Article 3[35] and include documentary checks, identity checks, and physical checks. Operators are under general duties to cooperate with the competent authorities.[36]

In addition to the general requirements regarding the competent authorities, official controls, and methods and techniques, the OCR contain specific requirements for areas covered by secondary substantive legislation,[37] such as products of animal origin, residues in food and feed, welfare requirements of animals, plant health, genetically modified organisms (GMOs), plant protection products, organic products, food quality schemes, and newly identified risks in relation to food and feed.

Methods used for sampling and for laboratory analyses, tests, and diagnoses during official controls and other official activities must comply with the EU rules establishing those methods or the performance criteria for those methods.[38] Operators subject to sampling, analysis, test, or diagnosis in the context of official controls have the right to a second expert opinion, at their own expense.[39] For products offered for sale through distance communication, competent authorities may order samples from operators without revealing their identity for the purpose of conducting official controls.[40] The competent authorities must designate official laboratories, which in turn are subject to obligations and audits, and may derogate from mandatory accreditation requirements only under specific conditions.[41]

6.3.1 *Official controls on animals and goods*

The official controls on animals and goods entering the Union will be organized based on risk to ascertain compliance with the rules referred to in Article 1(2) (and to which Articles 47 and 48 do not apply).[42]

However, to ascertain compliance with the rules referred to in Article 1(2), the competent authorities will perform official controls at the first point of entry into the Union at border control posts. However, there are certain exemptions[43] for specific categories of animals and goods as noted in Article 47(1).[44] These are all subject to documentary checks, and identity and physical checks are performed based on risk. There are further requirements for the establishment, listing, and

[35] ibid, art 3(41)–(43).
[36] ibid, art 15.
[37] ibid, arts 16–27.
[38] ibid, art 34.
[39] ibid, art 35.
[40] ibid, art 36; also see Jose Plana Casado (n 8).
[41] OCR, arts 37–42.
[42] ibid, art 43.
[43] ibid, art 48.
[44] ibid, art 47(1).

minimum standards of Member State border control posts[45] and the use of a Common Health Entry Document (CHED).[46]

Approval of pre-export controls by third countries is possible. Pre-export controls performed by third countries can be approved if a third country can demonstrate that the system of official controls in that third country is able to ensure that the main features of that system are effective and equivalent to EU standards.[47]

All authorities of the Member States dealing with animals and goods entering the Union are required to cooperate closely to ensure that the official controls on consignments of animals and goods entering the Union from third countries are performed in compliance with the OCR.[48]

6.3.2 *Non-compliance*

Actions must be taken in the event of suspicion of non-compliance and actual non-compliance of animals and goods entering the Union.[49] In cases where it is suspected that animals or goods entering the EU are non-compliant, the competent authorities will perform official controls in order to confirm or to eliminate that suspicion.[50] Non-compliant consignments of animals or goods entering the Union are placed under detention,[51] and the competent authorities will invalidate official certificates and take any necessary follow-up measures.[52] FBOs must comply with the measures ordered.[53] The OCR further stipulates how the handled consignments are to be treated.[54]

The Commission can adopt rules for specific official controls and for measures to be taken in relation to particular categories of animals and goods.[55]

6.3.3 *Financing and official certification*

Adequate financial resources for staff and other resources of the competent authorities performing official controls must be available.[56] The fees collected[57] are set at

[45] ibid, arts 59–64.
[46] ibid, arts 56–58.
[47] ibid, arts 73–74.
[48] ibid, art 75.
[49] ibid, art 65.
[50] ibid, art 65.
[51] ibid, arts 66–67.
[52] ibid, art 68.
[53] ibid, art 69.
[54] ibid, arts 71–72.
[55] ibid, art 77.
[56] ibid, art 78.
[57] ibid, arts 79–85.

cost price or according to the fees or charges for the official controls on consignments of animals and goods entering the Union specified in Annex IV.

Official certification must be issued by the competent authorities, and is subject to certain procedural safeguards, such as impartiality or accuracy.[58]

6.3.4 *Reference laboratories and reference centres*

An EU reference laboratory will be established where the effectiveness of official controls and other official activities also depends on the quality, uniformity, and reliability of the methods or the results of analysis, testing, or diagnosis.[59] The EU reference laboratories then contribute to the improvement and harmonization of those methods, for instance for use by national laboratories. There are over 40 laboratories on different topics in animal, food and feed, and plant health, for instance for mycotoxins and plant toxins at the Wageningen Food Safety Research in the Netherlands, and for GMOs at the Joint Research Centre of the European Commission. Alongside the reference laboratories, the OCR includes provisions for the designation of EU reference centres for animal welfare (EURCAWs), which aim to improve the enforcement of the legislation on animal welfare, which is one of the Commission's priorities. Examples include the first EU reference centre for animal welfare focusing on pigs, which supports the enforcement of EU pig legislation (such as transport and killing),[60] and the centre for the welfare of poultry and other small, farmed animals,[61] as well as the welfare of ruminants and equines.

6.3.5 *Administrative assistance and cooperation*

The competent authorities in the Member States concerned provide each other with administrative assistance,[62] such as, for instance, participation in joint on-the-spot official controls. Member States also designate a liaison body to facilitate the exchange of communication between competent authorities.[63] Member States can send a request for assistance for data or information from the competent authorities of another Member State.[64] Assistance without request in the event

[58] ibid, arts 86–91.
[59] ibid, art 92.
[60] Commission Implementing Regulation (EU) 2018/329 of 5 March 2018 designating a European Union Reference Centre for Animal Welfare [2018] OJ L63/13.
[61] Commission Implementing Regulation (EU) 2019/1685 of 4 October 2019 designating a European Union Reference Centre for Animal Welfare for poultry and other small farmed animals [2019] OJ L258/11.
[62] OCR, art 102.
[63] ibid, art 103.
[64] ibid, art 104.

of non-compliance that has implications for another Member State should be notified.[65] In the case of non-compliance creating a risk or a repeated or potentially serious infringement, the competent authorities will, without delay, notify the competent authorities of the Member State of dispatch and of any other concerned Member State.[66] The same should happen on the basis of information provided by third countries.[67] The Commission holds a residual role of coordinating assistance in cases where the competent authorities concerned are unable to agree on appropriate action to address the non-compliance.[68]

6.3.6 *Planning and reporting*

Member States must perform official controls on the basis of multi-annual national control plans (MANCP). They are managed by a single body tasked with coordinating the preparation of the MANCP across the various competent authorities responsible for official controls in a Member State, ensuring that the MANCP is coherent and collecting information.[69] The MANCPs contain information on the structure and organization of official control systems within Member States, including the prioritization, risk categorization, and organization across different sectors in a Member State and much more.[70] The MANCP is made public, unless disclosure undermines the effectiveness of control (for instance, because a specific sector will be chosen for priority inspection). The MANCP is regularly updated.[71]

In order to enable Union-wide targeted assessments on the state of application of the rules covered by the OCR or establishing the prevalence of certain hazards across the Union, the Commission may adopt coordinated control programmes and information and data collection measures.[72] The coordinated control programmes are a tool to better understand the practices in a certain sector.

Member States must submit an annual report,[73] as does the European Commission,[74] which takes into account the national annual reports and the results of the Commission controls. In addition, and for the application of the crisis management plan under the General Food Law Regulation (GFLR), Member States are required to draw up contingency plans for food and feed.[75]

[65] ibid, art 105.
[66] ibid, art 106.
[67] ibid, art 107.
[68] ibid, art 108.
[69] ibid, art 109.
[70] ibid, art 110.
[71] ibid, art 111.
[72] ibid, art 112.
[73] ibid, art 113.
[74] ibid, art 114.
[75] ibid, art 115.

6.3.7 Union activities (Title VI)

The Commission checks whether Member States are fulfilling their duties with respect to the enforcement of EU law under the OCR. Commission experts perform controls, including audits, in each Member State to ensure compliance with the set of rules covered by the OCR and to verify that the systems in place within Member States are functioning effectively overall.[76] The Commission can also conduct controls in third countries.[77] The Commission prepares a report on controls in Member States.[78] To plan the Commission's controls, it establishes an annual or multiannual control programme.[79] Member States take these controls into account and implement follow-up measures to remedy any shortcomings identified, provide documentation, and allow Commission access to premises.[80]

6.3.8 Conditions for the entry into the Union of animals and goods

The EU has strict conditions governing the entry into the Union of animals and goods. The Commission requests information on third countries' control systems from third countries.[81] It can also adopt additional conditions for entry into the Union of animals and goods from third countries by means of delegated acts,[82] including a list of third countries from which certain animals and goods may come.[83] The Commission can also prescribe special measures for certain animals and goods from third countries in cases of serious non-compliance or when there is a risk to human, animal or plant health, or concerning GMOs or the environment.[84] In certain areas, the Commission may recognize that measures applied in a third country are equivalent to the requirements laid down in those (EU) rules.[85]

Third countries that intend to export animals and goods to the Union must provide accurate and up-to-date information on the general organization and management of sanitary and phytosanitary control systems in their territory.

[76] ibid, art 116.
[77] ibid, art 120. These are largely based on risk, considering types of goods and information received and similar factors; see ibid, art 121. The Commission issues a report on these activities; see ibid, art 122, and has a Programme of Commission controls; see ibid, art 123.
[78] ibid, art 117.
[79] ibid, art 118.
[80] ibid, art 119.
[81] ibid, art 125.
[82] ibid, art 126.
[83] ibid, art 127.
[84] ibid, art 128.
[85] ibid, art 129.

6.3.9 *Information management system*

The Commission sets up and manages a computerized information management system for official controls (IMSOC)[86] where information regarding official controls is exchanged.[87] IMSOC enables the computerized handling and exchange of information, data, and documents, providing a mechanism for exchange. It also acts as a tool to collect and manage the reports on official controls, allowing for the production, handling, and transmission, including in electronic form, of the journey logs. Lastly, the IMSOC integrates the existing computerized systems managed by the Commission.[88]

6.3.10 *Enforcement action by competent authorities*

Articles 137 and 138 provide general obligations of the competent authorities as regards enforcement action and actions to be taken in the event of established non-compliance. According to Article 137(2), competent authorities will perform an investigation in order to confirm or to eliminate a suspicion of non-compliance. Moreover, Article 138 prescribes the actions to be taken in cases of non-compliance. Specifically, the public authority will take any action necessary to determine the origin and extent of the non-compliance, and will take appropriate measures to ensure that the operator remedies the non-compliance and prevents further occurrences of that non-compliance.[89] The measures that can be taken include a number of actions, such as restricting or prohibiting the placement on the market; ordering the recall, withdrawal, removal, and destruction of goods; authorizing, where appropriate, the use of the goods for purposes other than those for which they were originally intended; or ordering the killing of animals.[90] Member States must specify penalties for infringements of the Regulation, which must be effective, proportionate, and dissuasive.[91]

6.3.11 *Union enforcement action*

Lastly, the EU has some powers to trigger mechanisms that constitute proper Union enforcement measures. Where the Commission has evidence of a serious

[86] ibid, arts 131–136, further developed by Commission Implementing Regulation (EU) 2019/1715 of 30 September 2019 laying down rules for the functioning of the information management system for official controls and its system components (the IMSOC Regulation) [2019] OJ L261/37.
[87] OCR, art 131.
[88] ibid, art 132.
[89] ibid, art 138(1).
[90] ibid, art 138(2).
[91] ibid, art 139.

disruption in a Member State's control system and such disruption may constitute a widespread risk, then the Commission may adopt marketing prohibitions, special conditions, suspension of operation of border controls, or other appropriate temporary measures to contain that risk.[92]

6.4 Conclusions

The 2019 iteration of the OCR makes an important advancement in that it embraces the One Health approach and serves as an umbrella instrument extending beyond the food sector to cover the agri-food chain instruments in a holistic manner.

For food law, the OCR develops the embryonic mandate of Article 17(2) GFLR that tasks Member States with having an official controls system for the enforcement of food and feed law. In effect, the OCR stands out as an impressive achievement by coupling the various 'right systems' with an 'enforcement system' that can be said to venture deep into what is often termed the 'procedural autonomy of the Member States'.

In doing this, the OCR institutes a multilevel official controls system. It outlines the requirements that Member States have to fulfil, in a procedural and institutional manner. Member States remain the prime responsible actors for the actual design and implementation of an enforcement regime, within the framework of the OCR. However, the Union mechanisms take on a supervisory role. National official control activity is monitored and supervised by the Commission. The Commission controls the controllers.

Overall, EU law emphasizes the role of public controls in the enforcement landscape. Whereas in other sectors, private enforcement, that is, the enforcement of EU law by private individuals, plays a pivotal role, its role in the EU food sector is less prominent. Whereas food law is obviously flanked by private enforcement mechanisms such as consumer rights and product liability, these exist in parallel and are not significantly 'integrated' into the rationale of food law enforcement at EU level. Furthermore, it has empirically been shown that private enforcement, for instance through damages claims by individuals at national level, remains relatively marginal in practice in the food sector.[93] Instead of relying on private individuals to enforce their rights, the EU is oriented towards public enforcement, in which public authorities monitor, investigate, and enforce food law compliance. This aligns with the idea that food safety is essentially a public good that must ultimately be overseen by public actors.

92 ibid, art 141.

93 Tetty Havinga, 'The Influence of Liability Law on Food Safety on Preventive Effects of Liability Claims and Liability Insurance' (2012) Nijmegen Sociology of Law Working Paper 2010/02 <https://papers.ssrn.com/sol3/papers.cfm?abstract_id=2016115> accessed 14 October 2023.

PART III
FOOD TECHNOLOGY LAW

In the European Union (EU), food may be marketed if it is not unsafe.[1] However, for certain categories of food, safety requirements compromise food business operators' (FBOs) freedom to place products on the market. Part III on food technology law discusses pre-market restrictions to the internal market, that is, situations where foods require special pre-market authorization or generic approval at EU level. Special authorization procedures exist for specific categories of foodstuffs, such as novel foods (see Chapter 7), and genetically modified (GM) food and feed (see Chapter 8). Other substances must be approved at EU or national levels before they can be placed on the market, notably the various food improvement agents (see Chapter 9), and added micronutrients in food fortification and supplements (discussed in Chapter 17). The situations that require authorization are defined by food technological factors, such as the novelty of foods, genetic modification, the use of food improvement agents, or the addition of micronutrients. Although the latter has a technological component, the micronutrient legal framework has a strong link to nutrition, and we discuss it in Part VII on food nutrition law.

Exceptions to the 'free marketing of food principle'

The General Food Law Regulation (GFLR) enshrines an umbrella safety rule (see Chapter 5) that implies a 'free marketing of food principle'. Under this principle, foods are only subject to an *ex-ante* safety self-assessment conducted by the FBOs, which continues to apply *ex-post* as well. The 'free marketing principle' is, however, limited. Certain categories of food and substances are regarded as inherently hazardous, and for these types of foodstuffs the law does not assume *a priori* that they are safe. This is where approval and authorization procedures come into play. Approval and authorization procedures reverse the safety assumption for certain categories of foodstuffs, which cannot be marketed until assessed as safe.

[1] Regulation (EC) 178/2002 of the European Parliament and of the Council of 28 January 2002 laying down the general principles and requirements of food law, establishing the European Food Safety Authority and laying down procedures in matters of food safety [2002] OJ L31/1 (General Food Law Regulation (GFLR)), art 14(1).

Relationship to the precautionary principle

Requiring authorization prior to placing foodstuffs on the market is a way of applying the precautionary principle.[2] Specific product categories, such as genetically modified organisms (GMOs) or novel foods, are considered 'hazardous until proven otherwise'. The 'free marketing principle' is therefore reversed as a precaution, and authorization procedures must establish the safety of these products, before they are permitted on the market. In its *Communication on the Precautionary Principle*, the Commission emphasizes that the FBO is responsible for proof of food safety in such cases: such 'prior approval (marketing authorisation) requirements on products that they deem dangerous *a priori* reverse the burden of proving injury, by treating them as dangerous unless and until businesses do the scientific work necessary to demonstrate that they are safe'.[3] It is, however, important to bear in mind that the precautionary principle does not inherently require either FBOs or regulators to carry the scientific burden of establishing proof of safety. Rather, the distribution of the burden of proof is a result of the specific design of the EU risk regulatory architecture in a given legal instrument. As will become apparent, the EU authorization procedures are designed in a way that burdens applicants with the cost of providing scientific proof demonstrating that an *a priori* harmful substance is safe. This division is in part due to the limited capacities of risk assessors (European Food Safety Authority (EFSA) and those at Member State level) to generate scientific findings themselves (see Chapter 3, section 4.2).

Typical characteristics of authorization procedures

In EU food law, a sectoral approach emerged with distinct pre-market authorization systems in different legislations. Since the 1960s, authorization procedures at the EU level were established for 'synthetic foods', such as colours, sweeteners, and other additives, the earliest being the 1962 directive on colourings. Novel foods were regulated for the first time in 1997, and GMOs in 1990. Since the implementation of the GFLR, authorization rules have multiplied and been refined, for

[2] Commission, 'Communication from the Commission on the precautionary principle' (Communication) COM (2000) 1 final (Communication on the Precautionary Principle), point 6.4: '(...) by shifting responsibility for producing scientific evidence. This applies in particular to substances deemed "a priori" hazardous or which are potentially hazardous at a certain level of absorption. In this case the legislator, by way of precaution, has clearly reversed the burden of proof by requiring that the substances be deemed hazardous until proven otherwise. Hence it is up to the business community to carry out the scientific work needed to evaluate the risk. As long as the human health risk cannot be evaluated with sufficient certainty, the legislator is not legally entitled to authorize use of the substance, unless exceptionally for test purposes.'

[3] ibid.

instance for food supplements (2002);[4] GMOs (2004); addition of micronutrients to food (2006); enzymes and flavourings (2008); and a revision of the novel foods regime (2015).

An important aspect to note regarding terminology is that the concepts of 'authorizations' and 'approvals' do not have an inherent legal definition in EU law—instead, there are different procedures that regulate, restrict, and approve placing on the market of foodstuffs or substances; each with different characteristics, but referred to in this book indiscriminately as 'authorization procedures'.

Generic versus individual authorizations

Substances or foodstuffs can be approved for all market players (generic authorization) or they may be issued only for a specific company (individual authorization). GMO authorizations, such as those for Sugar beet (H7-1) are individual authorizations, as they are registered specifically to KWS Saat and Monsanto. The Novel Food Regulation (NFR) is a hybrid—ultimately, authorizations are generic, and after a novel food is successfully included in the Union list, all companies may place it on the market. For instance Chia seeds (*Salvia hispanica*) are included on the list of novel foods, and therefore any FBO may market them, subject to the specified conditions of use. However, there are proprietary rules about data protection and some novel food authorizations may enjoy exclusive individual marketing permission for five years, before turning generic. These individually authorized novel foods will become generically available only after the individual protection of the authorization has lapsed. EU law places the authorization costs on the applicant, a risk regulatory design choice that has an important effect on innovation and market structure.

Positive lists (approved/authorized items) and negative lists (bans)

Another common mechanism to restrict what can be placed on the EU food market is market regulation through laws that include positive and negative lists. These lists are by their nature generic, that is, they apply equally to all market participants. Positive lists specify permitted items, while negative lists detail prohibited ones. If approved, no specific individual authorization is necessary, and the *ex-ante* self-assessment in these cases remains. In order to include a new item on the list, depending on the legal instruments, FBOs or other actors (for instance, Member States) can apply through an authorization procedure to amend existing lists. An example of this is additives (see Chapter 12). Companies can use additives listed on the positive list if they take into account the specified conditions. If an

[4] Directive 2002/46/EC of the European Parliament and of the Council of 10 June 2002 on the approximation of the laws of the Member States relating to food supplements [2002] OJ L183/51.

additive is not on the approved list, companies or Member States can go through an authorization procedure get an additive approved.

Procedures

When examining the different authorization schemes, certain questions arise to understand the institutional design of the procedures. Who can apply? Where does an application request have to be lodged, with a national authority or the European Commission? Who has to provide scientific evidence? Which evidence is required? It is also important to remember the distinction between risk assessment and risk management, and how it is implemented in a given procedure. Who assesses the risks; is it EFSA (most EU authorization and approvals) or a national body (for instances such as the non-harmonized addition of vitamins and minerals to food)? Who makes the final authorization decision at risk management stage, is it through the Committee Procedure (novel food and GMOs), or is it taken at national level (plant protection products)? Lastly, more practical points will arise, such as how long an authorization is valid for, whether a re-approval may be required (in the case of GMOs, every ten years), or whether an authorization will be periodically reviewed (additive approvals)?

National versus EU authorization procedures

In the absence of EU harmonization, Member States can continue to regulate foodstuffs at national level, for example by maintaining national marketing restrictions and authorization systems. In fact, national authorization requirements are relatively common and one of the residual areas where the EU food market remains fragmented. These national rules, however, have to comply with general rules of primary law such as the free movement of goods. For instance, EU harmonization of supplements and the addition of micronutrients to food is incomplete, and many Member States retain national authorization schemes.[5]

While safety is the prime rationale for authorization requirements, the reversal of the *a priori* safety assumption in EU law is motivated by their innovative or technological character (safety–technology nexus). This is also the case for fortified foods and supplements, which also involve more human health-related elements than the other legal frameworks (safety–nutrition nexus). Although a tenuous distinction, we discuss the respective authorization and approval requirements in Part IV on food safety law and Part VII on food nutrition law.

[5] Lisa van der Meer and Hanna Schebesta, 'The Internal Market, Incomplete: EU, Dutch and Belgian Legislation on Maximum Food Fortification with Micronutrients' (2020) 3 European Food and Feed Law Review 201.

7
Pre-Market Authorizations of Novel Products
Novel Food Regulation

7.1 Introduction

The Novel Food Regulation (NFR) institutes a pre-market authorization requirement for foods that are considered novel food for the EU market. Therefore, only foodstuffs that have been on the EU market before 15 May 1997 enjoy a presumption of safety. By contrast, foodstuffs, substances, and processes not used before that date must undergo a safety assessment.

Food technology is making important advances. Examples that are widely discussed include novel food authorizations for insect food, algae, 3D-printed food, Cannabidiol (CBD) oils, and nanotech. On one hand, it appears logical to test such novel technical features for safety. On the other hand, the necessity of novel food authorization is often a subject of controversy, with arguments citing potential negative effects on innovation.

A prominent example is the case of insect foods. Insects and insect-derived foods are an appealing option that could play a role in the protein transition, as a protein source for use in both human nutrition and feed. However, insects are also an important source of a new allergen, and can be subject to microbiological contamination. Insects had an uneasy classification under the previous Novel Food Regulation, and Member States started to develop different national interpretations. Since the new novel food law entered into force in 2015, it has been clarified that insects are indeed considered novel food, and must therefore be authorized. To date, several insects have been authorized, namely the Tenebrio Molitor larva (mealworm),[1] the Locusta Migratoria,[2] and the Acheta Domesticus (house cricket).[3]

[1] Commission Implementing Regulation (EU) 2021/882 of 1 June 2021 authorising the placing on the market of dried Tenebrio molitor larva as a novel food under Regulation (EU) 2015/2283 of the European Parliament and of the Council, and amending Commission Implementing Regulation (EU) 2017/2470 [2021] OJ L194/16.

[2] Commission Implementing Regulation (EU) 2021/1975 of 12 November 2021 authorising the placing on the market of frozen, dried and powder forms of Locusta migratoria as a novel food under Regulation (EU) 2015/2283 of the European Parliament and of the Council and amending Commission Implementing Regulation (EU) 2017/2470 [2021] OJ L402/10.

[3] Implementing Regulation (EU) 2022/188 of 10 February 2022 authorising the placing on the market of frozen, dried and powder forms of Acheta domesticus as a novel food under Regulation (EU)

EU Food Law. Hanna Schebesta and Kai Purnhagen, Oxford University Press. © Hanna Schebesta and Kai Purnhagen 2024.
DOI: 10.1093/9780198901570.003.0008

Most countries regulate new food technologies and products, although the legal frameworks vary in their approach. For instance in the United States, the distinction focuses much more on whether a food contains or is a new substance that would be regulated as a food additive, in which case it is subject to market approval by the Federal Drug Authority (FDA), or whether it can be granted the status of generally recognized as safe (GRAS).[4]

Whereas the need for and costs of authorization procedures are typically discussed critically in the EU context, from a political point of view, the novel food risk management decisions are non-contentious, that is, expressing a positive vote in the Committee procedure and aligning with the EFSA recommendation. Novel foods, as opposed to GMOs, must be regarded as a consensual policy area.[5]

7.2 The Novel Food Regulation (NFR)

EU rules on novel foods were established on 15 May 1997.[6] The NFR of 2015, applicable since 2018, replaced these provisions,[7] and introduced major changes. Importantly, it centralized the authorization system at EU level, to be administered by the Commission.[8] Novel foods may only be marketed if they are included on a positive list, the Union list of authorized novel foods (Union list). To include novel foods on this list, FBOs follow an authorization procedure. Under the old rules, individual authorizations had to be made. A significant change under the 2015 regime is that the novel food authorization system is (in principle) generic, meaning that once a food is on the Union list, anyone may market that food in the EU. The new NFR also instituted an intellectual property rights regime that grants individual protection to applicants' proprietary data used during authorization,

2015/2283 of the European Parliament and of the Council, and amending Commission Implementing Regulation (EU) 2017/2470 [2022] OJ L30/109.

[4] Jessica Vapnek, Kai Purnhagen, and Ben Hillel, 'Regulatory and Legislative Framework for Novel Foods' in Shivani Pathania and Brijesh K Tiwari (eds), *Food Formulation: Novel Ingredients and Processing Techniques* (Wiley 2021) 285.

[5] Annalisa Volpato, 'Novel Foods in the EU Integrated Administrative Space: An Institutional Perspective' in Lucia Scaffardi and Giulia Formici (eds), *Novel Foods and Edible Insects in the European Union* (Springer 2022) 15.

[6] Regulation (EC) 258/97 of the European Parliament and of the Council of 27 January 1997 concerning novel foods and novel food ingredients [1997] OJ L43/1. In 2001, specific rules about information governance in the application procedure were passed, see Commission Regulation (EC) 1852/2001 of 20 September 2001 laying down detailed rules for making certain information available to the public and for the protection of information submitted pursuant to European Parliament and Council Regulation (EC) No 258/97 [2001] OJ L253/17.

[7] Regulation (EU) 2015/2283 of the European Parliament and of the Council of 25 November 2015 on novel foods, amending Regulation (EU) No 1169/2011 of the European Parliament and of the Council and repealing Regulation (EC) No 258/97 of the European Parliament and of the Council and Commission Regulation (EC) No 1852/2001 [2015] OJ L327/1 (Novel Food Regulation, NFR).

[8] Volpato (n 5).

leading to monopolized authorizations for the applicant for a five-year period. In addition to the full authorization procedure, there is also a simplified registration procedure for foods new to the EU that are traditional foods from third countries. This change should facilitate marketing of such products compared to the older regime, which required authorization procedures even for products that were commonly consumed on a large scale in non-EU countries.

In terms of risk governance, the safety assessments regarding the risks from novel foods is undertaken by EFSA, whereas the political risk management decision to authorize is made by the Commission through the Committee procedure (see Chapter 3).

7.3 Legal base and objectives

Article 114 of the Treaty on the Functioning of the European Union (TFEU)[9] on the establishment and functioning of the internal market serves as the legal base of the NFR. The purpose of the Regulation is 'to ensure the effective functioning of the internal market while providing a high level of protection of human health and consumers' interests'.[10] The NFR recognizes that novel food (processes) may prove to be unsafe and attempts to balance preventive market oversight with an authorization system that encourages new technologies and innovations in food production.[11]

7.4 Scope of the NFR

The NFR regulates the placing of novel foods on the market within the EU.[12] The Regulation excludes areas with their own specific legal framework from its application, and is not applicable to GMOs, food enzymes, food additives, food flavourings, and extraction solvents.[13] FBOs must verify whether foodstuffs they want to market fall within the scope of the NFR.[14] If foodstuffs are within its material scope, that is, they qualify as novel foods, then FBOs can only market them if they are included in the Union list of foodstuffs that may be marketed.[15]

[9] Consolidated version of the Treaty on the Functioning of the European Union [2012] OJ C326/47 (TFEU).

[10] NFR, art 1(2).

[11] ibid, Recital (29). On 'innovation' being an implicit regulatory goal of the NFR, see Alessandro Monaco and Kai Purnhagen, 'Risk Triggers as Innovation Triggers: Risk Analysis and Innovation's Promotion under the Novel Food Regulation' (2022) 17 European Food and Feed Law Review 219.

[12] NFR, art 1(2).

[13] ibid, art 2(2).

[14] ibid, art 4(1).

[15] ibid, art 6(2).

In order to qualify as novel food, both the 'food' definition under the GFLR and the 'novelty' aspect under the NFR must be met.[16] The cumulative conditions of 'novelty' are:[17]

- foodstuffs cannot demonstrate 'human consumption within the EU to a significant degree' before 15 May 1997 (ie the date of entry into force of the Regulation);
- foodstuffs must fall under one of the categories of the NFR in Article 3.

Regarding the first condition, a Commission guidance document[18] establishes criteria for testing whether the criterion on human consumption to a significant degree is met. These refer to geographical aspects (one Member State suffices); demonstrated quantity of use; intended purpose—which must be for food use only (not for drugs or cosmetics); specific population groups; usage of other forms (the consumption of the 'original form' does not count in order to establish consumption of selective extracts, new production processes, or new parts of the plants); availability (commercial availability to consumers, not just private individuals). To establish that food has indeed been consumed by humans, the food must have been consumed as a normal part of a diet, and not, for instance, only used as a supplement, medicine, or cosmetics. Regard will be had to whether it was available for purchase by consumers, that is, not only in pharmacies, health shops, or specific restaurants, and whether it was consumed for a long period of time, and in similar quantities. In addition, new forms/states of traditional foods will also be considered novel. This occurs when processing or a new production process alters the composition of the food to a significant degree, such as in the case of selective (non-traditional) extracts, or parts of plants that were previously not consumed. For instance, in coffee production, only the coffee fruit has been used; coffee pulp—in contrast—is currently considered a novel food. Likewise, the fruiting body of a mushroom, if regularly eaten, is not a novel food, while its mycelium is regarded as a novel food.[19]

Secondly, foods that fall within one of the listed food categories in Article 3 NFR qualify as novel food, and an FBO must therefore determine the applicable food category. The 2015 NFR amendment updated and clarified the categories of

[16] ibid, art 3.
[17] ibid, art 3(2)(a).
[18] Commission, *Human Consumption to a Significant Degree* (Information and Guidance Document). In order to support FBOs' assessment of whether a novel food has been consumed to a significant degree, the Commission had already issued this document under the old regime (Regulation (EC) No 258/97 (n 6)). This document is still valid, as the legal criterion remained unaffected by legal changes.
[19] Alessandro Monaco, Alexandra Molitorisová, and Kai P Purnhagen, 'An Analysis of the Regulatory Framework Applicable to Products Obtained from Mushroom and Mycilium' (Report for the Adalbert Raps Stiftung 2021).

food, including the inclusion of whole animals such as insects or engineered nanomaterial under the Regulation's scope. It also codified the case law that had been rendered by the Court of Justice of the European Union (CJEU) in determining whether foods were to be regarded as novel or not.[20] One of the more notable cases in this regard was the unresolved question whether whole insects would qualify as novel foods under the old NFR under the heading of 'food ingredients isolated from animals'. The case had caused significant regulatory fragmentation among Member States, with some regarding it as a novel food, and therefore prohibited without an authorization, while others allowing their marketing The CJEU held that under the old regime, whole insects would fall outside of the scope of the NFR. In contrast, the 2015 NFR explicitly states that whole insects do fall within its scope.

The listed food categories not only comprise new 'foods' understood as products, but equally novel molecular structures, derivatives, cell and tissue cultures, new production processes, and nanoengineering:[21]

- food with a new or intentionally modified molecular structure, where that structure was not used as, or in, a food within the Union before 15 May 1997;
- food consisting of, isolated from or produced from microorganisms, fungi or algae;
- food consisting of, isolated from or produced from material of mineral origin;[22]
- food consisting of, isolated from or produced from plants or their parts, except when the food has a history of safe food use within the Union and is consisting of, isolated from or produced from a plant or a variety of the same species obtained by: traditional propagating practices which have been used for food production within the Union before 15 May 1997; or non-traditional propagating practices which have not been used for food production within the Union before 15 May 1997, where those practices do not give rise to significant changes in the composition or structure of the food affecting its nutritional value, metabolism or level of undesirable substances;
- food consisting of, isolated from or produced from animals or their parts, except for animals obtained by traditional breeding practices which have been

[20] Case C-526/19 *Entoma SAS v Ministre de l'Économie et des Finances and Ministre de l'Agriculture et de l'Alimentation* EU:C:2020:769.

[21] NFR, art 3(2).

[22] Case C-448/14 *Davitas GmbH v Stadt Aschaffenburg* EU:C:2016:839 (*Davitas*); This category derives from Davitas, De Tox Forte, a food product the sole ingredient of which is clinoptilolite, a mineral substance of volcanic origin, which was classified as a novel food. The Court clarified that it fell within the definition of 'with a new (. . .) primary molecular structure', which covers not only foods or food ingredients the primary molecular structure of which 'was created ex novo or modified', but also those 'already existing in nature before that date'. It is now expressly included: '(i) New or intentionally modified molecular structure.'

used for food production within the Union before 15 May 1997 and the food from those animals has a history of safe food use within the Union;

- food consisting of, isolated from or produced from cell culture or tissue culture derived from animals, plants, micro-organisms, fungi or algae;
- food resulting from a production process not used for food production within the Union[23] before 15 May 1997, which gives rise to significant changes in the composition or structure of a food, affecting its nutritional value, metabolism or level of undesirable substances;
- food consisting of engineered nanomaterials as defined in point (f) of this paragraph;
- vitamins, minerals and other substances used in accordance with Directive 2002/46/EC, Regulation (EC) No 1925/2006, or Regulation (EU) No 609/2013, where: a production process not used for food production within the Union before 15 May 1997 has been applied as referred to in point (a) (vii) of this paragraph; or they contain or consist of engineered nanomaterials as defined in point (f) of this paragraph;
- food used exclusively in food supplements within the Union before 15 May 1997, where it is intended to be used in foods other than food supplements as defined in point (a) of Article 2 of Directive 2002/46/EC.

Determining the novel food status can be complex, and has resulted in litigation before the CJEU. Various forms and uses of the same primary foodstuff can have different novel food statuses, even if the primary foodstuff itself is a non-novel food. For instance, leaves of *Stevia rebaudiana Bertoni* in tea, herbal, and fruit infusions are not considered as novel. Other uses would require a novel food application. However, the use of extracts from leaves of *Stevia rebaudiana Bertoni* as a sweetener or as a flavouring fall within the scope of the Regulation on Food Additives[24] or the Regulation on Flavourings[25] instead, where they are authorized under the respective regime. Even ingredients deriving from a 'classic' food may be classified as novel, as is the case for coagulated potato proteins and hydrolysates.[26]

[23] Individual ingredients are not enough, a new production process can equally result in a novel product; see Case C-383/07 *M-K Europa GmbH & Co. KG v Stadt Regensburg* [2009] ECR I-00115 (*M-K Europe*): 'The fact that all the individual ingredients of a food product meet the requirement laid down in Article 1(2) of Regulation No 258/97, or have a safe history, cannot be regarded as sufficient for that regulation not to apply to the food product concerned. In order to decide whether that food product should be classified as a novel food within the meaning of Regulation No 258/97, the competent national authority must proceed on a case-by-case basis, taking into account all the characteristics of the food product and of the production process.'

[24] Regulation (EC) No 1333/2008 of the European Parliament and of the Council of 16 December 2008 on food additives [2008] OJ L354/16 (Regulation on Food Additives).

[25] Regulation (EC) No 1334/2008 of the European Parliament and of the Council of 16 December 2008 on flavourings and certain food ingredients with flavouring properties for use in and on foods and amending Council Regulation (EEC) No 1601/91, Regulations (EC) No 2232/96 and (EC) No 110/2008 and Directive 2000/13/EC [2008] OJ L354/34 (Regulation of Flavourings).

[26] Commission Decision of 15 February 2002 authorising the placing on the market of coagulated potato proteins and hydrolysates thereof as novel food ingredients under Regulation (EC) No 258/97

Food technology is increasingly experimenting with highly processed food, for instance when creating meat replacements, the use of new technologies such as nanoengineering, and in order to enhance nutritional properties of foodstuffs. In a recent case regarding the new NFR 2015, the CJEU determined that sprouted buckwheat flour produced from germination of buckwheat seeds in a nutrient solution containing spermidine was to be considered a novel food.[27] Specifically, the Court classified it as food 'consisting of, isolated from or produced from plants or their parts' under Article 3(2)(a)(iv). The provision contains an exception, and if two conditions are met, a food will not be considered novel. These conditions are: first, 'a history of safe food use within the Union' and, second, the food is 'obtained by traditional propagating practices' or 'non-traditional propagating practices' that do not give rise to significant changes in the composition or structure of the food affecting its nutritional value, metabolism, or level of undesirable substances. Accordingly, the CJEU found that there was no clear evidence confirming the safety of buckwheat flour based on compositional data and experience of continued use for at least 25 years in the customary diet of a significant number of people in at least one country of the European Union. Neither would it be regarded as being obtained by propagating practices within the meaning of that provision.

As companies try to avoid an authorization requirement, the qualification of a food product as a novel food is undesirable from a business perspective. The novel food status of food products and technology has therefore often been disputed and has been the subject of litigation before the CJEU throughout the different versions of the Novel Food Regulations. The Court has so far tended to interpret the food categories expansively,[28] thus rendering more foods subject to the NFR regime.

7.5 Consultation process to determine the novel food status

In many cases, FBOs are unsure about the applicability of the NFR. To support businesses, the 2015 Regulation formalized a new consultation mechanism.[29] Under

of the European Parliament and of the Council (notified under document number C(2002) 506) [2002] OJ L50/92.

[27] Case C-141/22 *TLL The Longevity Labs GmbH v Optimize Health Solutions mi GmbH* EU:C:2023:428.

[28] See *Davitas* (n 22) and *M-K Europe* (n 23). The extensive interpretation of (old) food categories has been criticized for defying the purpose of having two cumulative conditions; see Valeria Paganizza, '"New Primary Molecular Structure" and Novel Foods According to the Court: Constructive or Demolishing Interpretation? The EU Judgment in Case C-448/14' (2017) 3 Rivista di Diritto Alimentare 20, discussing *Davitas*.

[29] NFR, art 4(2), which is expanded upon in Commission Implementing Regulation (EU) 2018/456 of 19 March 2018 on the procedural steps of the consultation process for determination of novel food status in accordance with Regulation (EU) 2015/2283 of the European Parliament and of the Council on novel foods [2018] OJ L77/6.

this procedure, the FBOs can make a consultation request to the Member State to determine the status of a potential novel food. The Member States have designated competent authorities for these requests. For instance, in the Netherlands, the designated authority is formally the Ministry of Health, Welfare and Sports, and there is also a dedicated novel food assessment body, the Novel Food Unit of the Medicines Evaluation Board. The procedural steps for this national consultation procedure have been clarified.[30] The competent authority not only informs the FBO, but also the Commission, so that the Commission can update the novel food status on its website (currently the novel food catalogue[31]).

7.6 The marketing of novel foods is restricted to inclusion on the Union list

Only novel foods that are listed on the Union list may be placed on the EU market.[32] Therefore, companies that want to use novel foodstuffs that are not on the Union list need to start an authorization procedure to include new novel foods on the list.

The general rule is that the Commission should authorize novel foods that satisfy the following three general conditions: foods do not pose a safety risk to human health; do not mislead the consumer; and in the case of substitute foods, it is not nutritionally inferior.[33]

7.6.1 The content of the authorization legal act

The entries in the Union list consist of the specification of the novel food, and if necessary, the conditions of use, such as maximum intake levels; specific labelling requirements; and post-market monitoring measures (see the entry for UV-treated baker's yeast (Saccharomyces cerevisiae) in Table 7.1).

The content and updating of the Union list are undertaken by the Commission.[34] The Union list is compiled in an implementing regulation,[35] which is updated through additional amending Commission implementing regulations,[36] for

[30] Commission Implementing Regulation (EU) 2018/456.

[31] Commission, 'EU Novel Food Catalogue' <https://webgate.ec.europa.eu/fip/novel_food_catalogue/> accessed 9 August 2023.

[32] NFR, art 6.

[33] Commission Implementing Regulation (EU) 2018/456, art 7.

[34] NFR, art 9(1).

[35] Commission Implementing Regulation (EU) 2017/2470 of 20 December 2017 establishing the Union list of novel foods in accordance with Regulation (EU) 2015/2283 of the European Parliament and of the Council on novel foods [2017] OJ L351/72.

[36] NFR, art 10(5): 'The procedure for authorising the placing on the market within the Union of a novel food and updating the Union list as provided for in Article 9 shall end with the adoption of an implementing act in accordance with Article 12.'

Table 7.1 *Entry for 'UV-treated baker's yeast (Saccharomyces cerevisiae)' in the Commission implementing regulation authorizing this yeast as a novel food*

Authorized novel food	Conditions under which the novel food may be used		Additional specific labelling requirements	Other requirements
'UV-treated baker's yeast (*Saccharomyces cerevisiae*)	**Specified food category**	**Maximum levels of vitamin D_2**	The designation of the novel food on the labelling of the foodstuffs containing it shall be 'Vitamin D yeast' or 'Vitamin D_2 yeast'	
	Yeast-leavened breads and rolls	5 µg of vitamin D_2/ 100 g		

Source: Commission Implementing Regulation (EU) 2018/1018 of 18 July 2018 authorising an extension of use of UV-treated baker's yeast (Saccharomyces cerevisiae) as a novel food under Regulation (EU) 2015/2283 of the European Parliament and of the Council and amending Commission Implementing Regulation (EU) 2017/2470 [2018] OJ L183/9.

instance granting a new authorization. For easier reference, the Commission maintains an online database.[37]

There are two procedural authorization tracks: one is the regular formal authorization under the general rules in Article 10 NFR and subsequent articles, and the other is a notification as traditional food under Article 14 NFR and subsequent provisions.

7.6.2 Article 10 NFR procedure: General authorization procedure

The general authorization procedure is regulated under Article 10 NFR and the Commission adopted further guidance for applications.[38] It can either be initiated by the Commission or following an application by an FBO to the Commission. The application is submitted electronically through the online application system.[39] The Commission then decides on the validity of the application.[40] It is circulated to the Member States and a summary is made available to the public. If the Commission decides it is necessary, EFSA can be requested to give an opinion.

[37] Commission, 'Novel Food Catalogue' <https://ec.europa.eu/food/safety/novel_food/catalogue_en> accessed 28 July 2022.

[38] Commission Implementing Regulation (EU) 2017/2469 of 20 December 2017 laying down administrative and scientific requirements for applications referred to in Article 10 of Regulation (EU) 2015/2283 of the European Parliament and of the Council on novel foods [2017] OJ L351/64.

[39] ibid, art 3.

[40] ibid, art 6.

Figure 7.1 General authorization procedure around 17 months

Following that, the Commission submits a draft implementing act to be decided in the Committee procedure (see Chapter 3). The draft must be submitted seven months after an eventual EFSA opinion if there is a potential health impact, or, if no EFSA opinion was requested, seven months after the receipt of the application.[41] In drafting this proposal, the Commission is not bound by the EFSA opinion, but should take the EFSA risk assessment into consideration. Apart from the EFSA opinion, the Commission as risk manager should consider the general conditions. These are that foods do not, on the basis of the scientific evidence available, pose a safety risk to human health; do not mislead the consumer, and are not nutritionally disadvantageous. The Commission should also consider any relevant provision of EU law, including the precautionary principle of Article 7 GFLR, as well as any other legitimate factor.[42]

Without an EFSA opinion, the entire process takes seven months, plus an additional three months due to the committee procedure delay.[43] Where an EFSA opinion is required, the process takes up to seventeen months, plus three months due to the Committee procedure delay (see Figure 7.1 for an overview of the timeline of the general authorization procedure).[44]

7.6.3 *Article 14 NFR notification or Article 16 authorization application for traditional food from a third country*

The alternative procedural track to a full general authorization is the notification or authorization of a traditional food from a third country. The novel food definition is subject to a geographic bias in that it inherently favours EU products—after all, the definition relies on geographic consumption in the EU before 1997 for products to be marketable freely. From a trade perspective, this system significantly restricts products from third countries.[45] To alleviate some of this bias, a specific

[41] NFR, art 12(1) and (2).
[42] ibid, art 12(1)(a)–(d).
[43] ibid, art 12(2).
[44] ibid, arts 11(1) and 12(1).
[45] Michael Hermann, 'The Impact of the European Novel Food Regulation on Trade and Food Innovation Based on Traditional Plant Foods from Developing Countries' (2009) 34 Food Policy 499; Anu Lahteenmaki-Uutela, *European Novel Food Legislation as a Restriction to Trade* (106th Seminar, European Association of Agricultural Economists, Montpellier, France, 25–27 October 2007).

and simplified notification procedure for traditional foods from third countries has been created.[46]

Traditional foods, as defined in the Regulation,[47] are those that fall into the following categories: micro-organisms, fungi, or algae; plants or their parts; animals; cell culture or tissue culture derived from animals, plants, micro-organisms, fungi, or algae; and additionally derived from primary production.[48] The definition therefore excludes some novel food categories such as production processes or products made of nanoengineered material, which cannot be regarded as a traditional foods. Traditional foods must also exhibit a history of safe food use, meaning a continued use for at least 25 years.[49]

With respect to traditional food, there are two marketing tracks. One is the notification of placing on the market of a traditional food under Article 14 NFR, and the other is the slightly more burdensome procedure of an Article 16 authorization for traditional foods from a third country. In the notification procedure under Article 14 NFR, the Commission forwards valid applications within one month to the Member States and EFSA, who have four months to raise reasoned safety objections. If there are no objections, the Commission updates the Union list without delay.[50] If there are objections, the Commission may not authorize the novel food. Instead, the applicant can respond to the reasoned safety objections and submit an application for authorization of a traditional food from a third country under Article 16 NFR.[51] EFSA then issues an opinion within six months (extendable). The risk assessment is targeted at assessing the data concerning the safety of the traditional food. Within three months of an opinion, the Commission drafts an implementing act for the Committee procedure.[52]

Both procedures, the notification of traditional foods as well as the authorization procedure for traditional foods, have some procedural advantages in comparison to a regular full authorization procedure. It is faster, there is less risk of an EFSA opinion, and the documentation is less onerous (see Figure 7.2. for an overview of the timeline of the traditional foods authorization procedure).

[46] This was also in response to World Trade Organization concerns about the restrictive nature of the old scheme of novel food authorizations; see Daniele Pisanello and Giorgia Caruso, *Novel Foods in the European Union* (Springer 2018).
[47] NFR, art 3(2)(c).
[48] GFLR, art 3(17).
[49] NFR, art 3(2)(b).
[50] ibid, art 15(4).
[51] ibid, art 16.
[52] ibid, art 18, using the examination procedure referred to in art 30(3).

Figure 7.2 Traditional foods authorization procedure around 10 months

7.7 EFSA risk assessment procedures for novel food

Since 2018, there has been a centralized risk assessment process in which EFSA conducts risk assessments when requested by the Commission. All applications for authorization are submitted to the Commission, which decides on the validity of the application and whether to request an EFSA risk assessment.

For regular authorizations, the EFSA opinion is adopted within nine months. During the risk assessment, EFSA takes into account whether the novel food is as safe as food in a comparable food category already on the EU market; whether it poses a safety risk to human health; and whether a novel food intended to replace another food is not nutritionally disadvantageous for consumers.[53]

Specifically, the Authority's opinion includes (a) the identity of the novel food; (b) the assessment of the production process; (c) compositional data; (d) specifications; (e) the history of use of the novel food and/or its source; (f) the proposed uses and use levels and anticipated intake; (g) absorption, distribution, metabolism, and excretion (ADME); (h) nutritional information; (i) toxicological information; (j) allergenicity; (k) an overall risk assessment for the novel food under the proposed uses and use levels and highlighting uncertainties and limitations where relevant; (l) when the dietary exposure exceeds the health-based guidance value identified in the overall risk assessment, the dietary exposure assessment of the novel food shall be detailed, providing the contribution to the total exposure of each food category or foodstuff for which the use is authorized or has been requested; (m) conclusions.[54]

When EFSA gives an opinion on traditional foods from a third country in the context of an Article 16 NFR procedure, the agency has a slightly shorter timeframe of six months. In assessing the safety of traditional foods, EFSA considers whether the history of safe-food use in a third country is substantiated by reliable data submitted by the applicant in accordance with Articles 14 and 16; whether it poses a safety risk to human health; whether a novel food intended to replace another food is not nutritionally disadvantageous for consumers.[55] The safety assessment differs from the regular authorization with respect to the substantiation of the history of safe food consumption.

[53] ibid, art 11(2).
[54] Commission Implementing Regulation (EU) 2017/2469, art 7(1).
[55] NFR, art 17(2).

EFSA has issued guidelines on how to prepare the application for an authorization as novel food.[56] The guidelines for the old and the new authorization systems are relatively similar and have been criticized for not taking into account novel methodologies and for not sufficiently considering ways to minimize the need for animal testing.[57]

7.8 The new data ownership turn in novel food authorizations

Under the 1997 novel food regime, novel foods had been authorized through Commission Decisions that were individually addressed to the applicants. Under the current regime, they are authorized by means of an implementing regulation with general application.[58] This novel food authorization has been characterized as generic, as once a novel food has been authorized, any FBO can market it under the conditions specified. However, the new NFR follows the more general 'data ownership turn' in EU law.[59] Proprietary rights on the data used in an application may lead to a five-year exclusive right if the scientific evidence was marked as proprietary at the time of application, and the novel food assessment could not have been made without it.[60] In order to secure such protection, FBOs must submit a request for data protection in their novel food application.[61] Effectively, this system therefore creates a five-year exclusive monopoly on this authorization before other parties can benefit from it—this presumably acts as an incentive to companies to protect their investments in innovation. It also demonstrates the close relationship between novel food regulation and intellectual property rights.[62] Based on the authorized novel foods, protected novel food authorization procedures have become the norm rather than an exception.

[56] EFSA Panel on Dietetic Products, Nutrition and Allergies (NDA) and others, 'Guidance on the Preparation and Presentation of an Application for Authorization of a Novel Food in the Context of Regulation (EU) 2015/2283' (2016) 14(11) EFSA Journal <https://efsa.onlinelibrary.wiley.com/doi/full/10.2903/j.efsa.2016.4594> accessed 21 February 2019.

[57] Alie de Boer and Aalt Bast, 'Demanding Safe Foods—Safety Testing under the Novel Food Regulation (2015/2283)' (2018) 72 Trends in Food Science & Technology 125.

[58] This had important implications in terms of enforceability, in that decisions are only binding on the individual to whom they are addressed; see Daniele Pisanello and Giorgia Caruso, *Novel foods in the European Union* (Springer International Publishing 2018).

[59] NFR, Recital (30).

[60] ibid, Chapter V 'Data Protection'.

[61] ibid, arts 26 and 27.

[62] See Jessica Vapnek, Kai Purnhagen, and Ben Hillel, 'Regulatory and Legislative Frameworks for Novel Foods' in Shivani Pathania and Brijesh K Tiwari (eds), *Food Formulation: Novel Ingredients and Processing Techniques* (Wiley 2021).

7.9 Reflections

In many ways, the regulation of novel food 'represents how society has chosen to deal with the unknown consequences of new technologies and materials'.[63] In this sense, the EU NFR remains very safety oriented. However, the area of novel food—in contrast to GMOs—is relatively depoliticized and technical in nature.

Nevertheless, literature often portrays the NFR as a regulatory burden, with relatively high costs imposed on companies, so high that they may stand in the way of innovation,[64] and even sustainable consumption. For example, obstacles for advancing 'circular' innovations from a resource perspective can be food-law related. An example is the case of the dried fruit pulp (cascara), which was regarded as a novel food in need of an authorization before it could be marketed in the EU. Despite its mundane use, it took a relatively long time to receive authorization.[65] Many small and medium-sized enterprises (SMEs) are working towards the validation of biomass for various 'circular' products, however innovations can become blocked if authorizations are too costly and time-consuming. The current NFR may, therefore, dampen the 'transformative potential of novel foods in Europe' for instance of alternative proteins such as single-cell proteins, plant-based novel proteins, cultured meat, macroalgae, and insects.[66]

The new NFR attempts to encourage new technologies and innovations in food production[67] by making it easier to introduce traditional foods from third countries and by allowing for the potential establishment of a five-year monopoly for successful authorizations if requested, in order to protect investments made by companies.

Nevertheless, the costs and efforts of authorizations appear to be quite prohibitive to companies, who have to bear the expenses of safety assessments. This mechanism can prevent useful food technologies from being developed or marketed in the EU, potentially stifling societal responses to global challenges such as the protein transition or circularity. Without necessarily changing the design of the authorization system, a redistribution of the costs for safety assessments in cases where there are foreseeable benefits for society should be sought. This could be achieved by, for instance, creating specific special-purpose authorization funding

[63] ibid.

[64] ibid.

[65] Commission Implementing Regulation (EU) 2022/47 of 13 January 2022 authorising the placing on the market of Coffea arabica L. and/or Coffea canephora Pierre ex A.Froehner dried cherry pulp and its infusion as a traditional food from a third country under Regulation (EU) 2015/2283 of the European Parliament and of the Council and amending Commission Implementing Regulation (EU) 2017/2470 [2022] OJ L9/29.

[66] Anu Lähteenmäki-Uutela and others, 'Alternative Proteins and EU Food Law' (2021) 130 Food Control 108336.

[67] NFR, Recital (29).

instruments, giving benefit assessments more weight in the authorization procedure, or establishing sand-box systems to assess potential benefits.

Interestingly, the issue of innovation may come to the forefront in the context of the 2023 proposal for New Genomic Techniques (NGT).[68] The NFR exempts 'classic' GMO foods, as they are already subject to the scrutiny of the GMO authorization risk assessment process. However, given that the NGT proposal does not outline an authorization procedure for all new genomic techniques, it seems logical that these techniques would then fall within the scope of the novel food authorization requirement in order to safeguard the objectives of the NFR.

[68] Commission, 'Proposal for a Regulation of the European Parliament and the Council on plants obtained by certain new genomic techniques and their food and feed, and amending Regulation (EU) 2017/625' COM (2023) 411 final.

8

Genetically Modified Food

8.1 Introduction

One of the most contentious issues in food law is the topic of genetically modified organisms (GMOs), characterized by highly polarized public debate and political standpoints across Member States. In European Union (EU) public opinion, GMOs once had a notoriously bad reputation—consumers were wary of genetically modified (GM) food, perceiving it as risky, unnatural, and potentially harmful to the environment.[1] In 2011, a majority of EU consumers (61%) disagreed with the idea that the development of GM food should be encouraged.[2] From that point, one can trace a more positive shift in consumer attitudes towards the use of GMOs[3] with the reluctance towards GMOs decreasing to 27%.[4] At the same time, surveys consistently show that a large part of the population is ignorant regarding GMOs, and new biotechnologies in particular. A survey[5] from 2022 found that only a third of EU consumers had heard about the use of new biotechnology in food production, confirmed by a later study that revealed that only 40% of respondents across the EU had heard about gene editing techniques.[6] In this sense, while for those interested in the topic, GMOs are heavily divisive, there exists a silent majority of the population that is not consciously aware of the topic at all. Nevertheless, consumers do value their freedom of choice when it comes to consuming GMOs. Almost all consumers (86%) believe that food made from GM crops should be labelled accordingly, which also holds true for gene editing, particularly among 68% of those consumers who were already familiar with gene editing. This is a clear sign of the importance of regulation enabling free choice.

Among those in favour of GMOs, a new narrative has emerged from industry and some scientists, which emphasizes the potential of GMOs and points to the promises that modern biotechnology holds for improving yield and crop

[1] European Commission, *Biotechnology* (Special Eurobarometer, Eurobarometer 73.1, 2010).

[2] ibid.

[3] Mihael Cristin Ichim, 'The More Favorable Attitude of the Citizens toward GMOs Supports a New Regulatory Framework in the European Union' (2021) 12 GM Crops Food 18.

[4] EFSA, *Food Safety in the EU* (Special Eurobarometer, Eurobarometer 97.2, 2022).

[5] ibid.

[6] IPSOS, 'Opinion Poll on the Labelling of GM Crops' (*the GREENS/EFA*, 30 March 2021) <https://www.greens-efa.eu/en/article/news/opinion-poll-on-the-labelling-of-gm-crops> accessed 28 July 2022.

EU Food Law. Hanna Schebesta and Kai Purnhagen, Oxford University Press. © Hanna Schebesta and Kai Purnhagen 2024.
DOI: 10.1093/9780198901570.003.0009

characteristics for the benefit of society.[7] This change in discourse marks a shift from an emphasis on the 'innovation paradigm', that played on regulatory responsibility to keep companies competitive and technological development up to date, towards a 'sustainability paradigm', where the main rhetorical argument is no longer a self-interested one, but rather rooted in claims of the altruistic features of GM technologies for the good of society as a whole. In this vein, the evolving Green Deal policy regarding GMOs has been marked by a radical change of narrative, which now portrays GMOs as a potential tool for achieving a sustainable food system. This vision had already been hinted at by, for instance, the United Nations (UN) World Food Systems Summit of 2021 and appears to have heavily influenced the design of the new regulation at EU level.

To what extent a reluctant or supportive stance towards GMOs is backed up by scientific evidence is heavily debated. However, any pretence of a broad scientific consensus on the safety of GMOs must be considered an overstatement.[8] The main scientific health concerns regarding adverse effects of GMO food consumption are carcinogenesis, teratogenesis, lethal effects, and negative influences on fertility.[9] The main identified adverse environmental implications of GM cultivation include unintended gene flows; the fate of naked DNA in, for example compost or manure; chemical toxicity (natural as well as novel); and the potential for transgene recipient establishment as weeds in the environment. All of these mechanisms could lead to potential indirect impacts on soil and water, biodiversity, pests, disease and weed control, and herbicide/insecticide resistance.[10] Alongside health and environmental concerns, the introduction of GMOs can also have wide socio-economic effects that deserve reflection.

Currently, EU law institutes an authorization system for GMOs. Consequently, GMOs and GM food and feed may only be marketed in the EU if they are authorized for cultivation and/or use in food and feed.

Historically,[11] the regulation of biotechnology in the EU has been nothing short of turbulent. In the mid-1970s, a scientific debate arose in the UK and Europe on whether rDNA research should proceed, and the Commission in 1978 presented a regulatory approach[12] that would have required notification and authorization

[7] Kai Purnhagen and others 'Europe's Farm to Fork Strategy and its Commitment to Biotechnology and Organic Farming: Conflicting or Complementary Goals?' (2021) 26 Trends in Plant Science 600.

[8] Angela Hilbeck and others, 'No Scientific Consensus on GMO Safety' (2015) 27 Environmental Sciences Europe 4.

[9] Chen Shen and others, 'Evaluation of Adverse Effects/Events of Genetically Modified Food Consumption: A Systematic Review of Animal and Human Studies' (2022) 34 Environmental Sciences Europe 1.

[10] Aristidis M Tsatsakis and others, 'Environmental Impacts of Genetically Modified Plants: A Review, Environmental Research' (2017) 156 Environmental Research 818.

[11] This section is based on the overview of the history of the biotechnology regulation in the EU by Shane H Morris and Charles Spillane, 'EU GM Crop Regulation: A Road to Resolution or a Regulatory Roundabout?' (2010) 1 European Journal of Risk Regulation 359.

[12] Commission, 'Proposal for a Council Directive establishing safety measures against the conjectural risks associated with recombinant DNA work' COM (78) 664 final.

by national authorities for activities involving recombinant rDNA. Whereas the UK passed legislation, the Commission proposal was dropped in favour of a non-binding recommendation.[13] In 1983, a Commission communication addressed biotechnology in greater detail,[14] followed by another communication in 1986.[15] In the meantime, several Member States had adopted national legislative frameworks. In 1988, the Commission followed suit and published two proposals[16] that followed the famous 'process' approach to biotechnology, that is, distinguishing safety according to the technique used for producing a modification, instead of assessing the safety of the changes produced in the final product. Even at that time, there was substantial criticism regarding this decision. In 1990, the first set of GMO directives were adopted.[17] In terms of harmonization, the 1990s set of GMO directives quickly failed, as several Member States invoked the so-called 'safeguard clause' to prevent the release of GMOs on their territory. Politically, GMOs remained a contentious issue, culminating in what is commonly referred to as a de-facto moratorium on GMOs in the EU between 1998 and 2004.[18] The majority of Member States (12 of 15) declared their unwillingness to authorize GMOs, and the Commission halted the submission of authorizations. Consequently, from 1998 no more GMO authorizations were issued. In 2001, there was sufficient political consensus to pass new Directive 2001/18 (GMO Deliberate Release Directive).[19] Meanwhile, internationally, the EU GMO moratorium was successfully challenged at the World Trade Organization (WTO) level.[20]

The controversy flared up again in 2018 with the landmark judgment in the *GMO* case,[21] in which the Court of Justice of the European Union (CJEU) held that

[13] Council Recommendation of 30 June 1982 Concerning the Registration of Work involving recombinant Deoxyribonucleic Acid (DNA) [1982] OJ L213/15.

[14] Commission, 'Biotechnology in the Community'(Communication) COM (83) 672 final.

[15] Commission, 'A Community Framework for the Regulation of Biotechnology' (Communication) COM (86) 573 final.

[16] Commission, 'Proposal for a Council Directive on the contained Use of genetically modified Microorganisms. Proposal for a Council Directive on the deliberate Release to the Environment of genetically modified Organisms' COM (88) 160 final.

[17] Council Directive 90/220/EEC of 23 April 1990 on the deliberate release into the environment of genetically modified organisms [1990] OJ L117/15; Council Directive 90/219/EEC of 23 April 1990 on the contained use of genetically modified organisms [1990] OJ L117/1.

[18] See Sarah Lieberman and Tim Gray, 'The So-Called 'Moratorium' on the Licensing of New Genetically Modified (GM) Products by the European Union 1998–2004: A Study in Ambiguity' (2006) 15 Environmental Politics 592. The moratorium was not an official legal act, rather it was the result of a political block that manifested very clearly from 1999 when a number of Member States agreed to form a blocking minority against any GMO approval, but was sustained by inaction of the Commission.

[19] Directive 2001/18/EC of the European Parliament and of the Council of 12 March 2001 on the deliberate release into the environment of genetically modified organisms and repealing Council Directive 90/220/EEC—Commission Declaration [2001] OJ L106/1 (GMO Deliberate Release Directive).

[20] WTO, *European Communities—Measures Affecting the Approval and Marketing of Biotech Products* (19 March 2010) WT/DS291, 292, and 293.

[21] Case C-528/16 *Confédération paysanne and Others v Premier Minister and Ministre de L'agriculture, de L'agroalimentaire et de la Forêt* EU:C:2018:583 (*GMO*).

certain novel mutagenesis techniques, such as CRIPR-CAS would be subject to the GMO Directive, and hence an authorization requirement. The Court made a clear nod to the legislator, suggesting that the legal framework was outdated. The judgment resulted in vehement calls by regulators, industry, scientists, and civil society to reform the—by now—outdated legal framework.[22] The Commission has since introduced the term 'New genomic techniques' (NGT) to complement the abbreviation GMO, probably in order to leave some of the stigma of the GMO discussions behind. After years of preparation, the new NGT proposal[23] was published in 2023 and will presumably become subject to heated debate during the legislative phase. It proposes excluding some new techniques (the so-called NGTs) from the general GMO authorization. According to the proposal, the NGT would act as a *lex specialis* in respect of the existing GMO legislation, which would continue to apply to other techniques. In this chapter, we outline the current legal framework before discussing the proposed changes under the NGT proposal.

8.2 The EU GMO legal framework

The EU has a set of legal instruments that jointly deal with various aspects of GMOs.[24] In terms of authorization procedures, the GMO Deliberate Release Directive regulates the release of GMOs into the environment and the cultivation of GMOs. Specific rules that are applicable for food and feed are laid down in the GM Food and Feed Regulation.[25] Authorizations can be requested either for only one purpose, or for both at the same time, under the 'one door-one key' principle. All GMO and GM food and feed must be authorized; the authorizations are then included in the GMO Community register.[26]

[22] Dennis Eriksson and others, 'Options to Reform the European Union Legislation on GMOs: Scope and Definitions' (2020) 38 Trends in Biotechnology 231.

[23] Commission, 'Proposal for a Regulation of the European Parliament and the Council on plants obtained by certain new genomic techniques and their food and feed, and amending Regulation (EU) 2017/625' COM (2023) 411 final.

[24] Regulation (EC) 1830/2003 of the European Parliament and of the Council of 22 September 2003 concerning the traceability and labelling of genetically modified organisms and the traceability of food and feed products produced from genetically modified organisms and amending Directive 2001/18/EC [2003] OJ L268/24; Directive 2009/41/EC of the European Parliament and of the Council of 6 May 2009 on the contained use of genetically modified micro-organisms (Recast) [2009] OJ L125/75; Regulation (EC) No 1946/2003 of the European Parliament and of the Council of 15 July 2003 on transboundary movements of genetically modified organisms [2003] OJ L287/1. This broad legal framework is complemented by a number of implementing acts and administrative documents. A comprehensive overview (excluding the 2015 amendment) is given by Margaret Rosso Grossman, 'Traceability and Labeling of Genetically Modified Crops, Food, and Feed in the European Union' (2005) 1 Journal of Food Law & Policy 43.

[25] Regulation (EC) 1829/2003 of the European Parliament and of the Council of 22 September 2003 on genetically modified food and feed [2003] OJ L268/1 (GM Food and Feed Regulation).

[26] Set up in accordance with GMO Deliberate Release Directive, art 28. See also European Commission—Health and Food Safety, 'Genetically Modified Organisms' <https://webgate.ec.europa.eu/dyna/gm_register/index_en.cfm> accessed 28 July 2022.

GMO is a polarized and controversial topic across the Member States. This makes it next to impossible to reach a political compromise. Prior to the novel NGT proposal, initial efforts to reform the legal system focused on attempts to re-nationalize GMO decision making by granting Member States greater risk management powers. This suggests that because Member States would have more freedom to block GMOs under individual opt-outs at national level, they would be less reluctant to authorize GMOs at EU level. Along these lines, the GMO Deliberate Release Directive was successfully amended in 2015 to allow Member States to prohibit the cultivation of GMOs on their territory.[27] The hope that this option would lead to more EU authorizations for GMO cultivation, however, did not materialize. A similar proposal for GM food and feed was unsuccessful and is still pending.[28] This means that to date all Member States must allow GM food and feed on their territory.

8.2.1 *Legal base, objectives, and main aims*

Despite the fact that most secondary legislation concerning the regulation of GMOs is focused on environmental protection, Article 114 of the Treaty on the Functioning of the European Union (TFEU)[29] on the approximation of laws has been chosen for the harmonization of GMOs.[30] The GMO Deliberate Release Directive covers 'the deliberate release into the environment of genetically modified organisms' and 'the placing on the market genetically modified organisms as or in products'.[31] It aims to align Member State laws and protect human health and the environment in accordance with the precautionary principle. The GM Food and Feed Regulation aims to ensure a 'high level of protection of human life and health, animal health and welfare, environment and consumer interests in relation to genetically modified food and feed, whilst ensuring the effective functioning of the internal market'.[32] It lays down procedures for the authorization, the supervision, and the labelling of GM food and feed.

[27] Directive (EU) 2015/412 of the European Parliament and of the Council of 11 March 2015 amending Directive 2001/18/EC as regards the possibility for the Member States to restrict or prohibit the cultivation of genetically modified organisms (GMOs) in their territory [2015] OJ L68/1 (GMO Cultivation Directive).

[28] Commission, 'Proposal for a Regulation of the European Parliament and the Council amending Regulation (EC) No 1829/2003 as regards the possibility for the Member States to restrict or prohibit the use of genetically modified food and feed on their territory' (Proposal) COM (2015) 177 final.

[29] TFEU, art 114.

[30] For the implications of this choice, see Kai P Purnhagen, 'How to Manage The Union's Diversity: The Case on the Regulation of New Plant Breeding Technologies Confédération Paysanne and Others' (2019) 56 Common Market Law Review 1379.

[31] GMO Deliberate Release Directive, art 1.

[32] GM Food and Feed Regulation, art 1.

8.2.2 Scope of the GMO deliberate release and GM food and feed frameworks

The most contentious issue in GMO regulation at EU level concerns the legal categorization of a product or substance as a GMO. The legal definition and the understanding in natural science may not necessarily align, as illustrated most prominently by the debate surrounding the legal status of 'new plant breeding techniques' and whether they qualify as GMOs, an issue that came under heavy scrutiny after the *GMO* case[33] of 2018.

8.2.2.1 What is a GMO

The definition of GMO is given in the GMO Deliberate Release Directive,[34] which states that 'genetically modified organism (GMO) means an organism, with the exception of human beings, in which the genetic material has been altered in a way that does not occur naturally by mating and/or natural recombination'. In addition, the Deliberate Release Directive contains a positive list of techniques (Annex I A) that result in genetic modification, and exemptions under Article 3(1) which are listed in Annex 1 B, including mutagenesis. This is why it is often said that the EU employs a 'process-based' authorization system where essentially the method used for modification determines the GMO status. This can be contrasted with other countries, where the product is regarded as more important.[35]

A landmark ruling regarding the interpretation of the mutagenesis exemption was issued in *Confédération paysanne and Others* (or simply the *GMO* case).[36] The CJEU provided a conservative interpretation of the exemption from the scope of application of the Directive for mutagenesis techniques: only organisms obtained by means of techniques/methods of mutagenesis which have conventionally been used in a number of applications and have a long safety record are excluded from the scope of the Directive. The CJEU interpreted this limitation on the exemption by following the wording of Recital 17 of the Directive, which explained the exemption, and stated that the GMO Release Directive should not apply to certain techniques of genetic modification which have conventionally been used in a number of applications and have a long safety record. The CJEU found that the legislator intended to exempt mutagenesis because at the time it was a conventionally used, safe technique. Following the referring national court, the CJEU found that *new* mutagenesis techniques pose risks similar to regulated techniques, and therefore, on a purposive interpretation, the legislator had not intended to exempt

[33] *GMO* case (n 21).

[34] GM Food and Feed Regulation, art 2, point 5, referring to GMO Cultivation Directive, art 2(2).

[35] Alan McHughen, 'A Critical Assessment of Regulatory Triggers for Products of Biotechnology: Product vs. Process' (2016) 7 GM Crops & Food 125.

[36] *GMO* case (n 21); Kai P Purnhagen and others, 'The European Union Court's Advocate General's Opinion and New Plant Breeding Techniques' (2018) 36 Nature Biotechnology 573.

such techniques.[37] On the basis of this judgment, many novel gene-editing techniques such as CRISPR–Cas9 would fall within the scope of the Directive and therefore require an authorization.

The judgment was fiercely contended and triggered widespread consensus on the need to reform the GMO legal framework.[38] The current GMO definition emphasizes the 'technique' used to create an organism, rather than the organism itself. Critics suggest that the focus should instead be on the resulting organism as the trigger for the regulation, rather than solely on the process used in its development. This could involve setting up different risk-based categories of organisms and/or techniques.[39] In addition, it has been suggested that new protocols for risk assessment should incorporate selected aspects of traits and gene functions.[40]

In 2021, the Commission published a study on NGTs that also criticized the existing regulatory framework.[41] As a consequence, the Council has tasked the Commission with submitting a proposal for the sector, and the NGT proposal was tabled in 2023.[42] The proposal suggests creating exemptions for NGT plants obtained through targeted mutagenesis or cisgenesis. Among these, it presents different categories of plants. The first category, 'category 1 NGT plants', refers to plants that could have been obtained naturally or by conventional breeding techniques. NGT plants that are not in category 1 are 'category 2 NGT plants', and would remain subject to the requirements of the Union GMO legislation, however with some specific exceptions as specified in the proposed law. Overall, the proposal creates a new category of GMOs, which would (partially) escape the application of the GM legal framework.

[37] See Hanna Schebesta, 'Confédération Paysanne Case (C-528/16): Legal Perspective on the GMO Judgment of the European Court of Justice' (2020) Revue européenne de droit de la consommation 369. For a study of the legislative process on how the mutagenesis exemption was included in the Directive, see Kathleen Garnett, 'Hold Your Pipettes: The European Court of Justice's Findings in *Confédération Paysanne & Others* stirs GMOtions' (2019) 28 Review of European, Comparative & International Environmental Law 349.

[38] The judgment was fiercely criticized; for an overview of reactions, see Martin Wasmer, 'Roads Forward for European GMO Policy-Uncertainties in Wake of ECJ Judgment Have to be Mitigated by Regulatory Reform' (2019) 7 Frontiers in Bioengineering and Biotechnology 132.

[39] Dennis Eriksson, 'Recovering the Original Intentions of Risk Assessment and Management of Genetically Modified Organisms in the European Union' (2018) 6 Frontiers in Bioengineering and Biotechnology 52.

[40] ibid; Charlotta Zetterberg and Karin Edvardsson Björnberg, 'Time for a New EU Regulatory Framework for GM Crops?' (2017) 30 Journal of Agricultural and Environmental Ethics 325.

[41] Commission, 'Study on the status of new genomic techniques under Union law and in light of the Court of Justice ruling in Case C-528/16' SWD (2021) 92 final.

[42] Commission, 'Proposal for a Regulation of the European Parliament and the Council on plants obtained by certain new genomic techniques and their food and feed, and amending Regulation (EU) 2017/625' COM (2023) 411 final.

8.2.2.2 *GM food and feed regulation*

Alongside the GMO Directive, the GM Food and Feed Regulation contains provisions that are specific to GM Food and Feed, which is broadly defined as[43] (a) GMOs for food use, meaning a GMO that may be used as food or as a source material for the production of food;[44] (b) food containing or consisting of GMOs, meaning food containing, consisting of, or produced from GMOs;[45] and (c) food produced from or containing ingredients produced from GMOs, meaning derived, in whole or in part, from GMOs, but not containing or consisting of GMOs.[46]

In *Bablok* (Honey judgment),[47] the Court clarified these categories further. A beekeeper had beehives around 500m from a plot of land on which the German region Bavaria had cultivated MON810 maize for research purposes. The MON 810 maize pollen (substance produced by seed plants) was found in the honey. The Court held that pollen which has lost its ability to reproduce and is totally incapable of transferring the genetic material which it contains, no longer constitutes a GMO. However, honey or food supplements containing such pollen must be regarded as being 'produced from GMOs' within the meaning of Article 3(1)(c) of the GM Food and Feed Regulation and therefore cannot be marketed without a prior authorization.[48]

8.3 Main requirements of GMO deliberate release and GM food and feed frameworks

The GMO Deliberate Release Directive institutes a duty on Member States to act in accordance with the precautionary principle and to ensure that all measures are taken to avoid adverse effects on human health and the environment which might arise from the deliberate release or market placing of GMOs. GMOs may only be deliberately released or placed on the market in compliance with the Directive, either for purposes other than market placement (Part B) or for the market placement (Part C).[49]

The GM Food and Feed Regulation, in turn, stipulates a direct prohibition that no person may market GM food or feed unless it is covered by an authorization.[50]

[43] GM Food and Feed Regulation, art 3 on the scope of the GM Food and Feed Regulation. See Eriksson (n 39).

[44] GM Food and Feed Regulation, art 2, point 8.

[45] ibid, art 2, point 6.

[46] ibid, art 2, point 10.

[47] Case C-442/09 *Karl Bablok and Others v Freistaat Bayern* [2011] ECR I-07419 (*Bablok*); see also Kai Purnhagen and Justus Wesseler, 'The "Honey" Judgment of Bablok and Others Versus Freistaat Bayern in the Court of Justice of the European Union: Implications for Co-existence' in Nicholas Kalaitzandonakes and others (eds), *The Coexistence of Genetically Modified, Organic and Conventional Foods: Government Policies and Market Practices* (Springer New York 2016).

[48] *Bablok* (n 47), paras 70–71.

[49] GMO Deliberate Release Directive, art 4(1).

[50] GM Food and Feed Regulation, art 4(2).

Food and feed may not have adverse effects on human health, animal health, or the environment; mislead the consumer; or differ from the food which it is intended to replace to such an extent that its normal consumption would be nutritionally disadvantageous for the consumer.[51]

8.3.1 *The content of an authorization*

One of the most promoted aspects of the GMO regime for both deliberate release and food and feed is the 'one door-one key' principle. It implies that an authorization for the deliberate release of GMOs either takes place under the GMO Deliberate Release Directive or if an authorization for both cultivation and food and feed is sought, under the GM Food and Feed Regulation. While the possibility of combining authorization procedures embodies the 'one door-one key' principle, cultivation is rarely a realistic option anymore, and will only be allowed in those few Member States that did not oppose cultivation under any circumstances.[52]

Applicants can choose to apply for an authorization for cultivation, or for food and feed, or for both simultaneously. Successful authorizations for cultivation are not common; those for food and feed are authorized more often. With the introduction of the 2015 amendment to the GMO Deliberate Release Directive, EU Member States can additionally restrict the geographical scope of a GMO application or authorization by requesting an adjustment to the geographical scope of an authorization.[53]

Very few authorizations for GMO crop cultivation have ever been granted. Amflora was a potato with modified starch that had been authorized for cultivation, but the authorization decisions were later annulled by the Court in *Amflora*.[54] This was because the Commission had failed to follow the procedure for authorization. BASF Plant Science GmbH, through one of the subsidiaries, requested authorization for cultivation from Swedish authorities. Several Member States submitted observations, leading to the Commission taking charge of the authorization process, following the committee procedure.[55] The European Food Safety Authority (EFSA) had given a favourable opinion on the crop in 2005. However, in the face of some scientific inconsistencies, the Commission decided to request

[51] ibid, art 4(1).

[52] Bernd van der Meulen and Neshe Yusuf, 'One-Door-One-Key Principle: Observations Regarding Integration of GM Authorization Procedures in the EU' (2015) 118 Pennsylvania State Law Review 877.

[53] GMO Deliberate Release Directive, arts 26b and 26c. The demand will be communicated to the Commission no later than 45 days from the date of the assessment report's circulation under art 14(2) of the Directive, or from receiving the opinion of EFSA under arts 6(6) and 18(6) of Regulation (EC) 1829/2003.

[54] Case T-240/10 *Hungary v European Commission* EU:T:2013:645 (*Amflora*).

[55] In this case, two committees were responsible: the Regulatory Committee on the Release into the Environment of Genetically Modified Organisms, established by Directive 2001/18/EC, and the Standing Committee on the Food Chain and Animal Health, referred to in Regulation (EC) 1829/2003.

a consolidated scientific opinion from EFSA. This was published in 2009, and was generally favourable, but included minority opinions conflicting with the overall conclusions. Subsequently, the Commission failed to draft a new decision, and did not submit the consolidated opinion to the committees in charge of the authorization decision; the decision to grant both authorizations was taken in 2010 on the basis of the old documents. The Court held the view that the outcome of the procedure could have been substantially different, given that EFSA's consolidated opinion expressed more uncertainties than the prior risk assessment. Consequently, the authorization decision of the Commission was annulled. The case has reaffirmed the Commission's reputation as the sole authority in authorizing GMO crops for cultivation in the EU. The only other crop commercialized for cultivation in the EU was the long-standing authorization of GM maize MON 810, initially authorized in 1998 on the basis of the old Directive.[56] However, 19 Member States used the option to prohibit[57] the cultivation of MON 810 in all or part of their territory. Currently, MON 810 is pending re-authorization. However, some non-crop plants are permitted for cultivation under the Deliberate Release Directive, notably several carnations (flowers) that are genetically modified for colour or herbicide resistance.

A number of authorizations for GM food and feed have been granted, namely for cotton, maize, oilseed rape, soybeans, and sugar beet. One example of an authorized GM food and feed is sugar beet (H7-1), with the unique identifier KM-ØØØH71-4, the authorization holders being KWS SAAT and Monsanto. This authorization is for: (1) foods and food ingredients produced from KM-ØØØH71-4 sugar beet and (2) feed produced from KM-ØØØH71-4 sugar beet. The GM sugar beet expresses the CP4 EPSPS protein after insertion of the cp4 epsps gene from Agrobacterium sp. strain CP4 into sugar beet (Beta vulgaris subsp. vulgaris). The CP4 EPSPS protein confers tolerance to glyphosate containing herbicides.[58] EFSA published its opinion in December 2006[59] and the sugar beet was originally authorized in October 2007 through a Commission Decision.[60]

[56] Council Directive 90/220/EEC (n 17) by Commission Decision 98/294/EC; Commission Decision of 22 April 1998 concerning the placing on the market of genetically modified maize (Zea mays L. line MON 810), pursuant to Council Directive 90/220/EEC [1998] OJ L131/32.

[57] GMO Deliberate Release Directive, art 26c.

[58] European Commission—Health and Food Safety, 'Genetically Modified Organisms, entry for KM-ØØØH71-4' (Community register of GM food and feed) <https://webgate.ec.europa.eu/dyna/gm_register/gm_register_auth.cfm?pr_id=27> accessed 29 July 2022.

[59] EFSA, 'Opinion of the Scientific Panel on genetically modified organisms [GMO] related on an application (Reference EFSA GMO UK 2004 08) for the placing on the market of products produced from glyphosate tolerant genetically modified sugar beet H7-1, for food and feed uses, under Regulation (EC) No 1829/2003 from KWS SAAT AG and Monsanto' (2006) 4(12) EFSA Journal <http://www.efsa.europa.eu/en/efsajournal/pub/431> accessed 29 July 2022.

[60] Commission Decision of 24 October 2007 authorising the placing on the market of food and feed produced from genetically modified sugar beet H7-1 (KM-ØØØH71-4) pursuant to Regulation (EC) No 1829/2003 of the European Parliament and of the Council (notified under document number C(2007) 5125) [2007] OJ L283/69.

The authorization was subsequently renewed in 2018 through a Commission Implementing Decision.[61]

8.3.1.1 GMO applications under Directive 2001/18/EC

Applications for authorizations under the GMO Deliberate Release Directive are submitted to a national competent authority in whose territory the release is to take place. This country becomes the lead country.

The GMO Deliberate Release Directive distinguishes between procedures for the 'deliberate release for other purposes than placing on the market' (Part B, Articles 5–11) and 'placing on the market' (Part C, Articles 12–24). 'Deliberate release' means any 'intentional introduction into the environment of a GMO or a combination of GMOs for which no specific containment measures are used to limit their contact with and to provide a high level of safety for the general population and the environment'.[62] In contrast, 'placing on the market' means 'making available to third parties, whether in return for payment or free of charge'.[63]

There is a standard authorization procedure for deliberate release (Part B-type),[64] as well as differentiated procedures,[65] where a written consent by the competent national authority is granted upon notification by a notifier. This notification must contain specific information, in particular: (a) a technical dossier supplying the information specified in Annex III necessary for carrying out the environmental risk assessment of the deliberate release and (b) the environmental risk assessment and the conclusions required in Annex II, section D, together with any bibliographic references and indications of the methods used.[66] The competent authorities send a summary to the Commission, which it forwards to the other Member States. Other Member States may present observations through the Commission or directly.[67] The decision-making process is therefore decentralized.

For the placing on the market (Part C-type), the notification procedure[68] applies. The notification should contain the information required in Annexes III and IV; the environmental risk assessment and the conclusions required in Annex II; the conditions for the product's placement on the market, including specific conditions of use and handling; a proposed period for the consent no longer than ten

[61] Commission Implementing Decision (EU) 2018/1113 of 3 August 2018 renewing the authorization for the placing on the market of food and feed produced from genetically modified sugar beet H7-1 (KM-ØØØH71-4) pursuant to Regulation (EC) No 1829/2003 of the European Parliament and of the Council (notified under document C(2018) 5029) [2018] OJ L203/32.

[62] GMO Deliberate Release Directive, art 2(3).

[63] ibid, art 2(4).

[64] ibid, art 6.

[65] ibid, art 7.

[66] ibid, art 6(2).

[67] ibid, art 11.

[68] ibid, art 13.

years; a monitoring plan; a proposal for labelling; a proposal for packaging; and a summary of the dossier.[69]

One of the key notification requirements is that under Annex II of GMO Deliberate Release Directive, an environmental risk assessment must be carried out, as referred to in Articles 4 (Part B-type) and 13 (Part C-type). The objective of the environmental risk assessment is

> on a case by case basis, to identify and evaluate potential adverse effects of the GMO, either direct and indirect, immediate or delayed, on human health and the environment which the deliberate release or the placing on the market of GMOs may have. The [environmental risk assessment] should be conducted with a view to identifying if there is a need for risk management and if so, the most appropriate methods to be used.[70]

The conditions for the environmental risk assessment have been laid down in an implementing act.[71] In addition, Annex III specifies that the following data must be included in the notification (for both Part B- and C-type): the summaries and results of the studies referred to in the notification, including an explanation regarding their relevance to environmental risk assessment where applicable. For Part C-type notifications, detailed information on those studies, including a description of the methods and materials used or the reference to standardized or internationally recognized methods and the name of the body or bodies responsible for carrying out the studies is required.

The lead country prepares an assessment report within 90 days, indicating whether it recommends allowing or not to allowing the placing on the market for the GMO in question.[72] The assessment report is sent to the Commission which forwards it to the EU countries for comments. An exemption from the geographical scope of a written consent or notification/authorization can be requested by Member States.[73] The decision moves into the committee procedure if at least one EU country raises one or more reasonable objections based on the assessment report.[74]

69 ibid, art 13(2).

70 Commission Decision of 24 July 2002 establishing guidance notes supplementing Annex II to Directive 2001/18/EC on the deliberate release into the environment of genetically modified organisms and repealing Council Directive 90/220/EEC (notified under document number C(2002) 2715) [2002] OJ L200.

71 Commission Directive (EU) 2018/350 of 8 March 2018 amending Directive 2001/18/EC of the European Parliament and of the Council as regards the environmental risk assessment of genetically modified organisms [2018] OJ L67/30.

72 GMO Deliberate Release Directive, art 14.

73 ibid, arts 26b and 26c. The demand will be communicated to the Commission no later than 45 days from the date of the assessment report's circulation under art 14(2) of the Directive, or from receiving the opinion of the EFSA under arts 6(6) and 18(6) of Regulation (EC) 1829/2003.

74 GMO Deliberate Release Directive, art 18.

8.3.1.2 GM Food and Feed application

The procedure is laid down in GM Food and Feed Regulation and Commission Implementing Regulation (EU) 503/2013[75]. In order to obtain a GM food and feed authorization, a notification must be submitted to the competent national authority of a Member State, which forwards it to EFSA and informs the Commission and the Member States.[76] The application must contain specific information,[77] which EFSA verifies. Within six months, EFSA gives an opinion, although it may request additional information.

The application must also comply with the requirements set out in Commission Implementing Regulation (EU) 503/2013 on applications for authorization of GM food and feed.[78] This includes all relevant data, studies, and analysis of the results; the purpose and scope of the GMO; the monitoring plan; the labelling proposal; the detection method; and indications of confidential information.

8.3.2 Risk assessment phase

Under the GM Food and Feed Regulation, EFSA issues an opinion under Article 6(6) for GM food and Article 18(6) for GM feed. EFSA issues its risk assessment opinion within six months.[79] It may request the food assessment body in a Member State to evaluate the safety of the food and a community laboratory to test and validate the method of identification of the transformation and samples of the food. The opinion must include, in the case of being favourable, a proposal for labelling, marketing conditions, or restrictions. EFSA will send the opinion to the Commission, to the Member States, and to the applicant.

The adequacy of the EFSA risk assessment is frequently subject to criticism. Among the issues raised is EFSA's reliance on a comparative safety assessment between GM and non-GM varieties which is regarded as inadequate for predicting adverse biological, toxicological, and ecological effects.[80] It is also regarded as unnecessarily reliant on animal studies. For instance, 90-day animal feeding studies

[75] Commission Implementing Regulation (EU) 503/2013 of 3 April 2013 on applications for authorisation of genetically modified food and feed in accordance with Regulation (EC) No 1829/2003 of the European Parliament and of the Council and amending Commission Regulations (EC) No 641/2004 and (EC) No 1981/2006 [2013] OJ L157/1 (Commission Implementing Regulation (EU) No 503/2013).

[76] GM Food and Feed Regulation, art 5, on the application for authorization.

[77] ibid, art 5(3) describes what documentation must accompany the application (information on the applicant, the food in question, the detailed description of how it was produced, the conditions for marketing the food, use and handling, an assessment of the risk to human health and the environment, food samples and their control samples, etc).

[78] Commission Implementing Regulation (EU) No 503/2013.

[79] GM Food and Feed Regulation, art 6, risk assessment opinion by EFSA.

[80] Angelika Hilbeck and others, 'GMO Regulations and Their Interpretation: How EFSA's Guidance on Risk Assessments of GMOs is Bound to Fail' (2020) 32 Environmental Sciences Europe 1.

are required with whole food/feed for most GMOs, and critics argue that the value of such studies is therefore unnecessary and inefficient.[81] By contrast, the environmental risk assessment is regarded as lacking clarity, and needs better definitions of harm and operational protection goals.[82]

The risk assessment of EFSA is not conclusive as to whether or not an authorization application will be successful. For the application of maize TC1507 by Pioneer, EFSA issued three positive opinions concluding that there was no risk to human health or the environment, but the risk management process did not follow this positive assessment: a qualified majority by the Member State representatives in the committee procedure persistently failed.[83] Risk assessment is not binding on risk managers, and in that sense it is legitimate that risk management decision deviate from risk assessment outcomes. This is because in the risk management phase other aspects may be taken into account, including social factors. One of the obvious tensions in the current regime is whether the risk management process adequately protects societal values such as environmental and human health. Some argue that blocking authorizations is irrational in cases where there is a positive EFSA assessment, as this should be sufficient evidence that a technology is safe.

8.3.3 *Risk management phase*

In formal legal terms, the decision to authorize is an implementing act taken by the Commission; the implementing act is adopted by following the committee procedure. First, the Commission prepares a draft legal act to grant the marketing authorization. National representatives then vote on the Commission proposal by qualified majority in the Standing Committee on Plants, Animals, Food and Feed. If the Committee does not approve or rejects the proposal by a qualified majority, the Commission may convene an Appeals Committee. If the Appeals Committee does not reach an opinion by a qualified majority, the Commission must assume responsibility for the final decision (see Chapter 3).

In reality, the committee procedure in the field of GMOs (both GMO and GM food and feed) has never resulted in a qualified majority among Member States either in favour of or against draft Commission authorizations that were up for

[81] See Dennis Eriksson and others, 'Options to Reform the European Union Legislation on GMOs: Risk Governance' (2020) 38 Trends in Biotechnology 349, referring especially to the principle of Replacement, Reduction and Refinement (3R) in animal feeding trials, and Directive 2010/63/EU of the European Parliament and of the Council on 22 September 2010 on the protection of animals used for scientific purposes [2010] OJ L276/33, art 4. See also Harry A Kuiper, Esther J Kok, and Howard V Davies, 'New EU Legislation for Risk Assessment of GM Food: No Scientific Justification for Mandatory Animal Feeding Trials' (2013) 11 Plant Biotechnology Journal 781.

[82] Eriksson and others (n 81); this is despite the amendment of the Directive of environmental risk assessment of GMOs Commission Directive (EU) 2018/350.

[83] Case T-164/10 *Pioneer Hi-Bred International, Inc. v European Commission* EU:T:2013:503 (*Pioneer Hi-Bred International*), para 12, in which the applicant lodged a suit for failure to act.

vote. However, Article 41 on the right to good administration of the Charter of Fundamental Rights (CFR) and case law[84] require the Commission as risk manager to make a decision on an application for authorization in a reasonable period of time.[85] Therefore, the Commission had significant discretion in making authorization decisions. When GMO authorization in terms of food is at stake, the Commission's discretion is guided by Article 6(3) of the General Food Law Regulation (GFLR) to take into account the opinions of EFSA, and the arguments brought forward by the Member States in the committee procedure as 'other legitimate factors on the matter'.

8.3.4 *Validity and renewal*

Authorizations will be valid throughout the Community for a period of ten years, and renewable for a further ten years.[86] Authorizations are renewable[87] for ten-year periods on application to the Commission by the authorization-holder, submitted no later than one year before the expiry date of the authorization. For instance, Bayer CropScience successfully applied to renew the authorization for placing products from oilseed rape T45 on the market.[88]

8.4 Traceability and labelling of GM food

The GM Food and Feed Regulation was accompanied by a specific GMO Traceability and Labelling Regulation,[89] which is meant to facilitate the withdrawal of products where unforeseen adverse effects are discovered, examine potential

[84] Judgment of the General Court of 26 September 2013 in Case T-164/10 *Pioneer Hi-Bred International, Inc v Commission* EU:T:2013:503.

[85] Commission, 'Proposal for a Regulation of the European Parliament and of the Council amending Regulation (EU) No 182/2011 laying down the rules and general principles concerning mechanisms for control by Member States of the Commission's exercise of implementing powers' (Communication) COM (2017) 085 final (Commission Proposal for amending Regulation (EU) No 182/2011).

[86] GMO Food and Feed Regulation, art 7, detailing the procedure to grant authorization.

[87] ibid, art 23, on renewal of authorizations.

[88] During the renewal procedure, the EFSA GMO Panel concluded that there was no evidence for new hazards, modified exposure, or scientific uncertainties to change the conclusions of the original risk assessment on oilseed rape T45 by EFSA in 2008. Commission Implementing Decision (EU) 2019/2081 of 28 November 2019 renewing the authorisation for the placing on the market of products containing or produced from genetically modified oilseed rape T45 (ACS-BNØØ8-2), resulting from the commercialisation of this oilseed rape in third countries until 2005, pursuant to Regulation (EC) No 1829/2003 of the European Parliament and of the Council (notified under document C(2019) 7480) C/2019/7480 [2019] OJ L316/57.

[89] Regulation (EC) 1830/2003 of the European Parliament and of the Council of 22 September 2003 concerning the traceability and labelling of genetically modified organisms and the traceability of food and feed products produced from genetically modified organisms and amending Directive 2001/18/EC [2003] OJ L268/24.

effects on the environment, and support the implementation of risk management measures in accordance with the precautionary principle.[90]

At the first stage of placing a product on the market consisting of or containing GMOs, operators must inform the receiving operator in writing (a) that it contains or consists of GMOs and (b) the unique identifier(s) assigned to those GMOs.[91] The unique identifier is a code which serves to identify a GMO on the basis of the 'authorised transformation event'.[92] These are non-consumer specific information requirements. The general labelling requirements for products consisting of, or containing GMOs, are the words 'This product contains genetically modified organisms' or 'This product contains genetically modified [name of organism(s)]', which must appear on a label for pre-packaged products (or on the display of non-pre-packaged products for the final consumer).[93]

The GM Food and Feed Regulation contains more specific labelling rules that apply to foods for consumers or mass caterers that (a) contain or consist of GMOs or (b) are produced from or contain ingredients produced from GMOs.[94] Foods containing material which contains, consists of, or is produced from GMOs in a proportion no higher than 0.9% of the food ingredients considered individually or food consisting of a single ingredient, are exempt from the labelling rules, provided that this presence is adventitious or technically unavoidable.[95] However, operators must be able to provide evidence that they have taken appropriate steps to avoid the presence of such material.

The foods must be labelled to indicate the presence of GMOs: (a) where the food consists of more than one ingredient, the words 'genetically modified' or 'produced from genetically modified (name of the ingredient)' should appear in the list of ingredients in parentheses immediately following the ingredient concerned; or (b) where the ingredient is designated by the name of a category, the words 'contains genetically modified (name of organism)' or 'contains (name of ingredient) produced from genetically modified (name of organism)' should appear in the list of ingredients. They may also appear in a footnote of at least the same size as the list of ingredients. If there is no list of ingredients, the words 'genetically modified' or 'produced from genetically modified (name of organism)' must appear clearly on the labelling. For non-pre-packaged food or pre-packaged food in small

[90] GMO Traceability and Labelling Regulation, Recital (3).

[91] ibid, art 4B.

[92] ibid, arts 3(4) and 8. The system is established in Commission Regulation (EC) 65/2004 of 14 January 2004 establishing a system for the development and assignment of unique identifiers for genetically modified organisms [2004] OJ L10/5.

[93] GMO Traceability and Labelling Regulation, art 4.

[94] ibid, art 12.

[95] EFSA, 'Guidance for the risk assessment of the presence at low level of genetically modified plant material in imported food and feed under Regulation (EC) No 1829/2003' (2017) 15(11) EFSA Journal <https://efsa.onlinelibrary.wiley.com/doi/full/10.2903/j.efsa.2017.5048> accessed 29 July 2022.

containers, this information must be permanently and visibly displayed either on the food display or immediately next to it, or on the packaging material.[96]

Under the new rules on NGT, the traceability and labelling framework would acquire even greater significance. With no authorization requirements, transparency in the market would rely solely on labelling. However, as currently proposed, many NGTs would not require specific labelling, therefore preventing consumers from ascertaining their presence in food altogether.

8.5 Proposal on plants obtained by certain new genomic techniques and their food and feed

The new NGT proposal on plants, and their food and feed, was tabled by the Commission in 2023. An NGT plant is defined as a genetically modified plant obtained by targeted mutagenesis or cisgenesis. The proposal distinguishes category 1 and 2 NGTs, where category 1 includes NGTs that meet criteria equivalent to conventional plants, and category 2 comprises NGTs that do not meet this criteria. Category 1 NGTs must get a status verification decision, which is tested by EFSA, and the GMO rules will not apply to them. The plants must bear a label indicating 'cat 1 NGT'. Category 2 NGTs must be authorized. For category 2 plants, the existing GMO legal framework would generally apply, but there will be some derogations specified in the NGT proposal. For instance, after the first renewal, the authorization will be valid for an unlimited period. The new proposal introduces regulatory incentives if NGTs contribute to sustainable cultivation and use according to the Regulation on the production and marketing of plant reproductive material in the Union.[97] Examples of these incentives are shorter time limits, or exemption for laboratory fees for small and medium-sized enterprises, where category 2 products possess traits relevant for sustainability. However, for organic foods, NGTs will be treated the same as GMOs, meaning that organic food cannot contain either NGTs or GMOs.

The NGT proposal is essentially deregulatory in nature. If the proposal is adopted as is, it means that in the future some plants, food, and feed, as well as their products, will circulate on the market without requiring full authorization. The proposed system would still rely on classifying techniques, coupled with the concept of 'conventionality'. Under the guise of sustainability claims, the proposal will significantly promote and encourage the use of genetic techniques. This is very

[96] GMO Food and Feed Regulation, art 13.

[97] As defined in art 52 of the Commission, 'Proposal for a Regulation of the European Parliament and of the Council on the production and marketing of plant reproductive material in the Union, amending Regulations (EU) 2016/2031, 2017/625 and 2018/848 of the European Parliament and of the Council, and repealing Council Directives 66/401/EEC, 66/402/EEC, 68/193/EEC, 2002/53/EC, 2002/54/EC, 2002/55/EC, 2002/56/EC, 2002/57/EC, 2008/72/EC and 2008/90/EC' COM (2023) 414 final.

much in line with the agenda advocated by the pro-GMO lobby, particularly following the *GMO* judgment, and consequently the proposal has been welcomed by major players in the agri-food industry. In terms of the Green Deal, it certainly seems that the Commission has embraced ecological modernism, where technology, rather than conservation and restoration efforts, will deliver a sustainable future.

8.6 Discussion

The societal controversy surrounding GMOs is reflected in the EU legislative framework, which adopts a general precautionary approach on behalf of the EU and enshrines a risk regulatory framework that tends to prohibit GMO authorizations. This means that societal and political resistance to GMOs can outweigh positive scientific risk assessments. Overall, the incoherent and outdated EU GMO legal framework needs to be recast to better accommodate novel technologies and enhance legal certainty.

The logic of the risk regulation is premised on the idea that GMOs may pose risks to human health and the environment and therefore need strict control measures. In this vein, a notable issue is the increasingly idiosyncratic nature of the EU GMO definition. A second issue is the premise itself. Rather than focusing on the regulation of GMOs, an alternative approach would be to move to a regulation of risks to the environment and human health, acknowledging that these may arise irrespective of whether an organism is created by techniques classified as genetic modification, or not. That said, applicability of the GMO Directive only results in an authorization requirement, not a straightforward ban on GMOs on the EU market, as often presented. This is complicated by the fact that politically, in the risk management phase, Member States mostly decline to authorize GMO cultivation.

One EU response to past deadlock has been the renationalization of the area. Risk management decisions in GMO cultivation and GM food and feed are addressed in the Committee Procedure, where they are habitually blocked (see Chapter 3). It has been argued that risk management decisions should therefore be transferred back to the Member States.[98] Indeed, the GMO Opt-Out GMO Cultivation Directive allows Member States to prohibit cultivation on their own territory, which is a first step towards a decentralized system. However, the corresponding proposal for GM food and feed is still pending and unlikely to be passed, meaning that GM food and feed authorizations will continue to be regulated at a harmonized level.

[98] Eriksson and others (n 81).

Given that renationalization did not lead to more authorizations for GMO cultivation, the approach of the new NGT proposal is to (partially) bypass the existing GMO authorization procedure altogether. GMOs had been notably omitted from the Farm to Fork Strategy's legal action points, but the Commission began efforts to create a new legal framework for NGTs. The NGT proposal as tabled makes a concerted effort to align with not only the Farm to Fork Strategy, but also other Green Deal strategies. In this, the proposal subscribes uncritically to unsubstantiated normative views regarding the sustainable nature of NGTs, and their perceived positive role in the EU's future food system.

9

Food Improvement Agents (Additives, Enzymes, Flavourings), and Use of Extraction Solvents

9.1 Introduction

The use of food improvement agents often revolutionize the way food is made or consumed; they have numerous applications, for instance food preservation and innovations in taste and texture, that make them highly appealing. Some concerns regarding the increased use of food improvement agents relate to the potential health effects of these artificially added substances. This links to an ongoing debate between proponents of 'natural' food consumption as opposed to 'artificial' food, wherein ultra-processed products are 'associated with unhealthy dietary nutrient profiles and several diet-related non-communicable diseases'.[1]

Substances that are added to food or used in it for technological purposes are therefore regulated at European Union (EU) and national level. At EU level, there is legislation on enzymes, additives, flavourings, and extraction solvents. Processing aids, in contrast, do not have a dedicated legal framework, and are only regulated incidentally. The legal framework is the so-called 'Food Improvement Agents Package' (FIAP), which covers the Food Additives Regulation,[2] the Enzymes Regulation,[3] the Flavourings Regulation,[4] and the Common Procedure

[1] Carlos Monteiro and others, 'The UN Decade of Nutrition, the NOVA Food Classification and the Trouble with Ultra-Processing' (2018) 21 Public Health Nutrition 5.

[2] Regulation (EC) 1333/2008 of the European Parliament and of the Council of 16 December 2008 on food additives [2008] OJ L354/16 (Food Additives Regulation).

[3] Regulation (EC) 1332/2008 of the European Parliament and of the Council of 16 December 2008 on enzymes and amending Council Directive 83/417/EEC, Council Regulation (EC) No 1493/1999, Directive 2000/13/EC, Council Directive 2001/112/EC and Regulation (EC) No 258/97 [2008] OJ L354/7 (Enzymes Regulation).

[4] Regulation (EC) 1334/2008 of the European Parliament and of the Council of 16 December 2008 on flavourings and certain food ingredients with flavouring properties for use in and on foods and amending Council Regulation (EEC) No 1601/91, Regulation (EC) No 2232/96 and (EC) No 110/2008 and Directive 2000/13/EC [2008] OJ L354/34 (Flavourings Regulation).

EU Food Law. Hanna Schebesta and Kai Purnhagen, Oxford University Press. © Hanna Schebesta and Kai Purnhagen 2024.
DOI: 10.1093/9780198901570.003.0010

Regulation[5] with a joint common authorization procedure. The use of extraction solvents is regulated separately in the Extraction Solvents Directive.[6] As the EU harmonization of food improvement agents is not yet fully complete, certain aspects of food improvement remain unregulated or only subject to Member States' law.

9.2 Food Improvement Agents Package (Additives, Enzymes, Flavourings)

The legal basis for the FIAP is Article 114 Treaty on the Functioning of the European Union (TFEU) on the approximation of laws of the Member States. The FIAP is dedicated to the effective functioning of the internal market whilst ensuring both a high level of protection of human health and a high level of consumer protection. Consumer protection is specified to include the protection of consumer interests and fair practices in food trade, taking into account, where appropriate, the protection of the environment.[7]

Arguably, the strongest *raison d'etre* of the FIAP is food safety. The package includes a common authorization procedure for all substances, which have to undergo stringent safety evaluations. For each of the improvement agents, a positive Union list is drawn up that specifies which substances are approved for use in the EU, and what their respective conditions of use are. These lists are of general application, meaning that any food business operator (FBO) complying with the law can market approved food improvement agents and foodstuffs containing them.

From a food technological perspective, there is a latent normative approach in the legal framework to limit the use of food improvements. Their use must confer a genuine advantage and be limited to what is necessary for achieving specific functions. Furthermore, there is some protection for the conservation of natural or traditional products; food improvement agents should generally not be used for unprocessed foods, and traditional foods may receive special protection at the national level.

In terms of consumer protection, there is a general duty not to mislead consumers, primarily manifested through labelling requirements. In addition, the use of, for instance, additives must have advantages and benefits for the consumer. The

[5] Regulation (EC) 1331/2008 of the European Parliament and of the Council of 16 December 2008 establishing a common authorisation procedure for food additives, food enzymes and food flavourings [2008] OJ L354/1 (Common Procedure Regulation).

[6] Directive 2009/32/EC of the European Parliament and of the Council of 23 April 2009 on the approximation of the laws of the Member States on extraction solvents used in the production of foodstuffs and food ingredients [2009] OJ L141/3 (Extraction Solvents Directive).

[7] Food Additives Regulation, art 1.

issue of consumer protection in food technology regulation is challenging, as it is an area where consumers are less literate, both in terms of processing information and making nutritional choices.

9.3 Food additives

Food additives are substances not normally consumed, but rather added to food for various technological purposes, such as preservation, to improve texture, or provide colour. With the rise of processed food, the use of additives has also risen.

Historically, there have been numerous food controversies regarding health risks associated with the consumption of additives. Intense disagreement regarding the safety of chemicals is common both at scientific and political levels. One notable example is the case of saccharin,[8] an artificial sweetener, which was found to be carcinogenic in some studies. Saccharin was initially banned in the US. However it was subsequently permitted again. Similarly, it is still permitted in many products in the EU market under the e-number label E954. In the same way, the conclusions on the carcinogenicity of aspartame (E951) are divided, with the World Health Organization (WHO) cancer research agency classifying the non-sugar sweetener now as 'possibly carcinogenic to humans' and establishing acceptable daily intakes (ADIs).[9] In most cases, the demonstration of conclusive long-term negative effects of specific chemicals is scientifically challenging, resulting in substantial scientific time lags and divided conclusions on safety. An example of a risk that was recognized only after years of being on the market is titanium dioxide (E171), which was only banned in the EU in 2022.

In the EU, food additives are governed by Regulation (EC) 1333/2008 (Food Additives Regulation). Additives are subject to the common authorization procedure in order to be added to a positive list of approved food additives in Annex II (food additives) and Annex III (food additives, enzymes, and flavourings). The lists contain the name of the food additive and its E number and conditions for use, as well as specifying categories of food to which the food additives may be added. Commission Regulation (EU) 231/2012[10] established specifications for food additives listed in Annexes II and III.

[8] Richard M Cooper, 'Saccharin—Of Risk and Democracy Food' (1985) 40 Drug, Cosmetic Law Journal 34.

[9] Elio Riboli and others, 'Carcinogenicity of Aspartame, Methyleugenol, and Isoeugenol' (2023) 24 The Lancet Oncology 848.

[10] Commission Regulation (EU) 231/2012 of 9 March 2012 laying down specifications for food additives listed in Annexes II and III to Regulation (EC) No 1333/2008 of the European Parliament and of the Council [2012] OJ L83/1.

9.3.1 *Scope, definition, and basic obligations*

What is a food additive from a legal perspective? A food additive is defined[11] as a substance that is (1) not normally consumed as food; (2) intentionally added for a technological purpose; and (3) remains in the product. Additionally, the Food Additives Regulation lists a number of substances that by definition are not considered food additives, such as starch or edible gelatine. Furthermore, the Food Additives Regulation does not apply to specific substances, notably processing aids.[12] To some extent, the definition of additives can therefore give rise to counter-intuitive classifications, for example the colouring extract of spirulina is not considered to be a food additive, while the enzymes Invertase (E1103) and Lysozyme (E1105) are classified as food additives.[13]

The fundamental rule of the Food Additives Regulation is that no person shall place on the market a food additive or any food containing it if its use does not comply with the Regulation.[14]

9.3.2 *Substantive conditions*

The Food Additives Regulation establishes functional classes for additives.[15] These are listed in Annex I, which distinguishes almost 30 different functional classes for different additives. Functional classes categorize food additives based on the specific technological role they play within the foodstuff; such as sweeteners, colours, preservatives, antioxidants, modified starches, gelling agents, emulsifiers, stabilizers, and anti-caking agents.

The Food Additives Regulation outlines a number of general substantive conditions with which an additive must comply:[16] there must be no concerns regarding its safety, there must be a reasonable technological need for it, and its use may not mislead the consumer. A food additive must have benefits, and serve one of the listed purposes. These include preserving the nutritional quality; meeting special dietary needs; enhancing the shelf life, stability, or organoleptic properties of a food; or aiding

[11] Food Additives Regulation, art 3(2)(a).
[12] Food Additives Regulation, art 2(2).
[13] Moisés Chong Sakihara, 'Food Ingredients with Technological Properties: The Four Rules for Classification as Food Additives or other Legal Categories of Food Substances' (2018) 13(5) European Food & Feed Law Review <https://www.jstor.org/stable/90026220?seq=1> accessed 29 July 2022.
[14] Food Additives Regulation, art 5.
[15] ibid, art 9.
[16] ibid, art 9.

in any step food production. There are also specific rules for particular classes of additives, such as sweeteners[17] and colour.[18]

The additional class-specific general rules for 'sweeteners' state that they may only be used to: (a) replace sugars for the production of energy-reduced food, non-cariogenic food, or food with no added sugars; (b) to increase the shelf life of food; or (c) to produce a food intended for particular nutritional uses.[19] To illustrate, Steviol Glycoside became authorized under the functional class of sweetener.[20] Energy reduction, however, requires the energy value to be reduced by at least 30% compared to the original or similar food.[21] Practically implementing a 30% reduction in energy value through the use of Steviol Glycoside in food reformulation has proven challenging. This is because Steviol Glycoside lacks bulking properties, and often has a taste that is disliked by many consumers.

The additional class-specific general rules for colours state that colours must have one of the following purposes: it must (a) restore the original appearance of food where the colour has been affected during food production; (b) make food more visually appealing; and (c) provide colour to food otherwise colourless.[22] The use of colours for markings is especially regulated.[23]

The carry-over principle[24] covers food additives that end up in food products incidentally, for example when they are used in another ingredient. Annex II lists the foods where the presence of additives due to carry-over is not allowed. Otherwise, the presence of a food additive is permitted under certain conditions,[25] for instance when it is present in a food exclusively because it was contained in one of the other ingredients, provided that it serves no technical function in the final product.

[17] ibid, art 6.
[18] ibid, art 8.
[19] ibid, art 7.
[20] Commission Regulation (EU) 1131/2011 of 11 November 2011 amending Annex II to Regulation (EC) No 1333/2008 of the European Parliament and of the Council with regard to steviol glycosides [2011] OJ L295/205.
[21] Food Additives Regulation, art 3(2)(f).
[22] ibid, art 8.
[23] ibid, art 17.
[24] ibid, art 18(1)(a).
[25] Specifically, '(a) in a compound food if the food additive is permitted in one of the ingredients of the compound food; (b) in a food to which a food additive, food enzyme or food flavouring has been added, where the food additive: (i) is permitted in the food additive, food enzyme or food flavouring in accordance with this Regulation; and (ii) has been carried over to the food via the food additive, food enzyme or food flavouring; and (iii) has no technological function in the final food; (c) in a food which is to be used solely in the preparation of a compound food and provided that the compound food complies with this Regulation'.

9.3.3 Union list of approved food additives and their conditions of use

A Union list of approved food additives is found in Annexes II and III. These Union lists collect what additives are allowed, in what foods, with what level of purity, and assigns them an E number and specific conditions of use. The lists have also been converted into a more user-friendly online database to provide information about the approved food additives for use in the EU and their respective conditions of use.[26] Annexes II and III are elaborated on in an additional Commission regulation,[27] and there is specific guidance on the food categories in Annex II.[28] The inclusion in the positive list is a generic authorization, which means that any FBO can use it.

These Union lists can be amended through the procedure in the Common Procedure Regulation under the common authorization procedure for food additives, food enzymes, and food flavourings (see section 9.7). Food additives that were permitted before 20 January 2009 are subject to a re-evaluation programme and undergo a new risk assessment by the European Food Safety Authority (EFSA).[29]

9.3.4 The permissible level of use of additives

The Food Additives Regulation establishes that the level of use[30] should be the lowest use necessary to achieve the desired effect. For some additives, the Regulation sets maximum levels (MLs), while for others the *quantum satis* principle applies. The *quantum satis* principle means that 'no maximum numerical level is specified and substances shall be used in accordance with good manufacturing practice, at a level not higher than is necessary to achieve the intended purpose and provided the consumer is not misled'.[31]

[26] European Commission's Directorate-General for Health and Food Safety, 'Food Additives Database' <https://webgate.ec.europa.eu/foods_system/main/?sector=FAD&auth=SANCAS> accessed 29 July 2022.

[27] Commission Regulation (EU) 231/2012 of 9 March 2012 laying down specifications for food additives listed in Annexes II and III to Regulation (EC) No 1333/2008 of the European Parliament and of the Council [2012] OJ L83/1.

[28] Commission, *Guidance document describing the food categories in Part E of Annex II to Regulation (EC) No 1333/2008 on Food Additives* (2017).

[29] Commission Regulation (EU) 257/2010 of 25 March 2010 setting up a programme for the re-evaluation of approved food additives in accordance with Regulation (EC) No 1333/2008 of the European Parliament and of the Council on food additives [2010] OJ L80/19, which in turn has been complemented by the Commission Implementing Regulation (EU) 2021/148 of 8 February 2021 amending Regulation (EU) No 257/2010 setting up a programme for the re-evaluation of approved food additives in accordance with Regulation (EC) No 1333/2008 of the European Parliament and of the Council on food additives [2021] OJ L44/3.

[30] Food Additives Regulation, art 11.

[31] ibid, art 3(2)(h).

Unless explicitly allowed, no additives may be used in unprocessed foods.[32] Member States may also prohibit the use of certain categories of food additives in some traditional foods produced on their territory.[33] For instance, the Regulation contains an exception for the German ban on additives in beers labelled traditional German beer (*Bier nach deutschem Reinheitsgebot gebraut*). In addition, the use of additives in foods for infants and young children is prohibited, unless explicitly allowed.[34]

9.3.5 *Labelling*

The Food Additives Regulation specifies informational rules that apply to sales to the final consumer.[35] Additionally, in contrast to the Food Information to Consumers Regulation (FICR),[36] it also stipulates requirements for sales not intended for the final consumer, such as business-to-business transactions.[37]

In addition, the general food information to consumer rules apply. Food additives are considered ingredients under the FICR,[38] and must be designated by the name of their category, followed by their specific name or, if appropriate, E number.[39] Food additives solely present due to the 'carry-over principle' can be omitted from the list of ingredients, as can food additives used as processing aids.[40] Additives are also exempt from the nutrition declaration.[41]

Table-top sweeteners have specific labelling rules; they must include the term '(. . .) -based table-top sweetener', using the name(s) of the sweetener(s) used in its composition. In addition, sweeteners containing polyols and/or aspartame must use the following warnings: (a) polyols: 'excessive consumption may induce laxative effects'; (b) aspartame/aspartame-acesulfame salt: 'contains a source of phenylalanine'.[42]

32 ibid, art 15.

33 Annex IV of Additives Food Regulation contains a list of traditional foods for which certain Member States may continue to prohibit the use of certain categories of food additives.

34 Food Additives Regulation, art 16 and Annex II.

35 ibid, art 23.

36 Regulation (EU) 1169/2011 of the European Parliament and of the Council of 25 October 2011 on the provision of food information to consumers, amending Regulation (EC) No 1924/2006 and (EC) No 1295/2006 of the European Parliament and of the Council, and repealing Commission Directive 87/250/EEC, Council Directive 90/496/EEC, Commission Directive 1999/10/EC, Directive 2000/13/EC of the European Parliament and of the Council, Commission Directives 2002/67/EC and 2008/5/EC and Commission Regulation (EC) No 608/2004 [2011] OJ L304/18 (Food Information to Consumers Regulation, FICR).

37 Food Additives Regulation, art 22.

38 FICR, art 2(2)(f).

39 ibid, pt C of Annex VII.

40 ibid, art 20(b).

41 ibid, point 11 of Annex V.

42 Food Additives Regulation, art 23(3).

There are also specific labelling requirements for foods containing certain food colours.[43]

9.3.6 *Specific procedural aspects of additives*

The common authorization procedure applies (see section 9.7) for authorizations. The authorization procedure has been updated by the Transparency Regulation,[44] to ensure the respective transparency to the public, the mandatory submission of studies, and included confidentiality and data protection provisions.[45] During the re-evaluation programme, EFSA could not confirm the safety of all food additives due to insufficient data, for instance for all uses. The Commission has therefore established additional implementing rules for additives that allow supplementary data collection in order to address remaining safety uncertainties as identified in EFSA opinions.[46] Parties may also request a pre-admission advice as to the requirements of an application.[47]

9.4 Food enzymes

Enzymes are proteins with catalytic functions—that is, they affect biochemical reactions without changing themselves. Enzymes are extensively utilized in food technology, commonly in baking, dairy processing, meat products processing, fermentation, and beverage processing. For instance, Amylase can be used to enhance bread volume and texture, Tannase is used to improve the flavour of tea and avoid clouding, and Protease can be used to influence foam quality in beer. In these applications, enzymes may become an integral part of the food product (eg yeast in bread), or merely induce a functional change. Classification and nomenclature of enzymes is based on the reactions they catalyse, however enzyme classification remains a major challenge.[48] The EU follows the nomenclature of the International Union of Biochemistry and Molecular Biology (IUBMB).

[43] ibid, art 24, as specified in Annex V.

[44] Regulation (EU) 2019/1391 of the European Parliament and of the Council of 20 June 2019 on the transparency and sustainability of the EU risk assessment in the food chain and amending Regulations (EC) No 178/2002, (EC) No 1829/2003, (EC) No 1831/2003, (EC) No 2065/2003, (EC) No 1935/2004, (EC) No 1331/2008, (EC) No 1107/2009, (EU) 2015/2283 and Directive 2001/18/EC [2019] OJ L231/1 (Transparency Regulation).

[45] Transparency Regulation amendments and additionally through the Commission Implementing Regulation (EU) 2021/148, arts 7c, 7d, 7e, and 8.

[46] Commission Implementing Regulation (EU) 2021/148, art 7a.

[47] ibid, art 7b.

[48] John F Roland, 'Regulation of Food Enzymes' (1981) 3 Enzyme and Microbial Technology 105.

Enzymes do not typically pose safety hazards,[49] and those that exist are regarded as well-understood.[50] Safety concerns stem in part from the fact that the industrial processing is not chemically pure.[51] Known enzyme hazards include 'plant toxins (eg, ricin), animal toxins (eg, prions), allergens (eg, gluten protein, Ara H2), antinutrients (eg, trypsin inhibitors, lectins), and pathogenic bacterial toxins (eg, shiga toxins, botulinum)'.[52] In addition, occupational safety concerns arise for those regularly exposed to enzymes, as they are known as inhalation sensitizers that may cause allergic reactions.[53]

In the US, enzymes were regulated relatively early on. They were regarded as food additives, and began undergoing evaluations by the US Federal Drug Administration under the Food, Drug and Cosmetic (FDC) Act as early as 1957.[54] In contrast, in the EU, only enzymes used exclusively in the production of food additives are governed as food additives—attention to enzymes as an independent type of food improvement agent was first raised in the 1990s due to controversy regarding the increasing use of genetically modified microorganisms to produce enzymes.[55] Unlike food additives and flavourings, food enzymes not used as food additives were thus largely[56] unregulated in the EU. It was only in 2008 that the Enzymes Regulation was passed, governing the use of food enzymes for technological purposes. The Commission is still in the process of establishing a Union list for authorized enzymes. Until the Union list is finalized, the Regulation does not apply and only Member States' law is applicable.[57] To date, Denmark[58] and France[59] have national legislation on enzymes, while Germany, Switzerland, and Austria have had safety reviews. Consequently, enzymes remain virtually unregulated in the EU.

[49] Gregory S Ladics and others, 'Safety Assessment and Regulation of Food Enzymes' in Selim Kermasha and Michael NA Eskin (eds), *Enzymes: Novel Biotechnological Approaches for the Food Industry* (Academic Press 2021).

[50] ibid.

[51] Roland (n 48).

[52] Ladics and others (n 49).

[53] Armin Spök, 'Safety Regulations of Food Enzymes' (2006) 44 Food Technology and Biotechnology 197.

[54] ibid.

[55] ibid.

[56] Subject to very specific exceptions: Council Directive 83/417/EEC of 25 July 1983 on the approximation of the laws of the Member States relating to certain lactoproteins (caseins and caseinates) intended for human consumption [1983] OJ L237/25 (repealed); and regulations on cheese, wine, and fruit juices, where, for example, Council Regulation (EC) 1493/1999 of 17 May 1999 on the common organisation of the market in wine [1999] OJ L179/1 (repealed) authorizes the use of urease, betaglucanase, and lysozyme in wine.

[57] Enzymes Regulation, art 24.

[58] Bekendtgørelse om tilsætninger mv. til fødevarer 1) [2020].

[59] Arrêté du 19 octobre 2006 relatif à l'emploi d'auxiliaires technologiques dans la fabrication de certaines denrées alimentaires [2006] JORF 279.

9.4.1 *Scope and definition*

A food enzyme is in the law is defined as

> a product obtained from plants, animals or micro-organisms or products thereof including a product obtained by a fermentation process using micro-organisms if they satisfy two cumulative conditions, (i) containing enzymes capable of catalyzing a specific biochemical reaction; and (ii) added to food for a technological purpose.[60]

Only enzymes that are added to food to perform a technological function are covered by the Enzymes Regulation; enzymes that are intended for human consumption, such as enzymes for nutritional or digestive purposes, are not regulated at EU level.[61] The Enzymes Regulation does not apply to microbial cultures that are traditionally used and that incidentally produce enzymes. Food enzymes used to produce food additives or processing aids are also not governed by the Enzymes Regulation;[62] if used exclusively in the production of food additives they fall within the scope of the Food Additives Regulation. This is why, for example, the enzymes Invertase (E1103) and Lysozym (E1105) are classified as food additives.

In order to support FBOs in determining the status of an enzyme either as an ingredient or as a processing aid, and consequently whether it needs to be included in the list of ingredients, the Standing Committee on the Food Chain and Animal Health has issued an (informal) guidance document.[63]

9.4.2 *Approval of enzymes at EU level is pending—the missing Union list*

Once the Regulation applies, food enzymes can only be placed on the market and used in foods when they are included in the Union list and comply with their respective specifications and conditions of use. The Union list is amended in accordance with the Common Procedure Regulation (see section 9.7).

[60] Enzymes Regulation, art 3(2)(a).
[61] ibid, Recital (4).
[62] ibid, art 2(2).
[63] Standing Committee on the Food Chain and Animal Health, *Guidance Document on Criteria for Categorisation of Food* Enzymes (2014).

As the Union list is not yet complete, there is only a register of enzymes for which a valid application has been made. The final Union list will be drawn up once all of the over 300[64] registered valid food enzyme applications have been assessed for safety.

An example of an evaluated enzyme is a food enzyme known as a xylanase. Xylanase is used in starch processing, alcohol distillation, and baking processes. It is produced by fermenting a strain of Aspergillus oryzae, which has a long history of safe use, but also potentially produces mycotoxins as secondary metabolites. To avoid this, the Aspergillus used to produce this food enzyme has been genetically modified. EFSA, after a full risk assessment, concluded that there were no safety concerns.[65]

9.4.3 *General principles of use and specific conditions*

The Regulation stipulates three general conditions for inclusion in the Union list: enzymes may not pose a safety concern, there must be a reasonable technological need to use them, and the use may not mislead the consumer. Misleading the consumer includes issues related to the nature, freshness and quality, naturalness, and nutritional quality of the enzyme.[66]

The entry in the Union list contains the specific conditions for utilizing food enzymes: the name and the specifications of the food enzyme, including its origin, purity criteria, and any other necessary information; the foods to which it may be added; and the conditions under which the food enzyme may be used. An ML of use may be fixed, otherwise the food enzyme should be used in accordance with the *quantum satis* principle. Where necessary, labelling conditions may be set. In addition, there may be restrictions on selling directly to the final consumer.[67]

[64] Marie Deckers and others, 'Food Enzyme Database (FEDA): A Web Application Gathering Information about Food Enzyme Preparations Available on the European Market' (2021) 2021 <https://academic.oup.com/database/article/doi/10.1093/database/baab060/6385791> accessed 29 July 2022.

[65] EFSA Panel on Food Contact Material, Enzymes, Flavourings and Processing Aids (CEF), 'Scientific Opinion on Xylanase from a Genetically Modified Strain of Aspergillus oryzae (strain NZYM-FB)' (2014) 12(5) EFSA Journal <https://efsa.onlinelibrary.wiley.com/doi/abs/10.2903/j.efsa.2014.3645 > accessed 29 July 2022.

[66] Enzymes Regulation, art 6.

[67] ibid, art 7.

9.4.4 Labelling

The Enzymes Regulation stipulates labelling requirements for food enzymes intended for sale to the final consumer, and some that apply in a business-to-business context.

In addition, the FICR defines enzymes as ingredients,[68] which must be indicated in the list of ingredients. However, enzymes that are present because they were contained in an ingredient and which do not serve a technological function do not need to be specified in the list of ingredients, for example enzymes used as processing aids may be omitted.[69] Flavourings, food additives, processing aids, and food enzymes are also exempt from requiring a nutrition declaration.[70]

Enzymes are listed in the ingredient list by naming their category followed by their specific name or E number. Where an ingredient belongs to more than one of the categories, the category of the principal function must be indicated.[71]

9.5 Food flavouring

Food flavourings have been commercially branded since the end of the eighteenth century, when, for instance, flavoured chewing gum was marketed for the first time.[72]

Since 1988, flavourings and source materials have been subject to harmonization under the approximation of law of the Member States mandate of Article 100a TFEU.[73] Regulation (EC) 2232/96[74] then set the main rules on flavourings in foods within the EU and initiated a procedure to establish an EU list of flavourings. The safety of thousands of flavourings was evaluated by EFSA, resulting in a list of over

[68] FICR, art 2(2)(f).

[69] ibid, art 20(b)(i) and (ii).

[70] ibid, Annex V.

[71] ibid, pt C of Annex VI.

[72] IGH Flavours & Technology, 'Food Flavours: 13 Key Steps in History' (14 October 2020) <https://igharoma.com/en/food-flavours-13-key-steps-in-history/> accessed 29 July 2022.

[73] Council Directive 88/388/EEC of 22 June 1988 on the approximation of the laws of the Member States relating to flavourings for use in foodstuffs and to source materials for their production [1988] OJ L184/61; Council Decision 88/389/EEC on 22 June 1988 on the establishment, by the Commission, of an inventory of the source materials and substances used in the preparation of flavourings [1988] OJ L184/67.

[74] Regulation (EC) 2232/96 of the European Parliament and of the Council of 28 October 1996 laying down a Community procedure for flavouring substances used or intended for use in or on foodstuffs [1996] OJ L299/1 (repealed).

2,000 flavourings that are considered safe for human consumption in the evaluation programme for food flavourings.[75]

As part of the FIAP, food flavourings are now governed by the Flavourings Regulation and the Common Procedure Regulation that introduced the common approval procedure for FIAP. Flavourings that are approved for use with foodstuffs are listed in the Union list, adopted in October 2012[76] and contained in Annex I of the Flavourings Regulation. This information is accessible on the online food flavouring database,[77] making it easier to access and reference.

In addition there is a specific Commission Implementing Regulation (EU) 1321/2013 on smoke flavourings.[78]

9.5.1 Scope

The Regulation covers flavourings which are used in or on foods; food ingredients with flavouring properties; food containing flavourings and/or food ingredients with flavouring properties; and the source materials (see Table 9.1 for an overview of flavouring categories).[79] Legally, flavourings are defined as products

> (i) not intended to be consumed as such, which are added to food in order to impart or modify odour and/or taste; and (ii) made or consisting of the following categories: flavouring substances, flavouring preparations, thermal process flavourings, smoke flavourings, flavour precursors or other flavourings or mixtures thereof.[80]

[75] Commission Regulation (EC) 1565/2000 of 18 July 2000 laying down the measures necessary for the adoption of an evaluation programme in application of Regulation (EC) No 2232/96 of the European Parliament and of the Council [2000] OJ L180/8 (repealed). This Regulation will remain in force until a number of substances for which the EU risk assessment have not been completed at the time of entry into force of Commission Implementing Regulation (EC) No 872/2012 of 1 October 2012 adopting the list of flavouring substances provided for by Regulation (EC) No 2232/96 of the European Parliament and of the Council, introducing it in Annex I to Regulation (EC) No 1334/2008 of the European Parliament and of the Council and repealing Commission Regulation (EC) No 1565/2000 and Commission Decision 1999/217/EC [2012] OJ L267/1, have been fully evaluated and added to the Union list. At that time, the authorization procedure for flavourings under the Common Procedure Regulation will be fully applicable.

[76] Commission Implementing Regulation (EU) 872/2012 (n 75).

[77] European Commission's Directorate-General for Health and Food Safety (n 26).

[78] Commission Implementing Regulation (EU) 1321/2013 of 10 December 2013 establishing the Union list of authorised smoke flavouring primary products for use as such in or on foods and/or for the production of derived smoke flavourings [2013] OJ L333/54.

[79] Flavourings Regulation, art 2(1).

[80] ibid, art 3.

Table 9.1 Overview of flavouring categories

Flavouring category	Legal definition	Examples[81]
Flavouring substances	a defined chemical substance with flavouring properties	Menthol, ethyl butyrate
- Natural flavouring substance	'natural flavouring substance' shall mean a flavouring substance obtained by appropriate physical, enzymatic or microbiological processes from material of vegetable, animal or microbiological origin either in the raw state or after processing for human consumption by one or more of the traditional food preparation processes listed in Annex II. Natural flavouring substances correspond to substances that are naturally present and have been identified in nature.	Vanillin, menthol obtained by fractioned distillation from mint oil; Limonene obtained by steam distillation from oranges
Flavouring preparations	a product, other than a flavouring substance, obtained from: (i) food by appropriate physical, enzymatic or microbiological processes either in the raw state of the material or after processing for human consumption by one or more of the traditional food preparation processes listed in Annex II; and/or (ii) material of vegetable, animal or microbiological origin, other than food, by appropriate physical, enzymatic or microbiological processes, the material being taken as such or prepared by one or more of the traditional food preparation processes listed in Annex II.	Vanilla or mint extract; Orange oil or black pepper oleoresin
- natural flavouring preparation		
Thermal process flavourings	a product obtained after heat treatment from a mixture of ingredients not necessarily having flavouring properties themselves, of which at least one contains nitrogen (amino) and another is a reducing sugar; the ingredients for the production of thermal process flavourings may be: (i) food; and/or (ii) source material other than food.	

[81] Examples derive in part from the FoodDrinkEurope, 'Guidelines on Flavourings' (8 October 2019) <https://www.fooddrinkeurope.eu/wp-content/uploads/publications_documents/Guidelines_on_Flavourings_-_FoodDrinkEurope.pdf> accessed 10 August 2022.

Smoke flavourings	a product obtained by fractionation and purification of a condensed smoke yielding primary smoke condensates, primary tar fractions and/or derived smoke flavourings as defined in points (1), (2) and (4) of Article 3 of Regulation (EC) No 2065/2003.	
Flavour precursors	a product, not necessarily having flavouring properties itself, intentionally added to food for the sole purpose of producing flavour by breaking down or reacting with other components during food processing; it may be obtained from: (i) food; and/or (ii) source material other than food;	Carbohydrates, oligopeptides, amino acids
Other flavourings	a flavouring added or intended to be added to food in order to impart odour and/or taste and which does not fall under definitions (b) to (g).	Rum ether is a 'complex flavour mixture' (therefore not a flavouring preparation)
Food ingredient with flavouring properties	a food ingredient other than flavourings which may be added to food for the main purpose of adding flavour to it or modifying its flavour and which contributes significantly to the presence in food of certain naturally occurring undesirable substances.	Cinnamon (contains Coumarin) in bakery wares
'source material'	material of vegetable, animal, microbiological or mineral origin from which flavourings or food ingredients with flavouring properties are produced; it may be: (i) food; or (ii) source material other than food;	Unprocessed food (Fruits, vegetables, mushrooms, meat, fish, rose petals, spices, aromatic plants) or processed food (black soya beans (fermentation/torrefaction), Cheese (enzymatic action), Green Tea (torrefaction).

Source: Flavourings Regulation.

The Regulation does not apply to substances which have exclusively a sweet, sour, or salty taste; raw foods; and non-compound foods.[82]

9.5.2 *General and specific conditions*

The general conditions are that flavourings may not pose a safety risk to consumer health, and that their use may not mislead consumers.[83]

Other substances are subject to specific conditions, the 'Regulated Substances'. The Regulation regulates the presence of substances, it prohibits 15 substances that may not be added to food,[84] and sets maximum MLs for 11 'naturally present' substances by reference to specific compound food.[85] Source materials are also regulated, either by prohibiting them,[86] or by setting conditions of use.

9.5.3 *Basic requirement*

Flavourings and foods that do not comply with the Regulation may not be placed on the market.[87] There are some flavourings and food ingredients with flavouring properties that do not require evaluation and approval (see Table 9.2), as long as they comply with the general conditions of use.

For the remaining flavourings and source materials, only those included in the Union list may be placed on the market as such and used in or on foods under the conditions of use specified.[88]

Specifically, the substances in Table 9.3 require approval.

9.5.4 *Union list*

The Regulation contains a Union list of approved flavourings and source materials for use in and on foods, conditions of use, and rules on the labelling of flavourings.[89] This list can be updated through the common authorization procedure (see section 9.7).

[82] Flavourings Regulation, art 2(2).
[83] ibid, art 4.
[84] ibid, pt A of Annex III.
[85] ibid, pt B of Annex III.
[86] ibid, Annex IV.
[87] ibid, art 5.
[88] ibid, art 10.
[89] ibid, Annex I.

Table 9.2 *Flavourings and food ingredients with flavouring properties for which evaluation and approval are not required*

(a) **flavouring preparations** referred to in Article 3(2)(d)(i);	(d) 'flavouring preparation' shall mean a product, other than a flavouring substance, obtained from: (i) food by appropriate physical, enzymatic or microbiological processes either in the raw state of the material or after processing for human consumption by one or more of the traditional food preparation processes listed in Annex II; and/or (...)
(b) **thermal process flavourings** referred to in Article 3(2)(e) (i) which comply with the conditions for the production of thermal process flavourings and maximum levels for certain substances in thermal process flavourings set out in Annex V;	(e) 'thermal process flavouring' shall mean a product obtained after heat treatment from a mixture of ingredients not necessarily having flavouring properties themselves, of which at least one contains nitrogen (amino) and another is a reducing sugar; the ingredients for the production of thermal process flavourings may be: (i) food; (...)
(c) **flavour precursors** referred to in Article 3(2)(g)(i);	(g) 'flavour precursor' shall mean a product, not necessarily having flavouring properties itself, intentionally added to food for the sole purpose of producing flavour by breaking down or reacting with other components during food processing; it may be obtained from: (i) food; (...)
(d) **food ingredients with flavouring properties.**	(i) 'food ingredient with flavouring properties' shall mean a food ingredient other than flavourings which may be added to food for the main purpose of adding flavour to it or modifying its flavour and which contributes significantly to the presence in food of certain naturally occurring undesirable substances.

Source: Flavourings Regulation, art 8.

9.5.5 Labelling

In addition to the general labelling requirements in the FICR, the Flavouring Regulation lays down consumer and business-to-business labelling rules, and special rules for use of the term 'natural'.

The specific rules for the labelling of flavourings in and on foods apply when sold to the general public[90] and from business-to-business.[91]

[90] ibid, art 17.
[91] ibid, arts 14 and 15.

Table 9.3 Flavourings and source materials for which an evaluation and approval is required

(a) flavouring substances;	a defined chemical substance with flavouring properties
(b) flavouring preparations referred to in Article 3(2)(d)(ii);	(d) 'flavouring preparation' shall mean a product, other than a flavouring substance, obtained from: (...) (ii) material of vegetable, animal or microbiological origin, other than food, by appropriate physical, enzymatic or microbiological processes, the material being taken as such or prepared by one or more of the traditional food preparation processes listed in Annex II. Example: orange oil.
(c) thermal process flavourings obtained by heating ingredients which fall partially or totally within Article 3(2)(e)(ii) and/or for which the conditions for the production of thermal process flavourings and/or the maximum levels for certain undesirable substances set out in Annex V are not met;	(e) 'thermal process flavouring' shall mean a product obtained after heat treatment from a mixture of ingredients not necessarily having flavouring properties themselves, of which at least one contains nitrogen (amino) and another is a reducing sugar; the ingredients for the production of thermal process flavourings may be: (...) (ii) source material other than food.
(d) flavour precursors referred to in Article 3(2)(g)(ii);	(g) 'flavour precursor' shall mean a product, not necessarily having flavouring properties itself, intentionally added to food for the sole purpose of producing flavour by breaking down or reacting with other components during food processing; it may be obtained from: (...) (ii) source material other than food.
(e) other flavourings referred to in Article 3(2)(h);	(h) 'other flavouring' shall mean a flavouring added or intended to be added to food in order to impart odour and/or taste and which does not fall under definitions (b) to (g);
(f) source materials other than food referred to in Article 3(2)(j)(ii).	(j) 'source material' shall mean material of vegetable, animal, microbiological or mineral origin from which flavourings or food ingredients with flavouring properties are produced; it may be: (...) (ii) source material other than food.

Source: Flavourings Regulation, art 9.

9.5.5.1. Using the term 'natural'

The specific conditions for using the term 'natural' are valid both in the business-to-business and the consumer labelling context. If the term 'natural' is used to describe a flavouring, the word 'flavouring' or a more specific name or description

Table 9.4 The term 'natural' and flavourings

How 'natural' may be used	Rule	Example of use
'natural flavouring substance(s)'	A flavouring substance obtained by appropriate physical, enzymatic, or microbiological processes from material of vegetable, animal or microbiological origin either in the raw state or after processing for human consumption by one or more of the traditional food preparation processes listed in Annex II. Natural flavouring substances correspond to substances that are naturally present and have been identified in nature;[94] May only be used for flavourings in which the flavouring component contains exclusively natural flavouring substances.[95]	
'natural "food(s) or food category or source(s)" flavouring'	'Natural' may only be used in combination with a reference to a food, food category, or a vegetable or animal flavouring source if the flavouring component has been obtained exclusively or by at least 95% by w/w from the source material referred to.	If flavouring component has >95% banana, then 'natural banana flavouring' Banana is a food, red berries are a food category.
'natural "food(s) or food category or source(s)" flavouring with other natural flavourings'	May only be used if the flavouring component is partially derived from the source material referred to, the flavour of which can easily be recognized.	If flavouring component is partially <95% from banana, but the flavour profile is banana, then 'natural banana flavourings with other natural flavourings'.
'natural flavouring'	May only be used if the flavouring component is derived from different source materials and where a reference to the source materials would not reflect their flavour or taste.	If flavouring component is 0% banana, but the flavour profile is banana, then 'natural flavouring'.
'natural flavouring preparation'	According to the definition obtained from food and material of vegetable, animal, or microbiological origin[96] in ways that result in them always regarded as natural.[97]	

Source: Flavourings Regulation, art 3. Examples derive in part from the FoodDrinkEurope, 'Guidelines on Flavourings' (8 October 2019) <https://www.fooddrinkeurope.eu/wp-content/uploads/publications_documents/Guidelines_on_Flavourings_-_FoodDrinkEurope.pdf> accessed 10 August 2022.

of the flavouring must be used.[92] 'Natural' may only be used for the categories 'flavouring preparations' and/or 'natural flavouring substances' (see Table 9.4 for the term 'natural' and flavourings).[93]

[92] ibid, art 16(1).
[93] ibid, art 16(2).
[94] ibid, art 3(2)(c).
[95] ibid, art 16(3).
[96] ibid, art 3(2)(d)(ii).
[97] European Commission, 'FAQ: Food: EU adopts list of approved flavouring substances' (1 October 2012) <https://ec.europa.eu/commission/presscorner/detail/en/MEMO_12_723> accessed 29 July 2022.

In practical applications, the 'natural' distinction remains difficult, even where it is regulated, such as flavourings. EFSA, for instance, advises against using the term 'natural' in combination with smoke flavourings to avoid misleading the consumer as to the naturalness of the product or production process.[98] From a conceptual point of view, 'natural' is used in opposition to 'artificial' flavours, which is a distinction largely dependent on the original raw materials used.

9.5.6 The special case of smoke flavourings

Due to the specific safety concerns they raise, additional rules apply to smoke flavourings. The Smoke Flavouring Regulation[99] governs the evaluation and authorization of primary smoke condensates and primary tar fractions for use as such in or on foods or in the production of derived smoke flavourings for use in or on foods, and establishes an authorization list for these substances.[100]

The Regulation contains rules on smoke flavourings used or intended for use in or on foods; source materials for the production of smoke flavourings; the conditions under which smoke flavourings are prepared; and foods in or on which smoke flavourings are present.[101]

The general conditions are that smoke flavourings may only be authorized if they pose no risks to human health, and do not mislead consumers. Each authorization may be subject to specific conditions of use.[102] Smoke flavourings or products using them must comply with the Regulation, otherwise they cannot be marketed.[103]

There are special conditions for production.[104] For instance, wood used for primary production must not have undergone chemicals treatment within six months prior to felling, unless the non-toxicity of those substances is demonstrated. The conditions for the production of primary products are further specified in Annex I.

The Regulation also establishes the positive Union list of authorized primary products and their conditions of use.[105]

To be included in the positive list of authorized smoke flavourings, an application must be made to the Member State authority.[106] The Regulation therefore does not follow the common authorization procedure of the FIAP. The Member

[98] EFFA, 'Guidance Document on EC Regulation on Flavourings' (July 2019) <https://cdn2.assets-servd.host/aggressive-shelduck/production/Documents/Guidance/effa-guidance-document-on-the-ec-regulation-on-flavourings-updated-july-2019.pdf> accessed 29 July 2022, 22.

[99] Regulation (EC) 2065/2003 of the European Parliament and of the Council of 10 November 2003 on some flavourings used or intended for use in or on foods [2003] OJ L309/1 (Smoke Flavouring Regulation).

[100] ibid, art 1(2).

[101] ibid, art 2.

[102] ibid, art 4.

[103] ibid, art 4(2).

[104] ibid, art 5.

[105] ibid, art 6.

[106] ibid, art 7.

State informs EFSA to request an opinion, and other Member States and the Commission. EFSA generally gives its opinion within six months, and forwards it to the Commission, the Member States, and the applicant. The Commission either proceeds to prepare a draft regulation for the authorization or a draft decision on the refusal for authorization.[107] Applications are renewable for a ten-year period.[108]

Applications for authorization, supplementary information from applicants, and opinions from the Authority must be made public,[109] unless a successful confidentiality request has been made by the applicant. This cannot cover information that is relevant in order to protect public health.[110] The data used by an applicant is proprietary and may not be used for other applications.[111]

At the first stage of placing an authorized primary product or smoke flavouring on the market, FBOs must ensure traceability and provide detailed information to the FBA receiving the product.[112]

9.6 Processing aids

In order to apply the legal framework, substances that are used in the food or production process need to be classified according to their legal category. It is important to note that from a food technology perspective, the legal definitions do not perfectly align with their technological use; however, in order to classify which legal framework is applicable, the legal categories take precedence. Processing aids are particularly challenging to categorize within this framework.

Processing aids are substances that are not consumed in the food itself, and are intentionally used to fulfil a certain technological purpose during the processing stage, even though unavoidable residues may be present in the final product.[113] A processing aid is therefore not deliberately added to the food (despite unavoidable residues), whereas food additives are deliberatively incorporated and become a component of the food.

Consequently, food processing aids are explicitly excluded from the Food Additives Regulation.[114] In contrast, food enzymes used as processing aids are—legally speaking—enzymes.[115]

The Regulation on the addition of vitamins and minerals and of certain other substances to foods equally excludes processing aids. This is because 'other

[107] ibid, art 9(1).
[108] ibid, art 12.
[109] ibid, art 14.
[110] ibid, art 15.
[111] ibid, art 16.
[112] ibid, art 13.
[113] Food Additives Regulation, art 3(2)(b).
[114] ibid, art 2.
[115] Enzymes Regulation, art 1.

substances' are defined as substances other than vitamins or minerals that have a nutritional or physiological effect while this is not the case for processing aids.[116]

There may be an interest in regulating processing aids more closely in the future. For instance, there are research studies that show processing aids have a significant impact on the elemental composition of foodstuffs. Filtering aids, such as bentonite, are often composed of mined minerals, and can release trace elements that include heavy metals.[117]

9.7 Common authorization procedure: Commission Regulation (EU) 234/2011

Regulation (EU) 234/2011[118] created a common procedure for updating the Union lists for food additives, enzymes, and flavourings. Updating means adding, removing, or changing the conditions to which substances are subject.[119]

9.7.1 Procedural aspects

The main stages of the common procedure to update the Union lists are the following:[120] the procedure for updating the lists can be taken by the Commission either on their own initiative, or the application of an EU Member Sate or another party. The Commission requests an EFSA opinion, unless an update has no health effects. EFSA issues the opinion within nine months,[121] but can request additional information for the risk assessment with extended timelines.[122] Within nine months of receiving the EFSA opinion, the Commission presents a draft regulation to update the Union lists to the Standing Committee on the Food Chain and Animal Health established by Article 58 of Regulation (EC) 178/2002.[123] The

[116] Regulation (EC) 1925/2006 of the European Parliament and of the Council of 20 December 2006 on the addition of vitamins and minerals and of certain other substances to foods [2006] OJ L404/26, art 2(2).

[117] Benjamin W Redan, 'Processing Aids in Food and Beverage Manufacturing: Potential Source of Elemental and Trace Metal Contaminants' (2020) 68 Journal of Agricultural and Food Chemistry 13001.

[118] Commission Regulation (EU) 234/2011 implementing Regulation (EC) No 1331/2008 of the European Parliament and of the Council establishing a common authorisation procedure for food additives, food enzymes and food flavourings [2011] OJ L64/15 (Common Procedure Regulation).

[119] ibid, art 2(2).

[120] ibid, art 3.

[121] ibid, art 5.

[122] ibid, art 6.

[123] Regulation (EC) 178/2002 of the European Parliament and of the Council of 28 January 2002 laying down the general principles and requirements of food law, establishing the European Food Safety Authority and laying down procedures in matters of food safety [2002] OJ L31/1.

draft regulation then follows the Committee Procedure (see Chapter 3). Legally speaking, the update of the Union lists is handled through separate Commission regulations, such as Commission Regulation (EU) 2022/63, which banned the previously approved additive E171 (Titanium Dioxide) for use in foodstuffs, because it was no longer considered safe.[124]

9.7.2 *Transparency and confidentiality*

The Transparency Regulation introduced a requirement for EFSA to publish applications and supporting information.[125] Applicants can request that certain parts of the information submitted remain confidential, which is assessed by EFSA according to the Transparency Regulation updates. In addition to general information that may be protected, certain information can be kept confidential. This includes information about starting substances and starting preparations, as well as how they are used to manufacture the substance subject to the authorization; detailed information on the nature and composition of the materials or products that the applicant intends to use, except for information which is relevant to the assessment of safety; and analytical information on the variability and stability of individual production batches of the substance. However, information that is relevant to the assessment of safety cannot be made confidential.[126]

9.8 Extraction solvents

Extraction is used to separate (extract) soluble components from raw materials by dissolving them in an extraction solvent. Common extraction processes are, for instance, to decaffeinate coffees and teas, the extraction of sugar from sugarbeets, oil from seeds, and generally separate other compounds, such as vitamins, proteins, aroma, and flavours.

Differences between Member States' laws on extraction solvents were seen as obstacles to the free movement of foodstuffs. Therefore, extraction solvents have been regulated in the EU since 1988[127] on the basis of Article 100a TFEU for the approximation of laws of the Member States. The most recent recast of the Directive was adopted in 2009.[128]

124 Commission Regulation (EU) 2022/63 of 14 January 2022 amending Annexes II and III to Regulation (EC) No 1333/2008 of the European Parliament and of the Council as regards the food additive titanium dioxide (E 171) [2022] OJ L11/1.

125 Transparency Regulation, art 11.

126 ibid, art 12.

127 Council Directive 88/344/EEC of 13 June 1988 on the approximation of the laws of the Member States on extraction solvents used in the production of foodstuffs and food ingredients [1988] OJ L157/28 (repealed) (Extraction Solvents Directive).

128 ibid.

The Extraction Solvents Directive sets common standards with the double objective of ensuring the free movement of foodstuffs and safe food processing.

9.8.1 Scope

The Extraction Solvents Directive applies to extraction solvents used in the production of food additives, vitamins, and other nutritional additives, unless such food additives, vitamins, or nutritional additives are listed in Annex I. An extraction solvent is defined as

> a solvent which is used in an extraction procedure during the processing of raw materials, of foodstuffs, or of components or ingredients of these products and which is removed but which may result in the unintentional, but technically unavoidable, presence of residues or derivatives in the foodstuff or food ingredient.[129]

9.8.2 Basic requirement

Only the use of specific extraction solvents that are listed in Annex I of the Extraction Solvents Directive is permitted in the EU. The Directive is directed towards the Member States and creates an obligation to authorize the Directive's extraction solvents under the conditions stipulated. Member States may not prohibit extraction solvents that are compliant with the Directive, and they may not authorize other extraction solvents. The law is therefore an example of exhaustive harmonization. As it is a Directive, Member States must implement it at national level.

9.8.3 General conditions for extraction solvents

The Extraction Solvents Directive stipulates overarching general conditions for extraction solvents. They must (a) not contain a toxicologically dangerous amount of any element or substance; (b) not contain more than 1mg/kg of arsenic or more than 1mg/kg of lead, unless specific purity criteria are mentioned in the Directive; and (c) satisfy specific purity criteria in the Directive.[130]

[129] ibid, art (1)(2)(b).
[130] ibid, art 3.

9.8.4 Permitted solvents and solvents with conditions of use and purity criteria

The Annexes further distinguish between permitted solvents and solvents for which conditions of use are specified. Permitted solvents are Propane, Butane, Ethyl acetate, Ethanol, Carbon dioxide, Acetone (if not for olive-pomace oil), and Nitrous oxide.[131]

For solvents for which conditions are specified, the Annex lists conditions of use (summary description of extraction) and maximum residue limits in the extracted foodstuff or food ingredient.[132] Extraction solvents used for the preparation of flavourings from natural flavouring materials stipulate maximum residue levels separately.[133]

The Directive prescribes which extraction solvents may be used, what the conditions of use are, and eventual maximum residue limits in the extracted foodstuff. For instance, Hexane for defattening protein products may be present only up to 30mg/kg in the defatted soya products.[134]

An extraction solvent is deemed compliant with good manufacturing practice if its use only results in the presence of residues or derivatives in technically unavoidable quantities that pose no risk to human health.[135]

9.8.5 Labelling

Extraction solvents can only be marketed if they comply with labelling rules. Specifically, their packaging, containers, or labels must specify (a) the commercial name; (b) a clear indication that the material is of a quality suitable for use for the extraction of food or food ingredients; (c) the batch reference for identification; (d) business address information; (e) the net quantity; and (f) if necessary, the special storage conditions or conditions of use.[136]

9.8.6 Procedural elements

The Commission has powers to amend the Annex, that is, to include or exclude extraction solvents, and set rules governing their marketing; methods of analysis necessary to verify compliance with the general and specific purity criteria; and the procedure for sampling and analysis through the Committee Procedure.[137]

[131] ibid, pt I of Annex I.
[132] ibid, pt II of Annex I.
[133] ibid, pt III of Annex I.
[134] ibid, pt II of Annex I.
[135] ibid, Annex I part I fn 2.
[136] ibid, art 7.
[137] ibid, art 4.

9.9 Discussion

The regulation of food improvement agents falls under food technology law. This is because the FIAP generally requires a technical function. The FIAP primarily regulates for food safety, with some specific attention to consumer protection, and in certain aspects to nutritional viability. From a technical standpoint, the FIAP may be perceived as somewhat 'old-fashioned'. However, increasingly, compounds are utilized not just for their technical function in food production, but also for improving their health-promoting effects.

Given the narrow functional focus of the food improvement agent framework, the persisting uncertainty regarding 'natural' compounds is surprising. To date, 'natural' remains an only partially regulated characteristic, and there is—for instance—no definition of what a 'natural colour' is.

Even from a technical perspective, the framework for food improvement agents remains incomplete with significant gaps in EU regulation, most notably the ongoing re-evaluation of additives and the incomplete status of the enzyme authorizations. Apart from occasional definitional issues, there is no major critique of the FIAP as a framework from a *legal* perspective—rather there appears to be a problem with the capacity of EFSA and the processes needed to keep up with safety assessments of an ever-evolving food technological landscape. In this sense, the main concerns expressed are actual food safety issues.

Lastly, as a strictly food safety oriented framework, the Farm to Fork Strategy has overlooked the inclusion of food improvement agents. This represents a small, but missed opportunity. First, the environmental aspects of added substances are not considered. For instance, a millilitre of food aromas (used in food and beverages) 'requires [not only] between 10 and 1000 g of fresh aromatic herbs or dry spices as raw material (which became a chemical waste) but also a large quantity of solvents (n-hexane to produce the concrete and then alcohol to produce the absolute), energy (fossil) to evaporate the large quantity of solvents and water as cooling and cleaning agent which become chemical waste water'.[138] It may therefore be timely to start considering green production of food improvement agents. Second, given the emerging connection between processed food and health issues, the Farm to Fork Strategy fails to fulfil its promises of creating a healthier food system in this regard.

[138] Aurore Filly and others, 'Alternative Solvents for Extraction of Food Aromas. Experimental and COSMO-RS Study' (2015) 61 LWT—Food Science and Technology 33.

PART IV
FOOD SAFETY LAW

The General Food Law Regulation (GFLR) contains the overarching safety clause that food may be marketed if it is not unsafe.[1] For specific topics, this general safety clause is complemented by more in depth secondary legislation on specific aspects of food safety. In European Union (EU) food law, it is common to distinguish between different types of food hazards. These are biological hazards, such as bacteria, viruses, parasites, or molds; chemical hazards, such as pesticides, processing chemicals, drug residues, or allergens; and lastly physical hazards, which could either be naturally present in a food, for example pits, bones, and bugs, or could be in a food as a result of handling or processing of material, for example glass or hair. This distinction stems from the GFLR, which defines 'hazard' as 'a biological, chemical or physical agent in, or condition of, food or feed with the potential to cause an adverse health effect'.[2]

Broadly speaking, the more specific EU food safety legislation follows a hazard-based categorization system. Biological hazards are primarily addressed through EU hygiene legislation, namely the General Hygiene Regulation and the Hygiene Regulation for Animal Origin, which are complemented by the more specific Commission Regulation on Microbiological Criteria (Chapter 10). Chemical hazards are addressed based on their 'route of inclusion' with legal frameworks distinguishing between unintentionally added contaminants and so-called avoidable substances. For unintentionally added substances, there is EU legislation on contaminants. Avoidable or 'intentionally added substances' are addressed in specific frameworks on the use of pesticides, veterinary medicinal products, biocidals, and hormones in meat (Chapter 11). These horizontal legal instruments are complemented by issue-based legislation, for instance Food Contact Materials (FCM), which is a practically highly relevant field for food and which addresses the chemical risks of food packaging (Chapter 12).

All of these food safety fields are governed by the GFLR's food safety institutions, processes, and risk regulation architecture.

[1] Regulation (EC) 178/2002 of the European Parliament and of the Council of 28 January 2002 laying down the general principles and requirements of food law, establishing the European Food Safety Authority and laying down procedures in matters of food safety [2002] OJ L31/1 (General Food Law Regulation (GFLR)), art 14(1).

[2] ibid, art 3.14.

10
Hygiene Legislation and Microbiological Criteria for Food

10.1 Introduction

The European Union (EU) food safety architecture is a multi-layered legal construct. The General Food Law Regulation (GFLR) creates an encompassing general safety paradigm: food that is unsafe may not be placed on the market. This umbrella provision is elaborated on in additional legal frameworks that cover transversal safety requirements. In EU food law, there is a distinction between biologically and chemically oriented frameworks. This chapter addresses food hygiene legislation which aims to safeguard food safety from a process-based perspective, as well as legislation on microbiological criteria for food that stipulates biological safety requirements for the final product. These frameworks therefore focus on the prevention of biological hazards.

The international Codex Alimentarius standards (see Chapter 18) are particularly influential to food safety law making, including hygiene. They receive quasi-legal status in certain areas where the standards are explicitly referenced in EU laws. The Codex General Principles of Food Hygiene[1] were adopted in 1969, and later revised in 1997 and 2003 in line with the science-based food safety paradigm (see Chapter 1). The latest revision in 2020 introduced the principle of a 'food safety culture' in food business operator (FBO) management, thereby 'acknowledging the importance of human behaviour in providing safe and suitable food'.[2] This 'human behaviour' centred approach to food safety processes has been codified in the EU hygiene legislation in 2021, and signals a significant evolution from the science-based paradigm of the 2000s.

10.2 Hygiene legislation

EU food law recognizes the critical role of processes in ensuring food safety. In 2004, the EU adopted three legal instruments that were jointly termed the 'Hygiene

[1] Codex Alimentarius: International Food Standards—General Principles of Food Hygiene (1969) CXC 1-1969.
[2] ibid.

EU Food Law. Hanna Schebesta and Kai Purnhagen, Oxford University Press. © Hanna Schebesta and Kai Purnhagen 2024.
DOI: 10.1093/9780198901570.003.0011

Package', comprising a general hygiene regulation for all foodstuff including foodstuff of animal origin, a special hygiene regulation for foodstuff of animal origin only, and an official controls regulation. This official controls regulation has now been replaced by the Official Controls Regulation (see Chapter 6) applicable to all food law.

The 2004 Hygiene Package aimed to simplify the existing food hygiene frameworks and 'introduced a shift in approach to food hygiene policy' that focuses on objectives to be achieved by FBOs rather than prescribing overly detailed requirements.[3]

10.3 The General Hygiene Regulation

The General Hygiene Regulation[4] defines 'food hygiene' as the set of measures and conditions necessary to control hazards and to ensure that a foodstuff is fit for human consumption taking into account its intended use.[5] The objective of the hygiene regulations is to fulfil the requirements outlined in Article 14 GFLR,[6] and more generally to achieve food safety objectives.

The scope of the General Hygiene Regulation is comprehensive, encompassing all food (including those of animal origin), at all stages of production, processing, and distribution.[7] However, the General Hygiene Regulation also includes a significant amount of 'flexibility provisions'; there are numerous exemptions, exceptions, and exclusions from the scope of the regulation. In addition, the margin for the Member States is wide, and the General Hygiene Regulation sometimes allows Member States to derogate from certain provisions, or adapt them. The Commission in principle also has the competence to institute derogations. This is the case for Article 13(2) General Hygiene Regulation, which grants the Commission a right to draw up a derogation from the hygiene requirements for 'small businesses', although this provision has so far not been used. In addition, much of the language of the General Hygiene Regulation is indicative or even

[3] Commission, 'Report from the Commission to the Council and the European Parliament on the experience gained from the application of the hygiene Regulations (EC) No 852/2004, (EC) No 853/2004 and (EC) No 854/2004 of the European Parliament and of the Council of 29 April 2004 {SEC (2009) 1079}' (Report) COM (2009) 403 final.

[4] Regulation (EC) 852/2004 of the European Parliament and of the Council of 29 April 2004 on the hygiene of foodstuffs [2004] OJ L139/1 (General Hygiene Regulation).

[5] ibid, art 2(1)(a).

[6] Regulation (EC) 178/2002 of the European Parliament and of the Council of 28 January 2002 laying down the general principles and requirements of food law, establishing the European Food Safety Authority and laying down procedures in matters of food safety [2002] OJ L31/1 (GFLR).

[7] As the CJEU confirmed in *Reindl*, mere distributors are also subject to the full hygiene regime, including microbiological requirements; see Case C-443/13 *Ute Reindl v Bezirkshauptmannschaft Innsbruck* EU:C:2014:2370 (*Reindl*).

subjective, such as 'adequate', 'where necessary', or 'as quickly as possible'. Open norms are therefore an important feature of the hygiene rules.

Firstly, the General Hygiene Regulation does not apply to all food producers. A notable exclusion exists for primary production for private use and for private domestic consumption. The General Hygiene Regulation further exempts 'the direct supply, by the producer, of small quantities of primary products to the final consumer or to local retail establishments directly supplying the final consumer'.[8] This also applies to sales made by local retail establishments directly supplying the final consumer. Therefore, the sale of raw milk, honey, eggs, fruit, and vegetables from farms can benefit from this exclusion. It is important to note that the rules for implementing this 'direct supply exclusion' must be set at the national level.[9]

10.3.1 Food safety management system: principles, general and specific requirements, and HACCP

The EU hygiene laws are based on several general principles. The most important ones are that food businesses are responsible for food safety, and that food safety must be ensured throughout the food chain.[10] This echoes the GFLR's approach of attributing compliance responsibility on all links in the food chain.

The main legal obligation is on FBOs to ensure that at all stages of production, processing, and distribution of food under their control meet the relevant hygiene requirements laid down in the General Hygiene Regulation.[11]

In addition, there are a number of general and specific requirements. FBOs must comply with the general hygiene requirements specified in Annexes I (for primary production) or II (any stage after primary production),[12] and specific hygiene requirements for food of animal origin if applicable.[13] The general and specific hygiene requirements are also known as prerequisite programmes (PRPs).[14]

In addition, FBOs must have a permanent procedure based on hazard analysis and critical control point principles (HACCP).[15] PRPs, together with the HACCP procedures, form an integrated food safety management system (FSMS) for FBOs. In recent years, guidance by the Commission has shifted from an exclusive focus

[8] General Hygiene Regulation, art 1(2)(c).
[9] ibid, art 1(3).
[10] ibid, art 1.
[11] ibid, art 3.
[12] ibid, art 4.
[13] Regulation (EC) 853/2004 of the European Parliament and of the Council of 29 April 2004 laying down specific hygiene rules for food of animal origin [2004] OJ L139/55 (Animal Origin Hygiene Regulation).
[14] This is to bring the EU terminology in line with international standards, notably the language used by the Codex Alimentarius, where PRPs are referred to as 'Codes of Practice' or 'GHPs'.
[15] General Hygiene Regulation, art 5.

on HACCP, towards advocating an integrated approach that covers both PRPs (so, the EU general and specific hygiene requirements) and HACCP within one FSMS.

10.3.1.1 The general requirements in Annex I—primary production and associated operations

FBOs in primary production and associated operations (ie operations related to transport[16]) are only required to comply with the general hygiene provisions in Annex I of the General Hygiene Regulation and any specific requirements provided for in the Animal Origin Hygiene Regulation. 'Primary production' is defined as 'the production, rearing or growing of primary products including harvesting, milking, and farmed animal production prior to slaughter. It also includes hunting and fishing and the harvesting of wild products.'[17]

The General hygiene provisions (Part A of Annex I) oblige FBOs to protect primary products from contamination, to control for hazards, and to implement a number of hygiene measures. In addition, FBOs have to keep specific data on record. In addition there are recommendations for guides to good hygiene practices (Part B of Annex I).

10.3.1.2 The general requirements in Annex II—general hygiene requirements (post-primary production stage)

Annex II does not apply when Annex I applies; meaning that Annex II only applies to FBOs that are active in the food chain after the primary production stage. Annex II enumerates the general hygiene requirements, and consists of 12 chapters, each often addressing a distinct scope of application.[18] The Annex lists rules on: general requirements for food premises (other than those specified in chapter III),[19] requirements for rooms where foodstuffs are prepared, treated, or processed,[20] requirements for movable and/or temporary premises,[21] rules for transport,[22] equipment requirements,[23] redistribution of food,[24] food waste,[25] water supply,[26] personal hygiene,[27] and specific rules for foodstuffs,[28] wrapping and packaging,[29] heat

[16] ibid, Annex I, pt A, I.
[17] GFLR, art 3(17).
[18] General Hygiene Regulation, Annex II, Introduction.
[19] ibid, Annex II, ch I.
[20] ibid, Annex II, ch II.
[21] ibid, Annex II, ch III.
[22] ibid, Annex II, ch IV.
[23] ibid, Annex II, ch V.
[24] ibid, Annex II, ch Va, added by the Commission Regulation (EU) 2021/382 of 3 March 2021 amending the Annexes to Regulation (EC) No 852/2004 of the European Parliament and of the Council on the hygiene of foodstuffs as regards food allergen management, redistribution of food and food safety culture [2021] OJ L74/3 (Amending Regulation 2021).
[25] ibid, Annex II, ch VI.
[26] ibid, Annex II, ch VII.
[27] ibid, Annex II, ch VIII.
[28] ibid, Annex II, ch IX.
[29] ibid, Annex II, ch X.

treatment,[30] the food safety culture,[31] and training.[32]

Member States may pass national measures that adapt the requirements laid down in Annex II. These shall serve to enable the continued use of traditional methods or to accommodate the needs of food businesses situated in regions that are subject to special geographical constraints. Other adaptations may only relate to the construction, layout, and equipment of establishments.[33] The national adaptations are subject to a notification requirement.[34]

In 2021, the EU passed a substantive amendment to the General Hygiene Regulation, reflecting the latest amendment of the Codex Alimentarius Commission of its global standard General Principles of Food Hygiene.[35] Accordingly, the EU Amending Regulation 2021 covered food allergen management at the primary production stage, included the redistribution of food, and enshrined the new principle of food safety culture. The principle of food safety[36] prescribes that management and employees should commit to the safe production and distribution of food, emphasizing, among other points, the importance of communication and training. This new principle recognizes the behavioural element of food safety, and therefore institutes an organizing principle that attributes responsibility to the individuals involved in food processes.

10.3.1.3 ***Specific requirements and specific hygiene measures***

The General Hygiene Regulation mandates compliance with both the general and the specific requirements. The specific requirements include those laid down for food of animal origin in the Animal Origin Hygiene Regulation (see section 10.4), and, in addition, the General Hygiene Regulation obliges FBOs to comply with overarching hygiene measures to be laid down by the Commission in delegated acts.[37] The list of other hygiene measures comprises the following aspects:

- compliance with microbiological criteria for foodstuffs; these are contained in the Regulation on Microbiological Criteria[38] (see section 10.5);
- procedures necessary to meet targets set to achieve the objectives of this Regulation;
- compliance with temperature control requirements for foodstuffs; specific temperature control requirements are specified in the Animal Origin Hygiene

[30] ibid, Annex II, ch XI.
[31] ibid, Annex II, ch XIa, added by the Amending Regulation 2021.
[32] ibid, Annex II, ch XII.
[33] ibid, art 13(3).
[34] ibid, art 13(5).
[35] CXC 1-1969.
[36] General Hygiene Regulation, Annex II, ch XIa, added by the Amending Regulation 2021.
[37] ibid, art 4(3).
[38] Commission Regulation (EC) 2073/2005 of 15 November 2005 on microbiological criteria for foodstuffs [2005] OJ L338/1 (Commission Regulation on Microbiological Criteria).

Regulation, the Regulation on Microbiological Criteria, and in some product-specific requirements (eg poultrymeat marketing standards);
- maintenance of the cold chain;
- sampling and analysis.

10.3.1.4 ***HACCP***

HACCP requirements apply only to FBOs active in food production stages *after* primary production and the associated (transport) operations listed in Annex I of the General Hygiene Regulation.

Business operators must implement a procedure based on HACCP principles,[39] which comprises the following seven steps, namely: identify hazards; identify critical control points; establish critical limits; establish monitoring procedures; establish corrective actions; verification; and documentation.

In terms of administration efforts, FBOs must provide their competent authority with evidence of their compliance 'in the manner that the competent authority requires, taking account of the nature and size of the food business'. They must ensure that these documents are updated and that records are maintained for an appropriate amount of time.[40]

As the Commission has broadened its reliance on HACCP to a more holistic approach that encompasses FSMS, Commission guidance on HACCP procedures is now contained in the Food Safety Management Systems Commission Notice (see section 10.3.2.1).

10.3.1.5 ***Official controls, registration, and approval***

FBOs are required to cooperate with competent authorities.[41] Specifically, they must register each food establishment under its control with the national competent authority, in the manner that the national system requires.[42] Where required under national law, FBOs must obtain an approval. Both registration and approval requirements are predominantly set at national level, for instance for FBOs handling products of animal origin. A list of approved food establishments is published by the Commission.[43] For a limited number of FBOs there is an approval requirement at EU level.[44]

[39] General Hygiene Regulation, art 5.
[40] ibid, art 5(4).
[41] ibid, art 6(1).
[42] ibid, art 6(2).
[43] Commission, 'Approved EU food establishments' <https://ec.europa.eu/food/safety/biological-safety/food-hygiene/approved-eu-food-establishments_en> accessed 28 July 2022.
[44] Commission Regulation (EU) 210/2013 of 11 March 2013 on the approval of establishments producing sprouts pursuant to Regulation (EC) No 852/2004 of the European Parliament and of the Council [2013] OJ L68/24.

10.3.2 *Guides to good practice (Chapter III)*

The role of guidance tools in implementing the hygiene rules is very important. While the Hygiene Regulations elaborate on the basic structure of obligations, the guides are practical tools that facilitate compliance by FBOs in a practical and applied way. Guides to good hygiene practice are legally recognized instruments to ensure FBO compliance with hygiene requirements;[45] this extends to both national[46] and EU guides.[47]

Member States must notify national guides,[48] which can be accessed through the Commission registration system,[49] while the guidance platform showcases a selection of representative full guides at both EU and national levels.[50] Hygiene is also an area where the Commission has issued a number of relevant substantive guidance documents. The abundance and diversity of relevant sources of law contributes to the complexity of the field, and arguably an overhaul of the Hygiene Regulations to consolidate the different rules is desirable to make compliance easier for FBOs.

Since 2015, the former Food and Veterinary Office (FVO) of the Commission's Health and Food Safety Directorate-General, two European Food Safety Authority (EFSA) opinions,[51] and Member State experts have emphasized the need to improve the functioning of the Hygiene Regulations in practice, notably by providing better guidance. In response, the Commission has issued a number of documents, of which two important ones are covered in sections 10.3.2.1 and 10.3.2.2.

[45] General Hygiene Regulation, art 4(6).
[46] ibid, art 8.
[47] ibid, art 9.
[48] ibid, art 8.
[49] Commission, 'National Guides to Good Hygiene Practice for Food and Feed: Register of national guides to good hygiene practice' <https://webgate.ec.europa.eu/dyna2/hygienelegislation/> accessed 28 July 2022.
[50] Commission, 'Food hygiene: Guidance platform' <https://ec.europa.eu/food/safety/biological-safety/food-hygiene/guidance-platform_en> accessed 28 July 2022.
[51] EFSA adopted two opinions. In 2017, it adopted the first—EFSA, 'Hazard Analysis Approaches for Certain Small Retail Establishments in View of the Application of their Food Safety Management Systems' (2017) 15(3) EFSA Journal <https://www.efsa.europa.eu/en/efsajournal/pub/4697> accessed 28 July 2022, focusing on butcher shops, groceries, bakeries, fish shops, and ice cream shops. In 2018, EFSA adopted the second opinion—EFSA, 'Hazard Analysis Approaches for Certain Small Retail Establishments and Food Donations: Second Scientific Opinion' (2018) 16(11) EFSA Journal <https://www.efsa.europa.eu/en/efsajournal/pub/5432> accessed 28 July 2022, focusing on distribution centres, supermarkets and restaurants (including pubs and catering) and addressing, within the hazard analysis, potential additional hazards relating to food donations at retail level. This opinion, adopted on 27 September 2018, states that food donations present several new food safety challenges at retail level and therefore it recommends several additional general hygiene requirements. It is thus necessary to lay down certain requirements in order to promote and facilitate redistribution of food, while guaranteeing its safety for consumers.

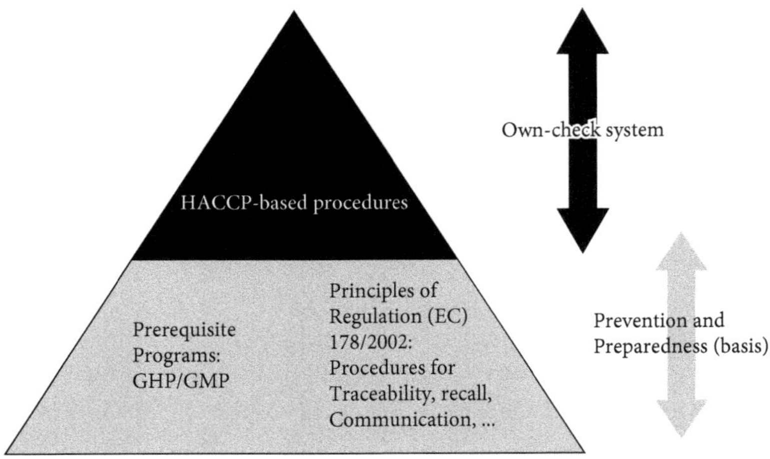

Figure 10.1 Elements of a Food Safety Management System (FSMS)
Source: FSMS Commission Notice, 3

*10.3.2.1 **Food Safety Management Systems Commission Notice (2016)***

The calls for improving the EU hygiene regime have resulted in the Commission Notice on the implementation of food safety management systems (see Figure 10.1) covering PRPs and procedures based on HACCP principles, including the facilitation/flexibility on the implementation in certain food businesses, adopted in 2016 (FSMS Commission Notice).[52]

The purpose of the FSMS Commission Notice is to support the implementation of the EU requirements on PRPs and HACCP-based procedures.

The FSMS, put simply, comprises all legal obligations and therefore includes PRPs. PRPs are defined as good practices,[53] such as good hygiene practices (GHPs) or good manufacturing practices (GMPs), and the obligations under the Hygiene Regulations.[54] In addition to PRPs, the FSMS comprises the general legal obligations, for instance under the GFLR on traceability. Alongside these, the HACCP procedures[55] constitute an 'own-check system'. In the FSMS, PRPs are conceived

[52] Commission Notice on the implementation of food safety management systems covering prerequisite programs (PRPs) and procedures based on the HACCP principles, including the facilitation/flexibility of the implementation in certain food businesses [2016] OJ C278/1 (FSMS Commission Notice).

[53] The PRPs depend on the food chain sector and the type of activity. Activity-specific codes at different stages of food production are good agriculture practices (GAPs), good veterinarian practices (GVPs), good manufacturing practices (GMPs), good hygiene practices (GHPs), good production practices (GPPs), good distribution practices (GDPs) and good trading practices (GTPs); see Retail Sector Commission Notice, section 4.

[54] Implementation of General Hygiene Regulation, art 4 and Annexes I and II, and product-specific provisions in Animal Origin Hygiene Regulation, Annex IIII.

[55] Implementation of General Hygiene Regulation, art 5.

as 'the foundation for effective HACCP implementation' and should therefore precede the establishment of any HACCP-based procedures.[56]

The FSMS Commission Notice contains guidance on the connection between PRPs and HACCP-based procedures within an FSMS, the implementation of PRPs (Annex I), the implementation of (classical) HACCP-based procedures (Annex II), and the flexibility provisions for certain food establishments (Annex III). With it, the European Commission takes a decidedly integrative approach to explaining how different elements of food safety interact with one another.

10.3.2.2. ***Food Retail Guidance (2020)***

In 2020, the Commission issued a Commission Notice providing guidance on food safety management systems for food retail activities, including food donations.[57] The purpose is to streamline retail activities, so that retailers only need to be aware of groups of hazards (biological, chemical, physical, or allergen).

Generic hazard analyses have been established by the Commission in order to facilitate compliance with hygiene requirements, and to offer guidance on how food retail businesses can comply with the law. The examples covered are for establishments including butcher shops, grocery shops (selling fruit and vegetables), bakery shops, fish shops, ice cream shops, distribution centres (including food banks), supermarkets and restaurants, catering services and pubs, and food donations.[58]

For example, consider the PRPs for retail activities (see Table 10.1) in general. Note how the PRPs are structured based on control infrastructure and activities and combine a variety of different safety clusters.

Similarly, the Commission elaborated requirements related to food donation that supplement the EU guidelines on food donation, and further elaboration to clarify how food donations can comply with the necessary hygiene rules in Annex II of the General Hygiene Regulations.

While the respective guidance documents aim to support FBOs in implementing their hygiene obligations under EU law, one should not underestimate the level of detail with which different issues are regulated. This regulatory complexity has also been criticized as standing in the way of food donations, which could otherwise contribute to the EU food system's circularity ambitions.

[56] FSMS Commission Notice, Annex I.

[57] Commission Notice providing guidance on food safety management systems for food retail activities, including food donations [2020] OJ C199/1.

[58] Commission Notice C199/1.

Table 10.1 A summary of PRPs relevant for retail activities based on the 2016 Commission Notice and the EFSA opinions

Control infrastructure/ activities	Monitoring	Record keeping (yes/no)	Corrective action
PRP 1 Infrastructure (building and equipment, including movable or temporary premises)			
Hygienic infrastructure and fit for purpose building and equipment	Monthly visual check based on checklist of infrastructure (hygiene and condition)	Yes, but only when there is remedial work required	Proper maintenance of premises and equipment
PRP 2 Cleaning and disinfection			
Cleaning and disinfection schedule and/or 'clean as you go' policy	Spot visual checks. Daily visual checks. Regular microbiological testing. Frequency may depend on the size of the establishment and results of previous testing.	Yes, when there is a non-compliance	Cleaning and disinfection of area/ equipment affected. Review and if necessary retrain staff and/or revise frequency and method of disinfection.
PRP 3 Pest control: focus on prevention			
Pest control activities	Weekly in-house check	Yes, but only when there is remedial work required or logbook when using external company	Revise and/or renew pest control activities
PRP 4 Technical maintenance and calibration.			
Maintain all equipment. Calibrate measuring devices (e.g. thermometer, balance, etc.)	On-going monitoring of equipment. Periodic calibration status or back-up check by using different thermometer	No. Yes, status of calibration/back-up check.	Repair or replace equipment as necessary. Review maintenance and calibration programme.
PRP 5 Physical and chemical contamination from production environment			
Ensure all materials are stored correctly Ensure all surfaces are properly rinsed/wiped after disinfection in accordance with manufacturer's instructions	Visual check during processing Monthly check based on checklist or visual inspection of infrastructure (hygiene and condition)	Yes, but only when there is remedial work required	Review storage, cleaning and disinfection procedures, etc.

Table 10.1 Continued

Control infrastructure/ activities	**Monitoring**	**Record keeping (yes/no)**	**Corrective action**
For bakery products, high temperatures will promote acrylamide formation			
Ensure correct baking (T/duration) conditions	Visual check during processing and of end-product	No	Disposal of 'over-cooked' products
PRP 6 Allergens			
Control the absence of unintentional allergens in raw materials. Keep an up-to-date inventory of food products with potential allergens including sources (e.g. raw material, cross-contamination, etc.). Potential sources of cross-contamination identified and controlled	Raw material specifications from suppliers. Activities to prevent cross-contamination are implemented on a continuous basis.	No. Some records should be kept (at least on corrective actions) if an allergen incident occurs	Stop using potentially 'contaminated' raw materials. Review suppliers/ supplier requirements. Revise acceptance criteria. Review and correct activities designed to prevent cross-contamination. If despite all actions mentioned above cross-contamination cannot be avoided, following a risk assessment FBOs should evaluate whether to provide information on the possible and unintentional presence of allergens in food.
PRP 7 Waste management			
Complete separation of waste from raw materials or foods. Comply with the specific legal requirements for the storage and disposal of waste for foods of animal origin (animal by-products).	Routine visual check to ensure the food business's policy on waste management is being fully complied with	No	Remove waste without undue delay from areas where food is handled. Review and revise current waste management activities. Retrain staff as required.

(continued)

Table 10.1 Continued

Control infrastructure/ activities	Monitoring	Record keeping (yes/no)	Corrective action
PRP 8 Water control, including ice making (if other water is used than supply of potable municipal water)			
Control of source and good condition of water distribution infrastructure with absence of toxic contact materials	Ongoing monitoring of water treatment. Periodic microbiological and chemical testing	Yes, results of microbiological and chemical testing	Revise water treatment
PRP 9 Personnel (hygiene, health status)			
Presence of hygiene rules and agreements with personnel adapted to the nature of the activities. Health status of personnel.	Daily visual check during processing. Medical check and awareness training for all personnel.	Documentation of hygiene instructions. Medical check and training record keeping.	Address any personnel issues immediately. Advise and inform personnel.
PRP 10 Raw materials (supplier selection, specifications)			
Raw materials are fulfilling legal requirements. Retailers have acceptance criteria based on, preferably written specifications (e.g., odor, smell)	Presence of specifications from suppliers or presence of labels of packaged materials. Acceptance criteria are checked upon each delivery.	Yes, but only when there is a non-compliance, e.g., the raw materials were not delivered at the correct temperature	Do not use affected raw materials. Review suppliers/ supplier requirements. Revise acceptance criteria.
PRP 11 Temperature control of storage environment			
Temperature of storage environment (cooling or deep freezing) is adequate to reach product temperature requirements	Automatic monitoring with alarm and/or automated record keeping. Manual monitoring/ daily check or more checks of the temperature of storage facilities and product.	As appropriate (See 2016 Commission notice)	Replace/repair/reset chilling/freezing equipment. Based on the extent of the non-compliance consider disposal of the affected product.

Table 10.1 Continued

Control infrastructure/ activities	Monitoring	Record keeping (yes/no)	Corrective action
PRP 12 Working methodology			
Personnel following clear, preferably written, work instructions, (standard operating procedures (SOP)), including instructions with regards to products approaching the end of shelf-life. For bakery products, where high temperatures will promote acrylamide formation, instruction on the disposal of 'over-cooked' product should be added.	Daily visual check	No	Retrain personnel
PRP 13 Product information and consumer awareness			
All products at retail level should be accompanied by sufficient verbal or written information to promote proper handling, storage and preparation by consumers. Allergen and shelf-life information should also be provided if appropriate.	Routine checks to ensure this information is provided	No	Review and revise the information as necessary

Source: Commission Notice C199/1.

10.4 The Hygiene Regulation for Animal Origin

The Hygiene Regulation for Animal Origin contains hygiene requirements for foods of animal origin as specific requirements. The basic obligation to comply with the Animal Origin Hygiene Regulation stems from the General Hygiene Regulation.[59] It is important to note that both hygiene regulations apply to food of animal origin in parallel.

[59] General Hygiene Regulation, art 4(2).

The Animal Origin Hygiene Regulation applies to both unprocessed and processed products of animal origin.[60] It does not apply to private domestic use, domestic preparation for domestic consumption, and more importantly, the direct supply of small quantities to final consumers or local retailers directly supplying consumers, and hunters.[61] The direct supply exemptions and the exemption for hunters must be established through national law.[62] Unless expressly indicated to the contrary, the Regulation does not apply to retail.[63]

The main general obligation on FBOs is to comply with the rules in Annex II and Annex III.[64] Foods of animal origin may only be placed on the market if they are in compliance with the rules, and handled by FBOs that have been registered and, where necessary, approved.

Annex I contains the definitions of animal origin products, which also covers, for example honey. Annex II prescribes the use of identification marking (section I), objectives of HACCP procedures (section II), food chain information (section III), and requirements applicable to frozen food of animal origin (section IV). Annex III contains the specific requirements for particular types of animal origin food, including hygiene in slaughterhouses or vessels used for fishery harvest, health requirements, processing requirements such as heat treatment, and documentation requirements. For instance, FBOs cannot use any substance other than drinking water to remove surface contamination from products of animal origin, unless use of the substance has been approved by the Commission.[65]

10.5 Microbiological criteria for foodstuffs

A specific legal instrument governs microbiological criteria for foodstuffs. The General Hygiene Regulation recognizes the importance of microbiological criteria and temperature control requirements based on a scientific risk assessment.[66] The Commission adopted the Regulation on Microbiological Criteria as a specific hygiene measure, mandated under Article 4(3)(a) General Hygiene Regulation. It complements the (sometimes) open norms of the two Hygiene Regulations with a

[60] Animal Origin Hygiene Regulation, art 1.
[61] ibid, art 1(3).
[62] ibid, art 1(4).
[63] ibid, art 1(5)(a).
[64] ibid, art 3.
[65] See ibid, art 3(2). Those measures, designed to amend non-essential elements of this Regulation, by supplementing it, shall be adopted in accordance with the regulatory procedure with scrutiny referred to in art 12(3). See the example of Case T-568/19 *Micreos Food Safety BV v European Commission* EU:T:2020:647, which concerned an application for Listex™ P100 that was not authorized as a decontaminant to reduce the presence of Listeria monocytogenes in animal-derived ready-to-eat food.
[66] General Hygiene Regulation, arts 1(1)(f) and 4(3)(a).

Table 10.2 *Examples of food safety criteria*

Food category	Micro-organisms/their toxins, metabolites	Sampling plan		Limits		Analytical reference method	Stage where the criterion applies
		n	c	m	M		
1.29 Sprouts	Shiga toxin producing *E. coli* (STEC) O157, O26, O111, O103, O145 and O104:H4	5	0	Not detected ◄ in 25 grams		CEN/ISO TS 13136	Products placed on the market during their shelf-life

Source: Commission Regulation on Microbiological Criteria, Annex I, ch 1.

'hard law' framework on microbiological criteria, which for many businesses may constitute a more cumbersome, but also more predictable legal framework.

The Commission Regulation on Microbiological Criteria establishes rules for compliance by FBOs when implementing the general and specific hygiene measures referred to in Article 4 General Hygiene Regulation.

As a general requirement, FBOs must comply with the specific microbiologic criteria (set out in Annex I).[67] For this reason, FBOs must conduct testing against the mircrobiological criteria, at a frequency that they decide, unless a statutory frequency is stipulated in the Annex of the Regulation;[68] these tests must be performed in compliance with the specific rules for testing and sampling.[69] Where the results are unsatisfactory, the Regulation delineates the measures that FBOs must take.[70]

The Annex containing the specific requirements comprise three chapters: food safety criteria, process hygiene criteria, and rules for sampling and preparation of test samples. The general food safety criteria (Chapter 1) are categorized by food type, and describe the limits for specific micro-organisms, their toxins, and metabolites (see Table 10.2).

The process hygiene criteria (Chapter 2) are also categorized by food type (see Table 10.3), and describe limits and actions in the event of unsatisfactory results.

Chapter 3 contains rules for sampling and preparation of test samples, specifically meat and seeds. In the absence of specific rules, the International Organization for Standardization (ISO) and guidelines of the Codex Alimentarius should be used as reference methods.[71]

[67] Commission Regulation on Microbiological Criteria, art 3.
[68] ibid, art 4.
[69] ibid, art 5.
[70] ibid, art 7.
[71] ibid, Annex I, ch. 3.1.

Table 10.3 *Examples of food safety criteria*

Food category	Micro-organisms	Sampling plan		Limits		Analytical reference method	Stage where the criterion applies	Action in case of unsatisfactory results
		n	c	m	M			
2.2.1 Pasteurised milk and other pasteurised liquid dairy products	Entero-bacteriaceae	5	0	10 cfu/ml		EN ISO 21528-2	Products placed on the market during their shelf-life	Check on the efficiency of heat-treatment and prevention of recontamination as well as the quality of raw materials

Source: Commission Regulation on Microbiological Criteria, Annex I, ch 2.

Much like the other hygiene laws, for microbiological criteria, highly specific topical legislation or guidance complements the main EU legal instruments, one example of which is the 2017 Commission notice on guidance document on addressing microbiological risks in fresh fruits and vegetables at primary production through good hygiene.[72]

10.6 Discussion

The main legal instruments governing hygiene at EU level are the General Hygiene Regulation and the Hygiene Regulation for Animal Origin. The framework followed a 'new approach to hygiene' by focusing on objectives to be reached rather than prescribing detailed requirements. This can possibly explain the surprisingly technical role of the Court of Justice of the European Union (CJEU) in hygiene cases:[73] for instance, the Court held that the chilling of meat after slaughter must be carried out in the slaughterhouse itself until the meat has reached a temperature throughout of no more than 7°C before loading the meat into a refrigerated truck;[74] that the concept of 'contamination' includes not only contamination by faeces, but also contamination by crop contents and by bile and that a poultry carcass must no longer contain any visible contamination after the cleaning stage and

[72] Commission notice on guidance document on addressing microbiological risks in fresh fruits and vegetables at primary production through good hygiene [2017] OJ C163/1.

[73] To date, there are roughly 20 cases at EU level dealing with the EU hygiene legal framework.

[74] Animal Origin Hygiene Regulation, Annex III, Section I, ch VII, points 1 and 3, and Case C-98/18 *T Boer & Zonen BV v Staatssecretaris van Economische Zaken* EU:C:2019:355.

before the chilling stage;[75] that the hygiene rules must be interpreted as not requiring that a washbasin within the meaning of that provision be used exclusively for washing hands or that it be possible to use the water tap or hand-drying material without touching by hand;[76] that in case of containers used for self-service retail of bread and bakery products, the fact that a potential purchaser could conceivably have touched the foodstuffs offered for sale by hand or sneezed on them does not automatically mean that those foodstuffs were not protected against any contamination;[77] and that a product obtained by the mechanical removal of meat from flesh-bearing bones after boning or from poultry carcases must be classified as 'mechanically separated meat' within the meaning of Hygiene Regulation of Animal Origin.[78] These cases are just the tip of the iceberg, and its reasonable to presume that there are many similar interpretations of the legal frameworks across the Member States.

Indeed, the Hygiene Regulations are marked by the deliberate and pervasive use of different types of flexibility provisions.[79] These provisions are intricate exclusions and exemptions from the scope of the Regulations; possible Commission derogations from the rules;[80] national adaptions of the rules;[81] and not unimportantly, the openly worded nature of many requirements, such as 'where this is necessary', 'as far as possible, or 'as adequate'. The goal of the flexibility provision has been 'to protect food diversity and to serve consumers and the needs of small-scale producers. In accordance with the principle of subsidiarity, Member States are best placed to find appropriate solutions based on local situations and on appropriate levels of hygiene in businesses, without compromising the objective of food safety'.[82] The open and flexible approach has not been without its

[75] Animal Origin Hygiene Regulation, Annex III, Section II, ch IV, points 5 and 8, and Case C-347/17 *A and Others v Staatssecretaris van Economische Zaken* EU:C:2019:720.

[76] General Hygiene Regulation, para 4 of ch I of Annex II, and Case C-381/10 *Astrid Preissl KEG v Landeshauptmann von Wien* [2011] ECR I-09281.

[77] General Hygiene Regulation, para 3 of ch IX of Annex II, and Case C-382/10 *Erich Albrecht and Others v Landeshauptmann von Wien* [2011] ECR I-09295.

[78] Animal Origin Hygiene Regulation, points 1.14 and 1.15 of Annex I, and Case C-453/13 *The Queen, on the application of: Newby Foods Ltd v Food Standards Agency* EU:C:2014:2297.

[79] For an excellent overview, see James Lawless, 'The Complexity of Flexibility in EU Food Hygiene Regulation' (2012) 7 European Food and Feed Law Review 220.

[80] General Hygiene Regulation, art 10(2): (a) to facilitate the fulfilment, by small businesses, of the requirements laid down in the Annexes; (b) to enable the continued use of traditional methods at any of the stages of production, processing, or distribution of food; (c) to accommodate the needs of food businesses situated in regions that are subject to special geographic constraints; (d) to facilitate the work of establishments producing raw material which is intended for the production of highly refined food products and which has undergone a treatment ensuring its safety.

[81] General Hygiene Regulation, art 10(3), allows Member States to adopt national measures adapting the requirements to support traditional methods or regions with special geographical constraints; in other cases only construction, layout, and equipment of establishments requirements may be modified. This is subject to notification requirements; see General Hygiene Regulation, art 10(5).

[82] Commission, 'Report from the Commission to the Council and the European Parliament on the experience gained from the application of the hygiene Regulations (EC) 852/2004, (EC) No 853/2004,

critics,[83] and at the same time compliance with hygiene rules remains a significant legal challenge, especially for smaller FBOs.[84] In this respect, the Commission has increasingly tried to 'do the work' for businesses, and provided extensive guidance documents to facilitate FBO's compliance with hygiene rules. Nevertheless, it is argued that food hygiene regulation has strongly favoured the food industry, while marginalizing small farmers, artisanal processes, and short food supply chains.[85]

In recent years, the Commission emphasizes the idea of an integrated FSMS, which combines both PRPs and HACCP. The idea of a systemic approach aligns with the introduction of the concept of 'food safety culture', a human behaviour-centred approach that transcends the science paradigm of 2000s. It also harmonizes with the idea of a food systemic approach.

and (EC) No 854/2004 of the European Parliament and of the Council of 29 April' (Report) COM (2009) 0403 final. See Lawless (n 81).

[83] Lawless (n 81).

[84] Lazar Živkovig and others, 'Exploring Regulatory Obstacles to the Development of Short Food Supply Chains: Empirical Evidence from Selected European Countries' (2022) 11 International Journal of Food Studies 138.

[85] Francesca Galli and Gianluca Brunori, *Short Food Supply Chains as Drivers of Sustainable Development: Evidence Document* (Laboratorio di studi rurali Sismondi 2013).

11
Chemical Safety of Food Products

11.1 Introduction

Broadly speaking, European Union (EU) food laws address biological (see Chapter 10) and chemical food safety hazards through different frameworks. In the regulation of chemical food safety,[1] the legal framework distinguishes unintentionally added contaminants from so-called avoidable substances.

Chemical contamination refers to the presence of unintentionally added substances in foodstuff. These are regulated by the Contaminants Regulation, except those falling under Regulation (EC) 2073/2005 on microbiological criteria.[2] Contaminants can occur naturally or be the result of anthropogenic activity. Examples of contaminant groups are heavy metals; industrial and environmental contaminants; 'natural' toxins produced by fungi, plant, or marine algae; and residues of veterinary medicinal products such as antibiotics. In addition, processing may result in the formation of contaminants, for instance acrylamide or furan, or polycyclic aromatic hydrocarbons (PAHs) in traditionally smoked meat. Contaminants that 'unintentionally' end up in food products can originate from diverse sources: for example, crops might become contaminated if they are grown in soil with a high heavy metal concentration, or if artificial fertilizers resulted in a high nitrate concentration in the soil. Regarding contaminants, EU law largely disregards the source of contamination and focuses on the end results; EU contaminants law prescribes maximum levels (MLs) for unintentionally added substances that can be present in final food products (see section 11.2).

In contrast, the regulation of avoidable chemical substances is undertaken with a view to covering all aspects of the chemical; the market authorization of the source substance, conditions on the use of products containing the substance, and maximum residue levels (MRLs) left in the end product. The presence of avoidable chemical substances in food typically originates from pesticides (see section 11.3.1), veterinary medicinal products (see section 11.3.2), biocides (see section 11.3.3), food contact materials (see Chapter 12), or food improvement agents (see Chapter 9). These are regulated along different pathways. An example of the

[1] Literature on legal aspects of chemical food safety is relatively scarce. See, for instance, Daniele Pisanello, *Chemistry of Foods: EU Legal and Regulatory Approaches* (Springer 2014).

[2] Commission Regulation (EC) 2073/2005 of 15 November 2005 on microbiological criteria for foodstuffs [2005] OJ L338/1.

EU Food Law. Hanna Schebesta and Kai Purnhagen, Oxford University Press. © Hanna Schebesta and Kai Purnhagen 2024.
DOI: 10.1093/9780198901570.003.0012

regulatory approach taken with respect to avoidable substances is the pathway for pesticides: the active substance, such as glyphosate, requires an authorization at EU level that establishes the eventual conditions of its use. Additionally, the deployment of authorized active substances in plant protection products (PPP) is regulated, and PPPs require an authorization by Member States, which can also establish conditions for their use. Therefore, a PPP such as Roundup that uses glyphosate needs to be authorized at Member State level. Alongside the specific regulatory conditions of use accompanying the active substance and PPP authorizations, further general conditions of use derive from the Integrated Pest Management Principles, and particularly the Sustainable Use of Pesticides.[3] In addition, the permissible residue in the final end product, that is, food, is also regulated: foodstuffs may contain pesticide residues only up to an MRL.

The use of chemicals on, in, and around food is abundant in today's food production, processing, and packaging industry. From a chemical perspective, not all hazards have been identified and not all risks have been assessed; significant gaps in regulation remain. Particular attention has been drawn to the presence of the so-called 'forever chemicals', or per- and polyfluoroalkyl substances (PFAS), a class of chemicals that does not break down. PFAS have been found pervasively in the environment, ground- and drinking water, and on food contact materials. Although the problem extends beyond food, it is of course a major concern that humans are exposed to highly toxic substances through the food and water they consume. To illustrate the extent of the problem, the Organisation for Economic Co-operation and Development (OECD) PFAS definition includes over 10,000 substances.[4] The debate surrounding PFAS may, however, shift the focus of food safety regulation towards addressing chemical aspects more comprehensively. This might lead to discussions about regulating chemicals themselves, rather than only their presence in the final food product.

11.2 EU legal framework for contaminants (unintentionally added substances)

The EU contaminants framework covers any substance that is unintentionally added to food as a result of operations during production or environmental contamination. The current regulatory framework for contaminants was established in 1993 and was reformed in 2008. MLs for contaminants are not fully harmonized

[3] Directive 2009/128/EC of the European Parliament and of the Council of 21 October 2009 establishing a framework for Community action to achieve the sustainable use of pesticides [2009] OJ L309/71.

[4] Any substance that contains at least one fully fluorinated methyl (CF3-) or methylene (-CF2) carbon atom (without any H/Cl/Br/I attached to it).

in the EU; for non-harmonized substances, national legislation may therefore exist, while other substances are simply unregulated.

11.2.1 *Regulation 315/93/EEC 'Procedures for Contaminants'*

The general Contaminants Regulation[5] outlines the procedures for contaminants. 'Contaminants' are defined as substances not intentionally added to food which are present in food as a result of the production, manufacture, processing, preparation, treatment, packing, packaging, transport, or holding of such food, or due to environmental contamination. Extraneous matter, such as insect fragments and animal hair is not covered by this definition.[6]

Food containing a contaminant of an amount unacceptable from a public health perspective and in particular at a toxicological level, will not be placed on the market.[7] As a main general rule, contaminant levels must be kept as low as can reasonably be achieved (ALARA) following good practices.[8] In addition, the Commission sets MLs for contaminants, which include limits for the same contaminant in different foods, analytical detection limits, and the sampling and analysis methods to be used.[9]

While certain contaminants MLs are set in the Union list at the EU level, other contaminants of concern are only subject to recommendations and 'joint risk management' approaches that are coordinated among Member States.

11.2.2 *Commission Regulation (EU) 2023/915 'Maximum Levels for certain contaminants'*

MLs have been set at EU level for certain contaminants, primarily listed in the Maximum Level Commission Regulation.[10] This means that there are no 'zero' tolerances, nor is there a default ML.

The regulated contaminant groups are (by order of appearance in the Annex): mycotoxins (aflatoxins, ochratoxin A, patulin, deoxynivalenol, zearalenone, fumonisins, citrinin, ergot sclerotia, and ergot alkaloids); plant toxins (erucic acid, including erucic acid bound in fat, tropane alkaloids, hydrocyanic

5 Council Regulation (EEC) 315/93 of 8 February 1993 laying down Community procedures for contaminants in food [1993] OJ L37/1 (General Contaminants Regulation).
6 General Contaminants Regulation, art 1.
7 ibid, art 2(1).
8 ibid, art 2(2).
9 ibid, art 2(3).
10 Commission Regulation (EU) 2023/915 of 25 April 2023 on maximum levels for certain contaminants in food and repealing Regulation (EC) No 1881/2006 [2023] OJ L 119/103 (Maximum Level Commission Regulation).

Table 11.1 *MLs for certain contaminants in foodstuffs*

6.1 Nitrates		**Maximum levels (mg NO_3/kg)**	
6.1.1	Fresh spinach (*Spinacia oleracea*)	3 500	The maximum level does not apply for fresh spinach for processing, which is directly transported in bulk from field to processing plant.
6.1.2	Preserved, deep-frozen or frozen spinach	2 000	

Source: Maximum Level Commission Regulation, Annex, Section 6.1: Nitrate.

acid, including hydrocyanic acid bound in cyanogenic glycosides, pyrrolizidine alkaloids, opium alkaloids, delta-9-tetrahydrocannabinol (Δ9-THC) equivalents); metals and other elements (lead, cadmium, mercury, arsenic, tin (inorganic)); halogenated persistent organic pollutants (dioxins and PCBs, perfluoroalkyl substances); processing contaminants (polycyclic aromatic hydrocarbon (PAHs), 3-monochloropropane-1,2-diol (3-MCPD), sum of 3-monochloropropanediol (3-MCPD) and 3-MCPD fatty acid esters, expressed as 3-MCPD, glycidyl fatty acid esters, expressed as glycidol); and other contaminants (nitrates, melamine, perchlorate). An example of the MLs for nitrates in specific foodstuffs is given in Table 11.1.

MLs are set for selected foods. In dried, diluted, processed, or compound foods changes of the contaminant's concentration caused by drying, dilution, or processing must be considered. The Regulation sets rules on dried, diluted, processed, and compound foods,[11] and the 2023 version of the Regulation includes a novel prohibition on detoxification.[12] The Commission has also set harmonized methods for sampling and analysis[13] at EU level.[14]

[11] Maximum Level Commission Regulation, art 3.
[12] ibid, art 4.
[13] For details on the analytical methods used in sampling, see Pisanello (n 1).
[14] Commission Regulation (EC) 401/2006 of 23 February 2006 laying down the methods of sampling and analysis for the official control of the levels of mycotoxins in foodstuffs [2006] OJ L70/12; Commission Regulation (EC) 1882/2006 of 19 December 2006 laying down methods of sampling and analysis for the official control of the levels of nitrates in certain foodstuffs [2006] OJ L364/25; Commission Regulation (EC) 333/2007 of 28 March 2007 laying down methods of sampling and analysis for the control of the levels of lead, cadmium, mercury, inorganic tin, 3-MCPD and benzo(a) pyrene in foodstuffs [2008] OJ L88/29; Commission Regulation (EU) 2015/705 of 30 April 2015 laying down methods of sampling and performance criteria for the methods of analysis for the official control of the levels of erucic acid in foodstuffs and repealing Commission Directive 80/891/EEC [2015] OJ L113/29; Commission Regulation (EU) 2017/644 of 5 April 2017 laying down methods of sampling and analysis for the control of levels of dioxins, dioxin-like PCBs and non-dioxin-like PCBs in certain foodstuffs and repealing Regulation (EU) 589/2014 [2017] OJ L92/9.

In addition to contaminant MLs, some additional MLs are set in specific legislation, for instance for carry-over feed additives[15] or with respect to specific foodstuffs, such as lead in caseins intended for human consumption.[16] Authorized novel foods may also have an individual ML in their product specifications.

11.2.3 Other risk management measures for contaminants

Alongside setting formal MLs, there are other EU actions available to target substances identified as hazardous.

One tool is to address specific hazards in specific legal instruments. The Acrylamide Commission Regulation,[17] for instance, sets out mitigation measures to ensure that acrylamide levels are as low as reasonably achievable below the benchmark levels for the foodstuffs specified.[18] Acrylamide is a process-contaminant that forms when starchy foods are baked, fried, or roasted, and is a probable carcinogen in humans. This Regulation became (in)famous for its focus on the 'Maillard reaction' (the browning of heated foodstuff) in certain food products (bread, potato-based items, and coffee) and prescribes that French fries should no longer be fried above 175 degrees Celsius, and exhibit an optimal 'pale' colour according to a 'frying colour guide'.[19] Such substance-specific regulation is in part a reaction to the solidification of scientific understanding regarding the risks associated with certain hazards, and in part they address issues that reach a certain threshold of public demand for regulatory action.

A second tool is the adoption of Commission Recommendations, which may generally recommend monitoring for the presence of specific substances. This approach has been used with respect to mineral oil hydrocarbons (MOH),[20] which may be present due to, for instance, environmental contamination or lubricants

[15] Commission Regulation (EC) 124/2009 of 10 February 2009 setting maximum levels for the presence of coccidiostats or histomonostats in food resulting from the unavoidable carry-over of these substances in non-target feed [2009] OJ L40/7.

[16] Directive (EU) 2015/2203 of the European Parliament and of the Council of 25 November 2015 on the approximation of the laws of the Member States relating to caseins and caseinates intended for human consumption and repealing Council Directive 83/417/EEC [2015] OJ L314/1.

[17] Commission Regulation (EU) 2017/2158 of 20 November 2017 establishing mitigation measures and benchmark levels for the reduction of the presence of acrylamide in food [2017] OJ L304/24 (Acrylamide Commission Regulation).

[18] Acrylamide Commission Regulation, Annex IV.

[19] ibid, Annex II, Part A.

[20] Commission Recommendation (EU) 2017/84 of 16 January 2017 on the monitoring of mineral oil hydrocarbons in food and in materials and articles intended to come into contact with food [2017] OJ L12/95.

used in machinery; perchlorate;[21] dioxins and PCBs;[22] and PFAS.[23] In addition to the official Commission Recommendations, the Standing Committee in 2014 agreed on recommendations for monitoring specific plant toxins and mycotoxins.[24]

Action levels (ALs) serve as an early warning tool. ALs are usually a fraction of the MLs, and they imply that the food can still be marketed, but that the Member States, in cooperation with FBOs, should aim to identify and reduce or eliminate the source of contamination. For instance, the Recommendation for reduction of dioxins and polychlorinated biphenyls (PCBs)[25] has a monitoring recommendation, but additionally defines ALs for dioxins and dioxin-like PCBs (DL-PCBs).

Even in the absence of MLs set at the EU level, established risks for certain contaminants can still be made actionable through a joint risk management statement and the general food safety requirements of Article 14 General Food Law Regulation (GFLR).[26] This happened with MOHs: according to the European Food Safety Authority (EFSA) Opinion, they may be mutagenic and carcinogenic. In addition to the Commission Recommendation,[27] further evaluations were conducted by EFSA in particular with respect to infant and young child formula. This, for instance, led to a joint risk management statement that in infant formula, follow-on formula, foods for special medical purposes intended for infants and young children, and young child formula, concentrations of 1mg/kg MOAH per MOAH C-fraction are considered a health concern, and that measures should be taken under Article 14 of GFLR.[28]

In addition, contaminant risks are communicated through the Rapid Alert System for Food and Feed (RASFF). For this purpose, EFSA developed the Rapid Assessment of Contaminant Exposure (RACE) tool[29] to support Member State authorities in deciding whether they should notify contaminations in RASFF. The

[21] Commission Recommendation (EU) 2015/682 of 29 April 2015 on the monitoring of the presence of perchlorate in food [2015] OJ L111/32.

[22] Commission Recommendation (EU) 2013/711 of 3 December 2013 on the reduction of the presence of dioxins, furans and PCBs in feed and food [2013] OJ L323/37.

[23] Commission Recommendation of 17 March 2010 on the monitoring of perfluoroalkylated substances in food [2010] OJ L68/22.

[24] Standing Committee on Plants, Animals, Food and Feed, *Compilation of Agreed Monitoring Recommendations as Regards the Presence of Mycotoxis and Plant Toxins in Food* (2014).

[25] Commission Recommendation 2013/711/EU.

[26] Regulation (EC) 178/2002 of the European Parliament and of the Council of 28 January 2002 laying down the general principles and requirements of food law, establishing the European Food Safety Authority and laying down procedures in matters of food safety [2002] OJ L31/1 (General Food Law Regulation, GFLR).

[27] Commission Recommendation (EU) 2017/84.

[28] Agreed at the meeting of the Standing Committee on Plants, Animals, Food and Feed, section Novel Food and Toxicological Safety of the Food Chain on 23 June 2020.

[29] EFSA, 'Risk Evaluation of Chemical Contaminants in Food in the Context of RASFF Notifications: Rapid Assessment of Contaminant Exposure tool (RACE)' (2019) 16(5) EFSA Supporting Publications <https://efsa.onlinelibrary.wiley.com/doi/abs/10.2903/sp.efsa.2019.EN-1625> accessed 28 July 2022.

risk evaluation is based on toxicological properties and dietary exposure, and establishes risk categorizations (no risk; low probability of adverse health effects or low concern for public health; potential risk; or risk).

Overall, in addition to the establishment of MLs, the EU implements a number of complementary risk management measures to address contaminants. This can be viewed as good practices of 'reflexive governance', or as is the case in some industries, as illegitimate and unpredictable de facto rule setting.

11.3 'Intentionally added' substances

In addition to contaminants, defined as 'unintentionally added' substances, there are various EU legal frameworks that regulate what could be called intentionally added substances, referred to predominantly as 'avoidable substances'. Avoidable substances in foodstuffs have different applicable frameworks depending on their source of origin. In this context, regulatory frameworks for pesticides, veterinary medicinal products, biocides, and hormones were developed.[30] In this section, we focus only on the legal requirements regarding the presence of avoidable substances in foods, specifically focusing on the final product.

11.3.1 Maximum pesticide residue levels (MRLs): Regulation EC 396/2005

The use of pesticides—technically 'plant protection products' (PPP)—can result in residues of active substances[31] (the substance itself, metabolites, and/or breakdown and reaction products) in foodstuffs. Pesticides are regulated at the EU level in a multi-layered legal framework comprising laws regarding the authorization of active substances, PPPs themselves, their use,[32] and how much of the pesticide residues may be present in or on final food and feed products. In this wider framework, the EU Pesticide MRL Regulation[33] sets MLs of pesticide residues (MRLs)

[30] Pesticides and biocides have been regulated since the 1990s. Originally Council Directive 91/414/EEC of 15 July 1991 concerning the placing of plant protection products on the market [1991] OJ L230/1; Directive 98/8/EC of the European Parliament and of the Council of 16 February 1998 concerning the placing of biocidal products on the market [1998] OJ L123/1, no longer in force.

[31] The applicable technical definitions are to be found in Regulation (EC) 1107/2009 of the European Parliament and of the Council of 21 October 2009 concerning the placing of plant protection products on the market and repealing Council Directives 79/117/EEC and 91/414/EEC [2009] OJ L309/1, art 3.

[32] 'Good agricultural practice' (GAP) means the nationally recommended, authorized, or registered safe use of PPPs under actual conditions.

[33] Regulation (EC) 396/2005 of the European Parliament and of the Council of 23 February 2005 on maximum residue levels of pesticides in or on food and feed of plant and animal origin and amending Council Directive 91/414/EEC [2005] OJ L70/1 (Pesticide MRL Regulation).

Table 11.2 *Products of plant and animal origin referred to in Article 2(1) to which MRLs apply.*

Code number	Category	Group / Subgroup	Main product of the group or subgroup (1)	Scientific names	Part of the product to which MRLs apply
(1)	(2)	(3)	(4)	(5)	(6)
0100000	Fruits, fresh or frozen; Tree nuts				
0110000		Citrus fruits			Whole product after removal of stems

Source: Pesticide MRL Regulation, Annex I, Part A.

and outlines the EU risk assessment procedure. There are MRLs for 315 fresh products covering around 1,100 pesticides currently or formerly used in agriculture in or outside the EU.[34]

Active substances must be authorized at EU level, and PPP formulae using active substances must, in turn, also be authorized by Member States. The PPP Regulation requires, where appropriate, the setting of MRLs for the agricultural products affected in accordance with the Pesticide MRL Regulation.[35]

The Pesticide MRL Regulation governs the setting of harmonized MRLs for all products specified in Annex I, which also indicates which part of the product MRLs apply to (Table 11.2).

The food categories must comply with the MRLs specified, as listed in Annex II (Table 11.3) and temporary MRLs in Annex III.[36]

Annex IV defines a list of active substances for which no MRLs are required,[37] for instance acetic acid, limestone, and orange oil (Table 11.4).[38]

If there is no specific MRL, a generic limit of 0,01mg/kg applies.[39]

For processed and composite products,[40] the Pesticide MRL Regulation prohibits the use of non-compliant ingredients in composite products.[41] The MRL for

[34] Directorate-General for Health and Food Safety of the European Commission, 'EU legislation on MRLs' <https://ec.europa.eu/food/plants/pesticides/maximum-residue-levels/eu-legislation-mrls_en> accessed 28 July 2022.
[35] Pesticide MRL Regulation, art 29.
[36] ibid, art 18(1)(a).
[37] ibid, art 5.
[38] ibid, Annex IV.
[39] ibid, art 18(1)(b).
[40] ibid, art 20.
[41] ibid, art 19.

Table 11.3 *Pesticide residues and maximum residue levels (mg/kg)*

Code number	**Groups and examples of individual products to which the MRLs apply**	**1,1-dichloro-2,2-bis (4-ethylphenyl)ethane**	**1,2-dibromoethane (ethylene dibromide)**	**1,2-dichloroethane (ethylene dichloride)**	**M161 1-methylcy clopropene**	**M40 2,4-DB (sum of 2,4-DB, its salts, its esters and its conjugates, expressed as 2,4-DB)**
(1)	(2)	(3)	(4)	(5)	(6)	(7)
0100000	1. Fruit fresh or frozen; Nuts	0,01	0,01	0,01	M91 0,01	M40 0,05

Source: Pesticide MRL Regulation, Annex II.

Table 11.4 *Examples of active substances of PPPs evaluated under Directive 91/414/EEC for which no MRLs are required, referred to in Article 5(1)*

Benzoic acid
Cow milk
Laminarin
Methyl decanoate (CAS 110-42-9)
Pepino Mosaic Virus, EU strain, mild isolate Abp 1
Pepper
Pseudomonas chlororaphis, strain MA342

Source: Pesticide MRL Regulation, Annex IV.

processed foods should be calculated taking into account changes in the levels of pesticide residues caused by processing. There is a mandate for the Commission to establish specific concentration or dilution factors for certain processing and/or mixing operations in an Annex VI that does not yet exist. The issue of processed and composite products, therefore, is marked by some legal uncertainty, for instance regarding the use of peeling factors or default drying factors for dried products.

As MRLs are set per product category and pesticide residue, the legal text is operationalized through the Commission's Pesticide residue database (v 2.2).

11.3.1.1 ***Risk assessment***

The risk assessment is undertaken by EFSA. EFSA uses estimates on chronic (long-term) and acute (short-term) exposure to pesticide residues in consumer diets, following a calculation model (PRIMo—Pesticide Residue Intake Model[42]) that uses data provided by Member States on national food consumption and unit weights.

Cumulative risk assessments are one of the frontier issues in risk assessment. EFSA presented its first pilots in 2020 assessing cumulative risk by establishing cumulative assessment groups (CAG) of pesticides to assess their combined toxicity for special effects, such as chronic effects on the thyroid system, and acute effects on the nervous system. It then proceeded with a cumulative exposure assessment, and subsequently conducted a cumulative risk characterization.[43] However, the issue of so-called 'stacking' remains a serious concern that is not sufficiently addressed in the regulatory framework.

11.3.2 MRLs of veterinary medicinal products

Similarly to pesticides, the EU legal framework for veterinary medicinal products encompasses a number of legal instruments that regulate different aspects of the authorization of pharmacologically active substances, the use of the products, and the residues of substances in the respective 'food producing' animal species. The novel Veterinary Medicinal Products Regulation[44] covers the authorization, use, and monitoring of veterinary medicinal products. The procedures to establish

[42] EFSA, 'Pesticide evaluation: Tools' <https://www.efsa.europa.eu/en/applications/pesticides/tools> accessed 38 July 2022.

[43] EFSA, 'Cumulative risk assessment of pesticides: FAQ' (2020) <https://www.efsa.europa.eu/en/news/cumulative-risk-assessment-pesticides-faq> accessed 28 July 2022.

[44] Regulation (EU) 2019/6 of the European Parliament and of the Council of 11 December 2018 on veterinary medicinal products and repealing Directive 2001/82/EC [2019] OJ L4/43.

Table 11.5 *Allowed substances*

Pharmacologically Active Substances	**Marker residue**	**Animal Species**	**MRL**	**Target Tissues**	**Other Provisions** *(according to article 14(7) of Regulation (EC) No 470/2009)*	**Therapeutic Classification**
Abamectin	Avermectin B1a	Bovine	10 µg/kg20 µg/kg	Fat Liver	NO ENTRY	Antiparasitic agents/Agents acting against endo—and ectoparasites
		Ovine	20 µg/kg50 µg/kg25 µg/kg20 µg/kg	Muscle Fat Liver Kidney	Not for use in animals from which milk is produced for human consumption	

Source: Veterinary Medicinal Products Regulation, Annex f—Table 1.

the MRLs[45] are set in the maximum concentration of a residue of a pharmacologically active substance which may be permitted in food of animal origin. These substances are risk-assessed by the European Medicines Agency, not EFSA. The applicable MRLs are listed in the Regulation on pharmacologically active substances and their MRLs (Table 11.5).[46]

11.3.3 Biocides—balancing chemical and microbial safety

Not only pesticides, but biocides too may leave residues in food or feed. The Biocidal Product Regulation (BPR)[47] covers 'biocidal products', defined as substances or mixtures with an active substance intended to exert a controlling effect

[45] Regulation (EC) 470/2009 of the European Parliament and of the Council of 6 May 2009 laying down Community procedures for the establishment of residue limits of pharmacologically active substances in foodstuffs of animal origin, repealing Council Regulation (EEC) No 2377/90 and amending Directive 2001/82/EC of the European Parliament and of the Council and Regulation (EC) No 726/2004 of the European Parliament and of the Council [2009] OJ L152/11 (Veterinary Medicinal Products Regulation).

[46] Commission Regulation (EU) 37/2010 of 22 December 2009 on pharmacologically active substances and their classification regarding maximum residue limits in foodstuffs of animal origin [2010] OJ L15/1.

[47] Regulation (EU) 528/2012 of the European Parliament and of the Council of 22 May 2012 concerning the making available on the market and use of biocidal products [2012] OJ L167/1 (Biocidal Product Regulation (BPR)).

on any harmful organism. The BPR specifies that biocidal products will be authorized provided that, where appropriate, MRLs for food and feed have been established.[48]

The legal framework remains incomplete in addressing certain risks that have become widely acknowledged. For instance, the Commission has so far failed to comply with the obligation[49] to adopt a delegated act to set a specific scientific criterion to identify substances which have endocrine disrupting properties. This was confirmed by the Court of Justice of the European Union (CJEU),[50] which found the Commission to be in breach of EU law.

So far, the Commission has only followed up with a Note for agreement with Competent Authorities for Biocidal Products, which shaped an interim approach to endocrine disruptors. It also clearly stated that the establishment of MRLs for active substances originating from biocides would have to wait for the next overhaul of the primary legislative instruments.[51]

11.3.4 Prohibition on certain hormones in meat

Hormones are chemicals that usually function as messengers between different body parts; they are therefore often called 'chemical messengers'. In the US, hormones are commonly used to increase animal production. In contrast, since well into the 1980s, the EU has banned hormones in stockfarming,[52] later extended to combat contentious uses of beta-agonists in livestock-rearing that stimulate the growth and yield of animals.

The Hormone Directive[53] prohibits the administration of certain substances in livestock, as well as the holding or placing on the market of the animals or foodstuffs derived from them. The prohibited substances are thyrostatic substances, stilbenes, stilbene derivatives, their salts and esters, and oestradiol 17β and its

[48] BPR, art 19(1)(e).

[49] ibid, art 5(3).

[50] Case T-521/14 *Kingdom of Sweden v European Commission* EU:T:2015:976.

[51] Health and Food Safety Directorate General of the European Commission, *Note for agreement with Competent Authorities for Biocidal Products: An interim approach for the establishment of maximum residue limits for residues of active substances contained in biocidal products for food and feed and specific migration limits in food contact materials* (2017).

[52] Council Directive 81/602/EEC of 31 July 1981 concerning the prohibition of certain substances having a hormonal action and of any substances having a thyrostatic action [1981] OJ L222/32; Council Directive 88/146/EEC of 7 March 1988 prohibiting the use in livestock farming of certain substances having a hormonal action [1988] OJ L70/16; whilst conceding derogations Dir 81/602/EEC, Dir 88/146/EEC, and Council Directive 88/299/EEC of 17 May 1988 on trade in animals treated with certain substances having a hormonal action and their meat, as referred to in Article 7 of Directive 88/146/EEC [1988] OJ L128/36.

[53] Council Directive 96/22/EC of 29 April 1996 concerning the prohibition on the use in stockfarming of certain substances having a hormonal or thyrostatic action and of beta-agonists, and repealing Directives 81/602/EEC, 88/146/EEC and 88/299/EEC [1996] OJ L125/3 (Hormone Directive).

ester-like derivatives. Beta-agonists are prohibited with derogations (Annex II), and substances having oestrogenic (other than oestradiol 17β and its ester-like derivatives), androgenic, or gestagenic action are provisionally prohibited (Annex III).

The EU not only banned the use of substances with hormonal action for promoting growth in farm animals but also their trade, which was highly contested in the World Trade Organization (WTO) arena.[54]

11.4 Discussion

The current system for regulating chemical substances in foodstuffs is in need of a regulatory overhaul. It is characterized by incomplete harmonization (not all substances or foods are covered), certain points of legal uncertainty (for instance regarding processed and composite products), regulatory gaps (PFAS and endocrine disruption), and an outdated risk assessment system (sustainability and combined effects).

Additionally, the food-sector specific approach has drawbacks, resulting in insufficient synergies between the pharma, food, and veterinarian risk assessments. In this context, the literature has called for work on joint exposure assessments. The 'European Exposure Science Strategy 2020–2030'[55] recommends the creation of 'a common scientific framework for exposure assessment interfacing EU chemical policies for environment, health, safety/risk and sustainability assessments, with particular emphasis on different exposure aspects, including common terminology, common principles and a suite of accepted data, methods and tools'. An emergent issue for contamination is micro- and nano-plastics in soil.[56]

Much of this overhaul will come under the auspices of the Green Deal policies. Actions under the Farm to Fork Strategy include the agricultural use of certain substances: the Commission has tabled a proposal[57] for a regulation on the sustainable use of pesticides, which would repeal and replace Directive 2009/128/EC,

[54] WTO, *Measures concerning meat and meat products (Hormones)* (12 July 1999) WT/DS26; WTO, *Measures affecting livestock and meat (Hormones)* (12 July 1999) WT/DS48; WTO, Continued Suspension of Obligations in the EC-Hormones Dispute (16 October 2008) WT/DS320; WTO, *Continues Suspension of Obligations in the EC-Hormones Dispute* (16 October 2008) WT/DS321.

[55] Yuri Bruinen de Bruin and others, 'Enhancing the Use of Exposure Science across EU Chemical Policies as Part of the European Exposure Science Strategy 2020–2030' (2022) 32 Journal of Exposure Science & Environmental Epidemiology 513.

[56] EFSA Panel on Contaminants in the Food Chain (CONTAM), 'Presence of Microplastics and Nanoplastics in Food, with Particular Focus on Seafood' (2016) 14(6) EFSA Journal <https://efsa.onlinelibrary.wiley.com/doi/10.2903/j.efsa.2016.4501> accessed 28 July 2022.

[57] Commission, 'Proposal for a Regulation of the European Parliament and of the Council on the sustainable use of plant protection products and amending Regulation (EU) 2021/2115' COM (2022) 305 final.

and set legally binding targets at EU level to halve the use and the risk of chemical pesticides by 2030. Other relevant Green Deal strategies are the Chemicals Strategy[58] and the Circular Economy Action Plan[59] to ensure chemicals are safe for both health and the environment. In addition, Europe's beating cancer plan,[60] Hydrogen Strategy,[61] and the Pharmaceuticals' Strategy[62] are expected to have implications for the food safety regulatory system.

For the food safety system, and a possible integration of food with other sectors, the Chemicals Strategy will likely prove more significant than the Farm to Fork Strategy.[63] It comprises a very ambitious plan of 85 actions with a number of topics that have been on the table for a significant amount of time, for instance the phasing out of per- and polyfluoroalkyl substances (PFAS) by introducing limits in the legislation on food contaminants in the Food Contaminants Commission Regulation (Comitology) in 2022. It also addresses endocrine disruptors,[64] as well as cocktail effects of chemicals. It further foresees institutional novelties, such as the 'one substance one assessment' process for the risk and hazard assessment of chemicals. This is in addition to other major legal actions, such as the revision of the Regulation on the Registration, Evaluation, Authorisation and Restriction of Chemicals (REACH); revision of EU legislation on hazard classification, labelling, and packaging of chemicals (CLP); revision of EU rules on food contact materials; revision of the Industrial Emissions Directive; and last but not least the Sustainable Product Initiative.

[58] Commission, 'Communication from the Commission to the European Parliament, the Council, the European Economic and Social Committee and the Committee of the Regions on Chemicals Strategy for Sustainability Towards a Toxic-Free Environment' (Communication) COM (2020) 667 final (Chemicals Strategy).

[59] Commission, 'Communication from the Commission to the European Parliament, the Council, the European Economic and Social Committee and the Committee of the Regions: A new Circular Economy Plan for a cleaner and more competitive Europe' (Communication) COM (2020) 98 final (Circular Economy Action Plan).

[60] Commission, 'Communication from the Commission to the European Parliament and the Council: Europe's Beating Cancer Plan—A new EU approach to prevention, treatment and care' (2021) <https://health.ec.europa.eu/system/files/2022-02/eu_cancer-plan_en_0.pdf> accessed 28 July 2022.

[61] Commission, 'EU Hydrogen Strategy' (2020) <https://ec.europa.eu/commission/presscorner/detail/en/FS_20_1296> accessed 28 July 2022.

[62] Commission, 'Pharmaceutical Strategy for Europe' (2020) <https://health.ec.europa.eu/system/files/2021-02/pharma-strategy_report_en_0.pdf> accessed 28 July 2022.

[63] Hanna Schebesta and others, 'Tour de Table: Farm to Fork Law Update' (2022) 17 European Food and Feed Law Review 208.

[64] Commission, 'Commission Staff Working Document Fitness Check on endocrine disruptors Accompanying the document Communication from the Commission to the European Parliament, the Council, the European Economic and Social Committee and the Committee of the Regions Chemical Strategy for Sustainability Towards a Toxic-Free Environment' SWD (2020) 251 final.

12
Food Contact Materials

12.1 Introduction

Food contact materials (FCM) refers to any material that comes into contact with food. These can be containers, such as cups, lids, and stirrers for coffee to go; or processing machines, such as a juice presser. In FCM, many substances are present either intentionally or non-intentionally (NIAS, non-intentionally added substances). The main health concern regarding substances used in the manufacture of FCM is that they migrate into foods, although their use may also present environmental concerns. Migration patterns are largely determined by the conditions of contact of the material and by the type of food (eg fatty versus dry foods).

A recent integrated food contact chemicals database lists 12,285 intentionally added food contact chemicals, whereas estimates range from between 40,000 and 100,000 for NIASs.[1] In the study on integrating intentionally added food contact chemicals, 608 were regarded as hazardous on the basis of authoritative sources, and another 1,411 chemicals presented reasons for concern. Moreover, the study revealed a significant lack of hazard data for approximately a quarter of intentionally added food contact chemicals. The safety issues associated with chemicals in food and beyond are therefore not only a regulatory gap, but also a real scientific gap.

FCM were regulated in the European Union (EU) as early as 1976 by Directive 76/893/EEC. Nowadays, the cornerstone of EU legislation is Regulation 1935/2004 on food contact materials.[2] It functions as a framework regulation (section 12.2), serving as the umbrella law for a system of subsequent legal acts on specific FCM materials (section 12.4).

12.2 'Food Contact Materials' Framework Regulation

FCMs are defined as materials and articles that are (intended to be brought) into contact with food, or where this can reasonably be expected. Covering or coating

[1] Ksenia Groh and others, 'Overview of Intentionally Used Food Contact Chemicals and Their Hazards' (2021) 150 Environment International 106225.

[2] Regulation (EC) 1935/2004 of the European Parliament and of the Council of 27 October 2004 on materials and articles intended to come into contact with food and repealing Directives 80/590/EEC and 89/109/EEC [2004] OJ L338/4 (FCMR).

EU Food Law. Hanna Schebesta and Kai Purnhagen, Oxford University Press. © Hanna Schebesta and Kai Purnhagen 2024.
DOI: 10.1093/9780198901570.003.0013

materials forming part of a food are outside the scope of the Regulation, as are antiques and fixed public or private water supply equipment.[3]

The main basic requirement of the Framework Regulation is that materials and articles must be manufactured in compliance with good manufacturing practices (GMPs) (see section 12.3) so that, under normal or foreseeable conditions of use, they do not transfer their constituents to food in quantities which could: (a) endanger human health; or (b) cause an unacceptable change in the composition; or (c) deteriorate the food's organoleptic characteristics. This requirement is also known as the 'the general inertness rule'.[4]

12.2.1 Commission powers to adopt specific measures

The FCM Framework Regulation grants the Commission powers to adopt specific measures for 17 FCM categories: active and intelligent materials and articles, adhesives, ceramics, cork, rubbers, glass, ion-exchange resins, metals and alloys, paper and board, plastics, printing inks, regenerated cellulose ('cellophane'), silicones, textiles, varnishes and coatings, and waxes.[5] The European Commission has only used its powers to draw up specific measures for some categories including plastics (see section 12.4.1), active and intelligent materials (see section 12.4.2), recycled plastic materials (see section 12.4.3), ceramics (see section 12.4.4), and regenerated cellulose film (see section 12.4.5). In the absence of this EU harmonization, the national Member States may adopt or keep their own national measures,[6] leading to fragmentation in the legal landscape for many FCM categories.

The category-specific measures typically encompass a Union list of substances authorized for use in the manufacture of articles and materials, along with purity criteria, conditions of use, migration limits, and any other rules to protect human health. These measures also include provisions for inspections and control, labelling, and traceability, all of which are set through the regulatory procedure.[7]

12.2.2 Performing the safety assessment

European Food Safety Authority (EFSA) will be consulted regarding any provision likely to affect public health.[8] Anyone can seek an authorization for substances not yet included in the Union lists. The application needs to be submitted to the

[3] ibid, art 1.
[4] ibid, Recital (3).
[5] ibid, Annex I.
[6] ibid, art 6.
[7] See ibid, arts 5(1) and 23.
[8] ibid, art 7.

Figure 12.1 EU Food contact material symbol
Source: Food Contact Materials Regulation

Member State authority, who forwards it to EFSA. Upon receipt of an opinion by EFSA, the Commission prepares a draft of the specific measure, which then follows the regulatory procedure to decide whether it will be approved or disapproved.

12.2.3 ***Labelling***

Articles and material must comply with labelling requirements.[9] FCM should include an indication of use, or mention the words 'for food contact' or the symbol in Figure 12.1, unless it is obvious that an article is used for food contact.

12.2.4 ***Declaration of compliance***

FCM for which specific measures have been adopted require a declaration of compliance.[10] The EU Commission Regulations on specific materials provide additional needed information on the declarations of compliance per material. Traceability mandates extend one link up and down, meaning it is required to trace both the origin of materials supplied and their destination.

[9] ibid, art 15.
[10] ibid, art 16.

12.3 The Regulation on Good Manufacturing Practices

Food business operators (FBOs) must follow good manufacturing practices for FCM. Commission Regulation (EC) 2023/2006[11] lays down the rules on GMPs for FCM to ensure legal compliance and quality standards appropriate for preventing risks to human health as well as compositional or organoleptic deterioration.

FBOs must comply with the general rules requiring a quality assurance system, a quality control system, and sufficient documentation;[12] and the detailed rules on GMP.[13] The detailed rules[14] cover special provisions for printing inks and plastic recycling processes.

12.4 EU legislation on specific materials

The European Commission only has legislation for the following FCM categories: plastics (section 12.4.1); active and intelligent materials (section 12.4.2); recycled plastic materials (section 12.4.3); ceramics (section 12.4.4); and regenerated cellulose film (section 12.4.5).

12.4.1 'Virgin' plastic materials

The majority of plastic used is single-use. Plastic has significant advantages in terms of food logistics and safety, in particular because it is functional and lightweight, and can improve logistics and increase shelf-life. However, there are serious human health and environmental concerns associated with its use.

The most comprehensive specific measure for FCM that has been adopted concerns 'virgin' plastics. Commission Regulation 10/2011[15] consolidates a number of old legal instruments,[16] and establishes requirements for the manufacture and marketing of plastic materials and articles intended for food contact.

'Plastic' means polymer to which additives or other substances may have been added, which is capable of functioning as a main structural component of final materials and articles. Commission Regulation 10/2011 applies to (a) plastics;

[11] Commission Regulation (EC) 2023/2006 of 22 December 2006 on good manufacturing practice for materials and articles intended to come into contact with food [2006] OJ L384/75 (GMPR).

[12] As provided for in ibid, arts 5, 6, and 7.

[13] As set out in ibid, Annex.

[14] ibid, Annex.

[15] Commission Regulation (EU) 10/2011 of 14 January 2011 on plastic materials and articles intended to come into contact with food [2011] OJ L12/1.

[16] The Commission Directive 2002/72/EC of 6 August 2002 (and its six amendments), the Council Directive 78/142/EEC of 30 January 1978, the Commission Directive 80/766/EEC of 8 July 1980, the Commission Directive 81/432/EEC of 29 April 1981, and the Council Directive 82/711/EEC of 18 October 1982 (and its two amendments).

(b) plastic multi-layered materials and articles held together by adhesives or by other means; (c) materials and articles referred to in points (a) or (b) that are printed and/or covered by a coating; (d) plastic layers or plastic coatings, forming gaskets in caps and closures, that together with those caps and closures compose a set of two or more layers of different types of materials; and (e) plastic layers in multi-material multi-layered materials and articles.

Plastic materials and articles may only be placed on the market if they adhere to[17] the regulations outlined in Regulation (EC) 1935/2004, ensuring compliance under intended and foreseeable use,[18] as well as meeting requirements for labelling[19] and traceability.[20] Additionally they must be manufactured according to GMPs.[21] Moreover, the specific Regulation sets compositional and declaration requirements in Chapters II, III, and IV.[22]

The compositional requirements stipulate that only authorized substances may be used in the manufacture of plastic FCM, subject to further requirements. Authorized substances are included in a Union list of substances permitted to be used in plastic materials and articles.[23] The Union list comprises (a) monomers or other starting substances; (b) additives excluding colorants; (c) polymer production aids excluding solvents; and (d) macromolecules obtained from microbial fermentation.

Generally, substances must be of a technical quality and a purity suitable for the intended and foreseeable use of the FCM, and the composition must be known to the manufacturer of the substance.[24] Specifically, substances must meet the migration limits (specific and overall), as well as any additional restrictions[25] and detailed specifications[26] in Annex I. Substances in nanoform may only be used if they are authorized and mentioned in the specifications. In addition, the general restrictions of Annex II must be respected.

For FCM, migration is a critical issue. Migration refers to the amount of a given substance released from a material or article into food. For this reason, the Regulation sets an overall migration limit (OML) and specific migration limits (SMLs).[27] As a general rule an OML[28] is set at 10mg/dm2 of the contact material.

[17] Commission Regulation (EU) No 10/2011, art 4.
[18] FCMR, art 3.
[19] ibid, art 15.
[20] ibid, art 17.
[21] ibid, art 3.
[22] Commission Regulation (EU) No 10/2011, Chapters II, III, and IV.
[23] ibid, art 5.
[24] ibid, art 8.
[25] ibid, Annex I, point 1, Table 1, column 10.
[26] ibid, Annex I, point 4.
[27] The 'specific migration limit' (SML) means the maximum permitted amount of a given substance released from a material or article into food or food simulants; ibid, art 3(13).
[28] The maximum permitted amount of non-volatile substances released from a material or article into food simulants; ibid, art 3(11).

The SMLs are set based on a risk assessment by EFSA regarding the toxicity of specific substances, through the Committee procedure. They may also stipulate additional restrictions, for example for the type of FCM or the type of food (eg only non-fatty[29]).

12.4.2 *Active and intelligent materials*

'Active materials and articles' extend the shelf-life or maintain or improve the condition of packaged food; they are designed to deliberately incorporate components that would release or absorb substances into or from the packaged food or the environment surrounding the food. 'Intelligent materials and articles' monitor the condition of packaged food or the environment surrounding the food. As active and intelligent materials by nature do not correspond to the inertness principle, they are subject to specific provisions. The general FCM framework Regulation contains special requirements for active and intelligent materials and articles. In addition, a Commission Regulation[30] lays down specific requirements for the marketing of active and intelligent materials and articles intended to come into contact with food.

Active and intelligent materials and articles may only be placed on the market if they are[31] suitable and effective for the intended purpose of use.[32] They must comply with both the general[33] and special[34] requirements, as well as with the labelling requirements[35] outlined in the FCM Framework Regulation. In addition, they must adhere to the compositional,[36] labelling, and declaration requirements[37] of the relevant Commission Regulation.

The Commission Regulation is not yet fully in force. Subject to some derogations, only substances which are included in the 'Community list' of authorized substances may be used in components of active and intelligent materials and articles. However, the Commission has not yet published the list, and therefore national provisions continue to apply until the date of application of the Union list.[38]

[29] 'Non-fatty food' means a food for which in migration testing only food simulants other than food simulants D1 or D2 are specified in Table 2 of Annex III to this Regulation; ibid, art 3(16).
[30] Commission Regulation (EC) No 450/2009 of 29 May 2009 on active and intelligent materials and articles intended to come into contact with food [2009] OJ L135/3.
[31] See the requirements of ibid, art 4.
[32] ibid, art 4.
[33] Regulation (EC) No 1935/2004, art 3.
[34] ibid, art 4.
[35] ibid, art 15(1)(e).
[36] Commission Regulation (EC) No 450/2009, Chapter II.
[37] ibid, Chapters III and IV.
[38] ibid, art 14.

Figure 12.2 'Do not eat' symbol
Source: Commission Regulation (EC) No 450/2009, Annex I

12.4.2.1 ***Labelling***

If materials or articles could be perceived as edible, they should be labelled with the words 'DO NOT EAT' and with the symbol in Figure 12.2[39] to allow identification by the consumer of the non-edible parts.[40]

12.4.3 ***Recycled plastic materials***

Plastics are among the most complex materials to recycle.[41] Additionally, food packaging is increasingly functional and complex, so that often food packages are made up of different layers of different polymers. [42] Another major challenge is that during waste treatment, plastics absorb other chemicals, which then end up in the food contact material unintentionally and may migrate into foods. While the recycling of plastic is essential to the EU's circular economy goals, it is presents significant food safety hazards. Consequently, the rules on recycled plastic materials and articles intended to come into contact with foods were overhauled in 2022.

Under the old regime, from 2008, Commission Regulation 282/2008[43] set the main requirement that recycled plastic materials and articles could only be placed on the market if recycled plastic is obtained from an authorized recycling process.[44]

[39] ibid, Annex I.
[40] ibid, art 11.
[41] Chris Matthews, Fintan Moran, and Amit K Jaiswal, 'A Review on European Union's Strategy for Plastics in a Circular Economy and its Impact on Food Safety' (2021) 283 Journal of Cleaner Production 125263.
[42] ibid.
[43] Commission Regulation (EC) 282/2008 of 27 March 2008 on recycled plastic materials and articles intended to come into contact with foods and amending Regulation (EC) No 2023/2006 [2008] OJ L86/9.
[44] ibid, art 3.

However, while EFSA had adopted almost 150 positive scientific opinions regarding applications for plastic recycling processes, the European Commission did not authorize a single process.

While no recycling processes were authorized under the old rules, the Regulation did include some notable exceptions to its scope of application. Recycled plastic materials made with monomers and starting substances, derived from chemical depolymerization of plastic materials and articles are exempt from the Regulation, as are recycled plastic materials made from unused plastic production offcuts and/or process scraps in compliance with Commission Regulation (EU) No 10/2011, that are recycled within the manufacturing site or are used at another site. In cases where these recycling processes are used, the FCM will only have to comply with the 'virgin plastic' Regulation. In addition, there is a notable provision stipulating that recycled plastic used behind a functional barrier[45] falls outside the scope of the Regulation. On the basis of these exceptions, recycled plastic made in an 'unauthorized' recycling process may be used as FCM.

The Commission repealed Regulation (EC) 282/2008 with a new Commission Regulation on recycled plastic materials and articles intended to come into contact with foods in 2022.[46] This new Regulation creates a fully harmonized regime, and aspires to regulate all aspects regarding the safety of recycled plastics. Under the new rules, the use of recycled FCM based on national legislation is no longer permitted.

As is apparent from the recitals of the new Regulation, EFSA highlighted important constraints on the use of recycled plastics with food, observing 'that it is impossible to predict the identity of contaminants potentially present in post-consumer polyethylene terephthalate (PET) used as input of a recycling process and therefore to ensure that they are not genotoxic', and also emphasizing that 'it also cannot be assumed that it is possible to risk assess contaminants in the same way as impurities are assessed under Regulation (EU) 10/2011, or that mixtures of chemically depolymerised materials are free of such contaminants, or that plastic functional barriers may fully contain them'.[47]

The basic obligation is that recycled plastic materials and articles shall only be placed on the market where the requirements of the Regulation are met during their manufacture.[48]

They must be manufactured using either a suitable recycling technology[49] or a novel technology.[50] The Regulation also sets requirements on collection and

[45] 'Functional barrier' means a barrier consisting of one or more layers of any type of material which ensures that the final material or article complies with art 3 of Regulation (EC) No 1935/2004 and with the provisions of this Regulation; Commission Regulation (EU) No 10/2011, art 3(15).

[46] Commission Regulation (EU) 2022/1616 of 15 September 2022 on recycled plastic materials and articles intended to come into contact with foods, and repealing Regulation (EC) No 282/2008 [2022] OJ L243/3 (Recycled Plastic Regulation).

[47] ibid, Recital (4).

[48] ibid, art 4.

[49] ibid, Annex I.

[50] ibid, art 3(6).

pre-processing,[51] requirements for decontamination,[52] and requirements on post-processing and use of recycled plastic materials and articles.[53] Overall, the Regulation aims to ensure that recycled plastic materials and articles are not only sufficiently inert but also microbiologically safe, therefore showing a marriage between chemical and microbiological safety concerns in one legal instrument. Recycled plastic materials and articles must also comply with the restrictions and specifications, such as migration limits, laid down in Regulation (EU) 10/2011.[54]

Generally, recycled plastic materials and articles should, in principle, only be produced using a technology which is sufficiently well understood to allow the Commission to determine whether it allows the recycling of waste plastic into plastic that meets the requirements of Regulation (EC) 1935/2004, and whether individual authorization of each of them are necessary. Specifically, the Regulation requires the decontamination of plastics by means of a suitable recycling technology. The list of suitable recycling technologies[55] cover post-consumer mechanical PET recycling and recycling from product loops which are in a closed and controlled chain. The corresponding decontamination technologies[56] are mechanical recycling and recycling from product loops which are in a closed and controlled chain. Of these, mechanical PET recycling processes are subject to an individual authorization requirement, as the treatment of the plastic input depends on specific configurations in the decontamination operations, and require a case-by-case evaluation. Recycling from product loops which are in a closed and controlled chain, by contrast, is not subject to an individual authorization.

12.4.4 Ceramics

In the production of ceramics, metal and metal oxides for technical or decorative purposes—in order to lower the melting point, or to influence appearance—are often used. Lead oxide is even an EU quality requirement,[57] with glassware only permitted to call itself 'lead crystal' when it contains at least 24% lead oxide.[58]

There is a legacy Directive on ceramics[59] dating from 1984, which had been adopted on the basis of Article 100 EEC. Ceramics means 'articles manufactured

[51] ibid, art 6.
[52] ibid, art 7.
[53] ibid, art 8.
[54] ibid, art 4(2)
[55] ibid, Annex I, table 1.
[56] ibid, Annex I, table 3.
[57] Council Directive 69/493/EEC of 15 December 1969 on the approximation of the laws of the Member States relating to crystal glass [1969] OJ L326.
[58] Commission, 'Migration limits for lead, cadmium and possibly other metals from ceramic and vitreous food contact materials' (Inception Impact Assessment) Ares (2019) 3505623, 29 May 2019.
[59] Council Directive 84/500/EEC of 15 October 1984 on the approximation of the laws of the Member States relating to ceramic articles intended to come into contact with foodstuffs [1984] OJ L277/12.

from a mixture of inorganic materials with a generally high argillaceous or silicate content to which small quantities of organic materials may have been added. These articles are first shaped and the shape thus obtained is permanently fixed by firing. They may be glazed, enamelled and/or decorated.'[60] The Ceramics Directive only regulates the migration of cadmium and lead. It also does not extend officially to glass and enamels (vitreous).

However, since 2009 and 2010 EFSA significantly lowered its recommendations regarding lead and cadmium in food, and observed that dietary exposure is the main source of intake of these heavy metals. Similar scientific evidence has become available for the toxicity of several other metals.[61]

The European Commission aims to adopt a new legislative act in 2023, which will likely propose lowering the limits for lead and cadmium; introduce regulatory limits for aluminium, arsenic, barium, cobalt, chromium, and nickel; and extend the legislation beyond ceramics to also cover vitreous materials.

12.4.5 Regenerated cellulose film

The Regenerated Cellulose Film Commission Directive[62] codifies an earlier directive from 1993.[63] It defines regenerated cellulose film as 'a thin sheet material obtained from a refined cellulose derived from unrecycled wood or cotton. To meet technical requirements, suitable substances may be added either in the mass or on the surface. Regenerated cellulose film may be coated on one or both sides.'[64] The Regulation covers uncoated and coated regenerated cellulose film, with coating derived from cellulose or coating consisting of plastics. Regenerated cellulose film (coated or uncoated) may be made only by using substances listed in the Annex. This includes any functional classes, maximum and minimum limit values, and other specified restrictions.[65] In cases of coatings consisting of plastics, these have

[60] ibid, art 1.

[61] EFSA, 'Safety of Aluminium from Dietary Intake—Scientific Opinion of the Panel on Food Additives, Flavourings, Processing Aids and Food Contact Materials (AFC)' (2008) 6 EFSA Journal 754; EFSA, 'Cadmium in Food—Scientific Opinion of the Panel on Contaminants in the Food Chain' (2009) 7 EFSA Journal 980; EFSA, 'Scientific Opinion on the Risks to Public Health Related to the Presence of Chromium in Food and Drinking Water' (2014) 12 EFSA Journal 3595; EFSA, 'Scientific Opinion on Safety and Efficacy of Cobalt Compounds (E3) as Feed Additives for All Animal Species: Cobaltous Acetate Tetrahydrate, Basic Cobaltous Carbonate Monohydrate and Cobaltous Sulphate Heptahydrate, Based on a Dossier Submitted by TREAC EEIG' (2012) 10 EFSA Journal 2791; EFSA, 'Scientific Opinion on the Risks to Public Health Related to the Presence of Nickel in Food and Drinking Water' (2015) 13 EFSA Journal 4002.

[62] Commission Directive 2007/42/EC of 29 June 2007 relating to materials and articles made of regenerated cellulose film intended to come into contact with foodstuffs [2007] OJ L172/71.

[63] Commission Directive 93/10/EEC of 15 March 1993 relating to materials and articles made of regenerated cellulose film [1993] OJ L93/27.

[64] Commission Directive 2007/42/EC, Annex I.

[65] The list is contained in Commission Directive 2007/42/EC, Annex II and can be consulted at <https://echa.europa.eu/regen-cellulose-film-subs?p_p_id=eucleflegislationlist_WAR_euclefportlet&p_p_lifecycle=0> accessed 9 September 2022.

to comply with the specific rules on plastic FCM.[66] Printed surfaces of regenerated cellulose film shall not come into contact with foodstuffs.[67]

12.5 Restrictions on the use of specific substances

In addition to the legislation on FCM material categories, there are restrictions on the use of specific substances. To date, these are bisphenol A, epoxy derivatives, as well as N-nitrosamines.

Bisphenol A (BPA, or '2,2-bis(4-hydroxyphenyl)propane') is a substance causing increasing regulatory concern. BPA is used in epoxy resins, for example for application on the interior of cans. In principle, Commission Regulation (EU) 10/2011 authorizes the use of BPA with an SML of 0,6mg of BPA per kg of food (mg/kg). However, over time, EFSA has revised its scientific opinion on BPA. BPA has been banned from polycarbonate plastic infant feeding bottles and drinking bottles intended for young children since 2011.[68] Since 2018, BPA has been restricted in varnishes and coatings intended to come into contact with food, to a specific migration limit of 0,05mg of BPA per kg of food (mg/kg).[69]

Certain epoxy derivatives are subject to special restrictions in all FCM,[70] either being subject to a full ban or specific migration limits.[71]

N-nitrosamines are specifically regulated in teats and suckers, showing the special attention of the regulator to baby products—with a limit for N-nitrosamines of 0,01mg in the total of N-nitrosamines released/kg of the parts of teat or soother made of elastomer or rubber.[72]

These restrictions are reactions to specific risk assessments and address particularly urgent substances and/or in FCM for particularly vulnerable groups (infants and young children) and are in part justified by the precautionary principle and the fact that no sufficient toxicological data are available.

[66] Commission Directive 2007/42/EC, art 4(3).

[67] ibid, art 5.

[68] Regulation (EU) 10/2011, Table 1 of Annex I, the entry concerning substance number 151 as amended by Commission Implementing Regulation (EU) No 321/2011 of 1 April 2011 amending Regulation (EU) No 10/2011 as regards the restriction of use of Bisphenol A in plastic infant feeding bottles [2011] OJ L87/1.

[69] Commission Regulation (EU) 2018/213 of 12 February 2018 on the use of bisphenol A in varnishes and coatings intended to come into contact with food and amending Regulation (EU) No 10/2011 as regards the use of that substance in plastic food contact materials [2018] OJ L41/6.

[70] Commission Regulation (EC) 1895/2005 of 18 November 2005 on the restriction of use of certain epoxy derivatives in materials and articles intended to come into contact with food [2005] OJ L302/28.

[71] Defined as 2,2-bis(4-hydroxyphenyl)propane bis(2,3-epoxypropyl) ether, referred to as 'BADGE' (CAS No 001675-54-3), bis(hydroxyphenyl)methane bis(2,3-epoxypropyl)ethers, referred to as 'BFDGE' (CAS No 039817-09-9); other novolac glycidyl ethers, referred to as 'NOGE'.

[72] Commission Directive 93/11/EEC of 15 March 1993 concerning the release of the N-nitrosamines and N-nitrosatable substances from elastomer or rubber teats and soothers [1993] OJ L93/37.

12.6 Discussion

The FCM Regulatory Framework is clearly incomplete at the EU level. Further, it has not been subject to systematic modernization, and it is therefore regarded as being in need of reform in order to meet health and safety concerns for a number of reasons:[73] (1) legally binding provisions are limited to specific materials (ie 'virgin' plastic, active and intelligent materials, recycled plastics, ceramics, and regenerated cellulose film) and a substantial amount of FCM are unregulated at EU level, for example paper, ink, adhesive, and glue. While some EU FCM do have a positive list, the list for active and intelligent materials has not yet been published. Other groups of FCM (ie adhesives) do not have a positive list of food contact substances at the EU level, but Member States may have set their own lists. For a large part, FCM therefore remain either unregulated or regulated at Member State level, giving rise to a fragmented and erratic legal landscape.[74] (2) The risk assessment structures are partially insufficient. There are important health risks associated with endocrine disruptors, however the risk assessment structures do not assess endocrine disruption; and non-intentionally added substances (NIAS) or the so-called 'forever chemicals' PFAS (per- and polyfluoroalkyl substances) raise unassessed safety risks with respect to new recycling technologies, and recycled plastics. Further critiques have been raised on the current system of single-substance assessment and 'management approaches that do not incorporate the most current scientific understanding, which emphasises the importance of mixture toxicity, low-dose effects, and non-standard testing approaches'.[75] In this context, a shift in focus from starting materials to final materials is proposed.[76] (3) Many safety hazards have not been evaluated, in part due to systemic hazard identification blindspots or inertia. For instance, the internationally used GHS hazard classification system[77] does not consider endocrine disruption or persistence-related hazards.[78] The FCM legal framework is therefore problematic as it is not harmonized at EU level; often safety risks remain unregulated; and a wide range of FCM related hazards have not been subject to risk assessment.

FCM intersects with chemical regulation in the EU, and there are some opportunities for creating better synergies between the sectors. The REACH framework on chemicals classifies substances of very high concern (SVHC), some of which,

[73] Safe Food Advocacy Europe, 'SAFE response to Road map: Revision of EU rules on food contact materials' (27 January 2021) <www.safefoodadvocacy.eu/wp-content/uploads/2021/01/SAFE-Response-to-EC-feedback-session-on-FCM-regulation-revision.pdf> accessed 9 September 2022.

[74] Catherine Simoneau and others, *Non-harmonised food contact materials in the EU: Regulatory and market situation: BASELINE STUDY: Final report* (Publications Office of the European Union 2017).

[75] Groh and others (n 1).

[76] ibid.

[77] The Globally Harmonized System of Classification and Labelling of Chemicals (GHS) is an international standard for the classification of hazards of chemicals under the auspices of the United Nations.

[78] Groh and others (n 1).

however, are still used in FCM. For example, the European Chemicals Agency (ECHA) identified BPA as a SVHC because of its endocrine disrupting properties. In food, however, the bisphenol ban was not passed, instead resulting in lower permissible amounts from 0.06 mg/kg to 0.05 mg/kg. In the future, the ECHA and EFSA agencies are going to work together more closely.

The FCM legislation is also a part of the Green Deal policies, notably, the Action Plan for a Circular Economy, the Chemicals Strategy, and the Farm to Fork Strategy. The European Strategy for Plastics in a Circular Economy in 2018 (European Commission, 2018) announced that, by 2030, all plastic packaging placed on the EU market should be either reusable or can be recycled in a cost-effective manner—this objective is reflected in the proposed revision of the packaging and packaging waste directive.[79] The Farm to Fork Strategy includes an overhaul of the FCM framework, which is further elaborated upon in the Chemicals Strategy. Additionally, the Chemicals Strategy will be very influential on the FCM risk governance mechanisms, as it proposes a multi-sectorial overhaul to better integrate the 'Chemicals Strategy'.[80]

[79] Commission, 'Proposal for a Regulation of the European Parliament and of the Council on packaging and packaging waste, amending Regulation (EU) 2019/1020 and Directive (EU) 2019/904, and repealing Directive 94/62/EC' COM (2022) 677 final, 30 November 2022.

[80] Commission, 'Communication from the Commission to the European Parliament, the Council, the European Economic and Social Committee and the Committee of the Regions on Chemicals Strategy for Sustainability Towards a Toxic-Free Environment' (Communication) COM (2020) 667 final (Chemicals Strategy).

PART V
FOOD INFORMATION LAW

In European Union (EU) law, '(i)nformation regulation is generally perceived by the law as a less onerous and equally effective way of regulation [than] content-related measures'.[1] Departing from this insight as shaped by the Court of Justice of the European Union (CJEU), a comprehensive regime of food information regulation has been put in place at the EU level. Nowadays, its prominent role is expressly stated in Article 8(1) of the General Food Law Regulation (GFLR),[2] which stipulates that: 'Food law shall (. . .) provide a basis for consumers to make informed choices in relation to the foods they consume.' According to Article 2(2)(b) of the Food Information to Consumers Regulation (FICR)[3] '"food information law" means the Union provisions governing the food information, and in particular labelling, including rules of a general nature applicable to all foods in particular circumstances or to certain categories of foods and rules which apply only to specific foods'. As to the importance of information regulation in EU internal market law, the FICR sets out horizontally applicable provisions as well as some special laws regarding the food market (see Chapter 13). Health and nutrition claims also enjoy special regulation in EU food law (see Chapter 14).[4]

[1] Kai Purnhagen and Ellen van Kleef, 'Commanding to "Nudge" via the Proportionality Principle?' in Harry Bremmers and Kai Purnhagen (eds), *Regulating and Managing Food Safety in the EU* (Springer Nature 2018) 151, 158.

[2] Regulation (EC) 178/2002 of the European Parliament and of the Council of 28 January 2002 laying down the general principles and requirements of food law, establishing the European Food Safety Authority and laying down procedures in matters of food safety [2002] OJ L31/1 (General Food Law Regulation, GFLR).

[3] Regulation (EU) 1169/2011 of the European Parliament and of the Council of 25 October 2011 on the provision of food information to consumers, amending Regulations (EC) No 1924/2006 and (EC) No 1925/2006 of the European Parliament and of the Council, and repealing Commission Directive 87/250/EEC, Council Directive 90/496/EEC, Commission Directive 1999/10/EC, Directive 2000/13/EC of the European Parliament and of the Council, Commission Directives 2002/67/EC and 2008/5/EC and Commission Regulation (EC) No 608/2004 [2011] OJ L304/18 (Food Information to Consumers Regulation, FICR).

[4] 'Food Information Law' contains (updated) parts of our earlier study: Kai Purnhagen and Hanna Schebesta, *Food Labelling for Consumers—EU Law, Regulation and Policy Options* (2019).

Information paradigm

EU food information law has developed through the case law of the CJEU on the free movement of goods. It took shape through the *Cassis de Dijon* case[5] in internal market law.[6] Balancing the requirement of removing obstacles to trade in Member State laws and the maintenance of social protection norms for the provision of health and safety, the Court's judgment has been understood as proclaiming a preference for information-related rules over content-related measures in the internal food market.[7] When determining whether a national or Union measure which creates obstacles to free trade in foods (falling under the scope of Article 34 Treaty on the Functioning of the European Union (TFEU)), meets the proportionality test, preference should be given to an information-related rule.[8] Ever since, this 'information paradigm' has served as a benchmark for assessing the proportionality of legislative interventions into internal market consumer law,[9] especially in the area of foods.[10] Instead of prohibiting certain practices, providing information to consumers is considered a standard approach to consumer protection. Elsewhere it was noted that the Court had established a 'permit but inform' logic in the internal market regulation for foods.[11] In essence: 'In order to allow for the proper functioning of the internal market, re-regulation aiming at consumer information about product quality may justify infringements of fundamental freedoms.'[12]

This 'permit but inform' rationale has been endorsed by the Court in several cases. In a case concerning an Italian prohibition to limit the label 'vinegar' exclusively to vinegar made from wine, the Court held that 'affixing of suitable labels (...) would enable the consumer to make his choice in full knowledge of the facts and would guarantee transparency in trading and in offers to the public by providing an indication of the raw material used to make the vinegar' and would therefore be preferred over content-related regulation.[13] In *Rau*, the Court upheld this

[5] Case C-120/78 *REWE v Bundesmonopolverwaltung für Branntwein (Cassis de Dijon)* [1979] ECR 649.

[6] See the contributors to Albertina Albors-Llorens, Catherine Barnard, and Brigitte Leucht, *Cassis de Dijon—40 Years On* (Hart 2021); Kai Purnhagen, 'The Virtue of Cassis de Dijon 25 years later—It Is Not Dead, it Just Smells Funny' in Kai Purnhagen and Peter Rott (eds), *Varieties of European Economic Law and Regulation* (Springer Verlag 2013) 315.

[7] John Usher, 'Disclosure Rules (Information) as a Primary Tool in the Doctrine on Measures Having an Equivalent Effect' in Stefan Grundmann, Wolgang Kerber, and Steven Weatherill (eds), *Party Autonomy and the Role of Information in the Internal Market* (de Gruyter 2001) 151, 152–153.

[8] Albors-Llorens, Barnard, and Leucht (n 6).

[9] Purnhagen (n 6) 329–332. Critical to this end, see Geneviève Helleringer and Anne-Lise Sibony, 'Consumer Protection through the Behavioral Glass' (2017) 23 Columbia Journal of European Law 607.

[10] Purnhagen and van Kleef (n 1) 158–159.

[11] Jens-Uwe Franck and Kai Purnhagen, 'Homo Economicus, Behavioural sciences, and Economic Regulation: On the Concept of Man in Internal Market Regulation and its Normative Basis' in Klaus Mathis (ed), *Law and Economics in Europe: Foundations and Applications* (Springer Verlag 2013) 329.

[12] Kai Purnhagen, 'The Precautionary Principle in Food Law is an Information Tool!' (2015) 6 European Business Law Review 903.

[13] Case C-193/80 *Commission of the European Communities v Italian Republic* [1981] ECR 3019, para 27.

rationale by stipulating that, in contrast to content-related measures, '(c)onsumers may in fact be protected just as effectively by other measures, for example by rules on labelling, which hinder the free movement of goods less.'[14] In *Reinheitsgebot* (German beer), the Court stipulated that consumer protection 'may be ensured by means which do not prevent the importation of products (. . .), in particular, 'by the compulsory affixing of suitable labels giving the nature of the product sold'. By indicating the raw materials utilized in the manufacture of beer 'such as course would enable the consumer to make his choice in full knowledge of the facts and would guarantee transparency in trading and in offers to the public'.[15] In *Drei Glocken*, the Court also rejected arguments from the Italian government to uphold a ban for pasta not made with durum wheat, as it found an information rule to be less onerous and equally sufficient to meet consumer's needs.[16]

Secondary legislation has meanwhile taken up this rationale. In particularly, Article 8(1) GFLR stipulates that '(f)ood law shall (. . .) provide a basis for consumers to make informed choices in relation to the foods they consume'. This line of case law has been interpreted as a disclosure-only rationale, putting the burden of perceiving and processing information on the consumer.[17] Indeed, the Court's cases beg the question of which type of consumer EU food information law targets and what kind of behaviour is normatively expected from consumers when reading and processing information on foods.

The 'average consumer' benchmark

The Court has developed the 'average consumer' benchmark to determine the normative expectations regarding the processing capacity of consumers as recipients of information.[18] In this capacity, this benchmark also determines law's expectations towards businesses regarding how to design food information. The Court developed this benchmark from the rationale of the proportionality principle as a standard of EU primary law which confines domestic law that establishes obstacles to the free movement of goods as outlined in Article 34 TFEU. While the benchmark was first developed in cases of unfair competition law outside the food area,[19] in food information law it was first mentioned in *Mars* as the benchmark

[14] Case C-261/81 *Walter Rau Lebensmittelwerke v De Smedt PVBA* [1982] ECR 3961, para 17.
[15] Case C-178/84 *Commission v Germany (Reinheitsgebot)* [1987] ECR 1227, para 35.
[16] Case C-407/85 *3 Glocken GmbH and Gertraud Kritzinger v USL Centro-Sud and Provincia autonoma di Bolzano* [1988] ECR 4233, paras 16–22.
[17] Ernst Steindorff, *EG Vertrag und Privatrecht* (Nomos 1996) 195 et seq.
[18] Hanna Schebesta and Kai Purnhagen, 'Island or Ocean: Empirical Evidence on the Average Consumer Concept in the UCPD' (2020) 28 European Review of Private Law 293.
[19] Case C-315/92 *Verband Sozialer Wettbewerb eV v Clinique Laboratoires SNC et Estée Lauder Cosmetics GmbH* [1994] ERC I-317, para 16.

of the 'reasonably circumspect consumer'[20]. The Court did not explicitly outline the characteristics of such a 'reasonably circumspect consumer.' In the literature it was stipulated that the ruling 'served to strengthen the tendency to impose an obligation on the consumer to take responsibility for protecting his own interest. The consumer, who has a right to information [. . .], must also take note of this information and consider it.'[21] In *Gut Springenheide*, the Court subsequently endorsed this view of its interpretation of the consumer benchmark in EU food information law. The case concerned the labelling of ready-packaged eggs. When determining what can be expected from the consumer in terms of reading and processing the information on packaging, the Court summarized previous judgments as requiring an 'average consumer, who is reasonably well-informed and reasonably observant and circumspect.'[22] This consumer benchmark should be understood as normative, as common sense and research has shown that in most circumstances consumers behave differently than assumed by the Court.[23] It was noted in the literature that the internal market 'demanded' such an interpretation of the average consumer to accommodate the differences in consumer perceptions and business structures across the Union.[24] However, the 'average consumer' benchmark only provided a level playing field; if more consumer protection was needed, it was up to the Member States to provide for stricter protection in their national legislation to account for the differences across the Union.[25] However, research shows that national laws rarely made use of this opportunity.[26]

It was also noted that, according to this case law, consumer protection in the EU was categorical in the sense that '[w]hoever falls under the definition is entitled to protection, and to the same degree.'[27] A closer look into the case law does not endorse this statement. First, the 'average consumer concept provides leeway for differentiated levels of consumer protection by the use of the attribute "reasonably"'.[28] Second, the CJEU has made it clear that the level of attention that is expected from consumers may 'vary according to the category of goods or services

[20] Case C-470/93 *Verein gegen Unwesen in Handel und Gewerbe Köln e.V. v Mars GmbH* [1995] ECR I-1923, para 24.

[21] Reiner Schulze, Hans Schulte-Nölke, and Jacky Jones, *A Casebook on European Consumer Law* (Hart, 2002) 114.

[22] Case C-210/96 *Gut Springenheide GmbH and Rudolf Tusky v Oberkreisdirektor des Kreises Steinfurt—Amt für Lebensmittelüberwachung* [1998] ECR I-4657, para 31.

[23] See eg the experimental test of the *Mars* case conducted by Kai Purnhagen and Erica van Herpen, 'Can Bonus Packs Mislead Consumers? A Demonstration of How Behavioural Consumer Research Can Inform Unfair Commercial Practices Law on the Example of the ECJ's Mars Judgement' (2017) 40 Journal of Consumer Policy 217.

[24] Ernst Steindorff, *EG Vertrag und Privatrecht* (Nomos 1996) 195 et seq.

[25] Schebesta and Purnhagen (n 18).

[26] Hanna Schebesta and Kai Purnhagen, 'Is the "Behavioural Turn" in Consumer Law Taken by Dutch National Courts?' [2017] Tijdschrift voor Consumentenrecht & Handelspraktijken 272.

[27] Martijn Hesselink, 'European Contract Law: A Matter of Consumer Protection, Citizenship, or Justice?' (2007) 15 European Review of Private Law 323, 327.

[28] Franck and Purnhagen (n 11).

in question'.[29] This means that food information may be treated differently than information on hazardous substances. Third, the Court clarified that the benchmark of a 'reasonably well-informed and reasonably observant and circumspect' consumer does not apply in contexts where a 'mistake as to the product's characteristics [may] pose any risk to public health'.[30] Here, the 'average consumer' arguably needs to be interpreted differently, perhaps in the form of a more vulnerable consumer. Fourth, a systematic analysis of most average consumer cases illustrated the variety of interpretations the Court has given to the 'average consumer', leading to significantly varying levels of protection and rationales.[31]

Beyond the realm of public health and looking at food cases specifically, subsequent case law has added more substance to the expectations placed on consumers regarding food labels. Most cases can be described as endorsing the view presented in the literature that *Mars* established a duty on consumers to read and process information on labels. In *Commission v Italy*, the Court held that other regulatory measures to protect consumers than providing information are not permissible under EU law.[32] In essence, EU law requires consumers to read the list of ingredients. This view was subsequently explicitly endorsed in *Darbo*.[33] Some years later, however, the Court has altered the definition of the 'average consumer' when it serves as a benchmark to determine information on foodstuff. In *Alberto Severi v Regione Emilia-Romagna*,[34] the Court interpreted provisions of Directive 2000/13/EC[35] and Regulation 2081/92[36] related to mandatory information requirements on foods:

> (I)n order to assess the capacity to mislead of a description to be found on a label, the national court must in essence take account of the presumed expectations, in light of that description, an average consumer who is reasonably well informed, and reasonably observant and circumspect, as to the origin, provenance, and quality associated with the foodstuff, the critical point being that the consumer must not be misled and must not be induced to believe, incorrectly, that the product has an origin, provenance or quality which are other than genuine.[37]

[29] Case C-342/97 *Lloyd Schuhfabrik Meyer v Klijsen Handel* [1999] ECR I-3819, para 26.

[30] Case C-220/98 *Estée Lauder* [2000] ECR I-117, para 28; see also Case C-99/01 *Linhart and Biffl* [2002] ECR I-9375, para 31.

[31] Schebesta and Purnhagen (n 18).

[32] Case C-51/94 *Commission of the European Communities v Federal Republic of Germany* [1995] ECR I-3599, para 36.

[33] Case C-465/98 *Verein gegen Unwesen in Handel und Gewerbe Köln eV v Adolf Darbo AG* [2000] ECR I-2297, para 22.

[34] Case C-446/07 *Alberto Severi v Regione Emilia-Romagna* [2009] ECR I-8041.

[35] Directive 2000/13/EC on the approximation of the laws of the Member States relating to the labelling, presentation and advertising of foodstuffs [2000] OJ L109/29.

[36] Council Regulation (EEC) 2081/92 of 14 July 1992 on the protection of geographical indications and designations of origin for agricultural products and foodstuffs [1992] OJ L208/1.

[37] *Alberto Severi v Regione Emilia-Romagna* (n 34) para 61.

While 'induced to believe' shifts some responsibility for the presentation of information on foodstuffs to producers, this modified test is still very much in line with the traditional behavioural model of the average consumer. According to this model, if the average consumer 'is reasonably well informed, it is due to his or her own behaviour'.[38] Interestingly, neither Directive 2000/13/EC, nor Regulation 2081/92 mention the average consumer, therefore the Court has interpreted the provisions of both measures in light of EU primary law to determine the benchmark.

In *Teekanne*, however, the Court extended the introduced line 'induced to believe' further. According to the Court, the 'ingredients list' line of case law only provided for the requirement of an accurate and comprehensive list of ingredients. Such a list in itself is, however, not sufficient, to preclude that consumers are being misled through other labelling elements.[39] The Court stipulated that the correctly displayed list of ingredients 'does not in itself preclude the possibility that the labelling of those goods and methods used for it may be such as to mislead the purchaser'.[40] Labelling comprises 'any words, particulars, trademarks, brand name, pictorial matter or symbol relating to a foodstuff and placed on its packaging. Some of those items may in practice be misleading, erroneous, ambiguous, contradictory or incomprehensible'.[41] In such cases the list of ingredients may be insufficient to correct a "'consumer's erroneous or misleading impression.'[42] Therefore it is the impression of the overall labelling 'taken as a whole',[43] and not only the list of ingredients, which must be taken into account when determining whether packaging is misleading, in particular 'the words and depictions used as well as the location, size, colour, font, language, syntax and punctuation of the various elements on the (...) packaging'.[44] *Teekanne* case further emphasizes that the burden of processing information is not solely on consumers. Elsewhere, the authors have emphasized that the *Teekanne* judgment indeed parallels insights from behavioural consumer science regarding the potential of consumers to be misled.[45]

Taking these (and many more) judgments into account, it has been observed in the literature that the concept of the average consumer remains vague in terms of determining what kind of behaviour is expected from a consumer.[46] This lack of clarity is concerning from the perspectives of both businesses and consumers.

[38] Case C-363/18 *Organisation juive européenne, Vignoble Psagot Ltd v Ministre de l'Économie et des Finances* EU:C:2019:494, para 48.
[39] Schebesta and Purnhagen (n 18).
[40] Case C-195/14 *Bundesverband der Verbraucherzentralen und Verbraucherverbände - Verbraucherzentrale Bundesverband e.V. v Teekanne GmbH & Co. KG* EU:C:2015:361 *(Teekanne)*, para 38.
[41] ibid, para 40.
[42] ibid, para 40.
[43] ibid, para 41.
[44] ibid, para 43.
[45] Schebesta and Purnhagen (n 18).
[46] ibid.

Both place trust in the predictability of the EU's legal system; consumers expect protection and businesses expect market access at consistent costs. The current 'bits and pieces' concept of the average consumer model[47] risks jeopardizing this trust, as consumers may not be adequately protected by information (as EU law neglects the real world consumer) and businesses do not know how to label their products in a legally predictable way. These shortfalls may challenge the acceptance of the EU legal system as a whole.

In EU food law, the legislator has made use of the Court's reasoning in *Lloyd Schuhfabrik Meyer*, where the Court stipulated that the level of attention expected from consumers may 'vary according to the category of goods or services in question'.[48] Research has described the moment of making a purchase decision for foods and the moment of consuming them as 'The Moments of Truth'.[49] Packaging can have a decisive influence on eating behaviour in both situations,[50] which gives special weight to food information laws and the normative expectations towards consumers. In shopping situations, in particular when consumers are pressed for time and hungry, they are less inclined to engage with information.[51] Many dimensions of the food environment have been shown to influence perceptions and food intake, such as portion and unit size, texture, and shape and packaging images.[52] The desire for unhealthy foods is believed to be driven by the increasing number of situations in which people are confronted with easy accessible and tempting food cues, such as snacks. Moreover, taste and satiety evaluations can be suggestible. For example, some consumers overgeneralize nutrition claims when it is inferred that the food is lower in calories, which can result in overeating.[53] These insights support the unique character of food as a product and the assumption that consumers' level of attention during food purchase and consumption are systematically different, which the legislator has also used as a means to depart from the classical notion of the 'average consumer' in the area of food information law.

The traditional average consumer benchmark requires the consumer to actively search for the information they want and to process the information they are provided with. The provisions of the GFLR still reflect this understanding. Article 8(1) GFLR therefore stipulates that 'Food law shall aim at the protection of the interests

[47] ibid.

[48] Case C-342/97 *Lloyd Schuhfabrik Meyer v Klijsen Handel* [1999] ECR I-3819, para 26.

[49] Pierre Chandon, 'How Package Design and Packaged-based Marketing Claims Lead to Overeating' (2013) 35 Applied Economic Perspectives and Policy 7, 8.

[50] ibid; Hans van Trijp and Ivo van der Lans, 'Consumer Perceptions of Nutrition and Health Claims' (2007) 48 Appetite 305.

[51] Peggy Liu and others, 'Using Behavioral Economics to Design More Effective Food Policies to Address Obesity' (2014) 36 Applied Economic Perspectives and Policy 6.

[52] Ellen van Kleef, Christos Kavvouris, and Hans van Trijp, 'The Unit Size Effect of Indulgent Food: How Eating Smaller-Sized Items Signals Impulsivity and Makes Consumers Eat Less' (2014) 29 Psychology & Health 1081.

[53] Véronique Provencher, Janet Polivy, and C Peter Herman, 'Perceived Healthiness of Food. If it's Healthy, You Can Eat More!' (2009) 52 Appetite 340.

of consumers and shall provide a basis for consumers to make informed choices in relation to the foods they consume'. Article 16 GFLR specifies that applies to all aspects of the 'presentation' of food products, understood in a wide sense, including 'the labelling, advertising and presentation of food or feed, including their shape, appearance or packaging, the packaging materials used, the manner in which they are arranged and the setting in which they are displayed, and the information which is made available about them through whatever medium'. While the information under scrutiny by food law is therefore to be understood widely, the GFLR has not made any attempt to deviate from the traditional average consumer benchmark.

The FICR builds upon the principles outlined in the GFLR and stipulates that food information law will provide a basis for final consumers to make informed choices. This includes not only making informed choices about the food they consume, but also using food in a safe way, in particular regarding health, economic, environmental, and ethical considerations.[54] Article 3(1) FICR therefore already legally qualifies information preferences of consumers. Article 7(2) FICR furthermore stipulates that '(f)ood information shall be accurate, clear and easy to understand for the consumer'. This can be interpreted as the first deviation from the classical notion of the average consumer benchmark, as this provision ensures that the respective consumer is not solely responsible for processing information on their own. Rather, in EU food law, information needs to be presented in such a way that the processing of information is easy for the consumer. Other legal acts of food law deviate even more explicitly from the traditional notion of the average consumer benchmark: Article 5(2) Nutrition and Health Claims Regulation (NHCR) stipulates that claims are only permitted if the average consumer 'can be expected to understand the beneficial effects as expressed in the claim'. The NHCR's Recitals 1, 3, and 10 make it even more clear that the 'average consumer' benchmark in EU food information law is to be understood as one that is more vulnerable, particularly to the pitfalls from choice architecture.[55]

Charter of Fundamental Rights

Article 15(1) Charter of Fundamental Rights (CFR) grants the right to engage in work and to pursue a freely chosen or accepted occupation. Article 16 CFR guarantees the freedom to conduct a business. Article 35 CFR requires that a high level of human health protection is ensured in the definition and implementation of EU

[54] FICR, art 3(1).

[55] Kai Purnhagen, Eva van Herpen, and Ellen van Kleef, 'The Potential Use of Visual Packaging Elements as Nudges—An Analysis on the Example of the EU Health Claims Regime' in Klaus Mathis and Avishalom Tor (eds), *Nudging—Possibilities, Limitations and Applications in European Law and Economics* (Springer 2016).

policies and activities. Article 38 CFR requires roughly the same for consumer protection. The former three provisions (and logically also the latter provision[56]) each have an impact on EU food information law, as the Court stipulated in *Weintor*.[57] The case concerned a German wine labelled as 'easily digestible'. According to Regulation 1924/2006,[58] which harmonizes rules governing nutrition and health claims made about food, such labelling in connection with wine is prohibited. The referring Court asked whether this restriction was compatible with the CFR. In essence, it highlighted the fact that labelling on foods is not only measured against consumers' rights to information and health, but also against the rights of businesses, such as their freedom to conduct business or their right to free speech.[59] The Court named some of the corresponding rights of the CFR.[60] It could have easily added Articles 11 and 38. The Court also made it clear that, in light of the determination of the legality of the food labelling, it needs 'to reconcile the requirements of the protection of those various fundamental rights protected by the Union legal order' and to 'strike a fair balance between them'.[61] Subsequently, concerning the particular case of alcohol, the Court found that consumers' health protection outweighed the freedom to conduct business, and therefore deemed the provision in the Health Claims Regulation to be compatible with EU law. The Court ruling was generally found to be a helpful way to deal with the CFR in freedom of goods cases.[62] For EU food information law the case conveys the message that the rights of the CFR complement Article 34 TFEU and the proportionality principle both as a legal basis and a limitation. Food information law is no longer only a commercial right of consumers and an obligation of businesses, but also an issue of fundamental rights.[63]

Other provisions (Articles 168, 169 TFEU)

Article 168(1) TFEU stipulates that '(a) high level of human health protection shall be ensured in the definition and implementation of all Union policies and activities'. Read together with the Court's reasoning in *Affish*, ensuring a high level of

[56] Steven Weatherill, 'Why There is No 'Principle of Mutual Recognition' in EU law (and Why that Matters to Consumer Lawyers)' in Kai Purnhagen and Peter Rott (eds), *Varieties of European Economic Law and Regulation* (Springer Science 2014) 401, 415: 'The Court did not cite Article 38 on consumer protection-it could have easily done so.'

[57] Case C-544/10 *Deutsches Weintor eG v Land Rheinland Pfalz* EU:C:2012:526 (*Weintor*).

[58] Regulation (EC) 1924/2006 of the European Parliament and of the Council of 20 December 2006 on nutrition and health claims made on foods.

[59] Eva van der Zee, 'Legal Limits on Food Labelling Law: Comparative Analysis of the EU and the USA' (2016) European Business Law Review 295.

[60] CFR, arts 15(1), 16, and 35.

[61] *Weintor* (n 57) para 47.

[62] Weatherill (n 56) 415.

[63] See van der Zee (n 59).

health protection means that health 'must take precedence over economic considerations'.[64] Article 168 TFEU also defines special actions to achieve that aim. However, as health policy is a sensitive area for each Member State, Article 168(7) TFEU establishes a rather weak limit to 'respect the responsibilities of the Member States for the definition of their health policy' when formulating and executing health policy at EU level. Article 169(1) TFEU stipulates that '(i)n order to promote the interests of consumers and to ensure a high level of consumer protection, the Union shall contribute to protecting the health, safety and economic interests of consumers, as well as to promoting their right to information, education and to organise themselves in order to safeguard their interests'. Subsequently, Article 169 TFEU stipulates additional measures for achieving this goal. There has been some discussion about the legal nature of this norm, whether it is only a policy objective, whether it grants a subjective right to information for consumers, and whether it[65] can be classified as a competence norm. The majority of these issues can be understood as having little to no practical relevance, as the respective results can also be achieved by other, more established means. For example, even if Article 169(2) TFEU did not classify as a competence norm, the same result (secondary law with the aim of a high level of consumer protection) can be achieved directly through Article 114 TFEU.

General food law information provisions

Articles 5–10 and 16 GFLR set out in its general horizontal requirements applicable to food information law in the EU and Member State laws and to all participants in the food chain who sell food in the EU.[66] Article 8(1) GFLR is the major provision that assigns consumer information a key role in the internal food market, which is applicable in a horizontal manner to all public and private addressees concerned with the marketing of foodstuffs in the EU.[67] Food law should provide the knowledge base to consumers so they can make informed decisions regarding their consumption. This includes the prohibition of deceptive and misleading information.[68] It should be noted that information here refers to 'consumer interest' and not to objective information. Hence, information needs to be provided with a view to enable consumers to satisfy their interest—and these do not

[64] Case C-183/95 *Affish BV v Rijksdienst voor de Keuring van Vee an Vlees* [1997] ECR I-4362, para 43; approved Case C-221/10 *Artedogan GmbH v European Commission* [2012] ECR I-0000, para 99.

[65] In particular Consolidated Version of the Treaty on the Functioning of the European Union [2012] OJ C326/47 (TFEU), art 169(2).

[66] GFLR, art 4(1)(2).

[67] See Case C-636/11 *Berger vs Freistaat Bayern* EU:C:2013:227, where this provision was used to interpret several provisions of national and EU food law and also rendered the obligation of the Food Business Operator.

[68] GFLR, arts 8(2) and 16.

necessarily coincide with public policy goals.[69] Article 16 GFLR specifies EU food law's wider understanding of information. It is the 'presentation' of food products, understood in a wide sense, including 'the labelling, advertising and presentation of food or feed, including their shape, appearance or packaging, the packaging materials used, the manner in which they are arranged and the setting in which they are displayed, and the information which is made available about them through whatever medium'. Furthermore, information serves as 'risk communication'[70] as an important component of 'risk analysis', which is the major basis for regulatory intervention into the EU food market.[71] In this capacity, food information serves mainly as public information,[72] where public authorities are responsible for communicating certain risks to consumers openly.

Outside of the horizontally applicable provisions, food information serves as a proxy to determine the 'unsafeness' of foods as outlined in Article 14(2)(a) GFLR. When 'the information provided to the consumer, including information on the label, or other information generally available to the consumer concerning the avoidance of specific adverse health effects from a particular food or category of foods' is not correct, this may have the effect that the mislabelled food is categorized as 'unsafe' under Article 14(2)(a) GFLR.[73] This triggers many consequences, from inspection to withdrawal duties. The majority of food information law is, however, regulated outside the scope of the GFLR.

[69] Purnhagen (n 12).
[70] GFLR, art 3(13).
[71] ibid, art 6.
[72] ibid, art 10.
[73] ibid, art 14(3)(b).

13
Food Information to Consumers Regulation

13.1 Introduction

The Food Information to Consumers Regulation (FICR) is the food-specific legal instrument governing food information that is provided in a consumer context. This makes the FICR a consumer centred legal instrument. It primarily ensures consumer protection by setting legal requirements on the information that must be provided by food business operators (FBOs) to consumers.[1]

Food information has been regulated at European Union (EU) level since the early days of European integration (see Chapter 1). The current FICR consolidated two prior Directives, namely Directive 2000/13/EC on the labelling, presentation and advertising of foodstuffs[2] and Directive 90/496/EEC on the nutrition labelling for foodstuffs.[3]

From a regulatory point of view, the FICR is a horizontal regulation that provides rules for food information for all food products. In addition to the FICR, more specific legal provisions may be applicable, for instance labelling rules stemming from a novel food or genetically modified organism (GMO) authorization, or special rules regarding products subject to an EU marketing standard such as eggs.

13.2 The Food Information to Consumer Regulation

The European Commission is given extensive powers to pass implementing and delegated acts in the FICR. The FICR implements a maximum harmonization approach, which means that Member States cannot implement more ('gold-plating') or less protective measures than the ones stipulated by the FICR. At the same time, there are many provisions that expressly reserve the right for Member States to adopt national measures.

[1] This chapter includes selected and updated parts of our earlier study: Kai Purnhagen and Hanna Schebesta, *Food Labelling for Consumers—EU Law, Regulation and Policy Options* (2019).

[2] Directive 2000/13/EC of the European Parliament and of the Council of 20 March 2000 on the approximation of the laws of the Member States relating to the labelling, presentation and advertising of foodstuffs [2000] OJ L109/29.

[3] Council Directive 90/496/EEC of 24 September 1990 on nutrition labelling for foodstuffs [1990] OJ L276/40.

EU Food Law. Hanna Schebesta and Kai Purnhagen, Oxford University Press. © Hanna Schebesta and Kai Purnhagen 2024.
DOI: 10.1093/9780198901570.003.0014

The Commission adopted several notices that clarify and explain rules of the FICR, notably on application in general,[4] substances or products causing allergies[5], and quantitative ingredients declaration.[6]

13.2.1 *Legal basis and framework of the FICR*

The FICR is based on the power to harmonize the internal market in Article 114 Treaty on the Functioning of the European Union (TFEU). It formulates detailed requirements about the information that FBOs must provide for foods intended for supply to the final consumer and mass caterers.

The FICR is structured in six chapters that in large parts mirror the structure of the General Food Law Regulation (GFLR). It contains general provisions, including scope and definitions, and elaborates on general principles regarding food information (Chapters I and II). Additionally, the FICR stipulates the basic requirements, namely, to provide food information to consumers and mass caterers in compliance with its provisions. It outlines what fair information practices are and attributes responsibilities associated with them. The FICR distinguishes between information that *must* be included, the so-called 'mandatory particulars' (Chapter IV) and rules about the provision of voluntary information (Chapter V). Furthermore, it covers the possibility of taking national measures (Chapter VII) and details the institutional arrangements of the Regulation (Chapter VIII).

13.3 Objective, scope, and definitions

13.3.1 *Scope*

The FICR 'provides the basis for the assurance of a high level of consumer protection in relation to food information, taking into account the differences in the perception of consumers and their information needs whilst ensuring the smooth functioning of the internal market'.[7]

[4] Commission Notice on Questions and Answers on the application of the Regulation (EU) No 1169/2011 of the European Parliament and of the Council on the provision of food information to consumers [2018] OJ L196/1.

[5] Commission Notice of 13 July 2017 relating to the provision of information on substances or products causing allergies or intolerances as listed in Annex II to Regulation (EU) No 1169/2011 of the European Parliament and of the Council on the provision of food information to consumers [2017] OJ C428/1.

[6] Commission Notice on the application of the principle of quantitative ingredients declaration (QUID) [2017] OJ C393/5.

[7] Regulation (EU) 1169/2011 of the European Parliament and of the Council of 25 October 2011 on the provision of food information to consumers, amending Regulation (EC) No 1924/2006 and

The FICR covers all foods intended for the final consumer, including foods delivered by mass caterers, and foods intended for supply to mass caterers.[8] In terms of personal scope, the Regulation applies to FBOs at all stages of the food chain, where their activities concern the provision of food information to consumers.[9] This reflects the ambition of EU food law to cover the entire food chain and hold all actors responsible.

13.3.2 *Definitions*

For the food law key terminology, such as 'food', 'food law', and 'food business operator', the FICR refers to the definitions of the GFLR,[10] while for specific terminology defined in other legislative acts of the EU, such as 'processing', 'food enzyme', and 'meat preparations', the FICR refers to the respective legal acts for their definition.[11] Many other key provisions are defined in Article 2(2) FICR.

Most importantly, 'food information' is defined very widely as 'information concerning a food and made available to the final consumer by means of a label, other accompanying material, or any other means including modern technology tools or verbal communication'.[12] Not only is packaging part of food information law, but other sources of information are as well, for instance advertisements of food including those on the television, the Internet and on billboards. It also covers verbal communication, such as interactions with a salesperson at a grocery store or a waiter in a restaurant.

The applicable definitions are discussed together with the articles that reference a given concept.

13.4 The principles of food information law

13.4.1 *General objectives*

Article 3 FICR states the general objectives of the Regulation. The Regulation aims to ensure a high level of consumer protection relating to consumers' health and interests.[13] It will enable consumers to make informed choices and utilize

(EC) No 1295/2006 of the European Parliament and of the Council, and repealing Commission Directive 87/250/EEC, Council Directive 90/496/EEC, Commission Directive 1999/10/EC, Directive 2000/13/EC of the European Parliament and of the Council, Commission Directives 2002/67/EC and 2008/5/EC and Commission Regulation (EC) No 608/2004 [2011] OJ L304/18 (Food Information to Consumers Regulation ((FICR), art 1(1).

8 FICR, art 1(3).
9 ibid, art 1(3).
10 ibid, art 2(1)(a).
11 ibid, art 2(1)(b)–(g).
12 ibid, art 2(2)(a).
13 ibid, art 3(1).

food in a safe way, particularly regarding health, economic, environmental, and ethical considerations.[14] EU food information law thus extends beyond the inherent safety-focus of food law and encompasses concerns regarding other credence characteristics of foodstuffs.[15] Whether Article 3(1) FICR extends non-safety concerns only to those connected to the consumption of food or if it also enables consumers to exercise political choices is not evident from the text.[16] It is clear that ethical concerns connected with food consumption, such as religious eating rules, vegetarianism,[17] and treatment of animals before slaughter,[18] are covered by this provision. AG Hogan's opinion suggests that the provision also extends to 'wider ethical considerations which may inform the thinking of certain consumers prior to purchase',[19] which includes political consumerism.[20] Reading Article 3(1) FICR in conjunction with Article 8(1) GFLR[21] suggests that AG Hogan's interpretation is not necessarily definitive. Article 8(1) GFLR stipulates an obligation for food law to provide consumers with information 'in relation to the foods they consume'. This focus on consumption suggests that Article 3(1) FICR should be interpreted in the context of food consumption exclusively. However, while Article 8(1) GFLR only provides a minimum standard for interpretation, it does not preclude a more extensive interpretation of Article 3(1) FICR.

Other interests beyond those of consumers are also protected by the FICR: food information should facilitate the circulation of food products in the EU market, while also taking into account the interests of producers.[22] While Article 3(2) FICR also highlights the contribution of food information law to the free movement of foods and requires 'taking into account, where appropriate, the need to protect the legitimate interests of producers and to promote the production of quality products', the FICR's emphasis is on the protection of the consumer.

[14] ibid, art 3(1).

[15] Eva van der Zee, *Sustainability Labels in the Shadow of the Law* (Springer 2022) 1.

[16] See in particular Case C-363/18 *Organisation juive européenne, Vignoble Psagot Ltd v Ministre de l'Économie et des Finances* EU:C:2019:494, paras 50, 51.

[17] ibid, para 50.

[18] Case C-497/17 *Oeuvre d'assistance aux bêtes d'abattoirs (OABA) v Ministre de l'Agriculture et de l'Alimentation and Others* EU:C:2019:137.

[19] Case C-363/18 *Organisation juive européenne, Vignoble Psagot Ltd v Ministre de l'Économie et des Finances* EU:C:2019:494, para 51.

[20] Dietlind Stolle and Michele Micheletti, *Political Consumerism: Global Responsibility in Action* (Cambridge University Press 2013).

[21] Such contextual reading is legally required by Regulation (EC) 178/2002 of the European Parliament and of the Council of 28 January 2002 laying down the general principles and requirements of food law, establishing the European Food Safety Authority and laying down procedures in matters of food safety [2002] OJ L31/1 (General Food Law Regulation (GFLR)), art 4(1)(2).

[22] FICR, art 3(2).

13.4.2 Principles governing mandatory food information (Article 4 FICR)

Food information law must adhere to some general principles when it comes to mandatory food information. Specifically, mandatory information must concern:

(a) information on the identity and composition, properties, or other characteristics of the food; or
(b) information on the protection of consumers' health and the safe use of a food (ie attributes that may be harmful to the health of certain groups of consumers; durability, storage, and safe use; health impacts, nutritional characteristics, including for special dietary requirements); or
(c) information on nutritional characteristics.

The FICR explicitly states that when considering the necessity for mandatory information, consideration should be given to whether 'a widespread need on the part of the majority of consumers for certain information to which they attach significant value or of any generally accepted benefits to the consumer'.[23] In substantiating the necessity to regulate food information, consumer studies are of paramount importance for examining and substantiating the need to introduce new mandatory food information.

Where food information affects public health, the European Food Safety Authority (EFSA) must be consulted.[24]

13.5 General food information requirements and responsibilities of FBOs

The FICR establishes the main basic requirement[25] that any food intended for supply to the final consumer or to mass caterers must be accompanied by food information that complies with the Regulation. The food information obligations can be divided in food information into a prohibition to mislead consumers (section 13.5.1), and specific mandatory food information requirements (section 13.6) and voluntary food information requirements (section 13.7).

The FICR attributes prime responsibility for food information compliance to the operator under whose name or business name a food is marketed (including businesses under their control) or the importer.[26]

[23] ibid, art 4(2).
[24] ibid, art 5.
[25] ibid, art 6.
[26] ibid, art 8.

13.5.1 *Fair information practices*

The Regulation details several fair information practices, which include advertising and the general presentation of foods.[27] On one hand, food information must not be misleading.[28] Specifically it must accurately present the characteristics of the food including its nature, identity, properties, composition, quantity, durability, country of origin, place of provenance, method of manufacture or production. It is prohibited to attribute effects or properties to the food which it does not possess, to suggest that the food possesses special characteristics when in fact all similar foods possess such characteristics, in particular by specifically emphasizing the presence or absence of certain ingredients and/or nutrients. It is also forbidden to suggest, by means of the appearance, the description, or pictorial representations, the presence of a particular food or an ingredient, while in reality a component naturally present or an ingredient normally used in that food has been substituted with a different component or a different ingredient.[29]

In addition to the prohibition on misleading information, there are clear information requirements, namely that food information 'shall be accurate, clear and easy to understand for the consumer'.[30] The FICR therefore combines a subjective, consumer-effect based approach to addressing information, which tests whether a consumer is misled with an objective, information-based approach that looks at the type and quality of the information provided.[31]

These provisions echo the wording of the Unfair Commercial Practices Directive (UCPD), but are more specific. The FICR's requirements for misleading practices significantly deviate in two ways from the general requirements of the UCPD: first, in order to establish whether information is misleading, the FICR does not require that deceptive practices must impact the transactional decision.[32] Second, unlike the UCPD, where untrue information does not constitute deceptiveness per se, false or inaccurate food information is independently prohibited under the FICR.[33] Whether the differing tests in Article 7 FICR can be considered *lex specialis* compared to the UCPD and hence preclude the applicability of the

[27] ibid, art 7(4).
[28] ibid, art 7(1)(a)–(d).
[29] ibid, art 7(1).
[30] ibid, art 7(2).
[31] Hanna Schebesta and Kai Purnhagen, 'Is the "Behavioural Turn" in Consumer Law Taken by Dutch Courts?' (2017) Tijdschrift voor Consumentenrecht en handelspraktijken 272.
[32] Eva van der Zee and Arnout Fischer, 'Green Pictograms on EU Foods: A Legal Study Informed by Behavioural Science' (2018) 7 Journal of European Consumer and Market Law 15; Kai Purnhagen and Erica van Herpen, 'Can Bonus Packs Mislead Consumers? A Demonstration of How Behavioural Consumer Research Can Inform Unfair Commercial Practices Law on the Example of the ECJ's Mars Judgement' (2017) 40 Journal of Consumer Policy 217.
[33] Hanna Schebesta, 'Control in the Label: Self-Declared, Certified, Accredited? On-Pack Consumer Communication about Compliance Control in Voluntary Food Schemes from a Legal Perspective' in Peter Rott (ed), *Certification—Trust, Accountability, Liability* (Springer 2019) 143.

UCPD's additional requirement of a causal link is not clear from the text. Article 7 FICR adds an additional, food-related layer to the deceptiveness test of the UCPD, which justifies the application of both provisions in parallel, the UCPD serving as a basis and the FICR providing additional specifications.[34]

13.6 Mandatory food information

At the heart of the requirements of mandatory food information is the 'list of mandatory particulars' which specifies what kind of information must be indicated on food. This list is usually the starting point for a systematic inquiry as to whether foods comply with the mandatory rules. The list must be read together with those articles that constitute the detailed counterpart of the listed items,[35] and the respective technical Annexes (I–XV). Furthermore, the provisions stipulate specifications as to the required context of their presentation.

13.6.1 The list of mandatory particulars (Article 9 FICR)

The mandatory particulars that need to be present in principle on all foods in the EU are:

(a) the name of the food;
(b) the list of ingredients;
(c) allergens;
(d) the quantity of (certain) ingredients;
(e) the net quantity;
(f) a date marking;
(g) any special storage conditions and/or conditions of use;
(h) the name and address of the food business operator;
(i) the country of origin or place of provenance (if necessary);
(j) appropriate instructions for use;
(k) beverages with more than 1.2% of alcohol, the actual alcoholic strength;
(l) a nutrition declaration (except foods listed in Annex V).

[34] Hanna Schebesta, 'Regulating Sustainability Claims on Seafood-EU Ecolabel, Unfair Commercial Practices Directive or Seafood Information Requirements?' (2016) 7 European Journal of Risk Regulation 784; Kai Purnhagen and others, 'Oversized Area Indications on Bonus Packs Fail to Affect Consumers' Transactional Decisions—More Experimental Evidence on the Mars Case' (2021) 44 Journal of Consumer Policy 385, 388–389; Eva van der Zee and Arnout Fischer, 'Green Pictograms on EU Foods: A Legal Study Informed by Behavioural Science' (2018) 7 Journal of European Consumer and Market Law 15.

[35] FICR, arts 10–35.

The mandatory particulars must be indicated with words and numbers; pictograms and symbols may only[36] be used as additional elements.[37] Behavioural research has shown that in most situations pictures are more effective for conveying information. Therefore some argue that EU food information law should allow for more extensive use of pictures.[38] The Commission already has the competence to do so, as it may adopt delegated acts to establish rules allowing certain mandatory particulars to be expressed through means other than on the package or label.

Additional mandatory particulars are required for specific kinds of food[39] listed in Annex III. The Commission draws up these additional mandatory particulars through delegated acts.

Under specific circumstances some mandatory particulars may be omitted;[40] this applies to glass bottles intended for reuse[41] and small packaging (less than $10cm^2$).[42] Additionally foods listed in Annex V are not required to provide a nutrition declaration. More surprising, perhaps, is that alcoholic beverages containing more than 1.2% by volume of alcohol are exempt from displaying a list of ingredients and the nutrition declaration.[43] This alcohol beverage exemption has faced criticism in recent years[44] and is currently being addressed by a policy initiative under Europe's Beating Cancer Plan.[45]

A major exception to the display of mandatory particulars is valid for non-prepacked foods, which are exempt from showing all mandatory particulars at EU level apart from allergens labelling.[46] However, Member States may enact national laws that do require mandatory particulars for non-prepacked foods, resulting in considerable variation in the area of non-prepacked food across EU countries. For allergens, Member States may specify rules regarding how allergen information is made available.

36 See Commission Notice Questions and Answers, point 2.4.5 for 'instructions for use'.
37 FICR, art 9(2).
38 Terry Childers and Michael Houston, 'Conditions for a Picture-Superiority Effect on Consumer Memory' (1984) 11 Journal of Consumer Research 643.
39 Foods packaged in certain gases; foods containing sweeteners, glycyrrhizinic acid, or its ammonium salt; beverages with high caffeine content or foods with added caffeine; foods with added phytosterols, phytosterol esters, phytostanols, or phytostanol esters; frozen meat, frozen meat preparations, and frozen unprocessed fishery products.
40 FICR, art 16.
41 ibid, art 16(1).
42 ibid, art 16(2).
43 ibid, art 16(4).
44 See Hanna Schebesta and Kai Purnhagen, 'Limits to Behavioural Consumer Law and Policy: The Case of EU Alcohol Labelling' in Klaus Mathis and Avishalom Tor (eds), in *Consumer Law and Economics* (Springer, Cham 2021).
45 Commission, 'Communication from the Commission to the European Parliament and the Council—Europe's Beating Cancer Plan' COM (2021) 44 final.
46 FICR, art 44.

13.6.2 *Availability and placement and presentation of mandatory food information*

Mandatory food information must be available and easily accessible. For pre-packed foods, it must be placed directly on the package or on an attached label.[47]

In terms of presentation, mandatory food information must be placed in a 'conspicuous place',[48] to be 'easily visible, clearly legible and, where appropriate, indelible'.[49]

Food information is subject to specific legibility requirements. As a general rule, the information size must be greater than 1.2mm; except for foods with a small surface, where the requirement is 0.9mm.[50] The information must be provided in a language easily understood by the consumers of the Member States where a food is marketed.

The particulars listed, including the name of the food, the net quantity of the food, and (if applicable) the actual alcoholic strength by volume, must appear in the same field of vision.[51]

13.6.3 *What are the specific rules of mandatory food information?*

The list of mandatory information has to be read together with the detailed rules covering each mandatory particular.

13.6.3.1 Name of the food (Article 9(1)(a), Article 17, definitions in Article 2, Annex VI)

The name of the food will be its legal name. In the absence of such a name, the name of the food will be its customary name, or, if there is no customary name or the customary name is not used, a descriptive name of the food will be provided.[52] The name may not be replaced with a name protected as intellectual property, a brand name, or a fancy name.

The legal name is 'the name of a food prescribed in the Union provisions applicable to it or, in the absence of such Union provisions, the name provided for in the laws, regulations and administrative provisions applicable in the Member State in which the food is sold to the final consumer or to mass caterers'.[53] Many of the 'legal

[47] ibid, art 8(7).
[48] ibid, art 13(1).
[49] ibid, art 13(1).
[50] ibid, art 13.
[51] ibid, art 13(5).
[52] ibid, art 17(1).
[53] ibid, art 2(1)(n).

names' of foods are enshrined in Regulation 1308/2013 establishing a common organisation of the markets in agricultural products (CMO Regulation)[54] testifying for the increasing overlap of rules on agriculture and foodstuffs in the secondary law.[55] Annex II Part VIII Nr 2 CMO Regulation, for example, stipulates a definition for 'chicks' as being 'live fowls, ducks, geese, turkeys and guinea fowls, each weighing not more than 185 grams'.

The application of the prerequisites of 'legal names' are strict, and the Court of Justice of the European Union (CJEU) has so far rejected all evolutionary interpretations concerning the provisions of 'legal names'. A particularly obvious category is the labelling of dairy products. According to *Diet Cheese*,[56] products, including 'cheese', can only be labelled 'milk products' if they are products derived exclusively from milk and provided that no milk constituent has been replaced, even partially, during the manufacturing process.[57] Only a strict ban on the use of the designation 'cheese' for products derived from milk from which the natural milk fat has been removed could with certainty prevent any confusion that might arise in the mind of the consumer as a result of the use of the word 'cheese', even if accompanied by written explanations.[58] In *Tofu Town*,[59] the CJEU stipulated that, whether in marketing or advertising, the term 'milk' and the designations reserved exclusively for milk products can only be used for products which meet the requirements laid down by the CMO.[60] These strict rules have been subject to criticism from FBOs developing alternative plant-based products meant to substitute dairy.[61]

Where there is no such legal name, FBOs should choose the customary name or if there is no customary name, the descriptive name of the product.

The customary name is 'a name which is accepted as the name of the food by consumers in the Member State in which that food is sold, without that name needing further explanation'.[62] The definition mandates an autonomous European interpretation. Any reference to national legal provisions, such as, for example, the *Lebensmittelbuch* in Germany, may, if at all, serve only as an indication for this

[54] Regulation (EU) 1308/2013 of the European Parliament and of the Council of 17 December 2013 establishing a common organisation of the markets in agricultural products and repealing Council Regulations (EEC) No 922/72, (EEC) No 234/79, (EC) No 1037/2001 and (EC) No 1234/2007 [2013] OJ L347/671.

[55] Kai Purnhagen, 'The Increasing Overlap of Agricultural, Free Movement and Competition Law in the EU' (2021) 46 European Law Review 20, 30.

[56] Case C-101/98 *Union Deutsche Lebensmittelwerke GmbH v Schutzverband gegen Unwesen in der Wirtschaft eV.* [1999] ECR I-8841 (*UDL/Diät-Käse*).

[57] ibid.

[58] ibid.

[59] Case C-422/16 *Verband Sozialer Wettbewerb e.V. v TofuTown.com GmbH* EU:C:2017:567 (*TofuTown*).

[60] Regulation 1308/2013, Annex VII, Part III.

[61] For an overview, see Anu Lähteenmäki-Uutelaa and others, 'Alternative Proteins and EU Food Law' (2021) 130 Food Control 108336.

[62] FICR, art 2(1)(o).

autonomous interpretation. The provisions furthermore mention only the view of customers as a benchmark to determine 'acceptance'. The benchmark applicable here is hence the one of the 'average consumer' as determined by EU food law. The view of other stakeholders in the food supply chain such as scientists, regulatory bodies, and the food industry is irrelevant. The application of such customary names allows the CJEU to be more flexible, providing an evolutionary interpretation. If a 'Sauce Hollandaise' or a 'Sauce Béarnaise', which are usually produced using butter, is produced using vegetable fats, the use of the designation 'Sauce Hollandaise' or 'Sauce Béarnaise' is nevertheless the usual designation and therefore not misleading if the replacement of the animal fat by the vegetable fat is referred to in the list of ingredients.[63]

Finally, the descriptive name 'is a name providing a description of the food, and if necessary of its use, which is sufficiently clear to enable consumers to know its true nature and distinguish it from other products with which it might be confused'. However, a complete description of all ingredients of a food is not required for a sufficient description, as this function is primarily fulfilled by the list of ingredients.[64]

Food can also be marketed under the legal name that is permitted in the Member State where the food product has been manufactured.[65] This provision stems from the principle of conditional mutual recognition in EU food law. The use includes both the original foreign language designation and its translation into the language of the Member State of marketing.[66] This is because, as per Article 9(1)(a) FICR, the name of a food is considered obligatory information. According to Article 15(1) FICR this information must be written in a language easily understood by consumers in the Member State of marketing. Therefore, the FBO must be free to translate the foreign name into the official language of the Member State of marketing, since the official language of the Member State of marketing fulfils the characteristic of 'easily understandable'.[67]

Annex VI contains specific technical rules regarding naming. The names must be mentioned together with any special physical condition of the food or the specific treatment which it has undergone (eg powdered, refrozen, freeze-dried, quick-frozen, concentrated, smoked). Foods treated with ionizing radiation must mention this. Additionally, specific rules apply for foods in which a component or ingredient that consumers expect to be normally used or naturally present has

[63] See Case C-51/94 *Commission of the European Communities v Federal Republic of Germany* [1995] ECR I-3599.

[64] Case C-383/97 *Criminal proceedings against Arnoldus van der Laan* [1999] ECR I-731.

[65] FICR, arts 3(1) and 17(2).

[66] Case C-366/98 *Criminal proceedings against Yannick Geffroy and Casino France SNC* [2000] ECR I-6579.

[67] Case C-369/89 *Piageme and others v BVBA Peeters* [1991] ECR I-2971.

been substituted with a different component or ingredient. Specific rules also apply for meat and fishery products, minced meat, and sausage casings.

13.6.3.2 ***List of ingredients (Article 9(1)(b), Articles 18–20, Annex VI, VII)***

The list of ingredients is headed or preceded by a heading with the word 'ingredients'. The list includes all ingredients, in descending order of weight.[68]

An ingredient is 'any substance or product, including flavourings, food additives and food enzymes, and any constituent of a compound ingredient, used in the manufacture or preparation of a food and still present in the finished product, even if in an altered form; residues shall not be considered as "ingredients"'.[69] Substances that have been used in the production process but have been completely removed (by filtration or other processes) are not ingredients. Yeast used in the production of alcohol-free beer is hence not regarded as an 'ingredient'. Products of ingredients produced by degradation or reaction are also considered 'ingredients'. When the substance used as an ingredient chemically converts into another substance by or after its use, the 'time of their use in the manufacture of the food'[70] is decisive. They are therefore to be indicated with the name of the ingredient used and not with the names of their degradation or reaction products. Natural components of ingredients are not 'ingredients' themselves. In cases where an ingredient has been altered many times along the supply chain, they have been used many 'time(s) (. . .) in the manufacture of the food'.[71] However, as they are to be listed in order of weight and an average consumer would expect the weight of the ingredient to be presented on the list according to the ingredient as it is present in the final product, preference shall be given to the form the ingredient has in the final product. Therefore, the last processing stage of the ingredient needs to be listed. Accordingly, a ready-made meal labelled 'spaghetti with tomato sauce' will list the final version of tomato purée as the ingredient, not peeled tomatoes.

There are an abundance of technical rules for indicating ingredients.[72] They cover rules on how to establish a descending order of ingredient weight, using category names rather than specific ingredients;[73] rules for the designation of ingredient categories that must also bear a specific name or e-number;[74] the designation of flavourings;[75] and the designation of compound ingredients.[76]

The list of ingredients consists of an enumeration of all the food ingredients used in the production of the food. Ingredients must be designated by their specific

[68] FICR, art 18(1).
[69] ibid, art 2(1)(f).
[70] ibid, art 18(1).
[71] ibid, art 18(1).
[72] See ibid, Annex VII.
[73] ibid, pt B of Annex VII
[74] ibid, pt C of Annex VII.
[75] ibid, pt D of Annex VII.
[76] ibid, pt E of Annex VII.

name as stipulated by Article 17 FICR and Annex VII.[77] Nano-engineered material must be specified.[78] In order to qualify as 'engineered nano-material', one or more of its dimensions need to be 100nm or less and it needs to be 'intentionally produced' as nano-material.[79] Particles of 100nm or less, which are a common outcome in some food production processes such as milling or smoking, are not 'intentionally' produced nano-material and therefore do not require specific labelling as such. Genetic modification of ingredients also needs to be indicated.[80] The ingredients must be stated in the order of their proportion by weight at the time of their use.[81] Later or earlier changes in weight—for example, due to enzymatic or physical processes—are irrelevant. As a rule, it will be possible to refer to the recipe to determine the weight. In contrast to the other ingredients, the weight of water and volatile ingredients is not to be determined by weight measurement, but must be calculated.[82] The list must be preceded by the word 'ingredients'; its use in conjunction with other words is permitted. The indication 'Contains' is mandatory for listing Annex II substances in foods when no list of ingredients is required.[83]

Some foods do not require an ingredient list,[84] for example fresh fruit and vegetables.[85] No other ingredients are used in their production, so a list of ingredients would be superfluous. 'Fresh' refers to foods that are not frozen or dried. Refrigeration is permitted as it is not considered 'treatment'. Carbonated water,[86] milk products,[87] foods consisting of a single ingredient,[88] and alcoholic beverages[89] are also exempted from the requirement to display an ingredient list. Criticism regarding the exemption of alcoholic beverages from this requirement has been recurrent.[90]

Equally, some constituents of food need not be mentioned, such as food additives and enzymes used as processing aids.[91] '(F)ood additive' means 'any substance not normally consumed as a food in itself and not normally used as a characteristic ingredient of food, whether or not it has nutritive value, the intentional addition of which to food for a technological purpose in the manufacture, processing, preparation, treatment, packaging, transport or storage of such food results, or may be reasonably expected to result, in it or its by-products becoming

[77] ibid, art 18(2).
[78] ibid, art 18(3).
[79] ibid, art 2(1)(t).
[80] Regulation (EC) 1829/2003, arts 12 and 13.
[81] FICR, art 18(1).
[82] ibid, pt A of Annex VII No 1.
[83] ibid, art 21(1).
[84] ibid, art 19.
[85] ibid, art 19(1)(a).
[86] ibid, art 19(1)(b).
[87] ibid, art 19(1)(d).
[88] ibid, art 19(1)(e).
[89] ibid, art 16(4).
[90] For a summary, see Schebesta and Purnhagen (n 44).
[91] FICR, art 20.

directly or indirectly a component of such foods'.[92] Important characteristics are the 'intentional' addition to the food and the existence of a 'carry over' effect. The latter refers to enzymes and food additives that have become part of the food but no longer have any technological effect.

Informed consumer choice is a major goal of EU food information law, and is consistently repeated in its provisions.[93] Case law has emphasized the crucial role of ingredient lists in enabling FBOs to meet this information obligation. In *Darbo*, the CJEU stated that 'consumers whose purchasing decisions depend on the composition of the products in question will first read the list of ingredients'.[94] In *Teekanne*, however, the Court stipulated that a list in itself is not sufficient to ensure consumers are not misled by other labelling elements.[95] Rather, the impression of the overall labelling 'taken as a whole',[96] not just the list of ingredients, must be considered when ascertaining whether packing is misleading.[97] While *Teekanne* diminished some of the prominence of the list of ingredients as a 'liability waiver' for FBOs, it is still seen as the major tool for communication between the consumer and the FBO.

13.6.3.3 ***Labelling of substances causing allergies or intolerances (Article 9(1)(c), Article 21, Annex II)***

Allergens must be indicated in the list of ingredients and emphasized through a typeset that clearly distinguishes them from the rest of ingredients.[98] In the absence of a list of ingredients, the allergen must be indicated by 'contains'. According to Annex II, the following foods are defined as allergens: cereals containing gluten; crustaceans; eggs; fish; peanuts; soybeans; milk and products thereof (including lactose); nuts; celery; mustard; sesame seeds; sulphur dioxide and sulphites; lupin; and molluscs.

13.6.3.4 ***Quantitative indication of ingredients ('QUID') (Article 9(1)(d), Article 22, Annex VIII, Commission Notice on QUID)***

Under specific circumstances, a quantitative indication of ingredients (QUID) is required. This means the quantity of an ingredient used in the food must be indicated when: the ingredient or category concerned is mentioned in the name of the food (eg strawberry yoghurt or fruit pie); the ingredient is emphasized on

[92] Regulation (EC) 1333/2008, art 3(2)(a).
[93] GFLR, art 8(1).
[94] Case 465/98 *Verein gegen Unwesen in Handel und Gewerbe Köln eV v Adolf Darbo AG* [2000] ECR I-2297 (*Darbo*), para 22.
[95] Schebesta and Purnhagen (n 31).
[96] Case C-195/14 *Bundesverband der Verbraucherzentralen und Verbraucherverbände - Verbraucherzentrale Bundesverband e.V. v Teekanne GmbH & Co. KG* EU:C:2015:361 (*Teekanne*), para 41.
[97] ibid, para 43.
[98] FICR, art 21.

the labelling in words, pictures, or graphics; or the ingredient is essential to characterize a food (such as, arguably, mayonnaise). This QUID is not required for foods consisting of a single ingredient, and in specific cases of pre-packed foods.[99] Annex VIII FICR and the Commission Notice on QUID[100] stipulate further requirements.

13.6.3.5 ***Net quantity (Article 9(1)(e), Article 23, Annex IX)***

Displaying the net quantity of a food will enable consumers to better assess the cost/performance ratio of food products and compare them accordingly.[101] The net quantity must be expressed using one of five units, namely litres, centilitres, millilitres, kilograms, or grams, as appropriate. What is appropriate depends on the aggregation state of the food. Liquid foods can be displayed as litres, centilitres, and millilitres, while firm foods can be displayed as kilograms or grams. When in doubt, the principle of proportionality applies.

13.6.3.6 ***Minimum durability date, 'use by' date, and date of freezing (Article 9(1)(f), Article 24, Annex X)***

Article 24 regulates details on the minimum durability date, best-before date, use by date, and date of freezing. '(D)ate of minimum durability' of a food means the date until which the food retains its specific properties when properly stored.[102] 'Specific properties' can be understood as defined by the Institute of Food Science and Technology, where food possesses the desired sensory, chemical, physical, and microbiological characteristics and substantially aligns with the nutritional claims made.[103] As very few foods have a static composition, slight changes are inevitable and acceptable as the life of a product progresses. The provisions regarding a good manufacturing practice and the product's formulation determine the shelf-life of a product. If applicable, the minimum durability date needs to be accompanied by the date of freezing. Highly perishable foods that after a short period of time may constitute an immediate danger to health must be labelled with a 'use by' date. Whether a food is highly perishable from a microbiological perspective is to be determined on a case-by-case basis by experts. Examples of highly perishable foods are fresh fruit; vegetable juices; pre-cut salads; fresh fish, eg raw salmon slices; or fresh meat, especially minced meat or poultrymeat. 'After the "use by" date a food shall be deemed to be unsafe in accordance with Article 14(2) to (5) GFLR.'[104]

[99] ibid, Annex VIII.

[100] Commission Notice on the application of the principle of quantitative ingredients declaration (QUID) [2017] OJ C393/05.

[101] Case C-3/99 *Cidrerie Ruwet SA v Cidre Stassen SA and HP Bulmer Ltd.* [2000] ECR I-8749; Case C-457/05 *Schutzverband der Spirituosen-Industrie eV v Diageo Deutschland GmbH* [2007] ECR I-8075.

[102] FICR, art 2(2)(r).

[103] Institute of Food Science and Technology (IFST), *Shelf Life of Foods: Guidelines for its Determination and Prediction* (IFST 1993).

[104] FICR, art 24(1) sentence 2.

There is some debate surrounding consumers' understanding of the difference between use by (safety) and minimum durability (quality), which has a connection with the food-waste policy agenda.[105] National legislation can make the application of a reduced VAT rate solely dependent on the criteria of the 'best before date' and the 'use by date'.[106]

The best-before-date labelling issue will further be expanded upon by a Farm to Fork Strategy action dedicated to the reduction of food waste.

13.6.3.7 ***Any special storage conditions and/or conditions of use (Article 9(1)(g), Article 25)***

The definition of the minimum durability date refers to the proper storage of the product.[107] The storage conditions stipulated in Article 25 FICR are therefore directly connected to the rules on the minimum durability date, as they determine the basics of their applicability. Special storage conditions or conditions of use must therefore be labelled, ensuring that consumers are aware of the prerequisites for applying the minimum durability date. If the food requires it, consumers need to be informed about the special storage conditions and/or conditions of use. Special storage conditions require indication only when they are applicable. When these additional requirements on storage information is warranted needs to be determined on a case-by-case basis. For class A eggs, the indication of special storage instructions for consumers are mandatory, stating that consumers should 'keep eggs chilled after purchase'.[108]

13.6.3.8 ***Country of origin labelling (COOL) and place of provenance (POP) labelling (Article 26, Annex XI, Commission Implementing Regulation (EU) 2018/775; Commission Implementing Regulation (EU) No 1337/2013 of 13 December 2013)***

Rules on country of origin labelling (COOL) or on the labelling of the place of provenance (POP) has the potential to discriminate against products on the grounds of their geographical origin. National information rules indicating the origin of products have been identified as a gross violation of the rules of the free movement of goods[109] and are therefore at odds with the very principle of internal market law. At the same time, consumers are increasingly interested in buying locally sourced food, leading to a demand for information regarding the origin of

[105] Commission, Directorate-General for Health and Food Safety, *Market study on date marking and other information provided on food labels and food waste prevention—Final Report* (Publication Office of the European Union 2018).

[106] Case C-499/16 *AZ v Minister Finansów* EU:C:2017:846.

[107] FICR, art 2(2)(r).

[108] According to Regulation (EC) 589/2008, art 12(1)(f).

[109] Case C-249/81 *Commission of the European Communities v Ireland* [1982] ECR I-4005 (*Buy Irish*).

products. This demand stems from the need for consumers to make an informed choice, a regulatory goal protected by EU food law. As a compromise between these two conflicting goals, Article 26 FICR stipulates that FBOs have to include the country of origin or place of provenance ('COOL'/'POP') on the ingredients list only if the consumer otherwise risks being misled.[110] This obligation extends to meat products only, which comprises pork, goat, sheep, and poultry.[111]

The Implementing Regulation of 2013 lays down more specific rules on the indication of the country of origin or place of provenance on the label of fresh, chilled, and frozen meat of swine; sheep or goats meat; and poultrymeat.[112] The country where an animal was reared and the country of slaughter must be labelled.[113] Minced meat may simply be labelled as 'EU', 'non-EU', or 'reared and slaughtered in EU and non-EU' countries.[114] Where the COOL/POP indicated is not the same as a food's primary ingredient, this must be specified either by mentioning the COOL/POP of the primary ingredient or with a generic statement that the origin/provenance of the primary ingredient is different from the indicated one.[115]

The Implementing Regulation of 2018 sets general rules and requirements regarding the indication of the country of origin or place of provenance of foods. It covers all indications of the COOL/POP of a food that is given by any means, such as statements, pictorial presentation, symbols or terms, and referring to places or geographical areas. It stipulates that the COOL/POP of the primary ingredient must be given if it is not the same as the food's COOL/POP.

For some products, such as beef, fresh fruit and vegetables, fishery products, honey, olive oil, and eggs, country of origin labelling is mandatory under specific vertical EU legislation.[116]

13.6.3.9 ***Alcoholic strength (Article 28, Annex XII)***

The alcoholic strength by volume must be indicated for beverages containing more than 1.2% in accordance with Annex XII, and for wine as specified in EU instruments.

13.6.3.10 ***Nutrition declaration (Articles 29–35)***

Nutrition declarations are part of the mandatory particulars of Article 9 FICR, and they are regulated extensively elsewhere, namely in Articles 29–35 FICR. Importantly, a number of foods are exempted from the nutrition declaration in Annex V. This is a detailed list that includes important exceptions, for example for

110 FICR, art 26(2)(a).
111 ibid, art 26(2)(b) in connection with Annex XI.
112 Commission Implementing Regulation (EU) No 1337/2013, art 1.
113 ibid, arts 5(1)(a), (b), and 6.
114 ibid, art 7.
115 FICR, art 36(3).
116 See ibid, Recital (32).

unprocessed products that comprise only a single ingredient (eg an apple), or food in packaging or containers the largest surface of which is less than 25cm^2 (eg small candy), or food, including handcrafted food, that is directly supplied by the manufacturer of small quantities of products either to the final consumer or to local retail establishments directly supplying the final consumer.[117]

The nutrition declaration *must* include the energy value and the amount of fat, saturates, carbohydrate, sugars, protein, and salt.[118] It *may* include monounsaturates; polyunsaturates; polyols; starch; fibre; vitamins; and minerals (if listed and present in significant amounts as defined in Annex XIII).[119]

The energy value is calculated using the conversion factors listed in Annex XIV. Generally, the energy value and the amounts of nutrients are expressed per 100g or per 100ml. Where vitamins or minerals are listed, they must also be provided as a percentage of the reference intakes set out in Annex XIII, per 100g/ml. The energy value and the amounts of nutrients may additionally be provided as a percentage of the reference intakes in Annex XIII per 100g/ml. In addition, the energy value and the amounts of nutrients can be expressed on a per portion basis or per consumption unit. These particulars must be included in the same field of vision and, if space permits, in tabular format with the numbers aligned.

The various options available to express portion sizes for indicated nutritional values have raised concerns at policy level, where it has been argued that these different options make comparison of energy intake difficult for consumers, potentially undermining efforts to promote a healthy diet.

13.6.3.11 ***How do particulars have to be presented (pictograms etc)?***

The particulars referred to must be included in the same field of vision and be presented together in a clear format. In addition, Annex XV provides specific regulations for the presentation of energy in certain units of measurement. The energy value, and the energy value together with the amounts of fat, saturates, sugars, and salt must be presented in the primary field of vision on the packaging.

The energy value and the amount of nutrients referred to in Article 30(1) to (5) FICR may be given by other forms of expression and/or presented using graphical forms or symbols in addition to words or numbers, provided that the following requirements are met:[120]

(a) they are based on sound and scientifically valid consumer research and do not mislead the consumer as referred to in Article 7;

(b) their development is the result of consultation with a wide range of stakeholder groups;

[117] ibid, Annex V.
[118] ibid, art 30(1).
[119] ibid, art 30(2).
[120] See ibid, art 35.

(c) they aim to facilitate consumer understanding of the contribution or importance of the food to the energy and nutrient content of a diet;
(d) they are supported by scientifically valid evidence of understanding of such forms of expression or presentation by the average consumer;
(e) in the case of other forms of expression, they are based either on the harmonized reference intakes set out in Annex XIII, or in their absence, on generally accepted scientific advice on energy or nutrient intake;
(f) they are objective and non-discriminatory; and
(g) their application does not create obstacles to the free movement of goods.

In order to inform consumers more effectively, EU food information law should use more pictures. This has become particularly relevant in discussions concerning the introduction of food health labelling such as the nutri-score.[121]

13.7 Voluntary food information

The FICR emphasizes mandatory food information that must be provided in a standardized way. However, FBOs can also choose to provide certain additional information about food products. These may be certain kinds of claims. In business practice, claims are often used to gain a comparative advantage over other companies stimulating consumer choice.[122] In cases of nutrition or health claims, the special Nutrition and Health Claim Regulation is applicable (Chapter 14). However, other types of information, claims, and labelling are often regarded as attractive information for consumers. Currently, the FICR has minimal regulation concerning this type of information, with only two articles addressing voluntary information.

13.7.1 What applies to all voluntary food information?

As a general rule, if the information listed in Article 9 or 10 is provided on a voluntary basis (eg where a food enjoys an exemption) then the information must be given in compliance with the applicable rules.[123]

In addition, any voluntary food information—including food labelling—provided in relation to foodstuff must not mislead the consumer; must not be

[121] BEAC, 'Factsheet—Nutriscore' (September 2019) <https://www.beuc.eu/sites/default/files/publications/beuc-x-2019-051_nutri-score_factsheet.pdf> accessed 11 August 2022.
[122] Harry Bremmers, Bernd van der Meulen, and Kai Purnhagen, 'Multi-Stakeholder Responses to the European Union Health Claims Requirements' (2013) 13 Journal on Chain and Network Science 161, 162.
[123] FICR, art 36(1).

ambiguous or confusing for the consumer; and must be appropriate and based on relevant scientific data.[124] The Commission is empowered to adopt implementing acts on substances causing allergies, vegetarian and vegan food, indication of reference intakes, and the presence of gluten in food.

Lastly, displaying voluntary information should never be to the detriment of mandatory information.[125]

However, voluntary food information must still adhere to general fair food information practices (section 13.4.1), that is, not be misleading and satisfying the positive food information requirements.

Nevertheless, the FICR only superficially addresses voluntary food information, and one may therefore conclude that this inaction is currently a regulatory gap that is only residually and indirectly framed by provisions of general consumer law, for instance on the prohibition of certain information practices under the Unfair Commercial Practices Directive, that may address this kind of information.

13.7.2 Labels and standard certification marks as voluntary food information

Since the 2000s, there has been a proliferation of consumer-facing labels that demonstrate a product's compliance with a specific scheme or standard. The use of labels on food products is regarded as a particularly attractive tool for food marketing. For instance, 'Fair Trade' labels or labels indicating animal welfare standards are increasingly prevalent on products.

In terms of the FICR, these labels are governed by the loose rules on 'voluntary food information'.

However, not all of these labels are, in fact, genuinely meaningful, leading to the risk of 'greenwashing'. What is often less clear for the consumer is that these labels vary significantly in terms of quality, depending on who sets the standard (a public body or the company itself) and how compliance with the standard is monitored. Public labels, such as the EU organic scheme, certify the adherence to the organic requirements laid down in the official EU Organic Regulation regime and involve an official system of control. Private standards and their labels, in contrast, each set their own standard and certification requirements. To understand private standardization, it is imperative to distinguish the activity of standard-setting from the process of certification and the notion of accreditation (Tripartite Standards Regime).[126] The standard-setter draws up the substantial requirements of a given scheme. Certification testifies that the substantial requirements of a scheme are

124 ibid, art 36.
125 ibid, art 37.
126 Schebesta (n 33).

being met. In addition, accreditation bodies control the certifiers, and they are governed by a regime of public control.[127] In the EU, Regulation (EC) 765/2008[128] (Accreditation Regulation) exercises this public control in the EU and aims to ensure the impartiality, functioning, objectivity, and competence of accreditation bodies.[129] Due to the important differences in the governance of standardization schemes, the reliability of different labels in terms of what they actually achieve, and whether standards are effectively monitored and enforced, varies between labels and can potentially mislead consumers.

So far, the topic of standards and labels is addressed only by a non-binding Commission document, the Commission best practice guidelines for voluntary certification schemes for agricultural products and foodstuffs (Guidelines).[130] It stipulates many governance conditions, for instance, that certification bodies should be independent of the standard-setter, which currently is often not the case.

However, under several Green Deal initiatives greater oversight for green and/or sustainability claims will be proposed.[131] For instance, the proposal for a directive aims to empower consumers for the green transition through better protection against unfair practices and better information,[132] which contains a significant overhaul of general EU information law, including the Unfair Commercial Practices Directive and the Consumer Rights Directive. The future directive will have a significant impact on the food sector, specifically by mandating much stricter rules regarding voluntary information through the strengthening of consumer protection against both unfair practices and heightened information requirements. It is accompanied by the proposal for a directive on substantiation and communication of explicit environmental claims (Green Claims Directive),[133] which provides more specific rules and complements the proposed changes to the Unfair Commercial Practices Directive. In addition, a future Framework for

[127] Spencer Henson and John Humphrey, 'Understanding the Complexities of Private Standards in Global Agri-Food Chains as They Impact Developing Countries' (2010) 46 Journal of Development Studies 1628.

[128] Regulation (EC) 765/2008 of the European Parliament and of the Council of 9 July 2008 setting out the requirements for accreditation and market surveillance relating to the marketing of products and repealing Regulation (EEC) No 339/93 [2008] OJ L218/30 (Accreditation Regulation).

[129] Schebesta (n 33) 147.

[130] See Commission Communication—EU best practice guidelines for voluntary certification schemes for agricultural products and foodstuffs [2010] OJ C341/5-11. Also noteworthy is the Commission, 'Communication from the Commission to the Council, the European Parliament and the European Economic and Social Committee—Contributing to Sustainable Development: The role of Fair Trade and non-governmental trade-related sustainability schemes' COM (2009) 215 final.

[131] Commission, 'Proposal for a Directive of the European Parliament and of the Council amending Directives 2005/29/EC and 2011/83/EU as regards empowering consumers for the green transition through better protection against unfair practices and better information' COM (2022) 143 final.

[132] ibid.

[133] Commission, 'Proposal for a Directive of the European Parliament and of the Council on substantiation and communication of explicit environmental claims' (Green Claims Directive) COM (2023) 166 final.

Sustainable Food Systems is expected to contain rules about the sustainability aspects of foodstuffs, and thereby address this important gap for the food sector specifically.

13.8 Discussion

Food labelling is almost exclusively regulated at EU level. The mandatory information displayed covers information about the food characteristics, as well as nutritional information.

Some efforts to reform the existing system have been proposed under the Farm to Fork Strategy. These concern a proposal for harmonized mandatory front-of-pack nutrition labelling to enable consumers to make health-conscious food choices. However, at the time of writing, there is a lack of political consensus on what type of scheme to be mandated.

In addition, there will be a proposal to require origin indication for certain products and a proposal for a revision of EU rules on date marking ('use by' and 'best before' dates) to prevent food waste. Both are relatively limited changes to the food information framework, and while potentially useful, they fall short of constituting a major overhaul of food information law.

The most significant gap that can be filled is the currently inadequate regulation of voluntary food information, in particular labels on food products. In this context, there were high hopes for a proposal for a sustainable food labelling framework to empower consumers to make sustainable food choices. This proposal was expected to be tabled in legislation for a Framework for Sustainable Food System legislation (Chapter 1). Overall, the details of this food labelling proposal are unknown, although it is clear that the Commission does not envision a full sustainability label. We must therefore wait to see whether and how a new Commission mandate will pursue the sustainability labelling initiative. Given these uncertainties, the most promising initiative in the medium term is the proposal for empowering consumers for the green transition through better protection against unfair practices and better information. Although not only directed at the food sector, the implications for voluntary food provision will be significant, given that the food sector is one of the major sectors to use labels to certify ethical, social, and environmental credence on goods.

From a purely food informational perspective it is clear that sustainability information poses one of the major and most pressing challenges due to the ambiguity of sustainability, and more specifically of what sustainable food really is. Although the Farm to Fork Strategy promises to take some steps towards clarifying the conceptualization of sustainable food, it is not clear how and when this will be achieved.

14
Nutrition and Health Claims

14.1 Introduction

The Nutrition and Health Claims Regulation (NHCR) regulates the provision of verifiable nutrition and health claims. This makes the Regulation a uniquely health-oriented legal instrument. The NHCR regulates the accuracy and scientific validity of claims made regarding nutrition and health, and its main aim is to enable consumer choice by protecting the availability and quality of information. In this regard, the NHCR goes beyond information governance as it sets detailed substantive requirements about the kinds of claim that can be made on food products. It transcends mere information governance and serves as an example of information regulation. The NHCR, in fact, stipulates a food information authorization requirement, where only authorized information may be placed on the product. Although it has been shown that nutrition and health claims enable consumers to eat more healthily by enabling their choices, the regulation does not attempt to steer consumers towards eating in a healthier way. Therefore, the NHCR classifies as a food information instrument.

Nutrition claims state, suggest, or imply that a food has a particular beneficial nutritional property, whereas health claims state, suggest, or imply that a relationship exists between a food category, a food, or one of its constituents and health.[1] In the European Union (EU), the use of nutrition and health claims is highly regulated, which means that—at least in comparison to other jurisdictions—consumers largely 'get what they read'. All nutrition and health claims that are used in the EU are scientifically substantiated, thereby offering 'publicly verified' information regarding the food product's nutritional and health properties. This regulatory approach is in stark contrast to the current 'laissez faire' rules governing general voluntary claims on food products, particularly regarding eco- and sustainability labelling.

[1] Regulation (EC) No 1924/2006 of the European Parliament and of the Council of 20 December 2006 on nutrition and health claims made on foods [2006] OJ L404/9 (Nutrition and Health Claims Regulation (NHCR)), art 2(2)(4)–(5).

EU Food Law. Hanna Schebesta and Kai Purnhagen, Oxford University Press. © Hanna Schebesta and Kai Purnhagen 2024.
DOI: 10.1093/9780198901570.003.0015

14.2 The Nutrition and Health Claims Regulation

The NHCR was last overhauled in 2006, rendering it a relatively dated instrument. In comparison, the Food Information to Consumers Regulation (FICR) was overhauled in 2011, meaning that the NHCR and its rules predate the main food information legal instrument. So far, there is no serious contemplation of an overhaul, although there is room for movement regarding the nutrient profiles and mandatory nutrition labelling schemes under the reforms initiated by the Farm to Fork Strategy.

14.3 Legal base, scope, and objective

The legal basis for the harmonization of nutrition and health claims in the NHCR is Article 114 Treaty on the Functioning of the European Union (TFEU)[2] on the approximation of laws. The NHCR contains specific rules for nutrition and health claims made on food. The NHCR's strong health objectives are summarized in its first recital, which reads:

> An increasing number of foods labelled and advertised in the Community bear nutrition and health claims. In order to ensure a high level of protection for consumers and to facilitate their choice, products put on the market, including imported products, should be safe and adequately labelled. A varied and balanced diet is a prerequisite for good health and single products have a relative importance in the context of the total diet. With the health objective co-exist the internal market rationale, high consumer protection, and the aim of harmonising the provisions laid down by law, regulation or administrative action in Member States.[3]

The NHCR applies to almost all food information, specifically to nutrition and health claims made 'in commercial communications, whether in the labelling, presentation or advertising of foods to be delivered as such to the final consumer, including foods which are placed on the market unpacked or supplied in bulk'.[4] Non-prepacked foodstuffs (including fresh products such as fruit, vegetables, and bread) when offered for sale to the final consumer or to mass caterers, as well as foodstuffs packed at the point of sale at the request of the purchaser or pre-packaged for immediate sale, enjoy an exemption. No mandatory nutrition information[5] or specific information regarding healthy diets[6] is required on these

[2] Consolidated Version of the Treaty on the Functioning of the European Union [2012] OJ C326/47 (TFEU), art 114.
[3] NHCR, art 1.
[4] ibid, art 1(2).
[5] ibid, art 7.
[6] ibid, art 10(2)(a)(b).

exempted foodstuffs. However, it is clarified that the NHCR also applies to foods intended for supply to restaurants, hospitals, schools, canteens, and similar mass caterers, albeit in a declaratory manner. A trademark, brand name, or fancy name which is construed as a nutrition or health claim does not require authorization if there is an accompanying nutrition or health claim on that packaging that complies with the provisions of the Regulation.[7]

14.4 Overview of the NHCR and definitions

Article 2 NHCR lists and defines the most important legal terms used in the Regulation. To ensure consistent application and in line with the horizontal approach of the General Food Law Regulation, reference is often made to the definitions and concept of other legislative acts, in particular to those in the general food law. Chapter II[8] stipulates the general principles for nutrition and health claims. Chapter III[9] lays down specific rules for nutrition claims, Chapter IV[10] for health claims. Nutrition and health claims are both subject to an authorization procedure. Once authorized, the nutrition claims are directly listed in the Annex to the NHCR. The health claims are listed in the Annex to Regulation (EU) 432/2012 containing the list of health claims, except for those claims which refer to the reduction of disease risk and to children's development and health. These are listed in the Annex to Regulation (EU) 1228/2014. The list of all authorized and non-authorized health claims are also available online in a digitalized EU register.[11]

Articles 15 to 19 detail the procedure for the authorization of health claims not yet listed. The prerequisites of these claims vary according to the type of claim.

The NHCR differentiates between nutrition claims, health claims, claims referring to the reduction of disease risk, and claims referring to children's development and health:

> 'nutrition claim' means any claim which states, suggests or implies that a food has particular beneficial nutritional properties due to: (a) the energy (calorific value) it (i) provides; (ii) provides at a reduced or increased rate; or (iii) does not provide; and/or (b) the nutrients or other substances it (i) contains; (ii) contains in reduced or increased proportions; or (iii) does not contain; (...)

[7] ibid, art 1(3).
[8] ibid, arts 3–7.
[9] ibid, arts 8 and 9.
[10] ibid, arts 10–19.
[11] Commission, 'EU Register of Health Claims' <https://ec.europa.eu/food/food-feed-portal/screen/health-claims/eu-register> accessed 22 December 2022.

> 'health claim' means any claim that states, suggests or implies that a relationship exists between a food category, a food or one of its constituents and health;
> (...)
> 'reduction of disease risk claim' means any health claim that states, suggests or implies that the consumption of a food category, a food or one of its constituents significantly reduces a risk factor in the development of a human disease.[12]

For consumers it may not always be easy to conceptually distinguish these claims from one another. The NHCR fuels this difficulty by, for example, categorizing claims related to 'slimming or weight-control or a reduction in the sense of hunger or an increase in the sense of satiety or to the reduction of the available energy from the diet' only as health claims,[13] while they could easily qualify as nutrition claims as well. From a consumer's perspective, health claims are associated with a number of properties, including reduction of disease risks and prevention.[14] Accordingly, it is difficult to distinguish claims referring to the reduction of disease risk from health claims, as it can be assumed that the buyers of food often associate claims referring to the reduction of disease risk with health. Likewise, claims regarding the reduction of the risk of disease are likely to be associated with ideas regarding disease prevention, treatment, or alleviation, that is, disease-related claims, which are prohibited under Article 7(3) FICR. It is equally difficult to distinguish claims referring to the reduction of disease risk from claims referring only to nutritional values; for example, a claim stating that a food is suitable for consumption by overweight individuals could be interpreted both as a claim regarding nutritional values and as a claim regarding the reduction of disease risk due associated with being overweight. In practice, it can be assumed that a claim may simultaneously fall under several categories. Consequentially, the same claim may be subject to different regulatory prerequisites, which need to be applied cumulatively.

14.5 Definition of claims

The NHCR defines claims as 'any message or representation, which is not mandatory under Community or national legislation, including pictorial, graphic or symbolic representation, in any form, which states, suggests or implies that a food has particular characteristics'.[15]

[12] NHCR, art 2(2)(4)–(6).
[13] ibid, art 13(1)(c).
[14] See Kai Purnhagen, Eva van Herpen, and Ellen van Kleef, 'The Potential Use of Visual Packaging Elements as nudges - An Analysis on the Example of the EU Health Claims Regime' in Klaus Mathis and Avishalom Tor (eds), *Nudging—Possibilities, Limitations and Applications in European Law and Economics* (Springer 2016).
[15] NHCR, art 2(2)(1).

Compulsory labelling, both on the basis of Union law and on the basis of national provisions, is excluded from the application of the NHCR. Such compulsory labelling also includes descriptive names of food.[16] If health or nutrition-related information is necessary according to the definition of a descriptive name and used as such, it will not qualify as a health or nutrition claim. Names such as 'juice made with our healthy oranges' would not qualify as a descriptive name and would therefore need authorization. Claims such as 'probiotic'—in as so far as they are a necessary part of the designation within the meaning of Article 3 FICR and used to designate the special property of, for example yoghurt—are not health-related claims.

A claim is only covered if it 'states, suggests or implies that a food has particular characteristics'. Therefore, claims need to mention particular characteristics such as that an ingredient is 'valuable' or 'sustainable'. Stating general characteristics are not covered, such as 'Food is life' or 'Fat is essential for nutrition'. However, it is difficult to draw a clear line in practice. Particular characteristics can also be indications of the very nature of the foodstuff(s), which are essential for consumers to distinguish them from other products. To determine this distinction, the presentation of the foodstuff as a whole must be considered. Using terms like 'states', 'suggests', and 'implies' casts a wide net to also cover those claims that may not directly refer to the property of the foodstuff.

In essence, any information within the meaning of a claim which can evoke associations with particular characteristics are within the ambit of a claim. Such an association could be represented, for example, by showing a muscular person alongside a chubby figure in an illustration. As the Court of Justice of the European Union (CJEU) held in *Weintor*: '[T]he concept of a "health claim" is deemed to refer not only to the effects of the consumption—in a specific instance—of a precise quantity of a food which is likely, normally, to have only temporary or fleeting effects, but also to those of the repeated, regular, even frequent consumption of such a food, the effects of which are, by contrast, not necessarily only temporary and fleeting.'[17] As would be 'apparent from a reading of recital 1 in conjunction with recital 10 in the preamble to Regulation No 1924/2006, it is established that, by indicating a nutritional, physiological or any other health advantage over similar products, claims promoting the foods on which they appear guide the choices made by consumers. Those choices directly influence the total selected intake of

[16] In the sense of Regulation (EU) 1169/2011 of the European Parliament and of the Council of 25 October 2011 on the provision of food information to consumers, amending Regulations (EC) No 1924/2006 and (EC) No 1925/2006 of the European Parliament and of the Council, and repealing Commission Directive 87/250/EEC, Council Directive 90/496/EEC, Commission Directive 1999/10/EC, Directive 2000/13/EC of the European Parliament and of the Council, Commission Directives 2002/67/EC and 2008/5/EC and Commission Regulation (EC) No 608/2004 [2011] OJ L304/18 (Food Information for Consumers Regulation (FICR)), art 2(2)(p).

[17] Case C-544/10 *Deutsches Weintor eG v Rheinland-Pfalz* EU:C:2012:526 *(Weintor)*, para 36.

individual nutrients or other substances, thereby warranting the restrictions imposed by that regulation in relation to the use of those claims.'[18]

14.6 Overarching requirements for nutrition and health claims

In essence, claims need to meet the several requirements, namely the overarching general requirements for nutrition and health claims, the specific requirements for nutrition claims and health claims respectively, and within health claims, the conditions for the specific type of health claim that must be met.

14.6.1 General principles for nutrition and health claims (Article 3)

Article 3 NHCR contains the regulatory basis for health and nutrition claims in the EU. Article 3(1) NHCR generally prohibits the use of all nutrition and health claims in the EU if they do not comply with the NHCR. The term 'use' is to be understood widely, and covers not only labelling but also all information connected to the product, such as on-pack information or accompanying documents.

As a general principle, claims may not be false, ambiguous, or misleading;[19] give rise to doubt about the safety and/or the nutritional adequacy of other foods;[20] encourage or condone excess consumption of a food;[21] state, suggest, or imply that a balanced and varied diet cannot provide sufficient nutrients ;[22] or refer to changes in bodily functions which could give rise to or exploit fear in consumers.[23]

14.6.2 Conditions for the use of nutrition and health claims (Article 4)

At the adoption of the NHCR it was foreseen that the Commission would establish specific nutrient profiles, which foods would have to comply with in order to bear nutrition or health claims. However, despite the provision requiring the Commission to do so by 19 January 2009, the nutrient profiles have not yet been established. Instead, they have now become part of the legislative agenda of the Farm to Fork Strategy. Nutrient profiles would restrict the use of nutrition and health claims on foods that are high in fats, sugars, and/or salt. This suggestion is made to combat the so-called 'halo effect' of nutrition and health claims, where one specific

[18] ibid para 37.
[19] NHCR, art 3(a).
[20] ibid, art 3(b).
[21] ibid, art 3(c).
[22] ibid, art 3(d).
[23] ibid, art 3(e).

claim on a food product implies that the entire product is healthy. This has been shown to easily mislead consumers, as seen in cases for where 'low-fat' yoghurts may have a very high sugar content, and yet be perceived as a healthy alternative.

Article 4(3) NHCR prohibits the use of health claims on beverages which contain more than 1.2% by volume of alcohol. There are some exceptions for claims specifically designed for alcohol: nutrition claims referring to low alcohol levels, or the reduction of the alcohol or energy content are permitted. The volume is to be determined according to Annex II Part IV Regulation 1308/2013.[24] The provision only covers beverages. Not all liquid food is considered a 'beverage'. If they are sold in small doses, available in pharmacies, accompanied by instructions for use, and designed to take in low quantities (such as sprays or drops), they are not considered 'beverages'.[25] Food such as alcoholic pralines are also not considered beverages and may therefore bear health claims.

14.6.3 General conditions for nutrition and health claims (Article 5)

Article 5 NHCR defines general conditions that must be fulfilled for the use of all health and nutrition claims. On one hand, the NHCR sets objective scientific requirements for nutrition and health claims, namely:

(a) that beneficial nutritional or physiological effects must be scientifically evidenced. This 'effect' has to be 'nutritional or physiological'. It is 'nutritional' if it sustains or improves the human organism through the consumption of the food. It is 'physiological', if it is triggered, prevented, or otherwise influenced by an event outside of the human body. This includes pharmacological effects. In foods, both terminologies are often indistinguishable, but also need not to be distinguished as they are both triggering the same legal effects.

(b) that the nutrient or substance is available in a significant or reduced quantity. The required 'significant quantity' is defined in Annex XIII of the

[24] It is unclear, however, whether the NHCR refers to the 'actual alcoholic strength by volume' or the 'total alcoholic strength by volume'. 'Actual alcoholic strength by volume' means the number of volumes of pure alcohol contained at a temperature of 20°C in 100 volumes of the product at that temperature. 'Total alcoholic strength by volume' means the sum of the actual and potential alcoholic strengths. The '(p)otential alcoholic strength by volume' means the number of volumes of pure alcohol at a temperature of 20°C capable of being produced by total fermentation of the sugars contained in 100 volumes of the product at that temperature: Regulation 1308/2013, pt IV no 13–15 of Annex II. As the NHCR's goal is to protect final consumers who consume the final product, claims need to refer to the food ready for consumption. Therefore, potential risks to consumers stem from the actual alcohol content of the product on the market. Hence, art 4(3) NHCR refers to the 'actual alcoholic strength by volume'.

[25] Case C-177/15 *Nelsons GmbH v Ayonnax Nutripharm GmbH und Bachblütentreff Ltd* EU:C:2016:474, Opinion AG Bobek, paras 28–42.

FICR.[26] These regulations are not suitable for application to all nutrients. It is on the food business operator to prove that the amount indicated has the effect claimed.[27]

(c) The nutrient or other substance for which the claim is made has to be in a form that is available to be used by the body ('bioavailability').[28]

(d) the quantity of the product can reasonably be expected to be consumed by a consumer.[29]

Claims may only be used if the average consumer can be expected to understand the beneficial effects as expressed in the claim.[30] This takes the average consumer as a central benchmark to determine consumer expectations and behaviour. The average consumer has been defined in the Court's judgment in *Gut Springenheide* as someone 'who is reasonably well-informed and reasonably observant and circumspect',[31] and has been used in many different functions and interpreted in many different ways in EU internal market law ever since.[32] In this regard, the NHCR deviates somewhat from the general notion of the well-informed, reasonably observant, and circumspect consumer, as it stipulates that claims are only permitted if the average consumer 'can be expected to understand the beneficial effects as expressed in the claim'. This deviation is supported by the fact that all food information in the EU has to be 'accurate, clear and easy to understand for the consumer'.[33] Read together with the requirements of the NHCR's Recitals 1, 3, and 10, it has been submitted that the 'average consumer' in the NHCR differs from that stipulated by the Court in *Gut Springenheide*.[34] It is more vulnerable, particularly to the pitfalls stemming from choice architecture.[35] This would imply that a different standard can be applied to the 'average consumer' in the NHCR. In order to prove that a consumer can be expected to understand the beneficial effects of a claim, results from consumer studies (in particular behavioural studies) can serve as valuable proof.

[26] FICR, pt A no 2 of Annex XIII; '(a)s a rule, the following values should be taken into consideration in deciding what constitutes a significant amount: - 15 % of the nutrient reference values specified in point 1 supplied by 100 g or 100 ml in the case of products other than beverages, - 7,5 % of the nutrient reference values specified in point 1 supplied by 100 ml in the case of beverages, or, - 15 % of the nutrient reference values specified in point 1 per portion if the package contains only a single portion.'

[27] NHCR, art 6(2).

[28] ibid, art 5(1)(c).

[29] ibid, art 5(1)(d).

[30] ibid, art 5(2).

[31] Case C-210/96 *Gut Springenheide and Tusky v Oberkreisdirektion Steinfurt* [1998] ECR I-4657, para. 37.

[32] Hanna Schebesta and Kai Purnhagen, 'Island or Ocean: Empirical Evidence on the Average Consumer Concept in the UCPD' (2020) 28 European Review of Private Law 293.

[33] FICR, art 7(2).

[34] Purnhagen, van Herpen, and van Kleef (n 14).

[35] ibid.

14.6.4 Scientific substantiation for nutrition and health claims (Article 6)

Nutrition and health claims will be based on and substantiated by generally accepted scientific data.[36] 'A claim should be scientifically substantiated by taking into account the totality of the available scientific data, and by weighing the evidence.'[37] The underlying data must have been collected using adequate methods as required by the individual case. The data must also be in a position to substantiate the claim, that is, establish a substantive link (cause–effect) between the scientific knowledge and the claim. The Annex to Regulation (EC) 353/2008[38] provides further details on the types of data and procedures for their collection that are applicable in EU law for scientific substantiation. It stipulates, inter alia, that substantiation requires:

> all scientific data, published and unpublished, in favour and not in favour that are pertinent to the health claim, together with a comprehensive review of the data from human studies in order to demonstrate that the health claim is substantiated by the totality of the scientific data and by weighing the evidence. Data from studies in humans addressing the relationship between consumption of the food and the claimed effect is required for substantiation of a health claim.[39]

Food business operators (FBOs) have the duty to justify the use of a claim.[40] According to the requirement to base and substantiate claims on scientific evidence,[41] the FBO's obligation to justify the use of the claim includes providing the relevant scientific evidence.

The competent authorities of the Member States may request an FBO or a person placing a product on the market to provide all relevant elements and data establishing compliance with the Regulation.[42]

14.6.5 Nutrition Information (Article 7)

It is mandatory to provide nutrition labelling for products on which a nutrition and/or health claim is made, with the exception of generic advertising.[43]

[36] NHCR, art 6(1).

[37] ibid, Recital (17).

[38] Commission Regulation (EC) 353/2008 of 18 April 2008 establishing implementing rules for applications for authorisation of health claims as provided for in Article 15 of Regulation (EC) No 1924/2006 of the European Parliament and of the Council [2008] OJ L109/11.

[39] Regulation (EC) 353/2008, no 1 of Annex 'General Principles for the scientific substantiation'.

[40] NHCR, art 6(2).

[41] ibid, art 6(1).

[42] ibid, art 6(3).

[43] ibid, art 7(1).

In addition, non-prepackaged foodstuffs offered for sale, and foodstuffs packed at the point of sale at the request of the purchaser or pre-packaged with a view to immediate sale are exempted from the obligation of carrying nutrition labelling.[44] Generic advertising, also excluded from the application of Article 7 NHCR, implies that the claim is not made in relation to one product, but to a group of products, for example in relation to 'fruit' and not to 'apple.'

14.7 Nutrition claims

A 'nutrition claim' means any claim which states, suggests, or implies that a food has particular beneficial nutritional properties due to the energy (calorific value) or the nutrients or other substances it contains or does not contain. Common nutrition claims are, for example, 'high in protein' or '30% less fat'.

A nutrition claim can refer to all nutrients and other substances.[45] Nutrients[46] are to be determined legally and cover the nutrients mentioned in the provision and their components. The listed categories are protein, carbohydrate, fat, fibre, sodium, and vitamins and minerals.[47] Fatty acids as components of fats or peptides and amino acids as components of protein are also considered nutrients in the legal sense. 'Other substances'[48] must have a nutritional or physiological effect, and cover, for instance, caffeine, lutein, glucosamine, and plant extracts.

Claims referring to the nature of the food or its ingredients which are not related to the nutritional value are not regarded as nutrition claims. Examples are 'isotonic', 'GMO free', 'gluten-free', and 'vegan'. It should also be noted that, if a product is classified as a medicinal product, it falls outside the scope of the Regulation.

The Nutri-score type of scheme is an interpretative scheme in that it attributes a positive message, therefore would also fulfil the requirements of a 'nutrition claim' as it provides information on the beneficial nutritional quality of a food. More generally, it may even be perceived as making a health claim because the green colour suggests a health benefit, and the categories provide an overall assessment of healthiness.

[44] ibid, art 1(2).

[45] In the sense of ibid, art 2(2)(2)–(4).

[46] In the sense of ibid, art 2(2)(2).

[47] As listed in Regulation (EU) 1169/2011 of the European Parliament and of the Council of 25 October 2011 on the provision of food information to consumers (the reference to the Annex to Directive 90/496/EEC must be construed as a reference to this Regulation).

[48] In the sense of NHCR, art 2(2)(3).

14.7.1 Specific conditions (Article 8) and comparative claims (Article 9)

Nutrition claims are only permitted if they are listed in the Annex and conform to the conditions outlined in the NHCR.[49] As all FBOs can use the listed nutrition claims if they fulfil the conditions specified, it can be considered a generic authorization system. Amendments to the Annex are adopted under the Committee procedure, in this case the regulatory procedure with scrutiny (See Chapter 3).

Nutrition claims can broadly be categorized into compositional nutrition claims and comparative nutritional claims. A compositional claim is, for instance, 'low sugars', which may only be made where the product contains no more than 5g of sugars per 100g for solids and 2.5g of sugars per 100ml for liquids.[50]

Comparative nutrition claims[51] compare the composition of the food in question with a range of foods in the same category that do not have a composition which allows them to bear a claim, including foods from other brands. Claims that compare the nutritional value of two foodstuffs are only allowed if those foods are from the same category and consider a range of foods in that category. An example of a comparative nutrition claim is, for instance, 'energy reduced'[52] or 'light/lite'. The purpose of such a comparison is to enable the average consumer to understand the beneficial effects of one food product over another for their purposes.[53]

14.8 Health claims

The NHCR defines health claims as 'any claim that states, suggests or implies that a relationship exists between a food category, a food or one of its constituents and health'.[54]

From this it follows that in general, 'health claims' are those claims that identify a property of the food as having advantages (or disadvantages) for human health. The claim needs to be connected, if only by broad association, to the property of a food, which means that the claim must refer directly or indirectly to the physiological effect of a food, its components, or a food category. This excludes general statements on health without a connection to the properties of a food (eg 'eat healthy!') from the definition of 'health claims'. Some information characterized by health claims may overlap with information covered by other provisions of EU

[49] ibid, art 8(1).
[50] ibid, Annex.
[51] ibid, art 9(1)–(2).
[52] A claim that a food is energy-reduced, and any claim likely to have the same meaning for the consumer, may only be made where the energy value is reduced by at least 30%, with an indication of the characteristic(s) which make(s) the food reduced in its total energy value; see ibid, Annex.
[53] ibid, art 5(2).
[54] ibid, art 2(2)(5).

law such as Regulation (EC) 609/2013 on infants' food. As long and as these claims are mandatory, they do not qualify as 'health claims'.

Claims stating benefits are also covered by the definition of 'health claims'. The term 'relationship' must be understood in a broad sense.[55] The word 'health' or similar wording does not need to be explicitly mentioned. Rather, it is sufficient that an average consumer associates the claims with health.[56] Accordingly, 'beneficial effects' are also covered by the definition of 'health claim'. As the Court held in *Weintor*, which concerned a claim that wine was 'easily digestible':[57]

> In the present case, the claim at issue suggests that, in view of the reduced acidity, the wine in question is particularly easy or pleasant to digest. Accordingly, the wine is said to produce a beneficial nutritional or physiological effect. It is common ground that, in so far as it is linked to the intake of a foodstuff in a specific instance, digestion can be regarded as a physiological process which, by definition, is limited in time, giving rise to only temporary or fleeting effects. On the basis of that finding, the referring court queries whether a description such as 'easily digestible' can be described as a 'health claim' even if it does not imply that the beneficial nutritional or physiological effect which the wine in question could produce leads to a sustained improvement in physical condition. In that regard it is apparent from the wording of Article 2(2)(5) of Regulation No 1924/2006 that the starting-point for the definition of a 'health claim' within the meaning of that regulation is the relationship that must exist between a food or one of its constituents and health. That being the case, it must be noted that that definition provides no information as to whether that relationship must be direct or indirect, or as to its intensity or duration.

14.8.1 Specific Conditions (Article 10)

All health claims on EU food products must be authorized. According to Article 10(1), health claims are by default prohibited in the EU, unless they comply with the general requirements for all claims (see section 14.4.1 in Chapter II NHCR), the specific requirements for health claims (Chapter IV NHCR), and are authorized in accordance with the NHCR and included in the lists of authorized claims provided for in Articles 13 and 14.[58]

In addition, health claims must be accompanied by mandatory information. Health claims are only permitted if the following mandatory information

[55] *Weintor* (n 17) para 34.
[56] See eg NHCR, art 13(c).
[57] *Weintor* (n 17) paras 31–33.
[58] NHCR, art 10(1).

is included in the labelling, or if no such labelling exists, in the presentation and advertising:[59]

> (a) a statement indicating the importance of a varied and balanced diet and a healthy lifestyle; (b) the quantity of the food and pattern of consumption required to obtain the claimed beneficial effect; (c) where appropriate, a statement addressed to persons who should avoid using the food; and (d) an appropriate warning for products that are likely to present a health risk if consumed to excess.

Generic references to general, non-specific benefits of the nutrient or food for overall good health or health-related well-being—such as 'good for your health'—may only be claimed in combination with an actual authorized health claim.[60]

Article 10(4) NHCR foresees the adoption of specific guidelines on the implementation of the specific conditions for health claims in Article 10 NHCR. The Commission has made use of this provision and issued an implementing decision 2013/63/EU adopting guidelines for the implementation of specific conditions for health claims laid down in Article 10 of the Regulation.[61]

14.8.2 Restrictions on the use of certain health claims (Article 12 NHCR)

Article 12 NHCR prohibits the use of certain health claims regardless of whether they comply with the other requirements of the NHCR. These are (a) 'claims which suggest that health could be affected by not consuming the food'.[62] This prohibition requires the claim to refer to a specific food. Reference to food in general is not prohibited. Phrases such as 'an apple a day keeps the doctor away' are therefore not prohibited. Also prohibited are (b) 'claims which make reference to the rate or amount of weight loss'.[63] This general prohibition is comprehensible, as it is difficult to attribute specific outcomes such as weight loss solely to the consumption of one food item. Lastly, (c) 'claims which make reference to recommendations of individual doctors or health professionals and other associations not referred to

[59] ibid, art 10(2).

[60] ibid, art 10(3). In Case C-524/18 *Dr Willmar Schwabe GmbH & Co KG v Queisser Pharma GmbH & Co KG* EU:C:2020:60 (*Schwabe/Queisser Pharma*) the CJEU had to interpret what accompany in this provision entails; see Hanna Schebesta, 'On Legal Value of Implementing Acts at the CJEU Case Note on Schwabe/Queisser Pharma (C-524/18)' (2020) 9 Journal of European Consumer and Market Law 248.

[61] Commission Implementing Decision 2013/63/EU of 24 January 2013 adopting guidelines for the implementation of specific conditions for health claims laid down in Article 10 of Regulation (EC) No 1924/2006 of the European Parliament and of the Council [2013] OJ L22/25.

[62] NHCR, art 12(a).

[63] ibid, art 12(b).

in Article 11'[64] are also prohibited. This prohibition covers references to recommendations, not the recommendations themselves.

14.8.3 Claims other than those referring to reduction of disease risk claims and to children's development and health (Article 13 NHCR)

Article 13 NHCR claims are often referred to as 'generic claims', as they are not reduction of disease risk claims or children's health claims. Generic claims refer to the role of a nutrient or substance in aspects such as growth, development, and body functions; psychological and behavioural functions; slimming and weight control, satiety, or reduction of available energy from the diet.[65] An example of such a claim is that magnesium contributes to a reduction of tiredness and fatigue.

These generic health claims may be made when they are indicated on the Union list for generic health claims, are based on generally accepted scientific evidence, and are well understood by the average consumer.[66]

The Commission was tasked with compiling a Union list of permitted health claims.[67] The entries on this Union list were initially based on submissions by the Member States, screened according to selection criteria, and a subsequent evaluation by European Food Safety Authority (EFSA). The Union list of permitted generic health claims was published in an Implementing Regulation in 2012.[68] However, many of the so-called Article 13(1) claims are still under consideration and factually 'on hold', most notably botanical claims (which concern around 1,548 botanical-related claims). This Union list is not yet definite, nor is it set in stone. It can and should be changed, amended, and added to by the Commission and Member States 'on a gradual basis'[69] when they see the need to do so 'either on the basis of generally established scientific data or newly developed scientific data'.[70]

New claims based on generally accepted scientific evidence can be added to the Union list either at the Commission's own initiative or following a request by a Member State by using the applicable Committee procedure and consulting the Authority.[71]

Following Article 13(5), FBOs that wish to include a new claim in the Union list can request the inclusion for new claims based on newly developed scientific

[64] ibid, art 12(c).
[65] ibid, art 13(1)(a)–(c).
[66] ibid, art 13(i)-(ii).
[67] ibid, art 13(3), by means of the regulatory procedure with scrutiny.
[68] Commission Regulation (EU) 432/2012 of 16 May 2012 establishing a list of permitted health claims made on foods, other than those referring to the reduction of disease risk and to children's development and health [2012] OJ L136/1.
[69] Case T-296/12 *The Health Food Manufacturers' Association and Others v European Commission* EU:T:2015:375, para 66.
[70] ibid, para 66.
[71] NHCR, art 13(4).

evidence and/or which include a request for the protection of proprietary data following the procedure as laid down in Article 18 NHCR.[72] Consequently, the use of general health claims may be authorized for specific applicants for a period of five years, if the appropriate procedure has been followed.

14.8.4 *Reduction of disease risk claims and claims referring to children's development and health (Article 14 NHCR)*

Article 14 NHCR concerns two specific types of health claims, namely (a) the reduction of disease risk and (b) claims referring to children's development and health. These need to undergo the regular authorization procedure according to Articles 15–19 NHCR and are subject to additional labelling provisions. These provisions require that 'the presentation or advertising shall also bear a statement indicating that the disease to which the claim is referring has multiple risk factors and that altering one of these risk factors may or may not have a beneficial effect'.[73]

A 'reduction of disease risk claim'[74] means any health claim that states, suggests, or implies that the consumption of a food category, a food, or one of its constituents significantly reduces a risk factor in the development of a human disease. Claims that specifically refer to the reduction of the risk of a disease itself are not covered. A successfully authorized reduction of disease risk is, for example, 'Plant sterols have been shown to lower/reduce blood cholesterol. High cholesterol is a risk factor in the development of coronary heart disease'.[75] Not permissible, however, would be the claim that the intake of plant sterols reduces the risk of coronary heart disease. The claim needs to reduce a risk factor 'significantly'. The claim does not need to 'necessarily contain the word "significantly" or a term having the same meaning'.[76] However, claims are assessed using the average consumer benchmark, and the law 'does not require that such a claim expressly states that the consumption of a food significantly reduces a risk factor in the development of a human disease. It is sufficient that that claim may give the average consumer who is reasonably well informed and reasonably observant and circumspect the impression that the reduction of a risk factor is significant'.[77]

[72] ibid, art 13(5).
[73] ibid, art 14(2).
[74] ibid, art 2(2)(6).
[75] Commission Regulation (EC) 983/2009 of 21 October 2009 on the authorisation and refusal of authorisation of certain health claims made on food and referring to the reduction of disease risk and to children's development and health [2009] OJ L277/3, Annex I.
[76] Case C-299/12 *Green—Swan Pharmaceuticals CR, a.s. v Státní zemědělská a potravinářská inspekce, ústřední inspektorát* EU:C:2013:501, para 25.
[77] ibid, para 24.

Article 14(1)(b) pertains to health claims concerning 'children's development and health'. An example of such a claim is that calcium is needed for normal growth and development of bones in children.[78]

Specific labelling is required according to the authorization, or where that does not exist, a statement 'indicating that the disease to which the claim is referring has multiple risk factors and that altering one of these risk factors may or may not have a beneficial effect'.[79]

14.8.5 *Application for authorization (Articles 15, 16, and 17 NHCR)*

Articles 15 to 17 stipulate the basic procedural rules for the authorization of claims on the reduction of disease risk and claims on children's development and health. Article 15 provides provisions on the initiative, and the formal and substantive structure of the authorization procedure. It also provides the legal basis for the Commission to initiate detailed implementing regulations and guidelines. Health claims as defined in Article 14 NHCR need authorization, as do certain claims falling under of Article 13 NHCR, referring to children's development and health.[80]

14.9 The application

The application needs to be submitted to the national competent authority.[81] The applicant has to choose the authority of the Member State where the applicant intends to place its food on the market. The application must include:

> (a) the name and address of the applicant; (b) the nutrient or other substance, or the food or the category of food, in respect of which the health claim is to be made and its particular characteristics; (c) a copy of the studies, including, where available, independent, peer-reviewed studies, which have been carried out with regard to the health claim and any other material which is available to demonstrate that the health claim complies with the criteria provided for in this Regulation; (d) where appropriate, an indication of the information which should be regarded as proprietary accompanied by verifiable justification; (e) a copy of other

[78] See Annex I of Commission Regulation (EC) 983/2009.

[79] NHCR, art 14(2).

[80] ibid, art 13(5).

[81] A list of competent national authorities is available in EFSA, 'List of competent authorities of the Member States within the framework of Regulation (EC) No 1924/2006 of the European Parliament and of the Council of 20 December 2006 on nutrition and health claims made on foods' (July 2023) <https://www.efsa.europa.eu/sites/default/files/efsa_rep/blobserver_assets/ndacompetentauthorities.pdf> accessed 13 August 2022.

scientific studies which are relevant to that health claim; (f) a proposal for the wording of the health claim for which authorisation is sought including, as the case may be, specific conditions for use; (g) a summary of the application.[82]

Commission Regulation (EC) 353/2008 provides additional details regarding the requirements for the respective application process.[83] The applicant may withdraw their application up until EFSA has finalized its scientific opinion.[84] The national competent authority acknowledges receipt within 14 days, and informs EFSA.[85] Before it submits the application to EFSA,[86] the national competent authority needs to conduct a validity check, as the national competent authority bears, together with EFSA, the responsibility for the validity of the application before submission to EFSA.[87] As a consequence, the national competent authority is not simply a 'postbox'[88] that forwards the application to EFSA for authorization. Rather, it needs to conduct an initial validity check by verifying that the required data is included and determining under which authorization procedure (Articles 15 or 18 NHCR) the applicant submits their application.[89] During this process the national competent authority may request further details from the applicant to accompany the application.[90] The national competent authorities need to finalize their assessment within a reasonable time limit, although what constitutes 'reasonable' needs to be determined on a case-by case basis..[91] Regardless of the circumstances of the individual case, a time period of seven months is considered too long.[92] In the event of a breach, however, EU law does not provide any sanctions.[93] If the national competent authority approves the validity of the claim, it submits the application to EFSA.

EFSA informs the other Member States and the Commission of the application.[94] EFSA then needs to prepare and provide its scientific opinion within a time limit of five months from the receipt of a valid application.[95] The national

[82] NHCR, art 15(3).

[83] Commission Regulation (EC) 353/2008 of 18 April 2008 establishing implementing rules for applications for authorisation of health claims as provided for in Article 15 of Regulation (EC) No 1924/2006 of the European Parliament and of the Council [2008] OJ L109/11.

[84] ibid, art 7(b).

[85] NHCR, art 15(2)(a)(i)-(ii).

[86] ibid, art 15(2)(a)(iii).

[87] ibid, art 16(1): EFSA's obligation to deliver its opinion within five months starts upon receipt of a 'valid application' from the national competent authority; see Case T-17/12 *Hagenmeyer and Hahn v European Commission* EU:T:2014:234 (*Hagenmeyer and Hahn*), para 136.

[88] *Hagenmeyer and Hahn* (n 87) para 134.

[89] Commission Regulation (EC) 353/2008, art 7(a).

[90] NHCR, art 16(2).

[91] *Hagenmeyer and Hahn* (n 87) para 149.

[92] ibid, para 151.

[93] ibid, para 160.

[94] NHCR, art 15(2)(b).

[95] ibid, art 16(1).

competent authorities and EFSA share the duty to check the validity of the application.[96] Consequently, before drafting its scientific opinion, EFSA conducts a second validity check ('completeness check') in addition to the one conducted by the competent national authority. During the completeness check, EFSA may request further details from the applicant to accompany the application.[97] EFSA may then issue a 'statement of validity', which also marks the start of the five-month period according to Article 6(1)(1) NHCR. At this point, it makes the application and any supplementary information supplied by the applicant available to the other Member States and the Commission[98] and makes the summary of the application referred to in Article 15(3)(g) NHCR available to the public.[99] If EFSA requests more information from the applicant at this stage of the procedure, a time period of two months is added to the five-month period.[100] When EFSA requests information, the time stops ('clock stop') until the requested information is with EFSA. The deadline is extended by two months following any request for additional information. The obligation ends with the publication of the opinion in the EFSA journal. No sanctions are imposed if EFSA does not provide its opinion in the designated time period.

14.10 EFSA's opinion

The verification of the application and the drafting of EFSA's opinion is a risk assessment measure conducted by EFSA.[101] Essentially, the Panel on Dietetic Products, Nutrition and Allergies (NDA Panel) is entrusted with this duty. Substantially, the NDA Panel needs to verify:

(a) that the health claim is substantiated by scientific evidence;
(b) that the wording of the health claim complies with the criteria laid down in this Regulation.[102]

If the assessment is positive, the opinion needs to comply with the criteria as set out in Article 16(4) NHCR. EFSA then needs to forward its opinion to the Commission, the Member States, and the applicant, including a report describing its assessment of the health claim and stating the reasons for its opinion and the information on which its opinion was based.[103]

[96] ibid, art 16(1): EFSA's obligation to deliver its opinion within five months starts upon receipt of a 'valid application' from the national competent authority, see *Hagenmeyer and Hahn* (n 87) para 136.
[97] NHCR, art 16(2).
[98] ibid, art 15(2)(b).
[99] ibid, art 15(2)(b)(ii).
[100] ibid, art 16(1).
[101] ibid, art 16(3).
[102] ibid, art 16(3).
[103] ibid, art 16(5).

14.11 Union authorization

After EFSA has submitted its opinion to the Commission,[104] the Commission may submit a draft decision on the lists of permitted health claims to the Standing Committee on the Food Chain and Animal Health[105] within a period of two months.[106] The decision regarding which claim will be included in the Union list is a risk management decision. Accordingly, the Commission considers not only the scientific opinion prepared by EFSA, but also 'any relevant provisions of Community law and other legitimate factors relevant to the matter under consideration'.[107] The legitimate factors that must be considered in risk management decisions, in addition to risk assessment, are 'societal, economic, traditional, ethical and environmental factors and the feasibility of controls'.[108] In practice, however, claims have been rejected on the grounds that they are 'inconsistent with generally accepted nutrition and health principles or if it encourages or condones excessive consumption of any food or disparages good dietary practice'.[109] Dismissing claims on these grounds has been explicitly endorsed by the CJEU.[110] The final decision on the authorization is to be made through a Committee procedure with control elements.[111] This authorization would in principle not expire. If the applicant wishes to protect proprietary data and therefore only seeks a preliminary authorization for five years, the 'lighter' procedure without the control element of Article 25(2) NHCR is applicable.[112] If the claim still fulfils the requirements of the regulation after five years, it may undergo the Article 25(3) NHCR procedure.[113]

When the decision is made, the Commission must inform the applicant without delay and publish its decision in the Official Journal of the European Union.[114] Once included in the lists provided for in Articles 13 and 14 NHCR, health claims may be used, in accordance with the conditions specified for them, by any FBO, unless they are restricted for use in accordance with the provisions of Article 21.[115]

[104] ibid, art 16(5).
[105] ibid, art 23(2).
[106] ibid, art 17(1).
[107] ibid, art 17(1).
[108] Regulation (EU) 178/2002 of the European Parliament and of the Council of 28 January 2002 laying down the general principles and requirements of food law, establishing the European Food Safety Authority and laying down procedures in matters of food Safety [2002] OJ L31/1 (General Food Law Regulation (GFLR)), Recital (19).
[109] NHCR, Recital (18).
[110] Case C-296/16 P *Dextro Energy GmbH & Co KG v European Commission* EU:C:2017:437.
[111] NHCR, art 17(3) in connection with art 25(3).
[112] ibid, art 17(3)(a).
[113] ibid, art 17(3)(b).
[114] ibid, art 17(4).
[115] ibid, art 17(5).

14.11.1 *Application for authorization according to Article 13(5) NHCR (Article 18 NHCR)*

FBOs can submit applications to add further claims to the Article 13 NHCR list. Initially, the Article 13 list was designed to give Member States and the Commission the opportunity to authorize certain health claims without undergoing the authorization procedures. When FBOs want to add claims to the list of approved health claims stipulated by the Member States and the Commission they need to apply the Article 18 procedure. The procedure is 'lighter' than the procedure for regular authorizations, as it only requires compliance with some of the requirements of Article 16 as a prerequisite for authorization through Article 18 NHCR.[116] This reduced amount of bureaucracy is intended to facilitate innovation.[117]

The authorization procedure is in large parts similar to the authorization procedure as stipulated in Articles 15 to 17 NHCR. The FBO intending to use the health claim submits its application to the national competent authority of a Member State, which must acknowledge receipt of the application in writing within 14 days of receiving it.[118] As the national competent authority is obliged to forward only a 'valid application' to EFSA,[119] the national competent authority checks the validity of the application.[120] If the assessment is positive, it passes the application on to EFSA, the Commission, and any other Member State. EFSA then conducts its own validity check, after which the time period of five months starts within which EFSA can issue its opinion.[121]

14.11.2 *Modification, suspension, and revocation of authorizations (Article 19 NHCR)*

The list of permitted health claims can and need to be changed 'on a gradual basis'.[122] Such a change can be initiated by the applicant or user of the claim[123] or by EFSA following a request from a Member State or the Commission.[124] The procedures for change largely resemble the procedures for authorization. EFSA needs to prepare an opinion, transmit it to the Commission, Member States, and to the applicant or user, if necessary, and publish it. The applicant or user can comment

[116] ibid, art 18(3)(2).
[117] ibid, Recital (26).
[118] ibid, art 18(1)-(2).
[119] ibid, art 18(3).
[120] Commission Regulation (EC) 353/2008, art 7(a), which distinguishes between the procedures of NHCR, arts 15 and 18.
[121] NHCR, art 18(3).
[122] Case T-296/12 *The Health Food Manufacturers' Association and Others v European Commission* EU:T:2015:375, para 66.
[123] NHCR, art 19(1).
[124] ibid, art 19(2).

within 30 days, before the Commission examines the opinion and comments and may modify the respective claim, if appropriate.

14.12 General and final provisions

The Commission is responsible for establishing and maintaining a Community register of nutrition and health claims made on food.[125] This health claim register can be accessed in a database on the internet.[126] Article 21 provides rules for data protection regarding the scientific data and other information submitted in the application process concerning claims under Article 15(3) NHCR. The provision, however, only provides protection under the conditions set out in Article 21(1)(a)–(c) NHCR. The provisions in the NHCR aim for maximum harmonization across all Member States; Member States may not introduce stricter measures.[127] If a Member State needs to deviate from the provisions of the NHCR (eg when new scientific evidence requires a Member State to take action according to Article 114(5) TFEU), it needs to notify the Commission and other Member States.[128] They will then initiate respective procedures. When a Member State believes that a health claim has been granted in breach of the rules of the NHCR or the scientific substantiation is not sufficient, the 'Member State may temporarily suspend the use of that claim within its territory'[129] and inform the Commission. Article 25 NHCR ensures that the authorization procedures follow the generally applicable rules of the Committee procedure, which govern almost all authorization procedures in the EU. Although the Commission was supposed to evaluate the provisions of the NHCR by 19 January 2013,[130] such an evaluation never took place. However, the NHCR has since been subject to the REFIT procedure, which compensates for the missing evaluation. The transition periods specified in Article 28 NHCR have all expired.

14.13 Conclusion

The NHCR is characterized by its regulation of food information concerning nutrition and health effects. The NHCR ensures that claims made about food products are scientifically substantiated. However, it does not intend to promote consumption of products with nutrition or health claims. In this sense, the concept

[125] ibid, art 20.
[126] EU Register of Health Claims (n 11).
[127] NHCR, art 22.
[128] ibid, art 23(1).
[129] ibid, art 24(1).
[130] ibid, art 27.

of preventive health, which advocates the idea of 'food as a medicine' has not been widely embraced in the legal framework on nutrition and health claims. In terms of health, the NHCR supports consumer choice by providing information, but does not promote or encourage the consumption of specific products.

From a future EU regulatory perspective, the EU Farm to Fork Strategy commits to a healthy food system. However, health has an uneasy place in EU law in terms of EU competence, and it is also a neglected topic in EU food law. In addition, it is not always evident to what extent health is included within the various dimensions of sustainability. In the past, issues at the intersection of nutrition and health have often been unresolved at the EU level, for example the implementation of nutrient profiles, which had been forecast by the NHCR for 2008 remains incomplete. The Farm to Fork Strategy does bring the topic of nutritional health back onto the agenda, and re-tables a formal proposal for the implementation of nutrient profiles.

The Farm to Fork Strategy exhibits only limited attention to the topic of nutrition and health claims. Future gains on the basis of this regulation could be made. First, the NCHR is incomplete with respect to some types of claims (such as botanicals), and other promising emerging areas (such as probiotics) lack sufficient studies to enable the authorization of health claims. In this respect, critics have noted that promising health claims are often rejected for 'lack of precision' of claimed health effects.[131] The market-driven mechanism relying on an applicant paying for authorization costs could be complemented by a health-driven mechanism that sees the Commission invest in promising nutrition and health benefits. Secondly, the extent to which consumers actually understand that nutrition and health claims on EU food products are, in fact, substantiated by scientific evidence is questionable and understudied. This could be clarified through the introduction of additional information items such as 'verified claims' along with the implementation of information campaigns. Lastly, the objective of the NHCR should be understood more widely in the context of health, and the potential in contributing to a preventive health agenda should be addressed in legislative initiatives beyond the Farm to Fork Strategy.

[131] Moritz Hagenmeyer and Andreas Hahn, 'EFSA's Secret Health Claims' (2013) 8 European Food and Feed Law Review 10.

PART VI

FOOD QUALITY LAW

There is no specific definition of food quality in European Union (EU) law, which has resulted in a highly multifaceted approach, where food quality is understood to encompass various aspects such as food safety, nutritional quality, origin and authenticity, ethics, aesthetics, sensory properties (taste), convenience, and functionality. Many of these aspects are addressed in the compositional requirements included in the EU marketing standards for specific agricultural products (see Chapter 1), and to a lesser extent in the early examples of vertical regulation, for instance concerning 'breakfast products', such as honey and milk (Chapter 1).

Among the EU laws that clearly govern specific food quality aspects are the Organics Regulation and Food Quality Schemes Regulation, covered in Part VI—Food Quality Law. The Organics Regulation lays down the EU legal requirements for the organic production and labelling of organic products (Chapter 15). The Food Quality Schemes Regulation lays down the rules for the EU food quality labels, namely the Protected Designation of Origin (PDO) and the Protected Geographical Indication (PGI), the Traditional Specialty Guarantee (TSG), and Optional Quality Terms (Chapter 16).

Nevertheless, it is important to bear in mind that alongside these public schemes, a plethora of private schemes have taken over the function of defining and guaranteeing a variety of food quality characteristics.

Conceptual clarifications around food schemes

Both the EU organic scheme and the food quality scheme are voluntary public schemes. They are 'voluntary' because producers are not forced to comply with the standards set in or through the legislation, and 'public' because the standard is set either directly or indirectly through public regulations. This distinguishes them from private standards, which are created by private bodies.

In this respect, some nuance on terminology is in order. When speaking about food schemes, it is conceptually useful to distinguish standardization, certification, and accreditation.[1] Standard-setting refers to the creation of the rules and

[1] Allison Loconto and Eve Fouilleux, 'Politics of Private Regulation: ISEAL and the Shaping of Transnational Sustainability Governance' (2014) 8 Regulation & Governance 166. In addition, the element of enforcement is not incorporated into the model. On enforcement of standards, see Paul

requirements that a certain scheme sets. Certification, in contrast, refers to the activity of checking compliance with a given standard. Lastly, accreditation controls the certifiers, and accreditation bodies are often public. In the EU, the Accreditation Regulation[2] is applicable and therefore accreditation is always linked to the exercise of public authority.[3]

The problem with private schemes is that there are no requirements on the governance design, and therefore on their credibility and accountability. This means that a food standard can even be set and certified by a company itself (self-declaratory). In the EU, private food schemes are only loosely regulated as voluntary information under the Food Information to Consumers Regulation. In 2010, the European Commission issued voluntary—and therefore non-binding—Commission Guidelines establishing a set of best practices for voluntary certification schemes for agricultural products and foodstuffs. [4] In addition, some practices of food schemes might be covered by the Unfair Commercial Practices Directive. Nevertheless, it is fair to say that in the highly regulated sphere of food information law, voluntary private schemes are the 'wild west' of food regulation.

Privatization: retailers as regulators

The global agro-food regime underwent significant transformation through corporatization and the rise of retailers.[5] Private food standards are the primary mode of governance in food supply chains,[6] making them a de facto precondition for participation in global[7] and domestic markets.[8] The proliferation of private schemes

Verbruggen, 'Gorillas in the Closet? Public and Private Actors in the Enforcement of Transnational Private Regulation' (2013) 7 Regulation & Governance 512.

[2] Regulation (EC) 765/2008 Setting out the Requirements for Accreditation and Market Surveillance Relating to the Marketing of Products, [2008] OJ L 218/30.

[3] Hanna Schebesta, 'Control in the Label: Self-Declared, Certified, Accredited? On-Pack Consumer Communication about Compliance Control in Voluntary Food Schemes from a Legal Perspective' in Peter Rott (ed), *Certification—Trust, Accountability, Liability* (Springer International Publishing 2019).

[4] European Commission Communication EU Best Practice Guidelines for Voluntary Certification Schemes for Agricultural Products and Foodstuffs, [2010] OJ C 341/5.

[5] Francis Snyder, 'Economic Globalisation and the Law in the 21st Century' in Austin Sarat (ed), *The Blackwell Companion to Law and Society* (Blackwell Publishing Ltd 2004).

[6] Linda Fulponi, 'Private Voluntary Standards in the Food System: The Perspective of Major Food Retailers in OECD Countries' (2006) 31 Food Policy 1, 31; Spencer Henson, 'The Role of Public and Private Standards in Regulating International Food Markets' (2006) 4 Journal of International Agricultural Trade and Development.

[7] Stefano Ponte and Peter Gibbon, 'Quality Standards, Conventions and the Governance of Global Value Chains' (2006) 34 Economy and society 1; Bernd van der Meulen, *Private Food Law. Governing Food Chains through Contract Law, Self-Regulation, Private Standards, Audits and Certification Schemes* (Wageningen Academic Publishers 2011).

[8] Thomas Reardon, Peter Timmer, and Julio Berdegue, 'The Rapid Rise of Supermarkets in Developing Countries: Induced Organizational, Institutional, and Technological Change in Agrifood Systems' (2004) 1 Journal of Agricultural and Developmental Economics 15.

that govern the food sector can be partially explained by the fact that private parties often employ much more sophisticated approaches to food quality regulation.

In the industrialized world, a fragmented regulatory space has emerged. Governance procedures such as private standard-setting supplement governmental command-and-control measures.[9] Safety standards are geared towards large quantities of produce of uniform quality. Costs of audits and certification are generally borne by the producer. The investments involved are not always attainable for small and medium-sized enterprises.

The relationship between public and private standards

The relationship between public and private standards has been subject to some debate. In a market-driven food sector, the importance of governments as regulators decreases and is replaced, or at least complemented, by retailers and certifiers as private standard-setters and enforcers.[10] With the rise of market-states,[11] the role of government regulation based on classic accountability models changes. In Market-state-regulatory-models retailers replace governments and regulation switches from top-down models to residual oversight and the provision of incentives.

Conversely, Arcuri uses the term 'publicization' to characterize the transformation of private standards into public standards.[12] In the EU, the most pertinent example of this is the EU organic standard laid down in the Organics Regulation (see Chapter 15). The organics sector used to be dominated by private labels, and hence private regulation. Over time, however, Member States acted and publicly regulated organic standards. In 1991, the EU followed suit with its own EU label for organics. Whereas the EU standard constitutes a minimum 'common denominator', private standards may set stricter standards—this model characterizes a coexistence of both public and private standards.[13] An example of this is the coexistence of the EU organic label and the 'Demeter' certification, which embraces a

[9] Christoph Möllers, 'European Governance—Meaning and Value of a Concept' (2006) 43 Common Market Law Review 313; Kai Purnhagen, *The Politics of Systematisation—Market, State, Integration, and Collectivity* (Springer 2013).

[10] Fabrizio Cafaggi, 'Private Regulation, Supply Chain and Contractual Networks: The Case of Food Safety' (2010) RSCAS 2010/10 Robert Schuman Centre for Advanced Studies—Private Regulation Series; Spencer Henson and John Humprey, 'The Impacts of Private Food Safety Standards on the Food Chain and on Public Standard-Setting Processes: Paper Prepared for FAO/WHO (2009); Spencer Henson and John Humprey, 'Chapter 5: Codex Alimentarius and Private Standards' in Bernd van der Meulen (ed), *Private Food Law. Governing Food Chains through Contract Law, Self-Regulation, Private Standards, Audits and Certification Schemes* (Wageningen Academic Publishers 2011).

[11] Dennis Patterson and Ari Afilalo, *The New Global Trading Order: The Evolving State and the Future of Trade* (Cambridge University Press 2010), Purnhagen (n 9).

[12] Alessandra Arcuri, 'The Transformation of Organic Regulation: The Ambiguous Effects of Publicization' (2015) 9 Regulation & Governance 144.

[13] ibid.

more far-reaching biodynamic approach. This situation is radically different in the United States (US), where the 'USDA organic' scheme prevents organizations from setting higher standards, therefore requiring them to choose either USDA organic or a different higher private scheme.[14] In the US context, a competitive relationship emerges between private and public regulation.

Sustainability as food quality?

It could be argued that the private sector is faster at responding to regulatory needs of consumers, especially with respect to sustainability characteristics of foodstuffs. This is why the food schemes are so successful, and can certify quality issues as diverse as fair trade, dolphin-free, or vegan. The private sector has also been more successful in developing multidimensional standards that aggregate different sustainability performance indicators into one scheme.

What role, then, should the EU public regulator take with respect to sustainability qualities of food products? Currently, there is also no clear definition of what sustainable food is. Sustainability links to a number of concepts that are discussed in relation to food quality, for instance healthy foods, unhealthy foods, local food, food produced in short food supply chains, plant-based food, fairly traded food, food with a low carbon footprint, and green food. These are largely without legal frameworks. The existing EU organic scheme and the EU quality schemes, as the only EU public food schemes, do not seem adequate for addressing sustainability quality holistically. Some advances towards defining 'green food' have been made in the area of public procurement, where the voluntary EU green public procurement criteria for food describe contract clauses for use in public governmental contracts. There is debate surrounding the expansion of the voluntary *green* public procurement criteria to include criteria for *sustainable* food.[15] The Farm to Fork Strategy promised a framework for sustainability labelling, which might have also involved definitions relating to what qualities sustainable food should possess. This would have depended on the approach chosen, as EU law is notoriously deeply committed to the information governance approach. A sustainability

[14] ibid.

[15] Hanna Schebesta and Plana Casado, 'Food: Mandatory EU Public Procurement Criteria for Food after the Farm to Fork Strategy' in Willem Janssen and Roberto Caranta (eds), *Mandatory Sustainability Requirements in EU Public Procurement Law: Reflections on a Paradigm Shift* (Bloomsbury Academic 2023); Hanna Schebesta, 'Revision of the EU Green Public Procurement Criteria for Food Procurement and Catering Services—Certification Schemes as the Main Determinant for Public Sustainable Food Purchases?' (2018) 9 European Journal of Risk Regulation 316; Hanna Schebesta, *Damages in EU Public Procurement Law* (Springer 2016) 235; Hanna Schebesta, 'EU Green Public Procurement Policy Modernisation Package, Eco-Labelling and Framing Measures' in Sarah Schoenmakers, Wouter Devroe, and Niels Philipsen (eds), *State Aid and Public Procurement in the European Union* (Intersentia 2014) 129.

labelling approach might therefore revolve around information governance (for instance that sustainability claims must be verifiable and scientifically proven), or they might take the shape of actual quality requirements. Until the public legislator acts, the area of defining sustainability as a component of food quality will remain reserved to the ambitions of private actors. This, in turn, has important ramifications on the choices that citizens are able to make about their food consumption, and whether consumers will find 'sustainable food' on the supermarket shelves at all.

15
Organic Food

15.1 Introduction

In practice, organic agriculture has of course got ancient roots, but it became more consolidated as an organic movement in rising opposition to industrial agriculture.[1] One of the early thinkers attributed to the organics movement is the Austrian Rudolf Steiner, who played a significant role in the development of the biodynamic movement in 1924.[2] In the United Kingdom, Lady Eve Balfour, who published 'The Living Soil' in 1943, and Sir Albert Howard, a scientist who similarly linked depleted soil to plant health and therefore to human health,[3] founded the British Soil Association in 1946. In these intellectual origins, the emphasis of the organic movement was largely on the holistic management of agricultural processes; an emphasis that has changed with the gradual codification of organics in regulation—over time, organics transitioned from a movement towards a more standardized approach.

Standardization and certification of organic products through private standards emerged in the 1970s.[4] In 1972, several initiatives united in the International Federation of Organic Agriculture Movements (IFOAM), attesting to the strongly transnational character of the organics private regulatory network. Arcuri attributes the rise of organic private regulation to an under-representation of interests valuing the environment and agro-ecological aspects, arguing that the 'lack of public regulation in these realms can be seen as the denial of a regulatory space to constituencies positively valuing sustainability, fair trade, and environmental protection'.[5] In this way, private regulation took on the role of filling a gap in public regulation.

Private regulation of organics was soon followed by governmental regulation, with Denmark being the first country to regulate organics in 1987. This process of 'publicization',[6] that is, the shift from private to public regulation, is unique to the

[1] Alessandra Arcuri, 'The Transformation of Organic Regulation: The Ambiguous Effects of Publicization' (2015) 9 Regulation & Governance 144.
[2] John Paull, 'The Secrets of Koberwitz: The Diffusion of Rudolf Steiner's Agriculture Course and the Founding of Biodynamic Agriculture' (2011) 2 Journal of Social Research & Policy 19.
[3] Gregory Barton, 'Sir Albert Howard and the Forestry Roots of the Organic Farming Movement' (2001) 75 Agricultural History 168.
[4] Arcuri (n 1).
[5] ibid.
[6] ibid.

EU Food Law. Hanna Schebesta and Kai Purnhagen, Oxford University Press. © Hanna Schebesta and Kai Purnhagen 2024.
DOI: 10.1093/9780198901570.003.0016

organics sector. Nowadays, this codification of organic requirements in first private and later public norms is a hallmark of the organic sector. What 'distinguishes organic from "sustainable" or "agroecological" management is that organic practices are well defined and in many countries regulated by laws. Regulation and certification is central to the current concept of organic agriculture in most countries'.[7] Whereas 'organics' may have lost some of its broader and holistic meaning, it has gained an unrivalled precision in terms of legal operationability.

In examining the detailed requirements of organic regulations, research has shown that 'across the board organic regulations define organic mainly in terms of 'natural' vs. 'artificial' substances that are allowed (or not) as inputs'.[8] The ideals of the original organics movement are nowadays reduced to the idea of 'chemical-free' farming, and therefore our current understanding of organic is 'largely void of broader environmental principles' and 'does not fully incorporate the original ideas of organic theoreticians who conceived it as a holistic farming system aimed primarily at improving soil health, thereby leading to improved animal, human, and societal health'.[9] The main idea behind organic agriculture as codified in regulations is therefore to avoid synthetic inputs, relying on natural substances instead.

The research by Seufert and others[10] also shows that—alongside the predominant idea of natural inputs—animal welfare and human health are organic principles that are more often found in regulations. In contrast, principles associated most with environmental sustainability, namely soil, water, and biodiversity were found to be 'not very prominent' in organic regulations. This general assessment is subject to some nuance due to specific exceptional countries; for instance India emphasizes biodiversity, and Australia water. In its regulatory version, the legal principles of organics, therefore, do not intrinsically pursue environmental concerns more broadly.

Indeed, it is argued that the definition of organics is driven by consumers.[11] Consumers' motives for purchasing organic food are diverse, ranging from health and nutritional concerns, superior taste, environmental concerns, lack of trust in the conventional food industry, animal welfare concerns, support for the local community, wholesomeness, nostalgia, and a sense of being fashionable.[12] However, among these motives, health stands out as the most important objective, followed by concerns about naturalness and the environment, and only then animal or social motives.[13]

[7] Verena Seufert, Navin Ramankutty, and Tabea Mayerhofer, 'What is This Thing Called Organic?—How Organic Farming is Codified in Regulations' (2017) 68 Food Policy 10.

[8] ibid.

[9] ibid.

[10] ibid.

[11] ibid.

[12] Renée Hughner and others, 'Who Are Organic Food Consumers? A Compilation and Review of Why People Purchase Organic Food' (2007) 6(2–3) Journal of Consumer Behaviour 94.

[13] Seufert, Ramankutty, and Mayerhofer (n 7).

The fact that the health properties of organic food is a prime consumer motivation raises the question whether organic food, from a nutritional perspective, is in fact healthier. The evidence is scientifically complex, and depends on various factors. A meta study linked demonstrable health benefits to levels of organic food consumption overall.[14] In addition, pesticide exposure has markedly decreased, although the same study found insufficient evidence to conclusively link it to positive health outcomes. A limitation of these studies is that consumption of organic food is often linked to overall healthier lifestyles, which weakens the ability to conclusively attribute health effects solely to organic food. When comparing the nutritional composition of organic and conventional foods, organic food is not by definition better. Nevertheless, organic food has proven to be a superior option in certain aspects of nutritional quality, for instance antioxidant activity, phenolic compounds, and omega-3 fatty acids.[15] Whereas the superior nutritional quality of organic food may be an incidental side effect of the organic production methods used, it is a not a legal requirement of organic food.

Overall, organics may therefore risk raising inflated expectations, for instance with consumers and policy makers, as to the health attributes or environmental and social characteristics associated with organic products. The extent to which such expectations are actually warranted depends on the design of respective organic law and the concrete legal requirements. Nevertheless, organics to date constitutes the most operational and legally practicable approximation of a definition of 'sustainable food', and it can therefore play an important role in shaping a more sustainable future food system. The following outlines the main protected features of the EU organic scheme, and how far these concerns are protected within it.

15.2 Organics Regulation

EU organic certification similarly transitioned from being governed by private schemes to being increasingly governed by public schemes.[16] Originally an issue governed by private regulation and private schemes, several Member States passed public organic regulations in the 1980s.[17] The first harmonized EU organic law was passed in 1991. There were subsequent amendments to the organic rules, with a

[14] Vanessa Vigar and others, 'A Systematic Review of Organic Versus Conventional Food Consumption: Is There a Measurable Benefit on Human Health?' (2019) 12 Nutrients 7.

[15] Faidon Magkos, Fotini Arvaniti, and Antonis Zampelas, 'Organic Food: Nutritious Food or Food for Thought? A Review of the Evidence' (2003) 54 International Journal of Food Sciences and Nutrition 357.

[16] Arcuri (n 1).

[17] France passed its organic legislation in 1980, Austria in 1983, and Denmark in 1987; see Susanne Padel, *The European Regulatory Framework and its Implementation in Influencing Organic Inspections and Certification Systems in the EU* (Certcost 2010).

'total'[18] or 'deep'[19] revision process starting in 2014. The outcome was Regulation (EU) 2018/848[20] (Organics Regulation), which applied from 1 January 2022.[21] The EU public organic scheme and private schemes coexist: the EU scheme formulates the minimum requirements, with private schemes, for instance biodynamic ones, exceeding the requirements set in EU legislation.

The Commission's proposal for the new Organics Regulation was originally based on both Article 42 Treaty on the Functioning of the European Union (TFEU) for competition in production of and trade in agricultural products and Article 43(2) TFEU on the Common Agricultural Policy (CAP). Later, the Committee on Legal Affairs recommended keeping Article 43(2) TFEU as the sole legal basis.[22]

The Organics Regulation establishes the principles and rules for organic production in the EU. It covers related certification procedures, requirements for labelling and production, as well as additional rules on controls. The new Organics Regulation acts as a 'Basic Act' or 'Framework Act', and important details of the legal framework still have to be developed in other legal acts (delegated acts and implementing acts). The extensive—if not excessive—reliance on non-legislative acts has led to criticism regarding the shift in power towards the executive.[23] It will almost certainly result in an EU organic scheme marked by complexity, based on a web of laws that amend the Basic Act numerous times (in the case of delegated regulations) and form a thick sub-layer (in the case of implementing regulations).

15.2.1 Scope of application

The Organics Regulation applies to products originating from agriculture, including aquaculture and beekeeping (Annex I TFEU) and to products originating from those products, if they are live and unprocessed agricultural products—animals, plants and seeds, mushrooms; processed food; and feed.[24] In addition, other products closely linked to agriculture (listed in Annex I of the Regulation)

[18] Hanspeter Schmidt, 'Regulation (EU) 2018/848: The New EU Organic Food Law' (2019) 14 European Food and Feed Law Review 15: criticizes the process as illegitimate as it used an important number of trilogues—privileged negotiations between the three EU institutions that precluded public participation in the process.

[19] Luca Leone, 'Lost in Translation? The EU Law Reform of Organic Farming' (2018) 13(5) European Food and Feed Law Review 421.

[20] Regulation (EU) 2018/848 of the European Parliament and of the Council of 30 May 2018 on organic production and labelling of organic products and repealing Council Regulation (EC) No 834/2007 [2018] OJ L150/1 (Organics Regulation).

[21] The original entry into force of the Regulation was postponed by one year. Regulation (EU) 2020/1693 of the European Parliament and of the Council of 11 November 2020 amending Regulation (EU) 2018/848 on organic production and labelling of organic products as regards its date of application and certain other dates referred to in that Regulation [2020] OJ L381/1.

[22] Leone (n 19).

[23] ibid.

[24] Organics Regulation, art 2(1).

can be certified as well.[25] The new Annex I also clarifies a list of additional products that are covered: specific yeasts, maté, vine leaves, palm hearts, hop shoots, silk-worm cocoons, natural gums and resins, essential oils, cork stoppers, raw cotton, raw wool, raw hides, and plant-based traditional herbal preparations. For instance, yeast was not previously considered an agricultural ingredient, but it is now. In addition, under the new rules, only organically produced substrates should be used in the production of organic yeast for use as food and feed. Furthermore, only certain products and substances should be allowed for use in the production, confection, and formulation of organic products. Food containing or consisting of engineered nanomaterials is also excluded.[26]

15.2.2 Objectives and general principles

The Regulation states ten different objectives,[27] testifying to the mixed and ambitious objectives to which organics are expected to cater. More concretely, organic production is defined as a sustainable management system that is based on certain general principles[28] and on more specific principles applicable to agricultural activities and aquaculture[29] and the processing of organic food[30] and feed.[31] For instance, organic food will exclude food containing, or consisting of, nanomaterials.[32] Overall, the objectives, as well as the general and the specific principles are indeed wide enough to incorporate much of the original organic movement's holistic ideas, and go beyond the simple idea of 'no chemical input'.

[25] ibid, art 2(1).
[26] ibid, art 7(e).
[27] Organic production will pursue the following general objectives: the environment and the climate; maintaining the long-term fertility of soils; biodiversity; a non-toxic environment; high animal welfare standards; encouraging short distribution channels and local production; rare and native breeds in danger of extinction; contributing to the development of the supply of plant genetic material adapted to the specific needs and objectives of organic agriculture; high level of biodiversity, in particular by using diverse plant genetic material, such as organic heterogeneous material and organic varieties suitable for organic production; fostering the development of organic plant breeding activities in order to contribute to favourable economic perspectives of the organic sector.
[28] Art 5, respect for nature's systems and cycles and the sustainment and enhancement of the state of the soil, the water, and the air, of the health of plants and animals, and of the balance between them; preservation of natural landscape elements; responsible use of energy and natural resources; production of a wide variety of high-quality food that respond to consumers' demand for sustainable goods; ensuring the integrity of organic production at all stages; the appropriate design and management of biological processes, based on ecological systems and using natural resources; restriction of the use of external inputs; local and regional the adaptation of the production process; exclusion from the whole organic food chain of animal cloning; observance of a high level of animal welfare respecting species-specific needs.
[29] Organics Regulation, art 6.
[30] ibid, art 7.
[31] ibid, art 8.
[32] ibid, art 7(e).

15.2.3 *Production rules*

Chapter III of the Organics Regulation specifies the production rules, divided into general production rules,[33] and production rules for specific categories of products, namely plants,[34] plant reproduction material,[35] livestock,[36] algae and aquaculture animals,[37] processed food[38] and feed,[39] wine,[40] and yeasts,[41] which in turn have dedicated Annexes to elaborate more detailed rules.

To illustrate the cascade of legal norms: soil-related crop cultivation and land-related livestock production has been defined as a basic organic farming principle.[42] Consequently, the general rules for plants[43] compel producers to comply with the detailed rules, which are in turn elaborated on in the Annex and stipulate that hydroponic production (the growing of plants in water solvent) should by default be prohibited (with few exceptions).[44]

The general production rules allow mixed farming, that is, conventional and organic farming may be combined (in separate streams), which initially had not been allowed in the Commission draft regulation. There are also detailed rules regarding the conversion from conventional to organic farming.[45]

EU organic production rules ban or limit the products and substances that may be used in organic production.[46] Beyond this, there is a prohibition on ionizing radiation,[47] animal cloning,[48] and nanotechnology in food. Genetically modified organisms (GMOs) are generally not permitted.[49] Composite organic products rely on labelling, therefore the value may not strictly be 0% as ingredients with a GMO trace of below 0.9% do not need to be labelled.

Overall, the production requirements are very input focused, but they are complemented by numerous requirements that emphasize aspects such as soil management, animal welfare, environmental impacts, and other related factors.

Among the category-specific requirements, these different dimensions are represented. For instance, regarding soil, some requirements enshrine a conservative

33 ibid, art 9.
34 ibid, art 12, Annex II
35 ibid, art 13, Annex II
36 ibid, art 14, Annex II
37 ibid, art 15, Annex II
38 ibid, art 16, Annex II
39 ibid, art 17, Annex II
40 ibid, art 18 Annex II
41 ibid, art 19 Annex II
42 ibid, art 5(f)(ii).
43 ibid, art 12.
44 ibid, pts 1 and 2 of Annex II.
45 ibid, art 10.
46 ibid, art 9(3).
47 ibid, art 10.
48 ibid, art 9(5).
49 ibid, art 11.

view on the necessity of soil for organic production, which means that crops must be grown in living soil,[50] and consequently of which hydroponics are prohibited in organic production. There are also requirements regarding soil management and fertilization,[51] as well as many requirements regarding animal welfare. These include general requirements, such as that 'any suffering, pain and distress shall be avoided and shall be kept to a minimum during the entire life of the animal'[52] and more tangible obligations such as that livestock must have permanent access to open-air areas.[53] The rules per species are more specific, and thus prevail. For instance, it is stipulated that poultry must have access to an open-air area for at least one third of their life.[54] Not more than 3,000 hens are allowed in a single compartment of a poultry house.[55] Nutrition is another aspect on which several requirements exist; for example, for bovine animals at least 70% of the feed must come from the farm itself or from other organic sources from the same region.[56] Similar obligations exist for other species. In several instances, the Organics Regulation therefore does in fact incorporate the ideas of close nutrition cycles advocated by the early proponents of the organic movement. In addition, on environmental protection, there exist numerous obligations, for instance new organic algae production must ascertain the conditions of the production unit and its immediate environment and likely effects of its operation,[57] and a sustainable management plan must be drawn up and monitored.[58] More specific requirements include rules such as that mangrove destruction is not permitted.[59]

Looking at the diverse dimensions underlying the rules, the new EU rules on organics are certainly more holistic than simply requiring non-chemical inputs. Nevertheless, the EU organic scheme falls short of a veritable agroecological approach. Currently, these more far-reaching ambitions are only feasible through additional private schemes.

15.2.4 Authorization of products and substances for use in organic production

A core feature of the Organics Regulation is the regulation of inputs. It therefore creates a framework for authorization of products and substances for use in

[50] ibid, Annex II, part I, 1.1 and 1.2.
[51] ibid, Annex II, part I, 1.9.
[52] ibid, Annex 1.7.7.
[53] ibid, Annex 1.7.3.
[54] ibid, Annex II, 1.9.4.4. (d).
[55] ibid, Annex II, 1.9.4.4. (n).
[56] ibid, Annex II, 1.9.1.1. (a).
[57] Directive 2011/92/EU of the European Parliament and of the Council of 13 December 2011 on the assessment of the effects of certain public and private projects on the environment [2012] OJ L26/1.
[58] Organics Regulation, Annex II, part III, 1.5.
[59] ibid, Annex II, part III, 1.4.

organic production.[60] It covers, first, all active substances to be used in plant protection products, complemented by an implementing regulation specifying which products and substances can be used in organic production.[61] Second, it specifies what fertilizers, soil conditioners, and nutrients may be used, equally elaborated on in an implementing regulation.[62] Beyond this, the Organics Regulation covers feed (non-organic feed material, and feed additives and processing aids). Third, the Regulation lays down which products can be used for cleaning and disinfection (animal production, plant production, and in processing and storage facilities). Lastly, it regulates food (additives and processing aids, non-organic agricultural ingredients,[63] and processing aids in the production of yeasts).

The authorization of active substances in plant protection products is elaborated on in an implementing regulation.[64] Active substances listed in its Annex may be contained in plant protection products used in organic production as long as they are authorized pursuant to Regulation (EC) 1107/2009 on plant protection products. Basic substances,[65] that is, substances that are not predominantly used for plant protection purposes and which are not substances of concern, can be used only if listed,[66] considering the conditions set by the respective review report[67] and any additional restrictions specified.[68] An example is vinegar, which is classified as a basic substance.[69] Equally, authorized low risk active substances can be used if specified in the Annex.[70] All authorized micro-organisms can be used as long as they are not GMOs, and other active substances may be used only if specified, and then according to the specified uses. Fertilizers, soil conditioners, and nutrients may only be used if listed in the Annex of the Implementing Regulation, and in compliance with the relevant Union and national legislations.[71] For instance, farmyard manure can be used, but its factory farming origin is prohibited.

[60] ibid, art 24.

[61] Implementing Regulation (EU) 2021/1165 of 15 July 2021 authorising certain products and substances for use in organic production and establishing their lists [2021] OJ L253/13.

[62] Implementing Regulation (EU) 2021/1165, art 24, Annex II lays down the list of fertilizers that can be used in organic production in the EU.

[63] Organics Regulation, arts 24(2)(b) and 25.

[64] Implementing Regulation (EU) 2021/1165, art 1, Annex I authorising certain products and substances for use in organic production and establishing their lists.

[65] Regulation (EC)1107/2009 of the European Parliament and of the Council of 21 October 2009 concerning the placing of plant protection products on the market and repealing Council Directives 79/117/EEC and 91/414/EEC [2009] OJ L309/1, art 23.

[66] Commission Implementing Regulation (EU) 540/2011 of 25 May 2011 implementing Regulation (EC) No 1107/2009 of the European Parliament and of the Council as regards the list of approved active substances [2011] OJ L153/1, Annex part C.

[67] Commission, 'Active substances, safeners and synergists' <https://ec.europa.eu/food/plant/pesticides/eu-pesticides-database/start/screen/active-substances> accessed 10 August 2022.

[68] Implementing Regulation (EU) 2021/1165, Annex I(1).

[69] Active substances, safeners and synergists (n 67).

[70] Implementing Regulation (EU) 2021/1165 authorizing certain products and substances for use in organic production and establishing their lists.

[71] Implementing Regulation (EU) 2021/1165, Annex II.

15.2.5 *Obligations on FBOs*

Food business operators (FBO) have a duty to act in the event of suspicion of non-compliance. This obligation would fall under the General Food Law Regulation (GFLR), but there is an additional specific obligation outlined in the Organics Regulation.[72] In addition, FBOs are required to take preventive and precautionary measures at every stage of production.[73] A novel production rule obliges organic farmers to take precautionary measures to avoid risks of contamination with non-authorized substances from conventional farming.[74] Under the 2007 rules, traces of non-authorized substances were inconsequential as long as there was no evidence that the organic farmer was actively using these substances. The 2018 Organics Regulation extends this obligation to cases where the organic operator has not taken the required precautionary measures. The obligation shapes a 'new kind of coexistence' between organic and conventional farmers that fundamentally departs from the 'Verursacherprinzip', that is, that the polluter is accountable.[75] FBOs must put in place and maintain measures that are proportionate and appropriate to identify the risks of contamination of organic production and products with non-authorized products or substances, including systematic identification of critical procedural steps.[76] In the future, this may ultimately lead to an approach similar to that used in the hazard analysis and critical control points (HACCP) approach for hygiene, but specifically tailored for contamination risks in the organics sector.[77]

15.2.6 *Labelling*

The Organics Regulation also has additional specific rules on labelling of organic products. The terms 'bio', 'eco', national versions ('organic') and derivatives are equivalent and refer to compliance with the Organics Regulation[78]—they may not be used on products that do not comply with the Organics Regulation. However, for products that fall outside the scope of the Regulation because they are not considered agricultural products or derivatives, these rules do not apply. 'Bio' and 'eco' may therefore be used in products such as detergents, although such products cannot claim to be certified by the EU organic food scheme. However, the EU organic label cannot be used on products like organic shea butter cream (which is a

[72] Organics Regulation, art 27.
[73] ibid, art 9(6).
[74] ibid, art 28.
[75] Schmidt (n 18).
[76] Organics Regulation, art 28(1)(b).
[77] Schmidt (n 18), calls this possibility an Organic Systematic Contamination Hazard Identification of Critical Steps (OSCHICS).
[78] Organics Regulation, art 30; for national language versions, see Annex IV.

cosmetic product).[79] This regulatory gap for non-food products may prove problematic as it potentially undermines consumer trust in the terms 'bio' and 'eco'.

For processed products, Article 30(5) of the Organics Regulation distinguishes three labelling situations: (a) full labelling permission, (b) limited labelling, and (c) labelling based on exceptions.[80] Full labelling (a) implies that the words 'organic' and derivatives may be used in the sales description and the list of ingredients. This is the case for products in full conformity with the rules and conditions applicable to the production of processed food and at least 95% of the ingredients of agricultural origin are organic. In the case of flavourings, ingredients are only used for natural flavouring substances and natural flavouring preparations and all flavouring components are organic. Limited labelling (b) implies that the words 'organic' and derivatives may be used only in the list of ingredients; this is if the ingredient complies with the production rules and the processed food with main production rules. In addition, there are other specific exceptions (c) that allow full labelling in the sales description and list of ingredients; for example fishing and hunting products can use 'organic' in both. The list of ingredients must always indicate which ingredients are organic. Furthermore, in cases (b) and (c), the list of ingredients must indicate the total percentage of organic ingredients in proportion to the total quantity of agricultural ingredients. In the list of ingredients, the words 'organic' or derivatives must be identical to the overall layout used in the list.

For products using 'organic', there are additional compulsory indications.[81] The code number of the control body must be indicated. Prepacked foods must display the EU organic logo, unless they are only allowed (b) limited labelling or fall under (c) exceptional labelling. If the EU organic logo is used, then the labelling requires an indication of origin regarding the place where the agricultural raw materials composing the product have been farmed. This is generally 'EU Agriculture', 'non-EU Agriculture', or 'EU/non-EU Agriculture'. The words 'EU/non-EU' may be replaced or supplemented by the name of a country, or by the name of a country and a region if it is the exclusive (legally: 95%[82]) place of origin.

15.2.7 Certification

FBOs placing organic products on the market must notify their activities to the competent authorities of the Member State where their business is conducted and where their undertakings are subject to the control system.[83] After notification,

[79] Commission, 'Frequently asked questions ON ORGANIC RULES' (17 July 2023) <https://ec.europa.eu/info/sites/default/files/food-farming-fisheries/farming/documents/organic-rules-faqs_en_1.pdf> accessed 10 August 2022.
[80] Organics Regulation, art 30.
[81] ibid, art 32.
[82] ibid, art 32(2).
[83] ibid, art 34.

undertakings receive an 'organic certificate' issued by the competent national authorities for compliance with the Organics Regulation.[84]

There is an exemption from notification and the organic certificate for FBOs that sell prepacked organic products directly to the final consumer or user. The direct sale must occur in the presence of both the operator or their sales personnel and the final consumer,[85] meaning that internet platforms cannot be regarded as engaging in 'direct sales' and therefore must comply with rules such as those for organic storage in Annex III Organics Regulation.[86] In addition, operators that sell unpacked organic products may be exempt at national Member State level if the sale does not exceed 5,000kg per year, generate a turnover of less than 20,000 EUR, or the certification costs exceed 2% of the organic products' turnover.[87]

Group certification is possible for groups of small farmers (and algae and acquaculture producers);[88] (i) where individual certification would amount to more than 2% of the turnover, with a turnover in organic production not surpassing 25,000 EUR or a standard output of organic production of not more than 15,000 EUR a year, (ii) for farmers with holdings of maximum of 5 hectares, 0.5 hectares for greenhouses, and 15 hectares for grassland. The group must comply with specific requirements and set up an internal controls system (ICS). An implementing regulation sets additional conditions, including that a maximum group size for economic operators is 2,000, and criteria for the internal system of controls.[89] Certified operators and groups have wide-ranging documentation duties and obligations to ensure compliance with the legal frameworks.[90]

15.3 Additional rules on official controls

The Organics Regulation establishes specific rules for official controls in an Official Controls Chapter. These apply in addition to the rules laid down in the Official Controls Regulation (EU) 2017/625 (see Chapter 6).

The additional rules on official controls and on actions to be taken by the competent authorities identify specific areas that need verification,[91] such as the

[84] ibid, art 35.

[85] Established case law; see Case C-289/16 *Kamin und Grill Shop GmbH v Zentrale zur Bekämpfung unlauteren Wettbewerbs Frankfurt am Main eV* EU:C:2017:758.

[86] Frequently asked questions ON ORGANIC RULES (n 79).

[87] Organics Regulation, art 35.

[88] ibid, art 36.

[89] Implementing Regulation (EU) 2021/279, art 5 laying down detailed rules for the implementation of Regulation (EU) 2018/848 of the European Parliament and of the Council on controls and other measures ensuring traceability and compliance in organic production and the labelling of organic products.

[90] Organics Regulation, art 39.

[91] ibid, art 38.

application of preventive and precautionary measures, as well as compliance with effective separation between organic, in-conversion, and non-organic foods. The official controls are based on the likelihood of non-compliance,[92] taking into account factors such as type, size, and structure of an operator or group, or the product category. Generally, at least one physical on-the-spot inspection is required per year, although a 'good compliance' record can lead to one inspection every 24 months.[93]

Member States must take additional actions in the event of suspected and established non-compliance, and compile a common catalogue of measures for cases of suspected non-compliance and established non-compliance.[94] An implementing regulation[95] stipulates that the national catalogue of measures must comprise various types of non-compliance and categorize them as minor, major, or critical. It also outlines which measures will correspond to each type of non-compliance.[96] An example classification that Member States may use is provided.[97] For instance, for a critical violation, possible sanctions include the limitation, suspension, or withdrawal of a certificate. In terms of consequences, non-compliance affecting the integrity of organic products results in a prohibition from referring to the entire lot as organic. Serious, repetitive, or continued non-compliance must result in a prohibition to market products and a suspension or withdrawal of the organic certificate.[98] Further to the Official Controls Chapter, Article 29 requires measures to be taken in the event of the presence of non-authorized products or substances. The suspicion of the presence of non-authorized products or substances is especially heavily regulated,[99] and requires a specific response by a control authority.[100]

[92] ibid, art 38(2).
[93] ibid, art 38(3).
[94] ibid, art 41.
[95] Implementing Regulation (EU) 2021/279, art 8 laying down detailed rules for the implementation of Regulation (EU) 2018/848 of the European Parliament and of the Council on controls and other measures ensuring traceability and compliance in organic production and the labelling of organic products.
[96] Organics Regulation, art 38.
[97] Implementing Regulation (EU) 2021/279, Annex I laying down detailed rules for the implementation of Regulation (EU) 2018/848 of the European Parliament and of the Council on controls and other measures ensuring traceability and compliance in organic production and the labelling of organic products.
[98] Organics Regulation, art 42.
[99] Hanspeter Schmidt and Manon Haccius, 'Analysis of Regulation (EU) 2018/848 on Organic Food: New Rules for Farming, Processing, and Organic Controls' (2020) 15 European Food and Feed Law Review 2: Schmidt and Haccius criticize the obligation as addressing 'only traces of substances used in conventional farming or processing, permitted to be used there but not in organic production. It does not address general environmental pollutants from waste incinerators, industry, nor traffic. And not substances that are not used at all in food and feed processing but present due to undesirable migration, for example MOSH/MOAH, mineral oil derivatives (Saturated Hydrocarbons/Aromatic Hydrocarbons), which originate from recycled substances'.
[100] Organics Regulation, art 29.

15.4 Trade with third countries

From 2026, all exported and imported products will have to comply with EU standards.[101] The new rules on imports are one of the most significant changes to the organics regime. EU producers' main criticism was the fact that EU produce had to comply with much more stringent rules than recognized third country products.[102] This means that now non-EU and EU producers have to comply with the same rules, thus levelling the playing field.

The import of organic and in-conversion products can now be undertaken through various trajectories. Firstly, the product complies with the Regulation and the FBOs are certified through a recognized body in the third country.[103] Alternatively, the product must come from a country that enjoys general recognition through a special trade agreement.[104] Another option is that the product originates from a third country which has been recognized for the purposes of equivalence (the recognition list expires in 2026).[105]

15.5 Procedural aspects

The Organics Regulation acts as a framework act that will be implemented and complemented by a high volume of tertiary acts. In this respect, the Commission enjoys very wide delegated powers to act, in almost thirty provisions. The Organics Regulation equally involves a significant amount of law making through the Committee procedure. In Committee procedures, the Commission is assisted by the 'Organic Production Committee' that acts as a committee within the meaning of Regulation (EU) 182/2011.[106]

15.6 Discussion

The 2018 Organics Framework overhauled the EU system on organic agricultural production. Overall, the production rules have been simplified and further harmonized by phasing out a number of exceptions and derogations. Further, the control systems are strengthened due to tighter precautionary measures and robust risk-based checks along the entire supply chain. This addresses suspicions

[101] ibid, arts 44 and 45.
[102] Regulation (EU) 2020/1693.
[103] Recognition of control authorities and control bodies in third countries is regulated in the Organics Regulation, art 46 and the Implementing Regulations.
[104] Organics Regulation, art 47.
[105] ibid, art 48.
[106] ibid, art 55.

regarding the potential abuse of the organics scheme. Producers in third countries have to comply with the same set of rules as producers in the EU. This is an important change as under the old regime, a mutual recognition of 'third country' organic regimes had been possible.

An important goal of the Organics Framework is to achieve pesticide-free production. In addition to this narrow aim, however, it incorporates many related values, such as environmental protection and animal welfare. There is also some emphasis on short distribution channels and local production and a stronger sense of 'organic' to imply 'natural', that is, non-artificial or technological, production. In this vein, production should be connected to soil (as a 'contribution to a non-toxic environment', 'long-term fertility', and 'biodiversity'), and the derogations for production in demarcated beds in greenhouses have been phased out. This means that organic production requires 'purely traditional' soil-based production. Such a choice could be questioned; organic production is difficult, and a very contained environment such as demarcated field agriculture could provide for a controlled production environment without the need of pesticides. Indeed, despite a general acceptance of the value of organic production, its precise boundaries are contested: this is true for organic greenhouse production[107] or the 'promise' of genetic modifications to contribute to pesticide-free production. In this context, for some, the Organics Regulation does not do enough and for others, too much. Balancing the various values associated with organics will inevitably lead to clashes between economic interests and ideologies.

At consumer level, the organics sector has a trust issue. It is well-known that consumers do not trust the enforcement of the organics framework, and these concerns are not entirely unjustified as there have been repeated reports of fraud in the organics sector. From a societal point of view, organic certification is very costly, and these costs are transferred to the consumers in the form higher prices for organic products. Therefore, organic diets are less affordable than conventional diets, contributing to structural food inequalities.

The Farm to Fork Strategy and the organic action plan[108] promise to boost organic production from an EU average of 8.5% to reach 25% of the EU's agricultural land use by 2030. The organic action plan addresses consumption of organic products to encourage farmers to convert to organics (Axis 1), incentives for production (Axis 2), and an improvement of the organic sector's contribution to sustainability and environmental challenges (Axis 3). The latter gives insights into the

[107] Fabio Tittarelli, 'Organic Greenhouse Production: Towards an Agroecological Approach in the Framework of the New European Regulation—A Review' (2020) 10 Agronomy 72, points out that 'knowledge gaps on the economic, social, ethical and environmental sustainability of organic greenhouse production still exist and researches on cropping system redesign for the individuation of innovative cropping systems at different latitudes and climatic condition are needed'.

[108] Commission, 'Communication from the Commission to the European Parliament, the Council, the European Economic and Social Committee and the Committee of the Regions on an Action Plan for the Development of Organic Production' COM (2021) 141 final.

Commissions vision of the future of organics, which sets the following goals: reducing the climate and environmental footprint, enhancing genetic biodiversity and increasing yields, finding alternatives to contentious inputs and other plant protection products, enhancing animal welfare, and making more efficient use of resources. In this context, the Commission implicitly recognizes that organics do not inherently align with all 'sustainability' goals and that the concept of EU organic certification is not congruent with 'sustainability' by definition.

Instead, the organics scheme must be considered as the most tangible and legally operationalized scheme that translates (some) sustainability dimensions on food. In this respect, organic food—probably for some time—will remain the closest that the EU will come to a legally workable definition of sustainable food in practice.

16
EU Food Quality Schemes

16.1 Introduction

A product's quality or reputation is often linked to where it comes from. Geographical indications (GIs) are a type of intellectual property protection that endows such geographical quality characteristics with legal protection. Examples of famous GIs are 'Champagne', 'Roquefort', and 'Parma ham'. Company brand names imply product quality by certifying a specific producer, and are legally protected as trademarks. Similarly, place names that identify products originating from specific territories and have the characteristics associated with the production in that place can be protected as geographical indications. However, non-geographical names can also be protected under specific circumstances. For example, Feta cheese is not named after a place but is so closely associated with Greece that it is considered an inherently Greek product.

From a historical perspective, the political nature of geographical indicators is clear. Geography implies a certain territory, and GI protection closely overlaps with the self-interest of States. Under international law, GIs have been legally protected for a long time.[1] The 1883 Paris Convention[2] covered 'Indications of source' and 'Appellation of origin', which were narrowly defined, prohibiting only 'false', but not 'misleading' indications. In 1891, the Madrid System[3] was established, which continues to operate under the auspices of the World Intellectual Property Organisation (WIPO) to this day, and which prohibits both false and deceptive indications of source. The 1958 Lisbon Agreement[4] protects Appellations of Origin, and extends protection to indications that are attributed not only to the geographic environment, but also to natural and human factors. Alongside these international treaties, geographical indications are additionally covered by the

[1] For an overview, see Bernard O'Connor, *The Law of Geographical Indications* (Cameron May 2004).

[2] Paris Convention for the protection of industrial property (adopted 20 March 1883, entered into force 7 July 1884) 828 UNTS 305 (Paris Convention).

[3] Madrid Agreement Concerning the International Registration of Marks (adopted 14 April 1891, entered into force 5 April 1892) 828 UNTS 389 (Madrid Agreement).

[4] Lisbon Agreement for the Protection of Appellations of Origin and their International Registration (adopted 31 October 1958, entered into force 15 February 1966) 308 UNTS 149 (Lisbon Agreement); Georg Miribung, 'Changes Happen Slowly—Some Comments on Geographical Indications between the Geneva Act and Regulation 2019/1753' (2020) 15 European Food and Feed Law Review 25.

EU Food Law. Hanna Schebesta and Kai Purnhagen, Oxford University Press.
DOI: 10.1093/9780198901570.003.0017

multilateral trading system in the form of the TRIPS/WTO Agreement,[5] which also applies to industrial or artisanal goods such as Meissner porcelain, Salzburger Mozartkugeln, and Sheffield steel. Recently, the European Union (EU) acceded to the Geneva Act of the Lisbon Agreement on appellations of origin and geographical indications.[6] The protection of GIs is therefore subject to a web of international obligations.

Over time, the legal protection of GIs has considerably widened, in that they not only address false indications, but increasingly misleading indications as well. Furthermore, the exclusive focus on geographic territory is softened, by extending GI protection to encompass natural and human factors more broadly.

For the governance of GIs, a number of different legal systems, such as national protection, the EU protected designation of origin (PDO) and protected geographical indication (PGI), the Madrid system, and the WTO TRIPS coexist. The governance of GIs therefore remains complex.

The purpose of GIs is to guarantee the specific characteristics of a given product, and as such they serve as an instrument to safeguard quality, and even 'food heritage'.[7] They further serve as a tool for product differentiation,[8] and are considered a mechanism for promoting rural development.[9] However, GIs are not always viewed positively.[10] GIs arguably lead to market protection, cartelization, excessive consumer prices, and even stifle innovation. The approach to this topic differs significantly between the US and the EU. The US is very trademark focused, and there is no intellectual property right protection for GIs. Instead, quality guarantees are achieved through trademark protection of specific companies. It is therefore not geographic provenance, but rather enterprises that safeguard the given quality of a product. In contrast, in the EU, geographical indications were historically widely recognized to guarantee consumer protection, and the protection of farmers and rural areas.

[5] Agreement on Trade-Related Aspects of Intellectual Property Rights (adopted 15 April 1994, entered into force 1 January 1995) 1869 UNTS 299 (TRIPS Agreement), art 22.

[6] Regulation (EU) 2019/1753 of the European Parliament and of the Council of 23 October 2019 on the action of the Union following its accession to the Geneva Act of the Lisbon Agreement on Appellations of Origin and Geographical Indications [2019] OJ L271/1.

[7] Floris de Witte, 'You Are What You Ate: Food Heritage and the EU's Internal Market' (2022) 47 European Law Review 647.

[8] Ramona Teuber, 'Geographical Indications of Origin as a Tool of Product Differentiation: The Case of Coffee' (2010) 22 Journal of International Food & Agribusiness Marketing 277.

[9] Giovanni Belletti and Andrea Marescotti, 'Origin Products, Geographical Indications and Rural Development' in Elizabeth Barnham and Bertil Sylvander (eds), *Labels of Origin for Food: Local Development, Global Recognition.* (CAB International 2011).

[10] For an in-depth discussion of the advantages and disadvantages, see Daniele Giovannucci and others, *Guide to Geographical Indications: Linking products and their origins* (Geneva: International Trade Centre 2009) 232.

16.2 Food Quality Systems Regulation

In 1992, the EU adopted Regulation 2081/92[11] for PDO and PGI and Regulation 2082/92[12] for TSG (traditional specialty guaranteed). Over the years these regulations have been amended and replaced several times, and subsequently consolidated into Regulation 1151/2012 (FQS Regulation).[13] The FQS Regulation protects several quality terms, most importantly the PDO/PGI scheme, but also the TSG, as well as optional quality terms (OQTs).

The legal basis of the Food Quality Schemes Regulation is Article 43(2) on agriculture and the first paragraph of Article 118 Treaty on the Functioning of the European Union (TFEU) on intellectual property rights.[14] The Court of Justice of the European Union (CJEU) further clarified that in relation to international intellectual property right treaties, the EU enjoys exclusive competence. This is because they have a direct and immediate effect on trade between the EU and third countries.[15] Exclusive competence of the Union is conferred on the EU by Article 3(1) TFEU in the field of the common trade policy. This means that the European Commission has sole responsibility for applications for international registration of GIs for products originating in an EU Member State.

16.2.1 Objective and scope

The FQS Regulation reconciles various objectives, namely fair competition for farmers and producers, consumer information, intellectual property, and the internal market. A key concept of the legal framework is the 'value-adding' characteristic or attribute of agricultural products,[16] and the EU system is explicitly designed to ensure the valorization of products' geographical origin, that is, 'to enable producers, in conditions of fair competition, to secure higher incomes in return for a genuine effort to improve quality'.[17] The CJEU has highlighted the concern for quality inherent in the FQS regime: 'EU legislation displays a general

[11] Council Regulation (EEC) 2081/92 of 14 July 1992 on the protection of geographical indications and designations of origin for agricultural products and foodstuffs [2006] OJ L93/12.

[12] Council Regulation (EEC) 2082/92 of 14 July 1992 on certificates of specific character for agricultural products and foodstuffs [1992] OJ L208/9.

[13] Regulation (EU) 1151/2012 of the European Parliament and of the Council of 21 November 2012 on quality schemes for agricultural products and foodstuffs [2012] OJ L343/14 (Food Quality Systems Regulation (FQS Regulation)).

[14] Georg Miribung, 'Changes Happen Slowly—Some Comments on Geographical Indications between the Geneva Act and Regulation 2019/1753' (2020) 15 European Food and Feed Law Review 25.

[15] Case C-389/15 *European Commission vs European Council* EU:C:2017:798; see Miribung (n 14).

[16] FQS Regulation, art 1.

[17] Case C-367/17 *S v EA and Others* EU:C:2018:1025; see also to that effect Case C-161/09 *Kakavetsos-Fragkopoulos AE Epexergasias kai Emporias Stafidas v Nomarchiaki Aftodioikisi Korinthias* EU:C:2011:110 (*Kakavetsos-Fragkopoulos*), para 34.

tendency to enhance the quality of products within the framework of the common agricultural policy, in order to promote the reputation of those products through, inter alia, the use of designations of origin which enjoy special protection.'[18] In addition, the CJEU has recognized the importance of being assured that products sold under the designation of origin are authentic.[19] The FQS Regulation is not solely an intellectual property rights instrument; it also serves other functions, notably product quality and valorization, but also the internal market and consumer protection.

The FQS Regulation covers agricultural as well as selected additional products, that is, agricultural products for human consumption listed in Annex I to the TFEU (see also Chapter 2) and other products listed in Annex I,[20] such as prepared meals, wool, and beeswax. It applies to beer, but not to spirits or grapevine products,[21] with the exception of wine-vinegars. The list of registered categories is led by vegetables and fresh fruit, followed by vegetables and cereals, meat products (fresh and processed), and cheeses.[22]

16.2.2 Protected designations of origin and protected geographical indications

PDOs and PGIs are intended to support products associated with a geographical area by securing fair returns, guaranteeing uniform protection of the names as intellectual property rights in the territory of the Union, and providing clear consumer information on the value-adding attributes of the products.[23]

The two main intellectual property schemes are designations of origin and geographical indications. A 'designation of origin' is a name that identifies (i) a product originating in a specific place, region or, in exceptional cases, country; (ii) whose quality or characteristics are essentially or exclusively due to a particular geographical environment with its inherent natural and human factors; and (iii) the production steps of which all take place in the defined geographical area. A 'geographical indication' is (i) a name, which identifies a product originating in a specific place, region, or country; (ii) whose given quality, reputation, or other

[18] *S v EA and Others* (n 17).

[19] Case C-108/01 *Consorzio del Prosciutto di Parma and Salumificio S. Rita v Asda Stores Ltd and Hygrade Foods Ltd* [2003] ECR I-5121, para 64.

[20] FQS Regulation, art 2.

[21] Regulation (EU) 1308/2013 of the European Parliament and of the Council of 17 December 2013 establishing a common organisation of the markets in agricultural products and repealing Council Regulations (EEC) 922/72, (EEC) 234/79, (EC) 1037/2001 and (EC) 1234/2007 [2013[OJ L347/671, pt II of Annex VII.

[22] See Tânia Albuquerque, Beatriz Oliveira, and Helena Costa, '25 Years of European Union (EU) Quality Schemes for Agricultural Products and Foodstuffs across EU Member States' (2018) 98 Journal of the Science of Food and Agriculture 2475.

[23] FQS Regulation, art 4.

characteristic is essentially attributable to its geographical origin; and (iii) at least one of the production steps of which takes place in the defined geographical area.[24]

The main difference between a PDO and PGI lies in the production steps. For a PDO, all production steps must take place in a particular region, whereas for a PGI, at least one production step must occur in the designated region.

Names of PDO and PGI may not be of generic nature, or conflict with names of plant varieties and animal breeds, with homonyms, and trademarks.[25] Geographical designations can 'over time and through use' become generic names where consumers perceive the name solely as a product name, rather than an indication of origin. This 'shift in meaning' occurred for 'Camembert' and 'Brie'.[26] The generic character of a name is assessed by taking into account the places of production of the product concerned both inside and outside the Member State of registration, the consumption of that product and consumer perceptions inside and outside that Member State, the existence of national legislation specifically relating to that product, and the way in which the name has been used in Community law.[27]

For each PDO and PGI, product specifications are compiled.[28] The product specification must include (a) the name and (b) a description of the product including the raw materials, if appropriate, as well as the principal physical, chemical, microbiological, and organoleptic characteristics; (c) a definition of the geographical area; and (d) evidence to suggest the product originates in the geographical area. Furthermore, (e) a description of the methods for obtaining the product and if applicable, the authentic consistent local methods is required. The (f) required link between the quality or characteristics of the product and the geographical environment is different for PDOs and PGIs. For PDOs, the specifications must establish outline how the geographical environment influences human factors. This may include details such as soil and landscape management, cultivation practices, or any other relevant human contribution to the maintenance of the natural factors of the geographical environment.[29] For PGIs, the specifications must establish the link between a given quality, the reputation, or other characteristic of the product and the geographical origin.[30]

The product specifications on the one hand act as a safeguard for quality. On the other hand, they function as enforceable intellectual property rights, potentially leading to exclusionary practices that protect narrowly defined local markets and may foster protectionism. Production specifications therefore have been subject to a number of legal disputes, for instance questioning the legality of a requirement

[24] ibid, art 5.
[25] ibid, art 6.
[26] Case C-132/05 *European Commission v Germany* EU:C:2008:117 *(Cambert and Brie)*.
[27] ibid; also see Joined Cases C-465/02 and C-466/02 *Germany and Denmark v Commission* [2005] ECR I-9115, paras 76–99.
[28] FQS Regulation, art 7.
[29] ibid, art 7(1)(f)(i).
[30] ibid, art 7(f)(ii).

imposing the slicing and packaging of ham within the production area.[31] These mandates may be allowed where they are a means to allow the PGI producers to control quality, for instance if they give rise to 'very precise technical and control interventions, on the authenticity, quality, hygiene and labelling' (as in the case of *Prosciutto di Parma*), but such product specifications would not be proportionate if they exceed what is 'customary in the ham trade or not going beyond the currently enforceable criteria concerning food hygiene'.[32]

A new aspect of the EU quality schemes entirely is that product specifications may contain a description of the contribution of the designation of origin or geographical indication to sustainable development.[33] In the future, this rule may be an important inroad for using the FQS for sustainability goals, and not only narrowly defined quality goals. To date, however, such sustainability product attributes are not specifically communicated to consumers, and the full effectiveness of the provision therefore depends on whether it will receive traction in subsequent amendments. A broader argument for the role that food quality schemes can play with regards to sustainability is the emphasis on territory, which is significant within these schemes, but, for instance, often absent from organic certification schemes.[34] It is questionable whether this positive view of the role that quality schemes can play for sustainability holds. On one hand, while organic schemes do consider local production of inputs to some extent, it is true that organics can also be marketed non-locally. This also, however, holds true for quality schemes, which, despite their geographically demarcated production, are destined to be marketed all over the world. In that sense, the link between more localized consumption of food as an element of sustainability and quality schemes is rather tenuous. In addition, even at the level of production, PGIs only necessitate one 'local' production step, thus significantly weakening arguments regarding the territorial locality of quality schemes as a whole.

16.2.3 The right to use and protection granted

The PDO and PGI quality schemes belong to the intellectual property (IP) rights arena as they confer an enforceable right on rights holders, and may conflict and

[31] See *S v EA and Others* (n 17); see, to that effect, *Prosciutto di Parma* (n 19) para 65.
[32] *S v EA and Others* (n 17) para 35.
[33] Regulation (EU) 2021/2117 of the European Parliament and of the Council of 2 December 2021 amending Regulations (EU) No 1308/2013 establishing a common organisation of the markets in agricultural products, (EU) No 1151/2012 on quality schemes for agricultural products and foodstuffs, (EU) No 251/2014 on the definition, description, presentation, labelling and the protection of geographical indications of aromatised wine products and (EU) No 228/2013 laying down specific measures for agriculture in the outermost regions of the Union [2021] OJ L435/262.
[34] Filippo Arfini and Valentin Bellassen, *Sustainability of European Food Quality Schemes* (Springer 2019) 3–22.

oppose other IP rights, in particular trademarks. One specific characteristic of this class of IP right is that it is not an individual right—instead, PDOs and PGIs can be used by any operator marketing a product conforming to the corresponding product specifications.[35] This is subject to the caveat that, of course, given the required geographical associations, not every operator *can* comply with the corresponding specifications.

The granting of an IP right gives rights holders specific enforceable privileges. Under the FQS Regulation, PDOs and PGIs are protected against[36] (a) direct or indirect commercial use of the registered name, (b) misuse, imitation, or evocation (also where accompanied by expressions such as 'style', 'type', 'method', 'as produced in', 'imitation', or similar), (c) any other false or misleading indication, and (d) any other practice liable to mislead the consumer as to the true origins of a product. The Court has explained that these provisions therefore contain a 'graduated list of prohibited conduct'.[37] As an intellectual property right, PGIs/PDOs enjoy strong protection, stronger even than EU trademarks in many respects.[38] This is because of the wider scope of protection offered to PDO/PGI, which not only covers the risk of confusion, but also protection against false or misleading indications. They also do not require a 'reputation within the EU', which is required for trademarks.

The Court has taken a broad approach in interpreting the provisions related to the protection offered to PDO/PGI. Point (a) of the prohibited practices concerns actions that use the protected name itself either directly or indirectly, whereas the other points protect PDO/PGI against practices that do not use the name directly. It is sufficient that the actions cause 'the consumer to establish a sufficiently close connection with that name'.[39] In *Morbier*, the Court held that:

> the concept of 'evocation', the decisive criterion is whether, when the consumer is confronted with a disputed designation, the image triggered directly in his or her mind is that of the product covered by the PDO, a matter which it falls to the national court to assess, taking into account, as the case may be, the partial incorporation of a PDO in the disputed designation, any phonetic and/or visual similarity, or any conceptual proximity, between the designation and the PDO.[40]

[35] FQS Regulation, art 12.
[36] ibid, art 13(1).
[37] Case C-490/19 *Syndicat interprofessionnel de défense du fromage Morbier v Société Fromagère du Livradois SAS* EU:C:2020:1043 (*Morbier*), para 24.
[38] For a more detailed comparison, see Yves van Couter and Florence d'Ath, 'Protecting the Origin of Foodstuffs in the European Union' (2016) 11 European Food and Feed Law Review 290.
[39] *Morbier* (n 37) para 25.
[40] ibid, para 26.

This means that a registered name may be evoked through the use of figurative signs, so that a prohibited action can be created through figurative signs and not just words.[41] In determining evocation, the Court looks at its effect on the consumer, as the CJEU had previously clarified in *Scotch Whisky Association*; it essentially requires the judge to ask whether 'when the consumer is confronted with the name of the product, the image triggered in his mind is that of the product whose geographical indication is protected'.[42] This interpretation relies on the presumed reaction of consumers based on the term or images used to designate the product at issue. In determining this reaction, the Court has recourse to general consumer case law, that is, the average European consumer who is reasonably well informed and reasonably observant and circumspect.[43]

It falls on the Member States to protect the rights granted by the legislation, and the FQS Regulation stipulates that Member States must take appropriate administrative and judicial steps to prevent or stop the unlawful use of protected designations of origin and protected geographical indications.[44] This means that violations of EU food quality schemes are safeguarded through public oversight. This public enforcement is one of the significant advantages of PDO and PGI protection compared to other IP rights, especially trademarks, which must be enforced by the right holder in courts at their own cost and risk.

16.2.4 Traditional specialty guarantee

Whereas PDOs and PGIs are traditional forms of intellectual property rights, the FQS Regulation also protects other categories of food quality schemes, which are not linked to geography and territory. Products can be registered as TSG if they originate from a traditional practice or are produced from raw materials or ingredients that are traditionally used.[45] In order to be 'traditional' there must be a proven history of use on the domestic market for a period of at least 30 years, allowing for transmission between generations.[46] A TSG must comply with product specifications, and registration comprises the name, product description, production method, and the key elements establishing the product's traditional character.[47]

[41] Case C-614/17 *Fundación Consejo Regulador de la Denominación de Origen Protegida Queso Manchego v Industrial Quesera Cuquerella SL and Juan Ramón Cuquerella Montagud* EU:C:2019:344.
[42] Case C-44/17 *Scotch Whisky Association v Michael Klotz* EU:C:2018:415 (*Scotch Whisky Association*), paras 45–46.
[43] Case C-75/15 *Viiniverla Oy v Sosiaali- ja terveysalan lupa- ja valvontavirasto* EU:C:2016:35, paras 25, 28, and 47.
[44] FQS Regulation, art 13(3).
[45] ibid, art 18.
[46] ibid, art 3(3).
[47] ibid, art 19.

Like PDOs and PGIs, TSGs are also registered and therefore protected against misuse, imitation, or evocation.[48]

The number of registrations under the TSG scheme are low.[49] One of the presumed reasons for this is that producers preferred to keep their recipes secret; registration does not lead to an exclusive use of the registered name ('non-exclusivity').[50] The old 2006 Regulation prohibited the registration of the same product under multiple schemes simultaneously.[51] This rule has been abolished, therefore concurrent registration of TSG and the PDO/PGI scheme now seems to be possible.[52] The TSG regime has faced criticism on functional grounds as it is not clear how it would support rural areas, given that the place of production is not a condition of registration. Consequently, the regime favours producers located in areas where replicating traditional processes is least expensive.[53]

*16.2.5 **Optional quality terms***

A novel scheme put forward by the FQS Regulation is that of optional quality terms (OQT). They are established 'in order to facilitate the communication within the internal market of the value-adding characteristics or attributes of agricultural products by the producers'.[54] OQTs relate to product characteristics or to farming/processing attributes applicable in specific areas. The use of the term must add value compared to products of a similar type and the term must have a European dimension.[55]

The OQT 'mountain product' is established in the FQS Regulation. It covers products where both the raw materials and the feedstuffs for farm animals come essentially from mountain areas. Additionally, for processed products, the processing must also take place in mountain areas.[56] A possible future OQT could be 'product of island farming'. The Commission is empowered to reserve new terms (and amend the conditions of use of existing ones) through delegated acts.

[48] ibid, art 24.
[49] See Albuquerque, Oliveira, and Costa (n 22).
[50] Matteo Gragnani, 'The EU Regulation 1151/2012 on Quality Schemes for Agricultural Products and Foodstuffs' (2013) 8 European Food and Feed Law Review 376.
[51] Council Regulation (EC) 509/2006 of 20 March 2006 on agricultural products and foodstuffs as traditional specialities guaranteed [2006] OJ L93/1, art 4.1.
[52] Gragnani (n 50).
[53] ibid.
[54] FQS Regulation, art 27.
[55] ibid, art 29.
[56] ibid, art 31.

16.3 Applications for PDO, PGI, and TSG and their placing on the market

The application procedure and registration process for PDO, PGI, and TSG are detailed in Chapter IV of the FQS Regulation. An implementing regulation contains additional rules on the application process.[57] Applications for registration of names may only be submitted by groups who work with the products with the name that is to be registered. The application is addressed to the authorities of the Member State. If, after assessment of any opposition received, the Member State considers that the requirements of the Regulation are met, it may lodge an application dossier with the Commission.[58] The application then undergoes scrutiny by the Commission,[59] generally within six months. After the publication of an application, any party may oppose a proposed registration. Any opposition can be made within three months from the date of publication.[60] The main reasons for opposing the registration for PDO and PGI are: non-compliance with conditions or product specifications;[61] conflicts with names of plant varieties and animal breeds, homonyms, and trademarks;[62] risking existing trademarks used for at least five years; the generic nature of the product.[63] The Commission registers the application through an implementing act. Where there are unresolved admissible objections, it adopts an implementing act using the examination procedure with involvement of the Agricultural Product Quality Policy Committee.

The European Commission creates a register of PDOs and PGIs,[64] and for TSG.[65] The register can be consulted via eAmbrosia for agricultural products and foodstuffs, wine, and spirits across the EU. Users can search for registered and protected products by product type, status, or country, among others. The database will generally link to the application file,[66] which contains the product specifications as well as the relevant legal EU instrument. This instrument enters a name in the register of PDOs and PGIs through an implementing regulation.

Before placing a PDO, PGI, or TSG on the market, the food business operator (FBO) must acquire verification by the Member State designated authorities that the product complies with the product specifications as registered.[67]

[57] Commission Implementing Regulation (EU) 668/2014 of 13 June 2014 laying down rules for the application of Regulation (EU) No 1151/2012 of the European Parliament and of the Council on quality schemes for agricultural products and foodstuffs [2014] OJ L179/36.
[58] FQS Regulation, art 49.
[59] ibid, art 50.
[60] ibid, art 51.
[61] ibid, art 5 or 7(1) not complied with.
[62] Contrary to ibid, arts 6(2), (3), or (4).
[63] Prohibition in ibid, art 6.
[64] ibid, art 11.
[65] ibid, art 22.
[66] Pursuant to ibid, art 50(2)(a).
[67] ibid, art 37.

16.4 Discussion

The uptake of quality scheme registration has been mixed—whereas PDO and PGI are successful (with a total of 699 PDO registrations and 958 in the agricultural products and foodstuffs register[68]), TSG has seen a relatively low uptake, with only 65 registrations.[69] The geographical distribution shows a concentration of registrations from southern EU countries, medium numbers from western EU countries, and few registrations from eastern and northern EU countries.[70] Only around 2% of registered PDO/PGIs are from non-EU countries.[71]

The EU quality scheme is a voluntary certification scheme with both public and private characteristics. The scheme is public in the sense that the conditions, required product specifications, conditions of use and protection, and the application process are all established by the EU Quality Schemes Regulation. Furthermore, the verification of product specifications and the enforcement of the schemes is undertaken by Member States public authorities. However, the PDO/PGI/TSG schemes also have private characteristics in the sense that the product specifications are compiled by the registering group of producers. The content of the specifications, and therefore ultimately the quality of the final product, is therefore determined by private parties.

The EU quality schemes transfer value from landscape to product (GIs, some OQTs) or capitalize on traditional processing (TSGs). By virtue of the common definition of product requirements, the quality schemes have an important quality signalling effect, and create added value by assuring the homogeneous quality of products. On the other hand, the PDO/PGI/TSG labels do not independently convey the product requirements and characteristics—they only communicate the originality of the product, and to some extent its origin. From a consumer perspective, the schemes appear less successful. It is hard to conceive how consumers can meaningfully distinguish between the three labels, and they are unlikely to be familiar with the finer legal distinctions of their significance. That said, studies do show—a somewhat unclear—impact of quality schemes on consumer decision-making processes.[72] Even when accepting the current philosophy behind the quality schemes, the current design of food information does not provide the consumers with clear, accurate, and understandable information. The consumer information interface of labels should be reconsidered, with a focus on how to make use of the sustainability dimension in quality schemes more apparent.

[68] See Commission, eAmbrosia <https://ec.europa.eu/agriculture/eambrosia/geographical-indications-register/> consulted 13 October 2023.

[69] ibid.

[70] See Albuquerque, Oliveira, and Costa (n 22).

[71] See ibid.

[72] Alexandra-Ioana Glogoveţan, 'Consumer Perception and Understanding of European Union Quality Schemes: A Systematic Literature Review' (2022) 14 Sustainability 1667.

The critiques of GIs are numerous. Due to its exclusionary nature, the use of the EU quality schemes creates market distortions, and leads to higher prices for consumers. The fixed nature of the product specifications can also impede innovation. At the same time, the run on indications of origin, and PDOs, and PGIs confirms a worrying trend in food identity politics that links to protectionism and 'gastronationalism',[73] reinforcing a territorial fragmentation of the EU's food identity, and a strengthening of national rather than European identities.

In the Farm to Fork Strategy, the Commission proposes to strengthen the legislative framework on geographical indications and include specific sustainability criteria. In principle, the new opportunity to include sustainability criteria might have opened up interesting novel ways for using the EU quality schemes, potentially providing an inroad to ultimately redefining what the EU considers as quality, by including a sustainability component. However, the tabled proposal,[74] while allowing producers to agree on sustainability undertakings, do not set or create clear incentives for them to do so. It is therefore unlikely that the EU food quality schemes will make an important step towards sustainability. At the same time, the proposal would significantly overhaul the current quality schemes and replace them with a unified registration of a 'geographical indication'. This move would lead to a closer alignment of the schemes with intellectual property rights regimes under international law.

[73] Michaela DeSoucey, 'Gastronationalism: Food Traditions and Authenticity Politics in the European Union' (2010) 75 American Sociological Review 432.

[74] Commission, 'Proposal for a Regulation of the European Parliament and of the Council on European Union geographical indications for wine, spirit drinks and agricultural products, and quality schemes for agricultural products, amending Regulations (EU) No 1308/2013, (EU) 2017/1001 and (EU) 2019/787 and repealing Regulation (EU) No 1151/2012' COM (2022) 134 final.

PART VII

FOOD NUTRITION LAW

17
Nutrition and Health in EU Food Law

17.1 Introduction

The main policy influences on European Union (EU) food law stem from agriculture, the internal market, food safety, and transparency, which is now complemented by the nascent sustainability reform in the Farm to Fork Strategy (see Chapter 1). In the past, nutrition and health have not received structural policy-making attention, with the consequence that its reflection in EU food law remains incidental and incomplete.

Health and nutrition are reflected in EU food law in a variety of ways. Health is an aspect that is protected through food safety—notably, the General Food Law Regulation (GFLR) prohibits unsafe foods, including foods that are injurious to health.[1] The majority of EU food law is, in fact, dedicated to the avoidance of health risks associated with food safety concerns. Another example of the food safety outlook on health in legislation is evident in the setting of maximum residue levels (MRLs), which sets limits on substances in food in order to avoid health risks.[2] These instruments do also have a somewhat hidden nutritional component, as the respective risk assessments rely on dietary information from reference populations.[3] In addition, nutrition considerations are latently present in much of EU food legislation. For instance, novel foods may not be nutritionally inferior to the products they replace.[4] In these cases, nutrition is not the major goal of an instrument, but nutritional objectives are incidentally protected. Only a few instruments prioritize nutrition and health objectives. One of these is the Nutrition and Health Claims Regulation,[5] which directly regulates information regarding nutritional

[1] Regulation (EC) 178/2002 of the European Parliament and of the Council of 28 January 2002 laying down the general principles and requirements of food law, establishing the European Food Safety Authority and laying down procedures in matters of food safety [2002] OJ L31/1 (General Food Law Regulation (GFLR)), art 14(2)(a).

[2] Regulation (EC) 396/2005 of the European Parliament and of the Council of 23 February 2005 on maximum residue levels of pesticides in or on food and feed of plant and animal origin and amending Council Directive 91/414/EEC [2005] OJ L70/1 (General Food Law Regulation (GFLR)).

[3] Regulation (EC) 396/2005, art 4(1).

[4] Regulation (EU) 2015/2283 of the European Parliament and of the Council of 25 November 2015 on novel foods, amending Regulation (EU) No 1169/2011 of the European Parliament and of the Council and repealing Regulation (EC) No 258/97 of the European Parliament and of the Council and Commission Regulation (EC) No 1852/2001 [2015] OJ L327/1 (Novel Foods Regulation (NFR)), art 7(c).

[5] Regulation (EC) 1924/2006 of the European Parliament and of the Council of 20 December 2006 on nutrition and health claims made on foods [2006] OJ L404/9 (Nutrition and Health Claims Regulation (NHCR)).

EU Food Law. Hanna Schebesta and Kai Purnhagen, Oxford University Press.
DOI: 10.1093/9780198901570.003.0018

and health characteristics of food. Nevertheless, the legislation is confined to information governance regarding nutrition and health claims, and it is therefore categorized more as food information law rather than nutrition and health law.[6] Lastly, there are legal frameworks that more stringently link to health and nutrition properties of food. These are the Regulation on Foods for Specific Groups and Purposes,[7] the Regulation on Food Fortification[8] (formally referred to as addition of vitamins, minerals, and other substances), and the Food Supplements Directive,[9] which could be loosely grouped together as 'nutrition food laws'.

As we show in this chapter, the topic of food for nutrition and health is contested, both between Member States and among stakeholders, and lacks a clear political vision and mandate. EU laws that are specifically dedicated to the content (rather than information) of nutrition and health are sparse and minimal, and address very specific topics without constituting a coherent and systemic approach.

17.2 Foods for Specific Groups and Purposes (FSGaP) Regulation

As early as 1976, Council Directive 77/94/EEC regulated foodstuffs for particular nutritional uses on the basis of Article 100 EEC, the approximation of laws of the Member States.[10] This framework was overhauled in 1989[11] and again in 2009 by the 'PARNUTS Directive',[12] a recast directive on particular nutritional uses. Finally, in 2013, the Regulation on Food for Specific Groups and Purposes (FSGaP Regulation) synthesized the fragmented legal landscape on nutrition in one directly applicable regulation: it consolidated the PARNUTS Directive',[13] which contained compositional and labelling requirements, and numerous non-legislative Union acts on foods intended for use in energy-restricted diets for

[6] ibid, art 7.

[7] Regulation (EU) 609/2013 of the European Parliament and of the Council of 12 June 2013 on food intended for infants and young children, food for special medical purposes, and total diet replacement for weight control and repealing Council Directive 92/52/EEC, Commission Directives 96/8/EC, 1999/21/EC, 2006/125/EC and 2006/141/EC, Directive 2009/39/EC of the European Parliament and of the Council and Commission Regulations (EC) No 41/2009 and (EC) No 953/2009 [2013] OJ L181/35 (Regulation on Foods for Specific Groups and Purposes (FSGaP Regulation)).

[8] Regulation (EC) 1925/2006 of the European Parliament and of the Council of 20 December 2006 on the addition of vitamins and minerals and of certain other substances to foods [2006] OJ L404/26 (Regulation on Food Fortification).

[9] Directive 2002/46/EC of the European Parliament and of the Council of 10 June 2002 on the approximation of the laws of the Member States relating to food supplements [2002] OJ L183/51.

[10] Council Directive 77/94/EEC of 21 December 1976 on the approximation of the laws of the Member States relating to foodstuffs for particular nutritional uses [1977] OJ L26/55.

[11] By Council Directive 89/398/EEC of 3 May 1989 on the approximation of the laws of the Member States relating to foodstuffs intended for particular nutritional uses [1989] OJ L186/27.

[12] Directive 2009/39/EC of the European Parliament and of the Council of 6 May 2009 on foodstuffs intended for particular nutritional uses (recast) [2009] OJ L124/21.

[13] ibid.

weight reduction[14] and dietary foods for special medical purposes,[15] processed cereal-based foods and baby foods for infants and young children,[16] infant formulae and follow-on formulae,[17] and foodstuffs suitable for people intolerant to gluten.[18] The consolidation process was unconventional in that the 2013 FSGaP Regulation covers fewer topics than the previous legal instruments. This deregulatory effect created some legal uncertainty, for instance with respect to the future of sports food[19] and milk-based drinks and similar products intended for young children.[20] The Commission also refrained from legislating on 'food for persons suffering from carbohydrate metabolism disorders (diabetes)', as it concluded that there was no scientific basis for producing specific EU legislation covering compositional requirements for this group of foods.[21] In essence, the limited approach taken by the Commission exemplifies an overall reluctance to engage with nutritional topics as central focuses of food regulation in the EU.

17.2.1 Food categories covered for specific groups or specific purposes

Regulation (EU) 609/2013 establishes compositional and information requirements for very specific food product categories only. These are (a) infant formula and follow-on formula; (b) processed cereal-based food and baby food for young children; (c) food for special medical purposes; and (d) total diet replacements for weight control. It also establishes a Union list that regulates substances that may be added to these categories of foods.[22]

The basic requirement is that only foods compliant with the FSGaP Regulation[23] and all other EU food law requirements may be placed on the market. The FSGaP

[14] Commission Directive 96/8/EC of 26 February 1996 on foods intended for use in energy-restricted diets for weight reduction [1996] OJ L55/22.

[15] Commission Directive 1999/21/EC of 25 March 1999 on dietary foods for special medical purposes [1999] OJ L91/29.

[16] Commission Directive 2006/125/EC of 5 December 2006 on processed cereal-based foods and baby foods for infants and young children [2006] OJ L339/16.

[17] Commission Directive 2006/141/EC of 22 December 2006 on infant formulae and follow-on formulae and amending Directive 1999/21/EC [2006] OJ L401/1.

[18] Commission Regulation (EC) 41/2009 of 20 January 2009 concerning the composition and labelling of foodstuffs suitable for people intolerant to gluten [2009] OJ L16/3.

[19] As tasked by FSGaP Regulation, art 13, the Commission evaluated the necessity of creating specific rules for food intended for sports people ('sports food'); see Commission, 'Report from the Commission to the European Parliament and the Council on food intended for sportspeople' COM (2016) 402 final.

[20] Commission, 'Report from the Commission to the European Parliament and the Council on young child formulae' SWD (2016) 99 final.

[21] Commission, 'Report from the Commission to the European Parliament and the Council on foods for persons suffering from carbohydrate metabolism disorders (diabetes)' COM (2008) 392 final.

[22] FSGaP Regulation, art 1.

[23] ibid, art 4.

Regulation is a *lex specialis* that prevails in the event of a conflict with other general requirements.[24]

The Regulation first stipulates general compositional and information requirements, including a number of nutritional and health-safety related conditions applicable to all foods covered by the Regulation.[25] The composition of the foods covered by the Regulation must be appropriate for satisfying the nutritional requirements of, and is suitable for, the intended persons, in accordance with generally accepted scientific data. The foods must not contain any substance that would endanger the health of the intended persons. For substances from engineered nanomaterials, this must be demonstrated on the basis of 'adequate test methods'. Substances added must be bio-available for use by the human body, have a nutritional or physiological effect, and be suitable for the persons for whom the food is intended. In addition, FSGaP foods may contain substances that have been subject to a novel food authorization, in accordance with the stipulated requirements therein. In terms of general information requirements, the labelling, presentation, and advertising of FSGaP foods must provide information for the appropriate use of such food, and 'shall not mislead, or attribute to such food the property of preventing, treating or curing a human disease, or imply such properties'.[26] Infant formula and follow-on formula is subject to an additional requirement, namely that it may not be designed in a way that discourages breast feeding, or that idealizes the use of formulae.[27]

In addition to the general requirements, specific requirements should be formulated in supplementary tertiary acts to be adopted by the Commission. The Commission is tasked with adopting specific compositional and information requirements for each product category through delegated acts in order to elaborate on the Regulation.[28] These are, for example, additional compositional requirements for FSGaP foods; specific requirements on the use of pesticides, including, inter alia, provisions to restrict the use of pesticides as much as possible; specific requirements on labelling, presentation, and advertising of food, including the authorization of nutrition and health claims in relation to them; eventual notification requirements for the placing on the market of food; requirements concerning promotional and commercial practices relating to infant formula; information provided on feeding infants and young children to ensure adequate information on appropriate feeding practices; and specific requirements for food for special medical purposes developed to satisfy the nutritional requirements of infants.[29]

[24] ibid, art 6.
[25] ibid, art 9.
[26] ibid, art 9(5).
[27] ibid, art 10.
[28] ibid, art 11.
[29] ibid, art 18.

The following discusses the four product categories of the Regulation and their respective tertiary, non-legislative acts.

17.2.2 *Infant formula and follow-on formula*

Infant formula and follow-on formula may only be placed on the market if it complies with the FSGaP requirements and the delegated regulation on infant formula and follow-on formula. The Regulation sets compositional requirements for formulae,[30] requirements on the suitability of their ingredients,[31] and requirements on pesticides.[32] It also stipulates specific requirements on food information[33] and the nutrition declaration.[34] Furthermore, there are rules for promotional and commercial practices for infant formula[35] and information relating to feeding infants and young children.[36] The marketing of infant and follow-on formulae may not discourage breast-feeding or idealize the use of such formulae. Nutrition and health claims may not be made.[37] Where protein hydrolysates were used as a source of protein, the old Directive allowed a health claim on the role of such formula in reducing the risk of developing allergy to milk proteins, a possibility that has now been phased out.[38] However, some statements relating to lactose and docosahexaenoic acid (DHA) are still possible.[39] The marketing of infant formula must always be notified to the Member State, while follow-on formula only needs to be notified if it uses protein hydrolysates or substances not listed in the Regulation.[40]

[30] Commission Delegated Regulation (EU) 2016/127 of 25 September 2015 supplementing Regulation (EU) No 609/2013 of the European Parliament and of the Council as regards the specific compositional and information requirements for infant formula and follow-on formula and as regards requirements on information relating to infant and young child feeding [2016] OJ L25/1. Commission Directive 2006/141/EC of 22 December 2006 on infant formulae and follow-on formulae and amending Directive 1999/21/EC Directive was applicable until 21 February 2022 to infant formula and follow-on formula from protein hydrolysates, art 2.

[31] Commission Delegated Regulation (EU) 2016/127, art 3.

[32] ibid, art 4.

[33] ibid, art 6.

[34] ibid, art 7.

[35] ibid, art 10.

[36] ibid, art 11.

[37] ibid, art 8.

[38] ibid, art 21.

[39] ibid, art 9.

[40] ibid, art 12.

17.2.3 Processed cereal-based food and baby food for infants and young children

So far, no delegated regulation has been adopted to address foods for infants and young children. Therefore, the legacy Directive of 2006 remains in force until the Commission passes the relevant non-legislative acts.[41] The rules include compositional rules for 'infants' (children under the age of 12 months) and 'young children' (aged between 1 and 3 years).[42] The Directive applies to foodstuffs for particular nutritional requirements of infants and young children in good health. They are intended for infants while they are being weaned, and young children as a supplement to their diet and/or for their progressive adaptation to ordinary food.[43] The foodstuffs covered are processed cereal-based foods (from one or more milled cereals and/or starchy root products) and baby foods, but it does not apply to milks. The Directive establishes compositional criteria,[44] permissible substances with their purity criteria,[45] and maximum residue levels of pesticides.[46] It specifies mandatory food information[47] and permissible nutrition information.[48]

17.2.4 Food for special medical purposes (FSMPs)

The (regulatory) distinction between food and medicine are hard to delineate (see section 17.2.4). A special category of food 'Food for special medical purposes' is designated,[49] that is, food for dietary management under medical supervision, 'intended for the exclusive or partial feeding of patients with a limited, impaired or disturbed capacity to take, digest, absorb, metabolise or excrete ordinary food or certain nutrients contained therein, or metabolites, or with other medically-determined nutrient requirements, whose dietary management cannot be achieved by modification of the normal diet alone'.[50] The Regulation distinguishes between nutritionally complete products with a standard formulation, nutritionally complete products with a nutrient-adapted formulation, and nutritionally incomplete products with a standard or nutrient-adapted formulation.

41 Commission Directive 2006/125/EC.
42 ibid, art 2.
43 ibid, art 1.
44 ibid, art 5, for processed cereal-based food Annex I, baby foods Annex II.
45 ibid, art 6.
46 ibid, art 7, Annex VI, Annex VII.
47 ibid, art 8(1).
48 ibid, art 8(2).
49 Commission Delegated Regulation (EU) 2016/128 of 25 September 2015 supplementing Regulation (EU) No 609/2013 of the European Parliament and of the Council as regards the specific compositional and information requirements for food for special medical purposes [2016] OJ L25/30.
50 FSGaP Regulation, art 2(2)(g).

FSMPs set nutritional compositional requirements.[51] They also contain pesticide residue levels for infants and young children.[52] The delegated regulation further sets specific requirements on food information[53] and the nutrition declaration.[54] Nutrition and health claims may not be made.[55] However, there is the option to make statements regarding the dietary management of a disease, disorder, or medical condition—interestingly, these have been observed to potentially 'act as an incentive for some food business operators to incorrectly place products on the market as FSMP'.[56]

Food business operators (FBOs) must notify the authorities of the Member State where the food is marketed.[57] Despite the novel FSMPs rules, Member State authorities have reported difficulties in enforcing the legal framework. An additional Commission Notice[58] has therefore been issued that clarifies the classification of FSMPs. This particularly focuses on the distinction between FSMPs and medicines, which must be done on a case-by-case basis.[59] If products are 'presented for the prevention of a disease', for example omega-3 fatty acids for cardiovascular disease, it is considered a medicinal product.[60] At the same time, 'products intended for consumers not suffering from any disease/disorder/medical condition should not be considered as FSMP'. In particular, this would cover food for healthy infants, healthy pregnant women, and sportspeople.[61] In the same vein, if a product can be used without medical supervision, it is not an FSMP. The Commission Notice further specifies what is meant by specially processed or formulated food, and the concept of 'modification of the normal diet'. The case law of the Court of Justice on the distinction of food from medicine remains pertinent in this regard (see Chapter 5).

[51] For foods developed for infants in Commission Delegated Regulation (EU) 2016/128, pt A of Annex I, and for people other than infants in pt B.

[52] Commission Delegated Regulation (EU) 2016/128 of 25 September 2015 supplementing Regulation (EU) No 609/2013 of the European Parliament and of the Council as regards the specific compositional and information requirements for food for special medical purposes [2016] OJ L25/30, art 3.

[53] ibid, art 5.

[54] ibid, art 6.

[55] ibid, art 7.

[56] Commission Notice on the classification of Food for Special Medical Purposes [2017] OJ C401/1 para (3).

[57] Commission Delegated Regulation (EU) 2016/128, art 9.

[58] Commission Notice on the classification of Food for Special Medical Purposes.

[59] Directive 2001/83/EC of the European Parliament and of the Council of 6 November 2001 on the Community code relating to medicinal products for human use [2001] OJ L311/67.

[60] Commission Notice on the classification of Food for Special Medical Purposes, para 43.

[61] Commission Notice on the classification of Food for Special Medical Purposes.

17.2.5 Total diet replacements for weight control

In order to lose weight, total diet replacement constitutes a method whereby all food is replaced with diet food products. In EU food law, 'total diet replacement for weight control' is defined as food specially formulated for use in energy restricted diets for weight reduction which, when used as instructed by the FBO, replaces the whole daily diet.[62] The Delegated Regulation lays down compositional requirements[63] and requirements for labelling, presentation, and advertising.[64] A compositional requirement is, for instance, that energy provided by total diet replacement for weight control products shall not be less than 2,510kJ (600kcal) and not more than 5,020kJ (1,200kcal) per daily ration.[65] There are also specific requirements concerning the nutrition declaration. Nutrition and health claims may not be made, with the exception of the nutrition claim 'added fibre'.[66] The statement 'low calorie diet' can be used if the energy content of the product is between 3,360kJ/day (800kcal/day) and 5,040kJ/day (1,200kcal/day), or 'very low calorie diet' if the energy content is below 3 360kJ/day (800kcal/day). The placing on the market of total diet replacement products must be notified to the Member State.[67]

17.2.6 Future development of the FSGaP Regulation

Overall, the FSGaP Regulation demonstrates a strong nutrition compositional approach to selected foods for specific groups and specific purposes, although it also contains information governance aspects. This approach recognizes the special vulnerability of infants and babies, and foods for special medical purposes and total diet replacements. The fact that only very specific food items are regulated, coupled with the deregulatory approach taken in the last consolidation of the FSGaP Regulation, illustrates that the nutritional health component of food is not easily regulated in the EU.

[62] FSGaP Regulation, art 2(2)(h).

[63] Commission Delegated Regulation (EU) 2017/1798 of 2 June 2017 supplementing Regulation (EU) No 609/2013 of the European Parliament and of the Council as regards the specific compositional and information requirements for total diet replacement for weight control [2017] OJ L259/2, art 3. The rules apply from 27 October 2022.

[64] Commission Delegated Regulation (EU) 2017/1798, art 5.

[65] ibid, Annex I.

[66] ibid, art 6.

[67] ibid, art 7.

17.3 Regulation on Food Fortification

The addition of substances to food is often referred to as food fortification or enrichment, and refers to the practice of deliberately adding certain substances, often micronutrients, to food products. It is regarded as an important nutritional tool with the potential to improve the overall diet of individuals, groups of populations, and even entire populations. While the addition of substances, such as micronutrients, can contribute to health, excess consumption may also have negative health effects. For instance, excess consumption of zinc may cause neurological diseases due to the interference with copper absorption,[68] and excess consumption of Vitamin A may cause skin disorders, nausea, vomiting, disorders of the musculo-skeletal system, and liver damage.[69] From a nutritional perspective, there is therefore both desirable minimum and maximum levels for these substances.

From a food technological perspective, one can distinguish different purposes for adding substances to food, namely (a) reconstitution (to restore the original nutritional composition that a food had prior to processing), (b) substitution (to imitate the nutritional properties of a food product that is being substituted, for instance the fortification of margarine as a substitute for butter), and (c) food fortification in the strict sense (adding substances to fortify the food).[70]

EU food law has a dedicated legal instrument on added substances, namely Regulation (EC) 1925/2006 on the addition of vitamins and minerals and of certain other substances to foods.[71] However, the regulatory legal framework is incomplete and therefore not fully operational.

17.3.1 Subject matter and scope

The Regulation was adopted with the purpose of ensuring the effective functioning of the internal market, whilst providing a high level of consumer protection.[72] The Regulation covers vitamins and minerals, as well as other substances with a nutritional or physiological effect,[73] and establishes both positive lists of substances that may be added, as well as substances that are prohibited, restricted, or under scientific evaluation. It does not apply to food supplements.[74]

[68] EFSA, 'Scientific Opinion on Dietary Reference Values for Zinc' (2014) 12 EFSA Journal 3844.

[69] EFSA, 'Scientific Opinion on Dietary Reference Values for Vitamin A' (2015) 13 EFSA Journal 4028.

[70] This section is in part adapted from Lisa van der Meer and Hanna Schebesta, 'The Internal Market, Incomplete: EU, Dutch and Belgian Legislation on Maximum Food Fortification with Micronutrients' (2020) 15 European Food and Feed Law Review 212.

[71] Regulation (EC) 1925/2006 of the European Parliament and of the Council of 20 December 2006 on the addition of vitamins and minerals and of certain other substances to foods [2006] OJ L404/26.

[72] ibid, art 1.

[73] ibid, art 2.

[74] ibid, art 1(2).

17.3.2 Positive and negative list of substances

The positive list contains permissible vitamins and minerals; these are listed in Annex I and may be added to foods in the forms provided in Annex II on purity criteria and use.[75] Vitamins and minerals must be bio-available to the human body and may be added to foods to address vitamin or mineral deficiencies or to enhance nutritional status. This should take account of evolving generally acceptable scientific knowledge on the role of vitamins and minerals in nutrition and consequent effects on the health of the population or specific population groups.[76] Vitamins and minerals may not be added to unprocessed foodstuffs, including fruit, vegetables, meat, poultry, and fish and generally not to beverages containing more than 1.2% by volume of alcohol.

The Regulation foresaw the establishment of maximum amounts of added substances by 2009. The maximum amounts should be set by establishing upper safe levels of vitamins and minerals, and by determining the intake of vitamins and minerals from other dietary sources.[77] For this purpose, the European Commission intended to establish tolerable upper intake levels (ULs), which are defined as 'the maximum level of total chronic daily intake of a nutrient (from all sources) judged to be unlikely to pose a risk of adverse health effects to humans'.[78] To date, due to the 'complex nature of the issue and the divergent views',[79] the European Commission has not set the maximum and minimum amounts of vitamins and minerals which may be added to foods in accordance with Article 6. Consequently, the full effect of the legislation has in fact not yet unfolded and there is a patchwork of national regulations in force on these matters.[80] For example, some Member States have laws with mandatory fortifications (eg mandatory iodine fortification of salt in Denmark), and/or prohibitions on fortifications (eg restrictions on the addition of vitamin A in the Netherlands).

The Regulation also contains a negative list of substances that are prohibited, restricted, or under EU scrutiny. These are listed in Annex III. This provision has received an interesting rejuvenation with the prohibition of trans fatty acids. Trans fats are primarily used in partially hydrogenated oils. They were used, for instance, in some margarines, which were marketed then as being a healthier alternative due to the absence of cholesterol. However, trans fat appears to distort

[75] ibid, art 3(1).

[76] ibid, art 3.

[77] ibid, art 6(3).

[78] European Commission Health and Consumer Protection Directorate-General, *Discussion paper on the setting of maximum and minimum amounts for vitamins and minerals in foodstuffs* (2006).

[79] Commission, 'Addition of vitamins and minerals' <https://ec.europa.eu/food/safety/labelling-and-nutrition/addition-vitamins-and-minerals_en> accessed 11 August 2022.

[80] The different Member State laws are listed in the Commission, 'Community Register on the addition of vitamins and minerals and of certain other substances to foods' (1 January 2021) <https://ec.europa.eu/food/safety/labelling-and-nutrition/addition-vitamins-and-minerals_en#register> accessed 11 August 2022.

the cell membranes, and therefore posed a risk of heart disease.[81] The European Food Safety Authority (EFSA) concluded that the consumption of trans fatty acids should be as low as possible.[82] Regulation (EU) 2019/649[83] added trans fatty acids, other than trans fats from animal origin, to the list of restricted substances under the list in Annex III, and the amount was set at a maximum of 2g per 100g of fat.

Considering the demonstrated adverse health effects, the decision by the United States Food and Drug Administration (US FDA) to regard trans fats as 'not generally recognised as safe', as well as the fact that many Member States had already limited trans fats, the EU's statutory limitation on trans fats proceeded relatively uncontentiously. At the same time, the use of Regulation 1925/2006 could be regarded as surprising, as it had previously been used only incidentally for highly specific substances, which were prohibited or limited under a net food safety rationale. In contrast, the regulation on trans fats adopts a holistic nutrition rationale, which aligns with broader public health objectives, and specifically the serious increase in the risk of heart disease.[84] Interestingly, the mandate to examine the relevance of trans fats was included in Regulation (EU) 1169/2011 on food information to consumers,[85] which obliged the Commission to prepare a report on the presence of trans fats in foods and in the overall diet of the Union population. One might therefore have expected a food information-based approach in tackling the issue, whereas the final result is a binding product compositional rule, which is one of the most far-reaching regulatory instruments available. This might mark the beginning of a new approach in EU food law, where compositional product requirements are established.

[81] Emil Ginter and Viliam Simko, 'New Data on Harmful Effects of Trans-Fatty Acids' (2016) 117 Bratisl Lek Listy 251.

[82] EFSA, 'Scientific Opinion on Dietary Reference Values for Fats, Including Saturated Fatty Acids, Polyunsaturated Fatty Acids, Monounsaturated Fatty Acids, Trans Fatty Acids, and Cholesterol' (2010) 8 EFSA Journal 1461; EFSA, 'Scientific and Technical Assistance on Transfatty Acids' (2018) 15 EFSA Supporting Publications 1433E.

[83] Commission Regulation (EU) 2019/649 of 24 April 2019 amending Annex III to Regulation (EC) No 1925/2006 of the European Parliament and of the Council as regards trans fat, other than trans fat naturally occurring in fat of animal origin [2019] OJ L110/17.

[84] ibid, Recital (3) and (4).

[85] Regulation (EU) 1169/2011 of the European Parliament and of the Council of 25 October 2011 on the provision of food information to consumers, amending Regulations (EC) No 1924/2006 and (EC) No 1925/2006 of the European Parliament and of the Council, and repealing Commission Directive 87/250/EEC, Council Directive 90/496/EEC, Commission Directive 1999/10/EC, Directive 2000/13/EC of the European Parliament and of the Council, Commission Directives 2002/67/EC and 2008/5/EC and Commission Regulation (EC) No 608/2004 [2011] OJ L304/18 (Food Information for Consumers Regulation (FICR)), art 30(7).

17.3.3 Labelling requirements

Nutrition labelling of products to which vitamins and minerals have been added is compulsory.[86] In addition, there should not be any mention stating or implying that a balanced and varied diet cannot provide appropriate quantities of nutrients.[87] Statements complying with the Nutrition and Health Claims Regulation may be used.[88]

17.3.4 Notification requirements

Member States must notify the Commission of existing or new national laws on the mandatory addition of vitamins and minerals, as well as prohibitions or restrictions on the use of certain other substances in the manufacture of specified foods.[89] In turn, Member States may require notification to their competent authority regarding the marketing of foods in their territory that have added vitamins and minerals and of foods containing substances listed in Annex III.[90]

The Regulation is intended to safeguard the free movement of goods, and expressly stipulates that Member States may not restrict trade in foods in compliance with the regulation and implementing acts.[91] Nevertheless, since the Regulation has failed to harmonize so many aspects, the issue of adding vitamins, minerals, and other substances is one that continues to produce a number of legal disputes under the Treaty articles. These articles apply in the absence of harmonization. There have been a number of cases challenging Member States' regulation in this regard. For example, issues have been raised regarding the vagueness of a blanket prohibition on enriched confectionary and drinks in France, as well as the unclear design of prior authorization schemes. However, in general terms, in the absence of EU harmonization, Member States are competent and have a wide margin of appreciation in designing national measures to address potential harm (see Chapter 4).[92]

[86] Regulation (EC) No 1925/2006, art 7.
[87] ibid, art 7(1).
[88] ibid, art 7(4).
[89] ibid, art 11.
[90] ibid, art 15.
[91] ibid, art 10.
[92] Van der Meer and Schebesta (n 70).

17.4 Directive 2002/46/EC on food supplements

The distinction between regular foodstuffs, medicines, and foods with medicinal purposes can be blurred. Directive 2002/46/EC[93] regulates food supplements, that is, concentrated sources of vitamins or minerals that are marketed as foodstuffs.[94] Food supplements are defined as 'foodstuffs the purpose of which is to supplement the normal diet and which are concentrated sources of nutrients or other substances with a nutritional or physiological effect, alone or in combination, marketed in dose form'.[95] Dose form refers to, for instance, capsules, pastilles, tablets, pills and other similar forms, sachets of powder, ampoules of liquids, drop dispensing bottles, and other similar forms of liquids and powders designed to be taken in measured small-unit quantities. The distinction between food supplements and medicine is particularly contested, and the Court of Justice of the European Union (CJEU) clarified that it would have to be undertaken by analysing whether the product is a medicinal product either by presentation or by function.[96] Although it is an incomplete legal framework, the Directive has succeeded in establishing a definition of food supplements that is valid throughout the EU.

Given that food supplements are governed by a directive, it is the obligation of Member States to 'ensure that food supplements may be marketed within the Community only if they comply with the rules laid down in this Directive'.[97] Only vitamins and minerals listed in Annex I, in the forms listed in Annex II, may be used in food supplements.[98] Annex II lists purity criteria. As long as these are not specified at EU level, generally acceptable purity criteria recommended by international bodies are applicable and national rules setting stricter purity criteria may be maintained.[99]

The Directive specifies rules on the setting of maximum amounts, taking into account upper safe levels of vitamins and minerals, as well as the dietary intake from other sources.[100] However, the minimum and maximum amounts of vitamins and minerals present in food supplements per daily portion of consumption[101] have not been set (as is equally the case for the addition of vitamin, minerals, and other substances to food). In this regard, the legal framework remains incomplete.

[93] Directive 2002/46/EC.
[94] ibid, art 1.
[95] ibid, art 2(a).
[96] These are the criteria of the medicinal product definition under Directive 2001/83, art 1(2); see Case C-319/05 *Commission of the European Communities v Germany* [2007] ECR I-9811.
[97] Directive 2002/46/EC, art 3.
[98] ibid, art 4.
[99] ibid, art 4(4)
[100] ibid, art 5.
[101] ibid, art 5.

Member States can restrict the marketing of a product in accordance with the requirements of that Directive if they are able to establish that the use of that product endangers human health.[102] The CJEU held that the fact that there is no nutritional need in the population of the Member State concerned does not suffice of itself to demonstrate the existence of such danger, and therefore it cannot justify a national ban.[103]

17.4.1 Labelling requirements

The legal name to be used in the food labelling is 'food supplements'. Generally, labelling of supplements 'must not attribute to food supplements the property of preventing, treating or curing a human disease, or refer to such properties',[104] or imply that a balanced and varied diet cannot provide appropriate quantities of nutrients.[105] It must also contain the product names; the recommended daily portion; a warning not to exceed the stated recommended daily dose; a statement that food supplements are not a substitute for a varied diet; and that the products should be stored out of the reach of young children.[106] The product must state the amount of nutrients or substances with a nutritional or physiological effect per portion recommended as the daily dose.[107]

17.4.2 Notification duty

There may be a notification duty on operators. Member States are allowed to request notification to their competent authority before placing a supplement on the market in their territory.[108] Currently food supplements only cover vitamins and minerals. Regulation for additional substances is intended, but is currently stalled. This means that for those substances, such as botanicals, pre-biotics, and amino acids, national legislation and the principle of mutual recognition apply.

[102] ibid, art 12.
[103] Case C-211/03 *HLH Warenvertrieb and OrthicaPara v Germany* [2005] ECR I-5141, para 72.
[104] Directive 2002/46/EC, art 6.
[105] ibid, art 7.
[106] ibid, art 6(3).
[107] ibid, art 8.
[108] ibid, art 10.

17.5 Discussion

Although the origins of nutritional food regulation dates back to the early beginnings of EU food law, harmonization in this area remains particularly ad-hoc and notably incomplete. EU law regulates the nutritional aspects of food composition for only very specific groups (infants and young children), and for very specific purposes (special medical purposes and total diet replacements). In addition, the EU legal frameworks of food fortification and food supplements are missing vital elements and are currently not fully operational. Due to the incomplete nature of this range of legal instruments, regulation in these areas still falls in part to the Member States, leading to a highly fragmented legal landscape across national jurisdiction. On one hand, this situation falls short of meeting the 'classic' internal market objective, and, on the other hand, it largely falls short of addressing the objective of promoting nutrition and health.

In industry applications, food is increasingly understood as integral to health, with nutrition playing an important role in preventive health behaviour. In food technology, a host of new food concepts are emerging, such as nutraceuticals, or more broadly speaking, functional foods. A predominant issue in practice is the uncertain classification and treatment of such products in the law. This is because 'under a given set of circumstances [these] may be named a dietary supplement, medical food, food for special dietary use or nutraceutical under different circumstances, depending on its ingredients (active components) and the claims reported on its label'.[109] For example, botanical food products are notoriously difficult to market, as some Member States tend to classify them as medicinal products, and they can also be regarded as food supplements depending on their function.[110] Innovative foods, therefore, face a complex and incomplete EU regulatory framework, which is complemented by a patchwork of national frameworks that often require notifications or authorizations in the nutrition food sector.[111]

From an EU perspective, food for health lacks a conceptual underpinning, and a coherent legal overarching framework for food health and nutrition has never

[109] Antonella Santini and others, 'Nutraceuticals: Opening the Debate for a Regulatory Framework' (2018) 84 British Journal of Clinical Pharmacology 659.

[110] Patrick Coppens, 'The Use of Botanicals in Food Supplements and Medicinal Products: The Co-Existence of Two Legal Frameworks' (2008) 3 European Food and Feed Law Review 93.

[111] For example, this author gives the following illustrative advice for Germany, see Moritz Hagenmeyer, 'Mad about the Food Supplements' (2006) 1 European Food and Feed Law Review 25: 'The main problem for foreign food operators wishing to import food supplements into Germany is probably the composition of their products. Labelling and notification can usually be carried out without much difficulty. If foreign supplements are merely composed of vitamins or minerals listed in the annexes of the European Food Supplements Directive 2002/46/EC, the products have the best chance to survive a critical examination by German food control authorities, provided the amounts of nutrients for daily consumption are not excessive and the preparations are not perceived as drugs by the consumer because of the way they are presented. If, however, other substances are being employed as ingredients, it is advisable to obtain premarketing advice on the legality of the food supplements in Germany.'

been created. One of the reasons for this is that the EU does not enjoy significant competence to regulate health issues autonomously. In fact, the validity of the Supplements Directive was challenged by several trade unions before the CJEU, alleging that it does not contribute to improving the conditions for the establishment and functioning of the internal market. Assuming that the relevant provisions are built on public-health considerations, the use of Article 95 EC would constitute a 'misuse of powers'.[112] Recalling earlier judgments, the Court rejected this argument and held that 'the Community legislature cannot be prevented from relying on that legal basis [Article 95 EC] on the ground that public health protection is a decisive factor in the choices to be made'.[113] Nevertheless, the fact that there is no autonomous legal basis for policies solely focused on human health means that ambitions for food legislation specifically targeting nutrition and health are somewhat curtailed.

In addition, nutrition needs to remain respectful of subsidiarity considerations, in that different geographies and diets give rise to diverging nutritional needs that may be addressed more suitably at local or national level. That said, the increasing recognition of individual nutrition, instead of a 'one size fits all' approach, encourages consideration beyond national or even EU diets alone. A first step would be to complement standard datasets with attention to transnational dietary patterns, such as veganism, vegetarianism, and others.

The Farm to Fork Strategy is—in fact—entitled 'Farm to fork strategy for a fair healthy and environmentally-friendly food system' and thus foreshadows greater structural attention to the topic of health in the food system. In this context, one might have assumed that it would set out to better align the food safety framework with health goals. Although health is regularly regarded as a dimension of sustainability, this is not entirely undisputed, as a traditional definition of sustainability encompasses economic, social, and environmental dimensions. The Framework for Sustainable Food Systems promised in the Farm to Fork Strategy should have clarified this dimension as being a part of sustainable food, and would ideally have anchored this objective more strongly in EU food law. However, the Farm to Fork Strategy did introduce certain technical measures aimed at addressing health aspects during the processing stages. These include: (a) an initiative to reformulate processed food, including setting maximum levels for certain nutrients, (b) nutrient profiles to restrict the promotion of food high in salt, sugars, and/or fat, and (c) nutrition labelling initiatives. The setting of maximum levels for certain nutrients, which was already used for trans fat, could be considered the initial emergence of a compositional approach to nutrition and health in food policy, and

[112] Joined cases C-154/04 and C-155/04 *The Queen, on the application of Alliance for Natural Health and Nutri-Link Ltd v Secretary of State for Health (C-154/04) and The Queen, on the application of National Association of Health Stores and Health Food Manufacturers Ltd v Secretary of State for Health and National Assembly for Wales (C-155/04)* [2005] ECR I-6451, para 25.

[113] ibid, para 30.

one that might be pursued further under the actions outlined in the Farm to Fork Strategy.

Whereas the thinking in the Farm to Fork Strategy nutrition proposals does take first steps beyond the health-safety nexus and towards the health-nutrition nexus, the proposed technical rules largely fight *unhealthiness* and aim to limit the known negative health effects of some nutrients. These restricted actions show that a systemic re-orientation through which a place for the positive relationship between food *for* health could be better constructed is currently not envisioned. In this context, the Farm to Fork Strategy not only overlooks the opportunity to integrate health into the current food safety paradigm at a systemic level, but it also more practically fails to keep up with food technological developments and consumer needs in this direction.

PART VIII

INTERNATIONAL FOOD LAW

18
Food in a Globalized World
International Food Law

18.1 Introduction

This chapter explores the relationship between European Union (EU) Food Law and international law. Traditionally, the primary connections have been established between World Trade Organisation (WTO) law (especially the Sanitary and Phytosanitary Measures (SPS) and Technical Barriers to Trade (TBT) Agreement) and EU food legislation. However, with a more comprehensive understanding of EU food law, other international law instruments such as the human right to adequate food and the United Nations (UN) on the sustainable development goals (SDGs) are increasingly important to the development and interpretation of EU food law.

Food regulations are (mostly) national or regional, yet trade is global, creating problems of 'linkage'[1] between the two levels. In a traditional interpretation, differing regulations on foods in various countries and regions are viewed as trade barriers, which may or may not need levelling by international law to ensure the smooth operation of supply chains and promote free trade. A closer look reveals a more complex picture. Domestic food regulations often influence regulation of the food market worldwide, resulting in de facto harmonization.[2] The EU acts as 'an external actor in transnational food regulation' that actively exports its safety standards.[3] In the EU this is known as the 'Brussels effect', and many countries align their food standards with the notoriously stringent EU food standards in order to facilitate trade of food products. In this way, national regulatory policies can be designed following regulations of other countries or regions, effectively aligning with their policy choices.[4] However, the same international standard can

[1] Dennis Patterson and Ari Afilalo, *The New Global Trading Order: The Evolving State and the Future of Trade* (CUP 2008) 86–93.

[2] Anu Bradford, 'The Brussels Effect' (2012) 107 Northwestern University Law Review 1, 3; Dominique Sinopoli and Kai Purnhagen, 'Reversed Harmonization or Horizontalization of EU Standards?: Does WTO Law Facilitate or Constrain the Brussels Effect?' (2016) 34 Wisconsin International Law Journal 92.

[3] Maria Weimer and Ellen Vos, 'The Role of the EU in Transnational Regulation of Food Safety: Extending Experimentalist Governance?' in Jonathan Zeitlin (ed), *Extending Experimentalist Governance?: The European Union and Transnational Regulation* (OUP 2015).

[4] Beth Simmons, 'The International Politics of Harmonization: The Case of Capital Market Regulation in Dynamics of Regulatory Change: How Globalization Affects National Regulatory Policies' in David Vogel and Robert A Kagan (eds), *Dynamics of Regulatory Change: How Globalization*

EU Food Law. Hanna Schebesta and Kai Purnhagen, Oxford University Press. © Hanna Schebesta and Kai Purnhagen 2024.
DOI: 10.1093/9780198901570.003.0019

have different domestic effects.[5] Domestic food laws may and probably should serve those public policy interests that respond best to specific domestic demands. However, domestic food laws are likely to have an impact on trade, and must therefore be compliant with the current international trade law regimes, notably WTO law. The tension between the free trade rationale and regulation for public policy interests, such as environmental or social concerns, is particularly apparent in the food sector.

From an international perspective, EU food law is considered regional, and as such is interwoven into international law. At a practical level, individuals within and outside the EU are dependent on the effective functioning of highly integrated international supply chains.[6] Regional food production in the EU alone cannot satisfy EU consumers' food demand, therefore food imports are vital for the EU's internal food market. Access to the EU food market can be crucial for foreign producers, as it can lead to increased revenues, especially for those whose livelihoods depend on access to supply chains that sell in the EU market. The EU is therefore one of the most potent players on the market and is known for de facto setting the highest standards for foodstuffs in the world.[7]

International food law for a large part can be subsumed under international economic law.[8] This traditional view of international food law relates to the import and export of food and the regulatory effects of them on the food system. This view, though trade related, acknowledges that a broader set of legal considerations such as those related to animal health, environmental protection, human rights considerations in production chains, and international trade law are meanwhile an integral part of international food law. The UN-developed international laws have shaped a binding human right to adequate food and led to the implementation of practically significant SDGs. In the absence of functioning international

Affects National Regulatory Policies (University of California Press 2004); Esteban Ferro, Tsunehiro Otsuki, and John S Wilson, 'The Effect of Product Standards on Agricultural Exports' (2015) 50 Food Policy 68. This is explicitly acknowledged in EU food law, which stipulates that EU food law needs to design 'objectives and principles for the contribution of the Community to developing international standards'. (Recital 25 Regulation (EC) 178/2002 of the European Parliament and of the Council of 28 January 2002 laying down the general principles and requirements of food law, establishing the European Food Safety Authority and laying down procedures in matters of food safety [2002] OJ L31/1).

[5] This is also true for food law within the framework of EU law; on the example of regulation of cheese made from non-pasteurized milk, see Fredrik Schauer, *Profiles, Probabilities and Stereotypes* (Belknap Harvard Press 2003) 279 et seq.

[6] EU primary law explicitly recognizes the importance of the functioning of supply chains in TFEU, art 122(1).

[7] Bradford (n 2).

[8] Bederman's definition of international economic law includes (i) the background rules of private international commerce on foodstuffs, (ii) the architecture of the global food trading systems, and (iii) the rules relating to international development and investment relating to food commerce; David Bederman, *International Economic Law* (New York Foundation Press 2001) 141.

governance institutions, however, the trade-related perspective is to date the most legally relevant instrument that effectively governs this wider set of legal considerations.

18.2 International food law and EU food law

The EU is commonly understood as an autonomous legal order in international law.[9] EU primary law considers international agreements or conventions as directly binding towards the Union and its Member States when they are concluded by the Union.[10] This is the case, for instance, with bilateral trade agreements, such as the Comprehensive Economic and Trade Agreement (CETA),[11] which contains numerous provisions that are directly applicable to food trade between Canada and the EU. Very few international treaties are dedicated to food specifically, a rare example being the Food Assistance Convention regarding food assistance that was adopted in 2012, which was ratified by the EU (although not by all of the EU Member States).

EU primary law grants legal value to international law beyond signed agreements and conventions in three ways. First, where treaties had been concluded by the Member States, but the Union had meanwhile assumed the powers exercised by Member States in that field.[12] Second, Article 3(5) of the Treaty on European Union (TEU)[13] obliges the EU to contribute 'to the strict observance and the development of international law, including respect for the principles of the United Nations Charter'. In this sense, international law, such as rules of customary international law, is binding on the EU institutions,[14] and can even develop indirect effects on food business operators (FBOs) through interpretation of provisions in EU food law.[15] Third, international law is considered binding on the EU when EU law refers to provisions of international law.[16]

References to international agreements are widespread in EU secondary food law. The General Food Law Regulation (GFLR), for example, declares 'narcotic

[9] See, inter alia, joined Cases C-402/05 and C-415/05 *P Kadi and Al Barakaat International Foundation v Council* [2008] ECR I-6351, para 282; for a critical appraisal, see Bruno de Witte, 'European Union Law: How Autonomous is its Legal Order?' (2010) 65 ZÖR 141.

[10] TFEU, art 216(2).

[11] Comprehensive Economic and Trade Agreement (CETA) between Canada, of the one part, and the European Union and its Member States, of the other part [2017] OJ L11/23.

[12] Joined Cases 21/72-24/72 *International Fruit Company and Others v Produktschap voor Groenten en Fruit* EU:C:1972:115; Case C-379/92 *Peralta* [1994] ECR I-3453.

[13] Consolidated version of the Treaty on European Union [2012] OJ C326/13 (TEU).

[14] Case C-162/96 *Racke GmbH & Co v Hauptzollamt Mainz* [1998] ECR I-3655, para 46.

[15] Case C-363/18 *Organisation juive européenne, Vignoble Psagot Ltd v Ministre de l'Économie et des Finances* EU:C:2019:954, para 56.

[16] On the example of WTO law, see Joined cases C-120/06 P and C-121/06 *P FIAMM and Others v Council and Commission* [2008] ECR I-6513, para 112.

or psychotropic substances' to fall outside the definition of 'food' and refers for the determination of these substances to the 'United Nations Single Convention on Narcotic Drugs, 1961, and the United Nations Convention on Psychotropic Substances, 1971',[17] adopting these conventions into EU law and making them *de jure* binding. At a more general level, regarding imports to the EU, the GFLR[18] declares provisions in specific agreements between the Union and an exporting country into the Union applicable to determine the rules for placing foods on the EU market. Where the food is exported from the EU, bilateral agreements between the Union or a Member State and a third country are directly binding in the event that the parties have agreed on specific provisions concerning the export of food from the Union.[19] Article 13 GFLR recognizes several obligations of Member States and the Union to contribute in various ways to the observance and development of international technical standards (see Chapter 5.4). While this provision has to our knowledge so far not been subject to judicial control at the EU level, it may well be that the Court chooses to apply a comparable approach to their legal interpretation as it adopted in relation to international law in Article 3(5) TEU.[20] Therefore, if there is room for interpretation in EU and Member State food law, a given provision may be interpreted in a way that helps to realize 'consistency between international technical standards and food law'.[21]

Overall, the relationship between international law and EU law is complex, which may be one of the reasons why the EU is not very invested in international law solutions in the food sector.

18.3 International law under the auspices of the UN

The law of the UN is important for EU food law in several ways. First, the principles of the United Nations Charter[22] and those that concern fundamental rules of international law may influence the interpretation of provisions in EU food law and guide food law making. Second, when the EU is party to a treaty concerning food, for instance under the auspices of the UN's specialized agencies—the Food and Agriculture Organization (FAO), the World Health Organisation (WHO), and the World Food Programme (WFP)—for providing food aid through the UN system,

[17] Regulation (EC) 178/2002 of the European Parliament and of the Council of 28 January 2002 laying down the general principles and requirements of food law, establishing the European Food Safety Authority and laying down procedures in matters of food safety [2002] OJ L31/1 (General Food Law Regulation (GFLR)), art 2(g).

[18] ibid, art 11.

[19] ibid, art 12(2).

[20] Case C-363/18 *Organisation juive européenne, Vignoble Psagot Ltd v Ministre de l'Économie et des Finances* EU:C:2019:954, para 56.

[21] GFLR, art 13(e), however, 'while ensuring that the high level of protection adopted in the Community is not reduced'.

[22] Charter of the United Nations (entered into force 24 October 1945) 1 UNTS XVI.

or United Nations Conference on Trade and Development (UNCTAD), the EU is bound by its international law obligations. Third, soft law such as, in particular, the model laws developed by the FAO/WHO (eg the FAO model food law[23] or FAO/WHO's guidance to develop food law[24]) and the SDGs developed by the UN have de facto influence on EU policy making, and by consequence, EU food law.

In 2015, the UN published the 17 sustainable development goals as part of UN Resolution 70/1. These SDGs will serve as a 'blueprint' for a sustainable future. As part of international law they are soft law, and therefore not directly legally binding. However, there is potential that they may become indirectly legally binding inside the EU through the mechanism deployed in Article 3(5) TEU, which calls for 'respect for the principles of the United Nations Charter'. While all SDGs have a potential impact on EU food law, in particular SDG 2 ('Zero Hunger'), 3 ('Good Health and Well-being'), 12 ('Responsible Consumption and Production'), and 13 ('Climate Action') are of immediate importance in food law. In the EU, the SDGs are implemented as part of the Green Deal, thus demonstrating the influence of the SDG agenda on policy agendas, and indirectly the resulting laws.

18.3.1 **Law of the UN**

The EU is member of the UN with enhanced participation rights, but no voting rights alongside the EU's 27 Member States.[25] Recognizing its important role in the world, the EU, nonetheless, adopted the internal obligation to contribute 'to the strict observance and the development of international law, including respect for the principles of the United Nations Charter'.[26] The obligation especially concerns international laws to which the EU is not a signatory. This is because international agreements or conventions signed by the EU are directly binding on the Union.[27] International law covered by Article 3(5) TEU concerns, in particular *ius cogens* norms, which 'reflect and protect *fundamental values of the international community*, are hierarchically superior to other rules of international law and are universally applicable'.[28]

An example of the relevance of international law in EU food law is the case *Organisation juive européenne*, which concerned the interpretation of EU food labelling law in light of *ius cogens*. The Court was tasked to decide whether the

[23] FAO, *Perspectives and Guidelines on Food Legislation: With a New Model Food Law* (2005), Annex.
[24] FAO/WHO, *Assuring Food Safety and Quality: Guidelines for Strengthening National Food Control Systems* (2003) Annex 6.
[25] UNGA Res 65/276 'Participation of the European Union in the Work of the United Nations' (2011) UN Doc A/RES/65/276.
[26] TEU, art 3(5).
[27] TFEU, art 216(2).
[28] International Law Commission (ILC), Report of the International Law Commission Seventy-first session (29 April–7 June and 8 July–9 August 2019) UN Doc A/74/10, para 56, conclusion 3.

omission of the indication 'Israeli settlement' was liable to mislead the consumer as to the place of provenance of that foodstuff and was therefore mandatory. It had been the predominant view that these settlements as 'occupied territories' indeed violated international law, and in particular the Palestinian's right to self-determination.[29] The right to self-determination is considered *ius cogens* in international law,[30] therefore its breach falls within the application of the obligations stipulated in Article 3(5) TEU. EU food law requires the mandatory indication of a country of origin or place of provenance of a food where an omission to do so might mislead the consumer as to the true country of origin or place of provenance of a food.[31] With direct reference to Article 3(5) TEU the Court stipulated that an 'omission of the indication that a foodstuff comes from an "Israeli settlement" located in one of the territories (in question) is likely to mislead consumers by suggesting that that food has a place of provenance other than its true place of provenance'.[32] To back up this claim, the Court also refers to the question of what kind of normative standard should be applied when testing the 'misleadingness' of consumers under the Food Information Regulation. When determining what kind of information needs consideration to test the potential misleadingness of the average consumer, Article 3(1) of the Food Information to Consumers Regulation (FICR) provides some normative standards. Information with regards to health, economic, environmental, social, and ethical considerations is required to enable consumers' 'informed choices'.[33] The Court emphasizes that this list presented in Article 3(1) FICR is non-exclusive and may also encompass 'other types of considerations, such as those relating to the observance of international law . . .'[34] The Court squarely endorses the view that consumers' purchasing decisions may be impacted by the production of foodstuff in settlements that are not recognized by international humanitarian law,[35] particularly if those breaches concern fundamental rules of international law.[36]

[29] UNGA Res 66/78 'Israeli settlements in the Occupied Palestinian Territory, including East Jerusalem, and the occupied Syrian Golan' (2012) A/RES/66/78; *Legal Consequences of the Construction of a Wall in the Occupied Palestinian Territory* (Advisory Opinion) [2004] ICJ Rep 136.

[30] ILC, Report of the International Law Commission Seventy-first session, Annex.

[31] Regulation (EU) 1169/2011 of the European Parliament and of the Council of 25 October 2011 on the provision of food information to consumers, amending Regulations (EC) No 1924/2006 and (EC) No 1925/2006 of the European Parliament and of the Council, and repealing Commission Directive 87/250/EEC, Council Directive 90/496/EEC, Commission Directive 1999/10/EC, Directive 2000/13/EC of the European Parliament and of the Council, Commission Directives 2002/67/EC and 2008/5/EC and Commission Regulation (EC) No 608/2004 [2011] OJ L304/18 (FICR), arts 26(2)(a) and 9(1)(1). Several additional provisions also exist which provide indication of country of origin requirements for specific types of food products. For an overview, see footnote 6 of Interpretative Notice on indication of origin of goods from the territories occupied by Israel since June 1967 [2015] OJ C375/4.

[32] Case C-363/18 *Organisation juive européenne and Vignoble Psagot* EU:C:2019:954, para 51.

[33] Case C-363/18 *Organisation juive européenne, Vignoble Psagot Ltd v Ministre de l'Économie et des Finances* EU:C:2019:494, Opinion of Advocate General, para 46.

[34] *Legal Consequences of the Construction of a Wall in the Occupied Palestinian Territory (Advisory Opinion)*, para 54.

[35] ibid, para 55.

[36] ibid, para 56.

Accordingly, EU food law needs to be interpreted against the background of the EU's obligation to comply with international commitments, in particular with *ius cogens* obligations, which facilitate the effective implementation of fundamental rules of international law.[37]

18.3.2 The Human Right to Food

Nowadays, the right to food is enshrined at international, regional, and national levels. Historically, the UN has played a pivotal role in championing the legal recognition of the right to food.[38]

The UN Universal Declaration of Human Rights of 1948 enshrines the right to food as part of the right to an adequate standard of living:

> Everyone has the right to a standard of living adequate for the health and well-being of himself and of his family, including food, clothing, housing and medical care and necessary social services, and the right to security in the event of unemployment, sickness, disability, widowhood, old age or other lack of livelihood in circumstances beyond his control.[39]

The Universal Declaration of Human Rights is not legally binding, although by now many of its provisions have been codified in other agreements, and generally at least some parts of the Declaration are regarded to be customary international law.

Among the numerous non-binding instruments of relevance for the right to food, the UN International Covenant on Economic, Social and Cultural Rights (ICESCR) of 1966 stands out, as it is a binding treaty. Article 11 of the Convention recognizes that the right to an adequate standard of living encompasses adequate food (Article 11.1), and also recognizes the right to be free from hunger (Article 11.2). Despite being a relatively 'old' right, it has been observed that 'efforts to develop and clarify its content are relatively recent'.[40] The Committee on Economic, Social and Cultural Rights (CESCR) further adopted General Comment No 12 'The Right to Adequate Food' only in 1999. While late, the document makes far-reaching interpretations of the right to food. 'The right to adequate food is realised when every man, woman and child, alone or in community with others, have

[37] Kai Purnhagen and others, 'Beyond Food Safety—EU Food Information Standards as a Facilitator of Political Consumerism and International Law Enforcement Mechanism' (2020) 45 European Law Review 553.

[38] Jarosław Kowalski and Aleksandra Kowalska, 'The Realization of the Human Right to Food: Preliminary Remarks on Assessing Food Security' (2022) 1 Przegląd Prawno-Ekonomiczny 9.

[39] Universal Declaration of Human Rights, UNGA Res 217 A (III) (10 December 1948), art 25.

[40] Christian Courtis, 'The Right to Food as a Justiciable Right: Challenges and Strategies' (2007) 11 Max Planck UNYB 317.

physical and economic access at all times to adequate food or means for its procurement. The right to adequate food shall therefore not be interpreted in a narrow or restrictive sense which equates it with a minimum package of calories, proteins and other specific nutrients.' It defined the core content of the right to food as: 'The availability of food in a quantity and quality sufficient to satisfy the dietary needs of individuals, free from adverse substances, and acceptable within a given culture; The accessibility of such food in ways that are sustainable and that do not interfere with the enjoyment of other human rights.'[41] The General Comment understood the normative content of the right to adequate food as covering the adequacy and sustainability of food availability and access, a progressive interpretation as it establishes an early link between the right to adequate food and sustainability. Later, in 2004, the FAO Council also adopted the first governmentally agreed document, namely the Voluntary Guidelines to support the Progressive Realization of the Right to Food, abbreviated to the Right to Food Guidelines.[42] These were recommendations for activities that governments should ideally undertake to safeguard the right to food. Finally, with the 2009 Optional Protocol to the International Covenant on Economic, Social and Cultural Rights, the right to food became justiciable at the international level, by allowing victims of violations of economic, social, and cultural rights to lodge complaints directly with the Human Rights Committee.[43]

In addition to protection at the UN level, the right to food can also be protected at the domestic level. However, the protection of the right to food at regional and national levels varies significantly. For instance, the right to food was recognized in 1988 through the Adoption of the right to food in the Additional Protocol to the American Convention on Human Rights in the area of Economic, Social, and Cultural Rights (the 'Protocol of San Salvador').[44] In contrast, the EU Charter of Fundamental Rights does not recognize the right to food, although food cases have been adjudicated with reference to human health protection, which is protected in the Charter.[45] At national level, some—but certainly not all—national constitutions enshrine the right to food explicitly, making it questionable whether it would qualify as a joint or common constitutional tradition of the Member States.

From the EU perspective, a rights-based treatment of food using a human right to food approach is hardly referenced at all in EU food law and policy making, and

[41] CESCR, 'General Comment No. 12' in 'The Right to Adequate Food (Art. 11) Adopted at the Twentieth Session of the Committee on Economic Social and Cultural Rights (12 May 1999) UN Doc E/C.12/1999/5.

[42] FAO/WHO, Voluntary Guidelines to support the progressive realization of the right to adequate food in the context of national food security (2004).

[43] UNGA 'Optional Protocol to the International Covenant on Economic, Social and Cultural Rights' (5 March 2009) UN Doc A/RES/63/117.

[44] OAS 'Additional Protocol to the American Convention on Human Rights in the Area of Economic, Social and Cultural Rights' (Protocol of San Salvador) (16 November 1999).

[45] Charter of Fundamental Rights of the European Union [2012] OJ C326/391, art. 35; Case C-544/10 *Deutsches Weintor eG v Land Rheinland-Pfalz* EU:C:2012:526 (*Weintor*).

is therefore inadequately accounted for. In practical terms, the SDGs have proven more influential than human rights-based approaches in EU food regulation.

18.3.3 FAO and WHO

The EU is a member of the FAO with voting rights to be coordinated with its Member States organized in accordance with the EU's competence regimes.[46] The EU is subject to several international arrangements approved by the FAO[47] and administered under the FAO's involvement. An example is the International Treaty on Plant Genetic Resources for Food and Agriculture, which aims to ensure the conservation and sustainable use of all plant genetic resources for food and agriculture, and devises mechanisms for the fair and equitable sharing of the benefits arising out of their use.[48]

The EU is not a member of the WHO, but has established a relationship of enhanced cooperation with the organization on the basis of an exchange of letters in 2001[49] and a document exchanged between the Commission and the WHO regional office.[50]

In the area of foods, the FAO and the WHO jointly collaborate in several institutions and projects. In terms of influence on food law, the most important institution is probably the Codex Alimentarius Commission (see section 18.3.4). The WHO and the FAO have also collaborated in the development of a number of soft laws, such as the FAO model food law,[51] the FAO/WHO's guidance to develop food law,[52] and the intellectual work behind these.[53]

18.3.4 International standards: Codex Code and the Codex Alimentarius Commission

International standards play a crucial role in governing the food sector. Three international intergovernmental food-related standards are 'primus inter pares'—they

[46] See Case C-25/94 *Commission v Council (FAO)* [1996] ECR I-1469.
[47] According to the Constitution of the food and agriculture organization of the United Nations (adopted 16 October 1945), art XIV.
[48] International Treaty on plant genetic resources for food and agriculture (adopted 3 November 2001, entered into force 29 June 2004) UNTS 2400.
[49] Exchange of letters between the World Health Organization and the Commission of the European Communities concerning the consolidation and intensification of cooperation [2001] OJ C 1/07.
[50] The objectives, principles, and modalities for continued cooperation between the European Commission and the WHO Regional Office for Europe (2015), available at <https://health.ec.europa.eu/system/files/2020-11/2020_who_euro_cooperation_en_0.pdf> accessed 11 August 2022.
[51] FAO Model Food Law (n 23).
[52] Guidelines for Strengthening National Food Control Systems (n 24).
[53] FAO Model Food Law (n 23).

are the CAC for food, the World Organization for Animal Health (WOAH, formerly OIE) for animals, and the International Plant Protection Convention (IPPC) for plant health. These international standards are recognized by the WTO, and although non-binding, compliance with them ensures a presumption of WTO law compliance (see section 18.4).

The CAC[54] had been established by the FAO in 1961 as part of the joint FAO/WHO International Food Standards Programme with a view to protecting consumers and producers in all countries (effectively reducing trade barriers), to simplify and integrate international food standards efforts (to avoid duplication and conflicting standards), and to effect economies in effort and expenditure. To achieve these aims, the main purpose of the CAC was identified as harmonizing the special requirements of regional markets with those of international food trade in general. To this end, an institutional structure has been established which comprises the Commission, the Executive Committee, and subsidiary bodies.

The CAC is an international organization, to be precise, it is an intergovernmental standard setting body with almost global membership. It develops and updates the standards in the Codex Alimentarius, a collection of international food standards. These standards cover foods at all stages of production, including processed, semi-processed, and raw. To achieve the objectives of the Codex, its scope of application is also extended to the materials used in the further processing of food products and the hygienic and nutritional quality of food, including microbiological norms, food additives, pesticides and veterinary drug residues, contaminants, labelling and presentation, and methods of sampling and risk analysis. The Codex contains general (horizontal) standards, for instance on labelling, food hygiene, additives, and pesticides, as well as food commodity specific (vertical) standards, for instance on cheese, meat, fish, and many others. In terms of documents, the Codex establishes food standards, guidelines, codes of practice, maximum residue levels, and other texts. These will be based on the principle of sound scientific analysis.[55]

The procedures for preparing standards can be outlined in the following steps: (1) proposal for a standard by a national government or subsidiary committee; (2) discussion paper; (3) decision to develop a standard; (4) preparation of a draft; (5) several iterations of comments; and (6) adoption. On adoption, a Codex standard is added to the Codex Alimentarius.[56]

The Codex works through committees, which include general committees on broad topics such as contaminants, food additives, food hygiene, food import and export inspection and certification systems, food labelling, general principles,

[54] Marielle Matthee, 'The Codex Alimentarius Commission and its standards' (Doctoral Thesis, Maastricht University 2006).

[55] FAO/WHO, *Codex Alimentarius Commission Procedural Manual* (2023).

[56] FAO/WHO, *Understanding the Codex Alimentarius, Food and Agriculture Organization of the United Nations, World Health Organization* (2018).

methods of analysis and sampling, nutrition and foods for special dietary uses, pesticide residues, and residues of veterinary drugs in foods. These are complemented by technical and commodity committees.

The CAC is very dedicated to the principles of scientific risk assessment, and develops its recommendations on the basis of the FAO/WHO scientific expert bodies. The expert bodies that support the scientific risk assessment are the Joint FAO/WHO Expert Committee on Food Additives (JECFA), the Joint FAO/WHO Meetings on Pesticide Residues (JMPR), the Joint FAO/WHO Expert Meetings on Microbiological Risk Assessment (JEMRA), the Joint FAO/WHO Expert Meetings on Pesticide Specifications (JMPS), and the Joint FAO/WHO Expert Meeting on Nutrition (JEMNU). Codex can also receive expert advice from ad hoc and external bodies, such as the WHO Nutrition Guidance Expert Advisory Group (NUGAG). The main principle that risk assessors should be separated from risk managers to the greatest practicable degree is enshrined in the Codex Working Principles for Risk Analysis for Application in the framework of the Codex Alimentarius.[57]

However, the WTO recognition had an important disruptive effect on the consensus culture within the Codex. It politicized its work and made compromise more difficult.[58] Technically, the CAC operates on the basis of formal decision rule within the Codex known as 'one country, one vote'.[59] Normally, votes are taken by a simple majority of votes cast by attending members, allowing them to set standards. The Codex rules of procedure were modified in order to strengthen the facilitation of consensus,[60] emphasizing that 'the Commission shall make every effort to reach agreement on the adoption or amendment of standards by consensus'.[61] Despite predictions to the contrary, in practice, consensus seems to prevail and there are relatively few instances of decisions taken by vote.

Membership of the FAO enables the EU to become a full member of the CAC.[62] The EU has been a full member of the CAC since 2003,[63] in addition to each of its Member States. To coordinate the *sui generis* character of the EU and its special relationship to its Member States, Annex II of Council Decision 2003/822/EC stipulates that voting rights as determined in Rule VI of the Rules of Procedure of

[57] Bernd van der Meulen, 'Impact of the Codex Alimentarius' (2019) 14 European Food and Feed Law Review 29.

[58] David E Winickoff and Douglas M Bushey, 'Science and Power in Global Food Regulation: The Rise of the Codex Alimentarius' (2010) 35 Science, Technology, & Human Values 356.

[59] *Codex Alimentarius Commission Procedural Manual* (n 56) Section 1, Rule VIII.

[60] ibid.

[61] ibid, Section 1, Rule XII.

[62] The CAC was established as a joint commission on the basis of Article VI.1 of the FAO Constitution (11th FAO Conference Resolution No. 12/61, 1961) and under Article 18 of the WHO Constitution (the 16th World Health Assembly Resolution WHA16.42, 1963). See FAO/WHO, *Statutes of the CAC* (2004) (n 55) art 2.

[63] Council Decision of 17 November 2003 on the accession of the European Community to the Codex Alimentarius Commission [2003] OJ L 309/14.

the CAC are to be exercised as a matter of principle in accordance with the competence regimes laid out in the Treaties the EU is based upon.[64] If these change, then the voting rights will change accordingly. In certain areas of competence, the EU has been explicitly granted competence to vote on agenda items in the CAC. These include items related to the harmonization of standards on certain agricultural products, foodstuffs, food additives, contaminants, veterinary drugs, pesticides, fish and fishery products, including labelling, methods of analysis and sampling, as well as codes and guidelines of hygiene practice, insofar as the Union legislation has harmonized either completely or to a large extent in the relevant fields within these areas. They also include issues of international trade to the extent that they relate to the objectives of the CAC, notably protecting the health of the consumers and ensuring fair practices in the food trade.[65] In turn, Member States were provided with explicit competence to vote on agenda items concerning organizational matters (eg legal or budgetary issues) and procedural issues (eg election of chairpersons, adoption of the agenda, and adoption of reports).[66]

Codex standards, guidelines, and codes of practice are legally non-binding. However, WTO law attaches preferable legal treatment to countries who comply with Codex Standards under the SPS and TBT Agreements. A recent example of Codex work is the global standards on food safety. In addition, in February 2022, the Council approved conclusions on food safety standards in international trade, calling for greater integration of sustainability concerns in the work of the CAC.

In the EU, the GFLR requires that international standards are 'taken into consideration in the development or adaptation of food law'.[67] The drafters of EU food law were aware of the risk that policy choices were being determined by Codex standards, potentially to the detriment of EU interests, and they took measures to shield EU food law from that risk: these standards shall not be taken into consideration 'where such standards or relevant parts would be an ineffective or inappropriate means for the fulfilment of the legitimate objectives of food law or where there is a scientific justification, or where they would result in a different level of protection from the one determined as appropriate in the Community'.[68] At the same time, the GFLR imposes a constructive EU approach towards international standards, requiring contribution to standards, coordination of work, promotion of recognitions of equivalence, consideration of the impact of international standards on developing countries, and the promotion of consistency between international standards and food law (while ensuring that the high level of protection in the Community is not compromised).[69]

[64] ibid, Annex II No 3.
[65] ibid, Annex II No 1.
[66] ibid, Annex II No 2.
[67] GFLR, art 5(3).
[68] ibid.
[69] ibid, art 13.

On the other hand, the Codex has a significant effect on EU law, both indirectly through its recognition in WTO law and also directly. For example, some regulations reference the Codex expressly, such as for setting maximum residue levels.[70] Other EU laws clearly echo or even replicate Codex provisions, and a 'considerable alignment' has been shown in terms of applicable definitions, the risk analysis architecture, and the substantive content of many regulations such as maximum residue levels.[71]

There is some, but not an abundance,[72] of Court of Justice of the European Union (CJEU) jurisprudence referring to Codex in a loose way, but the Court typically appears to respect that Codex documents are not directly binding, and largely uses them as referencing standards (unless they are granted effect through reference in EU legislation). The Codex can be relevant in assessing whether a name is defined as generic in trademark applications.[73] In the case law, it is widely recognized that the Codex Alimentarius is intended to provide guidance on defining the characteristics of certain foodstuffs; however, this guidance appears to serve as more of an orientation for the court than imposing strictly binding requirements.[74] For instance, in determining whether an additive is necessary, the principle of proportionality considers the results of international scientific research, in particular the work of the Scientific Committee for Food and of the Codex Alimentarius Committee of the FAO.[75]

Nevertheless, under the logic of EU law, the Codex is not binding, unless made so by a direct reference in secondary legislation. This was confirmed in a case on the reduction of disease risk claims under the Nutrition and Health Claim Regulation, where the CJEU argued that although Recital (7) of the Regulation references the Codex Guidelines for the use of nutrition and health claims—indicating that the legislature considered Codex definitions and conditions when formulating the

[70] Regulation (EC) 396/2005 of the European Parliament and of the Council of 23 February 2005 on maximum residue levels of pesticides in or on food and feed of plant and animal origin and amending Council Directive 91/414/EEC [2005] OJ L70/1, art 14(2)(e); even more explicitly and binding in Regulation (EC) No 470/2009 of the European Parliament and of the Council of 6 May 2009 laying down Community procedures for the establishment of residue limits of pharmacologically active substances in foodstuffs of animal origin, repealing Council Regulation (EEC) No 2377/90 and amending Directive 2001/82/EC of the European Parliament and of the Council and Regulation (EC) No 726/2004 of the European Parliament and of the Council [2009] OJ L152/11, art 14(3)(b).

[71] Van der Meulen (n 57).

[72] There are 23 judgments on Eur-Lex referencing 'Codex Alimentarius'.

[73] Case T-2/21 *Emmentaler Switzerland v European Union Intellectual Property Office* EU:T:2023:278; Case T-291/03 *Consorzio per la tutela del formaggio Grana Padano v European Union Intellectual Property Office* [2007] ECR II-3081.

[74] The classic court case is Case 286/86 *Ministère public v Gérard Deserbais* [1988] ECR 4907, para 15, which is still regularly cited; also Case C-448/98 *Criminal proceedings against Jean-Pierre Guimont* [2000] ECR I-10663.

[75] The classic case of reference here is the judgment in Case 174/82 *Criminal proceedings against Sandoz BV* [1983] ECR 2445; but also Case C-121/00 *Criminal proceedings against Walter Hahn* [2002] ECR I-9193.

Regulation—the legislature created its own definition, and therefore arguments based on the Codex were not relevant.[76]

18.4 WTO law and food

A large number of trade disputes brought before the WTO concern trade in foods,[77] and WTO law constitutes the legally most significant constraint to national and regional food law making. The WTO framework is trade oriented, and the provision of food safety and/or food quality, and the regulations of wider concerns beyond food safety—such as sustainability—were never a major objective in WTO law.[78] The WTO is primarily a rules-based settlement system for disputes between members. The fundamental objective of the dispute settlement system is to establish trade based on non-justifiable discrimination of trading partners as the norm.[79] In the context of global food trade, however, the WTO has been described in the literature as the major de facto international regulator.[80]

Numerous cases have successfully challenged EU food regulation in front of the WTO dispute settlement mechanism.[81] These are well-known cases, such as *EC-Bananas*,[82] also known as the banana war, which concerned the EU's preferential market for bananas from the African, Caribbean, and Pacific (ACP) countries and which was found to be illegal in 1997. The Commission proposed changes to legislation.[83] *EC-Hormones*[84] concerned an EU prohibition on the marketing of meat and meat products treated with certain hormones; it was also held to be illegal under WTO law, and the dispute was later ended through a bilateral agreement

[76] Case T-17/12 *Moritz Hagenmeyer and Andreas Hahn v European Commission* EU:T:2014:234, paras 82–83.

[77] Around 30% of the disputes initiated since the WTO's inception in 1995 involved food; see Marco Bronckers and Ravi Soopramanien, 'The Impact of WTO Law on European Food Regulation' (2008) 3 European Food and Feed Law Review 361. This number dates from 2008, but food remains a significant topic in WTO litigation

[78] Huei-chih Niu, 'A Comparative Perspective on the International Health Regulations and the World Trade Organization's Agreement on the Application of Sanitary and Phytosanitary Measures' (2006) 1 Asian Journal of WTO & International Health Land and Policy 513, 515.

[79] See Kai Purnhagen and Bernd van der Meulen, 'Consumer Protection Legislation' in Benjamin Caballero, Paul Finglas, and Fidel Toldrá (eds), *Encyclopedia of Food and Health* (Academic Press 2016) 296.

[80] Alessandra Arcuri, 'The Coproduction of the Global Regulatory Regime for Food Safety Standards and the Limits of a Technocratic Ethos' (2014) Robert Schuman Ctr for Advanced Studies, Paper No 97; Winickoff and Bushey (n 58).

[81] Chris Downes, *The Impact of WTO SPS Law on EU Food Regulations* (Springer 2014).

[82] WTO, *European Communities—Regime for the Importation, Sale and Distribution of Bananas* (8 November 2012) (WT/DS27).

[83] Commission, 'The banana case: Background and history' (Brussels, 11 April 2001) <https://ec.europa.eu/dorie/fileDownload.do;jsessionid=V1wJqrq8peM7gMomm_mDkqHnNFKXvwnLyjABU -82cdCXZ9-L9Iyo!-898031139?docId=391247 &cardId=391247> accessed 11 August 2022.

[84] WTO, *European Communities—Measures Concerning Meat and Meat Products (Hormones)* (25 September 2009) (WT/DS26).

for a mutually acceptable solution on implementation. The EU also lost in front of the WTO in the dispute *EC-GMO*[85] on the alleged de facto moratorium on approvals for biotech products; the case gained significant attention due to the contentious nature of GMO governance. While the EU will not always modify its domestic legislation in line with the WTO rulings, the WTO rules certainly serve as a boundary of legality that EU law makers strive to adhere to.

18.4.1 The relationship between WTO food law and EU food law

The EU and each of its Member States are members of the WTO. To avoid preferential treatment of the EU and its Member States, WTO law stipulates that, when the EU exercises its right to vote, it has an equal number of votes as the number of its Member States who are also members of the WTO.[86] As a general rule, the EU speaks and votes for its Member States even in areas where it does not have exclusive competence. Member States are only allowed to speak and vote individually on budgetary and organizational matters.

The EU is bound by the (former) GATT Treaty and the WTO agreements, however, the rules in the Treaty—due to their reciprocal, flexible, and open-ended character—do not enjoy direct effect in the EU legal order.[87] Consequently, the Union has, in principle, no obligation to compensate damages sustained from a breach of WTO law.[88] However, insofar as the Union intends to implement WTO obligations into its law,[89] or refers directly to the WTO agreement,[90] EU institutions are bound to these provisions of WTO law. Likewise, WTO law can serve as a source of inspiration for the CJEU when interpreting EU provisions either expressly,[91] in light of WTO law, or aligning interpretations with decisions of the WTO appellate body.[92]

[85] WTO, *European Communities—Measures Affecting the Approval and Marketing of Biotech Products* (WT/DS291; WT/DS292; WT/DS293).

[86] Agreement Establishing the World Trade Organization (Marrakesh Agreement) (adopted 15 April 1994, entered into force 1 January 1995) 1867 UNTS 154, 33 ILM 1144, art IX(1).

[87] On GATT, see *International Fruit Company* (n 12) paras 4–6; On WTO agreements, see Case C-149/96 *Portugal v Council* [1999] ECR I-8395.

[88] *FIAMM* (n 16).

[89] Case C-69/89 *Nakajima All Precision Co. Ltd v Council* [1991] ECR I-2069.

[90] *FIAMM* (n 16) para 112.

[91] Case C-83/94 *Criminal proceedings against Peter Leifer, Reinhold Otto Krauskopf and Otto Holzer* [1995] ECR I-3231, para 24.

[92] Marco Bronckers, 'Private Appeals to WTO LAW: An Update' (2008) 42 Journal of World Trade 245.

18.4.2 WTO food law under the GATT

The GATT governs international trade in goods. Article XX GATT provides for the right of WTO members to adopt measures for non-trade purposes, provided that the measure is adopted for one of the legitimate objectives listed and complies with the general conditions of the Article.[93] Article XX(b) GATT[94] provides general exceptions for members to justify the adoption of measures 'necessary to protect human, animal or plant life or health', and Article XX(j) GATT allows for measures 'essential to the acquisition or distribution of products in general or local short supply'. The decision as to when such a level is acceptable according to WTO law involves a regulatory element, effectively resulting in de facto regulation of food health and safety at the WTO level. To prevent leaving this significant decision solely to the discretion of members and the WTO dispute settlement body, the WTO Agreement on the Application of Sanitary and Phytosanitary Measures[95] provides more defined criteria determining the standards against which such measures may be justified.

18.4.3 WTO food law in the SPS Agreement

The SPS Agreement is applicable to the majority of food trade related measures. The SPS Agreement covers only national measures with the purpose of protecting (1) human or animal life risks arising from additives, contaminants, toxins, or disease-causing organisms in their food, beverages, and feedstuffs (contaminants include pesticide and veterinary drug residues and extraneous matter); (2) human health from animal- or plant-carried diseases; (3) animals and plants from pests or diseases; and (4) the territory of a country from other damage caused by the entry or spread of pests.[96]

According to WTO law, any national SPS measure influencing food trade needs to be preceded by a determination of the appropriate level of protection (ALOP) the member aims to pursue.[97] Paragraph 5 of Annex A of the SPS Agreement defines ALOP as 'the level of protection deemed appropriate by the Member establishing a sanitary or phytosanitary measure to protect human, animal or

[93] Lorand Bartels, 'The Chapeau of the General Exceptions in the WTO GATT and GATS Agreements: A Reconstruction' (2015) 109 American Journal of International Law 95.

[94] General Agreement on Tariffs and Trade (GATT), art XX(b), Agreement Establishing the World Trade Organization (Marrakesh Agreement) (adopted 15 April 1994, entered into force 1 January 1995) 1867 UNTS 154, 33 ILM 1144.

[95] Agreement on the Application of Sanitary and Phytosanitary Measures (adopted 15 April 1994, entered into force 1 January 1995) 1867 UNTS 493 (SPS Agreement).

[96] ibid, Annex A.

[97] WTO, *Australia-Measures Affecting Importation of Salmon—AB-1998-5—Report of the Appellate Body* (20 October 1998) WT/DS18/AB/R.

plant life or health within its territory'. The measures taken at national level, for example the stipulation of maximum residue levels, are then characterized as 'SPS measures'. SPS law obliges members to determine their ALOP *ex ante* of subsequent SPS measures.[98] Implicitly, members therefore have a duty to determine the ALOP.[99] To accommodate the socio-economic differences among its members, the standards against which the ALOP is set is left to the discretion of individual members.[100] Members need to exercise this discretion in a way that ensures the ALOP is established with the aim of minimizing negative trade effects.[101] This means, for example, that a Member must avoid arbitrary or unjustifiable differences in the levels it considers to be appropriate in different situations.[102] While the ALOP can be expressed in general, non-quantifiable terms, the WTO panel has stipulated that 'a more explicit and in particular a quantitative expression of a Member's ALOP would greatly facilitate the consideration of compliance with the SPS Agreement'.[103] While this poses challenges to developing countries,[104] economically developed regions such as the EU usually express their ALOPs with a view to implementing the concept of Food Safety Objective (FSO) as determined by food safety science.[105] Consequently, the EU, in particular, is known to have the highest ALOP in food trade compared to other countries.

A member's SPS measure is only in compliance with WTO law when it is appropriate to achieve the ALOP with the tools SPS law provides. As a general rule, the SPS Agreement stipulates a preference for the harmonization of measures among WTO members.[106] Consequently, the level of harmonization is preferably determined outside of WTO law by international standards, guidelines, or recommendations, where they exist.[107] The Annex further defines that in the area of food trade this provision refers primarily to 'the standards, guidelines and recommendations established by the CAC relating to food additives, veterinary drug and pesticide residues, contaminants, methods of analysis and sampling,

[98] ibid.
[99] ibid.
[100] WTO, *European Communities—EC Measures Concerning Meat and Meat Products (Hormones)—Report of the Appellate Body* (16 January 1998) WT/DS26/AB/R and WT/DS48/AB/R; Emily Reid, 'Risk Assessment, Science and Deliberation: Managing Regulatory Diversity under the SPS Agreement?' (2012) 3 European Journal of Risk Regulation 535; Michael Ming Du, 'Autonomy in Setting Appropriate Level of Protection under the WTO law: Rhetoric or Reality?' (2010) 13 Journal of International Economic Law 1077.
[101] SPS Agreement, art 5.4.
[102] ibid, art 5.5.
[103] WTO, *Australia—Measures Affecting Importation of Salmon-Recourse to Article 21.5 by Canada—Report of the Panel (Australia—Salmon 21.5)* (18 February 2000) WT/DS18/RW, para 7.129.
[104] Dasep Wahidin and Kai Purnhagen, 'Determining a Science-based Food Safety Objective/Appropriate Level of Protection for Application in Developing Countries' (2017) 8 European Journal of Risk Regulation 403.
[105] Casper de Swarte and Robert Donker, 'Towards an FSO/ALOP Based Food Safety Policy' (2005) 19 Food Control 825.
[106] SPS Agreement, art 3.1.
[107] ibid.

and codes and guidelines of hygienic practice'.[108] If measures of a member conform to these international standards, guidelines, or recommendations, they are deemed to be necessary within the meaning of Article XX(b) SPS Agreement.[109] Since the CAC was named as an organization capable of establishing international standards for food safety in the SPS Agreement, it has gained considerable legal authority in WTO law.[110] National legislators now 'have an incentive to bring Codex standards more closely in line with domestic policy goals since the negative domestic consequences of adopting an international standard are least when the divergence between the international standard and the optimal domestic regulation are smallest'.[111] It had been observed that consequently, Codex standards now have the potential to 'act to restrict and structure the policy choices of states'.[112]

18.4.4 WTO food law in the TBT Agreement

In addition to the SPS Agreement, the TBT Agreement can also be relevant to food regulation. The TBT Agreement aims to ensure that technical regulations, standards, and conformity assessment procedures are non-discriminatory and do not create unnecessary obstacles to trade. WTO members retain the right to adopt national measures to achieve legitimate policy objectives, such as the protection of human health and safety, the protection of the environment, or promoting consumer interests. Food labelling requirements, food packaging, nutrition claims, and food quality are typically not considered to be SPS measures and are therefore subject to the TBT Agreement. The issue of mandatory nutrition labelling and nutrition warnings have been particularly contentious within the WTO TBT Committee.

The TBT Agreement states that members will use relevant international standards as the basis for their own technical regulations.[113] However, unlike the SPS Agreement, the TBT Agreement does not specify the international standard-setting

[108] ibid, Annex A 3 a.

[109] ibid, art 3.2.

[110] See Michael A Livermore, 'Authority and Legitimacy in Global Governance: Deliberation, Institutional Differentiation, and the Codex Alimentarius' (2006) 81 New York University Law Review 766, 774; see also Ravi Afonso Pereira, 'Why Would International Administrative Activity Be Any Less Legitimate?—A Study of the Codex Alimentarius Commission' (2008) 9 German Law Journal 1693, 1703; Winickoff and Bushey (n 58); Grace Skogstad, 'The WTO and Food Safety Regulatory Policy Innovation in the European Union' (2001) 39 Journal of Common Market Studies 485, 495–496; Codex Alimentarium Commission, 'About Codex' <http://www.codexalimentarius.org/about-codex/en/> accessed 11 August 2022.

[111] Livermore (n 110).

[112] ibid.

[113] Agreement on Technical Barriers to Trade (adopted on 15 April 1995, entered into force 1 January 1995) 1868 UNTS 120 (TBT Agreement), art 2.4.

bodies whose standards are recognized, although it is generally acknowledged that at least the three international bodies mentioned in the SPS Agreement qualify.

In practice, in addition to the SPS Agreement, the TBT Agreement remains relevant in framing the policy space left to Member States for regulating in the food domain within the confines of international trade law.

18.4.5 The WTO Business Regulation

The EU has passed a law that facilitates the enforcement of international trade law. The Trade Barriers Regulation (TBR)[114] establishes Union procedures whereby any EU individuals, companies, associations, or EU countries claiming to have suffered injury or adverse trade effects due to trade obstacles can submit a complaint to the Commission. The objective of the TBR is to address obstacles to trade that impact the Union's market, with a view to mitigating the resulting injury. Additionally, it aims to address obstacles to trade that have an effect on the market of a third country, with a view to alleviating the adverse trade effects resulting from such obstacles. For this purpose, the TBR establishes procedures to enable EU industry, enterprises, and countries to request the Commission to examine alleged trade barriers put in place by non-EU countries that contravene international trade rules.

One of the challenges of international law is its justiciability or enforceability by private individuals. With the TBR, EU law provides a remedy that is open not only to EU Member States but also to private parties, such as trade associations or enterprises, to enable them to enforce international trade law obligations.

18.5 Discussion

In the arena of international law, two main influences on food regulation can be distinguished, international law under the auspices of the UN, on the one hand, and international trade law, especially WTO law, but increasingly free trade agreements, on the other hand. Within these, three main spheres of food law emerge: namely, the right to food, intergovernmental global standards, and international trade law.

A number of international law instruments of relevance to food were created under the auspices of the UN and related bodies and agencies (such as FAO

[114] Regulation (EU) 2015/1843 of the European Parliament and of the Council of 6 October 2015 laying down Union procedures in the field of the common commercial policy in order to ensure the exercise of the Union's rights under international trade rules, in particular those established under the auspices of the World Trade Organization [2015] OJ L272/1.

and WHO). These are often non-binding in nature. A notable exception is the International Covenant on Economic, Social and Cultural Rights (ICESCR), which is a binding treaty that recognizes the right to adequate food. Whereas from a legal perspective human rights-based approaches are proliferating, the right to food has received little legal and political recognition in EU food law and policy. In practical terms, the SDGs have had a much stronger impact on food policy implications in the EU through the Green Deal.

On the other hand, international trade law, and specifically WTO law, imposes quite a significant restriction on food regulation, including with respect to sustainability requirements. The free trade paradigm conflicts with measures that make the food system more sustainable, which can be regarded as barriers to trade. Increasingly, the predominant role of the WTO is being complemented by regional free trade agreements, which undermine the hegemony of the WTO law trading system. Along this trajectory, there may also be new opportunities for incorporating sustainability aspects into food law within free trade agreements, and even in forging connections between the right to food and international economic law.[115]

International law, therefore, can lead to both opportunities and barriers to the regulation of (sustainable) food at national and EU levels. Interestingly, to date there have only been a few tangible efforts aimed at establishing a global food law, which is why it may be warranted to characterize global international food law an 'emerging area of law'.[116]

[115] Giovanni Gruni, *The EU, World Trade Law and the right to Food: Rethinking Free Trade Agreements with Developing Countries* (Bloomsbury Publishing 2018).

[116] Michael Roberts, 'Understanding Modern History of International Food Law Is Key to Building a More Resilient and Improved Global Food System' (2021) 17 Journal of Food Law & Policy 56.

Future of Food Law—Conclusions and Outlook

In the introduction of this book, we argued that European Union (EU) food law is a mirror of our society, and that better understanding how EU law currently shapes our food system helps us to better understand EU society.

In this concluding chapter, we synthesize the main findings of the book across its different parts, and outline the main challenges that EU food law will face in shaping the future of food law. It is, however, the EU legislative system, and therefore ultimately the EU population and society, that will decide which EU food laws to adopt, and which path to pursue for the future.

Part I—European integration and food law

This book explores the correlation between the legal framework of European integration and the European Union with the development and gradual crystallization of EU food law, first as a policy sector, and later as a regulative domain. It emphasizes the role of the EU Treaties as structural constraints and facilitators that shape the scope of possibilities for EU food law making. EU food law is thereby placed in the wider context of general EU institutional law and the originally Treaty-based development of law on food through the internal market provisions contained therein.

Agriculture and food internal market law—the great divide

In explaining why EU food law is the way it is, we outlined the influence of four main political paradigms; agriculture, the completion of the internal market, food safety, and most recently sustainability. Two of the original objectives of European integration were already enshrined in the founding Treaties; these were the Common Agricultural Policy (CAP) and the internal market. At the inception of European integration, the Treaty provisions enshrined the Common Agricultural Policy and the establishment of the Common Market as parallel tracks. Initially, these were used conjointly; however, the establishment of a separate internal market competence resulted in an ever-stronger separation of these two areas. These tracks

EU Food Law. Hanna Schebesta and Kai Purnhagen, Oxford University Press.
DOI: 10.1093/9780198901570.003.0020

follow different legal systemic rules, and over time, their provisions have given rise to largely separate silos of harmonizing regulation for agriculture on one hand and food as a trade commodity in the internal market on the other hand. With the recent renationalization and opening up of the CAP to general internal market rules, and the simultaneous opening up of EU food law to areas traditionally reserved to the CAP, it is getting increasingly difficult to align and reconcile these two domains. This separation is not only enshrined in the legal frameworks, but has also manifested in the institutional arrangements within the European Parliament, European Commission, and to some extent European Council constellations.

All EU efforts for creating a unified and integrated food system approach, to this day, face this great divide. The call for a holistic food system approach, notably emphasized at the level of the United Nations (UN) and echoed in the European Union's Farm to Fork Strategy, is therefore notoriously difficult to implement in the EU legal context. Agriculture and food are—by virtue of their distinct legal bases in the EU 'constitutional' foundation—inherently separate realms of law.

Regulating the agri-food domain—a domain-based approach

EU Food law has developed in an organic way. In the absence of any special competence norm in the Treaties, it has travelled between the policy areas of agriculture, internal market, health, environment, competition law, and consumer law. As food holds unique characteristics compared to other tradable goods, these competence norms are also often exercised in a food-specific way. We observe that overarching EU legal frameworks, such as consumer protection and information rights, had to find specific expression in the food domain. A case in point is the many food-specific information rights for consumers or, in the area of competition law, the specific unfair trading practices within the food domain. Even the precautionary principle has found specific expression in the General Food Law, largely deviating from the general application of the principle. We also identify areas where such domain specific regulation has not yet occurred, notably in the realm of product liability. Here, the food domain typically presents with characteristics that are not effectively addressed by existing liability requirements, therefore depriving liability of its risk regulatory function. This development opens up the question as to whether it is time to consider a specific competence norm for the area of food, which is able to deal with the respective domain-specific competence areas and the requirements of the sector.

Nowadays, given the vision to regulate the food system holistically, the spread of EU food law over different policy areas is problematic. Due to the absence of a dedicated food competence in the Treaty, food law is based on an amalgam of different legal bases, and often has to be phrased in terms that allow harmonization for internal market purposes. The application of different competence regimes in isolation results in fragmentation and competence gaps.

The policy fragmentation, and particularly the disjunction of EU agricultural and food law, is one of the fundamental legal challenges of current EU food policy. In this book, we argue that it could be resolved by regulating EU (agri-)food law through a 'domain-based approach', rather than on the basis of clear competence divisions. Competence-based regulation pursues isolated policy interests, such as trade (internal market, international trade), environment, health, consumer protection, and agriculture. In contrast, an agri-food domain-based approach acknowledges the need to strike a balance between these diverse rationales and policy areas, and results in secondary legislation that institutes a specific compromise between these competing interests. In food law, this can be achieved by relying on the full spectrum of the 'web of competence', by using legal bases in a cumulative and complementary way. While particularly useful in potentially bridging the agriculture–food divide, there are some limitations to this approach. The Treaties pose substantive limitations on how food law can be regulated in the EU: this concerns, for example, the absence of a strong autonomous health competence, as well as the fact that sustainability is not enshrined as an integrative principle at Treaty level. The absence of a strong EU health competence obstructs the re-alignment of food law with health objectives. In addition, the right to food is neither enshrined nor currently read into the EU Charter. Consequently, a rights-based approach to EU food law is quasi absent.

The hostile intra-EU political climate makes any forthcoming Treaty change regarding changes to the policy competence allocation difficult, if not improbable. Therefore, the Lisbon Treaty has acquired a quasi-immutable status. The inflexibility inherent to the Treaty structure favours realistic short to mid-term solutions to policy fragmentation, which can be implemented through secondary legislation under a 'domain-based approach'.

The sustainability shift in EU law—the Farm to Fork Strategy and Beyond

The question remains, then: will EU food law fundamentally change, and when? The next decade will predictably be dedicated to responding to recent developments at EU political and geopolitical levels. Most legislative endeavours will arguably be concerned with achieving the sustainability goals in food legislation as set out in the Farm to Fork Strategy. However, the impact of the Covid pandemic and the war in Ukraine on food supply reminded us how vulnerable food supply is. As a result, food security will probably be given special attention alongside the sustainability goals stemming from the Farm to Fork strategy.

The Farm to Fork law-making process is ongoing, and some proposals for laws and amendments have already been tabled. One of the main sustainability gains of the Farm to Fork Strategy lies in the business accountability area, for instance in the new Corporate Sustainability Due Diligence Directive that has been proposed. And yet, as we have shown in the preceding chapters, the influence of the Farm to Fork Strategy on current food legislation is largely limited. Furthermore, the Farm to Fork Strategy made no indication that there is any intention to modify the General Food Law Regulation (GFLR), and therefore the core of contemporary EU food law. It is questionable when the Sustainable Food System Framework (SFSF) legislation, originally scheduled for the end of 2023, will be proposed in the next Commission mandate. It appeared that the SFSF proposal would—from a regulatory meta-perspective—remain inconsequential to the existing institutional structures that define legislative and non-legislative food law. The risk analysis processes appeared unlikely to undergo modification, although perhaps complementary processes related to sustainability could be devised under the SFSF. In addition, it appears that the mandate of the European Food Safety Authority (EFSA) was to remain confined to food safety, without extending it, or that of another agency, to sustainability. A different—and perhaps more desirable—scenario, however, would see the SFSF amend the GFLR. Sustainability aspects could be implemented into the general definitions. 'Sustainability' may be added next to the 'not unsafe' general obligation in Article 14 GFLR. Either way, 'safety' should no longer be the single prime goal of EU food law, which will raise questions regarding the relationship between the 'not unsafe' and the 'sustainability' goals. While the general 'safety' architecture will remain, 'sustainability' will need to be implemented as a complementary goal into EU food law.

Risk regulation and innovation

The science-policy interface in EU food law is reigned by the risk analysis principle. According to the GLFR, EU risk analysis is comprised of three main elements: risk assessment, risk management, and risk communication. Food risk assessment is to be conducted by risk assessors, such as EFSA, and food management is to be undertaken largely by the European Commission, but often with the involvement of the Committee Procedure Committees, and therefore Member State representatives. The largely strict separation of risk assessment and risk management echoes the approach in the Codex Alimentarius, and it can be regarded as a distinctive feature of EU risk regulation—other jurisdictions such as the United States or the EU Member States at domestic level have a much more mixed approach.

This risk management design, pervasive in EU food law, in practice proves unsatisfactory. On one hand, the incorporation of other social or societal factors aside from the food safety aspect is not structured, so that these factors are largely sidelined by the safety aspects. On the other hand, for polarized topics such as active substances for pesticides and genetically modified foods, the absence of consensus means that decisions are neither blocked nor authorized, and thus end up at the discretion of the Commission. A major gap in the risk analysis design is how sustainability may be integrated explicitly into or relate to these processes. One inroad might be the better regulation of risk management processes, an issue that was overlooked by the recent Transparency Regulation, which focused on improving aspects of risk communication and risk assessment.

An overhaul of the GFLR would also be warranted by factors other than just the oversight regarding sustainability. While the risk analysis paradigm has become pervasive in EU food law, it has also come of age. Risk analysis structures how science and politics interact when regulating the food market. While scientific regulation has had a rationalizing effect on food regulation, its judicial and administrative oversight is still limited. Exercising risk analysis for nearly 20 years illustrated both the strengths and the weaknesses of this approach. Availability of scientific evidence, choice of scientific evidence, managing different interpretations, and finally the realization that a clear-cut differentiation between risk assessment, risk management, and risk communication is often not as easy as envisaged. In this respect, the institutions and specifically EFSA are barely starting to digest the changes imposed by the Transparency Regulation.

It is even more surprising that despite these experiences, the Farm to Fork strategy did not address the General Food Law or EFSA as part of the reform agenda. The current institutional design, notably EFSA, is largely food-safety oriented. There are to date no profound changes at institutional or procedural level proposed by the Farm to Fork strategy, which will constitute an obstacle to the effective implementation and anchoring of the sustainability paradigm into mainstream EU food law.

The risk analysis paradigm operates in a state of tension with innovation. Innovation is not a goal *in se*, neither is it a panacea. However, the focus on 'risk' risks introducing a conservative approach to regulation, neglecting societal benefits; furthermore, current risk analysis mechanisms allocate the responsibility for risk science (and its costs) to food business operators (FBOs), whereas sometimes the risk analysis mechanisms fulfil a public function (food safety). In this context, it is time to think about how to overhaul the risk analysis paradigm, authorization procedures, and shift cost allocations in order to stimulate sustainable innovation while ensuring food safety. A main institutional design would address how we move from a legal framework that regulates innovation—in terms of limiting its risks and assigning responsibility for such risks (and resulting benefits)—towards a legal framework that actively encourages sustainable innovation while ensuring food safety and managing risks. Although a conceptually daunting task, an integration of the risk paradigm with a sustainability analysis may shape the way forward.

Has the internal market for food been completed?

The free movement of goods Treaty articles used to be an important source of food law developments; and main landmark decisions in EU law were habitually rendered on food products. The historical overview of the case law rendered by the Court of Justice of the European Union (CJEU) on food products demonstrated that classic narratives or schemes of the internal market tests deployed by the Court do not hold when looked at from a domain perspective. The Court has shown itself to follow erratic internal market tests and rationales, and specifically the significance of justifications, the proportionality testing, or 'certain selling arrangements' are decided on a case-by-case basis. Only the result seems clear—the Court has hardly accepted any justifications for trade obstacles in the area of food and it has a significant preference for the provision of information instead of other regulatory measures. The main exception to this general finding is when a genuine and recognized food safety issue is concerned.

The book therefore identified the fading relevance of the internal market Treaty provisions with respect to the free movement of goods in food, and outlines this to be due to three main factors. First, most issues in food have been subject to harmonization in secondary legislation, which typically pre-empts the application of the free movement of goods provision. Instead, litigation is increasingly based and resolved on the basis of secondary legislation. Second, the *ex-ante* notification of technical regulations, now under Directive (EU) 2015/1535, prevents the creation of obstacles, because critical draft Member State legislation can be identified and its compliance with Treaty principles checked prior to their entering into force. Third, the principle of mutual recognition has been codified in Regulation (EC) 764/2008 on mutual recognition for products not subject to harmonization and is now subject to a decentralized administration at Member State level. While the free movement of goods 'law' is still good law, it is applied in the procedural and administrative setting at Member States' level.

Nevertheless, some food law pockets remain where the free movement of goods provisions retain relevance; these are authorization procedures, which are excluded from the scope of the Mutual Recognition Regulation and which have become common practice in non-harmonized areas for instance with respect to food fortification. A future development to watch out for is domestic sustainability legislation. Given that we do not (yet) have an EU sustainable food law, many domestic measures to make national food systems more sustainable risk being tested against the free movement framework—in the future, the Treaty provisions might therefore re-emerge as a significant legal framework in the area of food regulation.

Part II—Food safety umbrella laws: the General Food Law Regulation and the Official Controls Regulation

The book explains the vital role of the GFLR in demarcating the EU food law domain and in instituting an overarching legal framework for all EU and national food law at any stage of production, processing, and distribution. It comprises principles (notably science-based risk analysis, the precautionary principle, transparency, and the protection of consumers' interests); it institutes the main food safety requirement and operator responsibilities and establishes EFSA and procedures for food rapid responses, emergencies, and crises. All of these elements are dedicated to food safety, and it is therefore justified to speak of a food safety oriented legal architecture of EU food law. The integration of food sustainability considerations into this general legal architecture is one of the major challenges that future EU food law will face.

However, the book also points to the need to think beyond food. The Official Controls Regulation (OCR) is the enforcement counterpart to the GFLR. Compared to the GFLR, it has a widened scope of application, as it applies not only to food and feed law, but also to rules on animal health and welfare, plant health, and plant protection products. In this respect the drafting of the Regulation is very compatible with an integrated food systems approach and could lead the way for future legislation. Thereby, the Regulation also resonates with a One Health approach, which emphasizes the interconnection of animal, environmental, and human health. This integrative thinking can prevent food law from becoming a silo of its own, and may orient integrative actions in the future with respect to veterinarian, pharmaceutical, cosmetic, and chemical EU legislation.

Parts III–VII—the food law *acquis*

In this book, we grouped the existing food secondary legislation into topical clusters, namely food technology law, food safety law, food information law, food quality law, and food nutrition law. Even though most of the laws discussed in the book belong and relate to the GFLR's food safety architecture, the clustering takes account of the other main purposes of a law (*ratio legis*) implemented in a given legislative framework.

Food technology law

One food safety concern originates from the application of food technology in food. Here, we see that food law uses authorization procedures as an implementation of the precautionary principle. Whereas the GFLR institutes a free marketing principle for all safe foods, subject only to the self-assessment of the FBOs, the specific food technology laws institute authorization requirements for certain substances or product categories, notably novel foods, genetically modified organisms (GMOs), and food improvement agents. The various authorization procedures have different designs, but the EU system largely shifts the burden of proof for safety to FBOs, which amounts to relatively substantive costs. This system is in part a consequence of the risk regulation architecture in the EU, which allocates EFSA little science-making powers, and confines EFSA to a science reviewer. Industry criticizes this system for being over-regulatory and standing in the way of innovation. Civil society criticizes this system for relying on science provided by industry, and therefore not being able to properly guarantee scientific independence and food safety. From a more fundamental perspective, it is not clear that a positive food safety evaluation should always be able to overcome other concerns, for instance with respect to the environmental or nutritional desirability of given techniques. An illustrative example is the contested nature of GMOs, where views on the future of our food system manifestly clash.

Opponents of the EU authorization systems habitually cite the more liberal United States (US) system, which allows many substances on the market. These arguments fail to take into consideration that the US has a more liberal '*ex ante*' system of regulation, but that it is paired with an incredibly strict liability and damages '*ex post*' regime, which the EU does not have. In that sense, the EU risk regulatory system can be regarded as proactive and preventive, whereas other systems are more reactive. Such systemic considerations must be taken into account when proposing modifications to the EU risk regulatory architecture. The food technology authorization systems might nevertheless be up for an overhaul. In light of the idea that food safety, and arguably food sustainability, is a public interest and a common good, at least in some cases the science and costs should be conducted at public and not necessarily private level.

Food safety law

The book shows that EU food law is generally dominated by food safety concerns and governed by a food safety-oriented institutional structure, principles, and processes. The food safety law part covers those secondary laws that ensure food safety in the strict sense, with respect to biological or chemical aspects. For biological safety these are the hygiene legislations and microbiological criteria for food, and for chemical safety these are the legal frameworks on intentionally and unintentionally added substances to food, as well as a separate regulatory framework on food contact materials.

EU food is regarded to be among the safest in the world, in that sense, the current EU food safety architecture appears to have achieved its main goals. At least this is true for food safety in a narrow and acute sense. A nuance to this assessment can be made for long-term and non-acute effects. Where indigestion over a long period of time causes illness, attribution and causation to substances becomes scientifically and legally challenging, as is the case for example for per- and polyfluoroalkyl substances (PFAS) and cancer. In this vein, the existing food safety network can be improved with respect to the identification of emergent food safety risks, and novel hazard identification such as endocrine disruption.

Further integrative efforts between pharmaceutical, veterinary, cosmetic, and food sectors are necessary in order to improve a holistic risk assessment approach. Inspiration can be found in the Chemicals Strategy, which designed a 'one substance—one assessment' approach to unite the different sectors, and furthermore proposed an essential use doctrine, whereby substances would be allowed on the EU market only when fulfilling an essential function. These are realistic and potentially effective suggestions that would do much to improve the state of the EU food safety risk architecture.

Food information law

Whereas the consumer and information nexus is governed by several important generalist EU law instruments, EU food law has a number of food-specific information legal frameworks. The Food Information to Consumer Regulation lays down mandatory and voluntary food information requirements, therefore taking a highly prescriptive approach to food information. This deviates to some extent from the frequent utilization of open norms in general EU consumer and information law, for example general obligations that consumers will not be misled. Regarding voluntary food information, the Nutrition and Health Claim Regulation lays down further detailed rules in the form of an authorization regime for nutrition and health claims on foodstuffs. This information governance system prescribes a standard for when certain nutrition claims can be used, and ensures that all health claims in the EU are both, scientifically validated and expressed on the packaging in a standardized formula. In these terms, EU food information law is highly prescriptive and regulated, and forms a specific pocket of law within general EU food information law. Within EU food information law, voluntary information law with respect to food certification and claims other than nutrition and health claims is left relatively unregulated. There is, to date, for instance no legal approach to sustainability labelling on food products, which in turn raises important questions. First, regarding how EU law should regulate sustainability claims, and whether specific requirements to make sustainability claims are better established in a food sector-specific approach or in a transversal general product approach. Secondly, there are important issues of scope between sustainability claims and green claims; the proposed food sustainability labelling framework under the Farm to Fork Strategy was potentially much more encompassing on substance than the ongoing general EU law proposals to regulate all green claims. Arguably, the current food information approach has shown the merits of sector-specific requirements, as overarching and general rules are often inadequate in order to capture the specificities of food products. In this vein, sector-specific rules on sustainable food claims are likely to be more efficient and tailored, and in terms of food information, constitute a regulatory gap that deserves to be filled.

Food quality law

There is no definition of food quality in EU law, which has resulted in a highly multifaceted approach, where food quality is understood to comprise dimensions of food safety, nutritional quality, origin and authenticity, ethics, aesthetics, sensory properties (taste), convenience, and functionality. For some agricultural and food products, a number of these aspects are addressed in specific 'vertical' food commodity legislation. Among the 'horizontal' EU laws that clearly and directly govern specific food quality aspects are the Organics Regulation, as well as the Food Quality Schemes Regulation. These schemes are public voluntary certification schemes, complementing private certification schemes that are more diverse in terms of the dimensions of quality that may be certified.

In this respect, the book highlighted that the 'organic' certification is the closest legally operational scheme linked to (some dimensions of) sustainable food—for instance, the attention to non-chemical input, to some extent soil agriculture, or the preference of local inputs covers certain aspects that could feature as sustainable food. Overall, however, EU organic certification to date lacks important sustainability aspects and must therefore be regarded as an incomplete proxy for sustainable food.

The Food Quality Schemes Regulation exhibits a different relation to quality. EU quality schemes are public certification marks. The quality requirements protected largely relate to geographic origin and authenticity, although other aspects such as traditional production may also be registered. These quality dimensions are not the only main goal of the Regulation, as it is a vehicle with which to ensure the organization of markets, producer premiums, trade advantages, and intellectual property protection. This is because the Regulation combines a 'classical' intellectual property protection regime for geographical indications (the EU protected designation of origin (PDO) and protected geographical indication (PGI)) with elements that certify more holistic elements, such as tradition or mountain origin. More encompassing and progressive recent efforts to enable producer groups to agree on sustainability quality aspects remained only voluntary, and seems of little actual impact on what EU quality schemes certify.

Clearly, a major unresolved challenge in relation to food quality is the lack of a joint definition or a common understanding of what would be sustainable food. In this respect, private certification schemes have developed both more holistic as well as more diverse issue-based certifications, therefore catering to the need for guaranteeing specific quality aspects in a given food product. Organic food certifies certain sustainable aspects in food, but is oblivious to others, and quality schemes may certify food origin and authenticity, but are not congruent to local food production or short food supply chains. The notion of sustainability links to a number of concepts that are discussed in relation to food quality, for instance healthy food, unhealthy food, local food, food produced in short food supply chains, plant-based food, fairly traded food, food with a low carbon footprint, and green food. These are largely without legal frameworks, and, in addition, sustainable food is more than the aggregate of all of these. The formulation of sustainable food criteria is, then, one of the priorities for the food quality agenda.

Food nutrition and health law

The relationship between EU food law and nutrition and health is uneasy. While nutrition and health are clearly recognized as important goals of EU food law, the book has shown that this is mostly limited to a negative conception, that is, the absence of detrimental nutritional or health effects. Food safety laws require the absence of negative impacts on health, or restrict the marketing of nutritionally inferior foods. A closer look at the food law *acquis* reveals a significant gap in substantive regulation concerning nutrition and health. A positive and prescriptive approach to food for nutrition and health is missing in the legislative frameworks with the following few exceptions. The Regulation on Foods for Specific Groups and Purposes sets compositional requirements for highly select types of food; this instrument does represent a fully fledged nutrition and health approach, but it is extremely limited in its target groups and thus does not amount to an overarching instrument that would govern aspects of nutrition and health in all EU food law. The Regulation on the addition of vitamins, minerals and other substances to food is an interesting example of an unfinished regulatory framework —key elements, such as the setting of maximum or minimum nutritional amounts could never be agreed. The same fate holds for the Directive on Food Supplements. These examples exhibit the political difficulty of implementing a nutrition and health approach whenever actual nutritional standards would be established. At the same time, the Regulation on the addition of vitamins, minerals, and other substances witnessed one of the more radical health and nutrition-oriented initiatives, by instituting a legally binding trans fat limit, which could well mark the inception of a new prescriptive approach to compositional requirements in food.

The realm of nutrition and health not only presents a significant gap in secondary legislation, it is also not well reflected as a positive paradigm in the general obligations of EU food law, particularly the GFLR. Food safety in the EU legal frameworks is negatively defined, that is, as the absence of dangers to health. The drafting of the general food legislation prior to the GFLR had proposed two paradigms; specifically, it had been suggested establishing a general obligation on food safety and wholesomeness. The more encompassing notion of 'wholesomeness', which could have played a key role in defining a positive approach to food safety and food as a preventive health component, is now missing. In future, it will be essential to develop and anchor a positive perspective on food in the EU food regulatory architecture, as consumers and the food industry increasingly look to food as a component of future health, and in order to carve out space for the positive valuation of food in the food system more broadly.

Overall, nutrition and health and their relationship to food remains one of the areas in which the internal market shows fragmentation through divergent Member State laws, and consequently the free movement of goods Treaty articles retain relevance as an arbiter of last resort.

Part VIII—international food law

The main challenge of the international and global angle on food law is the fragmentation across policy spheres. While largely consolidated spheres in their respective mandates, their co-existence obstructs the making of global food law and policy. The right to food manifests in the UN Declaration on Human Rights and later the International Covenant on Economic and Social Rights and related bodies. In the EU context, the human right to food is, however, not translated into the Charter of Fundamental Rights, and in EU legislation and policy, a human rights approach remains largely absent in discourses. In legitimizing and steering EU food policy, the sustainable development goals are currently exerting a greater influence compared to other frameworks. The absence of a strong recognition of the right to food in EU food law results in a policy blind spot when it comes to humans in the food system, and it is an opportunity to create stronger human rights scholarship within the EU food law making context.

In substantive terms, the Codex Alimentarius is the only fully global intergovernmental international standard-setting organization, and is highly influential and successful in setting global food safety standards in food. Nevertheless, the Codex work is limited to food safety, and thus precludes to a large extent standards on other issues, such as sustainability. The effective extension of Codex work to a more encompassing agenda that includes sustainability could greatly contribute to global food systems governance.

Lastly, World Trade Organization (WTO) law forms a separate track of international law that frames and sets limits on EU law in general, as well as EU food law in particular. Much like the EU internal market law, WTO law is dedicated to safeguarding free trade between its members. WTO law therefore constitutes an outer boundary of what kind of regulations the EU or Member States may take with respect to food. EU food regulation has raised trade concerns and disputes at WTO level numerous times, for instance with respect to the *Beef Hormones* and the *Genetically Modified Food* disputes. The upcoming sustainability regulation risks violating WTO law as well, necessitating strong justifications to withstand legal scrutiny. The standards set by the Codex Alimentarius Commission are subject to a special recognition in WTO law, which warrants the legality of domestic regulation in compliance with the Codex standards. This integration tool promotes coherence in international law. However, given that Codex standards are substantively limited to food safety, the creation and recognition under WTO law of global or regional standard setters on other subject matters relevant to food, such as food sustainability, is desirable.

Overall, we conclude that the dispersed international rights frameworks, the absence of sustainability in global intergovernmental standards, and the free trade orientation of the WTO law framework lack synergy and must be better streamlined to achieve a sustainable future food system governance.

Future-proofing food law—beyond food law

A major part of the current EU food law reform agenda concerns the implementation of sustainability in EU food law. In the long run, however, the future of food law arguably lies beyond sustainability and the food sector. The food domain has continuously undergone profound transformations; after World War II, food security and agricultural production were at the core of food-policy formation. This was followed by a strong political motivation to improve trade within the EU by completing the common, and later the internal market. Over time, EU food law included food quality and increasingly food safety concerns. The upcoming relevant trends for the food domain relate to sustainability, including societal and ethical considerations, the food-health nexus, coupled with a return to considerations of food security. Food has a geopolitical dimension, and food security remains a sometimes-unspoken premise of food law. The Covid pandemic illustrated how closely related our food chains and health are and that it is important to ensure that food chains remain open. Opening up supply chains is a major domain of EU competition law, which likewise needs to be considered in the future of food law. And alongside these are the individuals working in the food system, which brings to the fore issues of land and labour law. In addition to public regulation, food chains are to a major extent regulated by private standards. Here, contract law mingles with competition law and public law provisions, which equally need to be considered when looking at regulating the EU food market. At the same time, planetary boundaries keep on challenging our food system. The narrow focus of EU food law as it currently stands will and has to open up to many other legal areas to cope with the challenges the food system faces. Food production influences food consumption, both regulated in different areas (agriculture and food), which therefore need to be aligned. Climate change influences both areas, and creates the need to connect both areas to environmental legislation. Beyond sustainability, the One Health approach aims to shape a positive interrelationship between environmental, animal, and human health; a legal approach to it requires a broad grounding in environmental, pharmaceutical, veterinary, cosmetic, and other regulatory fields in addition to food. Food law alone cannot implement an integrative vision of the food system.

In essence, in order to future-proof EU food law, we must look beyond the Farm to Fork Strategy, and in order to future-proof the food system, we must look beyond food law.

Index

For the benefit of digital users, indexed terms that span two pages (e.g., 52–53) may, on occasion, appear on only one of those pages.

agricultural products 35, 117
authorization procedures 155, 156–58, 160–61, 214, 322
average consumer benchmark 46, 273, 311

Better Regulation 28, 68–70
Biocidal Product Regulation 251
Brussels effect 124, 383–84

Cassis de Dijon 83
certification marks 301–3
Charter of Fundamental Rights (CFR) 50–51, 55, 278, 390
Codex Alimentarius 391
Commission Directorates-General 57
Common Agricultural Policy 12, 14, 403
Common Market 7, 9–10, 11–13, 15–16
competence to act *see* principle of conferral of powers
completion of the internal market 7–8, 12, 15, 18, 80
consumer protection 45, 122
Contaminants Regulation 243
Council of the European Union (the Council) 59
Court of Justice of the EU 59, 76

Dassonville 82, 83
delegated act 70

Economic Community (EC) 10
environmental protection 47
EURATOM 9–10
European Coal and Steel Community (ECSC) 9–10
European Commission 56
European Council 55
European Economic Community (EEC) 7, 9–10
European Economic Community (EEC) Treaty 9–10, 15
European Food Safety Authority (EFSA) 128, 170, 256, 320–21
European integration 7, 8, 15, 17–18, 81, 103
European Parliament 58
European Union's advisory bodies 61–64
Extraction Solvents Directive 215

fair information practices 287
Farm to Fork Strategy 29
Food and Agriculture Organization (FAO) 391
Food Business Operators (FBOs) 127
  FBOs responsibilities 142
food contact materials 255
Food Contact Materials Regulation 255
Foods for Specific Groups and Purposes (FSGaP) Regulation 364
food for special medical purposes (FSMPs) 368
Food Fortification Regulation 371
food improvement agents 193
Food Improvement Agents Package (FIAP) 193–94
  Food Additives Regulation 195
  Enzymes Regulation 200
  Flavourings Regulation 204
  Common Procedure Regulation 214
Food Information to Consumer Regulation 282, 283, 284, 288, 300, 303
Food Quality Systems Regulation 351, 358
Food Safety Management System (FSMS) 230
Food Supplements Directive 375
free movement of goods 80, 85, 408

General Agreement on Tariffs and Trade (GATT) 398
General Food Law Regulation (GFLR) 113–25, 137, 138, 280
Geographical indication (GIs) 349–50
GM Food and Feed Regulation 177, 178, 181
GMOs 174–79
GMO Deliberate Release Directive 177–78, 181, 182, 184
good manufacturing practices regulation 258
Green Paper on the General Principles of Food Law in the European Union 8, 21–22, 113–14

HACCP 225–26, 228
harmonization 15, 16, 17, 18, 104
health claims 307, 309, 314
Hormone Directive 252
human health protection 48, 279–80
Hygiene Package 223–24
  General Hygiene Regulation 224
  Hygiene Regulation for Animal Origin 235

implementing act 71
infant formula and follow-up formula 367
intentionally added substances 247
internal market 42, 79, 80

Keck exemption 84, 98–99

legislative act 65–68, 66*t*
Lisbon Treaty 11

mandatory food information 288
market access test 84, 106–7
Maximum Level Commission Regulation 243
measures having equivalent effect to quantitative restrictions 81, 82, 85
microbiological criteria for foodstuffs 236
mutual recognition declaration 107
Mutual Recognition Regulation 106

'natural' 210
new genomic techniques 176–77, 190
non-legislative act 66*t*, 70–71
  delegated act (*see* delegated act)
  implementing act (*see* implementing act)
novel food catalogue 166
Novel Food Regulation (NFR) 159–72
Nutrition and Health Claims Regulation 304–24
nutrition claims 306, 307, 309, 313

Official Controls Regulation (OCR) 142
ordinary legislative procedure 68
Organics Regulation 336, 344, 346

Pesticide Maximum Residue Levels Regulation 247
precautionary principle 47, 120, 156
principle of conferral of powers 64
principle of proportionality 64, 84–85
  proportionality test 84–85
principle of solidarity 49–50
principle of subsidiarity 64
prior authorization 107
processing aids 213
product requirements 86
  certain selling arrangements 98
  genuine food safety requirements 93
  labelling 91
  mandatory descriptions and denominations 89
  packaging 92
  product compositional requirements 87
  requirements on origin indications 97
  restrictions on nutritional substances, enriched food, and supplements 96
protected designation of origin (PDO) 350, 352, 358, 359
protected geographical indication (PGI) 350, 352, 358, 359

quantitative restrictions to trade 80–81, 82–83

Rapid Alert System for Food and Feed (RASFF) 135
right to food 11, 50–51, 389–402, 414
risk analysis principle 118
  risk assessment 119, 170, 186, 256
  risk communication 119, 122
  risk management 119, 187

Sanitary and Phytosanitary Measures (SPS) Agreement 398
Schuman Declaration 9
Single European Act (SEA) 10
soft law 76
SOLVIT 107
Spaak Report (Brussels Report on the General Common Market) 9–10, 36
Standing Committees 58
sustainable development goals (SDGs) 384–85, 386–87

Technical Barriers to Trade (TBT) Agreement 400
traditional specialty guarantee (TSG) 356, 358, 359
transparency principle 124
Transparency Regulation 113, 131, 132–35
Treaty on the European Union (TEU) 11, 55
Treaty on the Functioning of the European Union (TFEU) 11, 34

Unfair Commercial Practices Directive 287–88, 302–3
unintentionally added substances 242
United Nations Charter 386, 387, 401

veterinary medicinal products 250
voluntary food information 300

White Paper on the Completion of the Internal Market 18
World Trade Organisation (WTO) 391, 397, 398, 401